Your Interpersonal Communication

Timothy P. Mottet
Texas State University—San Marcos

Sally Vogl-Bauer
University of Wisconsin—Whitewater

Marian L. Houser
Texas State University—San Marcos

PEARSON

Boston   Columbus   Indianapolis   New York   San Francisco   Upper Saddle River
Amsterdam   Cape Town   Dubai   London   Madrid   Milan   Munich   Paris   Montreal   Toronto
Delhi   Mexico City   São Paulo   Sydney   Hong Kong   Seoul   Singapore   Taipei   Tokyo

Editor-in-Chief, Communications: Karon Bowers
Senior Acquisitions Editor: Melissa Mashburn
Senior Development Editor: Carol Alper
Associate Development Editor: Angela Mallowes
Editorial Assistant: Stephanie Chaisson
Senior Managing Editor: Linda Mihatov Behrens
Associate Managing Editor: Bayani Mendoza de Leon
Marketing Manager: Blair Tuckman
Manufacturing Buyer: Mary Ann Gloriande
Image Permission Coordinators: Annette Linder/Lee Scher
Photo Researchers: Lynne Schulhafer/Maggie Fenton
Project Coordination, Text Design, and Electronic Page Makeup: Nesbitt Graphics, Inc.
Senior Cover Design Manager/Cover Designer: Nancy Danahy
Printer/Binder: R.R. Donnelley/Willard
Cover Printer: Lehigh-Phoenix Color/Hagerstown
Cover Images: JGI/Jamie Grill © Blend Images/Alamy

Credits and acknowledgments borrowed from other sources and reproduced, with permission, in this textbook appear on pages 389–390.

Library of Congress Cataloging-in-Publication Data

Mottet, Timothy P.
  Your interpersonal communication / Timothy P. Mottet, Sally Vogl-Bauer, Marian L. Houser.—1st ed.
    p. cm.
  ISBN 978-0-205-49440-8
  1. Interpersonal communication. I. Vogl-Bauer, Sally. II. Houser, Marian L. III. Title.
  HM1166.M65 2012
  153.6—dc23
                       2011020932

1 2 3 4 5 6 7 8 9 10—RRDW—14 13 12 11

PEARSON

ISBN 13: 978-0-205-49440-8
ISBN 10:   0-205-49440-4

Dedicated to . . .

My current and former graduate students from UTPA and Texas State—TPM

Eleanor Vogl—SVB

My many mentors and students from the University of Missouri–Columbia, Miami University, The University of Tennessee-Knoxville, and Texas State University–San Marcos—MLH

Brief Contents

Contents

Preface xiii

10 Self-Disclosure and Intimacy in Relationships 258

11 Family and Friend Relationships 282

12 Workplace Relationships 306

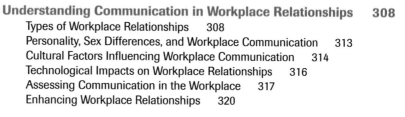

Preface

Psychologist Carl Jung once said, "The meeting of two personalities is like the contact of two chemical substances; if there is any reaction, both are transformed." At times, our relationships transform us for the better. At other times, unfortunately, our relationships can be challenging and, like a bad chemical reaction, can even become toxic. Interpersonal communication, the communication created between individuals, is the chemistry that forms, develops, and sometimes destroys relationships. Understanding the dynamics of interpersonal communication allows one to make communication choices that can transform the quality of every relationship and, consequently, the quality of one's life.

Our approach to interpersonal communication helps students to better understand the "chemistry" by showing how an individual's personality influences social style and interaction. We refer to the relationship between personality and communication as one's communication personality, which is as unique as a signature: No two are alike.

Our goal in this text is to provide students with the skills and knowledge they need to discover and understand their own communication personalities, a more comprehensive understanding of their own personal needs to connect and interact with other people, and an appreciation for the uniqueness of other people's communication personalities. The exercises and discussions in this text give students the opportunity to apply what they learn to their own relationships, thus polishing their social skills for communication success in the future. Successful relationships are based on the knowledge and understanding of what it takes to find a communicative balance between two very different people, laying the groundwork for effective interpersonal communication.

Personalized Learning

We have designed the following unique features to help students discover their individual interpersonal communication styles. Several boxed features offer specialized information. Icons located in the margins help readers to visually identify the different themes and content that will enhance their understanding of interpersonal communication.

Nature/Nurture Intersections of Interpersonal Communication

For students to enhance their social skills, they need to first understand why they communicate the way they do. For example, why do they always seem to avoid conflict? Or why do they share too much information too soon in their relationships? Understanding why they act the way they act and say the things they say allows students to pinpoint where and how they can improve their communication habits.

NATURE/NURTURE intersections

Fitting into Your Parents' Genes

Scholars continue to shed light on what is known about genetics, heredity, and the role of parents in the development of infants. These findings suggest that genetics/heredity, parental behaviors, and communicative interactions all make important contributions to the ways in which humans develop across the lifespan.[36]

It is understood that children inherit their genetic makeup from their biological parents. This led communication scholars to examine the degree to which someone's communication traits were linked to inherited cognitive brain structures. The results of these studies suggest that, depending on the communication trait, genetics explains a moderate to large portion of why we may be predisposed to communicate in certain ways.[37] While these findings are very important to the study of communication traits, this is just the beginning.

Researchers outside the field of communication are discovering that our brain structures have a great deal of plasticity (or flexibility) and can be shaped by the environment and our interactions with others, especially when humans are very young. This is when parents' verbal and nonverbal behaviors are instrumental in shaping how their children's genetic predispositions get reinforced, modified, or altered after birth.[38] These findings suggest two different types of parental contributions. First, biological parents contribute the genetic makeup for the brain systems that are associated with communication traits that their biological children receive. Second, in raising children, parents or caregivers (who may or may not be the biological parents) shape how the infants' brain systems develop, adapt, and respond to parent–child interactions.[39] Finally, the environment in which parents and children live often influences parental behaviors and thus child development.

On the surface, these connections might not seem highly controversial. As we learn more about how brain systems (a) influence communication trait development, (b) are modified by the communicative behaviors of parents (or other caregivers) with their infants, and (c) are studied in the environmental context within which they develop, the questions that scholars ask are beginning to change. It is no longer a case of nature versus nurture; rather, the question is how nature influences nurture and vice versa. But before these approaches could be merged into a more cohesive picture, *each of the above points had to be supported by research.* This required a great deal of time, energy, and sometimes controversy on the part of lots of individuals in various disciplines, and the learning is by no means complete.

As we learn more about genetics and brain systems, communication traits, and environmental factors, the role of parents and caregivers becomes even more important, not less for children. If parental verbal and nonverbal behaviors can modify how brain systems develop and adapt *after* birth, teaching parents how to interact with their children is more important than ever before.

We provide **Nature/Nurture Intersections** boxes as one way to help students begin this self-discovery process. Researchers often refer to the biological influence as "nature" and the developmental or learned influence as "nurture." Some communication researchers argue the nature perspective: that humans embody these communication abilities and tendencies naturally. Others argue the nurture perspective: that *we learn* how to communicate. Historically, most interpersonal communication textbooks have focused more on the nurture perspective than on the nature perspective, but *Your Interpersonal Communication* provides a balanced coverage of the research examining what influences communication behavior. We believe that communication behaviors are influenced by both nature and nurture, and we support an interactionist position. Rather than buying into an either/or dualism, we believe that both biology and what we learn influence communication. As a result, we talk about the contributions of both nature and nurture in our coverage of interpersonal communication.

Understanding the nature perspective is important for several reasons. First, it's important to understand the natural part of communication; that is, the portion that resides in the genes we inherited from our parents and grandparents. These inborn traits make us unique and allow us to have "one of a kind" personalities. Second, there are times when we need to work against what is natural to develop the communication skills that will allow us to have the relationships we need to be happy and successful. For example, if it's natural for you to always argue and debate other people's ideas, there are going to be times when you need to work against this natural communication tendency. Some people find argumentative people to be offensive and even rude. In fact some people may find your style to be verbally aggressive. They may even feel as though you are personally attacking them when this is not the case. Our approach to teaching interpersonal communication is to provide the following resources, which help students to develop their own approaches to interpersonal communication that are compatible with their individual personalities.

ASSESS YOUR communication personality

Rubin et. al.'s Interpersonal Communication Motives[42]

Log on to our self-assessment library, MyPersonalityProfile, found on MyCommunicationLab (www.mycommunicationlab.com), and assess your Interpersonal Communication Motives by completing this interactive assessment. Also, encourage your relational partner (i.e., close friend, colleague from work, family member) to do the same. Then you can compare and contrast your scores and begin to understand better how your interpersonal communication motives may influence your communication with others. Or you may use the following paper version of this assessment.

Directions:

Here are several reasons people give for why they talk to other people. For each statement, please circle the number that best expresses your own reasons for talking to others.

1. Because it's fun	Exactly 5	A lot 4	Somewhat 3	Not much 2	Not at all 1
2. Because it's exciting	Exactly 5	A lot 4	Somewhat 3	Not much 2	Not at all 1
3. To have a good time	Exactly 5	A lot 4	Somewhat 3	Not much 2	Not at all 1
4. To help others	Exactly	A lot	Somewhat	Not much	Not at all

Assessing Your Communication Personality

Throughout each chapter and online, self-assessments, called **Assess Your Communication Personality** allow students to study themselves and their communication personalities. By completing the self-assessments, they will be better able to determine . . .

- If they are nervous or fearful of communicating with others.
- If they're too needy and drive people away because of their communication behaviors.
- If they're too aggressive, assertive, or argumentative when communicating with others.
- If they have control over their emotions or if their emotions control them.
- If they disclose too much (or too little) information about themselves in their relationships.
- If they manage conflict appropriately or avoid it.

After students complete these self-report measures, we help students understand what their scores mean and provide a boxed feature titled **What Can I Do Now?** that offers follow-up guidance to assist students in making choices to develop, enhance, or modify their communication skills to improve the quality of their relationships.

Pearson's MyPersonalityProfile, found on the MyCommunicationLab website (www.mycommunicationlab.com; access code required), includes assignable, interactive assessments. Students can complete the assessments in the printed text or online, where automatic scoring and visual results provide insight into how their personality traits compare to those of their classmates and of students taking assessments nationally. Not only can students assess their own communication personalities, but they can also invite others with whom they communicate on a regular basis to do the same, initiating their understanding of the other people in their relationships. Students will learn more about their relational partners' social styles and why their partners communicate the way they do. When students compare scores from the self-tests, they begin to see how their communication personalities and those of their relational partners are similar and different. This information allows the students to immediately begin to understand others more clearly. An instructor can assign the self-tests as class projects and compare how various members of the class differ in their communication styles.

WHAT CAN I do now?

▶ *You could increase your awareness.* Understand that you and your partner's styles of communication are in part motivated or driven by needs. Rather than reacting to your partner's communication, try to understand what is motivating him or her to communicate in a particular manner. This is called perspective taking.[43] Attempt to consider all the possible reasons why your partner communicates the way he or she does.

▶ *You could attempt to meet your partner's needs.* No two people are alike. When your partner communicates, he or she needs something. If possible, try to meet the need, and your partner might believe you have mind-reading skills. If your partner needs attention, then give attention. If your partner needs control, then yield. Research clearly suggests that you can enhance the quality of your relationships by helping others to meet their interpersonal needs.[44]

▶ *You could increase your adaptability.* No two relationships are the same. Adapting your communication means that you and your relational partner make choices about what's best for the relationship.[45] Above, we recommended meeting your partner's needs as one way of enhancing your relationship. Here, we recommend taking it a step further and together adapting your communication to meet the needs of the relationship. This requires a conversation between you and your relational partner in which you openly discuss interpersonal needs and how best to meet these needs.

Gender/Sex, Culture/Diversity, Technology, and Personality Threads

Some interpersonal communication textbooks devote an entire chapter to gender/sex, culture/diversity, and technology. Because we believe that these topics are essential to students discovering their own interpersonal communication, we decided to thread these important influences throughout every chapter in the book. Whenever we make reference to how gender/sex, culture/diversity, technology, or personality may influence interpersonal communication, we include one of the icons (see below) in the margins of the text.

Gender/Sex Thread. Although sex (male/female) differences may be easier to identify than gender (masculine/feminine) differences (because it's easier to identify a person as male or female), gender differences represent the more important factor for consideration when it comes to interpersonal communication. Not all women are feminine, and not all men are masculine. Most people have a gender orientation in between these two poles that influences their communication. We assert that men and women sometimes don't understand each other, not because of their biological sex, but because of their gender orientation. To help students discover gender differences in their own interpersonal communication, we integrate research examining gender differences into each of the chapters to illustrate how being masculine or feminine influences the way in which people send and receive messages. When there are differences in communication because of a person's biological sex (male/female), we make a point of clarifying this important distinction.

Culture/Diversity Thread. As the world becomes more and more diverse, we interact and communicate with individuals from a variety of cultural backgrounds on a daily basis. Understanding some fundamental intercultural communication differences will allow students to better interact and respond to diverse individuals or groups of people. For example, understanding how high- and low-context cultures and individualistic and collectivistic cultures impact how we send and receive messages will instantly sensitize us to how we communicate with diverse others. This intercultural awareness along with communication skill development will enhance our ability to develop relationships and communicate across cultures. Throughout each chapter, students will learn how culture affects communication in areas such as perceiving others, sending and receiving verbal and nonverbal messages, and listening and responding to others.

Technology Thread. Students use multiple communication technologies daily to manage their lives, yet many students remain unaware of how technology usage impacts their interaction with others. One of the hottest areas of interpersonal communication research is how technology is influencing our interpersonal communication and how our interpersonal communication is influencing the development of technologies. This book integrates the most current and state-of-the art research examining technology and interpersonal communication not only in just one chapter, but in every chapter. Students will learn about how social networking sites and text messaging are influencing what's going on in their relationships with others. It's rare to look around and not see people texting, processing their email, or checking their Facebook status using smart phones, laptops, or iPads and in some of the most unusual places. Technology has changed the way we understand and handle our interpersonal relationships. Computer-mediated communication (CMC) is literally altering the norms of interpersonal interaction and creating a new system of messages by which people attempt to understand one another both verbally and nonverbally.

 Personality Thread. Because your personality plays an influential role in how you interact with others and how others interact with you, we are threading this theme throughout each of the chapters. Your communication is an expression of your personality; you reveal your personality through your communication. When you first meet others, you get a sense of their personalities through their communication or social styles. Your social style, or how you interact with others, is uniquely yours. Do others consider you the funny one? Do they perceive you to be warm and outgoing? Perhaps you're more quiet, but would like to be more outgoing and social. Regardless of your social style, your personality is partially responsible for your interpersonal communication. If you want to learn more about your communication, then you need to learn more about your personality.

Interpersonal Communication Ethics

One of the most important decisions you can make within your relationships is what is right and wrong or good and bad for another person or yourself. Ultimately, what you decide may either enhance or harm your relationships and trying to figure this out can get very complicated. Who gets to determine right versus wrong or good versus bad communication choices? The sender of the message? The receiver of the message? Society at large? Furthermore, when are interpersonal communication decisions considered ethical, especially if the lines between right and wrong are blurred?

    Ethics in Interpersonal Communication boxes present contemporary interpersonal communication situations with "questionable" ethics. You will read about ethics in perceptions and stereotyping, during conflict, within identity management, in the CMC context, and so on. Ethical dilemmas thrive in our daily interpersonal communication. Although we don't go so far as to present firm guidelines for what is and is not ethical communication, we do present scenarios that students may have experienced or that they may have recently read about in the news. The ethical questions that accompany each scenario will help students to think about how their communication choices, as well as the choices of others, could determine how or whether they consider these interactions to be fair or unfair, right or wrong, and even good or bad.

ETHICS in interpersonal communication

Can Your Personality Influence the Ethics of Your Communication?

Machiavellianism is a personality trait that influences not only your communication, but also the ethics of your communication. The concept of Machiavellianism is based on the 16th century writings of Niccolò Machiavelli, who offered advice on how to get other people to do things for you. Researchers are still uncertain about how a person acquires a Machiavellian personality trait, but like most, it's probably a combination of nature and nurture influences. People who are high in Machiavellianism (high Machs) differ from those who are low in Machiavellianism (low Machs) in that high Machs "manipulate more, win more, and are persuaded less . . . in situations in which subjects interact face to face with others."[26] High Machs believe that the ends justify the means. Put another way, high Machs do whatever it takes to be successful, including restricting others' choices and using misleading and false information in their communication.[27] High Machs tend to prevail in situations involving emotional involvement more often than low Machs do because high Machs have the ability to ignore how others are feeling and concentrate more on winning, whereas low Machs care about how others are feeling.[28] Additionally, high Machs often view unethical behaviors as being acceptable.[29]

The research examining Machiavellianism and communication introduces a number of interesting questions related to interpersonal communication. What do you think about the following questions?

- Can a personality trait actually cause someone to be unethical in his or her communication? Can't a person choose not to be unethical in his or her communication?
- Are all high Machs unethical in their communication?
- Can a person be held responsible for communication that may be unethical if it is personality-driven?
- Should a low Mach who is in a relationship with a high Mach be worried?
- Can a high Mach learn to become a low Mach? Can a low Mach learn to become a high Mach?

mycommunication**lab** Log onto our MyCommunicationLab Self-Assessment Library (www.mycommunicationlab.com) and assess your Machiavellianism by completing the interactive assessment. Encourage your relational partner to do the same. Then you can compare and contrast your scores and begin to understand better how your Machiavellianism may influence your interpersonal communication.

Using *Your Interpersonal Communication*

Your Interpersonal Communication includes a number of features that are designed to help students study and learn.

A Clear and Easy-to-Follow Organization

Dividing the text into three primary units ensures that students grasp the communication fundamentals. The first unit, "Interpersonal Communication Foundations," sets the stage for the perspective of this textbook and presents the link between communication and personality. The second unit, "Interpersonal Communication Skills," develops the interpersonal communication foundation and its elements—those that are basic to all relationships (e.g., verbal and nonverbal communication). This unit also presents these elements at work within critical interpersonal applications such as listening and displaying emotions. Finally, in the third unit, "Interpersonal Communication Dynamics," we pull together all the issues from the first two units and frame them within specific relational contexts. It is our hope that reviewing the specific interpersonal elements and applications within friendships, intimate relationships, and workplace relationships will provide a real-world perspective that will enable students to better understand these elements.

At the beginning of every chapter are **Chapter Objectives,** and each chapter concludes with **Take-Aways, Discussion Questions,** and **Building Your Skills** activities. Our unique opening Chapter Objectives represent three clusters, each organized to focus on a

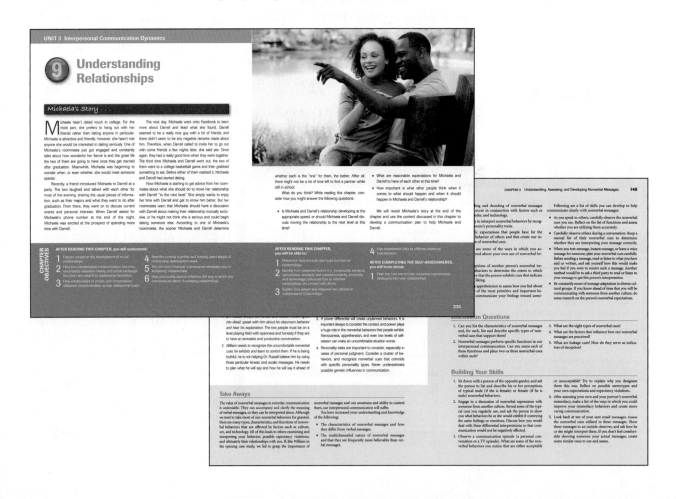

different post-assessment outcome: What students will understand; what students will be able to accomplish; and what students will know about themselves.

An Extensive Social Science Research Foundation

We have worked hard to review the scholarly contributions that have been made in communication as well as related disciplines so that students acquire an expansive understanding of what is being learned about interpersonal communication. In fact, we have even added a distinct chapter, "Interpersonal Communication Research," that focuses on conducting communication research to give students an idea of "how we know what we know" about interpersonal communication and add validity to the field and study of interpersonal as a whole. We cover the most current information about interpersonal communication and how this knowledge affects daily interactions, guidance for how to use and evaluate research, and how students can begin to engage in their own research projects. For example, if students read research that shows how the use of technology is changing how they communicate, then they might reflect more carefully on their own communication behaviors.

Integrated Chapter Case Studies

Case studies introduce and conclude each chapter, offering realistic and diverse examples to help students learn more about interpersonal communication. The case study at the beginning of the chapter illustrates a specific interpersonal communication problem or dilemma relating to the chapter content, followed by a series of questions for students to consider as they work through the chapter material. Then, at the end of the chapter, students are encouraged to answer the questions on the basis of what they have learned from the text and to compare their answers with the authors' suggestions for the characters in the case study. In this way, students learn how their unique approach to interpersonal problems may effectively incorporate what they have learned from the chapter. If their answers differ significantly from ours, they can determine why or how their initial solutions might have overlooked or inappropriately applied what they're learning about interpersonal communication. Or it could be that they would approach the communication situation in a different and valid way. Either way, the case study is an opportunity for students to become skilled in applying the concepts they are learning to a real-life situation.

Michaela's Story . . .

Michaela hasn't dated much in college. For the most part, she prefers to hang out with her friends rather than dating anyone in particular. Michaela is attractive and friendly; however, she hasn't met anyone she would be interested in dating seriously. One of Michaela's roommates just got engaged and constantly talks about how wonderful her fiancé is and the great life the two of them are going to have once they get married after graduation. Meanwhile, Michaela was beginning to wonder when, or even whether, she would meet someone special.

Recently, a friend introduced Michaela to Darrell at a party. The two laughed and talked with each other for most of the evening, sharing the usual pieces of information, such as their majors and what they want to do after graduation. From there, they went on to discuss current events and personal interests. When Darrell asked for Michaela's phone number at the end of the night, Michaela was excited at the prospect of spending more time with Darrell.

The next day, Michaela went onto Facebook to learn more about Darrell and liked what she found. Darrell seemed to be a really nice guy with a lot of friends, and there didn't seem to be any negative remarks made about him. Therefore, when Darrell called to invite her to go out with some friends a few nights later, she said yes. Once again, they had a really good time when they were together. The third time Michaela and Darrell went out, the two of them went to a college basketball game and then grabbed something to eat. Before either of them realized it, Michaela and Darrell had started dating.

Now Michaela is starting to get advice from her roommates about what she should do to move her relationship with Darrell "to the next level." She simply wants to enjoy her time with Darrell and get to know him better. But her roommates warn that Michaela should have a discussion with Darrell about making their relationship mutually exclusive, or he might not think she is serious and could begin dating someone else. According to one of Michaela's roommates, the sooner Michaela and Darrell determine

A Communication Development Plan for Michaela

To complete Michaela's story, recall that Michaela has recently begun dating Darrell. The relationship is progressing smoothly; however, Michaela is feeling pressure from her roommates to advance the relationship at a faster rate. She wants to continue to get to know him better, while her roommates are telling her that if she does not tell Darrell that she wants a mutually exclusive relationship, she might "lose him" to someone else.

What do you think?

Is Michaela and Darrell's relationship progressing at the right speed? Are Michaela's expectations for her relationship with Darrell reasonable? Does it matter what Michaela's roommates think about her relationship with Darrell?

RESOURCES IN PRINT AND ONLINE

Name of Supplement	Available in Print	Available Online	Instructor or Student Supplement	Description
Instructor's Manual and Test Bank (ISBN: 020506020X)	✓	✓	Instructor Supplement	This comprehensive Instructor's Manual portion, prepared by Meredith Marko Harrigan, State University of New York at Geneseo, has the following resources for each chapter: Learning Objectives, Concise Chapter Summary, Sample Answers for Discussion Questions, and suggestions for Activities and Assignments. The Test Bank portion contains a blend of fully reviewed assessments (multiple choice, true/false, completion, and essay questions), which are referenced by page and topic. Lecture outline handouts that match the PowerPoint™ presentation package are also included. Available for download at **www.pearsonhighered.com/irc;** access code required.
MyTest (ISBN: 0205060218)		✓	Instructor Supplement	This flexible, online test-generating software includes all questions found in the Test Bank section of the printed Instructor's Manual. This computerized software allows instructors to create their own personalized exams, to edit any or all of the existing test questions, and to add new questions. Other special features of this program include random generation of test questions, creation of alternative versions of the same test, scrambling of question sequence, and test preview before printing. Available at **www.pearsonmytest.com;** access code required.
PowerPoint™ Presentation Package (ISBN: 0205060226)		✓	Instructor Supplement	Prepared by Jason Pasqua, Laramie County Community College, this text-specific package provides a basis for your lecture with PowerPoint™ slides for each chapter of the book. The package also features selected figures and images from the book as well as additional discussion-launching questions embedded in the presentations. Available for download at **www.pearsonhighered.com/irc;** access code required.
Interpersonal Communication Video Library	✓		Instructor Supplement	Pearson's Interpersonal Communication Video Library contains a range of videos for adopters to choose from. Each of the videos features a variety of scenarios that illustrate interpersonal concepts and relationships. Some topics included in the library are nonverbal communication, perception, conflict, and listening. Please contact your Pearson representative for details; some restrictions apply.
Interpersonal Communication Study Site		✓	Student Supplement	This open access student resource features practice tests, learning objectives, and Web links organized around the major topics that are typically covered in the Interpersonal Communication course. Each topic is also correlated to the chapters in *Your Interpersonal Communication*. Available at **www.abinterpersonal.com.**
Study Card for Interpersonal Communication (ISBN: 0205514278)	✓		Student Supplement	Colorful, affordable, and packed with useful information, the Pearson Study Cards make studying easier, more efficient, and more enjoyable. Course information is distilled down to the basics, helping students to quickly master the fundamentals, review a subject for understanding, or prepare for an exam. Because the Study Cards are laminated for durability, students can keep them for years to come and pull them out whenever a quick review is needed. Available for purchase.
MyCommunicationLab		✓	Instructor and Student Supplement	MyCommunicationLab is a state-of-the-art, interactive and instructive solution for communication courses. Designed to be used as a supplement to a traditional lecture course or to completely administer an online course, MyCommunicationLab combines a Pearson eText, MySearchLab™, MediaShare, MyPersonalityProfile, multimedia, video clips, activities, research support, tests, and quizzes to completely engage students. MyCommunicationLab can be packaged with your text and is available for purchase at **www.mycommunicationlab.com;** access code required. See next page for more details.

Save time and improve results with mycommunicationlab

Designed to amplify a traditional course in numerous ways or to administer a course online, **MyCommunicationLab** for Interpersonal Communication courses combines pedagogy and assessment with an array of multimedia activities—videos, assessments, research support, and multiple newsfeeds—to make learning more effective for all types of students. Now featuring more resources, including a video upload tool (MediaShare) and the assessment tool MyPersonalityProfile, this new release of **MyCommunicationLab** is visually richer and even more interactive than the previous version—a leap forward in design with more tools and features to enrich learning and aid students in classroom success.

Teaching and Learning Tools

Pearson eText Identical in content and design to the printed text, a Pearson eText provides students access to their text whenever and wherever they need it. In addition to contextually placed multimedia features in every chapter, our new Pearson eText allows students to take notes and highlight, just like a traditional book.

Videos and Video Quizzes Interactive videos provide students with the opportunity to watch video clips that portray different communication scenarios, interviews with well-known communication scholars, and investigative news reports on interpersonal communication issues played out in real life. Many videos are annotated with critical thinking questions or include short, assignable quizzes that report to the instructor's gradebook.

Assessment Online self-assessments in MyPersonalityProfile, including SCAM, PRCA-24, and assessments that test introversion, shyness, and communication competence, help students learn about the different communication styles and assess their own. Instructors can use these tools to show learning over the duration of the course. In addition to MyPersonalityProfile, Pre- and Post-Tests are included in every chapter. The results from these tests create a customized study plan for further review and focus students on areas in which they need to improve.

ABC News RSS feed MyCommunicationLab provides an online feed from ABC News, updated hourly, to help students choose and research assignments, such as reflections on interpersonal skills demonstrated in news stories or features.

MySearchLab Pearson's MySearchLab™ is the easiest way for students to start a research assignment or paper. Complete with extensive help on the research process and four databases of credible and reliable source material, MySearchLab™ helps students to quickly and efficiently make the most of their research time. In addition to an extensive research database, MySearchLab™ also includes AutoCite, which assists in the creation of a "Works Cited" document.

Cutting Edge Technology

MediaShare With this new video upload tool, students are able to upload group assignments or interpersonal role plays for their instructor and classmates to watch (whether face to face or online) and provide online feedback and comments. MediaShare also includes the ability for instructors to attach a grade to an assignment, which can be exported into most learning management systems. Structured much like a social networking site, MediaShare can help to promote a sense of community among students.

Audio Chapter Summaries Every chapter includes an audio summary that can be streamed online, perfect for students reviewing material before a test or instructors reviewing material before class.

Online Administration

No matter what course management system you use—or if you do not use one at all but still wish to easily capture your students' grade and track their performance—Pearson has a **MyCommunicationLab** option to suit your needs. Contact one of Pearson's Technology Specialists for more information and assistance.

A **MyCommunicationLab** access code comes at no additional cost when packaged with select Pearson Communication texts. To get started, contact your local Pearson Publisher's Representative at **www.pearsonhighered.com/replocator.**

Acknowledgments

Any successful book is a team project involving many people. The three of us are grateful to our team, who helped us to make this book a reality. We are indebted to the scholars and teachers whose research and ideas form the basis for this book. We are thankful for our students, past and present, who have nurtured us and shaped how we approach teaching and learning. We are particularly thankful for the outstanding editorial support we have received from our colleagues and friends at Pearson/Allyn and Bacon. Karon Bowers, Editor-in-Chief, Communication, continues to be an important friend and mentor who is always there with needed support, information, and inspiration. Jeanne Zalesky, Senior Acquisitions Editor, supported our text through much of its development. Senior Development Editor, Carol Alper, has been there every step of the way with her years of experience and numerous track changes informing the development of this book. We would also like to thank the following hard working and incredibly talented individuals for their invaluable contributions to our book project: Melissa Mashburn, Senior Acquisitions Editor; Angela Mallowes, Associate Development Editor; Paul DeLuca, Senior Digital Media Editor; Lisa Dotson, Digital Media Editor; Stephanie Chaisson, Editorial Assistant; and Bayani de Leon, Associate Managing Editor.

We appreciate the many teachers who read the manuscript and helped us to get it right! We thank the following individuals for sharing their subject matter expertise with us:

Alicia Alexander, Southern Illinois University, Edwardsville

Patricia Amason, University of Arkansas

Natalie Bothwell, Lake Superior College

Nanci Burk, Glendale Community College

Kendra Burkey, Hesston College

Amy Capwell Burns, University of Toledo

Bobette Bushnell, Oregon State University

Rebecca Carlton, Indiana University, Southeast

Angela Cooke-Jackson, Eastern Kentucky University

Angela J. Cordova, Oregon University

Lisa Darnell, University of North Alabama

Karen Shearer Dunn, Queens University of Charlotte

Elaine Gale, California State University, Sacramento

Susan Hague, Delgado Community College

Meredith Harrigan, State University of New York, Geneseo

Pamela A. Hayward, Augusta State University

Sean Horan, DePaul University

Betty Kennan, Radford University

Marc Martin, San Francisco State University

Virginia M. McDermott, University of New Mexico

Rebecca Mikesell, University of Scranton

Laura Oliver, University of Texas at San Antonio

Michael P. Pagano, Fairfield University

Michele Poff, University of Washington

Marshall Prisbell, University of Nebraska at Omaha

Narissra Maria Punyanunt-Carter, Texas Technical University

Armeda Reitzel, Humboldt State University

Henry Rubin, Quincy College

Jennifer A. Samp, University of Georgia

Brian Simmons, Cascade College

Barbara J. Tarter, Marshall University

Maria Beatriz Torres, Minnesota State University at Mankato

Claire Van Ens, Kutztown University of Pennsylvania

Gust A. Yep, San Francisco State University

Phyllis S. Zrzavy, Franklin Pierce University

Each of us has been influenced by our villages, including colleagues, friends, teachers, and family members who have offered their support and inspiration for this project. Timothy Mottet is grateful for his many colleagues, graduate students, friends, and family members who have supported him throughout this book project. Timothy would like to thank Henry and Margaret Hauser, who, before their passing, endowed the Hauser Chair in Communication at the University of Texas–Pan American (UTPA). Mrs. Hauser, a high school speech teacher from Kansas, devoted her life to enhancing students' speaking skills. The Hausers' investment continues to enrich the Department of Communication at UTPA.

Timothy would like to thank his UTPA colleagues for their support: Yanrong Chang, Jane Cross, Cory Cunningham, Elizabeth Garcia, Jessica Raley, Dora Saavedra, Marisa Saavedra, Kimberly Selber, Jack Stanley, and Sharon Valdes. Timothy is especially fortunate to work under a very supportive and caring leadership team, including Dahlia Guerra, Paul Sale, and Ana Maria Rodriguez. Five graduate research assistants who deserve special recognition are Katrina Newell, Rebekha Sepulveda, Andrea Fuentes, Gil Castillo, and Monica Mercado. This impressive group of Hauser Graduate Research Assistants were instrumental in conducting research for this text.

Timothy would also like to thank his former colleagues at Texas State University–San Marcos for what he calls his "extended post-doc." It was there that many of the ideas reflected in this book were cooked. Special thanks are owed to Steve Beebe, Richard Cheatham, Sue Hall, Mary Hoffman, Marian Houser, Maureen Keeley, Phil Salem, Sue Stewart, and Lee Williams. Each of these individuals has influenced Timothy and his thinking in important ways. Timothy's friendships with Steve and Sue Beebe, Jim McCroskey and Virginia Richmond, Marilyn and Robert Root, and Chris and Jane Brayton serve as a constant source of encouragement and guidance. Timothy is grateful for the love of his family, including his parents Carol and Joe Mottet and other family members, including Julie and Rob Johnson, Dan and Barb Mottet, Doug and Jane Mottet, Maria and Alfredo Gonzalez, Prieto and Anita Gonzalez, and Emily and Birdie Gonzalez-Mottet. Finally, Timothy would like to extend a very special thanks to Rick Gonzalez for his love, patience, understanding, and support. Rick's intuitive understanding and practice of interpersonal communication has enriched Timothy's life in ways he never thought possible.

Sally Vogl-Bauer is incredibly grateful to her family and friends for their continued support throughout this journey. Not only did they make her laugh, they were also extraordinarily understanding when plans were repeatedly changed or canceled because of some pending deadline. Specifically, her husband John, mother Eleanor, and sisters

Cathy, Mary, and Sue (along with her beagle "girls") were essential to her sustained sanity. Although their due diligence at keeping her on task was not always what she wanted to hear at the moment, it helped her to keep her eye on the prize. She loves you and appreciates you more than you know.

In addition, Sally would like to thank her colleagues at the University of Wisconsin–Whitewater for the support provided to help with this project. Specifically, she would like to thank Denise Ehlen, John Stone, and Dick Haven for their assistance in helping to obtain research support for this project. She would also like to thank Barb Monfils and Barb Penington for all of their continued support and encouragement. Their understanding and friendship throughout this journey will not be forgotten.

There were also those who planted the seeds of Sally's love of interpersonal communication and learning long before this particular project germinated and eventually bore fruit. In particular, Nancy Burrell, Pamela Kalbfleisch, and Michael Beatty provided a strong foundation on which to build her career and develop the skills that would later be needed on this project. She learned much from each of them, and she can only hope that her work reflects well upon them.

Marian Houser would like to acknowledge the love and support of her family and friends during the writing of this book. As a new textbook author, she initially found this a daunting task. Her husband Steve was with her every step of the way with words of encouragement. And even though Marilyn, her mother, kept saying that she herself "could never accomplish something like writing a book," it is clear that Marian's love for writing and teaching come directly from Marilyn. Marian's friends Tim Mottet, Rick Gonzalez, Renee and DC Cowan, and Mary Hoffman created the perfect distractions at the perfect moments when relaxation was called for. Thank you, DivAmigos!

On a daily basis, Steve Beebe, Ann Burnette, Lee Williams, Cassandra LeClair-Underberg, Kristen LeBlanc, Alison David, and so many other Department of Communication members at Texas State University offered words of wisdom and guidance during this process. Graphic designer and colleague Malinda Murray provided invaluable talent in terms of translating many of my conceptual ideas into meaningful graphics. Equally important was the firm smile placed on Marian's face each and every day as her graduate students Brendan Radomski, Christina Fleuriet, Charles Rivas, Tony Longoria, Jason Estes, Dana Pedersen, Emily Honea, and so many others offered her new stories and ideas to add to her chapters. Their endless suggestions and comments sparked ideas for new material and examples.

None of this would have been possible without the initial guidance and inspiration of Marian's mentors, Ann Frymier, Gary Shulman, Marj and Larry Nadler, Paul Mongeau, and Jimmie Trent. These individuals at Miami University played a most valuable role by encouraging Marian to follow her dream. This process has continued with Marian's own group of mentees, Sean Horan, Renee Cowan, Lisa Furler, and Michael Burns, who have never lost touch and remain a part of her academic and her personal life. Their success makes this all worthwhile.

Timothy P. Mottet
Sally Vogl-Bauer
Marian L. Houser

About the Authors

Timothy P. Mottet is dean of the College of Fine Arts and Communication at Texas State University–San Marcos. Before returning to Texas State where he taught for several years, he chaired the Department of Communication at the University of Texas–Pan American (UTPA). In addition to being an award-winning teacher, Dr. Mottet is a nationally recognized communication researcher whose research examines the relationships among communication, personality, and cognitive functioning. Between 2002–2006, Dr. Mottet was listed among the top 20 most prolific researchers in the Communication Studies discipline.

Dr. Mottet has been an invited summer scholar at North Dakota State University and the University of Nebraska–Lincoln, where he taught graduate seminars in Communication, Learning, and the Brain. He is also a member of Harvard University's International Mind, Brain and Education Society. Away from the university, Dr. Mottet enjoys international travel, scuba diving, fitness, ballet, entertaining friends, and spending time with his partner Rick and two cats. If you have any questions for Dr. Mottet, please send him an email at tm15@txstate.edu. He enjoys hearing from students.

Sally Vogl-Bauer is professor in the Department of Communication at the University of Wisconsin–Whitewater (UWW). In addition to being an award-winning teacher, Dr. Vogl-Bauer has been recognized by the College of Arts and Communication at UWW for her research and service contributions. She is a former chair of the Department of Communication and has mentored numerous junior faculty members and students. She was one of the first Peer Coaches, a program designed to assist faculty and staff with their classroom instruction, as well as Scholar Mentors, a program designed to assist junior faculty in scholarly publishing, at UWW.

Dr. Vogl-Bauer is actively involved in learning and assessment practices and implementing the ideals of liberal education through the LEAP initiative (Learning Education and America's Promise) adopted at UWW and across the country. On a personal note, Dr. Vogl-Bauer enjoys landscaping, home renovation, bargain hunting, watching professional football (especially the Green Bay Packers), hanging out with friends and family, and spending time with her husband and two beagles. If you have any questions for Dr. Vogl-Bauer, feel free to email her at voglbaus@uww.edu.

Marian L. Houser is an associate professor in the Communication Studies Department at Texas State University–San Marcos. In addition to receiving numerous departmental teaching awards, Dr. Houser was the recent recipient of the President's Award for Scholarly and Creative Activities. In 2010, she received the Eastern Communication Association's Past-President's Award for her contributions to research and teaching.

Dr. Houser's primary research interest is in the area of communication in relationships with a focus on teacher–student relationships (traditional versus nontraditional students and face-to-face versus electronic) and student learning indicators as well as interpersonal communication with a focus on dating initiation and relational conflict. She was selected by the Dean and College Chairs to present her research at the 2011 Dean's Seminar. Though Dr. Houser has published and/or presented over sixty research studies, she takes great pride in the twenty-plus manuscripts she has published and/or presented with her students.

When Dr. Houser is not researching or mentoring students, she can be found relaxing with her husband and two Yorkshire terriers in the Texas hill country, kayaking down the Guadalupe River, or scuba diving around the world with the DivAmigos, daughter Staci, and son Drew. If you have any questions for Dr. Houser, feel free to email her at mh53@txstate.edu.

Your Interpersonal Communication

Interpersonal Communication and Personality

Simon, his wife Jill, and their two children, Monica and Seth, were invited to his parents' home to celebrate a special birthday. Simon's mother, Maria, was turning 70, and Simon's father, Marcus, had prepared a special dinner for the family. Marcus became quite frustrated and disappointed when, throughout the meal and afterward, he noticed that no one was paying attention to Maria. Rather than spending time with her and engaging her in conversation, Simon, Jill, Monica, and Seth all seemed to be distracted and obsessed with using their cell phones and laptop computers.

The next day, Marcus called his son in the evening to let him know how disappointed he was. Rather than the family communicating with each other and celebrating Maria's birthday, Marcus said, everyone appeared to be in their own little worlds and unaware that Maria was celebrating an important birthday. Marcus mentioned to Simon that Maria was feeling sad and disappointed, not because she wanted attention but because she wanted

to connect with her grandchildren and be a part of their lives.

Simon realized how each member of his family had a different type of personality that influenced not only that person's individual communication style, but also how they all interacted as a family. Simon wondered why and how his two children could be so different from one another when he and Jill had raised them similarly. Seth talks constantly and tries hard to control everyone else's behaviors. When he's not talking, he's texting or on Facebook. Monica, on the other hand, is exceptionally quiet and reserved. She rarely engages others in a conversation or adds anything to a conversation. She would rather be alone and playing video games. Jill, Simon's wife, is assertive, and many people unfortunately misinterpret her assertiveness as her being pushy or aggressive. Simon considers himself to be a quiet person, but he can easily communicate with others when necessary.

It wasn't until after this phone call from his father that Simon recognized the lack of interpersonal communication

CHAPTER OBJECTIVES

AFTER READING THIS CHAPTER, you will understand:

1 How interpersonal communication is defined and how both your biology and culture influence your interpersonal communication.

2 The components of the communication process: source, receiver, messages, channels, noise, feedback, and context.

3 The difference between the content and relational levels of interpersonal communication.

4 How to define and explain the five communication traits that make up the Big Five model of personality.

5 How your biology and personality influence your communication and the development of your communication skills and behaviors.

6 The six interpersonal communication motives and how these motives influence the communication in your relationships.

in his family and thought about how each family member's personality might be influencing their interpersonal communication. He also became aware of how his and Jill's use of communication technology at inappropriate times could be influencing how his children use their technology.

What do you think? While reading this chapter, consider how you might answer the following questions to help Simon:

- What are some of the reasons why Simon's family members failed to communicate in an appropriate way with each other around the dinner table?

- How will this lack of interpersonal communication eventually affect the family as well as individual family members?

- How can Simon address his concerns with his family without his children thinking that he is overreacting or not in touch with the 21st century family?

We will revisit Simon's story at the end of the chapter and use the content discussed in this chapter to develop a communication plan to help Simon.

AFTER READING THIS CHAPTER,
you will be able to:

1 Adapt your communication to accommodate your relational partner's interpersonal communication motives as well as to help your partner adapt his or her communication to accommodate your interpersonal communication motives.

2 Appropriately use communication technologies such as cell phones, social networking sites (e.g., Facebook, MySpace), and text-messaging.

AFTER COMPLETING THE SELF-ASSESSMENTS,
you will learn about:

1 You and your relational partner's interpersonal communication motive profiles.

2 You and your relational partner's interpersonal communication motives and how they influence your communication with each other.

This book is about the nature of communication that takes place between two people. When two people come together, they usually use communication as a way to understand and influence each other. They want to know why a person communicates and behaves the way he or she does. They want to understand what to expect from a person, including how a person will behave and possibly respond to a particular situation.

Using communication to create understanding and influence is more complex than most people think. For example, you send a message to a person with the intent that he or she will understand you. Put simply, you hope that Message Sent = Message Received.[1] However, sometimes the messages we send are not the messages that others receive. For some reason, our messages are misinterpreted. This misinterpretation can result in a number of unexpected outcomes, such as frustration, worry, hurt feelings, and disappointment. For example, suppose you said, "Let's meet at Taco Bell for lunch at noon," but you forgot to mention which Taco Bell. You assumed that the other person would understand the location, but this was not the case. He went to the other Taco Bell in town, and after waiting for an hour, he thought he had been stood up or that you had been in an accident. In other words Message Sent ≠ Message Received.

> The meeting of two personalities is like the contact of two chemical substances; if there is any reaction, both are transformed.
>
> —CARL JUNG

What's frustrating for most people is how such a simple message (Let's meet at Taco Bell for lunch at noon) that is missing one small but important piece of information (the specific location of the Taco Bell), can end up hurting or worrying another person. Unfortunately, it happens more often than you might think. What complicates the miscommunication is that we have a tendency to blame the other person for not understanding us, which only adds fuel to the relational fire. You might hear a person saying, "What didn't you understand?" or "I can't believe you were confused by my voice mail message" or "You knew which Taco Bell I was referring to." Rather than blaming others for not understanding you, we encourage you to take responsibility for your interpersonal communication. Instead of stating, "I can't believe you didn't understand what I was saying," you might say instead, "I have failed you in my communication."

Although there are a number of reasons why the messages we send don't always equal the messages others receive, there are consequences for miscommunication. You can inadvertently hurt someone's feelings when your intention was to help them, or you can be perceived negatively when someone "twists your words" in an argument. This book focuses on how to minimize the negative consequences of miscommunication by encouraging both relational partners to take responsibility for the interpersonal communication that is yielded from a relationship.

To help you begin to understand the interpersonal communication process, this chapter is divided into four sections. The first section defines interpersonal communication and discusses the influences of nature and nurture on our communication. The second section describes three characteristics that make interpersonal communication different from other types of communication. The third section explains how personality and communication are related and gives you the opportunity to assess your interpersonal communication motives. The fourth and final section focuses on how gender, culture, and technology influence interpersonal communication.

Understanding Your Interpersonal Communication

One of the goals of this book is to help you develop the interpersonal communication skills you need to be successful. We begin this process by defining interpersonal communication, identifying the influences of nature and nurture on your social skill development, and sharing information that will help you value your communication with others.

Defining Interpersonal Communication

Interpersonal communication *is a transactional process that occurs when two people use verbal and nonverbal messages to create understanding and to influence each other to manage the relationship.* Although there are a number of different terms in this definition that are important and need clarifying, creating understanding and influencing each other are two concepts that set interpersonal communication apart from other forms of communication. For example, Sarah and Leo are on two different pages in their relationship, and they don't understand each other. Through their communication, they're trying to get on the same page. Sarah would like more space in the relationship, and she communicates in a manner by which she hopes to influence Leo to give her some more breathing room. At the same time, Leo would like Sarah to be more respectful of his family. He influences Sarah to return his mother's phone calls and emails.

Transactional Nature of Interpersonal Communication. When you communicate with another person who is physically present, the communication is **transactional**, meaning that you send and receive messages simultaneously. As you talk to someone, you also respond to that person's messages, even while you speak.[2] Whether you're having an engaging conversation with your best friend in a coffee shop or trying to avoid a conversation with a person by avoiding eye contact and sticking to text-messaging, your nonverbal behavior provides information to others about your emotions and interest, or lack of interest. The transactional nature of communication suggests that you cannot *not* communicate. Ultimately, people judge you by your behavior, not by your intent. And since you behave in some way (even when you try to avoid a conversation by text-messaging), there is the potential for someone to make sense out of your behavior.

Interpersonal communication is a process in which two people send and receive messages to each other at the same time. As you talk to someone, you also respond to that person's nonverbal messages.

Components of Interpersonal Communication. Key elements of interpersonal communication include the source, receiver, message, channel, noise, feedback, and context. Figure 1.1 is one way to illustrate the interpersonal communication process.

■ *Source.* The **source** is the person who has a thought or a feeling and wants to express this idea and feeling to another person. Thinking about the best way to express oneself is referred to as **encoding**, which is the process of putting your thoughts and feelings into words and nonverbal cues. Encoding is an intentional act of thinking about your goals and the best way to meet your goals through your communication. When you ask yourself, "How can I say this without the other person taking it the wrong way?" you're engaged in the encoding process.

■ *Receiver.* The person listening to the message is the **receiver**. The receiver is responsible for **decoding** messages, which is a process of interpreting and evaluating the other person's messages. When you make sense out of other people's messages, you're decoding.

■ *Messages.* We communicate with others using both verbal and nonverbal messages. By **verbal messages**, we mean language. **Nonverbal messages** refer to any messages other than verbal, meaning that they're non-language-based.

FIGURE 1.1

The Interpersonal
Communication Model

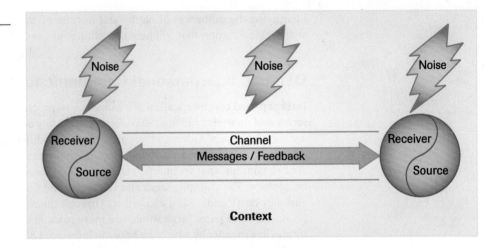

- *Channel.* Verbal and nonverbal messages are transmitted from source to receiver through the **channel**, which is the pathway that messages travel and usually includes our senses: visual/sight, auditory/hearing, tactile/touch, and olfactory/smell.
- *Noise.* Anything that distorts or interferes with the communication process is considered **noise**. From the physical noise of someone's cell phone vibrating in a backpack to the psychological noise of daydreaming or worrying about the amount of work that must be completed before you go home for the day, noise can disrupt the interpersonal communication process.
- *Feedback.* Your verbal and nonverbal responses to another person's message are referred to as **feedback**. Without feedback, communication is less likely to be effective. Feedback can seek additional information or simply confirm that the message has been interpreted.
- *Context.* The physical, historical, and psychological communication environment is referred to as **context**. All communication takes place in some context, and the context affects how people communicate. For example, suppose you are telling another person about a problem you're having with a colleague at work. The language choices you make and the nonverbal gestures you decide to use depend on where you're physically located (e.g., workplace, café, bedroom), on how long you've known the other person (historical), and the psychological contexts or the two personalities that two people bring to the conversation. For example, someone with very low self-esteem might interpret your messages in a defensive manner, and someone who is assertive will not be afraid to speak up and defend himself or herself.

Identifying Nature/Nurture Intersections of Interpersonal Communication

One of the features that makes this book unique is our focus on how nature and nurture work together to influence interpersonal communication. Researchers have labeled the biological influence as "nature" and the cultural influence as "nurture."[3] Some communication researchers argue that we're *born* with the ability to communicate effectively, which is the nature perspective. Others argue that we can *learn* how to communicate effectively, which is the nurture perspective. Although some researchers argue that biology (or nature) rather than culture (or nurture) plays the larger role in influencing our communication behaviors, we take an interactionist position, which means that our communication behaviors are influenced by both our nature and our nurture.[4] Rather than there being an "either/or" dualism, our communication is influenced by both our biology *and* our culture.

Nature Influences. Communication researchers are beginning to better understand how the genes you inherited influence your personality and communication behaviors.[5] When you hear people say that your voice or mannerisms are just like your mother's or father's, they're referring to the impact that your biology has on your communication. A large percentage of your communication behaviors is heavily influenced by how your brain functions; it's natural.[6] If you have ever wondered why you're shy or why you experience anxiety when communicating with others, we now know that you did not necessarily *learn* to become shy or anxious when communicating with others. Instead, you may have been *born* shy and anxious; it's a natural process that is a result of your brain functioning.[7]

One of the ways to study how nature influences your communication is to study your personality, which is one of the unique features of this textbook. Knowing how two people's personalities influence the communication that is created through a relationship allows us to better understand why the relationship works or doesn't work and, more important, what we need to do to enhance the relationship. Because personality is such a big feature in this book, you will see this icon in the margins whenever we're making reference to your personality and how it influences your interpersonal communication.

Included in this book are a number of self-assessment instruments that we encourage you to complete. They will allow you to better understand your communication motivations. We refer to this feature as *Assess Your Communication Personality*, since your personality plays an instrumental role in both your motivation for communicating and your communication behaviors. We encourage you to take the time to complete the self-assessment quizzes in the text or online. Once you have completed them, we help you to interpret your scores, and we provide you with a checklist of recommendations on how you can enhance your interpersonal communication in a "What Can I Do Now?" feature.

Nurture Influences. **Culture** is a learned system of knowledge, behavior, attitudes, beliefs, values, and norms that is shared by a group of people.[8] Through your nurturing, or how your parents and other family members raised you, you learned your culture. For example some parents teach their children how to greet another person by shaking the other person's hand and looking him or her in the eye, which is a common way of greeting others in the United States. Other parents may teach their children to bow or keep their eyes directed towards the floor when greeting an adult. Children are not biologically programmed to do so. It is a learned behavior.

Many communication researchers argue that communication behaviors are learned primarily by watching and modeling others' communication behaviors.[9] People have a tendency to imitate behavior. For example, communication researcher Kory Floyd found that the affection sons received from their fathers impacted the affection these sons expressed to their own children.[10] In other words, sons learn how to be fathers by modeling their own fathers' communication behaviors and the culture within their own family.

Being able to see and understand how culture influences your communication development is important when managing relationships, even those within your family. For example, family members who live and work in remote and rural parts of the country are likely to talk about experiences and events that are different from those who live in large urban centers.

Knowing that a part of your communication is influenced by your biology and your culture is the first step in becoming aware of how these factors influence communication and how you might need to adapt your communication to accommodate other people's biological and cultural differences.

Valuing Interpersonal Communication

Interpersonal communication skills are life skills. Regardless of your field of study or your personal and professional goals, you will use the skills that you learn from this book on a daily basis. If you're like most people, you depend on a number of relationships to get through your day. At home, you need family members to provide you with emotional support and to take part in managing the house and perhaps children. At work, you need your manager and co-workers to help you reach your goals. At school, you need your teachers to provide you with information and skills and with additional direction to help you complete the assignment. You need your friends to include you in their social activities so that you don't feel left out. Communication is an enormous part of what makes each of these relationships work. Without communication, your relationships would falter and eventually come to a halt. Not only will developing interpersonal communication life skills help you to stay physically and psychologically healthy, but these life skills will also help you at home and at work.

Enhances the Quality of Your Physical Health. People who have well-developed interpersonal communication skills are healthier than people with less-developed interpersonal skills. It has been shown that interpersonal communication skills reduce loneliness, and loneliness is positively related to a number of physical and psychological problems.[11] Although being married or in a committed relationship has a number of challenges, the research data consistently show that people who are coupled and in constructive relationships are significantly healthier than noncoupled people and therefore live longer.[12] For example, people in committed relationships are less likely to smoke or drink heavily than people who are single, divorced, or widowed. Being in a committed, healthy relationship has also been correlated with lower rates of cardiovascular disease, cancer, and respiratory diseases.

Enhances the Quality of Your Personal Life. Research suggests that parents who share their own thoughts and feelings with their children also have children who are academically, socially, and emotionally well adjusted.[13] A survey of 1,280 people ages 13 to 24 conducted by MTV and the Associated Press found that the number one answer to the question, "What makes you happy?" was spending time with family members.[14] Rather than spending time with friends or believing that money, cars, or trips will make a young person happy, they appear to be the happiest when spending time with members of their family. Also, teenagers and young adults have been found to be more susceptible to symptoms of depression when they perceive lower levels of trust and communication in their relationships with their parents.[15]

Enhances the Quality of Your Professional Life. The workforce is growing more diverse, and there is an increasing need for people with well-developed interpersonal communication skills who can work with different types of people. Researchers predict that by 2050, whites will make up only 46% of the U.S. population, and blacks will make up 15%. Hispanics, who make up about 15% of the U.S. population in 2010, will account for 30% in 2050. The percentage of Asians in the U.S. population, which is currently about 5%, is projected to increase to 9% by 2050.[16]

As the workplace becomes more diverse, you're going to need to be comfortable working with others who are unlike you in a number of important ways. Your colleagues might have a different belief system than yours. They might not share your attitudes and values. Their life experiences will probably be different from your experiences. Through your interpersonal communication skills, you will be able to appreciate their unique qualities while also being able to identify common goals and interests. In a recent survey of recruiters from companies with more than 50,000 employees, interpersonal communication skills were cited as the single most important decisive factor in selecting new employees.[17] The survey, conducted by the University of Pittsburgh's Katz Business School, points out that interpersonal communication skills that allow you the ability to work with diverse others are the main factor contributing to job success.[18]

CHECKING YOUR UNDERSTANDING
Models of Communication

Take a few minutes to check your understanding of key concepts in this part of the chapter by answering the following questions:

1. How is interpersonal communication defined and what does it mean when we say that interpersonal communication is transactional?

2. Differentiate the nature and nurture influences on interpersonal communication. What does it mean when researchers say that communication is influenced by nature and nurture? Do you agree with the researchers that both nature and nurture play a role in your communication development, or do you believe that one of these influences plays a larger role than the other? Explain.

3. How do the various components of the communication model fit together? To answer this question, do the following: (A) Develop a communication model that includes source, receiver, message, channel, noise, feedback, and context. (B) Define each of the terms.

4. Describe how interpersonal communication enhances the quality of your physical health as well as your personal and professional lives.

Characteristics of Interpersonal Communication

A number of important characteristics make interpersonal communication unique and different from other forms of communication. Three of the more important characteristics are content and relational levels, impersonal and intimate continuum, and irreversible and unrepeatable.

This popular film highlights the confusing nature of interpersonal relationships and how people misinterpret messages by not focusing on both the content and relational dimensions of a message.

Interpersonal Communication Creates Meaning on Content and Relational Levels

Messages create meaning on two different levels: content and relational.[19] The **content level** in your message is *what* your message is about and is usually conveyed by using verbal messages. The **relational level** focuses not on *what* is said but on *how* it's said. Relational meanings are usually created by using nonverbal messages, such as tone of voice, eye contact, and posture. Here's an example to illustrate the difference between content and relational levels of messages: Rudy and Sharon are on a first date. When saying good night, Rudy informs Sharon that he will give her a call. Unfortunately, Sharon pays attention only to the message's content ("I will give you a call") and not to the message's relational cues (Rudy's voice was insincere, and he did not make eye contact with Sharon). Sharon continuously monitors her phone to make sure she doesn't miss Rudy's phone call. The call never comes. If Sharon had paid as much attention to the relational cues in Rudy's message as to the content of his message, she probably would have interpreted his message more accurately and not expected him to call her.

The following is another example that illustrates the difference between content and relational levels of messages. Read the following verbal message aloud seven different times, each time stressing the word in boldface:

"**I** didn't say you had an attitude problem."

"I **didn't** say you had an attitude problem."

"I didn't **say** you had an attitude problem."

"I didn't say **you** had an attitude problem."

"I didn't say you **had** an attitude problem."

"I didn't say you had an **attitude** problem."

"I didn't say you had an attitude **problem**."

Do you hear how the content of the verbal message (*what you say*) can create seven different meanings based on your use of nonverbal messages (*how you say it*)? Your stressing the word in bold is a type of nonverbal message that can change how others interpret what you say. You will learn more about nonverbal messages in Chapter 5.

Interpersonal Communication Occurs on an Impersonal–Intimate Continuum

In your daily life, you encounter a wide variety of relationships. Although all relationships require communication, not all relationships require interpersonal communication. Figure 1.2 illustrates the relationship continuum. On one end (the blue zone) are impersonal relationships such as the ones you have with a checkout clerk at

FIGURE 1.2

The Relationship Continuum

the grocery store. Unless you know the checkout clerk, you might exchange a greeting, money, and a good–bye, and the relationship is over. Unfortunately, some of these impersonal relationships occur without any verbal messages and minimal nonverbal messages being exchanged. For example, have you ever walked into a convenience store, purchased an item, and exchanged money without speaking a word or even making eye contact with the person behind the counter?

On the other end of the continuum (the yellow zone) are highly intimate relationships such as the ones you typically have with your best friend, husband, wife, life partner, girlfriend, or boyfriend. Through your interpersonal communication, intimacy can be achieved in all types of relationships, including friendships, relationships between partners, and relationships among family members. As you and your relational partner begin sharing more information and more in-depth information with each other, you begin to perceive your relationship as being more intimate. You know that you're becoming intimate with another person when you are both motivated to spend time together and to interact with each other. You will learn more about relational development and intimate relationships in Chapters 8, 9, and 10.

In the middle of the continuum (the green zone) are the bulk of your relationships, some closer than others. As you move closer to the right, the relationships become more intimate. As you move closer to the left, the relationships become more impersonal.

Interpersonal Communication Is Irreversible and Unrepeatable

Because interpersonal communication is an ongoing process, it's both irreversible and unrepeatable. It's irreversible in that once you have communicated something, you can't take it back. At times, you might say something to another person that you wish you hadn't said. You quickly say, "I didn't mean that" or "Forget what I just said." Unfortunately, you can't unspeak your words once they've been spoken.

Interpersonal communication is also unrepeatable. If you've ever tried to recapture an intimate conversation or a special moment that you had with someone, you realize that it's next to impossible to recreate the moment. You try hard to recapture the evening, making sure the menu is the same. You play the same music and wear the same clothes. Unfortunately, the evening doesn't have the same feel. Why is this? There are a number of reasons. Even if only a week has passed, you and the other person are not the same two people you were one week ago. Much has happened. You have both lived through another seven days of life. You might not be feeling the same. You might have a slight headache. The other person might have new worries and anxieties about work that were not there last week. Your interpersonal communication is highly susceptible to all of these contextual and psychological factors, which make it difficult to recreate an interpersonal moment.

CHECKING YOUR UNDERSTANDING

Understanding Interpersonal Communication

It's time again to check your understanding of the key concepts that were discussed in this section of the chapter. How easy is it for you to answer the following questions?

1. What is the difference between the content and relational levels of interpersonal communication? Which level is more closely related to nonverbal messages?

2. How would you answer the following questions: Is all interpersonal communication intimate communication? Does interpersonal communication include impersonal communication? Explain.

3. Why is it important to understand that interpersonal communication is both irreversible and unrepeatable?

Personality and Interpersonal Communication

Your personality plays an important role in your interpersonal communication. Psychologist Carl Jung once said, "The meeting of two personalities is like the contact of two chemical substances; if there is any reaction, both are transformed." You know from first-hand experience that some relationships have chemistry where you and the other person are as Jung mentioned—transformed. You become better people as a result of the relationship. Unfortunately, other relationships are more like a failed chemistry lab experiment where there's no chemical reaction or the experiment blows up in your face. One way to get a better handle on the chemistry in your relationships is to examine personality.

Personality is the total psychological makeup of an individual—a profile that reflects experiences, motivations, attitudes, beliefs, values, and behaviors.[20] Your personality is a combination of various **traits**, which are distinguishable ways in which one individual differs from others.[21] In some ways, your personality is like a very specific mixture of chemicals or traits that make you as unique as your fingerprint. No one has a personality exactly like your own. Your communication is an expression of your personality. For example, listen to how your friends describe other people. It's common to hear them describing communication behaviors.

"She's very easy to talk to."

"He talks too much."

"She's very quiet."

"He's loud and funny."

"She's always defensive."

"He's so demanding."

"She's very warm and approachable."

"He's cold and distant."

Have you ever noticed how some people make communication look easy? They walk into a room, introduce themselves to others, carry on conversations with ease, and make others feel good about themselves. They're social magnets. People like them and are attracted to them. They have a number of high-quality relationships.

FIGURE 1.3

The Big Five Personality Profile for a Single Person

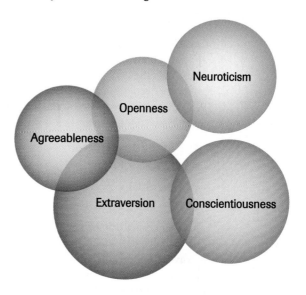

Students often ask, "How do they do it?" "Why are they so socially skilled and I'm not?" "Why do I have such a difficult time introducing myself or initiating a conversation with others without making a fool of myself?" "Why does it come so naturally for them and it's so unnatural for me?" These important questions deserve answers. One way to answer these questions is to more closely examine the role of personality in interpersonal communication, which is a unique feature of this particular textbook.

Understanding Your Personality

Psychologists Robert McCrae and Paul Costa are responsible for identifying and labeling a collection of personality traits known as the **Big Five personality model**, which includes openness, conscientiousness, extraversion, agreeableness, and neuroticism.[22] Although the exact number of personality traits has been questioned over the years, the McCrae and Costa Big Five personality model is widely accepted among today's psychologists and communication researchers.[23] Figure 1.3 illustrates the Big Five personality model for a single individual. According to McCrae and Costa, your personality is a composite of these five traits, with some traits playing a larger role than others in your communication behavior.

Openness. People who are **open** are intellectually curious, have an appreciation for art, and tend to be imaginative and creative. They tend to be more aware of their feelings. Individuals who are open to experience also tend to be highly individualistic and unconventional. They enjoy being unique. People with low scores on openness tend to have narrow and common interests. Put another away, they like what others like. They tend to prefer what's familiar rather than what's novel or unique. Here are a few items that describe a person with a high level of openness:

- I am full of ideas.
- I am quick to understand things.

- I have a vivid imagination.
- I spend time reflecting on things.
- I have a rich vocabulary.

Conscientiousness. People who are **conscientious** are goal-driven; they develop plans and work hard to achieve their goals. They are perceived to be intelligent and dependable. They "walk the talk," meaning that they do what they say they will do. They can also be compulsive perfectionists and workaholics. Some might perceive them to be stuffy and boring. People who are not conscientious are perceived to be unreliable, lazy, and living for the moment. Here are a few items that describe a person with a high level of conscientiousness:

- I am always prepared.
- I follow a schedule.
- I like order.
- I pay attention to details.
- I get chores done right away.

Extraversion. People who are **extraverted** like to talk and socialize. They tend to be high-energy and action-oriented individuals who like to say "Yes" to exciting opportunities. Extraverted individuals assert themselves and like to draw attention to themselves whenever possible. Low extraverted people (introverts) tend to be quiet and enjoy their own company. Unfortunately, their lack of social involvement is sometimes misperceived as their being shy or depressed. Here are a few items that describe a person with a high level of extraversion:

- I am the life of the party.
- I feel comfortable around people.
- I start conversations.
- I don't mind being the center of attention.
- I talk to a lot of different people at parties.

Your personality makes you unique. Even brothers and sisters who have the same parents and were raised in the same manner can behave and interact with others in an entirely different way. For example, she's highly extraverted and open to new ideas. Her brother, on the other hand, is highly conscientious and introverted.

Agreeableness. People who are **agreeable** tend to be positive. They get along with others and are considerate, friendly, generous, and willing to extend a helping hand when needed. Disagreeable individuals tend to be selfish and to be unconcerned about other people. Agreeable people tend to be more popular. Others are attracted to agreeable people and tend to avoid disagreeable people. Here are a few items that describe a person with a high level of agreeableness:

- I am interested in people.
- I am aware of others' emotions.
- I have a soft heart.
- I take time out for others.
- I sympathize with others' feelings.

Neuroticism. People who are **neurotic** tend to experience feelings of anxiety, anger, and depression. They are emotionally reactive, and their emotional reactions are usually intense. Highly neurotic individuals tend to perceive

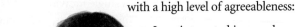

ordinary situations as threatening and have little patience. They have a negative attentional focus, which means that they tend to focus on the negative and overlook the positive aspects in their environments. Conversely, low neurotic individuals are less easily upset and are less emotionally reactive. They tend to be calm and emotionally stable. Here are a few items that describe a person with a high level of neuroticism:

- I am easily disturbed.
- I get irritated easily.
- I get stressed out easily.
- I have frequent mood swings.
- I worry about things.

Table 1.1 provides a quick review of the Big Five factors that comprise a personality.

Rather than having a single personality trait, you have a personality that is made up of a variety of traits, which form a personality profile. Some traits are so strong that they influence your communication behavior regardless of the situation you find yourself in.[24] For example if you're highly extraverted, you probably talk too much in libraries and theaters where most people tend to be quiet. On the other hand, being extraverted can allow you to be more adaptable in your communication behavior. By becoming aware of your personality and how it influences your communication behavior, you're better able to modify your communication behaviors making them appropriate for the situation or context.

Two questions that people often ask are "What personality profiles make the perfect relationship?" and "Can I change my personality or my significant other's?" There are no simple answers to these questions. People with all different types of personality profiles can work together. It depends on how well you and your significant other communicate with each other. Although personality influences how you communicate, it's your communication that ultimately influences the quality of your relationships.

In terms of the second question, the research suggests that your personality can change over your lifetime; however, the amount of change is a question that researchers are still investigating.[25] Rather than investing time in changing your personality or the other person's personality, it's probably better to invest that time in trying to learn as much as possible about each other's personalities and how these personalities influence the communication that is created in your relationship.

TABLE 1.1

Review of the Big Five Personality Model	
Trait	**Description**
Openness	Being curious, original, intellectual, creative, and open to new ideas.
Conscientiousness	Being organized, systematic, punctual, achievement-oriented, and dependable.
Extraversion	Being outgoing, talkative, and sociable and enjoying social situations.
Agreeableness	Being affable, tolerant, sensitive, trusting, kind, and warm.
Neuroticism	Being anxious, irritable, temperamental, and moody.

As we examine how personality impacts your interpersonal communication, we're also interested in better understanding what makes communication ethical. Throughout this book we introduce a number of different ethical issues as they apply to a particular concept in a boxed feature titled *Ethics in Interpersonal Communication*. An **ethic** is a belief, value, or moral principle by which we determine what is right and wrong. We use our ethics when making important decisions. Below is an ethical issue we would like you to think about since it's related to your personality.

Connecting Personality, Communication, and Biology

For several decades researchers have been interested in better understanding why we communicate the way we do. The general belief was that our communication behavior

ETHICS **in interpersonal communication**

Can Your Personality Influence the Ethics of Your Communication?

Machiavellianism is a personality trait that influences not only your communication, but also the ethics of your communication. The concept of Machiavellianism is based on the 16th century writings of Niccolò Machiavelli, who offered advice on how to get other people to do things for you. Researchers are still uncertain about how a person acquires a Machiavellian personality trait, but like most, it's probably a combination of nature and nurture influences. People who are high in Machiavellianism (high Machs) differ from those who are low in Machiavellianism (low Machs) in that high Machs "manipulate more, win more, and are persuaded less . . . in situations in which subjects interact face to face with others."[26] High Machs believe that the ends justify the means. Put another way, high Machs do whatever it takes to be successful, including restricting others' choices and using misleading and false information in their communication.[27] High Machs tend to prevail in situations involving emotional involvement more often than low Machs do because high Machs have the ability to ignore how others are feeling and concentrate more on winning, whereas low Machs care about how others are feeling.[28] Additionally, high Machs often view unethical behaviors as being acceptable.[29]

The research examining Machiavellianism and communication introduces a number of interesting questions related to interpersonal communication. What do you think about the following questions?

- Can a personality trait actually cause someone to be unethical in his or her communication? Can't a person choose not to be unethical in his or her communication?
- Are all high Machs unethical in their communication?
- Can a person be held responsible for communication that may be unethical if it is personality-driven?
- Should a low Mach who is in a relationship with a high Mach be worried?
- Can a high Mach learn to become a low Mach? Can a low Mach learn to become a high Mach?

mycommunicationlab Log onto our MyCommunicationLab Self-Assessment Library (www.mycommunicationlab.com) and assess your Machiavellianism by completing the interactive assessment. Encourage your relational partner to do the same. Then you can compare and contrast your scores and begin to understand better how your Machiavellianism may influence your interpersonal communication.

A child's behavior and communication style is the product of nature/nurture influences. Parents contribute to the genetic makeup of their children's brain structures and how they raise their children shapes how brain systems develop, adapt, and respond to parent–child interactions.

was learned through our nurturing at home as well as our involvement with different social groups, such as friends, co-workers, and community organizations. This perspective became known as the learning paradigm of communicative behavior.

Recently, researchers have challenged this learning paradigm, arguing that our biology is largely responsible for our communication behavior.[30] Researchers Michael Beatty and Jim McCroskey have developed what has become known as the communibiological paradigm for understanding the causes of communicative behavior.[31] Through a program of research, Beatty, McCroskey, and their colleagues have provided convincing evidence that our communication behavior or our social style is in large part genetically influenced and inherited from our parents and grandparents.

Beatty and McCroskey began their research program by linking communication behaviors to specific neurological brain structures.[32] They made this connection in an interesting way. First, they demonstrated how our communication behavior is a function of our psychology. Second, they revealed how our psychology (personality) is related to our biology and specifically neurology (i.e., brain circuitry), which is largely influenced by the genes we inherited from our family members. Figure 1.4 shows these relationships.

To illustrate the relationships between neurology, psychology, and communication and to show why they're important, we're going to share the following example of Peter, a compulsive talker. His compulsive talking irritates most people and as a result, he has few friends. In an effort to make more friends, Peter tends to talk more, thus leading him through a vicious cycle that results in greater loneliness. How can someone like Peter break the cycle?

FIGURE 1.4

The relationships between neurology, psychology, and communication

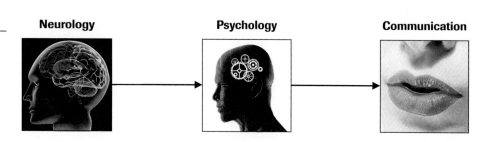

We believe that Peter talks a lot because he has a very hyperactive extraverted personality trait that motivates him to talk too much.[34] This hyperactive personality trait is the result of specific brain structures that are a part of Peter's DNA he inherited from his parents and grandparents.[35] Put another way, Peter's biology (neurology) is influencing his psychology (personality), which is influencing his social style (communication).

Learning that his compulsive talk behavior is, in part, influenced by his biology allows Peter to better understand himself and why he is the way he is. In addition to wanting to learn more about his biology and personality, he is more aware of his social style and he tries very hard to monitor his compulsive nature to talk. When others learn that Peter has an awareness of his personality and communication behaviors, they become more understanding.

Assessing Your Interpersonal Communication Motives

One of the ways in which you can begin assessing your interpersonal communication is by understanding your **interpersonal communication motives**, which are relatively stable, personality-like characteristics that explain *why* people communicate with others

NATURE/NURTURE intersections

Fitting into Your Parents' Genes

Scholars continue to shed light on what is known about genetics, heredity, and the role of parents in the development of infants. These findings suggest that genetics/heredity, parental behaviors, and communicative interactions all make important contributions to the ways in which humans develop across the lifespan.[36]

It is understood that children inherit their genetic makeup from their biological parents. This led communication scholars to examine the degree to which someone's communication traits were linked to inherited cognitive brain structures. The results of these studies suggest that, depending on the communication trait, genetics explains a moderate to large portion of why we may be predisposed to communicate in certain ways.[37] While these findings are very important to the study of communication traits, this is just the beginning.

Researchers outside the field of communication are discovering that our brain structures have a great deal of plasticity (or flexibility) and can be shaped by the environment and our interactions with others, especially when humans are very young. This is when parents' verbal and nonverbal behaviors are instrumental in shaping how their children's genetic predispositions get reinforced, modified, or altered after birth.[38] These findings suggest two different types of parental contributions. First, biological parents contribute the genetic makeup for the brain systems that are associated with communication traits that their biological

children receive. Second, in raising children, parents or caregivers (who may or may not be the biological parents) shape how the infants' brain systems develop, adapt, and respond to parent–child interactions.[39] Finally, the environment in which parents and children live often influences parental behaviors and thus child development.

On the surface, these connections might not seem highly controversial. As we learn more about how brain systems (a) influence communication trait development, (b) are modified by the communicative behaviors of parents (or other caregivers) with their infants, and (c) are studied in the environmental context within which they develop, the questions that scholars ask are beginning to change. It is no longer a case of nature versus nurture; rather, the question is how nature influences nurture and vice versa. But before these approaches could be merged into a more cohesive picture, *each of the above points had to be supported by research*. This required a great deal of time, energy, and sometimes controversy on the part of lots of individuals in various disciplines, and the learning is by no means complete.

As we learn more about genetics and brain systems, communication traits, and environmental factors, the role of parents and caregivers becomes even more important, not less for children. If parental verbal and nonverbal behaviors can modify how brain systems develop and adapt *after* birth, teaching parents how to interact with their children is more important than ever before.

and *how* people communicate to satisfy their needs.[40] What motivates one person to communicate and to get involved in a relationship might not be the same as what motivates another person to get involved in a relationship. It's also important to understand that just because your motives are stable or resistant to change, this doesn't mean that you can't override your motives when necessary. For example, when communicating with your boss, you consciously get command of your control needs and yield to your boss. Your ability to adapt and override your personality, when needed, is a very important part of what this book is about. *By becoming aware of your personality, you learn to have more control over your personality.* Before reading any further, we recommend that you assess your interpersonal communication motives by completing the measure in the self-assessment box on pages 20–21.

Communication researcher Rebecca Rubin and her colleagues identified a set of six interpersonal communication motives, the ones you just assessed in the self-assessment instrument, that influence you to communicate in a particular way to satisfy your relational needs.[41] Again, your interpersonal communication motives are related to your personality in that your motives are unique and distinguish you from other people. According to Rubin, a need is something that is lacking in your relationships, and a motive is a reason for action. Put another way, your motive is your goal or plan for fulfilling your need. Here are a couple of examples to illustrate the difference between a need and a motive:

- Ellen always has an agenda when she interacts with her friends. She is always telling her friends what to do rather than asking them for their input. She has a *need* for things to go her way in her relationships. She is *motivated* to fulfill this need by communicating in a controlling manner by telling people what to do rather than asking them for their advice.

- Sam desperately wants to be your friend. He's always calling and inviting himself over to your house. He works too hard to be your friend. You avoid him, which only causes him to communicate more. Sam has a *need* for companionship; he's lonely. He is *motivated* to fulfill this need by getting himself included in your life.

The examples above illustrate two (control, inclusion) of the six interpersonal communication motives that Rubin and her colleagues identified. **Pleasure** is when you communicate to be entertained. You communicate with others to have fun and for excitement. **Affection** is when you communicate to express love toward others or to be loved by others. You have a need to initiate and maintain relationships based on love, adoration, and devotion. **Inclusion** is when you communicate to be a member of a group, to be affiliated with others, or to have friends and companions. You communicate to establish and maintain satisfactory relationships with others. **Escape** is when you communicate to avoid other activities and worries by communicating with someone. You avoid potentially stressful situations by starting up conversations. **Relaxation** is when you communicate to unwind, rest, or feel less tense. You communicate with others to calm down. **Control** is when you communicate to have others perform tasks for you, to tell others what to do, or to acquire things you need.

You can identify a person's motives by paying attention to his or her communication behaviors. If a person is always trying to influence and persuade others to do the things he or she wants done, then chances are this person has a high control motive to communicate. This was the case with Ellen above. If a person is always asking questions in an attempt to get himself or herself invited to social or company functions or frequently invites others to socialize after work, then chances are this person has a high inclusion motive to communicate. This reflects Sam's motivation for communicating with others. Although most people are driven to communicate for a combination

ASSESS YOUR **communication personality**

Rubin et. al.'s Interpersonal Communication Motives[42]

Log on to our self-assessment library, MyPersonalityProfile, found on MyCommunicationLab (www.mycommunicationlab.com), and assess your Interpersonal Communication Motives by completing this interactive assessment. Also, encourage your relational partner (i.e., close friend, colleague from work, family member) to do the same. Then you can compare and contrast your scores and begin to understand better how your interpersonal communication motives may influence your communication with others. Or you may use the following paper version of this assessment.

Directions:

Here are several reasons people give for why they talk to other people. For each statement, please circle the number that best expresses your own reasons for talking to others.

		Exactly	A lot	Somewhat	Not much	Not at all
1.	Because it's fun	5	4	3	2	1
2.	Because it's exciting	5	4	3	2	1
3.	To have a good time	5	4	3	2	1
4.	To help others	5	4	3	2	1
5.	To let others know I care about their feelings	5	4	3	2	1
6.	To thank them	5	4	3	2	1
7.	Because I need someone to talk to or be with	5	4	3	2	1
8.	Because I just need to talk about my problems sometimes	5	4	3	2	1
9.	Because it makes me feel less lonely	5	4	3	2	1
10.	To put off something I should be doing	5	4	3	2	1
11.	To get away from what I am doing	5	4	3	2	1
12.	Because I have nothing better to do	5	4	3	2	1
13.	Because it relaxes me	5	4	3	2	1

14. Because it allows me to unwind	Exactly 5	A lot 4	Somewhat 3	Not much 2	Not at all 1
15. Because it's a pleasant rest	Exactly 5	A lot 4	Somewhat 3	Not much 2	Not at all 1
16. Because I want someone to do something for me	Exactly 5	A lot 4	Somewhat 3	Not much 2	Not at all 1
17. To tell others what to do	Exactly 5	A lot 4	Somewhat 3	Not much 2	Not at all 1
18. To get something I don't have	Exactly 5	A lot 4	Somewhat 3	Not much 2	Not at all 1

Scoring Instructions:

To compute the Pleasure Motive, add items 1 + 2 + 3.
To compute the Affection Motive, add items 4 + 5 + 6.
To compute the Inclusion Motive, add items 7 + 8 + 9.
To compute the Escape Motive, add items 10 + 11 + 12.
To compute the Relaxation Motive, add items 13 + 14 + 15.
To compute the Control Motive, add items 16 + 17 + 18.

Place the total for each motive in the column titled "Score." If your individual motive score is ≥ 9, then circle *high* in the column titled "Motivation Level." If your individual motive score is ≤ 8, then circle *low*. Once finished, circle the score below for each motive.

SCORE		MOTIVATION LEVEL	
Pleasure:	_____	Low	High
Affection:	_____	Low	High
Inclusion:	_____	Low	High
Escape:	_____	Low	High
Relaxation:	_____	Low	High
Control:	_____	Low	High

Low Pleasure	3	4	5	6	7	8	9	10	11	12	13	14	15	High Pleasure
Low Affection	3	4	5	6	7	8	9	10	11	12	13	14	15	High Affection
Low Inclusion	3	4	5	6	7	8	9	10	11	12	13	14	15	High Inclusion
Low Escape	3	4	5	6	7	8	9	10	11	12	13	14	15	High Escape
Low Relaxation	3	4	5	6	7	8	9	10	11	12	13	14	15	High Relaxation
Low Control	3	4	5	6	7	8	9	10	11	12	13	14	15	High Control

TABLE 1.2

Interpersonal Communication Motives Profiles (Opposite)													
Low Pleasure	3	4	5	6	7	8	9	[10]	11	12	(13)	14	15	High Pleasure
Low Affection	3	4	5	[6]	7	8	9	10	11	12	13	14	(15)	High Affection
Low Inclusion	3	4	5	[6]	7	8	9	10	11	12	13	14	(15)	High Inclusion
Low Escape	3	(4)	5	6	7	8	9	10	11	12	[13]	14	15	High Escape
Low Relaxation	3	(4)	5	6	7	8	9	10	11	12	[13]	14	15	High Relaxation
Low Control	3	[4]	5	6	7	8	9	10	11	12	13	(14)	15	High Control

of interpersonal communication motives, not all of the motives may be equally dominant. For example, some people may have a higher need for control and a lower need for inclusion.

Assessing your interpersonal communication motives can help you better understand relational conflict or the struggles and stressors that are a part of relational life. For example, in Table 1.2, assume that you have the profile (set of interpersonal communication motives) that includes the circles and your partner (boyfriend/girlfriend, spouse, best friend) has the profile with the squares. You would anticipate there being some natural conflict in this relationship, since you and your partner's interpersonal communication motives are very different. You are motivated to communicate to meet your pleasure, affection, inclusion, and control needs, while you partner is motivated to communicate to meet escape and relaxation needs. The communication behaviors that you would use to meet your needs look and sound different from the communication behaviors that your partner would use to meet his or her needs. For example, you would communicate to get work done (control) and to accomplish specific goals and tasks, such as planning a party for friends (pleasure, affection, inclusion). Your partner might communicate to avoid work (escape) and to make plans that would enable him or her some unstructured time (relaxation).

A question that students often ask is "Can the relationship illustrated in Table 1.2 work?" Of course it can work, but it requires awareness and open communication. In many ways, you complement one another. Where you're high, your partner might be low, allowing you to help each other out. It's important to remember that one profile is not necessarily better than the other, just different. Being aware of each other's motives is invaluable information that allows us to better understand each other's communication behavior.

Now assume that the profiles reflected in Table 1.3 reflect you and your partner's interpersonal communication motives. This relationship would look different from the one in Table1.2. Rather than being opposite, your interpersonal communication motives are quite similar. Your communication with each other might feel a bit more comfortable, since you have the same motives to communicate. It could also be that you're more competitive with each other because your motives are similar. Again, it's important to understand that one set of interpersonal communication motives is not necessarily better than another, just different.

TABLE 1.3

Interpersonal Communication Motives Profiles (Similar)														
Low Pleasure	3	4	(5)	[6]	7	8	9	10	11	12	13	14	15	High Pleasure
Low Affection	3	4	(5)	6	[7]	8	9	10	11	12	13	14	15	High Affection
Low Inclusion	3	(4)	5	6	[7]	8	9	10	11	12	13	14	15	High Inclusion
Low Escape	3	4	5	(6)	[7]	8	9	10	11	12	13	14	15	High Escape
Low Relaxation	3	4	5	(6)	[7]	8	9	10	11	12	13	14	15	High Relaxation
Low Control	3	4	(5)	[6]	7	8	9	10	11	12	13	14	15	High Control

Another way in which you can use your assessment data (and your partner's assessment data) to enhance your interpersonal communication is to work to meet each other's needs. You are encouraged to have your partner complete the same Interpersonal Communication Motives measure that you completed located in the Assessing Your Communication Personality box or to go online and complete the same instrument. Once it has been completed, have your partner chart the scores in the same manner that you did when you completed the measure.

 WHAT CAN I **do now?**

▶ *You could increase your awareness.* Understand that you and your partner's styles of communication are in part motivated or driven by needs. Rather than reacting to your partner's communication, try to understand what is motivating him or her to communicate in a particular manner. This is called perspective taking.[43] Attempt to consider all the possible reasons why your partner communicates the way he or she does.

▶ *You could attempt to meet your partner's needs.* No two people are alike. When your partner communicates, he or she needs something. If possible, try to meet the need, and your partner might believe you have mind-reading skills. If your partner needs attention, then give attention. If your partner needs control, then yield. Research clearly suggests that you can enhance the quality of your relationships by helping others to meet their interpersonal needs.[44]

▶ *You could increase your adaptability.* No two relationships are the same. Adapting your communication means that you and your relational partner make choices about what's best for the relationship.[45] Above, we recommended meeting your partner's needs as one way of enhancing your relationship. Here, we recommend taking it a step further and together adapting your communication to meet the needs of the relationship. This requires a conversation between you and your relational partner in which you openly discuss interpersonal needs and how best to meet these needs.

CHECKING YOUR UNDERSTANDING
Personality and Interpersonal Communication

Before going any further, check your understanding by answering the following questions:

1. Define *personality* and *personality traits*.

2. Differentiate among the Big Five personality factors: Openness, Conscientiousness, Extraversion, Agreeableness, and Neuroticism.

3. What does it mean when researchers claim that a part of your communication style is neurologically influenced? To answer this question, discuss the relationships between neurology, psychology, and communication.

4. What are the six interpersonal communication motives, and how do you see your motive profile and your partner's motive profile influencing the communication you have with each other?

Gender, Culture, Technology, and Interpersonal Communication

Three factors that influence your interpersonal communication are gender, culture, and technology. Because of their pervasive impact on all aspects of your interpersonal communication, we have decided to thread these three factors throughout the entire book. Whenever we discuss how gender/sex, culture/diversity (race, ethnicity), or technology affect or are affected by your interpersonal communication, we will highlight this by placing the appropriate icon pictured in Figure 1.5 in the left-hand margin. Before going any further, we would like to introduce you to these important factors and to define and explain concepts that we will be referencing throughout the chapters.

Gender and Interpersonal Communication

Men and women use verbal messages differently.[46] You probably already know this to be true from your own relationships challenging. Your becoming aware of these differences is just another way in which you can enhance your interpersonal communication with others.

Although sex and gender are related and the two terms are often used interchangeably, there are some distinctions that we would like to make. **Sex** refers to biological characteristics that are present from the time of birth. Different pairs of chromosomes—XX for females, XY for males—provide clear genetic coding for how the body will develop, including the body's reproductive organs. We use the terms *male* and *female* to describe our biological sex.

Gender refers to the cultural and psychological characteristics that are associated with our biological sex; it is a cultural construction of what it means to be a man or woman. The terms *masculine* and *feminine* are used most often in referring to gender. In many ways, gender is an implicit rulebook that tells you how you are to behave and communicate as a male or a female. Unlike sex, which is biological or natural, gender is learned or developed through the nurturing process and through your interactions in your culture.

Although popular culture would have us believe that men and women (sex differences) communicate in such drastic ways that we're not even from the same planet,[47] academic research does not necessarily support these bold assertions.[48] Research does suggest that there are differences between masculine and feminine (gender

FIGURE 1.5

Icons Reflect Coverage of Issues Related to Gender/Sex, Culture/Diversity, and Technology

Gender/Sex

Culture/Diversity

Technology

differences) styles of communicating in that feminine styles are more geared to establishing and maintaining relationships and masculine styles are more geared toward reaching task-related goals.[49] In this book, we make every effort to identify if the communication difference is between men and women or between masculine and feminine.

Culture and Interpersonal Communication

Your ability to develop relationships and communicate across cultures is going to become a necessity as the global economy evolves and your hometown communities become more diverse. As was discussed above, your culture is a learned system of knowledge, behavior, attitudes, beliefs, values, and norms that is shared by a group of people.[50] Most people don't fully recognize their culture until they're no longer in it. This often occurs when you travel out of your city, state, or country. After some time away, you begin to miss home. You begin to miss the food, music, and everyday routines that are familiar to you. Put simply, you miss your culture.

You also belong to a number of **co-cultural groups**, which is a cultural group within a larger culture. Within the United States, a number of co-cultures exist based on age, class, ethnicity, religion, sexual orientation, and other defining characteristics that bring a group together. Members of smaller co-cultural groups usually share a style of communication that is unique to the group. For example, researchers have identified a unique language that gays and lesbians use to form community.[51] People who become members of service and social fraternities and sororities usually go through an initiation period during which they learn not only the Greek alphabet, but also secret handshakes, sayings, and songs.

Intercultural communication occurs when individuals or groups from different cultures or co-cultural groups attempt to communicate. You don't need to travel the globe to experience intercultural communication. If you are white, heterosexual, and Christian, you might experience intercultural communication when troubleshooting a computer problem with a customer service representative from India, while attending a gay pride parade in your local city, or when celebrating the Christmas holiday with Jewish friends. If you're like some people, intercultural situations can put you outside your comfort zone and allow you to feel a number of different emotions, including anxiety, frustration, or excitement. Some people become frustrated and impatient with their inability to communicate effectively across cultural groups. The messages they send don't always equal the messages that others receive, a situation that can result in intercultural misfires.

Technology and Interpersonal Communication

You don't need to be an expert in communication to know that technology is changing the way you communicate and how you interact in your relationships. For example, nearly 80% of all 14- to 16-year-olds have cell phones, and 90% of teenagers use their cell phones more for texting than for talking.[52] People who use social networking sites, such as Facebook and MySpace, spend an average of about 20 minutes a day on the site and may have between 150 and 200 friends listed on their profile; two-thirds of users log in at least once a day.[53]

Not everyone is pleased with how people are using technology to communicate. Consider the following examples:

- Have you ever been in a face-to-face conversation with someone who interrupts the conversation to take a call on his or her cell phone? Why does the cell phone always seems to take priority over face-to-face conversation?

- Have you ever been in a face-to-face conversation with someone who began texting a friend while also talking with you?

- Have you ever spent an evening at home with your partner and found that your partner was spending most of his or her time on the Internet rather than talking to you or doing things with you?

If you have ever been in one of the above situations, you know how frustrating it is to try to communicate with others when they're using technology. Table 1.4 identifies some ways in which you can enhance your interpersonal communication when using technology.

TABLE 1.4

Using Technology Appropriately When Communicating with Others

Guidelines for Using Cell Phones[54]

- *Excuse yourself before taking a call.* The call may be important to you, but realize that you are also important to the person in front of you. Taking a call signals that the person you are with is less important than the person calling. If that's not the impression you want to give, don't take the call. The caller can always leave you a voicemail.
- *Don't talk on your cell phone in front of someone who expects your attention.* Supermarket clerks and cashiers at drive-through windows deserve the respect of having your attention.
- *Don't yell while talking on your cell phone.* Have you noticed how some people scream when using the cell phone? Lower your voice or move to a quieter place to continue the call.
- *When in close distance to others, such as in an airplane, checkout line, elevator, keep it short.* Call the person back when you have more privacy.

Guidelines for Text-Messaging[55]

- *Don't use text-messaging to convey important information.* Put simply, don't dump your boyfriend or girlfriend using a text message. Instead, have a face-to-face conversation. Text-messaging is designed for casual information.
- *Don't text-message anything confidential, private, or potentially embarrassing.* You never know when someone might be looking over the recipient's shoulder—or, worse, when your message might be sent to the wrong person.
- *If you text-message someone who doesn't have your phone number, introduce yourself.* Start your message by stating who you are: "Hi—it's Tim from work. Call me when you get a sec."
- *Don't use text-messaging when informing someone of sad news, business matters, or urgent meetings unless it's to set up a phone call on the subject.* This type of information needs to be conveyed in a phone call or face-to-face.

Guidelines for Using Social Networking Sites[56]

- *Make sure that your content is suitable for the eyes of your family members, employers, and casual acquaintances.* Your mother could be logging in, employers and prospective employers may be checking you out, or they might ask their children to search your social networking site(s).
- *Be as careful when you chat online about your studies, work, personal life, or social events as you would when talking to a stranger.* Your posts on newsgroups and online communities may be publicly available in archives where they can be found years later.
- *Make only comments about a named individual that would be acceptable if made face to face.* Laws on bullying, stalking, and defamation all apply online, and the penalties can be severe.
- *Be careful when discussing details of your whereabouts.* It is important, for your own safety, that you keep private where you are planning to go and when you will not be at home.

CHECKING YOUR UNDERSTANDING
Technology and Interpersonal Communication

Assess your understanding of the content of this section by answering the following questions:

1. Describe the similarities and differences between sex and gender.
2. How would you describe your culture to someone? What is a co-cultural group to which you belong? Describe an intercultural communication problem you recently encountered. Describe the two cultures that were involved.
3. How do you see communication technologies, such as cell phones, social networking sites (e.g., Facebook, MySpace), and text-messaging affecting your interpersonal communication?
4. How would you inform a good friend about how to use cell phones, social networking sites, and text-messaging appropriately so as to not negatively influence communication with others? What would your advice be?

A Communication Development Plan for Simon

To complete Simon's story, you will recall how Marcus, Simon's father, was disappointed by his family's behavior when they were invited to dinner to celebrate Maria's 70th birthday. Simon now recognized the problem and was upset by the lack of attention he and his family had given to his mother. He also realized that he and his wife Jill were partially responsible. Both of them had been answering phone calls and responding to emails while at dinner. Simon was embarrassed by the poor example he and Jill were setting for their children, Monica and Seth, and by his children's communication behaviors. Seth talks too much and is overly controlling in his communication behavior, and Monica talks too little and is withdrawn. Even though his family was in the same physical space, there was minimal interpersonal contact. Simon also knows that his mother was feeling sad and disappointed, because she wanted to connect with her family members and be a part of their lives.

After reading this chapter, you might have some new answers to the questions we posed at the beginning:

What are some of the reasons why Simon's family members failed to communicate in an appropriate way with each other around the dinner table?

Possible Explanations

There are a couple of ways to explain the communication dynamics that occurred at the dinner table. *First, Simon needs to realize that his family members have different personalities and motivations for communication.* Monica is an introvert, which means that she prefers not to talk. It doesn't necessarily mean that she isn't interested in others. Seth is an extravert, has control needs, and tends to communicate to control his environment. This can be good and bad depending on the situation. Seth needs to become aware of his communication personality and how others perceive his. Jill's assertiveness is not necessarily a problem, but it can become one if others perceive her to be demanding.

Second, Simon and his family members are allowing communication technologies to negatively affect how they interact with others. If communication technologies are not used well, they can negatively influence communication within a family.[57] Simon also realized that his children are imitating both his and Jill's use of cell phones and laptops at inappropriate times.

How will this lack of interpersonal communication eventually affect the family as well as individual family members?

Possible Explanations

It appears that family members are self-absorbed, living in their own worlds and unaware of each other. The family appeared to be uninterested in Maria's 70th birthday. Also, the family didn't understand how important this birthday party was to Marcus. Put simply, they're not paying attention to how others might be feeling. Over time, this inattention will become normative and usual, and rather than there being a collective family, there will be a series of individuals who get together on occasion.

How can Simon address his concerns with his family without his children thinking that he is overreacting or not in touch with the 21st century family?

There are a number of communication strategies that Simon can use to enhance the communication within his family.

1. *Simon, with his wife Jill, needs to develop family rules for when and how to use communication technologies appropriately when spending time together as a family.* As parents, Simon and Jill must follow their own rules and insist that their children do the same. For example, cell phone use and text-messaging should be off limits during a meal or other family functions unless there is an emergency. Family members need to understand that talking on the phone or text-messaging while having a meal together is rude because it sends a clear message that others are more important and take priority over family members.

2. *Simon can help his family members to see how others might interpret their communication behaviors.* For example, Simon can help Monica to see how people might interpret her being quiet as her not being interested in oth-

ers. Simon can help Seth understand his control needs and how they are conveyed through his communication. He can suggest to Jill how her assertiveness can sometimes be perceived as too demanding. He can also let his family know about his own communication style. Perhaps others—maybe even members of his own family—perceive his being quiet as his being weak and uncaring. Sharing this information with his family will help them to become more self-aware and understand how their personality is related to their communication behaviors.

3. *Simon can help his family members become more competent communicators.* Simon can share with his family members the knowledge, skills, and motivations they need to be both effective and appropriate in their communication. Specifically, he can help them to do the following:

   - Be aware of how their different personalities influence not only their own communication behaviors, but also how they interact as a family.

   - Acknowledge others by giving them full attention, especially during special occasions that honor another person.

   - Take perspective by considering others' needs rather than their own needs.

   - Engage others in conversations. Instead of talking about themselves, ask others questions about how they are doing, what they are doing, and what they are thinking.

   - Monitor their use of communication technologies. There is a time and a place for appropriate use of communication technologies. Talking on a cell phone or texting while celebrating a family member's 70th birthday is probably inappropriate.

Take-Aways

This book is about the communication that takes place between two people. Using communication to create understanding is more complex than most people think. The following list of knowledge claims summarizes what you have learned in this chapter:

- Interpersonal communication is a process that occurs when two people use verbal and nonverbal messages to create understanding and to mutually influence each other to manage the relationship.

- Interpersonal communication is influenced by both nature (biological) and nurture (cultural) influences that work together to affect social skill development.

- Interpersonal communication has content and relational dimensions, occurs on an impersonal–intimate continuum, and is irreversible and unrepeatable.

- Interpersonal communication skills help you to stay physically and emotionally healthy as well as helping you to enhance your effectiveness at home and at work.

- Your personality plays an important role in your interpersonal communication. Understanding your personality traits means understanding what makes you and others distinctly unique and different from each other.

- Your personality is a composite of five traits: openness, conscientiousness, extraversion, agreeableness, and neuroticism.

- Your interpersonal communication motives (pleasure, affection, inclusion, escape, relaxation, and control) allow you to better understand what's driving your own and others' communication.

Following are some of the ways in which you learned more about how your personality influences your interpersonal communication:

- By completing the Interpersonal Communication Motives Scale, you learned about why you communicate the way you do in your relationships.

- By completing the Interpersonal Communication Motives Profile, you learned about how you and your partner or spouse's motives interact to affect the communication that your relationship yields.

- When using your cell phone, excuse yourself before taking a call, don't talk on a cell phone in front of someone who expects your attention, and keep your conversations short when in a public setting.

- When text-messaging, don't convey important, confidential, or private information.

- When using social networking sites, restrict access to your profile page to people you know and trust, and be careful when discussing details of your whereabouts.

Discussion Questions

1. How is interpersonal communication defined and what does it mean when researchers say that your interpersonal communication is part nature and part nurture?

2. What are the components of the interpersonal communication process?

3. What is the difference between the content and relational levels of interpersonal communication?

4. What are the five traits that make up the Big Five model of personality? How are these traits related to your communication behavior?

5. How are your biology (neurology), psychology (temperament), and communication behaviors related? Would you consider your communication style to be learned, influenced by the genes you inherited by your family members, or both? Explain.

6. How do the six interpersonal communication motives influence the communication in your relationships?

Building Your Skills

1. Sit with your partner and think of a time when you got into an argument in which matters were resolved. Discuss and write what you worked out and what you could have done differently. Are you more aware of you and your partner's communicative motives?

2. Observe and make a list of ten communicative misbehaviors that occur while talking on a cell phone, using a social networking site (e.g., Facebook, MySpace),

and text-messaging, and write what that individual could have done differently.

3. Think of a person with whom you often get into conflicts. This can be a family member, significant other, or co-worker. Then with a classmate discuss two criteria of being a competent communicator that you most need to work on with that individual.

2 Understanding Self, Personality, and Communication

Rick works as an assistant buyer for the Nordstrom department store chain in Seattle. He is responsible for assisting the lead buyer of men's suits and formal wear. For the past two years, he has been analyzing data and customer purchasing trends. He's a number cruncher. Rick's job is to keep his buyer informed of what is and is not selling in men's suits and formal wear. The buyer then uses the data when purchasing clothes that will eventually appear in Nordstrom stores throughout the country. Although Rick enjoys his job, he would like to be promoted.

Rick has applied for a couple of lead buyer positions and was turned down both times. The new positions would require him to interact and develop relationships with designers from all over the world. Rick admits that he is the analytical type and not necessarily the most warm and fuzzy person around. He is very quiet, and communicating with strangers makes him nervous. He doesn't know why. In fact,

he becomes very frustrated when he sees his colleagues walking into the offices of top designers and comfortably initiating conversations. He wants to be able to do that, but he can't. When he tries, he becomes so nervous that he begins to stutter, and this makes him feel self-conscious, embarrassed, and frustrated.

Rick considers himself interpersonally challenged because of the awkwardness and anxiety he experiences when interacting with others. He doubts himself and his abilities. He feels stupid. These feelings of self-doubt usually cause him to become even more anxious about his interactions with others, especially in the workplace. He also feels weak because he has not been able to overcome this communication problem that he thinks is preventing him from being promoted despite his perfect work record.

Although Rick understands that a new position would require him to be more social, meaning that he would need

CHAPTER OBJECTIVES

AFTER READING THIS CHAPTER, you will understand:

1 The differences between self-concept and self-esteem.

2 How self-concept and self-esteem affect communication.

3 The difference between personality and communication traits.

4 How your communication apprehension affects your interpersonal communication.

5 The difference between assertiveness and responsiveness.

6 The four social styles that comprise your socio-communicative orientation: amiables, analyticals, drivers, and expressives.

7 How to differentiate between the identity management characteristics of public and private self, of pragmatic and principled self, and of high and low monitors.

8 Each of the identity management strategies.

to communicate and develop relationships with others in order to do the job, he still wants to continue trying for the promotion.

What do you think? While reading this chapter, consider how you might answer the following questions to help Rick:

- Why can't Rick overcome his fear of communicating with strangers? Is that fear normal?

- Rick has been very successful as an assistant buyer. Why does his inability to communicate with strangers make him feel stupid?

- How would you advise Rick? Would you advise him to continue applying for the buyer position? Why or why not?

We will revisit Rick's story at the end of the chapter and use the content discussed in this chapter to develop a communication plan to help him.

AFTER READING THIS CHAPTER, you will be able to:

1 Enhance your self-concept and self-esteem.

2 Manage your communication apprehension.

3 Adapt your social style to other people's social styles.

4 Manage your identity.

AFTER COMPLETING THE SELF-ASSESSMENT INSTRUMENTS, you will learn about:

1 Your level of communication apprehension and how your level of communication apprehension compares to that of other people.

2 Your social style and that of others: amiables, analyticals, drivers, and expressives.

Interpersonal communication is a process of two people sharing themselves with each other. This process begins with you. Who are you? Try answering some of the following questions:

- How do I define myself?
- What do I believe in?
- What abilities and competencies do I possess?
- Do I value my abilities and myself?
- Am I pleased with the person I am becoming?
- How do I describe my personality and am I aware of how it affects my behavior?
- Am I aware of how I communicate and interact with other people?

If you can answer these questions easily, then chances are you understand yourself. Most people, however, struggle with these questions. Their answers are influenced by a variety of factors, including how their parents raised them, the media they watch and interact with, how their friends treat them, and how they compare themselves to others.

> If one is estranged from oneself, then one is estranged from others too. If one is out of touch with oneself, then one cannot touch others.
> —ANNE MORROW LINDBERGH

The purpose of this chapter is to help you answer these questions, give you new ways to think about who you are as a person, and help you better understand others. The first part of the chapter focuses on understanding the self, paying particular attention to self-concept, self-esteem, developmental influences, and their impact on our communication. The second part allows you to self-assess two communication traits that are associated with your personality and provides you with some strategies for developing these communication personality traits. The third section of the chapter introduces you to identity management, including characteristics, influences, and strategies.

Understanding the Self

Understanding the self begins with knowing the difference between your self-concept and self-esteem. **Self-concept** is the sum total of a person's knowledge and understanding of his or her self.[1] It is one's mental and conceptual understanding of who one is as a person. According to psychologist and philosopher William James, the individual has many different selves.[2] Some people's self-concept is influenced by their material possessions. They are what they own. "I drive a Lexus and wear designer clothes." Some people self-identify by their friends, social networks, and careers. When interacting with them, you might hear them talking about a group they belong to, or you might hear them define themselves by their jobs or careers. "I belong to Kappa Kappa Kappa, and I am a fashion designer." Other people's self-concepts are heavily influenced by their spiritual selves, which are their internal thoughts and introspections about their values and moral standards. "I am a devout Buddhist." For most people, their self-concept is a combination of these various aspects and dimensions of a person's life.

Self-esteem reflects a person's overall self-appraisal of his or her worth. According to psychologist Morris Rosenberg, self-esteem is a feeling of self-worth and fundamental respect for oneself.[3] Rosenberg characterized low self-esteem as a lack of respect for oneself and feelings of unworthiness, inadequacies, and deficiencies.[4] "I'll never measure up enough to get a better job." Whereas your self-concept is descriptive (i.e., it's how you describe yourself), your self-esteem is evaluative (i.e., it's how much you value yourself). When you describe yourself as being a single mother of two who works part-time as a cashier at Barnes and Noble and is working on a degree in communication at the university, you're describing your self-concept. When you say that you feel that you're a good mother who is making a difference in the lives of her children by also being a competent employee and successful student, you're revealing your self-esteem, which is an evaluation of your self-concept.

Self-Concept

Your sense of who you are as a person is learned and is always developing and evolving from birth. This section explains both of these important characteristics.[5]

Self-Concept Is Learned. You learn about who you are as a person through your self-perceptions, social comparison, peer group influence, and reflected appraisals.[6] **Self-perceptions** include your own assessments of your abilities and talents. Psychologist Albert Bandura defined individuals' **self-efficacy** as their personal assessments of their ability to perform in a certain manner and their ability to reach their goals.[7] When you say, "I can do this," when confronted with a challenging task, you have a high degree of self-efficacy, meaning that you believe you can do what it takes to accomplish the task. When you say, "There's no way I can do this," then your self-efficacy is low. How you think about your ability to accomplish goals shapes your conceptions of self.

Social comparisons occur when you compare yourself to others. For example, young children who are short don't recognize their height until taller children surround them. This type of social comparison is an important source of self-knowledge. At times, we consider ourselves to be successful or unsuccessful in terms of how we compare with others who are similar to us. We use others, especially those we identify with in terms of age, education level, ethnicity, race, sex, and socioeconomic status, as benchmarks. If you have a friend who has reached a number of personal and professional goals, you might compare your accomplishments to this person's accomplishments. The research suggests that we interact with people we consider superior others when we need motivation to excel and with people we consider inferior others when we need to feel good about ourselves.[8] How you compare to others influences your self-concept development.

Peer group influence involves the impact that your friends have on your self-concept development. Your peer group is a collection of people of approximately the same age, social status, and interests as yours.[9] Put simply, your peer group is your potential friendship network. Psychologists Judith Harris and Steven Pinker's research confirmed what all parents feared: Their children's friends have more influence on their children's self-concept and behavior than they do as parents.[10] Most parents intuitively understood this conclusion before it was published. This is why your parents are usually quite concerned about the company you keep and the friends you hang around with. These relationships play a role in the development of your self-concept.

Reflected appraisals are assessments you make about yourself based on how you believe others see and behave toward you. Sociologist Charles Cooley used the metaphor of a mirror to illustrate the self-concept as a reflected appraisal.[11] If you see others reacting positively to you and wanting to be with you, then your self-concept as a potential friend slowly begins to develop. One of your authors clearly remembers his first professional position upon graduating from college as a trainer for an international airline. During a meeting with a group of airline executives, his colleagues treated him like a professional even when he didn't see himself in this new role. Over time, he started identifying as a professional because others perceived him in this manner and treated him as a professional.

Self-Concept Is Multifaceted. Some researchers argue that the self-concept is organized, stable, and unchanging.[12] Others argue that it is unorganized and changes over time.[13] In reality, both of these perspectives are correct.[14] Some people see themselves in a particular manner and then arrange their lives accordingly so that this core conception of who they believe they are is supported. For example, some politically conservative people arrange their environment to ensure that their conservative identity is preserved.[15] They might live in a neighborhood or region of the country that is known to support their politics; socialize only with conservative-minded neighbors; homeschool their children; and attend a church that supports their conservative beliefs, values, and attitudes. For some individuals, their self-concepts are so solid and unchanging that they are willing to defend their self-concept through aggressive behavior. Some men have what researchers refer to as "hyper-masculine" self-concepts and exhibit extreme and exaggerated forms of masculinity, virility, and physicality. They tend to become aggressive when anyone challenges their masculine self-concept.[16]

Portions of your self-concept are also flexible and evolving. People have a tendency to try on different identities and find out whether they fit. Some identities work; others don't. Our self-concept becomes what we would like to be rather than what we see ourselves being. Some researchers refer to the self-concept as a "working self-concept," meaning that it is evolving and developing on the basis of your life experiences; there is no beginning or ending.[17] In many ways, your self-concept is similar to a software program that is constantly being developed. Every few months, there's a new update that allows your self-concept to change and develop.

Self-Concept Is Socially Constructed. Clinical psychologist George Kelly's personal construct theory is one way of understanding how the self-concept may change because of life experiences.[18] According to Kelly, you have certain labels (or constructs) that you place on your experiences; over time, these labels reflect your self-concept and identity, and you use these constructs to help interpret your experiences. For example, some young gay teenagers who have not self-identified as gay learn that being gay is not a good thing. At school, they're called names. Since some young gay teens don't have the opportunity to interact with other gay people, the only constructs and labels they have are negative.[19] They develop what sociologist Erving Goffman referred to as a "spoiled" identity, which is a flawed self-concept.[20] Unfortunately, these negative self-constructs keep these young people from self-identifying as gay, which leads some gay teens to self-destructive behavior. Kelly argues that people have the ability to reconstruct their identities. When young gay teens can interact with other gay teens and other positive gay role models, they learn new labels and constructs. Not all gays fit the negative stereotypes; gay people can live normal and healthy lives. Because of their exposure to other gay people who have healthier self-concepts, their spoiled identity is lessened. They begin to reconstruct a new self-concept that is more authentic and more empowering.

Self-Esteem

Your self-esteem, or your overall self-appraisal of your worth and value, is a multidimensional psychological concept that influences your interpersonal communication in meaningful ways.[21] New research also suggests that biology, in addition to your environment, plays a significant role in the development of your self-esteem.[22]

Self-Esteem Is Multidimensional. Some researchers suggest that three major dimensions of self-esteem affect how people communicate and interact in their relationships. **Cognitive self-esteem** is your self-evaluation regarding your ability to learn, process, and use information and knowledge. **Social self-esteem** is your self-evaluation regarding your ability to interact and relate to others as well as your ability to develop and maintain friends. **Physical self-esteem** is your self-evaluation regarding your body image and attractiveness.

Another way in which researchers study the multidimensionality of self-esteem is by researching it as a state or a trait. When your self-esteem fluctuates from situation to situation, you have *state* self-esteem. The situation affects how much you value yourself. You may have high self-esteem when interacting with your friends but low self-esteem when interacting with your colleagues at work. There is something about the situation or the types of relationships that causes you to value yourself differently. When your self-esteem remains constant or consistent regardless of the situation, you have *trait* self-esteem. This type of self-esteem is unchanging and is not affected by the situation or types of relationships.

Researchers wonder whether there are differences between men's and women's levels of self-esteem. Communication researchers Mike Allen, Erin Sahlstein, and their research colleagues conducted a meta-analysis of the effects of sex (male and female) on self-esteem. This research method allows researchers to identify trends across a number of different studies. After collapsing the findings of 103 studies that examined sex differences in self-esteem into a single study, Allen and his colleagues found the following:[23]

- In examining self-esteem, the data suggest that overall, women have slightly higher self-esteem than men do.

- In examining *cognitive* self-esteem, women have slightly higher self-esteem than men do.

- In examining *social* self-esteem, men have slightly higher self-esteem than women do.

- In examining *physical* self-esteem, men have slightly higher self-esteem than women do.

According to Allen and Sahlstein, the data suggest that there are only small differences between men's and women's levels of self-esteem. However, even minimal differences may have important implications for the mental, physical, and relational health of individuals and couples.

Self-Esteem Is Affected by Nature and Nurture Factors. Researchers have found that your biology, that is, your genes, is partially responsible for your level of self-esteem. In fact, researchers have found that about 52% of your self-esteem is based on the genes you inherited from your parents and grandparents.[24] According to this group of researchers, 48% of your self-esteem is learned, while 52% of your self-esteem is genetically inherited. If you struggle with low self-esteem, chances are others in your family have also struggled with low self-esteem. Another way to recognize the power of your self-esteem genes occurs when you work hard to enhance your self-esteem and nothing seems to work. For example, you lose weight, excel in your studies, and help your team win the championship, and you still experience low self-esteem. What you're feeling at this moment is the 52% of your self-esteem genes that are stubborn and resistant to change. The good news is that a large portion of your self-esteem can be enhanced through your environment or your nurturing.

Your environment, including the relationships you have with your parents, friends, and teachers as well as your exposure to certain forms of media also influences your self-esteem development. Researchers have found that negative self-esteem develops when children are neglected by their parents, grow up with parents who struggle with depression, or are exposed to negative parenting practices.[25] Lowered self-esteem is also the result of negative interpersonal experiences with friends, such as when your friends provide negative feedback about your competence, physical appearance, and family.[26]

Researchers have found that teachers play a significant role in the development of students' self-esteem, but they disagree on whether males or females benefit more from the attention that teachers give to students. Educational researchers Myra and David Sadker argue that the educational system disadvantages girls.[27] Their data suggest that instructors teach male and female students differently. For example, teachers pay more attention to male students, call on male students more often, and allow male students to interrupt female students more often. Because of differences in teaching styles, male and female students leave the classrooms with differing levels of self-esteem.

By contrast, psychologist Leonard Sax argues that the educational system disadvantages male students, in particular young boys. He argues that teachers and their teaching practices are ineffective with boys and young men. According to Sax and other researchers, young men are being left behind in the educational system, resulting in fewer men attending college.[28] Regardless of which sex's self-esteem benefits more because of the attention teachers pay to students, teachers play a role in the development of their students' self-esteem.

Self-Concept and Self-Esteem Affect Your Communication

Now that you have an understanding of self-concept and self-esteem and how they develop, let's consider how self-concept and esteem affect communication.

Affect Motivation to Communicate. Your sense of who you are and your self-esteem influence your motivation or desire to communicate. Communication researchers have found that what motivates people to communicate is not so much their "real" or "actual" communication abilities, but how they perceive their abilities.[29] If you have ever watched performers auditioning for *American Idol*, you have seen the difference. Some of the performers who audition for the show perceive themselves to be excellent singers. The judges, however, pan the performances and give the contestants thumbs down. During follow-up interviews, the contestants are often dumbfounded to learn that the judges did not consider their talent to be worthy of continuing to the next round.

Researchers found the same result for communication behavior.[30] What motivates people to communicate is not so much their actual abilities, but their self-perceived abilities. Some individuals who perceive themselves as competent communicate too much. Others who actually are competent, perceive themselves to be incompetent and communicate too little. The amount of talk is influenced by how one perceives the self.

Affect Self and Other Expectations. Your sense of who you are and your self-esteem influence the expectations you have for yourself and others. **Self-expectations** are the goals you set for yourself or how you believe you ought to behave and what you ought to accomplish. Self-esteem has an important effect on the prophecies people make. A **prophecy** is a prediction about a future event. Sociologist Robert Merton is credited with the expression "**self-fulfilling prophecy**," which is the idea that what you believe about yourself often comes true because you expect it to come true.[31] Have you ever expected that your first date with someone was going to go well . . . and it did. What about a job interview? Have you ever had the expectation that you're not going to do well in a job interview and then performed incredibly poorly during the interview?

People with lower self-esteem are more likely to develop prophecies that include rejection and failure. For example, researchers found that when people expect rejection, they are more likely to behave in ways that lead others to reject them.[32] You begin communicating in more negative ways, and you start believing your own words. You become the person you talk about in your own communication.[33] On the other hand, people with higher self-esteem are more likely to develop positive prophecies or predictions that include success. For example, researchers found that individuals with high self-esteem were more likely to be engaged in their studies and to experience success as a result of their motivation and engagement.[34] They communicate in more empowering ways and believe the feedback they receive from their own voices.

Your self-esteem also influences **other-expectations**, which are the standards you set for others or how you believe others should behave in certain situations.[35] On the basis of these expectations, you communicate and interact with people in a manner that tends to make these expectations come true. The teacher-student relationship is a unique relationship that has been studied extensively in terms of other-expectations. Here are a few research findings that reveal how the teacher–student relationship is different depending on the expectations teachers have for their students:[36]

- Teachers respond to low-expectation students' incorrect answers by giving the student the answer or calling on another student to answer the question.
- Teachers respond to high-expectation students' incorrect answers by giving the student additional time, repeating the question, providing a clue, or asking a new question.
- Teachers criticize low-expectation students more frequently.
- Teachers are less likely to praise low-expectation students when these students provide a correct answer.
- Teachers are less nonverbally responsive (less eye contact, less smiling) to low-expectation students.

Affect How Messages Are Interpreted. Your sense of who you are and your self-esteem influence how you interpret other people's messages. For example, people with lower levels of self-esteem don't interpret constructive feedback well. Regardless of how well the constructive feedback was discussed with them, they interpret the feedback in a very personal manner. Therefore, they experience feelings of hurt, stress, and sometimes embarrassment.[37] In many interpersonal relationships, this can be a source of conflict that, if not managed well, can affect the quality of the relationship.

Another way in which your conceptions of yourself affect how you interpret messages is in your ability to be influenced and persuaded. Are you easily persuaded? Communication researchers have been able to determine that people with high and low levels of self-esteem are not persuaded as easily as are people who have moderate levels of self-esteem.[38] People with high self-esteem are confident in their ability to critically listen and interpret information in order to make a decision that's right for them. People with low self-esteem are less confident in their ability to critically process and interpret information and are too concerned about what others think. Therefore, they have a tendency to avoid or ignore persuasive messages.

Finally, your sense of who you are and your self-esteem influence how you interpret situations. Table 2.1 illustrates how two different people interpret their relational success and failure differently depending on their level of self-esteem. Relational success could be anything from your asking someone out on a date and this person accepting your invitation to your having a good relationship with your supervisor at work.

TABLE 2.1

The Effect of Self-Esteem on Relationships: Success or Failure		
	High Self-Esteem	**Low Self-Esteem**
Cory: Relational Success	"I'm deserving of this relationship!"	"I got lucky with this relationship; it will probably not last."
Seth: Relational Failure	"There's always another relationship."	"I wasn't deserving of the relationship."

A Cory with high self-esteem interprets his relational success to his being a good person and deserving of the relationship. A Cory with low self-esteem interprets his relational success quite differently. Rather than believing that he is worthy and deserving of relational success, he interprets his relational success to his being lucky. He even questions whether the relationship will last.

A Seth with high self-esteem interprets his relational failure by shrugging it off and moving on to the next relationship. In fact, he is not devastated or upset by the relational failure. A Seth with low self-esteem, by contrast, blames the relational failure on his not being worthy or deserving of the relationship in the first place. You might hear someone with low self-esteem saying, "It was too good to be true, and I didn't think it would ever work in the first place."

Enhancing Your Self-Concept and Self-Esteem

Because your self-concept and self-esteem affect your communication, it's best to continually find ways to enhance and develop your self-concept and self-esteem. Here are some strategies that you might find helpful.

Develop Supportive Relationships. Since the company you keep influences your self-concept and how you feel about yourself, it's important that you initiate, develop, and manage constructive relationships with others who can support you. Enhancing a positive self-concept begins by surrounding yourself with people who are interested in taking the time to understand you. They are more likely to become interested in understanding you if you're equally interested in understanding them. This mutual desire to understand each other lays the foundation for supportive relationships.

Taking a course in interpersonal communication is one way in which you can learn how to develop supportive relationships. Through your study, you will learn how relationships work and the role that communication plays in developing and managing relationships. Additionally, reading this textbook will help you to begin developing new communication skills and to polish skills that you're currently using to enhance your relationships.

It's also important to get yourself out of destructive relationships. Unsupportive relationships harm self-concept and self-esteem and, over time, can have a devastating effect. Although it is not always an easy thing to do, it is healthy to end these relationships. Again, this textbook along with a course in interpersonal communication will provide you with the skills you need to take this important step if necessary. You will see an enhanced self-esteem emerge simply by ridding yourself of unsupportive relationships that prevent you from reaching your goals.

It's not the quantity of friends you have but the quality of your friendships that influences self-concept and esteem. Perhaps it's time you took inventory of your friendships.

Develop Realistic Expectations. Developing realistic expectations begins by understanding the difference between the "real" self and the "ideal" self. The **real self** is your honest assessment of your current abilities. The **ideal self** is what you strive to become. Having expectations for yourself is important; however, it is important to set realistic expectations. For example, Javier has set expectations for himself that are outside of his abilities. He is an overachiever. Regardless of how hard he works, his goals are probably unreachable. Alexander, on the other hand, is an underachiever. His expectations for himself are too low; he can reach his goal with minimal effort. Unfortunately, both Javier and Alexander have unrealistic expectations that are likely to negatively influence their self-concept and self-esteem.[39] Jillian has established expectations that are within her reach. She understands her abilities, skills, and talents and has some goals that are challenging but attainable.

Develop New Competencies. Learning and self-esteem are related.[40] As was discussed earlier, your belief that you can learn and influence your own thoughts and behaviors is referred to as self-efficacy.[41] For example, many college students who successfully complete a semester of college leave with a level of self-confidence that they did not possess when they started the semester. Students leave with an "I can do it" attitude, which enhances their self-concept and self-esteem. Their sense of self-efficacy increases, as does their confidence in their ability to influence and take control of their lives. Rather than letting life happen *to* them, they begin to believe that they can make life happen *for* them.

Becoming proficient at a new skill allows you to feel productive. When you feel that you have something to offer others, your life is enriched. For example, many colleges and universities are becoming more accessible to community members by offering evening, weekend, and summer courses in cooking, various languages (e.g., Sign, French, Spanish, Japanese, Russian), public speaking, accounting, and massage therapy, to name a few. These courses allow people from the community to learn new skill sets or to fine-tune or polish their skills making them more proficient.

What is it that you would like to learn? What skills would you like to acquire? One of your authors has an annual New Year's resolution, which is to do something for the

Tim's self-concept and self-esteem were enhanced when he learned a new set of skills and helped others after Hurricane Katrina.

first time. One year, he volunteered with Habitat for Humanity and spent a summer learning how to build homes in hurricane-ravaged New Orleans. He left South Texas with minimal carpentry skills and returned home two months later with a new set of carpentry skills, an enriched self-concept, and enhanced self-esteem.

Develop Rational Beliefs. You can enhance your self-concept and self-esteem by thinking differently. A number of people with low self-esteem and self-concept live with illogical, irrational beliefs; these thoughts are often exaggerated and extreme. You can begin by evaluating your own beliefs. Would you consider them irrational or rational? To get you started, consider some of the irrational beliefs showcased in Table 2.2. Do you see how replacing these irrational beliefs with rational beliefs could enhance your self-concept and self-esteem?

Cognitive restructuring is the process that one goes through when one replaces debilitating irrational beliefs with empowering rational beliefs.[42] There are a number of self-help books in the marketplace that can help you with this restructuring process.[43] Although some people can learn how to replace their irrational beliefs with rational ones on their own, others have a more difficult time in changing their belief systems and might need

TABLE 2.2

Examining Differences between Irrational and Rational Beliefs	
Irrational Beliefs	**Rational Beliefs**
I must be loved or approved by everyone I consider significant.	I want to be loved and approved by most people, and I will try to act in a respectful manner so that they will love and approve of me. However, I must be respectful of those who don't love or approve of me. My self-esteem cannot depend on the whims of others.
I must be competent and perfect in all that I do.	I will strive to do my best rather than to be the best. I can enjoy doing things even if I'm not particularly good at them. I'm not afraid to try things in which I might fail. Taking risks is courageous and is necessary if I am to grow.
I must live in fear of the unknown and always be prepared for the worst to happen.	It is probably in my best interest to face the unknown and render it less dangerous, and if that is impossible, I will stop obsessing about it and being fearful. Worry will not stop it from occurring. Even if it does occur, I can manage and cope with it.
I must avoid life's difficulties and responsibilities.	I'll do those necessary things no matter how much I dislike them. Avoiding difficulties prevents me from living my life to the fullest. Difficulties and responsibilities are a major part of life.

Source: Adapted from: Schiraldi, G. R. (2001). *The self-esteem workbook.* Oakland, CA: New Harbinger Publications.

some professional assistance. For many people, their lowered self-concept and self-esteem are the culmination of many years living with their own irrational beliefs or with others who have irrational beliefs about them. For example, your parents might believe that you're the perfect child and that you will one day achieve great success because of your moral values and intelligence, and no other future seems possible or acceptable. Over time, you internalize these irrational beliefs of perfectionism. Striving to become perfect becomes your reality.[44]

Develop Plan B. It's important that you prepare for setbacks when you are organizing and planning your life. A **setback** is something that reverses or delays your progress in reaching your goal. Setbacks are a part of life. They can paralyze people with low self-esteem and cause it to plummet further into an abyss. It's important that you learn how to cope and manage setbacks. You do this by developing an alternative plan, or a plan B. Although disappointing at first, some setbacks have a silver lining, meaning that in time, you will be glad they occurred. Other times, however, these setbacks are unfortunate, frustrating, and very disappointing. A part of enhancing your self-esteem and self-concept is learning how to anticipate, cope with, and learn from your setbacks. Here are a few guidelines for processing setbacks:[45]

- *Anticipate setbacks.* Setbacks are a constant in life. Don't obsess about them, but realize that they could occur. There is always more than one way to achieve your goals. Expand your options.

- *Take responsibility.* Admit your role in the setback. Identify the behaviors or lack of behaviors that resulted in the setback.

- *Refocus.* Rather than focusing and obsessing on the setback, which is in the past, refocus on the future. Develop ways to repair the setback, or develop alternative plans.

- *Learn from your setbacks.* Take a few minutes to ask yourself the following questions, which will allow you to learn from the setback: Did certain things go well? What are the advantages of not getting what I want right now? What coping skills could I learn from this setback? Were there signs of an impending setback that I did not see? If a similar event occurred again, what could I do differently?

 ## CHECKING YOUR UNDERSTANDING
Self-Concept and Self-Esteem

Before reading any further, take a few minutes to assess your learning by writing answers to the following assessment items:

1. Describe how self-concept and self-esteem are different and how they affect your interpersonal communication. To do this, describe how self-efficacy, social comparison, and reflected appraisals affect the development of your self-concept.

2. Explain how the cognitive, social, and physical dimensions of self-esteem are different.

3. How do your biology and environment influence the development of your self-esteem?

4. List and explain the five ways in which a person can maximize his or her self-concept and self-esteem.

Understanding Communication Traits

Similar to personality traits, we also have **communication traits**, which are enduring consistencies and differences in message-sending and message-receiving behaviors among individuals.[46] Some people are very talkative, whereas other people are quiet and prefer not to talk. Like our personality traits, our communication traits tend to be consistent ways of behaving. Communication researchers have identified a number of communication traits that influence how we relate and interact with others and our relationships.[47] Two of these traits that are particularly important to understanding self are communication apprehension and socio-communicative orientation.

Communication Apprehension

If you have ever experienced a bit of stage fright, then you've experienced **communication apprehension**, which is "an individual's level of fear or anxiety associated with either real or anticipated communication with another person or persons."[48] Before you read any further, we want you to become aware of your level of communication apprehension when communicating with others. Please take a few minutes to complete the communication apprehension measure in the following self-assessment box.

 ASSESS YOUR **communication personality**

McCroskey's Personal Report of Communication Apprehension (PRCA-24)[49]

Log onto our self-assessment library, MyPersonalityProfile, found on MyCommunicationLab (www.mycommunicationlab.com), and assess your communication apprehension by completing the interactive assessment, or use the assessment below. Also, encourage your relational partner (a friend, coworker, family member, or romantic partner) to do the same. This way, you can compare and contrast your scores and begin to understand better how your communication traits may influence your interpersonal communication.

Directions:

This instrument, the PRCA-24, is composed of twenty-four statements concerning your feelings about communication with other people. Please indicate in the space provided the degree to which each statement applies to you by marking whether you (1) *strongly agree*, (2) *agree*, (3) *are undecided*, (4) *disagree*, or (5) *strongly disagree* with each statement. There are no right or wrong answers. Many of the statements are similar to other statements. Do not be concerned about this. Just work quickly, and record your first impression.

_____ **1.** I dislike participating in group discussions.
_____ **2.** Generally, I am comfortable while participating in a group discussion.
_____ **3.** I am tense and nervous while participating in group discussions.
_____ **4.** I like to get involved in group discussions.
_____ **5.** Engaging in a group discussion with new people makes me tense and nervous.
_____ **6.** I am calm and relaxed while participating in group discussions.
_____ **7.** Generally, I am nervous when I have to participate in a meeting.
_____ **8.** Usually, I am calm and relaxed while participating in meetings.
_____ **9.** I am very calm and relaxed when I am called upon to express an opinion at a meeting.

_____**10.** I am afraid to express myself at meetings.

_____**11.** Communicating at meetings usually makes me uncomfortable.

_____**12.** I am very relaxed when answering questions at a meeting.

_____**13.** While participating in a conversation with a new acquaintance, I feel very nervous.

_____**14.** I have no fear of speaking up in conversations.

_____**15.** Ordinarily, I am very tense and nervous in conversations.

_____**16.** Ordinarily, I am very calm and relaxed in conversations.

_____**17.** While conversing with a new acquaintance, I feel very relaxed.

_____**18.** I'm afraid to speak up in conversations.

_____**19.** I have no fear of giving a speech.

_____**20.** Certain parts of my body feel very tense and rigid while I am giving a speech.

_____**21.** I feel relaxed while I am giving a speech.

_____**22.** My thoughts become confused and jumbled when I am giving a speech.

_____**23.** I face the prospect of giving a speech with confidence.

_____**24.** While giving a speech, I get so nervous that I forget facts I really know.

Scoring Instructions:

The PRCA-24 permits computation of one total score and four subscores. The subscores are related to communication apprehension in each of four common communication contexts: group discussions, meetings, interpersonal conversations, and public speaking. To compute your scores, merely add or subtract the scores for each item as indicated below.

SUBSCORE DESIRED	SCORING FORMULA
Group discussion	18 + scores for items 2, 4, 6; − scores for items 1, 3, 5
Meetings	18 + scores for items 8, 9, 12; − scores for items 7, 10, 11
Interpersonal conversations	18 + scores for items 14, 16, 17; − scores for items 13, 15, 18
Public speaking	18 + scores for items 19, 21, 23; − scores for items 20, 22, 24

To obtain your total score for the PRCA-24, simply add your four subscores together. Your score should range between 24 and 120. If your score is below 24 or above 120, you have made a mistake in computing the score.

Scores on the four contexts (groups, meetings, interpersonal conversations, and public speaking) can range from a low of 6 to a high of 30. Any score above 18 indicates some degree of apprehension. If your score is above 18 for the public speaking context, you are like the overwhelming majority of Americans.

NORMS FOR PRCA-24	AVERAGE
For total score:	65.6
Group:	15.4
Meeting:	16.4
Dyad (interpersonal):	14.5
Public:	19.3

NATURE/NURTURE intersections

Does Your Brain Make You Shy?

Did you know that a part of shyness has been linked to brain activity? Dr. Carl Schwartz of Harvard Medical School found that shyness has roots in an almond-shaped brain region call the amygdala, which is known to control emotions such as fear (see Figure 2.1).[53]

The study used a tool called functional magnetic resonance imaging to look for differences in how the brains of introverts and extraverts reacted to pictures of unfamiliar faces. Schwartz and his team of researchers examined subjects who had been classified as shy or outgoing 20 years earlier, when they were toddlers. Adults who had been clas-

sified as shy as children had a higher level of blood flow in the amygdala than the level of those who had been labeled as outgoing. "We found that individual differences in temperament (personality) are associated with persistent differences in the responsivity of the amygdala after more than 20 years of development and life experience," Schwartz says. Put simply, a part of shyness is linked to brain activity. Even after 20 years of experience interacting and relating to people, individuals continue to experience shyness in a consistent manner. Schwartz commented that this study demonstrated a relationship between brain activity and shyness; however, the study did not prove a direct cause-and-effect relationship.

FIGURE 2.1

The Amygdala: The Portion of the Brain That Controls Emotions Such as Fear

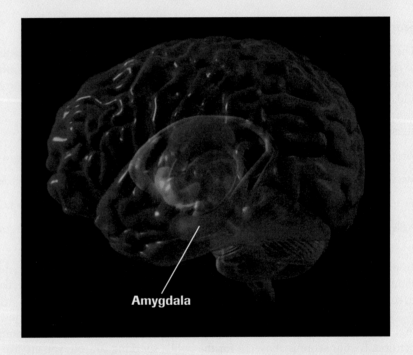

Amygdala

Understanding Your Communication Apprehension. Research suggests that one in five Americans experience an abnormally high level of communication apprehension.[50] You might have seen television commercials advertising social anxiety medication. Communication apprehension is a form of social anxiety. People who are high in the communication apprehension trait experience fear when communicating with others in a variety of contexts, including meetings, small groups, public presentations, and relationships. People who are low in the communication apprehension trait rarely experience fear when communicating with others. Research suggests that a high level of communication apprehension has a tendency to negatively affect all types of important interpersonal relationships, including parent–child, teacher–student, doctor–patient, workplace, and our intimate and sexual relationships.[51]

To help you understand how your communication is affected by your communication apprehension, consider the following questions. [52]

- *Do you avoid communicating with others?* Rather than informally socializing with others, do you make excuses for not attending social events?

- *Do you withdraw from communication?* Rather than getting more involved in conversations with friends or colleagues, do you have a tendency to pull away from these conversations and social opportunities?

- *Do you experience communication disruptions?* Rather than talking in a clear manner, do you have a tendency to mispronounce words and use too many vocal disfluencies or interrupters, such as "uhh," "ahh," "um," and "like"?

- *Do you overcommunicate?* Rather than having a discussion in which there is give and take in the conversation, do you have a tendency to dominate the conversation?

The more questions you answered yes to, the more likely you are to experience high levels of communication apprehension. The following section provides you with some ways to manage your apprehension when it comes to communicating with others.

 WHAT CAN I **do now?**

If you scored 18 or higher on any of the subscores of the PRCA-24:

▶ *You could avoid the triggers that activate your communication apprehension.* Try reducing the number of unfamiliar or formal situations. Also, try limiting situations in which people pay excessive attention to you or in which you are evaluated.[54]

▶ *You could make sure that your personality, communication, and environment are in sync.*[55] In other words, don't put yourself into situations that require excessive amounts of communication if you have a choice.

▶ *You could get skills training in communication.* You're already taking the first step in reducing your communication apprehension by reading this book and taking communication courses.[56]

▶ *You could remember to visualize success.* Although it might seem a bit too simple, studies have found that if you take the time to imagine yourself being successful, the brain has a way of making you feel more confident and less anxious. [57]

▶ *You could seek out professional assistance.* A variety of professional therapies and treatments have been shown to reduce communication apprehension.[58] Your medical doctor can even prescribe social anxiety medication (e.g., Prozac, Zoloft, Paxil) if you have an extremely high level of communication apprehension.[59]

Socio-Communicative Orientation

Your **socio-communicative orientation (SCO)** is how you perceive your levels of responsiveness and assertiveness when communicating with others. It's similar to your handwritten signature in that it is unique; no one has a signature that's exactly like yours. Your socio-communicative orientation is also unique; no one has a SCO that's exactly like yours. What is your social signature? To find out, take a few minutes to assess your socio-communicative orientation.

 ASSESS YOUR **communication personality**

Richmond and McCroskey's Socio-Communicative Orientation Assessment[60]

Log onto our self-assessment library, MyPersonalityProfile, found on MyCommunicationLab (www.mycommunicationlab.com), and assess your socio-communicative orientation by completing the interactive assessment. Also, encourage your relational partner (a friend, coworker, family member, or romantic partner) to do the same. This way, you can compare and contrast your scores and begin to understand better how your communication traits may influence your interpersonal communication.

Directions:

The following questionnaire lists twenty personality characteristics. Please indicate the degree to which you believe each of these characteristics applies to you while interacting with others by marking whether you (5) *strongly agree* that it applies, (4) *agree* that it applies, (3) are *undecided*, (2) *disagree* that it applies, or (1) *strongly disagree* that it applies. There are no right or wrong answers. Work quickly; record your first impression.

_____ 1. Helpful
_____ 2. Defends own beliefs
_____ 3. Independent
_____ 4. Responsive to others
_____ 5. Forceful
_____ 6. Has strong personality
_____ 7. Sympathetic
_____ 8. Compassionate
_____ 9. Assertive
_____10. Sensitive to the needs of others
_____11. Dominant
_____12. Sincere
_____13. Gentle
_____14. Willing to take a stand
_____15. Warm
_____16. Tender
_____17. Friendly
_____18. Acts as a leader
_____19. Aggressive
_____20. Competitive

Scoring Instructions:

To score your responses, add what you marked for each item as follows:

Assertiveness = 2 + 3 + 5 + 6 + 9 + 11 + 14 + 18 + 19 + 20

Responsiveness = 1 + 4 + 7 + 8 + 10 + 12 + 13 + 15 + 16 + 17

Scores above 34 indicate high assertiveness or responsiveness. Scores below 26 indicate low assertiveness or responsiveness. Scores between 26 and 34 indicate moderate levels of assertiveness or responsiveness.

To identify the quadrant that most accurately reflects your socio-communicative orientation, map your assertiveness and responsiveness scores using the matrix in Figure 2.2. First, place an X on the vertical axis that reflects your assertiveness score. Second, place an X on the horizontal axis that reflects your responsiveness score. Now connect the two scores. For example, if you scored a 35 on assertiveness and a 46 on responsiveness, you would fall within the "Expressive" quadrant.

FIGURE 2.2

Assertiveness/Responsiveness Matrix

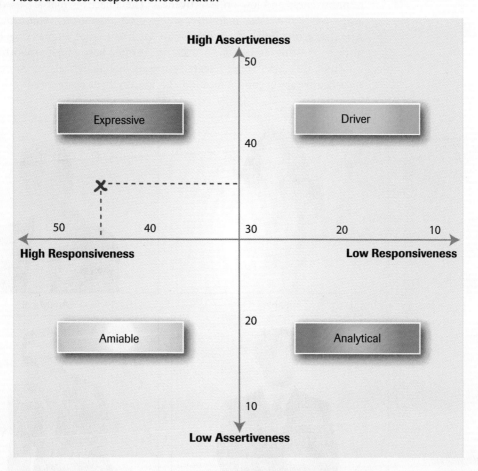

Source: Richmond, V. P., & McCroskey, J. C. (1990). Reliability and separation of factors on the assertiveness and responsiveness scales. *Psychological Reports, 67*, 449–450.

Understanding Your Socio-Communicative Orientation. Your social style is a composite of two communication factors: assertiveness and responsiveness. **Assertiveness** is the capacity to make requests; to actively disagree; to express positive or negative personal rights and feelings; to initiate, maintain, or disengage from conversations; and to stand up for one's self without attacking another.[61] Put simply, it is your ability to express your needs, wants, and desires in a firm, but polite manner. **Responsiveness** is the capacity to be sensitive to the communication of others, to be seen as a good listener, to make others comfortable in communicating, and to recognize the needs and desires of others.[62] When these two factors are combined, four distinct social styles emerge. The following list will help you to interpret your scores and describe some of the characteristics of these four social styles:[63]

Amiables. The **amiables** are considered relationship specialists and are high on responsiveness and low on assertiveness. The adjectives that are used to describe amiables are *conforming, unsure, pliable, dependent, awkward, supportive, respectful, willing, dependable,* and *agreeable.* Amiables seem to be most comfortable working in environments in which they can provide services and be supportive and helpful in their relationships with others. We often find these people in careers such as teaching, human resources, social work, psychology, and other helping professions.

Analyticals. The **analyticals** are considered technical specialists and are low on responsiveness and low on assertiveness. The adjectives that are used to describe analyticals are *critical, indecisive, stuffy, picky, moralistic, industrious, persistent, serious, exacting,* and *orderly.* Professions such as science, engineering, construction work, accounting, and certain aspects of law often have a high proportion of people who have this style. Some research suggests that analyticals are more likely to be apprehensive about communication and, as a result, be more withdrawn and quiet.[64]

Amiable

Analytical

Driver

Expressive

What is your social style? How does it influence how you communicate with others and how others communicate with you?

Thus, analyticals may be less effective communicators than people who have the other styles and more resistant to attempts to interact with them.

Driver. The **drivers** are considered control specialists and are low on responsiveness and high on assertiveness. The adjectives that are used to describe drivers are *pushy, severe, tough, dominating, harsh, strong-willed, independent, practical, decisive,* and *efficient.* These people might be in careers such as small-business ownership, top management, production management, administrative personnel, politics, and other decision-making management positions. Because of their ability to take responsibility and direct others, top management often puts these individuals into positions of control.

Expressive. The **expressives** are considered social specialists and are high on responsiveness and high on assertiveness. The adjectives that are used to describe expressives are *competent, excitable, versatile, reacting, ambitious, stimulating, enthusiastic, dramatic,* and *friendly.* People with expressive behavior are often found in sales, entertainment, advertising, art, music, and writing. These people know how to use their communication skills to gain recognition and attention, and they like being seen and noticed by others.

 WHAT CAN I **do now?**[65]

If you're an amiable, you could . . .

▶ Let others know what you need and desire.

▶ Make requests, such as "When time permits, would you please do this . . . ," rather than not asking for help.

▶ Learn to say no, and be careful that people do not take advantage of your willingness to help others.

When you're relating to an amiable, you could . . .

▶ Refrain from taking advantage of the person's willingness to help others.

▶ Talk about positive, people-oriented issues.

▶ Use responsive behaviors, such as vocal assurances (e.g., yes, okay, I hear what you're saying) and forward body leans to show your interest in the conversation.

If you're an analytical, you could . . .

▶ Let others know what you need and desire, making requests rather than demands.

▶ Increase your responsive behaviors by letting others know that you're listening and interested in what they're saying.

▶ Allow others to get to know you as a person by sharing more of yourself with them.

When you're relating to an analytical, you could . . .

▶ Talk about documented facts.

▶ Provide deadlines.

▶ Be patient, organized, and logical.

▶ Use task rather than relational communication, and focus on work rather than personal life.

continued

If you're a driver, you could . . .

▶ Listen more and talk less.

▶ Paraphrase what you hear other people saying; for instance, you could say, "Here's what I hear you saying. . . . Is my understanding correct?"

▶ Pay attention to other people's feelings and emotions, and acknowledge how others are feeling. Observe facial expressions, and listen to tone of voice. Usually, the face and the tone of voice reveal how the other person is feeling.

When you're relating to a driver, you could . . .

▶ Talk about task-related items, such as goals and objectives, in a direct manner.

▶ Encourage immediate action, and proceed rapidly with a degree of urgency.

▶ Behave in a professional and businesslike manner, especially remaining time conscious.

If you're an expressive, you could . . .

▶ Continue using assertive (making request of others to make sure your needs are met) and responsive (actively listening to others and confirming them) behaviors.

▶ Monitor others' behaviors to make sure you're not "too much" for some people. If others are using avoidant behaviors, such as looking away, sighing, or using a closed body orientation, they might want you to tone down your communication style.

When you're relating to an expressive, you could . . .

▶ Use animated gestures and an open body position.

▶ Use an expressive voice by altering the rate (speed) and volume (loudness) of your voice.

▶ Talk about people and opinions while being stimulating, flexible, and open.

CHECKING YOUR UNDERSTANDING
Communication Traits

Before reading any further, try answering the following questions:

1. What is a communication trait, and how is it similar to and different from a personality trait?

2. How does a person's communication apprehension affect his or her interpersonal communication? What can a person do to manage his or her communication apprehension?

3. How would you describe your socio-communicative orientation? Are you an amiable, analytical, driver, or expressive? How are assertiveness and responsiveness related to your social style?

4. How would you go about adapting your social style to another person's social style?

Managing Your Identity

Your **identity** is a set of characteristics that you recognize as belonging uniquely to you and no one else. Some of these characteristics include the concepts that you have been learning about in this chapter: self-concept, self-esteem, and communication traits, to name a few. Most people invest considerable time in managing their identities. If you're on Facebook or MySpace, how much time did you spend creating your profile, making sure you had the right picture and profile description? **Identity management**, also known as impression management, refers to the ways in which people try to control the impressions others have of them.[66] What parts of your self-concept and personality do you share with others? Are you successful in managing your identity? Answers to these questions will be addressed in the following three sections that examine identity management characteristics, influences, and strategies.

ETHICS in interpersonal communication

Is Identity Management Ethical?

Some researchers argue that identity management is an unethical communication act, while others suggest that identity management is ethical and a sign of a competent communicator.[67] A 2006 study of online dating relationships found that dating participants revealed a lack of honesty by engaging in deceptive forms of identity management.[68] When developing their online profiles, participants were more likely to present their "ideal" selves than their "real" selves. If the relationship developed further, they were faced with the prospect of "getting caught in the act" and being perceived as deceptive and dishonest in their self-presentation online.[69] In a study of sales representatives and their supervisors, representatives who engaged in impression management simply to get a better review from their supervisors were seen, by their supervisors, as deceptive on the basis of their purpose and motivation.[70]

To other researchers, identity management is a natural and adaptive communicative process and therefore is ethical.[71] For example, even if you feel that you can just "be yourself" around close friends and family members, you might find yourself acting quite differently—or presenting a somewhat different version of yourself—around your best friend than you do around your mother without really thinking about it. You might exhibit such different behavior not only because of your desire to be viewed somewhat differently by your friend and by your mother but also because your friend and your mother have different expectations or demands about what sort of person you should be. Thus, engaging in impression management can help to ensure that social interactions go smoothly.

Is it intention that makes identity management unethical? Is a person who intentionally uses identity management to be deceptive less ethical than a person who uses identity management unintentionally? What do you think? The above research suggests that it's the extent to which an individual engages in identity management and the motivation behind it that determine whether an identity management strategy is seen as a deceptive act or a strategic attempt at effective communication. Do you agree? Why or why not?

Identity Management Characteristics

The first characteristic of identity management is that most people construct and use both public and private identities in their interactions with others.[72] When talking to your close friends, you use your **private identity**, the person you believe yourself to be in moments of honest self-examination. When talking to a potential employer, you use your **public identity**, the way you want others to view you; it's your public image. How accurate is your Facebook or MySpace profile? Does it reflect your private or your public identity?

Sociologist Erving Goffman considered people's social interactions to be similar to a theatrical performance in which people use verbal and nonverbal messages to manage the roles they're playing in a particular context in order to make an impression.[73] Like an actor in a repertory company who plays different roles on different nights, you have different audiences for whom you perform throughout your day. Because of your different audiences, you have different identities. One way to illustrate how you use different identities for different audiences is to observe cell phone behavior. Someone talking to a friend on a cell phone quickly switches identity when accepting a call on the other line from a potential employer who wants to arrange a job interview. You see and hear a different person emerge from the conversation. The verbal and nonverbal messages you use with your close friends might not be the messages you use with a potential employer.

The second characteristic of identity management is that people have different beliefs about their identities that influence how they manage their identities. Some people endorse a pragmatic conception of self and identity management; others endorse a principled conception of self.[74] People who endorse a **pragmatic self** believe identity to be flexible and adaptive. They consider managing one's identity to be a practical way to reach their goals in an appropriate manner without violating norms or standards that others consider to be important. For example, if you're meeting your dating partner's parents for the first time and you endorse a pragmatic self, you will manage your identity in such a manner that you will not offend the parents. Your goal is to earn the parents' approval.

People who endorse a **principled self** believe that identity should not be altered or adapted to fit situations. They value consistency between their actions in social situations and relevant underlying attitudes, feelings, and beliefs. Being principled in terms of identity management means that one's identity is a reflection of how one feels and what one believes. Being authentic and true to one's self takes priority over the impressions that others might have of one. If you endorse this view and were meeting your dating partner's parents for the first time, rather than managing your identity for the parents, you would present yourself as who are with the hope that they would not find your authentic self to be offensive or inappropriate.

Identity Management Influences

Two major types of factors influence how you manage your identity: situational factors and personality factors. First, there are situational factors that influence your desire to manage your identity. For example, most people carefully manage their identities when interviewing for a position. In fact, research suggests that interviewees who manage their impressions by engaging in appropriate waiting room behavior, dressing appropriately, managing communication apprehension, using technology strategically, and making a professional introduction are perceived as socially skilled and desirable by interviewers.[75] You want to manage your identity well when there is a lot at stake—for example, when meeting and interacting with your significant other's parents and family members, your new neighbors, important clients at work, even teachers.

Second, there are personality factors that influence identity management. Psychologist Marc Snyder identified an individual difference in people that he referred to as **self-monitoring**, which is an internal process of being aware of yourself and how you are coming across to others. According to Snyder, "the self-monitoring individual is one who, out of a concern for social appropriateness, is particularly sensitive to the expression and self-presentation of others in social situations and uses these cues as guidelines for monitoring his own self-presentation."[76] Put simply, some people are high self-monitors, and others are low self-monitors.

ASSESSING on the web

Log onto our self-assessment library, MyPersonalityProfile, on MyCommunicationLab (www.mycommunicationlab.com), and complete Gangestad and Snyder's Self-Monitoring Scale online to determine your level of self-monitoring.[77]

Source: Gangestad, S. W., & Snyder, M. (2000). Self-monitoring: Appraisal and reappraisal. *Psychological Bulletin, 126,* 530-555.

High and low self-monitors differ in a variety of ways. High self-monitors pay attention to others' behaviors and use these behaviors as guide for their own communication and other behaviors. For example, high self-monitors might notice how others are constantly talking about sports, and regardless of whether they are sports fans, they quickly learn the language of sports and use it with fluency. High self-monitors are very observant and socially flexible.

High self-monitors are also very sensitive to social norms and make the necessary adjustments to present themselves in the best way possible. For example, high self-monitors notice the formality or informality of others' communication and then quickly adapt their own communication accordingly. It doesn't matter where they are, they fit in, and they feel comfortable in the various situations in which they find themselves. From the boardroom in the executive tower to working out in the field alongside volunteers rebuilding after an earthquake, high self-monitors adapt and make themselves similar to others in a particular situation.

Low self-monitors tend to pay more attention to their inner psychological states (i.e., feelings, attitudes, beliefs, personality traits) and use these states as guides for their communication and other behaviors. For example, low self-monitors who find themselves in a social function with hundreds of people quickly find a way out. Rather than mingling, socializing, and getting to know a lot of other people, low self-monitors are likely to single out a few people who are similar to them and then find a quiet corner where they can engage in a more intimate conversation. They're not necessarily shy; they just don't like spending a lot of time in an environment where they cannot be themselves.

Low self-monitors are consistent in their behavior. You know you're interacting with a low self-monitor when you see someone not adapting to a situation in a manner that you would consider normal. You might hear a friend of the low self-monitoring person saying, "That's just the way he is." Table 2.3 describes some of the research findings that differentiate high and low self-monitors.[78]

Identity Management Strategies

There are a number of strategies that you can use to manage your identity. When using these strategies, it's very important to consider your audience. You probably manage a number of relationships, including the ones you have with your parents, siblings, friends, and teachers and the ones you have at work with your supervisor and coworkers and with your employees if you're a manager or supervisor. You simultaneously manage several different identities; you're a son or daughter, student, employee, friend, campus leader, and member of a religious congregation. It's important to consider your goal when managing your identity. How do you want other people to see you? What behaviors would they consider appropriate?

 A large number of heterosexual people, especially men, continue to have and express negative attitudes toward gay and lesbian people.[79] Because of these negative attitudes,

TABLE 2.3

Differences between High and Low Self-Monitors	
High Self-Monitors	**Low Self-Monitors**
• Prefer variety in relational partners	• Prefer relational partners who are similar to them
• Prefer relationships that are flexible	• Prefer that others adapt to them
• Are adaptable in their relationships	• Have a single and unified social network; prefer being exclusive
• Have a number of segmented social networks; prefer being nonexclusive	• Prefer to commit to fewer friends and relational partners
• Have a tendency to not commit in relationships	• Tend to feel comfortable being intimate with others
• Tend to feel uncomfortable being intimate with others	• Prefer significant others who are willing to be intimate with them
• Fear that significant others will want them to be more intimate than they can be with the person	• Seek forgiveness from partners they have wronged

gays and lesbians manage their identities as a way to avoid various forms of physical and emotional abuse as well as discrimination. Unlike members of other minority groups who have physical characteristics that identify them as belonging to a minority group (e.g., skin color), gays and lesbians are invisible because physically they reflect the general population. Except in instances of "outing," in which an individual's sexual orientation is made public against his or her wishes by another person, identifying homosexual men and women depends largely on the communication skill of the gay and lesbian person and his or her use of identity management strategies. Here are a few of the identity management strategies that gay and lesbian people use to manage their identities:[80]

- *Passing*: When gays and lesbians "play it straight," they're passing. They intentionally lead others to believe that they're heterosexual. An example of this strategy would be a gay man pretending to have a girlfriend.

- *Covering*: When gays and lesbians prevent others from seeing them as homosexual, they're covering. Important information is omitted. The objective is not to pretend to be heterosexual, but to keep others from identifying them as homosexual. Examples of this strategy include monitoring use of pronouns (avoiding "he" or "she" and using "my friend") and removing nonverbal symbols that others might perceive to be homosexual such as photos, reading materials, bumper stickers, and rings.

- *Implicitly out*: When gays and lesbians discuss their personal lives openly and honestly without labeling themselves as gay or lesbian, they're using an implicitly out identity management strategy. This strategy allows others to make whatever sense of the personal information they choose.

- *Explicitly out*: When gays and lesbians share their homosexual identity to others, they're using an explicitly out identity management strategy.

How gay and lesbian people manage their identities has been shown to influence how others communicate and interact with them. One research study testing the explicitly out identity management strategy found that when learning about another person's sexual orientation during an initial encounter, heterosexual men and women liked the person less, were less likely to develop a relationship with the gay or lesbian person, and did not anticipate communicating with the person in the future. Other research studies have found that learning about a person's sexual orientation is less of an issue once a relationship has been established, suggesting that timing plays a role in identity management.[81]

There are some identity management strategies that apply to most relationships. Following are some strategies that you might find helpful in managing your appearance, first impressions, and online identity.

Manage Your Appearance. You begin managing your identity by first managing your **appearance**, or the personal factors that people use to shape an image of you. When managing their work or professional identity, most people wear clothing that is suitable for their profession or occupation. Because appearance is a highly personal identity management strategy, it's challenging to provide a list of strategies without a context for the strategies. Following is a list of identity management strategies using the context of appearance for a job interview or a semiformal business meeting or social gathering:[82]

- Wear clean and pressed clothes that cover the body appropriately and polished shoes.
- Be well groomed, including clean and styled hair, clean and appropriate length fingernails, and fresh breath.
- Wear a moderate amount of jewelry. Remove all hats, sunglasses, earphones, and chewing gum before entering the office where the interview is going to take place.
- Cover all tattoos, and remove nontraditional jewelry such as nose, tongue, or multiple ear studs.

Manage the First Impression. As you probably know, the first impression is the one that people tend to remember. For instance, you usually know within the first few minutes of meeting someone how the first date is going to end. Malcolm Gladwell coined the term "the blink" for this concept. In his bestseller, titled *Blink*, Gladwell describes how and why people have the ability to make important decisions in seconds. According to Gladwell, our instantaneous judgments are for the most part accurate and need to be trusted.[83] Here are a few communication strategies that you might want to try to enhance other people's first impression of you:

For most people, a first date is one of those events where people carefully manage their appearance and first impression.

- *Use a firm handshake.* A firm handshake is one that is strong (but not so strong as to cut off the blood supply), vigorous (meaning that it conveys an appropriate amount of energy), adequate in duration (not too brief or too long), and complete in grip (meaning that full hands are gripped, with palms touching).[84]

- *Use a confident voice.* A confident voice has energy and volume, a fast tempo, few and short pauses, varied pitch, expressiveness, and fluency.[85]

- *Use expressive gestures.* Dale Leathers, who studied nonverbal communication extensively, recommends five ways to effectively use gestures. Gestures should (1) be used to add emphasis to the points we are making; (2) be spontaneous, relaxed, and unrehearsed; (3) be used to signal that we wish to speak or that we want someone else to speak; (4) be kept away from the body, thus increasing the persuasive impact; and (5) indicate our feelings and emotions.[86]

- *Use responsive cues.* Nonverbally responsive behaviors that signal that you're paying attention to another person include using affirming head nods, maintaining eye contact, displaying an expressive face, showing interest by taking notes, sitting up and leaning forward, and using back channel cues that suggest that you understand what the person is saying.[87]

 Manage Your Online Identity. If you're a user of online social networking websites, such as Facebook or MySpace, it's important that you manage your online identity. There are an estimated 110 million monthly active users of social networking websites in the U.S., and these individuals have access to your identity through the profile you create for your website.[88] What would a potential employer learn about you from conducting an online search or reviewing your social networking profile? This was the case with administrators in the San Antonio, Texas, school district who were in the process of hiring new teachers for their schools. What they found were teacher applicants whose identities during the interview were inconsistent with their online identities.[89]

Here are a few strategies that you might want to try to ensure that your online identity is managed well:

- *Google yourself.* Go to a popular search engine (Google.com, Yahoo.com, or MSN.com will do), and type your name within quotation marks. If you find something that you would rather the world not see, contact the site's owner and ask that the item be removed.

- *Clean up your Facebook or MySpace page.* Some online social networking sites allow you to have multiple identities or profiles for different social networks. You might want to have two profiles—one for your personal network and one for your professional network.

- *Tune in to your blog buzz.* You can monitor your Web presence through sites such as Pubsub.com, which will alert you by email when your name is mentioned in Internet newsgroups, blogs, and securities filings.

- *Be in good company.* Research suggests that the online company you keep enhances your identity. One study found that your social capital increases as your number of online friends increases.[90] **Social capital** is how valuable you are perceived to be in terms of your connections. For example, the popular kids in high school had a lot of social capital. Others wanted to be their friends. The same seems to be the case for online social networks. As your network increases, your identity is enhanced.[91]

CHECKING YOUR UNDERSTANDING

Identity Management

Take a few minutes to check your understanding of the following assessment items:

1. What does it mean when the authors state that most people construct and use both public and private identities in their interactions with others?
2. What is self-monitoring? How do high and low self-monitors differ in their communication behaviors?
3. How do you manage a first impression, appearance, and an online identity?

A Communication Development Plan for Rick

To complete Rick's story, recall that he considers himself to be interpersonally challenged because of the awkwardness and anxiety he experiences when interacting with others. He doubts himself and his abilities. He feels stupid. These feelings of self-doubt usually cause him to become even more anxious about his interactions with others, especially in the workplace. He also feels weak because he has not been able to overcome this communication problem that he thinks is keeping him from being promoted despite his perfect work record.

What do you think about Rick's problem? What advice would you give him after reading this chapter?

Possible Explanations

Why can't Rick overcome his fear about communicating with strangers? Is that normal? It is normal for people with high levels of communication apprehension to feel frustrated when they're unable to overcome their fear of communicating and interacting with others. Scientific research suggests that Rick might never completely cure his fear of communicating. He can, however, learn to manage his fear by following some of the suggestions that were discussed in this chapter. Here's a quick review:

1. Rick can seek out communication skills training. He can take additional communication courses, in which he will learn more about himself, how and why communication works and doesn't work, and skills to enhance his communication effectiveness.

2. Rick can plan for social situations. Here are a few suggestions for how Rick might plan for situations that require him to interact with others. He should:[92]

   - *Prepare a self-introduction to be ready to introduce himself.* He should keep the introduction brief and mention his connection to the party, event, or function so that others know how to interact with him.

   - *Listen to people.* This is probably the easiest skill for those who find it difficult to engage in small talk. Rather than talking, Rick should actively listen to others, nodding his head, leaning forward, making eye contact, and asking questions for clarification.

   - *Prepare to meet people.* If he's attending a party or a company function, he should anticipate or ask the host who will be attending and then Google the other attendees and find out more about them. If it's a company function, he should use the organization's website.

   - *Determine what he has in common with other people.* He should ask simple questions to determine points of similarity: "Where are you from?" "What school did you attend?" "Where do you work?" "What are your hobbies?" These questions are usually safe and provide a point of departure in the conversation.

   - *Use conversational starters.* He should familiarize himself with current events and, when there is a lull in the conversation, refer to what's going on in the community, such as a sporting event, a concert or theatrical production, or a fund-raiser.

3. Rick can seek out professional assistance. There are a number of professional therapies and treatments that have been shown to reduce communication apprehension.

Why does Rick's inability to communicate with strangers make him feel stupid? He has been very successful as an assistant buyer. This is not an unusual feeling. Rick's self-concept and self-esteem are partially influenced by his communication skills and abilities. Regardless of the professional success that Rick has achieved, the challenge he faces when communicating and interacting with others is very personal to him and is a part of how he sees himself. It's important for Rick to understand that his fear of communication and his struggles to overcome it are not a personal weakness. Communication science suggests that Rick's high level of communication apprehension is linked to his genetics that were passed down to him from his parents and grandparents. Although he can modify his anxiety and learn to cope with it, it's uncertain whether he can completely rid himself of his communication apprehension.

Should Rick continue applying for a buyer position? It's important for Rick to find a job that is a good fit with his personality and communication abilities. Again, a good fit is one in which the environment fits a person's personality and communication traits. If he were to obtain a position as a lead buyer at Nordstrom, knowing that the position has a number of communication demands such as making presentations and developing relationships with clients and designers, would Rick be happy? Would he be effective? Does Rick want this particular position, or does he want a promotion and this seems to be the natural position for him, since he has been an assistant buyer. It might be wise for Rick to explore other promotion opportunities in which the position's communication requirements would better fit his personality.

Take Aways

Interpersonal communication begins with your understanding of who you are as a person. Most people do not live in isolation from others. You're a product of the relationships that you have with others as well as the personality and communication traits that you possess. The purpose of this chapter was to introduce you to some new ways to think about who you are as a person. When you understand yourself better, you also begin to understand others better. This level of understanding enhances interpersonal communication. The following list of knowledge claims summarizes what you have learned in this chapter:

- Your self-concept is the sum total of your knowledge and understanding of your self; it's descriptive. Self-esteem reflects your overall self-appraisal of your worth; it's evaluative.

- Your self-concept is complex and constantly evolving, and it develops through your self-perceptions, social comparisons, peer group influence, and reflected appraisals.

- Your self-esteem is affected by two large factors: biology and environment. A part of your self-esteem is inherited through the genes that have been passed down to you from your parents and grandparents, and a part of

your self-esteem develops through your relationships, your educational experiences, and your exposure to and interaction with various forms of media.

- Your self-concept and self-esteem affect your communication in that they influence your motivation to communicate, the expectations you have for yourself and others, your relational messages, and how you interpret messages.

- Communication traits are enduring consistencies and differences in message-sending and message-receiving behaviors among individuals.

- Most people manage their identities in order to reach their interpersonal communication goals.

- Your identity is a set of characteristics that you recognize as belonging uniquely to you and no one else: private and public identities, pragmatic and principled selves.

Following are some of the ways you learned about how your personality and communication traits influence your interpersonal communication:

- By completing the communication apprehension (PRCA-24) measure, you learned about the anxiety you experience when communicating with others.

- By completing the socio-communicative orientation (SCO) measure, you learned about your social style and how to adapt to other people's social styles.

Following are a list of skills you can develop to enhance your interpersonal communication:

- Enhance your self-concept and self-esteem by developing supportive relationships, realistic expectations, skill competencies, rational beliefs, and a plan B that will help you when there's a setback.

- Manage your communication apprehension by guarding against negative attentional focus, finding a good fit, seeking out communication skills training, visualizing success, finding professional assistance, and avoiding the things that trigger your communication apprehension.

- Manage your identity by using a variety of strategies, including managing first impression, appearance, and online identity.

Theory Discussion Questions

1. Differentiate between self-concept and self-esteem. How are they related to communication?

2. What is communication apprehension, and how does it affect your communication?

3. What are the four socio-communicative orientations? Provide an example of a person you know who exemplifies each style.

4. What is the difference between the public self and the private self, and what is the difference between the principled self and the pragmatic self?

5. How do situation and personality work together to influence impression management?

6. What are some identity management strategies?

Building Your Skills

1. Get together with a significant other, family member, or good friend with whom you communicate on a regular basis. Then both of you take all of the self-assessments in this chapter. Compare your results. What surprises you about yourself? About the other person?

2. After completing the socio-communicative self-assessment in this chapter, write a brief description of your particular social style. Now identify how you differ from people with other styles. How do you better understand the other styles? What are some ways in which you could improve your communication with people who represent each of the other communicative styles?

3. Pair up with another classmate. Discuss how you see the concepts in this chapter regarding self, personality, and communication working together to affect relationships. Can you see evidence of these factors working together in your own life? Use real-life examples.

4. Do a personal assessment of your own self-concept and self-esteem. How happy are you with your evaluation? Now write down some ways in which you could enhance your self-concept and self-esteem. Track your results over the course of the class. At the end of the semester, do another personal assessment. Are there any differences?

5. Get together with three other classmates, and prepare a skit in which each person acts out one of the socio-communicative styles in a social setting. Act out the skit in front of the class, and ask your classmates to guess who represents each style.

6. After reading the section on online impression management, do a self-assessment of your own online presence. Google yourself, evaluate your own Facebook or MySpace profile, and run a PubSub search on yourself. What do you find? Is there anything there that you might not want family members or potential friends, teachers, or employers to see? How could you "clean up" your digital dirt?

3 Understanding Your Perceptions of Others

Dr. Menger, a young assistant professor, was excited about teaching her first graduate class. She had gone to great lengths to plan her first lecture so that it would be well-organized and interesting to her new graduate students.

As Dr. Menger began her lecture, she noticed that at first the students seemed a bit subdued, but as the class progressed, most of them began to perk up and become more animated. One student, Shuntaro, however, seemed to be less than enthused. When Shuntaro would get a confused look on his face, he would scribble down comments and shove his notebook in front of the person next to him. This began to irritate Dr. Menger, who found herself becoming more animated in an effort to get her students' attention and, she hoped, grab Shuntaro's interest as well. After a while, however, she realized that Shuntaro wasn't going to get involved in class, so she began to ignore him.

After class, Dr. Menger decided she was going to need to speak to Shuntaro. As the students left for the evening, Professor Menger glared at Shuntaro and shook her head.

Shuntaro avoided eye contact and quickly scurried out of the class. When Dr. Menger returned to her office, she sent Shuntaro an email indicating her displeasure with his classroom behavior, and asking him to stop by during her office hours the next day.

When Shuntaro knocked on her door the next day, Dr. Menger opened it ready to lecture him on the expected behavior of graduate students. She told Shuntaro that what she observed was rude, insolent behavior that would not be tolerated. The look on Shuntaro's face was complete shock. He wondered what he had done to cause Dr. Menger to confront him in this manner. When his classroom behavior was described, Shuntaro suddenly realized what was going on. He quickly apologized and told Dr. Menger that he was very interested in her class and enjoyed the lecture and the activity. "I was trying to understand your interpretation of the assigned reading, so I was writing down questions for Brittany and Charles to help me follow along better."

This caught Dr. Menger completely off guard, so she asked Shuntaro why he didn't simply ask her for help.

CHAPTER OBJECTIVES

AFTER READING THIS CHAPTER, you will understand:

1 The perception process and the stages and attributions that create the process.

2 Three primary influences on the perception process.

3 The power of your inherent and individual influences on your perceptions.

4 The errors you can make in the perception process and how they affect your communication.

"This is my first class with you, and I didn't want you to think I wasn't trying or that I wasn't smart enough to be in your class. I work very hard to fit in, so I don't typically speak up. Getting others to help me understand some of the more difficult class concepts has been really great. I didn't know I was upsetting you last night. I really had no idea."

What perceptions did Dr. Menger have of Shuntaro after her class? Do you think her assessment, based on Shuntaro's behavior, was accurate? While reading this chapter, consider how you might answer the following questions to help both Shuntaro and Dr. Menger better understand the situation.

- Based upon Dr. Menger's comments to Shuntaro in her email message, what do you believe Dr. Menger's perceptions are?

- How might Shuntaro's communication behaviors have created these perceptions?

- What social or cultural influences might have contributed to Dr. Menger's perception of Shuntaro's behavior in her class?

We will revisit Dr. Menger and Shuntaro's story at the end of this chapter. As you read, see how many concepts you might be able to apply to their situation.

AFTER READING THIS CHAPTER, you will be able to:

1 Manage your perceptions by recognizing when social and/or cultural factors influence and control them.

2 Curb your use of stereotyping and prejudice by considering three methods of perception checking.

3 Become more accurate in your perceptions by following three steps of direct perception checking.

AFTER COMPLETING THE SELF-ASSESSMENTS, you will learn about:

1 The level of perceived attitude and background homophily that exists in your close relationship(s).

2 Your attributional confidence and how your score indicates errors in your perceptions.

We develop perceptions of others in our initial encounters with them, and these perceptions are invaluable in understanding our communication with others. What many people fail to recognize is that our perceptions are not always accurate. For example, recall a time when you might have decided that people you met were rude and you instantly disliked them. Did you stop and ask yourself exactly what they did that made you feel this way? Did they do or say something that led you to believe they were unfriendly? If you could not pinpoint the cause, perhaps you made a mistake in judging them. It is also possible that the explanation lies within your own self-perceptions. In other words, thoughts about yourself might have been projected onto the other people. For example, people who are unhappy in their personal relationships might hate seeing others getting along and being romantic. They might develop negative perceptions of happy couples that are really about their own unhappy relationships. It is essential to discover the basis of these initial impressions to avoid jeopardizing future relationships.

> We do not see things as they are.
> We see them as we are.
> —*THE TALMUD*

A primary goal of this chapter is to help you understand the perceptual process, the stages within the process, and the factors that influence it. Everyone moves through steps of the perception process, but not everyone recognizes his or her own inaccuracies along the way. This perspective is largely based on Glasser's **Choice Theory**, which asserts that we all have a personal framework for a "Quality World" and we constantly compare our real-world experiences to what we view as quality. Because of this, we might not be able to alter the behaviors of others, but we can change the way we perceive them.[1]

Understanding the Perception Process

Because humans are social creatures they constantly encounter others who are new and unfamiliar. To determine how to interact with them, we form rapid impressions. We look people over and make snap judgments about their communication behaviors: appearance, posture, facial expressions, vocal characteristics, and so on. We relate what we see to our previous experiences, and this sometimes clouds our perceptions.[2] For example, let's say you meet a man who is over seven feet tall and you instantly feel uncomfortable around him. As he introduces himself, you recall your third grade teacher, Mr. Davis, who used to stand tall over students and chuckle at their mistakes as they read aloud in class. As this tall man begins to talk about himself, you remain unresponsive and avoid eye contact. You have no interest in getting to know him because you feel that he is cocky and a bit of a know-it-all. In a split second, you have developed a negative perception of this man. Is your evaluation fair? Is it accurate? Whether you know it or not, your first impressions will guide your future behavior, and until you become more aware of them, your positive or negative biases will prevail. Scholars refer to the self-knowing that fosters competent perceptions as a component of **social intelligence**[3] or the "ability to act wisely in human relationships."[4] So if you do not have a clear awareness of yourself and how you communicate, it will be difficult to determine whether your perceptions and subsequent behaviors are accurate and appropriate.

Meeting someone for the first time can frequently be awkward, especially if you are unaware of your own communication.

Defining Perception

Perception may be defined as the process of observing things around us and making sense of them through our own frame of reference. **Interpersonal perceptions** develop when we observe and interpret the communication (verbal and nonverbal) of the people we encounter. Ultimately, we develop perceptions of another person, and these perceptions are either positive or negative. When we make these perceptions, they guide the way we send and receive messages. Research on speed dating, for example, suggests that people accurately evaluate the value of a future date with someone in less than 30 seconds.[5] The concept of "thin-slicing" suggests that speed daters can quickly evaluate others, develop perceptions, and make swift decisions based on attractiveness, similarities, and nonverbal cues.[6] To help you understand your own perceptions of others, let's now break down the perceptual process into its various stages (see Figure 3.1).

FIGURE 3.1

The Stages of Perception.

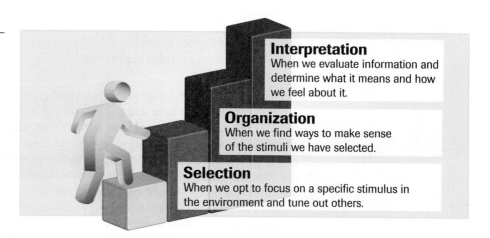

Interpretation
When we evaluate information and determine what it means and how we feel about it.

Organization
When we find ways to make sense of the stimuli we have selected.

Selection
When we opt to focus on a specific stimulus in the environment and tune out others.

Identifying Perception Stages

Although we can identify and separately depict the stages of the perceptual process, in reality, the stages occur rapidly and are so intertwined that most of us fail to recognize that we are experiencing each of them. Imagine yourself sitting in the airport waiting to board a plane. There are hundreds of people moving all around you. You don't stop and consciously think, "I believe I'll watch that man in the corner feeding his baby. He must be a great father." Your eyes are drawn to him, but more than likely you have no idea why you have decided to observe this scene when there are so many others to choose from. In a split second, you have experienced the three perceptual stages: selecting, organizing, and interpreting.

Selecting. The first stage, when you opt to focus on a specific stimulus in the environment and consequently tune out others, is known as **selecting**. You might not know exactly why you make this choice, but something draws your attention. You do this constantly throughout the day; you've probably even had this experience while you have been reading this chapter. Stop for a moment, and think about the past few minutes. Has there been a noise, a smell, or something that has drawn your attention away from the pages in front of you? If you recall the past five minutes, you will probably discover that something loud, sudden, interesting, or even annoying interrupted your reading. Though there are many reasons to select certain stimuli, the following three are quite common:

- *The stimulus is unique and stands out.* For example, most people stop and stare at individuals who are vastly different in their dress or behavior. This happens because these people draw our attention away from what we are doing. Neuroscientists explain that our brains are actually wired to alert us to anything unusual.[7]

- *The stimulus appeals to your level of interest or need.* If something or someone resonates with you and your interests or needs, you will most likely focus on it. Think about waking up in the morning, wanting to go back to sleep, and suddenly smelling freshly brewed coffee. "This is just what I need to get my day started!" you think. While the coffee might fulfill an early morning need, a newspaper headline or television bulletin running across the bottom of the screen may capture your interest.

- *You select on the basis of your expectations.* When you are confronted with new and unexpected information, it will capture your attention and elicit either a positive or a negative response.[8] For example, if you expect your instructor to come to class dressed professionally but he or she arrives wearing shorts and a tank top, your expectations have probably been violated.

Organizing. The second stage of the perceptual process, in which we find ways to make sense of the stimuli we have selected, is known as **organizing**. We are bombarded with stimuli; consequently, our world can become quite chaotic. To simplify and eliminate this chaos, also known as **entropy**, we begin to organize the information or stimuli we have selected.[9] To do this, we draw upon familiar experiences that exist in our minds—our **cognitive schemata**. These are our mental frameworks, or mental file folders, which are filled with our past knowledge and experiences (see Figure 3.2). For example, you might be surprised to see a man wearing an apron and cooking dinner because your experiences since you were young have involved women performing this task. However, your cognitive file folder for this activity has expanded, and you see men on television with their own cooking shows. What this means is that you now have a schema for

FIGURE 3.2

Cognitive Schemata are your mental file folders that help you interpret what you see in the world. They hold all of your past knowledge and experiences about people, places, feelings, and emotions.

dealing with this information. Our cognitive schemata allow us to classify and interpret information by associating the unfamiliar with the familiar.

Four schemata are primarily used to organize the information you select: physical, role, interaction, and psychological.[10]

- *Physical schemata help you to classify people you meet on the basis of their physical appearance.* Your classification of them is related to your previous experiences. We may recognize beauty, for example, based on what we see on television and in magazines. We recognize when someone is too heavy, wears too much makeup, or dresses inappropriately to meet our socially determined expectations. You have a mental file folder of information to help you organize physical attributes.

- *Role schemata help you to organize the communication behaviors of individuals in specific roles or social positions.* You have mental notes about the verbal and nonverbal communication of doctors, teachers, husbands, wives, grandparents, and so on. If you observe a woman your grandmother's age exhibiting abnormal behavior for her age, you might have negative perceptions of her based upon your existing role schemata.

- *Your **interaction schemata** allow you to organize people according to their social behaviors.* As a student, for example, you most likely have a schema for students' classroom interactions. Context plays a big role in perceptions of interactions because you interpret them according to location, time of day, and so on.

- *Psychological schemata reflect your personal dispositions and mental states.* You can typically look at someone and tell whether the person is nervous, worried, elated, or the like. Though some people are better at hiding their internal states than others, you have a basis for comparison and generally know how people are feeling at a given moment in time.

Though we discuss these four schemata separately, they rarely work in isolation. You draw upon them collectively at times to paint a more complete picture. In the late 1950s and early 1960s, a television program called *Leave It to Beaver* was very popular. In this program about a middle-class family, the mother, June Cleaver, was portrayed

The audience was outraged when Kanye West grabbed the microphone away from Taylor Swift during her acceptance speech at the MTV Video Music Awards.

as being a typical housewife at the time. Every day, she wore a dress and pearls. She cooked, cleaned, made her kids' lunches, and, on top of it all, seemed very pleased to do this every day. Mothers at this time imported these elements for their physical and psychological schemata. Though women's cognitive schemata have likely expanded and most women no longer emulate June Cleaver, mothers and women in general who were exposed to the program might still call upon these schemata to organize their perceptions and assign meaning to them.

Interpreting. The third stage, in which we evaluate information and determine what it means and how we feel about it, is known as **interpreting**. At the 2009 MTV Video Music Awards show, rapper Kanye West grabbed the microphone from 17-year-old Taylor Swift as she was accepting the award for best female video. He shouted that the video of Beyoncé Knowles (another female singer) was one of the best videos of all time. The people in the audience sat in stunned silence for a moment but eventually began to boo West. How might you interpret his behavior? In regard to role and interaction schemata, is this normal for a music artist attending an awards show? For people who regularly watch such shows, this sort of behavior is unusual for most artists but not new for Kanye West.

He had engaged in similar rude outbursts in the past, as in 2007, when he announced that he would never return to MTV after Britney Spears was selected over him to open the awards show, and in 2006, when he stormed the stage at the MTV Europe Music Awards after losing for Best Video. The press interpreted Kanye West's behavior and described him as an egotistical bully.

Though many factors may aid you in the interpretive process, three are quite common: your previous experiences and expectations, how well you know a person, and your degree of intimacy.

- *Your previous expectations and experiences allow you to relate new information to that with which you are already familiar.* For example, if you have seen Kanye West misbehave on other television shows, you might determine that he is again behaving inappropriately. In fact, you probably expect him to behave this way, and for him to act otherwise might seem abnormal.[11]

- *If you know someone well and are familiar with how that person communicates, you will interpret his or her behavior correctly.* Typical interpretations are that the behavior is positive or negative, normal or abnormal, appropriate or inappropriate, and so on.

- *The degree of relational intimacy also enhances the interpretive process.* If someone you have started dating only recently shows up late to pick you up, you might be skeptical of the reason the person provides for the delay. But if your relationship is more intimate (e.g., you have been dating for two years), you might be more understanding and forgiving. The closer you are to people, the more likely you are to interpret their behaviors correctly.

When you interpret another person's behavior as odd or unusual, it is common to seek the cause of his or her behavior. The perception process typically involves making attributions in order to explain unexpected behaviors and make sense of things.[12]

Explaining Perceptual Attributions

When we attempt to determine the cause for someone else's behavior, we are making **attributions** about them.[13] This is especially true when someone communicates in a negative or unexpected manner that catches us by surprise.[14] Attributions serve to create a more complete picture of the situation and provide a sense of comfort because we feel we know what is going on, even if our conclusions are incorrect. The attributions we make about others are based upon three critical factors: locus, stability, and controllability.[15] Each of these factors helps us to perceive someone's communication as positive or negative.

Locus of Attributions. Researchers define locus as either the internal or external location assigned to the cause.[16] In other words, you determine whether a person's actions are within that person's control and self-directed (internal locus) or a product of fate, destiny, or even good or bad luck (external locus). These sources of someone's behavior help us to determine the reasons behind the perceptions we hold. For example, if Monica has a date with Richard and he is late, Monica might ask herself, "Is he late because of the storm, or is it because he doesn't really want to go see the movie I suggested?" One reason—the weather—may be external, while the other—that he doesn't want to see the movie and decided that if he arrives late, they won't get there in time to see it—is internal. Locus can make a huge difference in our positive and negative perceptions and eventually can affect our relationships.

Causal Stability of Attributions. Another factor that helps to determine the cause behind another person's behavior is known as causal stability. This element involves the duration of the specific behavior. In the previous situation with Monica and Richard, if he was late because he consistently loses track of time at work rather than as the result of an inconsistent, unpredictable event such as a ten-car-pile-up on the interstate, she is less likely to be understanding. In this example, you can see that the stability factor can be assigned an internal or external locus, and together they create and exacerbate the positive or negative perceptions. In the classroom, instructors search to explain students' poor performance. For example, if Janis earns a D and an F on her first two exams, a stable explanation might be that she is unintelligent. However, if she informs her instructor that she did not study, the failing grade will likely be attributed to an unstable cause; she chose not to put forth effort to study. Researchers use the term **learned helplessness** to explain a person's inclination to use stable causes as a way to explain why bad things happen to them.[17]

Controllability of Attributions. When people attempt to determine whether a person's behavior is within his or her control, they are making judgments based upon the determined cause.[18] A good example of this is a study investigating perceptions people have of obese individuals. If Daniel's obesity is attributed to factors outside of his control (e.g., a thyroid condition) people are more sympathetic toward his condition—he can't help the way he is. However, if the cause for his weight is determined to be something within his control (e.g., eating fast-food every day), feelings of anger and a desire to distance oneself from him typically occurs.[19] Your assessment of whether you believe that a person's behavior is controllable will decide your attitude.

What you should notice with these three elements of the attribution process is the close link between each of them. In other words, they are rarely used in isolation. Your attributions—and ultimately your perceptions—are clearer when you consider all three. For example, if Jonas is failing sophomore English and his instructor attempts to determine the reason for this, the combined examination of locus, stability, and control may offer an explanation. So if the instructor decides that lazy behavior is the best explanation for Jonas's failure, an internal, stable, and controllable attribution is utilized (and the instructor is probably quite disgusted and irritated with Jonas). Of course, this does not mean that the teacher is correct. Fundamental attribution errors do occur, and we will discuss them later in the chapter.

CHECKING YOUR UNDERSTANDING
The Perceptual Process

Before reading further, take a few minutes to assess your learning by writing your answers to the following items:

1. What is the definition of *perception*, and why is important for successful interpersonal communication?
2. What are the three stages of the perceptual process? Briefly describe how they are sequential and work together.
3. What are attributions and the three primary elements in the attribution process? Be able to describe how attributions may be positive or negative depending upon the specific combination of the three elements.

Influences on Your Perception of Others

Another way to understand the factors that influence the perceptual process is to think of these factors as eyeglass lenses that transform the way we view the world. This is the role our culture, our social groups, and our own unique characteristics play in the development of our perceptions. They provide a lens through which we see and understand the behavior of those around us. Think about it this way: Eyeglass lenses can cause you to see things more clearly; blur your vision; or enlarge, reduce, or alter your overall focus. Thus, how you see the world around you and the way in which you perceive others and their communication depend on multiple factors. As you read about each of these influential elements, imagine the role they play in your own life and in the perceptions you develop every day.

Personality and Self

Our personality, our view of ourselves, and how we feel about ourselves all play a significant role in influencing perceptions. Though our perceptions are not always right, these "lenses" influence the way in which we see and interpret the communication of people around us. For example, let's say that you are an extremely organized person and you routinely fill in your day planner down to the minute. On the first day of class, you are assigned to work on a project with a group of four people. As you and the rest of your group plan your first few meetings together, you notice that one member is writing the dates and times on the palm of her hand. You are shocked

Because group work is very common today, recognizing how your own communication traits affect your views of others is important to your success within groups.

and wonder how you will ever be able to work with someone who is so unorganized and obviously a poor student. Your vision of yourself as a conscientious, organized person creates these negative perceptions of this group member. Each of us has elements of our personality, as well as social and cultural influences, that form our perceptual lens.

Personality Traits. The perception process is influenced by personality traits because they predispose us to engage in certain communication behaviors, emotions, and moods that influence our impressions of the people around us. Numerous studies over the past twenty years support the idea that we selectively attend to, view, and understand others in accordance with our own personality traits. This is especially true when it comes to emotional traits such as anger, anxiety, or happiness.[20] In other words, if you have an inherently positive and upbeat personality, you will perceive these traits in others and assume that they are like you. Recall from Chapter 1 the Big Five personality traits: openness, conscientiousness, extraversion, agreeableness, and neuroticism. Recently, scholars have conducted research that looks at the impact of these Big Five traits on our perceptions of others in initial interactions.[21] They found that when we first meet people, our perceptions of them are driven by the characteristics of our own personalities.

- *People who are high in extraversion are sociable, talkative, assertive, excited, and overall very emotionally expressive.* Extraverts elicit the greatest consensus between self and perceptions of others; therefore, they more readily notice their own traits in others.[22] When they meet others who are emotionally expressive, they quickly perceive these others to be similar in the amount of personal self-disclosure and talking that occurs. They view these interactions as smooth and relaxed, but they perceive low extraverts as awkward and interactions with them as forced and strained.[23]

- *People who are high in agreeableness are trustworthy, altruistic individuals who are kind and exhibit overall prosocial behaviors.* They smile, laugh, and look people in the eye when they engage in discussions with them. Agreeable individuals are quick to take note of those who are less friendly and open or who are disagreeable. Their positive perspective causes them to spend a great deal of time drawing individuals out of their shells. So while they might quickly perceive others as disagreeable, they are also able to communicate well with them.

- *People who are high in neuroticism are typically anxious and prone to sadness, irritability, moodiness, and emotional instability.* They do not particularly enjoy interpersonal exchanges and become frustrated with pointless conversations, though still viewing themselves as polite.[24] They perceive others to be poor listeners, probably because they are very apprehensive communicators who have trouble developing accurate perceptions of others. If they must interact with others, though, they typically let the other person's behavior guide their own.

- *Individuals who are high in openness have a broad imagination and range of interests in individuals with an imaginative outlook on behaviors and events in life.* Because they are open to new experiences and enjoy meeting people, they initiate conversations and are comfortable, verbally and nonverbally, having conversations. They perceive others who are both like and unlike them in conversational style as being behaviorally accommodating and believe that this is a good thing. Higher degrees of openness create a positive vision of others' willingness to adapt accordingly.

- *People who are high in conscientiousness focus more on external, environmental cues and are thoughtful, goal-directed, and organized.* They perceive individuals who do not have these traits as impulsive and careless and their lives as hectic and chaotic. The perceptual process for them is organized and thus fairly quick as their organizational skills allow them to carefully categorize others' behaviors and rapidly develop their perceptions of the others.

NATURE/NURTURE intersections

Turning On Your Brain

Recent research has established a link between our personalities and how our brains respond to environmental stimuli. It has come to light that people with different personalities—primarily within the extraverted and neurotic personality traits—create differential brain responses as detected by magnetic resonance imaging (MRI).[25]

Dr. Turhan Canli and colleagues from Stanford University reported that brains of people who are either extraverted or neurotic respond differently to stimuli and amplify specific experiences over others. The researchers exposed 19- to 42-year-old women to positive and negative emotional stimuli by showing them positive photos (puppies, a happy couple, ice cream, and a beautiful sunset) and negative photos (people angry or crying, a cemetery, and guns).

The MRI results showed that the females who are high rather than low extraverts have greater brain reactivity when observing positive stimuli rather than negative ones. The frontal parts of the brain that control emotions, such as the frontal cortex and amygdala, received higher blood flow, suggesting greater brain reactivity to these positive images. Women who scored high on neuroticism measures, on the other hand, had greater brain reactivity when observing *negative stimuli*. In contrast to the extraverts, their reactions did not occur in the brain areas controlling emotions; in fact, they experienced reduced blood flow to these areas.

Ultimately, these results show evidence that the personality controls brain activity and the way in which women perceive emotionally charged stimuli. The researchers summed up the results of this study by saying, "One group saw the cup as being very full while the other group saw it as very empty."

Self-Concept. As we read in Chapter 2, self-concept is our view of who we are, what our abilities are, and our level of knowledge and skills. Who we believe we are as individuals affects not only our perception of ourselves but also our perception of others and our communication with them. If you believe yourself to be a strong, authoritative person who takes control of situations, then you will compare others to this perspective. You might communicate with a powerful voice, maintain an erect posture, and engage in direct eye contact. On the basis of your self-concept, you would view others who do not have these characteristics as weak and easily influenced, and your communication will reflect these perceptions. It is your reflected appraisal of your self-concept that influences how you perceive and communicate with others.[26] Of course, it is possible that you have a strong sense of self but do not feel good about it. This describes your self-esteem, and like your self-concept, it has a direct impact on your interpersonal communication.

Self-Esteem. As we also learned in Chapter 2, our self-esteem, or our positive/negative self-impressions also impact our perceptions. The positive or negative impression we have of ourselves is known as self-esteem. How much we like ourselves is a powerful lens for our perceptions. Individuals who have higher self-esteem levels, for example, form more accurate perceptions of both the positive and negative characteristics of their significant others. There is a more balanced and enduring image of the other person. This is not always the case for people who are lower in self-esteem. Recent research suggests that these people have a tendency to view their relationships as either good or bad, and this varies over time as a reflection of how they are feeling about themselves.[27] So their perceptions of their partners and partners' communication are distorted. Ultimately, how you feel about yourself affects how you see others.

Social Influences

Every day, we play roles that we perceive are expected and accepted in society. We are men, women, sons, daughters, students, employees, and so on, all engaging in behaviors that reflect the roles we have assumed. We know how to communicate in these roles because society provides an abundance of information to influence us and our perceptions. We observe these roles on television, at work, in public, and everywhere else where society infiltrates our life, so the information is inescapable. Because we have opportunities to be influenced by images around us, we develop perceptions of ourselves and others based on societal standards.

 Gender/Sex Roles. From the time you were a small child, you most likely noticed (probably subconsciously) what it meant to be a man or a woman. Gender roles are socially learned behaviors. If you had traditional role models, your father was viewed as the "breadwinner" who was strong and made the important decisions for the family, and your mother was loving, emotional, and sensitive. These characteristics, while very stereotypical, also reflect gender traits more than sex or biological traits. Gender roles are not necessarily associated with anatomy. They reflect levels of feminine and masculine characteristics and are typically associated with the biological characteristics of males and females. Thus, the dichotomous sex types can exist on a continuum from masculine men to feminine women. In this view, it is possible for men to have a degree of femininity within their sex role. If a man becomes emotional and cries, that is often thought to be a feminine behavior and unacceptable in a masculine society's (e.g., U.S.) standards. Social learning tends to guide our sex role perceptions and tell us whether men and women are communicating appropriately according to their understood roles. Gender role differences have been magnified for marketing purposes in the popular press, yet research suggests that the differences in male/female communication are much more modest. Still, small social learning differences can have an impact.

Sandra Bem's Behavioral Sex Role Inventory depicts four differential gender roles: stereotypical masculine behaviors, stereotypical feminine behaviors, undifferentiated behaviors, and androgynous behaviors.[28] The gender style of your communication and how well it fits within societal norms impacts your perception of others and the way they view you. Some of the typical masculine communication behaviors are self-reliant, independent, and assertive while examples of feminine communication behaviors are shy, affectionate, and sympathetic. Undifferentiated communication behaviors are neither masculine nor feminine, and **androgynous** communication behaviors are a combination of highly masculine and highly feminine characteristics. Androgynous individuals are thought to be better communicators and, therefore, have more positive perceptions of themselves and others because they have an ability to reflect on both feminine and masculine characteristics—they can see both "sides" and determine when specific gender roles are most appropriate in specific situations. In a recent book entitled *Code Switching: How to Talk So Men Will Listen*, the authors assert that if men and women hope to get along and better understand one another in the workplace, they need to alter their more traditional masculine and feminine communication styles.[29] According to these authors, androgynous individuals are higher in self-esteem, and therefore, more positive in their perceptions of others, because they know how to express themselves around many different types of people and have more communication tools at their disposal.

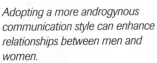

Adopting a more androgynous communication style can enhance relationships between men and women.

Occupational Roles. Your views of the world are influenced by your occupation and your perception of what is and is not acceptable. Regardless of our occupation, society has informed us of what we can expect from people who fill these roles. The media are some of the biggest contributors to our perceptions of communication behaviors associated with specific occupations, and we know we have expectations because we know when they are violated. For example, we expect most professionals to be well-spoken, articulate, and knowledgeable. When this does not happen, we are confused. Have you ever walked outside a hospital and witnessed nurses or doctors smoking? What was your perception of them? Chances are you developed some negative perceptions of their behavior based upon your view of their occupation as health professionals. There is an abundance of research to suggest that individuals who violate the occupational roles set forth by society engender negative reactions and unfortunate repercussions.[30] Ultimately, what this reveals is society's powerful effects on us. Whom and what we become and how we communicate and perceive others' communication are determined by societal influences.

 ## Cultural Influences

As with societal influences, cultural norms and values affect your perceptions of others. Every culture maintains a collection of customs, norms, rituals, and language, and these affect perceptions of the culture's own communication as well as that of other cultures. Cultural perception shapes and guides interactions, as we are easily influenced by our cultural (e.g., American) and co-cultural (e.g., Democrat) groups. When we communicate with others within our culture, we typically share similar attitudes, beliefs, and worldviews. We have customs and norms that link us together. Most Americans, for example, cherish the right and opportunity to voice opinions and support for certain political candidates and to vote for those individuals when the time comes. If you were raised in a politically active family and were surrounded by people who were active and involved citizens, you would see the value in emulating their behavior. Because of your cultural influences, you also might be intolerant of people who are apathetic and announce that their vote does not matter. Your perception of them might be that they are lazy, weak, or unintelligent. Your perceptions might even lead you to choose to separate yourself physically from people who do not share your cultural values.

Most of your customs are derived from your cultural and co-cultural groups. People within the U.S. culture are thought to be **individualistic** (as is true in Canada, Great Britain, and other countries as well) and therefore competitive, self-sufficient, and valuing immediate family. People within **collectivistic cultures** (e.g., Japan, China, and Korea), who value extended families and prefer to maintain a group orientation, misunderstand individualistic cultural groups. A recent study compared the perceptual differences between Western (American) and East Asian (Chinese) cultures and reported that the collectivist attitudes of the Chinese people enable them to be more adept at interpreting the actions of others.[31] Ultimately, this becomes a fundamental skill for positive social interactions.[32]

New brain research at MIT reveals that culture affects how people see the world—how they perceive others.[33] Brain scanners picked up differential levels of attention and effort for individualistic and collectivistic cultures. Subjects from individualistic cultures (e.g., Westerners) focused more on central objects than on their surroundings, while Easterners focused on both the context and the object. What these findings reveal is that perceptual differences are to be expected. Unfortunately, these differences can lead to negative perceptions and poor communication between individuals in these cultural groups. This is especially important to consider in organizations as the global marketplace expands and intercultural business dealings increase.

CHECKING YOUR UNDERSTANDING
Influences on Our Perceptions

Before reading further, take a few minutes to assess your learning by writing your answers to the following items:

1. Can you make a list of the Big Five personality traits and explain how each one can influence your perceptions?

2. In what ways do your self-concept and your level of self-esteem influence your perceptions? Can you provide a specific example showing the impact each of these can have on your perceptions?

3. What is the value of androgyny as a sex/gender role in creating your perceptions?

4. Are you from an individualistic culture or a collectivistic culture? How might your particular culture affect the way in which you perceive others? If you have ever traveled to another country, can you name specific objects you might have viewed differently from your own culture's perspective when you were there?

Inaccuracies in the Perception Process

Our personalities, how we view ourselves, and our social and cultural experiences are all factors that color what we see around us. They are a reflection of who we are, where we come from, and the people who are important in our lives—and they are often incorrect. If you ask someone from northern portions of the United States how they view people from the South, you might hear responses such as "slow," "backward," and "country." Conversely, people from the South might describe Northerners as "rude," "aloof," and even "standoffish." Of course, we know that these descriptions are not necessarily true, but for some reason, these ideas have been perpetuated and endure. Though it is not always possible to determine the exact source of our perceptions, recognizing that they are often wrong can aid communication in our relationships. The next sections will present examples and effects of inaccurate judgments within our perceptual processes.

Stereotyping and Prejudice Effects

Stereotypes are the categories we place people in based upon the groups to which they belong. We do this because it helps us to make sense of the world and plan our communication with others. Most people stereotype at some point in their lives, but if you disagree or find this thought offensive, there are two things you should know. First, stereotyping is not necessarily negative. Second, you probably do it almost every day but fail to recognize it. Although stereotyping might not be negative or mean-spirited, it can create inaccurate perceptions. We "think" we know how to converse with others if we can place them in a category such as a social class, occupation, or sexual orientation. For example, if you meet a very tall woman, you might instantly think, "I'll bet she played high school or college basketball." If it turns out that she didn't and you are aware that you have misjudged her, you can quickly divert the conversation if you had tried to talk about basketball with her. Unfortunately, more serious stereotypical misperceptions based on gender/sex, race, and occupation can occur, and these can be detrimental to you and the communication with other people you encounter.

 Gender Role Stereotypes. When we place men and women into certain behavioral categories, this is gender role stereotyping. Though this is extremely common in Western culture, applying these generalizations to specific individuals can be dangerous and even unethical. Common gender stereotypes are associated with personality traits: women tend to be **communal** (e.g., warm, emotional, nurturing) and men tend to be **agentic** (e.g., active, instrumental, competent). If we look at these characteristics across the entire population, we might find them to be fairly accurate.[34] However, when we apply these gender stereotypes to specific individuals, the accuracy of the stereotypes is drastically reduced, and this is when communication is negatively affected.[35]

Racial Stereotypes. Just as gender stereotyping is common, so is grouping individuals according to their race. These stereotypes are broad and cannot logically be applied to specific individuals, yet racial stereotypes are extremely common in Western culture. In the United States, for example, race is still understood as a black-white paradigm, with perceived differences in extremely broad categories such as income, motivation, and even overall intelligence.[36] A study conducted with college students revealed that white students perceive black students to be less intelligent. Even when high GPAs for black students were presented, students misremembered the grades and reported them to be lower than white students' GPAs.[37] The researchers explained that this response helped students to maintain their existing stereotypes and racial expectations.

Occupational Stereotypes. Categorizing people in certain occupations and employment positions on the basis of their sex, social status, intelligence, and other attributes is known as occupational stereotyping. Instead of assisting our communication with others, this categorization actually impedes the process. A recent article entitled "'If You Know He Is an Engineer, I Don't Need to Tell You He Is Smart': The Influence of Stereotypes on the Communication of Social Knowledge" suggests that stereotypes bias our perceptions to make them consistent with our expectations of social categories.[38] In other words, if

It is important to overcome outdated gender stereotypes to improve communication in the workplace.

Catherine reveals that she is a physician, an engineer, or a corporate executive, chances are you will place her into a category you have created for "smart people." Because of this presumption, you will communicate with Catherine in a way that matches what you expect from her. Your perceptions may be based on a bit of truth, but this certainly cannot tell you everything you need to know. Research findings in occupational stereotyping suggest their power and perpetuation. These inaccurate and stereotypical perceptions are most common between people who are accepted and typically in control (the in-group) and others who are viewed as outsiders and are unaccepted (out-group members), yet people in the in-groups typically claim that they are not prejudiced.[39]

Though **prejudice** may or may not be caused by stereotyping, prejudice and stereotyping are often linked. Just recognize that they are not the same concept. Exhibiting prejudice is associating a positive or negative judgment with a specific group of people. For example, after the bombing of the World Trade Center and the Pentagon in 2001, many Americans developed a negative view of Muslims, prejudice developed, and incidents of discrimination began to be depicted in the press. Following the invasion of Iraq, even when people in the United States did not know Muslim individuals personally, they determined that Muslims were dangerous and could not be trusted. In 2006, a Gallup poll revealed that approximately 40% of all Americans admitted to being prejudiced against Muslims and believed that Muslims needed to be held to stricter security standards than non-Muslims.[40]

A similar prejudice was held against Japanese-Americans after the bombing of Pearl Harbor in 1941. Although the prejudice began with American farmers' perception of labor competition with Japanese-Americans farmers along the West Coast, the attack on Pearl Harbor fueled the already extreme negative feelings. On the basis of anti-Japanese sentiments, approximately 120,000 people (more than two thirds of whom were American citizens) were hauled off to one of ten internment camps across the United States. Though prejudice is not always negative, some of the most common examples typically are (e.g., racism, sexism, ageism, and ableism). If you stop and think a moment about different experiences in your life, you can probably recall a time when either you or someone you know dealt with the difficulty of the prejudice of others. If examples do not come easily to you, perhaps reading the following case study will help. If not, perhaps you will find the next category of perceptual inaccuracies—primacy and recency effects—to be more common.

ETHICS in interpersonal communication

To Boost Business, Hotel Owner Forbids Spanish to Be Spoken [41]

In October 2009, Larry Whitten, a 63-year-old former Marine from Texas, purchased a hotel in Taos, New Mexico, to save it and the jobs of those who worked there. He had saved over twenty other distressed hotels across the country and, eager to continue his mission, he moved to Taos. Two things were different at the Paragon Inn: (a) Most of the employees were Hispanic and spoke Spanish—a language with which Larry Whitten was unfamiliar; and (b) employees were bitter because this was the fifth owner they'd worked for in a short time span.

Whitten felt that he had been successful in saving troubled hotels and was confident that he could do the same with the hotel in Taos. Because of the differences he encountered, he decided to do the following: ask all employees to refrain from speaking Spanish in front of him; request that employees who deal directly with hotel guests change their first names to make them easier to pronounce (e.g., *Marcos* would change to *Mark*, and the pronunciation *Mahr-TEEN* would change to *MAHR-tin*); and fire insubordinate employees who refused to abide by his rules.

Whitten said that he had made this decision for three reasons: Hostile employees would make the situation worse by speaking Spanish behind his back; making the names of employees easier to pronounce would assist guests with their requests and make them more comfortable interacting with employees; and insubordinate employees would create a hostile work environment and hurt the business he was trying to save.

The reactions to Whitten's decisions were disturbing. Employees of the Paragon Inn called him "a white" and a racist. Some employees picketed outside the hotel. Employees who were asked to change their names refused, and one man stated, "I don't have to change my name and language or heritage. I'm professional the way I am."

Because he is the owner, it does seem that Larry Whitten should have the right to create his own rules for his business. In addition, he has a track record of successfully reviving failing businesses. But does he have the right to ask employees to change their names in a state where Spanish is one of the primary languages and a town in which a large part of the population is of Hispanic origin?

What do you think? Is Larry Whitten displaying his own cultural insecurity by asking his employees to change their names? For example, if guests are uncertain how to pronounce the name "Jesus," is it ethical to ask an employee who has this name (and considers his name part of his identity) to change the spelling to alleviate their discomfort? Because Larry Whitten *can* do this as the boss, does it mean he *should*?

Taos artist Ken O'Neil summed up the situation as follows: "To make demands like he did just seems over the top. Nobody won here. It's not always about winning. Sometimes, it's about what you learn."

Primacy and Recency Effects

When you meet someone for the first time, it is highly likely that you make snap judgments about the person's appearance, trustworthiness, and overall competence. Another choice is to hold off, give a person the benefit of the doubt, and make an assessment after making multiple observations. Both are very common perceptual behaviors, especially in new situations with unfamiliar people. According to Princeton professor Alex Todorov, we tend to hold onto these initial perceptions, and they become ingrained within us.[42]

Primacy Effects. When we make an instant judgment based on our first impressions about others, it is the result of **primacy** effects. This is important to consider in your daily communication, for it suggests the need to put your best foot forward and strive to make a good impression at every opportunity. Researchers who looked at jury decisions during trial testimony found that when jurors tentatively (and anonymously) reported their early verdicts (before final testimony and evidence), they stuck to this decision regardless of what was later presented.[43] The earliest research on memory and judgment reported significant primacy effects; we place greater weight on the initial information we acquire about individuals.[44] In a study supporting primacy effects, Solomon Asch presented a list of descriptive adjectives to participants. The first word in the list was either positive or negative followed by a list of opposite descriptors (e.g., intelligent, impulsive, stubborn, and critical versus critical, stubborn, impulsive, and intelligent). What he discovered was similar to the jury research findings. Participants formed impressions based upon the initial word in the list (intelligent versus critical), and the remaining words had little influence. Thus, positive or negative impressions prevailed at the expense of later information that might actually be more informative.

Recency Effects. When we assign greater weight to the most current information we encounter, we succumb to **recency** effects. Though the power of first impressions cannot be denied, we frequently observe others' actions over time and change our perceptions of them. The impressions that we maintain, in this case, are the most recent. Research has found that this recent information is more accurate than earlier memories and experiences.[45]

There is some evidence, however, to suggest people utilize both primacy and recency in their decision making. If you realize that the initial information you have about someone is based on the unknown and there is no point of comparison, you might wait for more recent impressions to form. Therefore, one does not necessarily contradict the other—they work in unison.[46]

Individuals may be judged favorably or unfavorably on the basis of a single positive or negative characteristic; this is termed the halo effect when the judgment is positive or the reverse halo effect (or the devil effect) when the judgment is negative.[47] These effects are cognitive biases in which traits that we initially perceived influence our interpretation of people and our perceptions of the latter traits they exhibit. According to Solomon Asch and current research, physical attractiveness is the most common source of positive, halo effect impressions. Thus, attractive individuals are thought to have additional positive virtues compared to less attractive individuals.[48] One of the more powerful factors leading to the halo effect is similarity, frequently referred to as the *similar-to-me effect*. The more we perceive that others are like us, the more we tend to view them favorably. **Homophily** is a term coined by communication scholars that refers to the degree to which we believe we are similar to others. Perceived homophily affects whether people will attempt to communicate and whether the attempt will be viewed as successful. In essence, this perception of similarity can open or shut the door to initial communication interactions. The Perceived Homophily Measure was created to help people understand the degree to which they perceive another person to be similar to them in background traits and attitudes. Take a few minutes to complete the Perceived Homophily Measure. Think of an individual you have recently met but still consider an acquaintance. Complete the instrument as you think of that person. When you are finished, compute your score, and on the basis of your results, consider whether your perceived homophily with the person might affect your communication and elicit the halo effect.

Understanding Your Level of Perceived Homophily. The perceived homophily scale was created to help us understand whether the individuals we approach to ask for personal advice (opinion leaders) are similar to us. If a person were important enough for us to ask for advice, then he or she would probably share similar attitudes and perhaps even behaviors and background with us. This was precisely what research discovered. The opinion leaders on whom the participants reported were perceived as being more similar to the participants than others were.

You were asked to complete the perceived homophily instrument based on a new acquaintance. This next section will help you to understand your results. Depending on your score, you might discover that this new acquaintance you reported on is someone you will get to know better in the future, share information with, and seek advice from.

ASSESS YOUR **communication personality**

McCroskey, Richmond, and Daly's Perceived Homophily Scale[49]

Log onto our self-assessment library, MyPersonalityProfile, found on MyCommunicationLab (www.mycommunicationlab.com), and assess your perceived homophily. If it is possible, you might also encourage the person you are assessing to do the same. That way, you can compare and contrast your scores and begin to understand better just how similar you are as well as how accurate your perceptions of homophily are.

Directions:

On the following scale, indicate your feelings about a recent acquaintance. Circle the number that best represents your feelings. Numbers 1 and 7 indicate a *very strong feeling*. Numbers 2 and 6 indicate a *strong feeling*. Numbers 3 and 5 indicate a *fairly weak feeling*. Number 4 indicates that you *are undecided* or *don't know*. Please work quickly. There are no right or wrong answers.

_____ **(name of acquaintance)**

1. Doesn't think like me	1 2 3 4 5 6 7	Thinks like me
2. Is from a social class similar to mine	1 2 3 4 5 6 7	Is from a social class different from mine
3. Behaves like me	1 2 3 4 5 6 7	Doesn't behave like me
4. Has an economic situation different from mine	1 2 3 4 5 6 7	Has an economic situation like mine
5. Is similar to me	1 2 3 4 5 6 7	Is different from me
6. Has a status like mine	1 2 3 4 5 6 7	Has a status different from mine
7. Is unlike me	1 2 3 4 5 6 7	Is like me
8. Has a background different from mine	1 2 3 4 5 6 7	Has a background similar to mine

Scoring Instructions:

Items 2, 3, 5, and 6 are reversed. Therefore, before adding your score, reverse the number you circled on these items (e.g., change 1 to 7, 2 to 6, 3 to 5, etc.). Now add the circled numbers together for items 1, 3, 5, and 7 to get your attitude homophily score. Add the circled numbers together for items 2, 4, 6, and 8 to get your background homophily score. Scores on each of the two scales should range from 4 to 28.

Chances are the more you perceive you are similar to this person, the more likely it is that you will attempt to communicate and view the person favorably.

- First, because scores range between 4 and 28 on both of the scales (attitude and background), you should consider a score between 4 and 14 to indicate that you perceive this person to be dissimilar to you in attitude and/or background. If you scored between 15 and 20, you consider this person to be somewhat similar to you; and if you scored 21 or higher, you perceive this individual to be a great deal like you in attitude and/or background.

- Second, it is possible to score low in one area and higher in the other. For example, you might perceive this person to be unlike you in attitude but similar in background. Research has revealed, however, that a higher perceived similarity in both areas leads to increased perceptions of the other person's credibility and an increase in your interpersonal attraction, which, in turn, affects your communication attempts and the results of your communication experience.

- Third, just because you perceive that you are similar to another person does not make it so. It is possible that you made these assumptions too quickly and need more information to determine how alike you really are. Nonetheless, your perception of similarity will create or deter your communication interactions.

WHAT CAN I do now?

▶ *You could ask yourself how you feel about this person.* Do you seem alike in your attitudes and interests?

▶ *You could be careful not to avoid communicating with someone simply because you do not feel a high degree of homophily with that person.* Not everyone will share your attitudes and background.

▶ *You could refrain from making snap judgments (based on primacy effects) when someone is different from you.*

▶ *You could examine the source of your attributions.* Are your homophily perceptions due to your internal or external attributions?

▶ *You could try to maintain both cultural and gender sensitivity.*

Perceptual Filters and Biases

Each of us has a monitoring system in our subconscious that forces information we encounter to "fit in" with what we already know and have experienced. As we discussed earlier in this chapter, our schemata (or mental file folders) for other people's communication helps us to interpret what we see. But we also use perceptual filters, or **defense mechanisms,** to alter or distort the intended meaning of messages we receive. We do this because we like to keep things orderly and stable, and if this means that we change the information we are bombarded with daily, we are okay with that. Leon Festinger referred to this desire to keep our perceptions mentally organized as the **principle of consistency.** We do not like feeling an imbalance, or **cognitive dissonance,** in our perceptions.[50] According to Festinger, when we feel dissonance, we take steps to reduce it. Even though we might believe that we desire a change and seek to engage in new experiences that might alter what we like or what we know, when we face inconsistencies, we get nervous and feel a sense of dissonance. This is when we call upon our defense mechanisms (selective exposure, selective attention, selective perception, and selective retention) to put things back in order. Because they change the meaning of the messages we receive, defense mechanisms typically lead to inaccurate perceptions and create barriers to communication.[51]

- *Selective exposure.* When we seek out and allow ourselves to be exposed only to messages that reinforce our existing attitudes and beliefs, we are engaging in **selective exposure.** For example, perhaps you feel that you are experiencing too many arguments in your romantic relationship. You begin to wonder whether the relationship is doomed because you don't believe that arguing is a good sign for your future. To perceive your relationship differently, you purposefully seek friendships with couples who argue as much as or more than you do. Exposing yourself to similar relationships allows you to view yours as normal.

- *Selective attention.* When you pay attention only to messages that reinforce your beliefs, you are engaging in **selective attention.** In some cases, we want to believe something so badly that we tune out or ignore what should be very obvious. Using the previous example, you perceive that there is increasing turmoil in your romantic relationship and are fearful that the relationship might end. You pride yourself in being able to maintain healthy relationships, so to rid yourself of these dissonant perceptions, you decide to focus only on the good things in your relationship. When you avoid the negative issues and focus on the positive communication that occurs, the dissonance dissipates.

- *Selective perception.* When messages are understood through our current frame of reference, sometimes to the point of changing the intent of the message, this interpretive process is known as **selective perception**. If you or someone else has ever said that you "hear what you want to hear," this describes selective perception. Parents engage in selective perception, for example, when they determine that a teacher is praising their child for being assertive when they are called in to discuss disruptive classroom behaviors.

- *Selective retention.* When you remember only those parts of the message that reinforce and are consistent with your beliefs, you are engaging in **selective retention**. This differs from selective perception, in which words are twisted. In the above example of a parent–teacher conference, if the teacher included some compliments of the child along with the criticism that warranted the conference, the parents would leave recalling the compliments or with any information that reinforced their personal perceptions of the child.

CHECKING YOUR UNDERSTANDING
Problems in Perceiving Others

Before reading further, take a few minutes to assess your learning by writing your answers to the following items:

1. How do stereotypes differ from prejudice in terms of what is communicated to others? Can you describe why you might view prejudice as negative but view stereotyping as positive in some instances?

2. How is information perceived by people differently when we engage in the primacy effect and in the recency effect? How does homophily lead to the halo effect (or the reverse halo effect) and play an important role in either primacy or recency?

3. Can you name the four defense mechanisms that people use as perceptual filters? How do you use any of these to avoid feelings of cognitive dissonance?

Enhancing Your Perceptual Accuracy

Perceptions drive our communication with others. Therefore, it is essential to discover methods to determine how accurate our perceptions are as well as how to improve them. The final section of this chapter will describe and discuss how to avoid errors in the perceptual attribution process and provide suggestions and tools to assist you in checking perceptions.

Attribution Errors

Because we might not feel confident in our perceptual abilities, we frequently make mistakes in our attributions of others' communication behaviors. When we attribute other people's behavior to either external or internal factors and assume something incorrectly, this can have detrimental effects on our relationships.

Avoiding Attribution Errors. Though there are many examples of attribution errors, some of the more common ones that we will discuss are the fundamental attribution error, ultimate attribution error, self-serving attribution bias, and overattribution.

- *Fundamental attribution error.* When we fail to carefully examine all the possible reasons behind another person's actions, this is a **fundamental attribution error**. Instead we determine that someone is behaving a certain way because that is simply the "way he or she is." In other words, internal causes or personality factors are the culprit.[52] So instead of studying the situation carefully to determine whether other influential elements (e.g., context) are at work, people typically prefer to take the easy road and view internal elements as the root cause. Researchers have suggested that these internal attribution errors occur because there are fewer internal factors to examine, making it a simpler conclusion to draw.[53]

- *Ultimate attribution error.* Fundamental attribution errors are especially common when the behavior is negative; these are referred to as **ultimate attribution errors**. For example. Jesse, a high school senior, wants money to rent a limousine to take him and a group of friends to the prom. His parents say no, and he becomes extremely angry. "Why can't they understand how important this is?" he asks himself. "They're so boring. Just because they never do anything fun, they want to ruin my life!" So Jesse determines that the reason his parents refuse to give him the limo money is because they are uninteresting and miserable and they want his life to be just like theirs. There is nothing external in his perceptions. He bases their negative decision solely on internal causes, an ultimate attribution error.

- *Self-serving attribution bias.* When we select attributions on the basis of whether we believe our behaviors will help or hurt us, this is a **self-serving attribution bias**. There are two types of self-serving biases: The **self-enhancing bias** occurs when something positive happens and you take credit for the successes or the positive outcomes experienced. The **self-protecting bias** is used when a person, in attempting to explain why things have gone wrong, blames it on factors that are out of his or her control.[54] This example might help you to understand this bias better: You lost your job because your boss said you were constantly late. Your self-protecting bias would tell you that this unfortunate situation occurred because your boss has unrealistic expectations or you live so far from work that you never know how bad traffic is going to be. You determine that external factors cause the lateness, and you perceive that they are out of your control.

- *Overattribution.* From time to time, people who are having negative life experiences with others will latch onto two or three traits and blame everything on them. This is known as **overattribution**, and it can be a real hindrance to relationships. Married couples who are experiencing problems in their relationships tend to engage in over-attribution because they find a few internal characteristics that they determine are primarily responsible for their partners' negative behaviors. Research on married couples suggests that unhappy couples tend to see the worst in their partners and are able to come up with a list of internal characteristics when problems occur.[55] Research has also reported that poorly performing college students tend to attribute all negative instructor behaviors to internal causes.[56] Thus, a teacher who is late for class might provide a perfectly logical explanation, but students will choose to believe that the lateness is within the teacher's control and blame the behavior on traits such as lack of organization, incompetence, and an uncaring attitude.

One of the primary reasons we make attribution errors is because we lack confidence in our overall ability to make predictions about the communication of others. One method to determine whether you may be prone to attribution errors is by measuring your **attributional confidence** or the level of confidence you have in evaluating the facts about people. Take a few minutes to complete the attributional confidence scale on the next page. It asks you to consider a specific person and report your confidence or certainty in making attributions about them. To complete the scale, you must think of a good friend.

ASSESS YOUR **communication personality**

Clatterbuck's Attributional Confidence Scale[57]

Log onto our self-assessment library, MyPersonalityProfile, found on MyCommunicationLab (www.mycommunicationlab.com), and assess your own level of confidence in evaluating the behavior of someone close to you. Encourage your close friend or relational partner to do the same. That way, you can compare and contrast your scores and begin to better understand your attributional accuracy and how it might influence your interpersonal communication. Or take the written assessment below.

Directions:

The questions that follow will ask you to express how confident you are that you know a particular fact about the person who is your good friend. On these questions, the answers should be written as a percentage—anywhere from 0% to 100%. For example, if you are totally confident that you know a particular fact, you might write 100%. If you are slightly less confident, you might put a number such as 83%. On the other hand, if you are not at all confident, you might place a very low percentage, such as 5%, in the answer blank. If you are absolutely unable to answer a question and the answer would be a guess for which you had no basis at all, you might put 0%. Remember, you may use any evidence as a basis for your guess, even if the person has not explicitly told you the answer. The point is for you to report your confidence in the GUESS ONLY; do not give the actual answer to the question.

1. How confident are you of your general ability to predict how he/she will behave? _____

2. How certain are you that he/she likes you? _____

3. How accurate are you at predicting the values he/she holds? _____

4. How accurate are you at predicting his/her attitudes? _____

5. How well can you predict his/her feelings and emotions? _____

6. How much can you empathize with (share) the way he/she feels about himself/herself? _____

7. How well do you know him/her? _____

Scoring Instructions:

Sum all the percentages on items 1–7. Divide the sum by 7. This will be the percentage of attributional confidence you feel toward this person.

Understanding Your Level of Attributional Confidence. The attributional confidence scale was developed by Glen Clatterbuck as a way to recognize the uncertainty that occurs in relationships. He found that for our relationships to progress, we need to reduce uncertainty by becoming confident in our attributions. In other words, the more confident we are in our attributions, the more we are attracted to others interpersonally and desire to get to know them better. Once you have completed and obtained your score for the instrument, ask yourself, "Am I attracted to this person, and do I feel we have some similar attitudes and behaviors?" If you find that your results agree with the research on this instrument, then this should indicate to you that the more you like someone and feel similar to that person, the more confident you will be in your perceptual attributions. Individuals who score high on the instrument typically have an interpersonal attraction for the other person as well as feeling a sense of interpersonal similarity with them.[58] As was discussed earlier in this chapter, perceived homophily leads to increased communication and, according to studies of intercultural interactions, increased self-disclosure and attributional confidence.[59]

There are several factors to consider when assessing your attributional confidence. Your score will offer insight to your perceived similarity with this particular person as well as your own perceptual attributions of them. Here are some recommendations for making sense of your score based on the various attribution errors and, ultimately, finding ways to correct them.

- First, scores range between 0% to 100% on the scale; you should consider a score under 50% to be low, scores between 50% and 79% to be average, and scores above 80% to be relatively high in attributional confidence.

- Second, if you scored low on the attributional confidence scale, it is important to your friendship for you to determine why this has happened. It is most likely due to one or more of the attribution errors discussed earlier. If you reported that you are not very good at predicting your friend's emotions or attitudes, this could lead to the error of overattribution or deciding that you know more about your friend than you actually do. If you find yourself engaging in overattribution and or other incorrect assumptions about your friend, this can be very risky to relationships. However, it can be avoided. Take a look at your lowest scored responses, and think of specific ways in which you and your friend might work together to learn more in these particular areas. You should pay particular attention to ways to improve the perceptual process so that you can help others do the same. It is never too late to improve your awareness of the perceptions you have about people and their behaviors and work to alter these perceptions.

 WHAT CAN I **do now?**

▶ *You could reexamine this relationship and your perceptions of your friend. A low confidence score suggests that you may engage in attribution errors.*

▶ *You could try asking yourself what attributes, in particular, you like about your friend.*

▶ *You could be aware of the low-scoring categories and work to discover more about your friend in these areas.*

▶ *You could engage in self-disclosure to increase your attributional confidence as well as reduce your uncertainty about your friend's values and behaviors.*

Initiating Perception Checking

One of the clearest means to improving your perceptions and avoiding some of the mistakes previously discussed is to learn how to check them with indirect and direct perception checking. First, however, there are multiple factors to be aware of before actually checking your perceptions. Consider the following three areas to be precursors to the perception process and imagine their value in developing your perceptions and improving communication in your relationships.

- *Question your perceptual accuracy.* Stop and consciously think about your perceptions and feelings about someone, and question your interpretation of the behaviors you observe and can recall. Instead of automatically jumping to negative assumptions, stop and consider exactly what it was you heard, saw, tasted, or smelled. Have you allowed yourself to take in everything by looking for further suggestive cues, or have you stopped short at the simplest, negative response? This can also work with positive perceptions, which should be examined carefully as well.

- *Consider yourself and how you might be getting in the way of accurate social perceptions.* We discussed the importance of self-concept and self-esteem earlier in this chapter, and if you are uncertain of your value for another person, then it is possible your perceptions of that person will be negative. This is especially true if you are unhappy with yourself when you are with this person. In other words, your own self-awareness and management of your life and self can affect the perceptual accuracy you have of others in your life.[60] Similarly, it is important to develop your social intelligence skills, such as having empathy and understanding of others and their experiences.[61] Without this, you may be unable to put yourself in others' shoes or understand their behaviors and, in turn, might develop inaccurate perceptions of them.

- *Consider the context, such as which people are present, where they are, and what time of day it is.* Most people blot out the context and fail to consider that a person may be engaging in specific communication behaviors because of his or her surroundings. Do not jump to conclusions. You must consider the whole scene; failure to do so will certainly result in flawed perceptions.

Indirect Perception Checking. When you take a more careful look at the person you are observing to see whether there might be something you missed, you are engaging in indirect perception checking. This is a sort of "stop, look, and listen" process that will allow you to take in nonverbal cues to fill in perceptual gaps and discover additional and necessary information. Consider this example: Your friends Marty and Bob are arguing, and if your first inclination is to blame Bob, stop for a moment and observe his nonverbal behaviors. What sort of face is he making, and what sort of gestures does he use (e.g., wrings his hands)? You should also listen to his voice, as it is a valuable cue that researchers tell us "leaks" clearer thinking and feeling cues.[62] On the basis of these observations, you change your mind. However, even though you observe Bob's behaviors carefully, this is still indirect perception checking and therefore, subjective. You are observing behaviors and coming to conclusions without inquiring whether they are, in fact, correct.

Direct Perception Checking. Sometimes it is best to come right out and ask whether your perceptions are correct. This more straightforward means is known as direct perception checking. You're going to miss out on some valuable information by relying solely on indirect observations, so here is a bit of advice: When in doubt, just ask! Though this sounds logical and quite simple, it can also be dangerous. You can never quite predict what someone, especially someone who is unfamiliar to you, will tell you, and if the response does not align with your perceptions, you must figure out how to deal with this. On the other hand, getting a straight answer and confirming or clarifying your perceptions can enhance your communication with others. Speed dating is a good example of a context in which direct perception checking may be risky but also maximizes the time available. If you have six minutes to select a date and the best-looking person in the room is ignoring you, direct perception checking might be the best route to understanding and moving forward to a different date. Ask your speed date whether he or she is avoiding you and is disinterested. You might not like the response, but you will save time and energy.

Ultimately, the most helpful perception checking involves both indirect and direct methods within three simple steps. When you follow these steps, you can avoid attribution errors and perceptual biases.[63]

1. Observe and acknowledge a particular behavior.
2. Create two possible interpretations of the observed behavior.
3. Request clarification for your interpretation to determine accuracy.

If you cannot imagine following these three steps in the course of a conversation, look at the following example and try to identify the three steps:

Hey, Shannon, I've been calling you for the past two days, and I haven't heard back from you—even when I've left you several voicemail messages. I wasn't sure if your phone wasn't working or if you were irritated that I couldn't meet you for lunch on Monday. What's going on? Do you mind me asking?

Can you locate the first step—the observed behavior? If you said it was Jacob's statement "I haven't heard back from you," you are correct. In addition, it has been two days, and Jacob wants to understand why Shannon has not responded. Following step 1, you should be able to find Jacob's two interpretations: (1) phone malfunction or (2) irritation over the broken lunch date. It is a good idea that he did this for a couple of reasons. First, it gives Shannon an "out" if she has actually been avoiding Jacob. She can simply say, "Yeah, my phone has been on the fritz." Of course, this might be untrue, but she still has an option and doesn't feel backed into a corner by Jacob's interrogation. Second, she can simply admit that she was bothered that he cancelled their lunch date, and she didn't even have to bring it up because Jacob already figured it out on his own. Jacob is being proactive with this three-step perception-checking process, and it could actually soothe any hurt feelings Shannon might have. Finally, you should be able to locate the third step of clarification and accuracy checking. Frequently, if people are angry, they will avoid confrontations and hide their feelings. This is not an option for Shannon because Jacob directly asks her which perceptual interpretation of his is correct. Of course, there may be a third option that Jacob has not thought of, but at least his feelings are out there for the two of them to deal with.

Following these three steps in the perception-checking process will aid you in your relationships because they serve to clarify communication behavior and, if used correctly, are nonthreatening. If you are asking for clarification (unless, of course, you say it in a threatening tone of voice), it will be rare for the other person to be offended. Of course, you may not be successful with this perception checking method in every single interpersonal encounter, but it is certainly worth a try to improve communication.

CHECKING YOUR UNDERSTANDING

Enhancing Perceptual Accuracy

Before completing the chapter, take a few minutes to assess your learning by writing your answers to the following items:

1. Because attribution errors are quite common, can you name the four types and provide examples of each one? Which one of these do you think could be most detrimental to your interpersonal communication and relationships?

2. What are three perceptual considerations to address before checking your perceptions?

3. Can you describe the primary difference between direct and indirect perception checking? Under what circumstances might the indirect method be beneficial to you?

4. What are three steps you should follow in the direct perception-checking process? Can you think of an encounter in which you were uncertain of your perceptions of another person's behavior and outline what you might say in each of these steps?

A Communication Development Plan for Dr. Menger

To complete Dr. Menger's story, you will recall how Shuntaro exhibited some specific behaviors that led her to make some inaccurate perceptions of Shuntaro. After reading this chapter, see whether you can address these questions about the perceptual process and the attributions Dr. Menger developed.

What do you think?

Dr. Menger obviously developed inaccurate perceptions about Shuntaro. How would you suggest she be more accurate in the perceptual process with him. What are things she needs to consider in the future with students in her class? In addition, how would you suggest Shuntaro alter his communication behaviors so that he can create accurate perceptions of himself? Is it possible that there are some intercultural behaviors that are socially learned and cannot be changed but could be presented differently?

Possible Explanations

Both Shuntaro and Dr, Menger play roles in the faulty perceptions and attributions that have developed in their first meeting. We determine how we view others and choose to interact with them on the basis of our past experiences. Unfortunately, when we interact with people of different cultures or those who behave in ways with which we are unfamiliar, we fall back on what we know, even though these assumptions or interpretations are probably inaccurate.

Here is the advice we would offer Dr. Menger and advice for Shuntaro to help control "other perceptions."

1. Shuntaro needs to be more aware. He should carefully consider the culture he is a part of and the cultural group he is entering and becoming a part of. If he had stopped to think about the expectations of students in the college classroom, he might have behaved differently.

2. Dr. Menger needs to avoid jumping to conclusions. She is clearly focusing on her class and the lesson she worked so hard to prepare and fails to recognize the social and cultural differences that may have been affecting Shuntaro's behavior.

3. Dr. Menger needs to stop, look, and listen. In this process, she needs to ask questions and engage in direct perception checking. Remember that two interpretations should be generated before firming up your perceptions. Dr. Menger could have asked Shuntaro, after class, whether he was nervous or uncomfortable. Dr. Menger might have inquired about social and cultural differences that were possibly influencing classroom behaviors. If she had perceptions of Shuntaro, then she needed to check on whether they were correct before sending Shuntaro such a harsh email message. Shuntaro was clearly bothered by Dr. Menger's response, and had Dr. Menger been more aware and been more direct with Shuntaro, the incident could have been resolved earlier.

4. Ultimately, Dr. Menger needs to reflect on the three-step process to developing accurate perceptions.

Take Aways

This chapter focused on increasing your understanding, skills, and knowledge of perceptions and inaccuracies in the perceptual process. There are many factors that we consider when we develop our perceptions, and the elements discussed in this chapter should not be considered exhaustive. However, they are commonly experienced in interpersonal relationships. The following list of knowledge claims summarizes what you have learned in this chapter:

- The perception process and the three stages through which people move to develop their perceptions: selection, organization, and interpretation.
- The four schemata that play a role in how you choose to organize the communication behaviors you observe. These are physical, role, interaction, and physical schema.
- How the three perceptual attributions you use help to explain why someone behaves the way he or she does.

- The influence our individual personality traits, self-concept, self-esteem, our gender/sex roles, occupational roles, and culture have on our perceptions.

- The inaccuracies in perceptual processes you engage in and the positive/negative effects they have on you and those with whom you interact.

- The power of homophily and fundamental attribution error and their effects on the perceptual process.

Following are some of the ways in which you can enhance your understanding and skills associated with the processes you use to develop your perceptions of others.

- Examine the power of homophily on the perceptions you make about others.

- Use the four defense mechanisms to assess your perceptions and possible inaccuracies in them.

- Use the attributional confidence instrument to assess how sure you are about the behavioral attributions you have made about someone close to you.

- Follow the three steps of the direct perception-checking process to examine the conclusions you draw about the communication of others in your interpersonal relationships.

- Troubleshoot your perceptual accuracy by learning to evaluate the communication in your interpersonal relationships via three important considerations: questioning your own accuracy, yourself, and the context.

Theory Discussion Questions

1. When you engage in the three stages of the perceptual process, what role do your schemata typically play? Do you typically favor one of the four schemata?

2. What is the relationship between self-concept and self-esteem? Why are they so powerful in creating your perceptions?

3. Which of the three areas of perceptual influence (individual, social, and cultural) do you believe drive most Americans in forming their perceptions? Considering what you know about Western culture, why do you believe this to be true?

4. Is it possible for people to engage in stereotyping as a defense mechanism to filter their perceptions? Explain how this might be true for someone.

5. Do you believe that personality type (the Big Five) plays a role in a person's use of either of the two self-serving attributions (self-enhancing versus self-protecting)? Why or why not?

Building Your Skills

1. Break into groups between four and six people. Assign each person one of the four schema used to organize perceptions. As you sit in a circle, have each person think of and describe aloud an example of how they use their particular schema to organize their perceptions of someone with whom they have interacted with but knew little about.

2. Locate a video clip that displays a common stereotype being utilized. Categorize the probable influence (individual, social, and/or cultural) that you believe is responsible for creating the stereotype. Discuss why this influence is likely and, on the basis of the locus of the attribution, whether or not it is possible to change.

3. Create a "realistic" scenario in which you might engage in the three steps of the direct perception-checking process. Role-play this scenario; afterward, discuss how this can work in all sorts of relationships (e.g., romantic, friends, parents).

4 Assessing and Developing Verbal Message Skills

Maurice's Story . . .

Maurice recently moved with his family from Los Angeles to a small Midwestern town. Maurice's father accepted a new position as Director of Admissions for the local college, where Maurice is a sophomore. Maurice is unlike anyone else in his new town in his attitudes and beliefs, and because of this and his self-confidence, people find him interesting. They want to be his friend.

Although Maurice had no problem developing new friendships, he is having a problem keeping his friends. His friends find him to be too assertive and at times even hostile. When he disagrees with people, which is often, he has a tendency to lash out at them in an insulting manner.

While having dinner with his friends one evening, Maurice observed his friends having a healthy debate about the upcoming political election. Rather than engaging in the debate, Maurice called his friends "stupid idiots" for supporting a political candidate whom he disliked. When his friends called him on his behavior, he said, "I don't care what you think of me. I can't stand your small town mentality. This is who I am, and if you can't accept me, then that's your problem."

In reality, Maurice cares a great deal about what his friends think of him. He is bothered by how he treats other people. This is not the first time he has communicated in this manner. The results are always the same: He quickly loses his friends. Although he apologized to his friends for his behavior at the dinner and they accepted his apology, the relationships were damaged. He realizes that he will need to reestablish his trust with his friends and that this will take some time. He is also worried that this overly aggressive verbal behavior could happen again.

What do you think? While reading this chapter, consider how you might answer the following questions to help Maurice:

CHAPTER OBJECTIVES

AFTER READING THIS CHAPTER, you will understand:

1. How language is symbolic and rule-governed and how these characteristics of language affect your interpersonal communication.

2. How your personality is related to your communicator style.

3. How men and women use conversational rituals differently.

4. How sex differences affect verbal messages.

5. Culture and the various communication aspects of culture.

6. How your culture influences your verbal message styles.

7. The difference between assertiveness, argumentativeness, and verbal aggressiveness.

8. Your level of assertiveness and argumentativeness and how you can use assessment of these traits to enhance your interpersonal communication.

- Why does Maurice use aggressive verbal messages when he knows that he will lose his friends by doing so?

- Is Maurice's aggressive use of verbal messages the result of his personality, a trait he inherited from his parents and their ancestors, or something that he has learned over time?

- What communication skills can Maurice develop to help him communicate more constructively when he disagrees with people?

We will revisit Maurice's story at the end of the chapter and use the content discussed in this chapter to develop a communication plan to help him.

AFTER READING THIS CHAPTER,
you will be able to:

1 Adapt verbal message styles to various cultural contexts.

2 Develop and use assertive verbal messages appropriately.

3 Develop and use argumentative verbal messages appropriately.

AFTER COMPLETING THE SELF-ASSESSMENTS,
you will learn about:

1 Assertiveness, your level of assertiveness, and how to maximize your interpersonal communication effectiveness by developing assertive verbal messages.

2 Argumentativeness, your level of argumentativeness, and how to maximize your interpersonal communication effectiveness by developing argumentative verbal messages.

From the late-night intimate conversations we have with our loved ones to the more serious conversations we have with our parents, co-workers, or friends about our problems, most of our relationships are grounded in conversations. Our conversations consist of verbal and nonverbal messages that are exchanged between people. Because of their importance, we are devoting a chapter to both types of message. This chapter examines verbal messages, and Chapter 5 focuses on nonverbal messages. Recall from Chapter 1 that **verbal messages** include the words and language we use to communicate with others. From our first getting-acquainted remarks to our saying good-bye, the influence of verbal messages on relationships has been the topic of numerous research studies.[1]

> If we spoke a different language, we would perceive a somewhat different world.
>
> —LUDWIG WITTGENSTEIN

Communication researchers Maureen Keeley and Julie Yingling recently examined the influence of final conversations on our relationships. In essence, they examined peoples' recollections of the final verbal messages they had with their loved ones just before the loved ones died. They found final conversations with terminally ill people to be important in terms of helping family members process and make sense of the deaths.[2]

In many ways, our conversations serve as foundations to our relationships. As our conversations unfold, we decide what we would like to do with the foundation. Sometimes, it forms the basis for a relationship. In this chapter, we examine the verbal messages that form this relational foundation:

- We discuss what makes verbal messages unique: the characteristics of verbal messages, the influence these messages have on your relationships, and how your personality and use of technology influence your verbal messages.

- We examine how sex differences affect verbal messages. Men and women have been shown to use language differently. Although these differences are minimal and generalizations do not apply to all individuals, these differences can influence how men and women relate to each other.

- We focus on the relationships between culture and verbal messages. Culture influences how people use verbal messages, and sometimes these differences in verbal message style affect our communication across cultures.

- Finally, we pay particular attention to assertive messages and how you can use assertive and argumentative messages to enhance your interpersonal communication, which is a process of mutual influence.

Verbal Messages

Did you know that trained researchers can predict which relationships will last and which ones won't in part on the basis of the verbal messages that people use?[3] Since most people want positive and constructive relationships, we're going to begin by examining some aspects to verbal messages that will help you to see how we use them to communicate and connect with others.

Characteristics of Language

A **language** is characterized as a system of symbols governed by rules that we use to stimulate meanings in the minds of others.

Language Is Symbolic. A **symbol** is an artificial representation of an idea or an object. For example, the word "book" is a symbol containing four letters arranged in a particular order that English speakers use to represent the object that you're currently reading. Symbols have arbitrary meanings that, over time, became associated with the objects that represent the symbols. Symbols can sometimes be ambiguous. For example, if you don't understand English and you hear the word "book," it probably won't mean anything to you, or you might try to connect it to an object or concept in your own culture that has a similar-sounding name. Also, depending on the context, "book" can have different meanings. In business, the book can mean the financial balance sheet that the accountants prepare; at the police station, the book might mean the law; and in the library, it can mean a great piece of literature or the latest thriller or romance novel.

One way to better understand the artificial nature of symbols is to understand **signs**, which are natural and signal the presence of something else. For example, smoke is a natural sign for fire, and tears are a natural sign for a person's emotions. Regardless of where you're from or what language you speak, you probably interpret these signs similarly because they're natural representations and universally understood.

Language Is Rule-Governed. We're going to discuss four rules that govern the symbolic nature of language: phonological, semantic, syntactic, and pragmatic. **Phonological rules** govern how words sound when spoken. A variety of sources govern how people pronounce words. Most dictionaries include the phonetic spelling of words, which is a set of symbols that help people to voice a particular word. For example, the word "nuclear" is to be pronounced nū'-klē-ar and not *nū-kū-ler*. The culture of the region is another source for phonological rules. Different regions of the United States have distinct accents that reflect and create the culture. **Accents** are unique ways in which words are pronounced in a particular region, such as the so-called Southern accent (which is a generic version of a number of accents found in the southeastern United States).

Semantic rules govern how people assign meanings to words. People assign meaning to words in two different ways: denotatively and connotatively. When you interpret verbal messages in a **denotative** manner, you interpret them literally, using the dictionary's definition. When you interpret verbal messages in a **connotative** manner, you interpret them on the basis of your personal experiences. For example, a soldier returning home from war might assign a meaning to the word "patriot" that differs from the meaning that word has to a civilian.

In relationships, it's important that two people are assigning meanings to words in the same way. If not, misunderstandings can easily occur. For example, Sarah and Luke have been romantically involved for almost two years. When Luke introduced Sarah to Keith, his colleague from work, Luke referred to Sarah as his "friend." Being referred to as a "friend" and not his girlfriend was quite hurtful to Sarah, and Luke was embarrassed when she told him this. Perhaps you have made a similar semantic mistake.

Syntactic rules govern how words are organized or ordered in a sentence or utterance. They enhance a person's ability to decode and assign meaning to the language.[4] Consider the following two examples:

- Colorless green ideas sleep furiously.
- Furiously sleep ideas green colorless.

Although both of these sentences are nonsensical, the first sentence has a structure or sequence of words that is ordered in a more comprehensible manner. Linguist Noam Chomsky argued, in his influential book *Syntactic Structures*, that speakers of a language have a relatively intuitive knowledge of syntax rules such that people can identify sentences that look and sound correct to them without necessarily being able to explain why they make more sense than other sentences with words arranged in a different order.[5]

Pragmatic rules govern how verbal messages should be interpreted in a given context. For example, a neighbor who asks you, "How are you?" probably doesn't want a full report of your physical and mental health. Instead, your neighbor is using a common ritual. If you provide an answer that goes beyond "I'm fine and how are you?" you are probably violating a pragmatic rule for this type of a relationship.

Power of Language

There is power in language. It influences you and your relationships in interesting ways. For example, many first-generation college students have parents whose knowledge of English is limited. These bilingual students live and work in two cultural systems. At school, they speak, write, and think in English. At home, many of them speak, write, and think using their parents' language. Because language is so intricately connected to culture, value systems, and ways of thinking, parents and children often find themselves in conflict and not understanding each other. Following are additional ways in which language affects you and your relationships.

Language Influences What You Think About. Language is powerful in that it allows people to name and label experiences, which affects what people think about. For example, it is probably safe to say that people have been sexually harassing each other since the beginning of time; however, it wasn't until 1974 that the term "sexual harassment" was coined.[6] Did people talk about the phenomenon of sexual harassment before it was labeled "sexual harassment"? Probably so; however, the label has helped us to think about the issue in different ways. Now researchers are studying it. Legislators are writing and passing laws to prevent it. Employers are discussing it with their employees, and families are discussing it with their family members. When you have the power to label a phenomenon, you can influence what people think about. It gets the topic or phenomenon on people's radar screens.

Language Influences How Others Perceive You. Your use of language affects how others perceive you. In fact, every time you speak, you're revealing yourself to others. For example, have you ever heard a racist joke from an acquaintance that made you very uncomfortable? If so, you have an idea of how the use of language can reveal a person's attitudes, beliefs, and values.

One perception that is particularly influenced by your language use is credibility, which comes down to whether or not others perceive you to be a competent, trustworthy, and caring person. Your use of clear or concrete messages and vocabulary that is suitable for those who will receive your message can affect your credibility positively.[7] What hurts your credibility is using **biased language**, which implies assumptions about people, groups, or organizations, unnecessarily categorizing them.[8] Here are a few examples of biased language:[9]

- *Regional stereotypic language.* Inappropriately assigns qualities and characteristics to an entire region.

  Example: They come from the backwards South.

  Recommendation: They come from the South.

- *Exclusive language.* This type of biased language is often sex-exclusive, which leaves out one of the sexes.

Avoid	*Use*
chairman	chair
freshman	first-year student
fireman	firefighter
salesman	sales representative
mailman	mail carrier

- *Sexist language.* Treats the sexes unequally and often promotes stereotypes.

  Example: A mother should read to her child at bedtime.

  Recommendation: Parents should read to their children at bedtime.

Language Affects Your Relationships. Language influences your relationships with others in that it enhances affiliation, liking, and attraction. Research has demonstrated that you are attracted to others whose style of speaking is similar to your own.[10] Have you ever noticed how your language changes when you're with someone you find attractive? You might notice yourself adapting to the other person's use of language. For example, if the other person uses slang, jargon, or even profanity, you might find yourself using the same forms and types of language. Conversely, have you ever noticed how your language changes when you're with someone you don't find attractive? If this person uses slang, jargon, and profanity, you might find yourself using more formal types of language.

Language Affects Your Perceptions. The language you use has been shown to influence your perceptions and attitudes.[11] It has been reported that people within a culture who have a large vocabulary for color names also have the ability to recall and discriminate between different shades of the same color.[12] For example, some people do not see the difference between royal blue and sapphire blue because their culture doesn't have a varied vocabulary for color. In other cultures in which the language includes a rich vocabulary of color (e.g., blue, azure, sapphire, royal), people can easily see the difference between sapphire blue and royal blue. Because of their color vocabulary, they can perceive color differently than people in cultures that have a different color vocabulary do.

In another study, researchers found that people's perceptions and attitudes toward disabled people were more positive when they described these individuals using the terms "disabled" and "physically challenged" than when they used "crippled" and "handicapped."[13] Using language that stimulated more positive meanings influenced them to hold more positive attitudes.

Some companies have been successful in shaping how employees perceive the work they perform on a daily basis by influencing the language they use on the job. For example, all new employees of the Walt Disney Corporation take part in the Disney University, which is a training program for new employees.

While attending Disney University, new employees are introduced to the language of the theater. Employees are referred to as cast members who wear costumes rather than uniforms. While working, cast members are on-stage. During breaks, cast members invisibly disappear to secret, off-stage areas. Guests, who are not known as customers, are never exposed to these off-stage areas of Disney theme parks. According to Disney management, this strategic use of language helps customer service employees to perceive their jobs as more than just flipping burgers or picking up garbage. Instead, they perform in a carefully scripted production that, according to Disney executives, translates into high-quality guest relations at Disney theme parks throughout the world.[14]

Can you predict the personality types of the women shown in the photo?

Personality and Language

Although you've been acquiring language since your birth, how you use your language is in large part affected by your personality. Have you ever wondered why some people are verbally skilled while others aren't? From their opening pickup lines to their eloquent "I want to break up with you" email, some people have a gift for using language. What about you? Do you have an effective way of starting a conversation with someone you're interested in getting to know better, or do you stammer, trying to find the right words? Some people make it look easy and artful; others find it challenging, almost like a form of rocket science.

Your personality plays a role in how you use language. Researchers have found that a person's personality is related to how he or she uses humor and profanity, for example, to develop and manage relationships.[15] Communication researcher Robert Norton, was one of the first scholars to study communication style. Although he defined communicator style as including both verbal and nonverbal message variables, he found that the way in which people use language plays a large part in a person's communication style. Norton discovered eleven dimensions to a person's communicator style; the seven of these dimensions listed in Table 4.1 focus primarily on a person's use of verbal messages when interacting with others.[16]

Your communicator style is a combination of verbal style variables rather than a single style variable (see Table 4.1). For example, a person may communicate very often in a dominant, dramatic, and friendly manner; occasionally in an attentive and open way; and never in a style that is contentious or precise.

A person's communicator style has been shown to be related to a number of important outcomes in a variety of different types of interpersonal relationships. For example, patients were more satisfied with their relationships with their doctors if doctors were attentive, dramatic, and not too dominant or contentious.[17] Employees considered their managers to be more effective if they were open and dramatic.[18] Students were motivated to develop a relationship with their teachers if teachers were attentive, dramatic, and friendly.[19] Finally, people are considered more interpersonally attractive and likable if they use a communicator style that is open, attentive, and precise.[20]

What does this research mean for you, your communication, and your relationships? On the basis of this research, which focused on many different types of relationships, it

TABLE 4.1

Verbal Communication Styles	
Verbal Styles	**Description**
Dominant	Uses intense and opinionated language and verbal messages that direct and control conversations. Is perceived by others as in control, competent, confident, self-assured, forceful, and competitive.
Dramatic	Uses vivid language, sarcasm, metaphors, and satire when telling jokes and sharing anecdotes. Is perceived by others as memorable, visible, observable, attractive, and popular.
Contentious	Uses factual and logical verbal messages to argue while also challenging others' verbal messages. Is perceived by others to be either quarrelsome, competent, and confident or unpleasant, rude, and aggressive.
Attentive	Uses verbal messages that paraphrase what the other person has said. Uses verbal messages that reflect careful attention to what has been said in a conversation. Is perceived by others to be listener-oriented, caring, and empathic.
Open	Uses verbal messages in a conversational and informal manner. Expresses emotions and attitudes as well as reveals information about oneself including one's personal experiences. Is perceived by others as revealing, uninhibited, and unreserved.
Friendly	Uses humorous, encouraging, positive, and supportive messages while also expressing affection for another person. Acknowledges others' contributions while using their first names. Is perceived by others as being sociable, outgoing, and well liked.
Precise	Uses careful, directed, concise, and concrete verbal messages. Is perceived by others as being credible, meticulous, and exact.

Source: Adapted from Norton, R. (1983). *Communicator style: Theory, application, and measures.* Beverly Hills, CA: Sage.

appears that most people consider a communicator style that is open, dramatic, attentive, and friendly to be the most effective in terms of developing relationships. These particular communicator style variables include verbal messages that not only reveal your willingness to develop a relationship, but also make you attractive to others.[21]

Although some people are naturally open, dramatic, attentive, and friendly, others are not. Can you learn to use verbal messages in such a way that others perceive you to be open, dramatic, attentive, and friendly? Communication researcher Cary Horvath helps us to answer this question. She found that a portion of a person's communicator style is related to personality and inherited traits. This means that a portion of the way in which we use verbal messages is somewhat fixed and cannot necessarily be learned as easily as other style variables.[22] Two dimensions in particular—open and dominant—were strongly related to the genes we inherited from our parents and grandparents. This means that these two style variables come naturally for some and not for others. Even though we may work hard to develop these style variables, there is a chance that we will never feel completely comfortable communicating in an open and dominant manner.

Each person has a unique personality and communication style that is revealed in how people use language in conversations. Through her use of language, people probably perceive this person to be attentive, open, and friendly.

Technology and Language

The technology we use to communicate has had a significant influence on our language. Research suggests that 85% of teens ages 12–17 engage at least occasionally in some form of text-based electronic personal communication, which includes text messaging, sending email or instant messages, and posting comments on social networking sites.[23] Text-messaging, also known as texting, has affected how people use verbal messages to communicate. An interesting research finding examining texting is that young people do not consider it a written form of communication. Instead, they consider texting to be oral or spoken communication.[24] According to linguistic researchers, "texters write it as though they are saying it."[25]

Characteristics of Text Messages. Because texting is conducted by using small and mobile communication devices (e.g., cell phones, BlackBerrys) with miniature keyboards, the technology has forced people to use verbal messages in new ways. Text messages have a number of common characteristics:[26]

- *Text messages convey relational rather than task information.* Rather than conveying information (e.g., "Where's the nearest Starbucks?"), texters usually use texting to convey relational information, including friendly greetings ("How are you?"), social arrangements ("You up for dinner tonight?"), and friendship maintenance ("Are you mad at me?").

- *Text messages are brief.* The average text message is fourteen words per message, and these messages include, on average, three abbreviations. These abbreviations or shortcuts are becoming known in the popular culture as "textspeak." Although developed by teenagers, textspeak is being used by adults in their texts to their children, spouses, intimate and casual friends, and colleagues at work.[27]

- *Text messages are comprehensible.* Text messages are understandable and are equivalent to a note left on the fridge, on the dining room table, or next to the telephone. On average, text messages contain three abbreviations; abbreviations account for 20% of the content of text messages.[28]

Although texting is a written form of communication, texters consider it a spoken form, since they write it as though they are saying it. What do you think?

- *Text messages include minimal punctuation.* Most text messages don't include proper punctuation or capitalization. Researchers argue that the lack of punctuation is not because of laziness or lack of respect for proper punctuation. Instead, it allows texters to speed up the texting and turn taking—it keeps the conversation rolling at a natural speed.[29]

Effects of Text-Messaging. Although some people consider texting to be a complete waste of time, there are a number of clear benefits for certain groups of individuals. First, individuals who are shy and communication apprehensive usually experience difficulty in forming and maintaining relationships and experience loneliness. Texting allows socially anxious people to connect with others and to form "texting communities" and "texting buddies"; these have been shown to reduce feelings of loneliness.[30] Second, texting allows socially anxious people to be authentic and real—it allows them to be their "true selves."[31]

As with all forms of technology, texting has some drawbacks. First, some researchers argue that texting leads to social skill deficits or people who have trouble communicating in face-to-face situations.[32] What's uncertain about this research, however, is the cause-and-effect relationship. Second, texting encourages inappropriate writing styles that appear in students' school work. Research suggests that although teenagers say that they make a clear distinction between writing for school and texting for personal communication, textspeak does appear in their school work.[33]

The use of textspeak in the professional workplace is inconclusive and may depend on level of education.[34] One study found that college students include textspeak in informal writing samples but not in formal writing that one would use in the workplace.[35] Another study reported that corporate interviewers received text messages from interview candidates thanking them for interviews rather than formal thank you notes (e.g., "Thx for the IView! I Wud ❤2 Work 4 U!!").[36]

Third, some people in the psychological community worry that too much texting may be addictive in a way similar to Internet addiction disorder, which was identified in 1995.[37] According to some reports, symptoms of text addiction include feeling anxious and frustrated when one's phone is not in one's hand. In addition to these psychological problems, repetitive strain injury in the hands, shoulders, and wrists has been reported.[38]

 CHECKING YOUR UNDERSTANDING

Verbal Messages

Before reading further, take a few minutes to assess your learning by writing your answers to the following items:

1. Describe and provide an example of three characteristics of language. In your description, make sure to differentiate the following terms: phonological, semantic, syntactic, and pragmatic rules, and denotative and connotative meanings.

2. Using communication accommodation theory, explain how language affects your relationships.

3. Explain the relationships between language, perceptions, and behavior.

4. How is technology influencing our use of verbal messages?

Sex Differences and Verbal Messages

Men and women tend to use verbal messages differently.[39] You probably already know this to be true from your own relationships. There may be times when it's hard to get a member of the opposite sex to understand what you mean. You walk away frustrated, saying to yourself, "This shouldn't be so difficult to understand." Becoming aware of these differences and adapting your communication accordingly is just another way in which you can enhance your interpersonal communication with others.

Powerful/Powerless Language

Linguist Robin Lakoff was one of the first researchers to identify a power difference between men's and women's uses of language. She described these differences as powerful language and powerless language.[40] **Powerful language** is stereotypically masculine and is characterized by assertiveness. It tends to be task oriented, focused on getting things done. Powerful language focuses more on the information being exchanged (the *what*) than on the relational elements (the *how*) in the message. **Powerless language** is stereotypically feminine and is characterized by an emphasis on connecting with others and fostering harmonious relationships. Powerless language focuses more on the quality of the relationship between individuals than on the content of the information being exchanged. More emphasis is placed on facial expressions and gestures or *how* something is communicated than on the content or *what* is communicated.[41]

Here are a few examples of powerful and powerless verbal messages and how men and women use them differently:[42]

- *Women use slightly more hedges than men do.* A **hedge** is a statement that limits the speaker's responsibility. It softens or weakens the meaning of the idea. Examples of hedges include "somewhat, perhaps, possible, or maybe." Here is an example:

    Powerful verbal message: "They are entering our market. We need to develop a strategy that will prevent them from taking our customers."

    Powerless verbal message: "It seems *possible* that they are entering our market. *Perhaps* we should develop a strategy that prevents them from taking our customers."

- *Women use slightly more tag questions than men do.* A **tag question** is a combination of a sentence and a question, treated as a single unit. Here are a few examples:

    Powerful verbal message: "That's an interesting idea."

    Powerless verbal message: "That's an interesting idea, isn't it?"

- *Women use slightly more intensifiers than men do.* An **intensifier** is a word that is evaluative and emotive—it conveys emotions. Examples of intensifiers include "extremely," "tremendously," and "incredibly," to name a few. Here are examples to see the difference:

    Powerful verbal message: "I'm happy for you and your accomplishments."

    Powerless verbal message: "I'm *incredibly* happy for you and your *tremendous* accomplishments."

Although men and women have been shown to use only slightly different amounts of powerful and powerless language, this slight amount seems to affect how others perceive them, especially in terms of their credibility. After analyzing thirty research studies examining men and women's use of powerful and powerless language, communication

There is just enough difference in the way men and women encode and decode verbal messages for it to occasionally cause miscommunication in relationships. Understanding this small difference can have a large impact on enhancing your interpersonal communication.

Try using powerful forms of language, especially when you're in a leadership role, and see what happens.

researcher Lindsay Timmerman reported that "any time that women present ideas or attempt to influence others (e.g., in the classroom, at work, in personal relationships, etc.), they are in danger of being perceived as less credible and less persuasive than their male counterparts, solely due to the language they use."[43]

Research conducted in the workplace found similar findings, in that people who use powerless messages were perceived as having a lower social status as well as being less knowledgeable, trusting, and dynamic than people who use powerful messages.[44] In a workplace study, both male and female employees perceived female leaders as less effective if they communicated using powerless verbal messages.[45]

You can enhance how others perceive you, especially at work, where being perceived as credible is important, by using powerful language rather than powerless language— that is, by using fewer hedges, tag questions, and intensifiers.

Conversational Rituals

Deborah Tannen, a linguist at Georgetown University, examined how men and women communicate differently in conversations at work and at home.[46] Tannen argues that men and women use different **conversational rituals**, which are routine scripts that we have learned to use when talking and responding to others. The problem with conversational rituals is that they can sometimes misfire: The message that is sent doesn't always equal the message that is received. Tannen mentions that when people greet you in the United States, they often use the following conversational ritual: "Hi, how you're doing?" They expect the other person to interpret it ritually rather than literally. They expect "I'm fine. How are you?" When they get a complete health report, the ritual has misfired.

Here are a few of the conversational rituals that Tannen identified in her research:[47]

Apology Ritual. Women often say, "I'm sorry," meaning it not as an apology but as a conversational smoother or as a way of expressing concern. Like putting a drop of oil on a squeaky hinge, a conversational smoother allows a person to communicate more smoothly and with less friction. For example, during a neighborhood association meeting, Leona states, "Oh, I'm sorry, I have one more item that I would like to add to our agenda." With this statement, Leona is not apologizing but simply using ritual apology to appear less abrupt and possibly to express concern about other people's time. From the female perspective, Leona uses ritual apology as a way of connecting with others. Ritual apology may misfire when men interpret it as an actual apology. From the male perspective, Leona is undermining her authority by appearing less organized and weak.

Opposition Ritual. Men often play the role of devil's advocate in conversations with others, and this conversational ritual has been known to misfire when it occurs with women. The **devil's advocate role** is being used when someone criticizes or opposes something purely to provoke a discussion or argument. Consider the following conversation between Dean, who is the editor of a men's fitness magazine, and Sarah, who is a writer for the magazine. Sarah is pitching an idea for a feature article:

Sarah: "How about a story about men who are compulsive about fitness to the point that it's dangerous and unhealthy?"

Dean: "How does your idea fulfill the mission of the magazine, which is to promote health and fitness?"

Sarah: "Well, the article would conclude with a list of ways in which men can be fit and healthy in a balanced manner."

Dean: "But isn't compulsive fitness an issue that women face more than men?"

Many women interpret this conversation ritual as a challenge, whereas many men understand it as the use of ritual to tease out ideas and a way to explore ideas more critically. Sarah might no longer consider her idea a good one and might drop it. Dean, however, might not be opposed to the idea but wants to probe Sarah's thinking and understand her angle for the feature article.

Compliment Ritual. Exchanging compliments is a conversational ritual, especially for women. According to Tannen, when a woman compliments another woman, she expects to receive a compliment in return.[48] Again, the ritual is a way to relate to and connect with another person. The ritual misfire occurs when men don't reciprocate compliments. Consider the following conversation between Kimberly and Greg, who are married. Kimberly is a pianist and Greg is a violinist in the local symphony. Following a concert, Kimberly complimented Greg on his solo. Because Greg didn't reciprocate the compliment, Kimberly asked, "What did you think of my solo?" Rather than following the ritual and complimenting Kimberly, Greg provided a detailed critique of what he thought of her solo. This was clearly a ritual misfire. According to Tannen, men tend to interpret messages literally rather than ritually. Kimberly was not expecting a critique of her solo. Instead, she expected the ritual to be reciprocated with a compliment.

Small Talk Ritual. Men and women often use small talk to relate to others. **Small talk** is brief, informal conversations about matters of little importance that allow people to relate to each other. Put another way, small talk is a type of social lubrication that allows conversations to run more smoothly. According to Tannen, men and women have different small talk rituals; many women use rapport talk, and many men use report talk.[49] **Rapport talk** focuses on sharing information about relationships; **report talk** focuses on sharing factual or statistical information. Both forms of small talk (rapport and report) are used to relate to and connect with others; however, men and women go about their small talk rituals quite differently. Women tend to interpret men's report talk as too impersonal, and men tend to interpret women's report talk as too personal.[50]

If your relationships, especially in the workplace with the opposite sex, are not working as smoothly as you would like, the problems could be the result of conversational ritual misfires. Men's and women's conversational rituals can be equally effective. One ritual is not better or more effective than the other. Both have been shown to be effective in the workplace when they're interpreted ritually rather than literally.[51]

Adapting Verbal Messages to Sex Differences

Here are a few ways in which you can adapt your verbal messages to communicate more effectively with people of the opposite sex.[52]

- *Be aware that men and women have learned to use different conversational rituals.* If you're male and receive a ritual apology, it probably wasn't intended as an apology. If you're female and receive a ritual opposition, it probably wasn't intended as a one-up strategy to assert status or power.
- *If you're male and receive a compliment from a female, then offer a compliment in return.* If a compliment is unwarranted, try sharing at least one positive comment with her.
- *If you're female and don't receive a compliment, understand that it's probably because the male does not understand the conversational ritual.* Tell him how much you value compliments.
- *If you're male, try using ritual apology and rapport talk when communicating with a female.* Temporarily suspending ritual opposition and report talk rituals will be appreciated in communicating with a female.
- *If you're female, try using ritual opposition and report talk when communicating with a male.* Temporarily suspending ritual apology and rapport talk rituals will be appreciated in communicating with a male.

 CHECKING YOUR UNDERSTANDING

Sex Differences and Verbal Messages

Before reading further, take a few minutes to assess your learning by writing your answers to the following questions and explaining them to your study partner:

1. How do hedges, tag questions, and intensifiers differ? Why do researchers consider these to be powerless forms of language? How do men and women use them differently?

2. What is a conversational ritual? Describe the four rituals? What makes them unique? How do men and women use these rituals differently?

3. What are the effects of conversational ritual misfires? Do you see these ritual misfires affecting your relationships at work? If so, how?

Culture and Verbal Messages

We opened this chapter with a quotation that has been attributed to philosopher and mathematician Ludwig Wittgenstein: "If we spoke a different language, we would perceive a somewhat different world." If you speak more than one language, you understand Mr. Wittgenstein's message differently than those who only speak one language. You more clearly understand how language influences how you think and perceive the world around you. Your language abilities are going to allow you to communicate more effectively in what is becoming a global economy and society.

Culture and Verbal Message Styles

Your culture influences not only the language you use to communicate, but also how you use your language or **verbal message style**. A number of style variables are influenced by your culture and also affect your relationships with others.

Accents and Dialects. Your verbal message style is often characterized by your accent and dialect, which are influenced by your culture or the place where you grew up or where you have lived for a considerable period of time. An accent occurs when people pronounce a word differently or emphasize or stress a different syllable within a word. In parts of Boston, it's common to hear of pizza being pronounced "peetzer" and the name Linda pronounced as "Linder." People native to different regions of the United States pronounce words differently and stress different syllables, which produces the accent. A **dialect** is a regional difference in how people use language to express themselves, including vocabulary and grammar. Similar to accents, different parts of the country have different dialects. For example, in parts of Texas, it's common to hear the phrase, "fixin' to," which means "getting ready to," and across the South, "bless his [or her] heart" can be a message of concern or a sarcastic comment. In parts of the upper Midwest, it's common to hear the phrases "You betcha," which means "Yes, you're correct," and "Oki doki," which means "Okay."

A number of researchers have examined how accents and dialects influence the way in which people perceive each other. Researchers have found that American listeners form more favorable impressions of speakers who have American-accented speech.[53] Your accent and dialect influence how others perceive your social status.[54] One study found that jury members made decisions about a person's guilt or innocence on the basis of the person's accent and dialect.[55]

Regardless of where you're from, you probably have an accent and dialect that are unique to your geographic location and cultural group. When you're interacting with people from your own cultural group or geographic location, you use your accent and dialect as a way to show them that you're similar to them. Recall from Chapter 3 that people are attracted to what they perceive to be similar. Familiar accents and dialects mark you as "similar," which is good when you want a relationship to develop. By contrast, some people are sexually attracted by unique and different accents.[56] One of your authors found that many bloggers, especially females, agree that French and Spanish accents are considered the most attractive. What do you think?

When you're interacting and developing relationships, especially at work when you may be communicating with people from different regions of the United States, you want to minimize your regional accent if at all possible. You want your work colleagues and potential clients to pay attention to you and your message, not to your accent and dialect. Noticeable accents and dialects have been shown to negatively affect sales professionals' abilities to sell their products and services.[57] In these situations, communication educators recommend using what is known as the General American Dialect, also sometimes called Standard Midwestern, Standard Spoken American English, or American Broadcast English. The General American Dialect is one of the most homogenous and widespread accents in North America. Most Americans consider this accent to be neutral and free of regional characteristics, which means that the accent and dialect do not distract or negatively influence perceptions.

Direct/Indirect Verbal Messages. Your verbal message style is characterized by how direct you are in your use of verbal messages. **Direct verbal messages** are those in which you immediately and explicitly make a request, ask a question, or state a comment using specific information, leaving no doubt as to the intended meaning. People who live in low-context cultures tend to have a verbal message style that is more direct. **Low-context cultures** are those in which people rely more explicitly on language and the meanings of words and use fewer contextual cues to send and interpret information.[58] Figure 4.1 summarizes differences in communication style between high-context and low-context cultures.

In low-context cultures, there's usually no warmup period during which the conversation begins with standard social graces such as "How have you been?" or "How was your weekend?" When you're direct with others, you're being frank with them. In an effort to get directly to the point, Americans tend to take verbal shortcuts. "How are you coping since you lost your job?" is an example of a direct message.

FIGURE 4.1

High-context and
Low-context Cultures

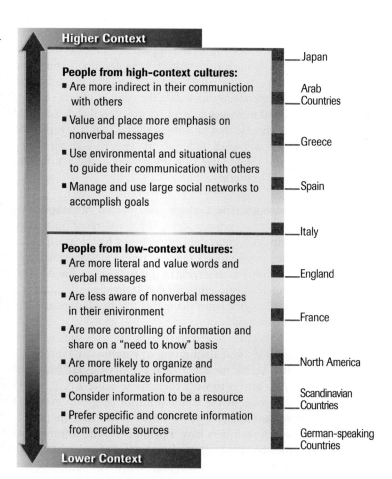

Higher Context

People from high-context cultures:
- Are more indirect in their communiction with others
- Value and place more emphasis on nonverbal messages
- Use environmental and situational cues to guide their communication with others
- Manage and use large social networks to accomplish goals

People from low-context cultures:
- Are more literal and value words and verbal messages
- Are less aware of nonverbal messages in their enivironment
- Are more controlling of information and share on a "need to know" basis
- Are more likely to organize and compartmentalize information
- Consider information to be a resource
- Prefer specific and concrete information from credible sources

Lower Context

Japan

Arab Countries

Greece

Spain

Italy

England

France

North America

Scandinavian Countries

German-speaking Countries

Indirect verbal messages are those in which you make your request, ask a question, or state a comment in an implicit or incomplete manner, allowing the context of the conversation to help you fill in the blanks. People who live in high-context cultures tend to have a verbal message style that is more indirect. **High-context cultures** are those in which nonverbal cues are extremely important in interpreting messages. Communicators rely heavily on the context for more subtle information, such as facial expression, vocal cues, and even silence, in interpreting messages. "So how are you doing with life's challenges?" is an example of an indirect message in which you skirt the issue; some people refer to this type of communication as "beating around the bush."

Certain/Uncertain Verbal Messages. Our culture influences the certainty of our messages, which is the degree of predictability that something will happen. **Uncertainty avoidance** is a measure of how accepting a culture is of a lack of predictability. Cultures in which people tolerate uncertainty have low uncertainty avoidance. People have learned to live with the fact that their ability to predict the future is limited. Many people from these cultures are more comfortable taking risks, and they tend to be more tolerant of others who engage in behavior that goes against what is considered normal. Cultures in which people don't like uncertainty have high uncertainty avoidance. People in these cultures have learned ways to structure their lives to provide as much certainty and predictability as possible. Cultures in which people need certainty to feel secure are more likely to develop and enforce rigid rules for behavior and establish more elaborate codes of conduct.

Certain verbal messages contain specific information that allow you to comfortably predict that something will happen; the expectation is clear. Verbal messages such as "Let's develop an action plan that includes the tasks that need to be completed, who is responsible for the task, and the deadlines" and "What are the rules and policies about this particular issue?" are messages that are indicative of cultures that generally do not like uncertainty, including the cultures of Greece, Portugal, and Guatemala.[59] **Uncertain verbal messages** contain information that is incomplete or vague; you cannot comfortably predict that something will happen. The expectation is unclear. Verbal messages such as "It will work itself out" or "Let's go with the flow" are indicative of cultures that are more comfortable with uncertainty, including those of Singapore, Hong Kong, Jamaica, and Denmark.[60]

Individualistic/Collectivistic Verbal Messages. Our cultural values also influence our verbal message styles. If you will recall from Chapter 3, people from individualistic cultures such as the United States, have learned to value their own interests more than the overall group's interest. Verbal messages such as "This is what I want . . .," "In my opinion, I'm deserving of this because . . .," and "My needs are not being met" reflect an individualistic cultural value. Individualistic cultures offer their members a great deal of freedom, the belief being that this freedom makes it possible for each person to achieve personal success.

People from collectivistic cultures such as Japan and other East Asian cultures, learn to value their group or community's interests more than their individual interests. Verbal messages such as "All of us are responsible for . . .," "We would like . . .," "Our goal is to work together to achieve . . .," and "We could not have accomplished this without the cooperation of all group members" reflect a collectivistic cultural value. Collectivistic cultures offer their members a close-knit social network in which members have a primary loyalty toward one another and the group to which they belong. Collectivistic cultures value what people do together and reward group achievement. In collectivistic cultures, to receive an individual honor would in many ways be considered dishonorable, since it would elevate the individual above the group. One of your authors, while working for an international airline, remembers a flight to Tokyo on which one of the employees of a Japan-based company refused his first-class seat so as to not dishonor his other group members who were flying in the coach cabin.

Informal/Formal Verbal Messages. Another way in which culture influences your verbal style is in the formality of your verbal messages. **Informal verbal messages** are casual, tend to be very familiar, and don't always recognize any status difference in the relationship. Informal verbal messages contain slang, jargon, and humor and often reveal personal information. "Hey, Emily, how ya doin'?" is an example of an informal message. **Formal verbal messages** are those in which language is used in its proper form and any status differences and titles are recognized. Slang and jargon are minimized. "Good morning, Dr. Hinojosa. I hope you are having a pleasant morning" is an example of a formal message.

People who were raised in the U.S. culture pride themselves on their informality and their quickness in getting on a first-name basis with others. People are known for striking up conversations with complete strangers. An example of this informality is the activity of Wal-Mart's infamous people greeters. Most Americans find this greeting to be a sign of friendliness and hospitality. In other countries, such informality is considered intrusive and inappropriate. In Germany, Wal-Mart reassigned the people greeters to other positions in their stores when the local people complained that they were uncomfortable being greeted by a complete stranger in such an informal manner.[61]

Adapting Verbal Messages to Cultural Differences

The following communication strategies will help you to adapt your verbal messages when you are interacting with people from different cultures:

- *Identify the other person's cultural background.* If you're about to interact with people who don't share your cultural background, it's beneficial to identify their cultural background. Are they from a traditionally low-context culture or a high-context culture? Figure 4.1 can help you identify the appropriate culture.

- *Develop verbal messages that are appropriate for the person's cultural background.* For example, "I don't care for the food at that restaurant. Can we eat at this one?" would be appropriate in a low-context culture but inappropriate in a high-context culture. The message is too direct. In high-context cultures, it's important to remain less direct and use the context and nonverbal cues to convey your message. Instead, you might simply pause for a few seconds, hesitate, and lower your eyebrows or turn down the corners of your mouth. These contextual cues would signal to the other person that you would rather not eat at the restaurant.

- *Interpret messages on the basis of cultural background.* Pay attention to what other people are trying to communicate to you through both their spoken messages and their unspoken messages. Read between the lines. What are they not telling you? Do their verbal messages match their gestures, tone of voice, facial expression, and amount of eye contact? For example, are they verbally communicating that the restaurant choice is fine with them while their facial expression and tone of voice are telling you that they would rather eat someplace else? If they are from a high-context culture, it's important to trust and decode their gestures, posture, eye contact, and tone of voice.

- *Tolerate ambiguity.* If you're from a cultural tradition that values certainty and you're uncomfortable with uncertainty, you might have to acknowledge the cultural difference. Be patient, and work at tolerating more ambiguity. Don't be in a hurry to have all of your questions answered. Remind yourself that the other person doesn't have the same attitudes about knowing the future or appreciating details.

CHECKING YOUR UNDERSTANDING
Culture and Verbal Messages

Before reading further, take a few minutes to assess your learning by writing your answers to the following assessment items.

1. What is a verbal message style? To answer this question, differentiate between the following concepts, and provide an example of each: accents/dialects, direct/indirect, certain/uncertain, individualistic/collectivistic, and informal/formal.

2. How do high-context cultures and low-context cultures differ in terms of verbal messages production and reception? Provide an example of a verbal message that reflects the high- and low-context cultural differences. What is the difference?

3. What are four ways in which you can maximize your verbal message effectiveness by taking into consideration another person's culture?

Enhancing Your Verbal Effectiveness

Did you know that people in the U.S. culture who use assertive and argumentative skills are considered effective communicators? Oprah Winfrey, President Obama, and President Reagan come to mind as individuals who use or used assertive verbal messages regularly. So why do many individuals consider assertive and argumentative people to be pushy, aggressive, and always fighting? Do you consider Oprah Winfrey and President Obama to always be fighting? What about Ronald Reagan? For the most part, President Reagan was perceived to be a kind and gentle person who also happened to be the president of the United States.

The purpose of this section of the chapter is to clarify these possible misperceptions and to help you develop assertive verbal messages that enhance interpersonal communication and relational development.[62] Verbally assertive and argumentative communication skills don't come naturally for many people; therefore, they have to develop these skills. Below, you have the opportunity to assess your natural tendencies to be assertive and argumentative as well as to develop both of these important interpersonal communication skills.

Assessing and Developing Assertiveness Skills

Assertiveness is an individual's ability to make requests; actively disagree; express personal rights and feelings; initiate, maintain, or disengage from conversations; and stand up for oneself without attacking others.[63] Put simply, your assertiveness is your ability to express your needs, wants, and desires in a firm but polite manner. Before you read any further, we recommend that you assess your communication by completing the following self-assessment instrument.

ASSESS YOUR **communication personality**

Rathus's Assertiveness Scale[64]

Log onto our self-assessment library, MyPersonalityProfile, found on MyCommunicationLab (www.mycommunicationlab.com), and assess your assertiveness by completing the interactive assessment. Also encourage your relational partner to do the same. Then you can compare and contrast your scores and begin to understand better how your assertiveness influences your interpersonal communication. If you prefer, use the assessment below.

Directions:

Indicate how descriptive of you each of the following statements is by using the following scale:

+3: extremely descriptive

+2: quite descriptive

+1: somewhat descriptive

−1: somewhat nondescriptive

−2: quite nondescriptive

−3: extremely nondescriptive

_____ 1. When food served at a restaurant is not done to my satisfaction, I complain about it to the server.

_____ 2. When I am asked to do something, I insist upon knowing why.

_____ 3. There are times when I look for a good, vigorous argument.

_____ 4. I strive to get ahead of most people in my position.

_____ 5. I enjoy starting conversations with new acquaintances and strangers.

_____ 6. If a famed and respected lecturer makes a statement that I think is incorrect, I will have the audience hear my point of view as well.

_____ 7. When I have done something important or worthwhile, I manage to let others know about it.

_____ 8. I am open and frank about my feelings.

_____ 9. If someone has been spreading false and bad stories about me, I see him or her as soon as possible to have a talk about it.

_____10. I complain about poor service in a restaurant and elsewhere.

_____11. If a couple near me in a theatre or at a lecture were conversing rather loudly, I would ask them to be quiet or to take their conversation elsewhere.

_____12. Anyone attempting to push ahead of me in a line is in for a good battle.

_____13. I am quick to express an opinion.

Scoring Instructions:

Add together all the positive (+) scores (+ subscore). Add together all the negative (−) scores (− subscore). If you have both (+) and (−) subscores, subtract the two from each other to form your Total Assertiveness Score. If your (+) subscore is larger than your (−) subscore, then place a (+) in front of your Total Assertiveness Score. If your (−) subscore is larger than your (+) subscore, then place a (−) in front of your Total Assertiveness Score. Your Total Assertiveness Score must range from +39 to −39.

0 = You tend to have an average level of assertiveness.

>0 = You tend to have an above-average level of assertiveness.

<0 = You tend to have a below-average level of assertiveness.

NATURE/NURTURE intersections

Your Brain's Chemical Hot Buttons

Do you know people who have explosive tempers? You never know what to expect from them. One minute, they're your friend; the next minute, they're your enemy. Where does the hostility, anger, and aggression originate? Researchers have been investigating this question for some time. Although some verbal aggression is learned in the home, in school, or at work, researchers have found that the source for most hostility is in a person's brain.[69]

Researchers have linked hostile communication behaviors to both brain chemicals and brain functioning.[70] Serotonin, which is a brain chemical linked to mood, plays a key role in regulating emotions such as aggression. When there is enough serotonin in the brain, hostile communication behaviors remain in check. If you ever get combative and cranky when you're hungry, you understand how this brain chemical works. When you're hungry, your body doesn't have the essential amino acids it needs for the body to create serotonin. Your brain misses the serotonin, and you become cranky and edgy. To remedy your crankiness, you fill your stomach with food, and this solves your emotional problem. Unfortunately, some people's bodies don't produce the amino acids necessary for the brain to have enough serotonin, even with the appropriate diet. Because of this, they have a difficult time regulating their hostility and verbally aggressive communication behavior.

Although most verbally aggressive behavior doesn't result in violence, neurologists have diagnosed a few individuals with what they refer to as intermittent explosive disorder (IED). Some of these individuals have a chemical imbalance that affects their brain's circuitry; others have problems with a part of their brain known as the prefrontal cortex, which is responsible for regulating and adapting communication behavior. Once the brain has short-circuited, because of either a chemical imbalance or damage to the prefrontal cortex, individuals who have IED engage in hostile and aggressive communication behaviors. Some neurologists believe that individuals with IED may be violent, as is the case with some episodes of road rage, which can result in accidents and severe injuries, including death.

Understanding Your Assertiveness. Some people are naturally assertive, while others aren't. What about you? Is it easy for you to speak up and let others know what you want and need, or do you sacrifice your needs to meet the needs of others? Of course, there is a time in all relationships when we must put aside our own needs to meet the needs of others. Parents do this on a regular basis. They first meet their children's needs, and if time and resources remain, then they meet their own needs. However, continuous neglect of your own needs is not good for you or your relationships. Numerous research articles discuss how constantly neglecting and sacrificing one's needs is detrimental to relationships.[65]

It's also important not to confuse assertiveness with aggressiveness. **Verbal aggression** (VA) is "the tendency to attack the self-concept of another person in face-to-face encounters, instead of, or in addition to, attacking one another's arguments."[66] You're verbally aggressive when you make it personal and make demands of the other person. Rather than making the communication about you, you make it about the other person. To illustrate the difference, compare and contrast the two verbal messages from Tara, who is working with her sister Elaine on the best way to care for their aging parents:

- "I would like you to take care of Mom and Dad on Mondays and Wednesdays so I can take care of my kids."

- "Since you don't have a husband or kids and watch television all day, you will take care of Mom and Dad on Mondays and Wednesdays."

The first verbal message is assertive because it directly addresses a need that Tara has in terms of her obligations: to take care of her kids on Mondays and Wednesdays. Tara is simply making a request that would allow her to meet her multiple obligations. In the second message, Tara is demanding (you will take care of Mom and Dad), and the tone of the message is more of a personal attack (since you don't have a husband or kids and watch television all day). Assertive verbal messages are phrased as a request. Aggressive verbal messages are phrased as demands and include personal attacks.

Another important part of being appropriately assertive is to be responsive. **Responsiveness** is an individual's ability to be sensitive to the communication of others. A responsive listener is seen as a good listener, makes others comfortable in conversations, and recognizes the needs and desires of others.[67] Whereas assertiveness focuses on us and our needs, responsiveness is other-focused and lets the receiver of our messages know that we are also aware of them. When they talk to us, we respond to what they are saying by leaning forward, nodding our heads, making direct eye contact, asking questions, responding to their questions, and paraphrasing or restating in our own words what we hear them saying and how we think they feel.

 WHAT CAN I **do now?**

Keeping in mind that the ability to develop assertive verbal communication skills may be easier for some people than for others simply because of personality type, we offer the following suggestions to help you enhance your communication effectiveness:[68]

▶ *Make requests rather than demands.* Requests begin with "I," and demands begin with "You." For example, "I would like to have the weekend off to go to the coast" is an example of a request, and "You need to give me the weekend off so I can go to the coast" is a demand.

▶ *Make requests succinct, and include a brief explanation using a firm but polite voice.* For example, "I would like to have the weekend off" is a succinct request, and "so I can look for a place to live when my lease expires" is the brief explanation.

▶ *Be sensitive to the other person's needs.* An example of a verbal message conveying sensitivity to the other person's needs might be "I realize this is going to put you in a difficult spot, since other employees want the weekend off too, but I would like to have the weekend off to go to the coast so I can look for a place to live when my lease expires."

▶ *Praise the other person.* Acknowledge something positive that the other person has done well. An example might be "I don't know how you do it, but you always seem to develop a schedule that fits everyone's needs. You're amazing."

▶ *Help to identify a mutually acceptable solution.* Allow the other person to know that you're willing to help him or her work the problem by finding an acceptable solution that is mutually beneficial. For example, you could say, "I'm willing to work the next three weekends; however, this weekend I need off."

▶ *Use responsive messages.* Responsive behaviors include eye contact, forward body leans, affirming head nods, and vocal cues. Nonverbally responsive messages have a tendency to take the edge off of verbally assertive messages; they add warmth to the assertive messages.

Assessing and Developing Argumentativeness Skills

Argumentativeness (ARG) is a communication trait in which people have a desire to advocate a position on an issue and criticize the positions that other people hold on these issues.[71] Before reading any further, take a few minutes to complete the argumentativeness self-assessment instrument.

 ASSESS YOUR **communication personality**

Infante and Rancer's Measure of Argumentativeness[72]

Log onto our self-assessment library, MyPersonalityProfile, found on MyCommunicationLab (www.mycommunicationlab.com), and assess your argumentativeness by completing the interactive assessment. Encourage your relational partner to do the same. Then you can compare and contrast your scores and begin to understand better how your argumentativeness level influences your interpersonal communication. If you prefer, you may use the instrument below.

Directions:

This questionnaire contains statements about arguing about controversial issues. Indicate how often each statement is true for you personally by placing the appropriate number in the blank to the left of the statement. If the statement is *almost never true* for you, place a 1 in the blank. If the statement is *rarely true* for you, place a 2 in the blank. If the statement is *occasionally true* for you, place a 3 in the blank. If the statement is *often true* for you, place a 4 in the blank. If the statement is *almost always true* for you, place a 5 in the blank. Remember, consider each item in terms of *arguing controversial issues*.

ALMOST NEVER TRUE	RARELY TRUE	OCCASIONALLY TRUE	OFTEN TRUE	ALMOST ALWAYS TRUE
1	2	3	4	5

_____ 1. While in an argument, I worry that the person I am arguing with will form a negative impression of me.
_____ 2. Arguing over controversial issues improves my intelligence.
_____ 3. I enjoy avoiding arguments.
_____ 4. I am energetic and enthusiastic when I argue.
_____ 5. Once I finish an argument, I promise myself that I will not get into another.
_____ 6. Arguing with a person creates more problems for me than it solves.
_____ 7. I have a pleasant, good feeling when I win a point in an argument.
_____ 8. When I finish arguing with someone, I feel nervous and upset.
_____ 9. I enjoy a good argument over a controversial issue.
_____10. I get an unpleasant feeling when I realize I am about to get into an argument.
_____11. I enjoy defending my point of view on an issue.
_____12. I am happy when I keep an argument from happening.
_____13. I do not like to miss the opportunity to argue a controversial issue.
_____14. I prefer being with people who rarely disagree with me.
_____15. I consider an argument an exciting intellectual challenge.
_____16. I find myself unable to think of effective points during an argument.
_____17. I feel refreshed and satisfied after an argument on a controversial issue.

_____**18.** I have the ability to do well in an argument.
_____**19.** I try to avoid getting into arguments.
_____**20.** I feel excitement when I expect that a conversation I am in is leading to an argument.

Scoring Instructions:

To compute the argumentativeness trait score, follow these steps:

1. Add scores for items 2, 4, 7, 9, 11, 13, 15, 17, 18, and 20. (A) Total = _____
2. Add scores for items 1, 3, 5, 6, 8, 10, 12, 14, 16, and 19. (B) Total = _____
3. Subtract your (B) total from your (A) total.

If the result is any number between $+14$ and $+40$, you have a high motivation to argue. If the result is any number between -4 and $+13$, you have a moderate motivation to argue. If the result is any number between -5 and -25, you a low motivation to argue.

Understanding Your Argumentativeness. Do you know people who like to argue? You might perceive them as always wanting to pick a fight when in reality, they simply like to argue about ideas. Communication researchers Dominic Infante, Charles Wigley, and Andrew Rancer were the first researchers to consider the desire to argue to be a communication trait. They found that for some people, arguing comes naturally. For others, it's like a foreign language that has to be learned.

Many people perceive arguing to be a destructive form of communication; they associate arguing with fighting and conflict. It's important that you understand the differences between being assertive, being argumentative, and being verbally aggressive:

- _You are being assertive_ when you let another person know your needs and desires without making demands on that person. You openly express your opinions while respecting the other person's opinions.

- _You are being argumentative_ when you advocate or support a position while also criticizing another person's position. You criticize the person's position and not him or her personally.

- _You are being verbally aggressive_ when you attack the person; you make it personal. Rather than criticizing the person's position, you attack him or her personally.

In many ways, arguing is a constructive form of interpersonal communication.[73] People who are argumentative critically think through situations and argue for or against particular proposals by using reasons and evidence. Research clearly indicates benefits to arguing on the job and in the home. At work, professionals who argue well are also considered more effective.[74] Specifically, individuals who are high in the argumentative trait, when compared to individuals who are low in the argumentative trait, tend to do the following:[75]

- Be in relationships that have fewer conflicts because arguing helps to prevent conflict.
- Be better at taking perspective or understanding another person's position on an issue.
- Be perceived as having more credibility, which allows them to be more persuasive and influential.
- Have a stimulated curiosity and learn more.
- Be more effective leaders who have followers who are more satisfied and committed to their jobs.

Research also suggests that in the home, couples who are more argumentative are also less verbally aggressive.[76] Verbal aggression has been shown to be a damaging form of domestic violence.[77] Although the headlines and stories in local newspapers usually reveal horrifying acts of physical domestic violence, which are visible to readers, researchers argue that verbal violence is equally horrifying. Verbal violence, which affects your psychology and is invisible to the public, receives less media attention.

 WHAT CAN I **do now?**

Although there are a number of benefits to being argumentative, people who are low in argumentativeness tend to perceive individuals who are high in argumentativeness as being verbally aggressive and overbearing at times. Following are a few recommendations for how you can adapt to low argumentative individuals to enhance your interpersonal communication.

▶ *Be aware that individuals who are low argumentativeness (−5 to −25) perceive individuals who are high in argumentativeness (+14 to +40) as being verbally aggressive.* If you get a defensive reaction from the other person when you begin to argue, recognize that he or she is probably interpreting your messages as being attacking.

▶ *Use **feed-forward messages,** which are messages that inform others of how to process information.* For example, you might say, "What I am about to say is not intended to be critical of you personally, but I would like to challenge your ideas."

▶ *Use responsive behaviors when listening to others argue.* Leaning forward, using direct eye contact, head nodding, and using back channeling cues (e.g,, "Uh-huh," "Okay," "Umm," and "Oh") are examples of responsive behaviors. These communication behaviors signal to others that you're actively listening to them and their arguments.

Because interpersonal communication is a process of two people influencing each other, it's important that you learn how to use verbal messages to argue. Following are four simple skills that can help you to argue more effectively and adapt to high argumentative individuals to enhance your interpersonal communication:

▶ *Inform. Tell others what you want them to believe and/or do.* When you argue, you're usually trying to persuade others that a problem exists and that changing their behavior or attitudes will help them to solve the problem. Make sure others know what the problem is.

▶ *Explain. Justify why this change is important to them.* Let others know why you want them to change their behavior or attitude. Let them see how changing their behavior or attitude will help to solve the problem and how this change will benefit them personally.

▶ *Support. Provide proof that the change works.* Usually, others are persuaded when they see evidence or proof that their behavioral change or attitude change will bring about change. Illustrate how behavioral and attitude change has worked in the past. Allow others to see directly how others have benefited from a change in behavior and/or attitude. They need to see proof or evidence that it works.

▶ *Disagree. Let others know when you disagree.* Openly share your disagreement, and let others know why you disagree. Make sure they know that you are disagreeing with their ideas and that your disagreement is not a personal attack on them.

CHECKING YOUR UNDERSTANDING
Using Assertive Verbal Messages

Before completing the chapter, take a few minutes to assess your learning by writing your answers to the following items:

1. Define *assertiveness*, *verbal aggressiveness*, and *argumentativeness*, and provide an example of each. To many people, these communication concepts appear similar. What makes them different from one another?

2. What are some of the benefits to having a high-argumentative communication style rather than a low-argumentative communication style?

3. What advice would you give a friend who wants to be more assertive? How would you teach your friend to be more assertive?

4. Explain how people who are high and low in argumentativeness perceive each other. How does this perceptual difference influence interpersonal communication?

A Communication Development Plan for Maurice

To complete Maurice's story, you will recall how Maurice has no problem developing new friendships but has a problem keeping his friends because of his hot temper and hostile communication style.

Why does Maurice use aggressive verbal messages when he knows that he will lose his friends by doing so?

Unfortunately, we all engage in behavior from time to time that we know is not in our best interests. Your brain's affective systems, which control and regulate emotions, hijack your thought processes.[78] In other words, your emotions (or what feels good) win out over what you know you should do. You *know* that eating fatty foods isn't good for you, but you eat them anyway. The same is true about your communication behaviors. You *know* that what you're about to say will probably hurt others, but you say it anyway.

What do you think?

Is Maurice's aggressive use of verbal messages the result of his personality, a trait he inherited from his parents and their ancestors, or something that he has learned over time?

Possible Explanations

It's probably a combination of factors. For many people, aggressive communication comes naturally at first, and because the behavior is rewarded in some manner, people learn to continue using the behavior. Your brain has what researchers have labeled the fight-or flight-activation system.[79] When confronted with a threat or a perceived threat, some people fight. Others get out of the way as soon as possible (flight). Research has shown that highly aggressive people have a sensitive fight system, which means that it doesn't take much of a threat (even a disagreement as in Maurice's case) for them to be activated into fight mode.[80] If this natural pattern of behavior is rewarded, then aggressive people learn to communicate using verbal aggression because they have learned that it works. They get what they want. In Maurice's case, he is probably naturally aggressive, meaning that his brain is wired for fight more than for flight. However, his needs are not being met. His verbally aggressive behavior is not being rewarded. In fact, he is being punished for it. He is losing his friends.

What communication skills can Maurice develop to help him communicate more constructively when he disagrees with people?

There are number of communication skills and strategies that Maurice can use to communicate more constructively when he disagrees with others.[81]

1. *Maurice can educate himself about his verbal aggression problem.* He can assess his own level of verbal aggression by completing the verbal aggression measure that is included on the interactive website that accompanies this textbook (www.mycommunicationlab.com). Once Maurice understands how serious his verbal aggression is, he can read about his communication problem. Communication researchers Andrew Rancer and Ted Avtgis have written a book titled *Argumentative and Aggressive Communication,*[82] which offers the most recent theory and research findings pertaining to people who have abnormal levels of verbal aggression.

2. *Maurice can develop argumentative skills.* One reason people are verbally aggressive is because they lack argumentative skills.[83] Maurice can begin this process by reading the section in this text about how to argue.

After reading this chapter, how would you teach Maurice to argue constructively?

3. *Rather than attacking people, Maurice should learn how to challenge people's ideas.* Rather than saying, "You're stupid for believing the way you do," Maurice should say, "I disagree with your ideas for the following reasons. First. . . . Second. . . . Third. . . ."

4. *Maurice can try to avoid the triggering events that activate his verbal aggression.* It could be particular topics, disagreements, or people who activate his verbal aggression. If discussions involving money trigger an aggressive response, then Maurice should find other ways to discuss this topic. It could also be a particular time of day or when Maurice is tired or hungry that triggers aggressive responses. Recall that the brain chemical serotonin plays a key role in regulating emotions such as aggression. Serotonin levels are low during periods of hunger or fatigue. Although these suggestions will not solve Maurice's aggression problem, they provide temporary relief and allow Maurice time to temporarily manage his communication.

5. *Maurice can be honest with his friends and inform them of his communication problem.* If he does this, his friends may be able to help him manage his communication. If nothing else, Maurice's friends will know not to take his outbursts personally.

Take Aways

This chapter focused on verbal messages, which are the foundation to the numerous conversations you have each day with your friends, family members, and work colleagues. The following list of knowledge claims summarizes what you have learned in this chapter:

- How language is characterized as a system of symbols governed by rules that we use to stimulate meanings in the minds of others.

- How language affects what you think about, how others perceive you, your relationships, and your perceptions.

- How sex differences influence your use of powerful and powerless language and conversational rituals.

- How powerless language includes hedges, tag questions, and intensifiers.

- How conversational rituals include apology, opposition, compliment, and small talk rituals.

- How culture influences your verbal messages in the following manner: accents/dialects, direct/indirect, certain/uncertain, individualistic/collectivistic, and formal/informal.

- How assertiveness is an individual's ability to make requests; actively disagree; express personal rights and feelings; initiate, maintain, or disengage from conversations; and stand up for oneself without attacking others.

- How verbal aggressiveness is the tendency to attack the self-concept of another person in face-to-face encounters instead of, or in addition to, attacking one another's arguments.

- How argumentativeness is a communication trait in which people have a desire to advocate a position on an issue and criticize the positions that other people hold on issues.

Following are some of the things you learned about how your personality influences your verbal communication:

- A person's personality affects his or her communication style, which includes seven different style variables: dominant, dramatic, contentious, attentive, open, friendly, and precise.

- Assertiveness, verbal aggressiveness, and argumentativeness are all communication traits that are influenced by personality.

Following is a list of skills you can develop to enhance your verbal communication effectiveness:

- To enhance how others assign appropriate meanings to your verbal messages, you are encouraged to use specific, precise, and concise words.

- To enhance your credibility, you are encouraged to avoid using biased language, such as regional stereotypes and exclusive language, and instead to use gender-free terms.

- To enhance your interpersonal communication when communicating with a person from a different culture, you are encouraged to develop verbal messages that are appropriate for the culture by using direct/indirect, certain/uncertain, individualistic/collectivistic, and formal/ informal messages, depending on the culture.

- To be assertive, you are encouraged to make requests rather than demands, make requests succinct and include a brief explanation using a firm but polite voice, be sensitive to the other person's needs, praise the other person, help to identify a mutually acceptable solution, and use responsive messages.

- To argue, you are encouraged to inform or tell others what you want them to believe and/or do, explain or justify why this change is important to them, support or provide proof that it works, and disagree or let others know when you disagree.

Theory Discussion Questions

1. What are the four rules that govern our use of language? Why are they significant?

2. How do sex and gender differ? Why is this important to our study of verbal messages?

3. What is a conversational ritual, and how do men and women use conversation rituals differently?

4. How are communication and culture related?

5. How do high-context and low-context cultures differ? How does the context influence verbal message styles?

6. How do argumentativeness and verbal aggressiveness differ?

Building Your Skills

1. Take both personal report measures in this chapter. Get together with a classmate or good friend, and compare scores. Did you score where you expected? Did anything surprise you? Explain.

2. Spend a day observing and taking notes on all the conversational rituals you observe. Then go over them in class, noting anything that was different from the norm.

3. Working in pairs or small groups, come up with a proposition for an argument. Then develop the whole argument, using reasons and evidence. Present your argument to the class.

4. Write down the characteristics of cultures (high context, uncertainty avoidance, etc.). Next, compose a list of cultures that fit the various cultural descriptions. Compare with a classmate. Are your observations the same? If not, how do they differ?

5. While watching your favorite TV program (sitcom, drama, or reality show), take note of all the verbal messages that reflect the use of a status lens and those that use a connection lens. Do you notice a difference in the way men and women communicate on television? If so, what is the difference?

6. Do a self-assessment of your own communicator style. Now write a few pages in your journal about how you see yourself in communication with others as well as ways in which you can adapt to others in communication.

Understanding, Assessing, and Developing Nonverbal Messages

William's Story . . .

William is a college student majoring in computer science. His grades are strong in his major, but he struggles in the interpersonal communication class that the university requires him to take. What troubles him most about this class is that he is expected to deliver a presentation on an interpersonal theory, and William detests formal presentations of any kind. As Dr. Kimberly Russell, William's professor, describes and explains the assignment enthusiastically, William sits slouched in the back of the room, rolling his eyes. To help the students plan their presentations, Dr. Russell divides them into groups for a brainstorming activity. William slowly drags his chair to his group's circle and doodles on a piece of paper as the other group members share ideas. Afterward, Dr. Russell goes around the room and asks each group to talk about the different presentation topics they came up with. Remaining uninvolved, William chuckles and shakes his head as a couple members of his group excitedly explain their ideas.

Two weeks later, the day before the theory presentations are to be given, William stops by Dr. Russell's office. He informs her that he will be unable to attend the next class. Hanging his head, he tells Dr. Russell that his father called to tell him that his mother had been rushed to the hospital with chest pains. He fidgets in the chair, sighs, and says, "They're not sure, but it looks like they might have to do surgery tomorrow." Dr. Russell stares intently at William and says, "I'm very sorry to hear about your mother's health problems. What do you think this will mean for your performance in class for the rest of the semester?"

William avoids direct eye contact with Dr. Russell and continues to stare down at the floor. Clearing his throat, he says, "Er . . . um . . . well . . . I don't think I'll be able to make it to class." Dr. Russell asks, "Does this means you won't be giving your presentation tomorrow?" William slowly nods his head up and down, indicating that this is exactly what he is saying. Dr. Russell sits up straight, stares at William, and says,

CHAPTER OBJECTIVES

AFTER READING THIS CHAPTER, you will understand:

1 The characteristics of nonverbal messages and how they differ from verbal messages.

2 The eight different types of nonverbal messages.

3 How nonverbal messages function in your relationships.

4 How culture, technology, and gender affect the encoding and decoding of nonverbal messages.

"William, this is a tough situation because the theory presentation is worth 100 points and is a significant portion of your grade." William cocks his head to the side and declares defensively, "Well, I can't help it that my mom is sick!" Dr. Russell responds, "I do understand this, but to be fair to the other students, I have to stick to the rules on the syllabus that clearly indicate no late work is accepted."

With a defiant look on his face, William blurts out, "Are you accusing me of lying?" Dr. Russell says, "William, I've been watching you in class, and I can tell that this is not an assignment you're excited about. So while I'd like to say that

I believe you, your classroom behavior leads me to doubt your honesty right now." Her response really sets William off, and he loudly exclaims, "So you're calling me a liar?!" His extreme defensiveness catches Dr. Russell off guard, as she has never seen intense emotions from William. She ends their conversation by saying, "I'm afraid I'm going to have to stick to the class policy. You'll need to attend class tomorrow and deliver your presentation, or you'll earn a zero on the assignment." Dr. Russell notices William getting tearful as he rises

continued on next page

AFTER READING THIS CHAPTER,
you will be able to:

1 Interpret varying nonverbal message cues within your relationships.

2 Interpret the meaning of nonverbal cues that denote pleasure, arousal, and dominance.

3 Evaluate the impact of violations of space and touch.

4 Understand the role of conversational involvement and how it enhances positive impressions.

5 Determine how and why your nonverbal expectations of others are violated.

AFTER COMPLETING THE SELF-ASSESSMENTS,
you will learn about:

1 The level of nonverbal immediacy that others in your life exhibit.

2 Your level of touch apprehension and how it affects your relationships.

slowly, saying, "Fine! This is ridiculous and unfair—". He pauses silently for a moment before muttering, "But I guess I'll see you tomorrow."

What do you think about this interaction? While reading this chapter, consider how you might answer the following questions to help William and Dr. Russell communicate clearly and effectively:

- What nonverbal behaviors did not seem to match William's verbal message?
- What nonverbal behaviors do you think were unintentional and led to Dr. Russell's perception that William

might be lying? Can you label the types of nonverbal cues he exhibited?

- What were the most important nonverbal messages that you believe leaked out and were decoded by Dr. Russell as clues to William's emotional state?

As you read, see how many concepts you might apply to their conversation to help determine why Dr. Russell did not trust William and why her response angered him. Think about how you might have used nonverbal messages differently if you were in William's shoes. If you were Dr. Russell, how might you have decoded William's behaviors?

Nonverbal messages are critical for effective communication in relationships. According to communication scholar Judee Burgoon, approximately 60–65% of the meaning in our messages is sent via nonverbal codes.[1] Although the percentage may vary, it is easy to see why miscommunication frequently occurs. The words that we utter in conversation are simply not enough to convey the total meaning of the messages we send to others. Nonverbal behaviors complete the message. This chapter will present and discuss the characteristics, types, and functions of nonverbal messages that will aid you in communicating in your relationships. If only 35–40% of the meaning in your messages is derived from the words you use, then it will benefit you to recognize, understand, and more carefully evaluate nonverbal communication.

> What you do speaks so loud that I cannot hear what you say.
> —RALPH WALDO EMERSON

Understanding Nonverbal Messages

Although nonverbal messages have been studied for decades, a common definition is difficult to find. One typical description is that nonverbal communication includes all messages other than words.[2] This is hardly clear or complete because not all behaviors are necessarily considered communication with assigned social meaning. For example, when you walk outside into the bright sunlight with a friend and squint your eyes to protect them from the harsh light, this behavior is not a nonverbal message that you have encoded; it is merely a physiological reaction. However, your friend might still decode your nonverbal behavior and assign meaning to it. Therefore, a more comprehensive definition of nonverbal communication might be the following: *messages other than words that stimulate meaning in the minds of others in specific contexts*.[3] With this definition in mind, by the end of the chapter, you should be able to identify different nonverbal codes and understand the characteristics that affect their interpretation.

Characteristics of Nonverbal Messages

Although there are many different types of nonverbal messages, they share some characteristics that help to differentiate them from verbal messages. This distinction is important to understand and recognize, though it is frequently difficult to separate verbal from nonverbal communication. To aid in this differentiation, take a look at the following five characteristics of nonverbal communication, and as you read them, try to figure out why they would not be considered characteristics of verbal messages.

Nonverbal Messages Are Inevitable. What this means is that nonverbal messages are going to be sent either intentionally or unintentionally. Whether you are aware of sending them or not, they come with the territory. Recall the meaning (from Chapter 1) of encoding and decoding, and examine this example: If Ben speaks softly and clears his throat as he searches for just the right words to explain why he has to cancel his date with his girlfriend Audrey, she might decode his nonverbal signals and determine that he is hiding something. Ben must realize that in face-to-face communication, there are multiple channels of information that Audrey can decode. Nonverbal messages are bound to occur in conversations; they are inevitable.

Nonverbal Messages Are Continuous. The saying "One can't not communicate" is found throughout the communication literature and expresses the idea that it is impossible not to communicate even when talking stops.[4] Although this might at first sound impossible, people have the ability to decode messages you are sending even when you are silent (e.g., they might say, "Oh, so you're giving me the silent treatment, huh?"). Nonverbal signals are constantly being sent and interpreted. This also reflects the inevitability of nonverbal communication that we discussed earlier. The continuous stream of nonverbal messages could be risky for relationships because the signals have multiple meanings; if they never end, there are frequent opportunities for decoding errors and miscommunication.

Nonverbal Messages Are Ambiguous. Nonverbal messages can mean different things, depending on the nature of the relationship between the people involved. If you have a long history with someone, it is highly likely that you will interpret cues accurately. If you do not know someone very well, however, there is a greater chance that you will decode incorrectly and base your interpretations upon previous similar interactions with someone else. A yawn, for example, can be an ambiguous nonverbal signal. Most people probably view a yawn as an indicator that someone is tired or bored, but this is not always the case. When multiple interpretations of a nonverbal message are possible, this adds to the ambiguity.

Nonverbal Messages Convey Believable Emotions. Nonverbal communication plays a powerful role in our relationships. Though we use words to tell someone how we feel about him or her, how we say the words frequently carries greater weight. Albert Mehrabian states that this is because nonverbal messages are the primary means of communicating emotions and feelings in relationships.[5] When we convey positive and negative emotions, research suggests that nonverbal messages are more believable indicators[7] because they are thought to reflect our true inner feelings.[6] When you say, "I love you" to your relational partner, how you say it and what you are doing when you say the words are very telling. Studies have shown that rather than trusting words, couples typically scan their partners' faces for expressions that convey the seriousness and depth of their feelings.[7] This makes it particularly important to be aware of your nonverbal expressions and make certain that they accurately reflect your verbal messages.

Although this might sound simple, it is actually very difficult, as we previously stated, owing to the fact that we can receive nonverbal messages through many different channels.

Nonverbal Messages Are Multichanneled. The fact that nonverbal messages can be conveyed simultaneously through a number of channels makes it vital for the listener to pay attention to many channels in order to fully understand messages. This can be especially useful in situations in which someone is trying to deceive you. Uncovering deception can be extremely difficult, but paying close attention to nonverbal messages within the various channels is one of the best ways to discover it.[8] We will discuss this in greater detail later in the chapter, but take a moment now to think about a time when you felt that someone was being untruthful. Most likely, something in the person's face, eyes, or voice made you question his or her honesty. When someone is sad, you probably figure it out by looking at the person's face and posture, and perhaps you hear it in the sound of the person's voice. Attending to all of these channels simultaneously allows you to decode the person's feelings.

Types of Nonverbal Messages

The characteristics that we have just discussed help you to interpret nonverbal communication. In this section, we present seven different types of nonverbal messages. Though some of the overarching categories may vary in the literature (e.g., body movement versus gestures), when they are broken down, the commonalities are clear. Once you understand the categories of ways in which nonverbal messages can be sent, it will be easier to understand how they function in your own interpersonal communication.

Kinesics. One of the largest categories of nonverbal codes is known as **kinesics**, which comprise all your gestures, body movements, and facial expressions. Paul Ekman and Wallace Friesen organized and classified five categories of kinesic behaviors, which are listed and described in Table 5.1.[9] As you review this table, try to think of your own examples of the five categories.

Vocalics. The sounds of the voice, often referred to as *paralanguage*, are known as **vocalics**. They pertain to how something is said rather than what is said. Examples of vocalics are speaking rate, volume, pitch, vocal qualities (e.g., rasping, harsh, breathy), accents, pauses, and speech hesitations. Vocalics enhance messages by supplementing or even contradicting the literal meaning. Think about the following examples of vocalics that may offer additional information. If someone asks you to go to a movie and you hesitate for just a moment, the person is likely to think that you are not interested. On the other hand, if you respond immediately, you talk quickly, and the pitch of your voice goes up significantly, the other person might detect excitement in your response. Do not underestimate the significance of vocalics in attributing meaning to words in everyday communication.

Proxemics. The nonverbal code that focuses on the study and use of space is called **proxemics**. Most of us place a high value on our space and are uncomfortable when it is invaded, so we frequently create territories that we protect. To help differentiate between territory and space, think about them this way: Space is the distance between people (e.g., standing in line at the ATM), and territories are the protected areas we own and occupy (e.g., your office) that are usually fixed. Anthropologist Edward T. Hall developed the concept of four spatial distances that correspond to the types of interactions in which we engage: intimate, personal, social, and public.[10]

TABLE 5.1

Five Categories of Kinesic Behaviors

Category	Description	Example
Emblem	Nonverbal movement with direct verbal translation. Most often used without verbal messages.	Placing your finger to your lips to indicate a desire for silence.
Illustrator	Nonverbal movement that accompanies a verbal message and complements, accents, or contradicts it.	Placing your hands high above your head as you describe how tall someone is.
Affect display	Nonverbal gesture and body movement that reflects feelings or emotions. Most often conveyed via facial expressions.	Sad people typically exhibit a slumped posture, hanging head, and the sides of lips dip down.
Regulator	Nonverbal gesture and body movement that controls or maintains speaking flow and rate of conversation.	Nodding your head and/or holding out your palm to indicate the other person's turn to speak. Glaring eyes to indicate a warning to stop speaking.
Adaptor	Nonverbal movement to help curb, control, or satisfy a personal behavior or emotion, or need. Discomfort and negative emotions are typical instigators.	Shifting your weight or placing your hands in your pockets to control nervousness during a speech.

Source: Ekman, P., & Friesen, W. V. (1969). The repertoire of nonverbal behavior: Categories, origins, usage, and coding. *Semiotica. 1,* 49–98.

Intimate space ranges from 0 (or touching) to 18 inches and is typically reserved for very close relationships. Romantic partners may kiss and caress, and good friends may console or share secrets. In this case, people in both of these relationships would experience intimate space. When someone invades your intimate space, it can be very awkward and perhaps even troubling.

Personal space ranges from 18 inches to 4 feet and is frequently referred to as our protective bubble because it is the space that gets invaded most often and the one that we are forced to protect the most often. Personal space is especially important when we are in public. For example, when you are at the ATM, you expect other people to stand at least four feet back from you, but what happens if someone is close enough to look over your shoulder? You might feel uncomfortable just imagining this scenario.

Social space ranges from 4 feet to 12 feet. Although this is a fairly broad range, there are times when a social situation would warrant that you position yourself at the lower end of this range (e.g., a company holiday party) and other situations in which you might place yourself at the higher end (e.g., a job interview). Regardless of where you fall in this range, the communication that occurs within social distances is rarely interpersonal and typically is considered impersonal.

Public space ranges from 12 feet to 25 feet and is extremely impersonal and typically acceptable for larger groups. This space commonly occurs in the classroom setting or any other audience–speaker type of environment.

These distance ranges are generally accepted in Western culture but vary in other cultures. We will discuss cultural influences on proxemics later in the chapter.

A primary factor influencing proxemic distance is the level of intimacy between individuals. According to **equilibrium theory** an inverse relationship exists between mutual eye gaze, intimacy, and space during social interactions. In other words, as intimacy and eye gaze increase, distance decreases.[11] However, sex differences are reported such that male eye gaze increases as distance increases and female eye gaze decreases as distances increase.[12] What this means is that eye contact may be a response to the degree to which males and females are comfortable with the interaction distance. This supports research that indicates that women are more relationally oriented and inclusive and therefore prefer closer spacing during interactions.

The space that we own or desire to own and protect is known as **territory**. When we want to own space, we work very hard to make certain others recognize that it belongs to us. As you can see in Figure 5.1, this is a three-stage, continuous process. The first stage involves marking territory to indicate ownership. Three typical markers to do this are central, boundary, and ear markers. *Central markers* are items that are placed to reserve our territory (e.g., placing your coat on a seat at a restaurant while you use the restroom). *Boundary markers* are set up to divide our territory from that of others (e.g., placing your personal items on either side of you at the movie theatre so no one sits next to you). *Ear markers* signal ownership of property (e.g., writing your name in a book or having a monogram embroidered on your shirt) or space (e.g., placing a name plate on a desk). A perfect example of a sort of imaginary marker for students is the classroom desk territory. Even though college classes rarely have assigned seats, students develop habits. They come to identify with where they sit and feel that they own the seat.

FIGURE 5.1

Protecting Our Territory

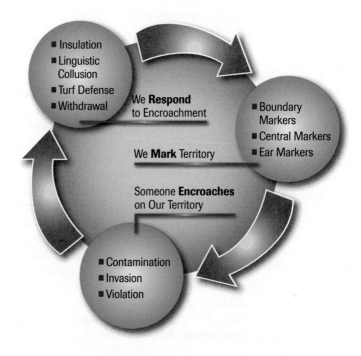

So what happens when you walk into class and someone has taken the seat you consider to be yours? This occurrence describes the second stage, known as territorial **encroachment.** If you feel uncomfortable and a little irritated because someone has taken your seat in class, then that person has encroached on your territory. There are several different forms of territorial encroachment: violation, invasion, and contamination.[13] **Violation** occurs when someone's territory is taken or used without permission, as when a sister enters her brother's bedroom that is clearly marked "boys only." **Invasion** is similar to violation but more extensive. If a person invades your territory, the meaning of the territory changes. A common example would be parents sitting in on their teenage daughter's party. The party takes on a whole new meaning and is no longer the "teen party in the basement." **Contamination** creates an impure territory and frequently leads to feelings of disgust and/or anger, as it can render the territory useless or unclean. An example would be a burglary; research reveals that homeowners feel violated and their home feels foreign to them after such an event.[14] How individuals react to encroachment incidents directly affects communication.

The third stage, therefore, is the response people have to encroachment. They can do any of the following: withdraw, insulate, engage in turf defense, or react with linguistic collusion. *Withdrawal* is perhaps the most obvious response to territorial encroachment because people leave the situation to avoid the discomfort or irritation. If someone took your seat in the classroom, you would probably just sit in another seat. *Turf defense* is just the opposite as individuals face the encroacher and defend their territory. For example, if someone invaded your personal space, you might confront them physically (push them back) or verbally (ask or tell them to move back). *Insulation* is creating a barrier to protect yourself and your territory. As mentioned earlier, it is fairly common in places such as movie theaters, where you might put your personal items in the seat next to you or even place your feet on the seat in front of you in hopes of preventing encroachment. Finally, *linguistic collusion* occurs when we speak in a language or jargon that excludes others from our conversations. Kids in school cliques frequently do this to exclude those they consider "uncool," but adults are also guilty of it, especially when they hope to gain control or assert their power (e.g., "You wouldn't understand").

Haptics.   Touch, also known as **haptics,** is vital to relationships. Touch is one of the first senses we experience as children, and it is vital for healthy physical and mental growth. The contact between a mother and her baby is, in fact, so beneficial that it is now used in neonatal intensive care units worldwide for premature infants.[15] In a study conducted with infants in a Korean orphanage, fifteen additional minutes of touch twice a day for four weeks significantly increased the infants' weight gain, body length, and head circumference, and after six months, these babies sustained fewer illnesses.[16] However, touch is also important as we grow and develop relationships because it is how we communicate our emotions and feelings. We hug, caress, shove, slap, pat, kiss, and embrace—and the list goes on—all to let someone else know how we feel. Though there is no blueprint for types of touching and how, where, when, and with whom a touch should be performed, researchers have managed to develop some overarching tactile categories. Table 5.2 presents the results of a touch study that examined over 1500 touches resulting in seven touch groups and their corresponding meanings: positive affect, playfulness, control, ritual, hybrid, task-related, and accidental.[17]

Chronemics.   The study of time and how time communicates is known as **chronemics,** and use of time is a valuable nonverbal cue. In our fast-paced society in which everything from eating to traveling happens quickly and information is accessed in mere seconds,

TABLE 5.2

Characteristics of Meaning for Individual Touches	
Categories	**Typical Examples and Enactment Styles**
Positive Affect Touches	
Support—serves to nurture, reassure, or promise protection	1. Knowing from a conversation the night before that a roommate is worried about a test, the toucher pats him on the shoulder when he sees him in the morning and says, "You'll do O.K." 2. After a friend expresses sadness about an event, the toucher silently reaches out and squeezes her arm. 3. Cuddling a crying child who is injured. (Hugs are rare events, reserved for a person who expresses strong distress.)
Appreciation—expresses gratitude	1. A boss touches a subordinate on the shoulder at the end of a day's work and says, "Thanks for the way you handled things." 2. A woman kisses a close male friend on the cheek after a meal he prepared and says, "Thanks a lot."
Inclusion—draws attention to act of being together; suggests psychological closeness	1. A couple walks down the street holding hands or with arms around one another. 2. A couple sits on a couch watching television with one person leaning against the other. 3. A male and a female who are close friends talk in a restaurant with knees touching.
Affection—expresses generalized positive regard beyond mere acknowledgement	1. (Highly intense form) Spontaneously hugging a romantic partner or close friend and saying words of endearment ("Hi, sweetheart," "I love you," etc.). 2. (Less intense, but more common type) Patting or caressing a close person when passing by in the room. 3. (Examples are varied and include hugs, kisses, and less involving, simple contacts.) The lack of a specific situation calling for touch—such as a sad event or a greeting—defines pure affection. (Rare between men.)
Sexual—expresses physical attraction or sexual interest	1. Movement from one to another type of holding and/or caressing (e.g., lovers embracing and caressing; multiple kinds of touching distinguish it from affection). 2. A simple hand touch to a sexual body part (e.g., reaching over and touching on the buttock).

TABLE 5.2 *(continued)*

Characteristics of Meaning for Individual Touches

Categories	Typical Examples and Enactment Styles
Playful Touches	
Playful affection—serves to lighten interaction; seriousness of affection qualified	1. A male saying, "How's about a kiss?" (I'm just kidding around) to a close female friend or romantic partner, followed by a quick kiss. 2. With others present, a male puts his arm around his male roommate, who is doing the dishes, and says, "You'd make a good wife" (I'm teasing about being affectionate).
Playful aggression—serves to lighten interaction; seriousness of aggression qualified	1. Aggressive touch with a comment that clarifies the intent as play (e.g., saying "Let's wrestle," and then performing a mock half-nelson to the other person notice the importance of the early verbal warning). 2. Aggressive comment with a touch play signal (e.g., a customer says to a waitress, "No, we don't want the check and tear it up," with a smile and light touch to her arm).
Control Touches	
Compliance—attempts to direct behavior and oftentimes also attitudes or feelings of another	1. A boss touches an employee on the shoulder and says, "Could you get this done by 5 o'clock?" (Touch translation: "I really want you to do it.") 2. Grabbing a companion by the upper arm and saying, "Let's hurry across the road."
Attention-getting—serves to direct the recipient's perceptual focus	1. Patting a companion on the shoulder and saying, "Look at this!" 2. Spot touching a stranger on the arm to say, "Excuse me, do you have the time?"
Announcing a response—calls attention to and emphasizes a feeling state of initiator; implicitly requests affect response from another	1. A woman touches her female friend and says, "Can you believe he did that?" (Translation: "I hope you feel the same way about him.") 2. A woman touches her male companion and says, "I'm so excited about today!"
Ritualistic Touches	
Greeting—serves as part of the act of acknowledging another at the opening of an encounter	1. (Formal) handshake greeting (mainly used between males). 2. (Slightly more informal) Hand to body part greeting, usually to shoulder or arm (mainly female–male or female–female touches).

(continued)

TABLE 5.2 *(continued)*

Characteristics of Meaning for Individual Touches	
Categories	**Typical Examples and Enactment Styles**
Departure—serves as part of the act of closing an encounter	1. Male pats male friend on shoulder when leaving. 2. Female touches lower back of female friend when leaving.
Hybrid Touches	
Greeting/affection—expresses affection and acknowledgement at the initiation of an encounter	1. Hug and/or brief kiss between male and female (usually close friends, romantic partners, or parent and son or daughter). 2. Hug between female friends. 3. Most common after a period of absence—most of a day or longer; rare between men.
Task-Related Touches	
Reference to appearance—a touch which points out or inspects a body part or artifact referred to in a verbal comment about appearance	1. A woman inspects a female friend's necklace and says, "This is pretty." A woman brushes a male friend's hair with her hand and says, "I like your haircut." 2. Males rarely use this touch, although they could, saying "Nice suit," while feeling the material at the lapel.
Instrumental Ancillary—a touch which occurs as an unnecessary part of the accomplishment of a task	1. Most common is handing an object to someone and allowing hand-to-hand contact (e.g., a clerk returning change to a customer).
Instrumental Intrinsic—touch which accomplishes a task in and of itself	1. Assisting a person in putting on a coat. 2. Placing a hand on a person's forehead to check for a temperature (implies support, but mainly accomplishes a task). 3. Putting suntan lotion on a person's back (may imply flirtation or affection).
Accidental Touches	
Accidental—touches which are perceived as unintentional	1. Brushing a person when passing by, getting up to go, etc. 2. Bumps or brushes between strangers are usually rejected, unless an apology is given.

Source: Jones, S. E., & Yarbrough, A. E. (1985). A naturalistic study of the meanings of touch. *Communication Monographs, 52,* 19–56.

time is vital. How you understand and use time communicates something about you to others. If you are habitually late, others may think you are lazy; if you procrastinate on a class project, your partners may think you don't care; and if you schedule your daily tasks down to the minute, people may view you as obsessive or a "control freak."

Although Americans typically move at a fast pace, scholars have determined that variations exist across the country. One study in 1990 found that the northeastern United States was faster-paced than the western United States. The three fastest-paced cities reported were Boston, Buffalo, and New York; the three slowest-paced cities surveyed were Shreveport, Sacramento, and Los Angeles.[18]

To better understand time as a form of nonverbal message, it is often organized into three areas: cultural time, biological time, and psychological time.[19] **Cultural time** is created on the basis of cultural values and whether a group views time as *technical* (precise, scientific time) and *formal* (organized by days, weeks, months, years, or moon phases, etc.) or *informal* (seen in vague terms such as soon, early, in a few). One of the most important informal time systems in Western culture is *punctuality*, or the time when we expect people to arrive. It is considered informal because there is no consensus about the definition of "punctual," which may be viewed as *diffused* (punctuality is an approximation) or *displaced* (punctuality has a specific end time). **Biological time** relates to our own body clocks and the way in which individuals respond to time. You probably know someone whom you would describe as an energetic "morning person" and a "night owl" who is most productive in the evening. Although you might consider yourself to have a consistent daily time pattern, biological time is actually cyclical and rotates with highs and lows or ups and downs through cycles of your life. **Psychological time** relates to our focus on, and the value we assign to, the *past* (emphasizing past memories), *present* (living in the moment), and *future* (focusing on what will/can happen).

Artifacts and Environment. This nonverbal category involves items and objects that are external to the physical appearance (e.g., beauty or body shape) as well as the mind. A great deal of research has been conducted on personal **artifacts and the environment** that reveal the value of the messages these nonverbal categories convey.

Artifacts Research. Items such as clothing, jewelry, hairstyle, the car you drive, and other personal possessions send messages because they reflect who you are—your attitudes, your beliefs, and even your values. A highly researched area of artifacts is clothing and the status connection. Innumerable books have been published on "dressing for success," and if you research the topic online, you will retrieve hundreds of websites that advertise books, organizations, and videos that were created to help people decide what to wear to get the job they want. Some articles have focused on the importance of teaching attire in particular. Whether an instructor is a professor or a graduate teaching assistant, more formal or professional attire is deemed more appropriate.[20] Studies have found that students are less prone to misbehavior, learn more, and give higher teacher ratings to instructors who dress professionally.[21] More specifically, faculty members who are formally dressed are perceived as more knowledgeable, more prepared, and better organized than are those who dress casually.[22] Regardless of where you are in life, clothing fosters impressions of status and power, so being mindful that what you wear communicates nonverbally is incredibly important.

Color of Artifacts Research. Nonverbal messages are constantly conveyed through the colors around you. You may have heard or read somewhere that people who drive red cars get more tickets or that babies whose rooms are painted yellow cry more. Color can make a difference in how we feel, what we think, and the way in which we react. According to recent research, color fundamentally affects our thoughts and behaviors through the associations we have learned over the course of our lives.[23] Red, for example,

FIGURE 5.2

Feng Shui: The Psychological Effects of Color. A blending of the five basic colors/elements reveals multiple colors that affect our moods both positively and negatively.

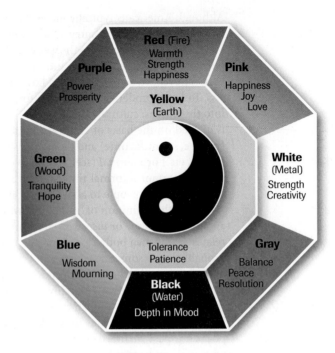

is frequently associated with negative experiences (e.g., errors circled on school papers) and blue with calm feelings (e.g., the peacefulness of the blue ocean). Feng shui, the traditional Chinese worldview that promotes harmony with the environment in order to maximize harmonious relationships, associates color with the five basic elements of the universe: water (black), fire (red), wood (blue/green), metal (white), and earth (yellow). Feng shui suggests that people's moods are affected by these five colors and color blends (see Figure 5.2).[24] Thus, ancient Chinese wisdom would tell us that the colors of the clothes we wear, the cars we drive, and the rooms we live and work in affect our thoughts and behaviors.[25]

Environmental Factors Research. When the way in which a room is arranged or laid out sends us a message and causes us to feel a certain way, environmental elements are at work. Visualize a professor's office you have visited. If the desk creates a sort of boundary that you do not cross, meaning that you sit directly across from the professor, this typically sends a very clear power message.[26] The chair of the department of one of the authors has a rocking chair beside his desk, which sends a message of comfort and equality. Restaurant owners have learned the importance of the environment as they plan the layout and physical features of their restaurants. Research in this area implies that the environment affects how people behave by incorporating both implicit and explicit rules for the interactions that take place there.[27] In other words, to truly understand people you must take the environment or context into account.[28]

Physical Appearance. The final nonverbal code that we'll discuss, **physical appearance**, is extremely relevant, especially in the United States, where beauty has become

The importance of physical appearance, often represented by weight, is documented on the national television series The Biggest Loser.

such a commodity. Women are purchasing bigger breasts and having their faces injected with Botox, while men are having hair transplants and investing in gym equipment in pursuit of the elusive "six-pack." The ideal body image exists, and we know what it is because we see it every day on television commercials and programs such as *The Biggest Loser*.

Of course, what is considered ideal or beautiful has changed over the years, but "thin" has pretty much always been "in," and the "fountain of youth" has been forever pursued. We learn the value of beauty at a very early age; one study revealed that adults and children alike viewed beautiful people as good and unattractive people as bad.[29] In addition, research has reported that attractive people are more popular, have higher self-esteem levels, and get better jobs than do people who are considered unattractive.[30] Two specific physical features that are reportedly important in determining level of attractiveness are symmetry (similarity in the two sides of the face and body) and body shape.[31] Three general body shapes are generally described in the literature: **endomorphs** (soft, chubby, fat), **mesomorphs** (slim, muscular, athletic), and **ectomorphs** (thin, skinny, frail) (see Figure 5.3).[32] When we see individuals who fall into one of these categories, we subconsciously associate certain personality traits with their body shapes. For example, ectomorphs are often described as anxious and shy, mesomorphs as cheerful and confident, and endomorphs as relaxed and warm. Such associations make it clear that physical appearance is judged by others around us and can be crucial to success in life.

FIGURE 5.3

Three General Body Shapes

Source: William Sheldon's Somatotypes, as cited in Phares, J. E. (1991). *Introduction to Personality* (3rd ed.). New York: HarperCollins.

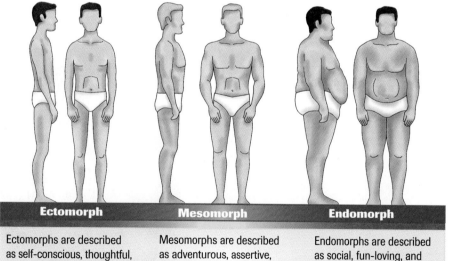

Ectomorph	Mesomorph	Endomorph
Ectomorphs are described as self-conscious, thoughtful, and introverted.	Mesomorphs are described as adventurous, assertive, and competitive.	Endomorphs are described as social, fun-loving, and even-tempered.

ETHICS in interpersonal communication

BeautifulPeople.com Kicks Out Overweight Members

BeautifulPeople.com is a website community that was created to link attractive people socially and professionally. To join, applicants must be evaluated by members of the opposite sex and receive an adequate number of positive votes. According to the site, "BeautifulPeople does not define beauty, it simply gives an accurate representation of what society's ideal of beauty is."[33] The basic notion is that people like to surround themselves with others who are like them, so attractive people like to be surrounded by other attractive people. But as everyone knows, looks can change

over time, and this can have negative repercussions for members of BeautifulPeople.com. No one knows this better than the some 5,000 people on the dating site who were kicked out for gaining weight over the holidays in 2009. Referred to as "fatties," they were flagged by other members who were angry that they were still on the site.[34] The company's response? The overweight members were emailed and told that they would have to reapply after they had "lost the holiday chunk."[35] Site founder Robert Hintze stated, "Letting fatties roam the site is a direct threat to our business model and the very concept for which BeautifulPeople.com was founded."[36]

Functions of Nonverbal Messages

Nonverbal messages are multichanneled, and because of this, they combine to create multiple meanings within social interactions. You might notice a smile, a hand gesture, and what time someone arrives at your house for dinner; together, these signals create an impression. Combined, nonverbal codes serve multiple functions (see Figure 5.4).

Nonverbal Messages Create Impressions. When we search for nonverbal message codes that fit together, we are creating impressions of others. Some examples may be how people are dressed, their posture, their speech patterns, and their gestures. Although your impressions may be based on stereotypes, they help to reduce uncertainty which, in turn, helps you to communicate in relationships.

Nonverbal Messages Manage Interactions. Nonverbal codes have been referred to as the "traffic cops" of interpersonal communication because they let us know when to

FIGURE 5.4

The Functions of Nonverbal Messages

engage, slow down, speed up, or halt interactions.[37] An example would be **back channel cues** (e.g., "uh-huh," "hmmm," "ahhh," head nods) that convey your level of interest and typically encourage continued conversation.[38]

Nonverbal Messages Express Emotions.   Though emotions are typically revealed on the face, they are also conveyed through vocalics or paralanguage. Some scientists believe that our basic emotions are inborn (e.g., happiness, reactions to pain) and that this is why we may encode and decode them similarly, while others believe that our display of emotions is a learned societal and cultural phenomenon. **Neurocultural theory** has been used to explain that a combination of the two is at work, contending that because all humans are born with the same neuromuscular structure (e.g., the same facial muscles controlled by the same areas of the brain), emotions may be encoded and decoded similarly.[39] Because emotions are so important to interpersonal communication, Chapter 7 is solely devoted to examining emotion and communication and how together they impact relationships.

Nonverbal Messages Create and Maintain Relationships.   Nonverbal messages help us to evaluate whether we should approach or avoid someone, and they eventually determine whether a relationship could be worthwhile. Recent studies examining nonverbal vocalics, for example, report that women find lower-pitched male voices to be more attractive[40] and judge men who have such voices to be stronger, more powerful, and definitely more masculine than men with lower-pitched voices are,[41] while men find higher-pitched voices in women more attractive than lower-pitched voices as well as making the woman seem younger.[42] An impression-forming concept known as "thin-slicing" (a brief excerpt of expressive behavior) indicates that both males and females place high value on **nonverbal immediacy** behaviors, which include cues such as eye contact, smiling, close proxemics, head nods, body relaxation, and vocal variety.[43] These nonverbal messages indicate liking and have been found to be especially useful in the context of speed dating.[44]

Nonverbal Messages Conceal and Deceive.   Some individuals are simply better at concealing their feelings and emotions, but clusters of nonverbal cues offer clues to determine whether someone is hiding information or lying, and there are simply no

A three- to six-minute speed date may be all the time you need to find that "special someone."

guarantees. The **leakage hypothesis** states that most of us unconsciously leak cues (e.g., shaky voice, speech hesitations) that reveal our true feelings, and according to researchers, these cues are the best indicators of deception.[45]

CHECKING YOUR UNDERSTANDING

Characteristics, Types, and Functions of Nonverbal Messages

Before reading further, take a few minutes to assess your learning by writing your answers to the following items:

1. What is the definition of *nonverbal communication*, and how important are nonverbal cues in determining what verbal messages mean?

2. What are the five characteristics of nonverbal messages? Briefly describe how each would not be a component in verbal communication.

3. What are the eight types of nonverbal messages? Offer specific examples of each one.

4. What are the definitions of the following theories and hypotheses that explain the functions of nonverbal communication: uncertainty reduction theory, neurocultural theory, nonverbal immediacy, and the leakage hypothesis?

Examining Factors That Affect Nonverbal Messages

A variety of factors can influence how nonverbal messages are delivered and interpreted. We will examine three factors in this section that can affect the way in which nonverbal messages are perceived. If these factors are not considered, miscommunication can occur and affect relationships.

The Impact of Culture

You have probably heard the phrase "America is a melting pot" and know that it refers to the many different cultural groups in our population. Look around your classes, and you will probably notice classmates who are not from your culture. The more obvious clues may be the color of their skin, the clothing they wear, or how they speak.

The cultural groups that people are part of influence the ways in which nonverbal codes are used and how they are interpreted. Nonverbal messages adhere to implicit rules and norms within cultures. For relationships to succeed, we must be aware and know how to adapt our communication to other cultures. We must avoid **ethnocentric** views that our own culture is superior and avoid judgments suggesting that our own communication and interpretations are always correct. Nonverbal messages vary from culture to culture, and this knowledge is certainly not new. You may have heard the saying "When in Rome, do as the Romans do." The original version of this statement was made in 387 C.E. by Saint Ambrose, bishop of Milan. When Saint Augustine came to Milan, he noticed that members of the Church in Milan did not fast on Saturdays, as Church members did in Rome. Augustine consulted Ambrose, who advised, "When I am at Rome, I fast on a Saturday; when I am at Milan, I do not. Follow the custom of the Church where you are." What Saint Ambrose recognized was that engaging in behaviors that are consistent with another person's culture makes you more interpersonally attractive.[46] There are many examples of cultural differences in nonverbal codes.

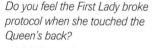

Gestures—specifically, emblems—vary greatly from culture to culture. A couple of examples are the raised middle finger and the "OK" sign with the thumb and forefinger forming a circle. The "OK" sign is widely recognized in America, but it is considered vulgar in Brazil, and in France it means that someone or something is worthless. In Western culture, extending the middle finger is considered a vulgar gesture that is typically interpreted as "up yours," but this message is indicated in Italy by a jerk of the forearm and in England by the palm-back V sign, which many people in the United States would interpret as a peace sign (even though the hand is reversed).

Chronemics play an important role in many cultures. Understanding the value of cultural time is necessary if you are going to forge a relationship with people from other cultures. In the United States as well as Germany and Scandinavia, time is very exact and specific. Many people use day planners and cell phones with calendars so that days, weeks, months, and years can be carefully structured. These are **monochronic** cultures in which events are scheduled one item at a time.[47] Though people from the United States are very punctual, they also use vague terms such as "early," "soon," and "late." But be warned that whatever terms such as "late" mean to you, you had better know the meaning that is understood by whomever you are meeting. Research suggests that showing up late sends a grievous nonverbal message about you.[48] Latin American and Middle Eastern cultures are **polychronic** and have several things going on simultaneously; they avoid rigid time structures. This can seriously affect corporations whose employees travel internationally and must learn to value the chronemics of other cultures.

Touch (haptics) and spatial distance (proxemics) also vary greatly among cultures. People in Latin American and Mediterranean countries, for example, value closeness and touch more than Americans do, regardless of sex. These are high-contact cultures that view touch and close proxemics as positive behaviors, and it is common to see men walking arm in arm. Although the United States is typically viewed as having a medium-contact culture, strong norms exist for touching and proxemic behaviors. Space is important to Americans. Walls and barriers are everywhere, and signs are posted that designate ownership. Cultures also have implicit norms for proxemics in various contexts (e.g., How close should you stand behind someone at the ATM?). Awareness is the key to success. Touch typically sends a message of power, and who is allowed to touch whom is invaluable information. The people of England, for example, were in an uproar when U.S. First Lady Michelle Obama briefly placed her hand on the back of Queen Elizabeth II as they talked during a reception in 2009. English traditionalists claimed that the First Lady broke protocol and should have known better. We must recognize that there is a price to pay for breaking nonverbal cultural norms. If the goal is to communicate effectively, then it is up to the individual communicator to become educated.

Do you feel the First Lady broke protocol when she touched the Queen's back?

The Impact of Sex Differences

Societal norms and expectations of gendered behaviors often create disparity in the nonverbal messages that males and females send. In other words, our social groups determine what is and is not appropriate behavior for our sex (e.g., women can cry, but men should not). To understand these differences, the context and the type of relationship must be considered.

Men and women display touch differently, and context is essential to understanding this. In romantic relationships, for example, touch differences do occur, but according to research, they depend upon the stage of the relationship.[49] The major sex difference is in touch initiation: Men initiate more touch in casual dating relationships, and women initiate more touch in married relationships. Males do less touching when the "honeymoon period" ends; women initiate more touch at this point.[50] Research suggests that men touch to assume power and control, so it makes sense that they would touch women earlier in the relationship. While women touch for affection and positive feelings, both sexes perceive that a man's touch toward a woman has sexual overtones.[51]

Much of the research on nonverbal sex differences revolves around a theme of dominance and submission. This is exhibited in male and female differences in gestures and eye contact. Women tend to smile more than men do and to engage in more eye contact and facial expressiveness when listening to men.[52] Scholars have suggested that this is due to the sex role stereotype of women having inferior status to men and goes back to sex role expectations and the idea that women are "supposed" to be more immediate.[53] Men tend to show dominance over women in their use of space by spreading out and sitting with legs wide to claim space. Men are also more dominant in protecting their territory. These assertive and aggressive nonverbal behaviors are attributed to social roles and behavioral expectations. Keep in mind that societal expectations for what is masculine and feminine are constantly changing, and a blurring of nonverbal differences is becoming more common.

The Impact of Technology

Although communication scholars once believed that nonverbal messages were typically not conveyed via computer-mediated communication (CMC), that perspective has changed.[54] Newer channels of CMC include text-messaging, instant messaging (e.g., AIM), social networking sites (e.g., Facebook), and online chat rooms and web forums. The study of nonverbal cues in CMC is relatively new. Three prevalent nonverbal cues that have been examined are kinesics, chronemics, and vocalics.

Even though it might at first seem impossible for individuals to communicate via CMC feelings and emotions that typically are communicated face to face, it does occur. This is typically accomplished through the use of emotion icons, or emoticons (such as :) or :( ).[55] If you include :(at the end of a text message that asks why a friend is late, this reveals your sadness or distress at the situation. Emoticons represent your facial expressions and clarify or add meaning to messages by conveying your mood or tone.[56] In face-to-face communication, some nonverbal cues leak out, but when emoticons are used, their messages are intentional and may be considered clearer.

Chronemics also affect messages in CMC, though message intent might not be as clear. Frequency of messaging, the duration and response time of messages, and the time of day messages are sent all indicate the important use of time.[57] Unfortunately, there are many opportunities for misinterpretation. A delay in your response to a text message, for example, might be perceived as rude or a sign of disinterest. Research also reveals the importance of time of day; text messages and emails that are sent at night, for instance, are thought to convey more intimacy and equality.[58]

Finally, vocalic cues, such as tone of voice, volume, accenting, and pausing, are possible in CMC.[59] CMC messages in all capital letters or with extra exclamation points and question marks (e.g., "What are you doing??!!!!") may indicate strong emotions and imply anger or excitement.[60] You should be very mindful of how you use punctuation and capitalization because misinterpretation is almost inevitable.[61] Remember that it is

NATURE/NURTURE intersections

The Science of Gaydar

Back in early 2000, Senator John McCain made a public statement about having been in the Navy with many gay men and knowing that they were gay (in spite of the ban on homosexuals in the military during his service) because of their nonverbal behaviors. Does this mean that McCain used "gaydar"?

Gaydar is a concept that is typically used within the gay and lesbian culture as a sort of superficial recognition device. It has even been depicted as a sixth sense or telepathic ability to recognize someone's sexual orientation by their masculine and feminine behaviors. Many people who claim to have gaydar abilities utilize what they claim are typical nonverbal cues that confirm sexual orientation labels. Kinesic behaviors such as hand gestures, posture, and walking style and vocalics such as vocal variety and pitch are thought to be common signals that gaydar picks up. Other people dismiss the idea of gaydar.

Recently, however, scientists have begun to claim that the gaydar may be real, and they attribute it to sensory interpretation. Geneticists at Pennsylvania's Monell Chemical Senses Center and researchers at Sweden's Karolinska University both report a scent-based ability to assess sexual orientation that is based in the limbic system (see Figure 5.5). In other words, individuals subconsciously use smell as a gaydar tool because we prefer the smell of people who have the same sexual orientation that we do. For gay men specifically, the chemical compound androsterone is detected through sweat and serves as a signal of potential partners. If this is the case, the nonverbal cues once thought helpful in detecting sexual orientation might not be the primary indicators. Instead, the clue may be in the smell—and in the brain.[62]

FIGURE 5.5

The Limbic System: Clues to sexual orientation may be linked to smell and emotional responses in the brain.

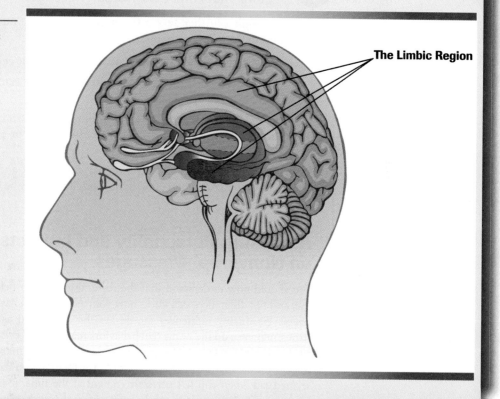

The Limbic Region

not only the words you write, but also the corresponding nonverbal cues that convey a positive or negative meaning. CMC contains nonverbal cues that can be manipulated and may work to your advantage (or disadvantage if misinterpreted) in your interpersonal relationships.[63]

An article in the *Wall Street Journal* entitled "Why Gen-Y Johnny Can't Read Nonverbal Cues" describes the current generation of students as incapable of deciphering and understanding most face-to-face nonverbal expressions.[64] Mark Bauerlein of Emory University writes that young people are so involved in text communication via cell phones, Facebook, and other technological tools that they are inexperienced in reading body language and understanding eye gaze, posture, and the like during face-to-face conversations. Students in classes are reporting difficulty in focusing their undivided attention on the teacher and classroom activities because of phones vibrating and computers "dinging" to signal awaiting messages. One study reported that in college classrooms across the United States, one third of all students spend the majority of their time in class playing video games on their phones and laptops.[65] Fearful that employees will perform inadequately at meetings and presentations, many companies are now banning the presence of these technological tools at their meetings in hopes of commanding the full attention of their employees.[66]

CHECKING YOUR UNDERSTANDING

Factors That Affect Nonverbal Messages

Before reading further, take a few minutes to assess your learning by writing your answers to the following items:

1. Why should avoiding ethnocentric views aid your communication with others?

2. How do chronemics differ by culture, and how can paying more attention to them help relationships?

3. Can you describe the primary ways in which men and women differ in nonverbal behaviors? Be able to explain how dominance or power is involved in these nonverbal cues.

4. How are kinesics (facial expressions), chronemics, and vocalics used in CMC? Be able to describe how different nonverbal cues may be interpreted.

Assessing Personality and Impacts on Nonverbal Messages

You should now understand that the cultural group you belong to, the technology you use, and sex differences can affect how your nonverbal behaviors are presented and perceived. Personality influences should also be considered as internal traits that have a strong influence on the nonverbal behaviors that are used every day. More often, however, we avoid thinking that smiles, gestures, and eye gaze are linked to personalities because it might indicate that we have little control over them. If you have ever been asked why you seemed sad when you felt perfectly content at the time, then you probably understand how nonverbal expressions can be unintentional and deeply connected to your inherent personality traits. Communication scholars refer to our personal repertoire of nonverbal signals as "identity badges" because they reflect our personality (as well as our culture, sex, etc.).[67] Traits such as extraversion, Machiavellianism, aggression, authoritativeness, and communication apprehension, and social skills such as high versus low self-monitoring are all reflected by nonverbal behaviors that are manifestations of personality.[68] Three specific nonverbal areas that have been connected to personality are immediacy, touch avoidance/apprehension, and deception.

Perceived Nonverbal Immediacy and Personality

Nonverbal immediacy is considered an important behavior to examine in relationships because it involves cues that convey interest, attention, and closeness and involvement to another person.[69] These emotions are conveyed through multiple nonverbal cues such as proxemics, haptics, eye contact, body movement, vocalics, and even chronemics.[70] Although you might be unaware of your own immediacy behaviors, you display them every day. You move closer to people who interest you and look away from those who do not. However, when people fail to convey nonverbal immediacy behaviors accurately, miscommunication occurs. A primary reason for the miscommunication is that nonverbal communication is multichanneled, making it difficult to control; another reason involves personality.

Nonverbal immediacy behaviors that convey feelings of closeness have been linked to personality traits such as sociability and extraversion.[71] These traits reflect interested, enthusiastic, and outgoing individuals who typically stand closer to others, engage in more direct eye gaze, and have more animated voices. Scientists explain that sociability is linked to levels of testosterone in the body[72] and extraversion is linked to the mesolimbic or the neural (nervous system) pathway of the brain, where behavioral responses are moderated when stimuli activate feelings of motivation.[73] What this means is that when you either display or fail to display nonverbal immediacy behaviors (e.g., you smile or frown, touch or move away), your behavior may be directly related to how predisposed you are to be sociable and extraverted.

To test this information on your own, think of someone with whom you have a close emotional relationship, and complete the nonverbal immediacy scale that follows.

 ## ASSESS YOUR **communication personality**

Richmond, McCroskey, and Johnson's Nonverbal Immediacy Scale—Observer Report[74]

Log onto our self-assessment library, MyPersonalityProfile, found on MyCommunicationLab (www.mycommunicationlab.com), and assess your perception of another person's nonverbal immediacy. Encourage the person you are assessing to do the same. This way, you can compare and contrast your scores and begin to understand better just how similar you are as well as how accurate your perceptions of each other's nonverbal immediacy are. If you prefer, you may use the instrument that follows.

Directions:

The following statements describe the ways in which some people behave while talking with or to others. Please indicate in the space at the left of each item the degree to which you believe the statement applies to a particular person with whom you have a close personal relationship, using the following scale:

1 = never

2 = rarely

3 = occasionally

4 = often

5 = very often

(continued)

_____ **1.** He/she uses her/his hands and arms to gesture while talking to people.

_____ **2.** He/she touches others on the shoulder or arm while talking to them.

_____ **3.** He/she uses a monotone or dull voice while talking to people.

_____ **4.** He/she looks over or away from others while talking to them.

_____ **5.** He/she moves away from others when they touch her/him while they are talking.

_____ **6.** He/she has a relaxed body position when he/she talks to people.

_____ **7.** He/she frowns while talking to people.

_____ **8.** He/she avoids eye contact while talking to people.

_____ **9.** He/she has a tense body position while talking to people.

_____**10.** He/she sits close or stands close to people while talking with them.

_____**11.** Her/his voice is monotonous or dull when he/she talks to people.

_____**12.** He/she uses a variety of vocal expressions when he/she talks to people.

_____**13.** He/she gestures when he/she talks to people.

_____**14.** He/she is animated when he/she talks to people.

_____**15.** He/she has a bland facial expression when he/she talks to people.

_____**16.** He/she moves closer to people when he/she talks to them.

_____**17.** He/she looks directly at people while talking to them.

_____**18.** He/she is stiff when he/she talks to people.

_____**19.** He/she has a lot of vocal variety when he/she talks to people.

_____**20.** He/she avoids gesturing while he/she is talking to people.

_____**21.** He/she leans toward people when he/she talks to them.

_____**22.** He/she maintains eye contact with people when he/she talks to them.

_____**23.** He/she tries not to sit or stand close to people when he/she talks with them.

_____**24.** He/she leans away from people when he/she talks to them.

_____**25.** He/she smiles when he/she talks to people.

_____**26.** He/she avoids touching people when he/she talks to them.

Scoring Instructions:

Step 1. Add the scores from the following items: 1, 2, 6, 10, 12, 13, 14, 16, 17, 19, 21, 22, and 25.

Step 2. Add the scores from the following items: 3, 4, 5, 7, 8, 9, 11, 15, 18, 20, 23, 24, and 26.

Total score = 78 + Step 1 − Step 2.

Norms:

Female mean = 96.7 S.D. = 16.1 High = > 112 Low = < 81

Male mean = 91.6 S.D. = 15.0 High = > 106 Low = < 77

Combined mean = 94.2 S.D. = 15.6 High = > 109 Low = < 79

This will help you to understand what nonverbal immediacy is and how your own personality contributes to the role nonverbal immediacy plays and the impact it has on your relationships.

Understanding Your Assessment of Nonverbal Immediacy. When the researchers created the observer report of nonverbal immediacy, their goal was to help individuals understand their perceptions of other people's nonverbal behaviors. Because nonverbal immediacy conveys feelings of closeness, the higher the score, the friendlier or closer we assume the other person to be. We use these nonverbal behaviors to develop our overall impression of others and how they feel toward us. This scale is particularly good for analyzing your perceptions of someone else's approach–avoidance behaviors, which can include eye contact, proximity, gestures, and body position. The higher the level of perceived nonverbal immediacy, the more this person wants to approach or get close to you. The scores listed at the end of the survey indicate that research has reported significant differences in the degree to which males and females utilize these nonverbal immediacy behaviors. If you were assessing a female when you completed the instrument, it is very likely that you observed more of these behaviors than you would have reported for a male. Look at your overall score, and try to understand it by considering these ideas:

- First, if you were reporting on a female, your final score was probably somewhere between 81 and 112. The higher the score, the more she smiles, touches, gestures, exhibits vocal variety, and is animated in conversations. If you were reporting on a male, the possible score range was between 77 and 106. Of course, you can see that there is an overlap in the possible scores for men and women, so it would be common to obtain a score for a man that falls within the female score range. As more men today are encouraged to "explore their feminine side," you shouldn't be surprised if this is what occurred with your score.

- Androgyny was described in Chapter 3 as a combination of highly feminine and highly masculine characteristics. It is frequently displayed via nonverbal immediacy behaviors. Because androgyny is indicative of effective communication, an overlap in male and female scores should be considered positive.

- If your perceptions of the person you were evaluating fell at the bottom end of the score range for either males (< 77) or females (< 81), it is important to think about why this may have occurred. First, think about the context you were using to analyze this individual's nonverbal behaviors. If it was a very serious or constrained situation, it is possible that closeness was not the primary goal. The nonverbal immediacy assessment instrument is intended to examine someone's overall nonverbal characteristics, so if you were placing them in one specific context, this might be why you scored them this way.

- The combined score is most often used because it actually incorporates the overlap between men and women and allows for it. In addition, using one score range to evaluate levels of nonverbal immediacy is simpler to understand. Therefore, if you encourage the person you evaluated to complete this instrument about you, this general range would probably be the simplest for him or her to understand. Just remember that the closer the score is to the high range, the more the individual is perceived to be exhibiting behaviors that reveal a desire to be close.

WHAT CAN I **do now?**

▶ *You could work on observing multiple nonverbal immediacy signals.* You can develop more accurate perceptions of someone's feelings toward you if you have multiple cues to evaluate.

▶ *You could practice using nonverbal immediacy behaviors to indicate similarity in status.* If you don't use immediacy behaviors, the other person might feel that you are superior to him or her, more powerful, or even egotistical.

▶ *You could use nonverbal immediacy behaviors to help reduce another person's uncertainty about you.*

▶ *You could incorporate nonverbal immediacy behaviors into your repertoire and practice using them to let others know that you like them.*

Touch Avoidance and Personality

Touch is one of the most important nonverbal cues we use to let someone know we are interested and have feelings of affection, love, and closeness.[75] People who avoid or are apprehensive about touch are often misunderstood because we tend to believe that they do not really care about us or do not want to get close. In reality, it could be their inherent predisposition to avoid touch, and as a result, miscommunication may occur that can damage relationships. Before reading any further, complete the touch apprehension measure on the next page to help you determine whether you are comfortable with touch or avoid it. When you have computed your final score, take a look back at this section to see whether some of the personality traits linked to touch describe you.

Touch avoidance is a trait that reflects your personal like or dislike of touching or being touched by others,[76] and it is a part of your personality because it is consistent across interactions and situations.[77] So whether you realize it or not, deep inside you have a certain level of affinity toward touching. Communication scholars have examined the link between touch avoidance and self-esteem and have reported that people who have lower levels of self-esteem avoid touch more than those with higher self-esteem levels do.[78] The same applies to extraverted individuals, who are outgoing and positive thinkers who enjoy interacting with others, close distances, and touch.[79] People with personalities that are opposite of this, such as individuals who are anxious, aggressive, or hostile, reportedly have a greater need for distance, leading to higher levels of touch avoidance.[80] Similarly, those who experience high levels of communication apprehension avoid close distances and, in turn, avoid touch.[81]

Additional research has linked the Big Five personality traits (conscientiousness, agreeableness, neuroticism, extraversion, and openness) to perceptions of touch and touch avoidance.[82] Individuals who display more openness and agreeableness tend to view touch more positively and therefore are lower in touch avoidance. Neurotic individuals, who are frequently described as tense, moody, and anxious, therefore often experience rocky relationships and have negative perceptions of touch.[83] If someone were to assess the degree to which you like to be touched, what would they learn?

Understanding Your Level of Touch Apprehension. Although touch is a nonverbal immediacy behavior, the lack of touch is not. Therefore, it is important to understand touch avoidance behaviors separate from immediacy. Because researchers have drawn a connection between touch and relational development, it is extremely important to

ASSESS YOUR **communication personality**

Richmond and McCroskey's Touch Apprehension Scale[84]

Log onto our self-assessment library, MyPersonalityProfile, found on MyCommunicationLab (www.mycommunicationlab.com), and assess your own levels of touch apprehension. Encourage someone close to you to do the same so that you can compare and contrast your scores. This should help you to understand how accurate your perceptions are of your own levels of touch. If you prefer, use the instrument below.

Directions:

Below are fourteen statements that people sometimes make about themselves. Please indicate whether or not you believe that each statement applies to you by using the following scale:

1 = strongly disagree
2 = disagree
3 = neutral
4 = agree
5 = strongly agree

_____ 1. I don't mind if I am hugged as a sign of friendship.

_____ 2. I enjoy touching others.

_____ 3. I seldom put my arms around others.

_____ 4. When I see people hugging, it bothers me.

_____ 5. People should not be uncomfortable about being touched.

_____ 6. I really like being touched by others.

_____ 7. I wish I were free to show my emotions by touching others.

_____ 8. I do not like touching other people.

_____ 9. I do not like being touched by other people.

_____10. I find it enjoyable to be touched by others.

_____11. I dislike having to hug others.

_____12. Hugging and touching should be outlawed.

_____13. Touching others is a very important part of my personality.

_____14. Being touched by others makes me uncomfortable.

Scoring Instructions:

To determine the score on the touch apprehension scale, complete the following steps:

Step 1. Add scores for items 1, 2, 5, 6, 7, 10, and 13

Step 2. Add the scores for items 3, 4, 8, 9, 11, 12, and 14

Step 3. Complete the following formula: Score = 42 + Total from Step 1 − Total from Step 2

Possible Score Range: 14–70

Scores > 50 indicate a high touch orientation (approacher).

Scores < 30 indicate a low touch orientation (avoider).

Scores between 30 and 50 indicate no strong touch orientation; the amount of touch will typically be that of the general culture.

understand what your score means. If you earned a high score (≥ 50), you are described as an approacher, or someone who prefers to get close and interact. Although touch can violate your expectations, touch is also necessary for a relationship to progress. If you scored low on this assessment (≤ 30), you avoid touch and therefore exhibit a degree of touch apprehension.

- Avoiders resist touch because they find it uncomfortable or even inappropriate. Much of the time, people resist it because they were not touched when they were children. If touch is not learned socially, then it is not a behavior they are comfortable performing. Unfortunately, avoiding touch can negatively affect interpersonal relationships because it is difficult to develop closeness without some form of touch.

- Approachers, on the other hand, prefer to develop a level of closeness and intimacy, and this is accomplished through different forms of touch. Of course, we are talking about positive touch here (e.g., stroking, massaging, love pats). There is a distinct difference between positive and negative touch. Positive touch sends messages of comfort, security, and closeness with others and is strongly encouraged to enhance relational development.

- Touch apprehension has been connected to high levels of communication apprehension.[85] Therefore, it appears that if you achieved a lower score on this instrument, you might also display a general discomfort when communicating in specific environments. This is something you might want to investigate, as it may be indicative of a general unwillingness to communicate, which can affect your success in school and the workplace as well as your relationships.

WHAT CAN I **do now?**

▶ *You could examine the touch in many of your interpersonal relationships.* If you scored in the low range on the touch apprehension assessment, ask yourself why increasing touch in certain situations would help your communication.

▶ *You could strive to feel more comfortable with touch.* Remember that touch breeds increased trust.

▶ *You could recognize that sex differences in touch exist.* It is more appropriate for women to touch both women and men than for men to touch either sex.[86]

▶ *You could understand and reflect on the development of your touch views.* Think back to your childhood, and recall the ways in which your close family members touched to assess your frame of reference of what is acceptable, appropriate, or even necessary.

▶ *You could recognize that touch communicates attraction and homophily.*[87] These are both positive contributors to relational development.

Deception and Personality

If, after reading about touch avoidance, you believe that it would be difficult to determine whether a particular behavior was situational or personality-based, you might be equally uncertain about nonverbal deception messages. Communication behaviors require careful attention and analysis. Although most people believe that they will know a lie when they see or hear it, there are many factors that refute this notion. This section will first discuss forms of deception, research on nonverbal deception clues, and links to personality traits.

Interpersonal deception theory was developed to help explain why people lie and how they utilize nonverbal messages to do so.[88] According to this theory, deceivers are trying to protect their image and at the same time maintain influence over other people. However, the greater the sending capacity a channel has for emitting nonverbal messages (e.g., the face has multiple areas to control), the easier it is to uncover deception there.[89] Scholars have suggested that the vocal channel, especially the tone of voice and how words are said, is better for lie detection because people are not good at hearing how their own voices sound.[90]

Though leakage cues are helpful in uncovering deception, they do not provide a foolproof method. Recently, psychologists and communication scholars have attempted to pinpoint specific personality types and traits that are more clearly linked to deception. Some traits that you have probably considered are nervousness, tension, or anxious feelings and behaviors. When people feel tense or nervous, they exhibit random body behaviors and arm movements. They may rock back and forth, shake a leg or foot as they are sitting, or fidget. Grouping these behaviors together is very helpful in lie detection, and they reflect specific personality types. According to scholars, there is a strong relationship between deception and neuroticism and psychoticism.[91] Individuals who are more likely to lie include people who are tense, nervous, and moody (neuroticism) and those who tend to be reckless, convey a disregard for conventional behavior, and show inappropriate emotional expressions (psychoticism). Of course, it would be inappropriate to go out and give everyone you suspected of lying a personality test, but if you know people who regularly exhibit these behaviors, you might want to think carefully about the information they provide.

Types of lies have also been linked to personality type. For example, social acceptance lies (lies that are told to help fit in or be liked by others) are connected to motivation for approval (a desire for positive evaluations and social approval from others). Self-gain lies (lies that materially benefit oneself) are reportedly related to Machiavellianism (self-serving individuals with little value placed on conventional morality)[92] and high self-monitoring (traits regulating expressive behaviors to achieve desired social appearance).[93] Therefore, if you recognize another person as constantly needing social approval, then the lies they would most likely tell would be those that would make others like them or help them to fit in.

CHECKING YOUR UNDERSTANDING
Assessing Personality and Impacts on Nonverbal Messages

Before reading further, take a few minutes to assess your learning by writing your answers to the following items:

1. What are nonverbal cues that indicate that a person is being nonverbally immediate, and what two personality traits are most frequently linked to people who are nonverbally immediate?

2. How are nonverbal immediacy and touch avoidance linked? Describe the personality traits associated (Big Five) with touch/touch avoidance.

3. What two common personality traits are linked to deception?

4. How do nonverbal leakage cues signal deception? How can interpersonal deception theory be used to support how people might deceive with nonverbal cues?

Enhancing Nonverbal Message Interpretation

While understanding the elements of nonverbal communication is an important first step toward being a competent communicator, the journey does not end there. If you expect your relationships to succeed, you must also know how to improve your interpretation of nonverbal messages. At this point, you should ask yourself how effective you are at reading other people's nonverbal cues. If you are like most people, your either miss or misinterpret valuable nonverbal messages. To avoid this, it is important to improve your abilities. Therefore, we will focus on two primary areas to enhance interpretation: Mehrabian's three-part framework for nonverbal communication and Burgoon's explanation of the violation of expectations we have for others' nonverbal communication.[94]

Interpreting Pleasure, Arousal, and Dominance Cues

All relationships consist of cues that help to explain the feelings people have for one another and how the relationship works for them. Nonverbal messages offer key insights into relationships. Albert Mehrabian reported that we synthesize and interpret nonverbal cues along three primary dimensions: **pleasure** (liking), **arousal** (interests), and **dominance** (status).[95] As you read through the discussion of nonverbal expressions within these three areas, think about how often you take the time to observe them and how often you are accurate.

- *Look for pleasure/liking cues.* When people like us or take pleasure in the topic they are discussing with us, they will exhibit nonverbal behaviors that signal this. If you are particularly observant, you will notice that they use some of the following behaviors: forward body leans, head nods, direct eye contact and smiling, open body

What are the nonverbal cues you see between these two women that indicate they are experiencing feelings of pleasure, arousal, and/or dominance?

orientation, and expressive gestures and vocalics.[96] Research tells us that nonverbal cues that signal liking are present in all stages of relationships and that people pay special attention to them in the initial stages. Recent research in a new relational environment of speed dating reveals the importance and value of nonverbal cues used to express interest and liking.[97] Individuals in this fast-paced environment have only minutes to determine whether or not someone is "for them" and whether they experience feelings of pleasure. Speed dating participants who like their partners exhibit positive nonverbal immediacy behaviors such as maintaining eye contact, appearing relaxed and interested, smiling, and speaking in an engaging voice. Of course, these nonverbal cues are important to recognize in all sorts of relationships and at every level. The key of course is to pay attention to them. Doing this can help you to avoid disastrous relational experiences and outcomes and might also prevent you from missing out on a perfect opportunity.

- *Look for arousal/interest cues.* When people are interested in others or have a passion for what is being discussed, they typically exhibit nonverbal behaviors that reveal their emotional arousal. Some of the many expressions that are typically present are changes in vocalic, kinesic, and proxemic cues.[98] The voice typically rises in pitch, and the speech tempo increases. Greater kinesic expressiveness occurs, including heightened dynamic gestures and excited or animated facial expressions. Proxemics also change, but people may be either considerably closer or farther away than usual—the key is to know what is "normal" for each individual. Considerable research has been conducted on nonverbal cues that signal the interest during stages of relational development. It is important to recognize and pay attention to them because they can work to either enhance or prevent relational intimacy.[99]

- *Look for dominance/status cues.* Even though these nonverbal cues might not seem particularly enhancing for relational success, they do play a pivotal role in our interpersonal communication. People who consider themselves or their ideas to be important during an interaction will more than likely display dominant nonverbal cues that indicate this view toward someone they perceive to be of lower status. The primary components of dominance are not all necessarily negative; they include strength, aggressiveness, persuasiveness, threat, dynamism, and self-control.[100] Because of the variance in positive and negative perceptions of these components, the nonverbal behaviors manifest themselves in multiple forms to communicate self-assurance (e.g., erect posture), conversational control (e.g., vocal control and intensity), confidence, and leadership (e.g., proximity). Some more specific and common nonverbal cues to look for to determine dominance within interpersonal relationships are gestures such as a downward head tilt; relaxed vocalics such as laughter, pitch variety, animation, and rate; and facial expressions such as less smiling. There is evidence that suggests that kinesic cues are significant predictors of dominance and status within interpersonal interactions.[101] Therefore, it is important to carefully examine where people sit, where they stand, whether they initiate touch, and whether they interrupt conversations. All of these nonverbal messages are necessary to evaluate nonverbal messages accurately.

Even though it is important to recognize these cues and interpret them accurately, there is always the possibility that you will make mistakes. This cannot be avoided, primarily because we are complex human beings and vary in our nonverbal expressions. The key is to have this arsenal of information available so that you recognize the three primary relational dimensions of nonverbal messages. Accurate interpretation of liking, interest, and status cues will aid you in examining and assessing interactions within your interpersonal relationships.

Interpreting Nonverbal Violations

While accurately interpreting nonverbal cues of liking, interest, and status is essential, it is also important to recognize that over the course of your life, you have developed expectations for when and how these cues are utilized. Unfortunately, when we have expectations for other's nonverbal cues (e.g., expecting people to look at us and nod their heads in understanding when we are talking), they are not always met. Nonverbal expectations are constantly violated; therefore, it is important to be aware that they exist, understand why we have the expectations (where they come from), and recognize how they are being violated. Judee Burgoon created the **expectancy violation theory** to explain our thoughts about the nonverbal communication we anticipate or expect from others.[102]

According to Burgoon and Hale, three factors influence how people react when others do not nonverbally behave as expected.[103] First, people have expectations for normative nonverbal behavior that is part of social interactions. Some women, for example, expect men to open the door for them as a gesture of courtesy. When this does not occur, expectations are violated.

Second, people experience increased arousal when others violate communication expectations. This resulting arousal leads to **orienting responses** in which people shift their attention from the interaction or conversation and focus on the other person in an attempt to interpret and evaluate the unexpected behavior. This evaluation then causes them to assign a valence to the behavior. In other words, when people interpret an unexpected behavior to be positive, then it has a **positive violation valence**. Conversely, when people deviate in a negative manner, this can produce less than favorable responses and the outcome is an expectancy violation that is **negatively valenced**.[104]

The third factor is **communicator reward valence**. When messages are ambiguous, people look to others and their relationships with these others to interpret violated expectations. A person is perceived to have a positive communicator reward valence if the person is interpersonally attractive, a judgment that is typically based on attractiveness, expertise, gender, socioeconomic status, perceived similarity, and communication style.[105] If the person violating the nonverbal expectation is perceived positively, then receivers have a tendency to grant the source permission to violate expectations. For example, if your boss is leading an important training session that is essential to your job performance and he or she constantly invades your personal space, it is likely that you will allow it. In this instance, you determine that your boss has positive reward valence. Conversely, if the person violating the expectation is perceived negatively, receivers have a tendency to socially sanction the source.[106]

Applying Your Knowledge. As was discussed in Chapter 2, it is important to manage impressions that others have of you. One way to ensure positive interpersonal encounters is to be aware of the nonverbal cues that, when violated, significantly influence how others view you. Research has identified three nonverbal strategies that should be considered:

- *Violations of space and touch directly affect violation valence.* What this means is that these two nonverbal codes lead to immediate interpretations and assigned valence. People are so sensitive to touch and space that they quickly become aware of their feelings when someone stands too close or too far and when they touch or fail to touch. Therefore, we need to be especially conscious of our physical distance from others and consider when and where a particular distance is appropriate. When in doubt, ask or at least watch the other person closely to ensure that your behavior is acceptable.

- *Consider the level of conversational involvement of others.* Ask yourself whether your conversation partner is physically and mentally involved during an interaction. People display this by being nonverbally immediate with forward body leans, touch, and eye gaze. They place the focus on you instead of on themselves, and they effectively manage the conversation by allowing you to talk as they listen. This is considered a positive expectancy violation that, regardless of their own reward valence, will enhance the impression they make on others. However, exceeding or falling well short of positive expectations can easily produce negative rewards. The advice, as with space and touch, is to be observant and attentive. We all like to be listened to. It validates us and makes us feel important. Just don't overdo it.

- *Consider your level of relaxation during conversations.* The ease with which you engage in discussions is a strong indicator of relational success. Two extremes of relaxation are hyperrelaxation and hyporelaxation. People who are hyperrelaxed exhibit poor posture, yawn, and avoid eye contact. They appear disinterested, uninvolved, and uncaring. Hyporelaxation, by contrast, is an excessively low level of relaxation in which people appear stressed, agitated, and even aggressive. Both of these levels negatively violate expectations, leading to negative evaluations and feelings of social discomfort. Although this might not be an area of nonverbal communication that you think about very often, research reveals its importance. Your level of relaxation during conversations is scrutinized, so you should be aware of the damage you may create conversationally if you fail to monitor it carefully.

CHECKING YOUR UNDERSTANDING
Enhancing Nonverbal Message Interpretation

Before completing the chapter, take a few minutes to assess your learning by writing your answers to the following items:

1. What are examples of nonverbal pleasure/liking cues, and why do they enhance interpersonal communication? Describe the research that lends support to the value of these cues.

2. What are some examples of arousal/interest cues, and why are they considered important in the stages of relational development?

3. How do people behave when they are feeling more dominant than the person with whom they are communicating?

4. What role do orienting responses and communicator reward valence play in expectancy violation theory?

5. What are the three nonverbal areas to which you should pay special attention in avoiding others' expectations and enhancing the impressions they have of you?

A Communication Development Plan for William

To complete William's story, recall that William was angry and felt that Dr. Russell was accusing him of lying. William might have been telling the truth, but his nonverbal cues sent a different message to Dr. Russell. Both people could benefit from understanding nonverbal message encoding and decoding to create a more positive conversation.

Was William consciously trying to deceive Dr. Russell? It seems apparent that William had no idea he was conveying clusters of nonverbal behaviors that were indicative of deception. It is doubtful that most people who hope to have a favor granted would fidget, sigh, hang their head, stare at the floor, and have such obvious strong vocal responses. Therefore, William might indeed be lying and the cues are leaking out. But we also know that nonverbal messages are multichanneled, and he uses many.

What specific nonverbal cues led Dr. Russell to conclude that William was being untruthful?

William obviously let his feelings leak out and was unaware that Dr. Russell observed them. He did not want to participate in the classroom brainstorming activity, he laughed at his group members' ideas, and his sullen attitude presented itself again in her office. Because of this, she read his nonverbal cues as deception, whether William was lying or not.

What do you think?

What could have improved the conversation between William and Dr. Russell?

Possible Explanations

Both of them need to develop a greater awareness of their own behaviors and perceptions. They need to be open and honest to encourage positive communication.

1. *Dr. Russell should be honest and, before William goes into detail, speak with him about his classroom behavior and hear his explanation.* The two people must be on a level playing field with openness and honesty if they are to have an amicable and productive conversation.

2. *William needs to recognize the uncomfortable nonverbal cues he exhibits and learn to control them.* If he is being truthful, he is not helping Dr. Russell believe him by using those particular kinesic and vocalic messages. He needs to plan what he will say and how he will say it ahead of

time and reflect on the perceptions of him that Dr. Russell may have already developed. Some helpful behaviors include interpreting pleasure, arousal, and dominance cues to help avoid misinterpretation of nonverbal messages.

After reading this chapter, what would you tell William to remember?

1. Remember the importance of pleasure/liking cues. Head nods, forward body leans, smiling, and direct eye contact are all examples of behaviors that signal your feelings of pleasure to others. Likability is incredibly important to create believability, and endearing yourself to others is extremely helpful in winning them over.

2. Always check your own and others' interest cues. Vocalic, kinesic, and proxemic behaviors indicate the amount of interest and level of desired involvement. When you are in an environment for a period of time, others begin to establish a baseline of what your "normal" nonverbal behavior is. Therefore, you should pay special attention to patterns that may be established by you and others.

3. A power differential will create unplanned behaviors. It is important always to consider the context, and power plays a huge role in the nonverbal behaviors that people exhibit. Nervousness, apprehension, and even low levels of self-esteem can make an uncomfortable situation worse.

4. Personality traits are important to consider, especially in cases of personal judgment. Consider a cluster of behaviors, and recognize nonverbal cues that coincide with specific personality types. Never underestimate possible genetic influences in communication.

Take Aways

The value of nonverbal messages in everyday communication is undeniable. They can accompany and clarify the meaning of verbal messages, or they can be interpreted alone. Although we tend to take most of our nonverbal behaviors for granted, there are many types, characteristics, and functions of nonverbal behaviors that are affected by factors such as culture, sex, and technology. All of this leads to others examining and interpreting your behavior, possible expectancy violations, and ultimately their relationships with you. If, like William in the opening case study, we fail to grasp the importance of

nonverbal messages and our awareness and ability to control them, our interpersonal communication will suffer.

You have increased your understanding and knowledge of the following:

- The characteristics of nonverbal messages and how they differ from verbal messages.

- The multichanneled nature of nonverbal messages and that they are frequently more believable than verbal messages.

- The encoding and decoding of nonverbal messages that must occur in conjunction with factors such as culture, gender, and technology.
- Your ability to interpret nonverbal behaviors by recognizing someone's personality traits.
- The specific expectations that people have for the nonverbal behavior of others and that create our interpretation of nonverbal cues.

Following are some of the ways in which you assessed and learned about your own use of nonverbal behaviors:

- Your perceptions of another person's nonverbal immediacy behaviors to determine the extent to which you perceive that the person exhibits cues that indicate caring and liking.
- Your touch apprehension to assess how you feel about touch, one of the most primitive and important behaviors to communicate your feelings toward someone else.

Following are a list of skills you can develop to help communicate clearly with nonverbal messages:

- As you speak to others, carefully observe the nonverbal cues you use. Reflect on the list of functions and assess whether you are utilizing them accurately.
- Carefully observe others during a conversation. Keep a mental list of their nonverbal cues to determine whether they are interpreting your message correctly.
- When you text-message, instant message, or leave a voice message for someone, plan your nonverbal cues carefully. Before sending a message, read or listen to what you have said or written, and ask yourself how this would make you feel if you were to receive such a message. Another method would be to ask a third party to read or listen to your message to get this person's interpretation.
- Be constantly aware of message adaptation in diverse cultural groups. If you know ahead of time that you will be communicating with someone from another culture, do some research on the person's nonverbal expectations.

Discussion Questions

1. Can you list the characteristics of nonverbal messages and, for each, list and describe specific types of nonverbal cues that support them?
2. Nonverbal messages perform specific functions in our interpersonal communication. Can you name each of these functions and place two or three nonverbal cues within each?
3. What are the eight types of nonverbal cues?
4. What are the factors that influence how our nonverbal messages are perceived?
5. What are leakage cues? How do they serve as indicators of deception?

Building Your Skills

1. Sit down with a person of the opposite gender, and ask the person to list and describe his or her perceptions of typical male (if she is female) or female (if he is male) nonverbal behaviors.
2. Engage in a discussion of nonverbal expressions with someone from another culture. Reveal some of the typical cues you regularly use, and ask the person to show you what behaviors he or she would exhibit if conveying the same feelings or emotions. Discuss how you would deal with these differential interpretations so that communication would not be negatively affected.
3. Observe a communication episode (a personal conversation or a TV episode). What are some of the nonverbal behaviors you notice that are either acceptable or unacceptable? Try to explain why you designate them this way. Reflect on possible stereotypes and your own expectations and expectancy violations.
4. After assessing your own and your partner's nonverbal immediacy, make a list of the ways in which you could improve your immediacy behaviors and create more caring communication.
5. Look back at ten of your sent email messages. Assess the nonverbal cues utilized in these messages. Show these messages to an outside observer, and ask how he or she might interpret them. If you don't feel comfortable showing someone your actual messages, create some similar ones to use and assess.

6 Assessing and Developing Listening and Responding Skills

Helen's Story . . .

Helen and Mark met when both were sophomores in college. Helen and Mark had a lot in common; they liked sports, especially football, enjoyed hanging out with friends, and had similar childhoods. They dated for a couple of years, got married two years after graduating from college, and have now been married for approximately four years. Although things are going pretty well for them, Helen feels that Mark doesn't really listen to her thoughts and opinions the way he once did.

Lately, it seems that whenever Helen wants to have a conversation with Mark, he is preoccupied with something else. It has reached the point at which Helen feels that Mark rarely, if ever, really listens to her, although Mark would most definitely deny that. Last weekend, Helen and Mark were relaxing, watching a random football game on TV, reading magazines, and waiting for their alma mater's homecoming football game to begin. Helen decided to ask Mark a question about their plans for Thanksgiving weekend. Her family wanted them to spend

the holiday with them, but Helen and Mark live a four-hour drive away, and Helen had some things that she wanted to do at home, so she wasn't sure she wanted to travel that far. When Helen asked Mark what he thought about spending the holiday with her family, Mark simply continued to read his magazine and then asked the score of the earlier game.

When Mark didn't even look up to acknowledge Helen's question about Thanksgiving, she just about lost it. She stood directly in front of Mark and confronted him on the fact that he had been ignoring her and her comments about the upcoming holiday. Mark, who was becoming equally frustrated, looked up from the magazine, told Helen that he had been listening to her, told her he didn't care what they did for the holiday, and then reminded her that she had not told him the score of the other football game. Therefore, could she please move so that he could see the television screen to learn the score?

At this point, Helen didn't know quite what to say, so she moved away from the screen, sat down in a chair, and let out

CHAPTER OBJECTIVES

AFTER READING THIS CHAPTER, you will understand:

1 The relationship between hearing and listening.

2 How verbal and nonverbal messages affect listening.

3 How listening styles and your reasons for listening may influence listening behaviors when you are interacting with others.

4 The challenges of information-processing and context barriers.

5 The options people have when providing listening responses to others.

a loud sigh of frustration. Technically, Mark did at least know the topic that she was trying to discuss with him, but the exchange was not very meaningful, nor did Mark's response leave Helen with a sense that he really understood how she felt about traveling over Thanksgiving. Furthermore, she was equally frustrated that Mark appeared to have ignored her remarks but was quick to let her know that she hadn't given him the requested information about the football score.

What do you think? While reading this chapter, consider how you might answer the following questions to help Helen:

- Was Mark really listening to what Helen was trying to say to him about the upcoming holiday?

- What types of listening barriers is Helen encountering in this conversation?

- How would you approach the situation if you were to advise Helen?

We will revisit Helen's story at the end of the chapter and use the content discussed in this chapter to develop a communication plan to help Helen.

**AFTER READING THIS CHAPTER,
you will be able to:**

1 Incorporate listening strategies that may make you a better listener.

2 Implement listening strategies that may make you someone who is more likely to be listened to by others.

3 Overcome numerous listening barriers that you experience in your interpersonal relationships.

**AFTER COMPLETING THE SELF-ASSESSMENTS,
you will learn about:**

1 What your preferred listening style(s) is (are) and how this influences your communication with others.

Despite the fact that listening is an essential tool for interpersonal relationships to thrive, much less survive, few of us take the time to listen well or know how to improve our listening abilities. Part of the problem may be that there are many misconceptions surrounding listening. Do any of these comments sound familiar?

- Listening is an innate skill; it is not something that needs to be learned.
- Not everyone or everything is worth listening to.
- Taking a listening course sounds really boring!
- You need to be a good listener only if you are a peon. Once you are in charge, you get to pick and choose whether or not you want to listen.

Because of the importance that listening plays in effective communication, the amount of total energy spent on the task of listening during effective communication should be 80%, while the energy exerted toward speaking should be 20%.[1] Historically, the primary focus when communicating has been on the speaker (or message sender). Therefore, we put significant amounts of energy into what messages we send and how we deliver our messages to others. But in doing this, we overlook the important role that listening plays in successful interactions. When we truly listen, we are better able to determine what to say to others. If we are poor listeners, we are more likely to say something that is not relevant to the person we are speaking to—or worse. As you can see in Figure 6.1, the percentages are reversed in ineffective communication: The 80% of energy is exerted for speaking, while 20% of energy is exerted for listening.[2] In a nutshell, we have misplaced where we should put our energies when interacting with others, and most of us have had to live with the consequences at some point in our interpersonal relationships.

> Listening, not imitation, may be the sincerest form of flattery.
>
> —DR. JOYCE BROTHERS

The purpose of this chapter is to help you understand more about listening, identify specific preferences you may have when listening to others, overcome listening barriers and apprehensions to become a better listener, and develop methods to improve how you respond to others and make it easier for others to listen to you. To accomplish these goals, the chapter has been divided into four sections. The first section examines the relationship between hearing and listening. The second section explores the relationships between your listening style, personality traits, and sex differences. The third

FIGURE 6.1

Energy Expended in Effective versus Ineffective Communication

Source: Data from Brownell, J. (2006). *Listening: Attitudes, principles, and skills* (3rd ed.). Boston, MA: Pearson.

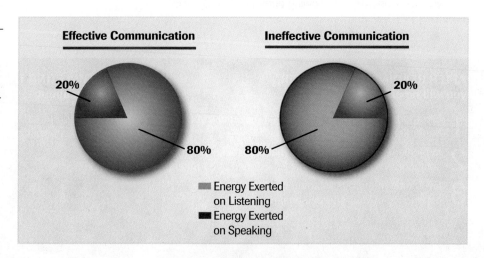

section looks at how to overcome or manage listening barriers in your relationships. The final section provides strategies to improve your own listening responses as well as enhance others' abilities to listen to you more effectively.

Understanding Listening

While it might seem that listening is as easy as turning a light switch on or off, a number of things can go wrong from a physiological perspective as well as from a psychological perspective. We will begin by addressing the physiological processes; then we will examine the psychological processes we engage in when we listen.

Hearing: A Physiological Process

Although hearing and listening are related, they are not interchangeable concepts. **Hearing** involves the physiological processing of sound waves.[3] Essentially, all sounds are composed of a series of vibrations. When interacting with someone, these sound vibrations are most typically generated when talking to another person. It is the combination or collection of sound waves that are grouped together to form words. The ear is the body's receptor for processing auditory inputs, or sound waves, starting by detecting the sound vibration and ending when the sound waves are transmitted into electrical nerve impulses that are sent to the brain for analysis and interpretation (see Figure 6.2).[4] Any listening that incorporates vocal communication messages requires the ability to hear.[5]

FIGURE 6.2

How Hearing Works

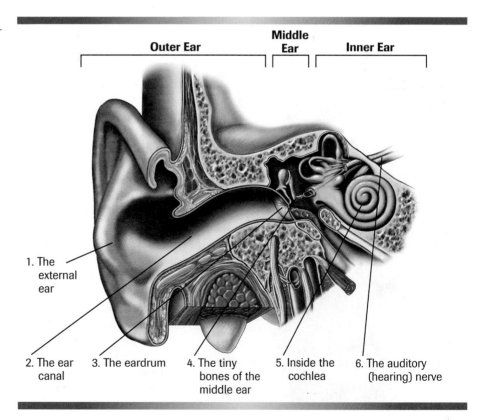

1. The external ear
2. The ear canal
3. The eardrum
4. The tiny bones of the middle ear
5. Inside the cochlea
6. The auditory (hearing) nerve

Within the brain, the collection of various sounds helps you to determine the particular word(s) someone has said. The sounds that we put together to form words are patterns that are learned. We learn over time that the combination of a particular set of sounds forms the word "talk" and not "walk."[6] If someone pronounces something in an unfamiliar way, mumbles, mispronounces words, or talks with a strong accent, the sounds that are transmitted through the ear and then interpreted in the brain lead us to perceive that the person may have said something else than what was intended.

Listening: A Psychological Process

Assuming that the ear was able to effectively process the sound waves it received, you are now able to begin the stages of listening. In 1996, the International Listening Association defined **listening** as "the process of receiving, constructing meaning from, and responding to spoken and/or nonverbal messages."[7] As a result, listening is often considered a psychological process, while hearing is often considered a physiological process. There are five stages to listening: selecting, attending, understanding, responding, and remembering. These stages can occur in very quick succession, especially the first three stages. The decisions that you make during each stage will play a major role in determining how you interpret the messages you receive.

Selecting. We are bombarded with sounds almost all the time. **Selecting** involves making choices about what auditory inputs to pay attention to and what auditory inputs to ignore. Just close your eyes for about ten seconds, and you will hear what I mean. There may be the sounds of a clock ticking, the hum of any technological devices that are running nearby, the sounds of heating or cooling systems, and perhaps the noises or shuffling of people moving around in the room or traffic passing by outside.

What sounds are you going to pay attention to? What are you going to ignore?

So far, this list does not take into account any voices you may hear in the background of others talking around you or perhaps the sounds coming from the television that is on in the other room. We have to pick and choose what sounds we wish to process further, since we are not very efficient when we try to select all of these sounds at the same time to focus on.

Two factors may help us to decide what messages we are going to select. The first factor is **auditory discrimination**, which refers to our ability to distinguish one sound from another.[8] Auditory discrimination helps us to decide whether any sounds are being received that may have special meaning to us. For example, when you hear birds chirping outside, are you able to identify whether the sound is a robin or a cardinal? When we are in a group with lots of people, we discriminate on the basis of the sound of a person's voice or laugh to help us know whether our brother or best friend is somewhere in the crowd.

The second factor is **auditory association**, which is applied when we are trying to establish connections or relationships between new incoming sounds and ones with which we are already familiar. We might do this when we are listening to a song for the first time and trying to determine what it has in common with previous songs by the same artist or from the same musical genre. Both auditory discrimination and auditory association are helpful when we are making choices about what sounds we are going to focus on in greater detail when we begin the attending stage.[9]

Attending. At times, one sound may hold more significance for us than another, leading us to pay attention to one sound while neglecting or ignoring others. **Attending** involves giving further attention to the sounds that we have selected.[10] For example, I can hear the sound my computer makes when it is turned on, and I can select this sound from the sounds in my immediate vicinity and make sure my computer sounds as it normally does when I am using it. However, when I hear my husband open the back door and enter the house when he gets home from work, I shift gears and either call his name from where I am in the house or get up to go meet him. As this example demonstrates, we can shift our attention from one sound to another in a split second. While this can be advantageous if there is a pending problem or a dangerous situation, it can be distracting if certain sounds can hold our attention or interest only for short periods of time.

Understanding. Trying to begin making sense of the messages or sounds on which you have chosen to focus requires **understanding**.[11] In other words, you want to interpret the message you have just selected and attended to. In the case of my computer, because it was making the same sound that it usually does when it is running, I interpreted this to mean that there were no problems with the machine. In the case of my husband, my initial interpretation was that he wanted me to greet him now that he was home. Although this is typically the case, the dogs often get to my husband first. As a result, he greets and pets our dogs and lets them outside before I enter the room he is in. I don't suspect that there is a problem between us just because he interacts with our dogs before he interacts with me. But if we have had a recent fight or disagreement, I could be wrong in my interpretation of his behavior. Things start to get more complicated once you begin trying to understand the messages you are receiving, since there may be significant room for multiple interpretations to explain or account for what something or someone said or did.

Responding. When **responding**, you are providing some type of reaction or feedback to the message.[12] Responses can include allowing the message to continue as it had been, or trying to offer feedback in an effort to provide an effective and appropriate answer to the message. In the case of my computer, my response was to save my document and keep working. Responding to my husband is trickier because my initial response is to greet him once he gets home. Although this is typically the correct response, I might be more hesitant to give him a hug immediately upon seeing him if he is in a bad mood.

Whether or not you have provided a successful response tends to be determined by the person you are listening to. Even if you think that you have given an appropriate response, the other person can still thwart your efforts to effectively process his or her message. If you have ever tried to please people by telling them what you think they want to hear and then they tell you that you are wrong, you will understand this predicament. Responding is inherently complicated and requires interpreting both verbal and nonverbal messages when listening if you want to provide a successful response.

Remembering. Retaining information that has been gained from processing the message so that we can refer to it (and the outcome reached) at a later point in time involves **remembering** information.[13] In the computer example, if I am successful in interpreting the message and the same thing occurs virtually every time I hear the sounds, my interpretation of this sound may become second nature to me. I rarely think about it or choose to select this sound unless the sounds generated by my computer vary significantly from what I have grown accustomed to.

Processing messages exchanged by individuals involves applying the same listening stages as when processing the sounds generated by computers. The primary difference lies in understanding that the messages we exchange with one another are significantly more complex than the sounds of a computer because the number of possible interpretations for why we do or say what we do tends to be much greater and more complicated. When we are listening to our friends or significant others, different strategies are available to help us get our interpretations right, respond appropriately, and remember these exchanges so that in the future we might be able to do so with greater efficiency and effectiveness. In the case of my husband coming home, the vast majority of the time, my greeting is positively received at the end of the day. But I am mindful to select and attend to his verbal and nonverbal cues to make sure that he is not preoccupied with something else when he first gets home. I remember that he could be tired or frustrated after a long day at work (for reasons that may or may not have to do with me). This affects the options I might want to select in the future.

Listening and Responding: A Communication Process

When listening to others, it is very common to exchange roles between being the sender and the receiver of the numerous verbal and nonverbal messages being exchanged between individuals. Let's examine the roles that verbal and nonverbal messages play when we listen and look at some of the things that are going on in the brain while we are involved in this listening exchange (see Table 6.1).

Processing and Interpreting Verbal Messages When Listening. Typically, when we think of hearing and listening, we focus on the processing and interpreting of verbal messages. This is understandable, since we associate hearing with listening, and hearing emphasizes the processing of sound-based messages.[14] Oral messages are the result of creating auditory outputs (pronouncing and speaking words) and processing auditory inputs (breaking the words down into numerous sound waves that are processed by the ear and then interpreted by the brain).

Processing and Interpreting Nonverbal Messages When Listening. Although we place significant emphasis on how verbal messages are processed and interpreted when we are listening, this can minimize the role of other sensory inputs when we listen to each other. Recall that the International Listening Association's definition of listening

TABLE 6.1

The Contributions of Verbal and Nonverbal Messages When Listening		
Verbal Messages +	**Nonverbal Messages =**	**Listening**
What people are saying	Vocalics used by the speaker (e.g., tone, rate, pitch, volume)	Choices made when processing verbal and nonverbal messages
Specific words used for emphasis by the speaker	Facial expressions Gestures/movement Physical appearance	What you do: Select Attend Understand Respond Remember

acknowledges the role of nonverbal messages in the listening process. When we send and receive messages while communicating, we simultaneously process nonverbal messages with any verbal messages. As a result, while the brain is interpreting auditory inputs, it is also interpreting visual inputs.

Our bodies have separate processing systems for handling visual and auditory inputs. Therefore, contradictions may be present if visual and auditory nerve pathways are sending conflicting information to the brain for processing.[15] For example, when we drastically change our appearance for a job interview or social gathering (e.g., a new haircut, different clothing choices), our friends may become confused when they recognize our voice but not our appearance. Furthermore, in humans, visual inputs tend to be more dominant than auditory inputs. As a result, it is important that we do not forget the significant role nonverbal messages may play when we are listening to others.

When we think back to the five stages of listening—selecting, attending, understanding, responding, and remembering—it becomes clear that we sometimes select and attend to some visual inputs (nonverbal messages) over auditory inputs (verbal messages) when someone is speaking to us. For example, have you ever been so distracted by someone's tattoo or body piercing that you didn't hear what the person was saying? In such a case, your selection and attending to a nonverbal message override your ability to select and attend to the verbal message. As a result, your ability to understand or provide an appropriate response may be limited. Because we rely heavily on nonverbal messages, we need to be mindful of problems that may surface when we try to focus equally on what someone is trying to say to us.

NATURE/NURTURE intersections

What Messages Do Our Brains Listen To?

A different way to approach the study of listening is to consider what some people might call a form of intrapersonal listening or subconscious information processing. Through the work of semanticists, philosophers, physicists, and others, we are learning that we might very well "become what we say we are," according to the electrical activity (measured in units of neuronal energy) that is occurring in our brains.

We have learned some things about the power of auditory inputs.[16] Let's assume the following:

- A *random thought* equals x (where x = a unit of neuronal energy).

- A *thought that you think about yourself* generates approximately 10 to 100 times more neuronal energy in your brain than a random thought does.

- When *you hear someone else say something about you*, this also generates approximately 10 to 100 times more neuronal energy in your brain than a random thought does.

- However, a *thought that you speak out loud about yourself* generates approximately 100 to 1,000 times more neuronal energy in your brain than a random thought does.

Although most people would agree that the messages you select, attend to, interpret, recall, and respond to *from others* are important, you probably don't realize how any negative thoughts *you* think about yourself (e.g., "This is never going to work!") or negative comments *you* say aloud about yourself (e.g., "Why am I even trying, I know I'm going to fail?") also get wired into your brain and psyche—and can be very powerful.[17]

Our brains don't discriminate when it comes to the positive or negative messages we think and say about ourselves. Our brains simply work with the messages we provide,[18] and then our brains select, attend to, interpret, recall, and respond in the same way that it would to other messages. The fact that we may be feeding our brains a diet of predominantly negative messages, especially if we are inclined to make a lot of negative comments about ourselves, gets lost in the translation.

We know that we should be mindful of how we process and interpret the comments others make about us. But perhaps even more important, we should think about the thoughts or remarks we make about ourselves. We could say, "I can do this" instead of "I can never get this done." On the plus side, if indeed our brains "listen" and interpret the inputs we provide, we could stack the deck in our favor and think and say more positive or constructive things about ourselves. This could improve our self-esteem and our attitudes or even help to change our behaviors. As a result, we could be making our brains a stronger partner in our daily lives.

Technological Impacts on Listening

Questions have been raised about the ways in which technology usage affects how we communicate with others in general and our listening behaviors in particular. On first glance, if you were to look at how we spend our time when we are interacting with others, you would see that we spend the majority of our time listening. In fact, in 2008, scholars reexamined how college students spent their time[19] and reported significant changes in the percentage of time spent listening since 1996 , as shown in Table 6.2.[20]

TABLE 6.2

How College Students Spend Time Communicating		
	1996	**2008**
Listening	46%	56%
Reading	15%	17%
Speaking	26%	16%
Writing	13%	11%

Source: Adapted from Emanuel, R. et al. (2008). How college students spend their time communicating. *The International Journal of Listening, 22,* 13–28; Wolvin, A., & Coakley, C. G. (1996). *Listening* (5th ed.). Madison, WI: Brown & Benchmark Publishers.

When examining this issue in greater detail, researchers found that college students listen to various types of media as much as they are engaged in listening to other people. Although these patterns were beginning to surface in earlier research,[21] the role of the media in college students' communication activities continues to evolve as more technology is integrated into college students' daily activities. For instance, as technologies become more portable, both interpersonal and mediated listening are likely to increase, since more technologies incorporate the ability to talk on the telephone as well as listen to music. Yet even when cell phone conversations are classified as interpersonal communication, students are spending a greater proportion of their listening day in nonsocial interaction activities (e.g., listening to music) than in social interaction. Therefore, while we may be spending more time listening, it is important to examine what we are listening to.

Furthermore, technological advancements may be forcing us to reconsider what it means to listen interpersonally as technologies become more interactive and "real-time" in their conversational capabilities. For example, instant messaging and text-messaging have both typing and reading components to them. But if individuals feel that they are really participating in a conversation when they engage in either activity, this may force us to reexamine what constitutes interpersonal listening.[22]

CHECKING YOUR UNDERSTANDING
Understanding Listening

Before reading further, take a few minutes to assess your learning by writing your answers to the following items:

1. What is the difference between hearing and listening? How do they work together?
2. What are the five stages of listening, and what occurs during each stage?

3. How do verbal and nonverbal messages influence the listening process? What are the contributions of each in terms of our ability to listen effectively?

4. How have college students' communication activities changed? In addition, how has technology influenced how we engage in listening activities?

Assessing Personality and Listening Preferences

It is difficult to assess how well someone listens. One of the first problems is that individuals tend to report that they are better listeners than either outcome data or personal observation and feedback suggest. This is known as a **social desirability bias**. Granted, when we reflect upon our own listening skills, this may be a natural inclination. Who wants to openly share that he or she is not very good at listening to others?[23] Listening is a very complex process, involving both the intent of the speaker and the impact the message was intended to have on the listener.[24] Therefore, rather than trying to assess our listening skills directly, we will help you to assess your listening style.

Assessing Listening Styles

Listening is a skill that is acquired, learned, and refined over time. Listening scholars Kittie Watson, Larry Barker, and James Weaver III studied the preferences people have when listening to others.[25] What is your listening style, and what does it say about you? You are encouraged to complete the listening preference profile on the next page to identify your listening style tendencies.

Researchers have examined the ways in which your listening style affects how you listen to others. The four listening styles are people-oriented, time-oriented, action-oriented, and content-oriented.

People-Oriented Listening Style. The relationship you have with the person you are talking to is the focus of the **people-oriented listening style**.[27] People-oriented listeners are focused on the relational elements of the relationship and seem better able to respond to emotional cues and expressed feelings of speakers. Therefore, people-oriented listeners tend to demonstrate signs of caring, compassion, and understanding when conversing with others. However, when two individuals dislike each other, there may be a tendency by either or both people to demonstrate levels of verbal aggressiveness, even though they may demonstrate a people-oriented listening style when around others.[28] In many respects, the people-oriented listening style is ideally suited to dyadic communication in interpersonal settings.

Individuals who demonstrate the people-oriented listening style need to be mindful of the following tendencies: being overly concerned about others' feelings, overlooking any faults in others, possibly intruding on others' privacy, being highly emotional when giving feedback, and failing to discriminate when developing relationships.

Time-Oriented Listening Style. The role time management plays in communicating with others is emphasized in the **time-oriented listening style**.[29] Time-oriented listeners want to hear focused, concise messages and sometimes look at their watches to monitor how much time is being spent during a conversation. They also tend to get irritated if others ramble on in their exchanges. As a result, time-oriented listeners may interrupt others to help them get to their point sooner or simply to end the conversation so that they can move on to other things. If a time-oriented listener told you that you had five minutes to make your point, you would want to directly address your main ideas, because this person may be unlikely to allocate thirty minutes to hear what you have to say.

ASSESS YOUR **communication personality**

Barker and Watson's Listening Preference Profile[26]

Log onto our self-assessment library, MyPersonalityProfile, found on MyCommunicationLab (www.mycommunicationlab.com), and assess your listening preferences by completing the interactive assessment. Encourage someone you communicate with regularly (e.g., friend, roommate, relational partner) to do the same. This way, you can compare your listening style preferences and begin to understand how each of your listening styles may influence your interpersonal communication. If you prefer, you can also use the following text-based version.

Directions:

Think of a specific listening role or situation that you are often in. For example, you may focus on your listening at work, as a friend, as a spouse, as a son or a daughter, or as a parent. (Note: You may complete the instrument more than one time, with different roles and situations in mind.) As you read the series of statements below, keep the particular listening role or situation you have chosen in mind. Circle the appropriate number on your answer sheet using the following key:

Always   5

Frequently   4

Sometimes   3

Infrequently   2

Never   1

1. I focus my attention on the other person's feelings when listening to them.   5 4 3 2 1
2. When listening to others, I quickly notice if they are pleased or disappointed.   5 4 3 2 1
3. I become involved when listening to the problems of others.   5 4 3 2 1
4. I try to find common areas of interest when listening to new acquaintances.   5 4 3 2 1
5. I nod my head and/or use eye contact to show interest in what others are saying.   5 4 3 2 1
6. I am frustrated when others don't present their ideas in an orderly, efficient way.   5 4 3 2 1
7. When listening to others, I focus on any inconsistencies and/or errors in what's being said. 5 4 3 2 1
8. I jump ahead and/or finish thoughts of speakers.   5 4 3 2 1
9. I am impatient with people who ramble on during conversations.   5 4 3 2 1
10. I ask questions to help speakers get to the point more quickly.   5 4 3 2 1
11. I wait until all the facts are presented before forming judgments and opinions.   5 4 3 2 1
12. I prefer to listen to technical information.   5 4 3 2 1
13. I prefer to hear facts and evidence so I can personally evaluate them.   5 4 3 2 1
14. I like the challenge of listening to complex information.   5 4 3 2 1
15. I ask questions to probe for additional information.   5 4 3 2 1
16. When hurried, I let others know that I have a limited amount of time to listen.   5 4 3 2 1
17. I begin a discussion by telling others how long I have to meet.   5 4 3 2 1
18. I interrupt others when I feel time pressure.   5 4 3 2 1
19. I look at my watch or clocks in the room when I have limited time to listen to others. 5 4 3 2 1
20. When I feel time pressure, my ability to concentrate on what others are saying suffers. 5 4 3 2 1

Scoring Instructions:

Tally the number of times you circled 4 or 5 for statements 1–5:
   People-oriented = _____
Tally the number of times you circled 4 or 5 for statements 6–10:
   Action-oriented = _____
Tally the number of times you circled 4 or 5 for statements 11–15:
   Content-oriented = _____
Tally the number of times you circled 4 or 5 for statements 16–20:
   Time-oriented = _____

You now have four scores, one for each of the four listener preferences: People, Action, Content, and Time. Now identify the types of listening preferences for which you have the highest scores. These scores say a lot about your preferred style of listening.
   To interpret your scores, use the following guidelines:

1. Preference strength is indicated by the number of scores in each of the listening preference types.

4 and 5 responses	high preference
3 responses	moderate preference
2 and 1 responses	low preference
0 responses	no preference

2. High scores (4 or 5) in two or more types suggest multiple listening preferences.
3. Zero scores in all the types suggest potential listening avoidance.

Source: www.innolectc.com

Individuals who demonstrate the time-oriented listening style need to be aware of the following challenges: being impatient with individuals whom they perceive as wasting time, interrupting others when they are speaking, letting time constraints affect their ability to concentrate, forcing other individuals to adhere to tight time limits, and rushing others to make any comments quickly.

Action-Oriented Listening Style. The task at hand and the goal that needs to be accomplished are the focus of the **action-oriented listening style**.[30] Action-oriented listeners look for organized, focused, and clear messages when communicating with others. Action-oriented listeners may get impatient when speakers go on tangents or fail to get to the point in a reasonable manner. These individuals would prefer to work from an outline and like to see a logical connection between ideas. Action-oriented listeners also tend to be good at identifying errors or inconsistencies in messages.

Individuals who demonstrate the action-oriented listening style need to be careful of the following tendencies: becoming impatient with speakers who ramble, jumping ahead to reach conclusions in advance of the speaker, getting distracted when speakers are unorganized, being overly critical of speakers, and underestimating emotional issues or concerns.

Content-Oriented Listening Style. The desire to look for details and to analyze problems or situations is highlighted in the **content-oriented listening style**.[31] Content-

What type of listening style do you think the student should be demonstrating? What about the instructor?

oriented listeners evaluate the quality of the message for clarity, accuracy, and understanding. Content-oriented listeners regularly strive to increase their knowledge base with additional objective information. Therefore, it would not be uncommon for content-oriented listeners to ask other people to expand on their ideas and to provide additional specifics when available, especially if the listener is processing complex information.[32] Content-oriented listeners also tend to stay calm and composed, even though others may be verbally aggressive to them, calling them names or making other personal attacks.[33] Content-oriented listeners would be excellent individuals to have if you ever needed to engage in an intellectual debate with someone on an issue or needed someone to do high-level problem solving.

Individuals who demonstrate content-oriented listening styles need to be careful of displaying the following behaviors: overemphasizing details, becoming intimidating when asking extremely direct questions, marginalizing information that is not of a technical nature, undervaluing information that comes from unknown sources, or requiring extended amounts of time to make decisions.

Understanding Your Listening Style Preference. Identifying your listening style preferences is an important step in understanding how you listen to and interact with others. But you also need to consider factors related to the person with whom you are speaking. Here are some recommendations for how to understand and apply what you are learning about your listening style:

- *Listening styles tend to vary on the basis of context, and some individuals may demonstrate co-listening style preferences.* Interestingly, even though it could be in our best interest to modify or adapt our listening styles to the context, we may not be very willing or receptive to changing.[34]

- *Your ability to maximize what your listening style has to offer is going to be contingent upon the communication style and needs of the other person.* If the person you are speaking to likes to share stories and you happen to be a people-oriented listener, your communication exchanges are likely to be more enjoyable than they would be if you had a time-oriented listening style.

- *Having different listening tendencies from your partner's doesn't make one of you the better communicator.* There is no listening style that is effective all the time with everyone.

- *There may be cultural preferences for certain listening styles.* If one culture reinforces the value of time-oriented listening while another culture encourages people-oriented listening, individuals in those cultures may have the tendency to judge or devalue the listening behaviors of others if it is different from their own.

WHAT CAN I do now?

▶ *You might want to assess whether you experiencing difficulties listening to some- one because of who the person is or because he or she seems to ramble on and on and never get to the point.* If you tune someone out because you don't like the person, that is a different issue than if you simply get frustrated because he or she has a hard time discussing specific issues.

▶ *You might want to reflect on how you can maximize the strengths of your listening style preference.* You may be able to provide important contributions to both your personal and professional relationships if you can take what your listen- ing style has to offer and use that toward accomplishing short- and long-term relational and professional goals.

▶ *Remember that you need to exert energy when demonstrating any of the listening preferences.* Although you may have listening tendencies, this does not mean that you will always demonstrate these behaviors consistently if you do not give every listening opportunity the time and effort necessary to be effective.

Enhancing Your Listening Goals

We listen for a variety of reasons. Our objectives may be very practical; we need to ac- complish some sort of goal. In that case, our listening intentions are very task-driven. We might also listen for relational reasons. We want to get to know someone better, or we care about what the other person may be experiencing. We will briefly discuss four particular reasons for listening. Then we will examine how our reasons for listening may interact with our listening styles.

Listening to Understand. When you **listen to understand**, you try to comprehend the content of someone's message.[35] This is needed if you are going to alter, retain, recall, or use the material shared by the speaker at a later time. It is common to listen for under- standing in numerous environments, such as class lectures, departmental meetings, or conversations. The primary focus tends to be on understanding content, with a sec- ondary emphasis on acquiring relational understanding.

Two listening styles may lend themselves very nicely to the objectives of listening to understand: action-oriented listening and content-oriented listening. Both styles focus on information shared by the speaker. The action-oriented listening style focuses on process- ing clear, organized messages in order to identify inconsistencies in speakers' messages to aid in processing and recalling what was said. The content-oriented listening style would also have the goal of listening to understand, since content listeners want to learn as much as possible about a subject. In both instances, people with action- and content-oriented lis- tening styles would be likely to select their reason for listening as the need to understand.

Listening to Evaluate. When you **listen to evaluate**, you are listening in an attempt to critically process what someone is saying.[36] When this is your goal or objective, you are going to look for patterns as well as inconsistencies in an attempt to assess the merits, value, or underlying intent of a message. Therefore, it would not be uncommon if listen- ers also examined speakers' verbal and nonverbal messages to identify any inconsisten- cies between what someone is saying and how the person is conveying that information.

When someone is hurt or disappointed, how we listen or respond may make the situation better—or worse.

Several listening styles stand out when you are listening to evaluate: action-oriented listening, content-oriented listening, and people-oriented listening. The action-oriented listening style is all about evaluating the content of messages. Although action-oriented listeners might not initially come in attempting to evaluate someone's message, it is the natural tendency of this listening style. People with the content-oriented listening style may also be inclined to listen to evaluate content, but they do so to establish a thorough knowledge base in an effort to sort out what to believe and what to ignore. Interestingly, someone with the people-oriented listening style might also engage in listening to evaluate when attempting to help others. In this case, people-oriented listeners may help others to find inconsistencies in their messages to help them uncover information that might not initially be apparent to them, especially if people-oriented listeners are trying to help others solve problems.

Listening to Build and Maintain Relationships. If your intent is to get to know another person or continue an already established relationship, it is imperative that you **listen to build and maintain relationships**. Most people are not likely to reveal great amounts of information, much less intimate information, if they think that others are not listening to what they have to say. When this occurs, most likely they will stop talking (although some people notice these signs sooner than others).

The people-oriented listening style is most closely related to this listening rationale.[37] When people-oriented listeners are successful at this, others are also more likely to open up more and feel a closer connection to the listener. Time-oriented listeners may have difficulty adjusting to this listening objective because it can not always be accomplished in preestablished blocks of time.

Listening to Help Others. When you **listen to help others** you hope to give others some form of assistance.[38] Listening to help others could serve a therapeutic function when someone needs help or guidance. There are numerous professions, ranging from therapists, medical professionals, and clergy to teachers, law enforcement officials, and managers that are firmly integrated in what would be called helping professions.

Two listening styles are likely to be used extensively for this listening objective: people-oriented listening and content-oriented listening. People-oriented listeners want to understand where others are coming from and how they can help others to overcome their problems. As a result, one of the bigger issues for people-oriented listeners might be emotional contagion. People-oriented listeners are likely to hear about all the problems others are facing, and it may become difficult for people-oriented listeners to separate the emotional elements of their professions from their personal lives. The content-oriented listening style could also work well for this listening objective, since it is important to be receptive to additional amounts of information when trying to help others; many problems have multiple layers and are not easily or quickly identified with limited knowledge.

Exploring Personality, Sex, and Listening Preference Differences

The relationship between personality, sex, and listening preferences tends to draw a great deal of interest as we try to understand why people's listening tendencies vary. Here, we review each area to examine the degree to which personality and sex differences play in the use of our listening styles.

Listening Styles and Personality Traits. Listening scholars have identified relationships between someone's listening style and two of the personality traits discussed in Chapter 1: extraversion and neuroticism. Here are some of their findings on personality traits and listening styles:

■ *People who report extraversion as their dominant personality trait are perceived by others as open, friendly, and receptive listeners, willing to offer support to others.* These individuals would be more likely to demonstrate either the people-oriented or content-oriented listening style, since people with these two listening styles tend to be both confident and patient when listening to others.[39]

■ *People who report neuroticism as their dominant personality trait are more likely to be perceived as acting indifferent when listening to others.* These individuals might end up becoming frustrated or impatient when listening to others and might want to control the interaction.[40]

■ *Three different listening styles—action, time, and content—are associated with high levels of neuroticism.* This suggests that when neuroticism is a dominant personality trait, there may be some sort of defense mechanism that kicks in with many of the listening styles in an attempt to manage conceivable threats by others during interactions.[41]

Listening Style Preferences and Sex Differences. There seems to be some confusion surrounding whether or not individuals listen differently if they are males or females. Although some people believe that males and females listen differently from one another,[42] research findings investigating the relationship between biological sex and listening style preferences paint a more complicated picture. If you take into account only someone's biological sex, there are some patterns that emerge with various listening styles:

■ Females report having higher people-oriented listening style scores than males.

■ Males report having higher content-, action-, and time-oriented listening scores than females.

These findings reinforce stereotypes that suggest that females are more likely to be kind, caring, and compassionate listeners, while males are more likely to be listening for specific information in an organized, timely fashion.[43]

However, someone's gender role orientation (e.g., whether he or she is masculine, feminine, or androgynous in approach) may be a more revealing indicator of someone's listening style than biological sex is.[44]

■ When individuals focus on other people and their relationships (e.g., a more feminine approach) by being open, kind, compassionate, and caring toward others, they are also more likely to utilize the people-oriented listening style.

■ When individuals focus on themselves and are more independent in their relationships (e.g., a more masculine approach) by demonstrating assertiveness, goal-setting, and the desire to master or control things, they are more likely to utilize the content-, action-, or time-oriented listening styles.

■ How individuals approach their interactions with others is more important than whether they are male or female.

One of the more unusual findings pertained to the people-oriented listening style. Individuals reporting high levels of femininity *or* high levels of masculinity were more likely to report using the people-oriented listening style. These findings suggest that "a people-oriented style of listening is not primarily a 'touchy-feely' matter of attending just to how other people feel. People-orientation in listening also seems to focus on getting things done at the same time, hence the association with masculinity."[45] As a result, your listening style may have more to do with behavioral tendencies than with whether you are male or female.

CHECKING YOUR UNDERSTANDING

Assessing Personality and Listening Preferences

Before reading further, take a few minutes to assess your learning by writing your answers to the following items:

1. What are the four listening style preferences? What does each listening style preference focus on? What are some things to be mindful of with each listening preference?

2. Four listening goals were highlighted. What is each of these goals, and why would someone select a particular goal when listening?

3. How are personality traits and listening style preferences related? What are some of the specific findings that have been reported?

4. What are some of the sex differences that have been noted in examining listening style preferences? What are some of the gender differences that have been noted?

Identifying Listening Barriers

Although we are not intentionally poor listeners, there are numerous listening barriers we can encounter. Some barriers may be widespread in your interactions with others; others may pop up only with a particular person and under particular circumstances. Regardless, listening challenges abound when we interact with others.

Listening Barriers Associated with Information Processing

Information-processing listening barriers are those things that are centered within ourselves that affect our ability to process messages effectively when we receive them. Here, we highlight six information-processing barriers.

Preoccupation. When we demonstrate **preoccupation**, we are focused on things other than the person we are listening to. Types of preoccupation can range from thinking about things you need to do later in the day, other thoughts or ideas that have your attention, to simply wanting to be somewhere other than where you are. If you have ever heard a person say that he is thinking about something else, this individual might be demonstrating preoccupation. Another indicator of preoccupation may be when someone asks you to repeat yourself several different times during the same conversation.

Multitasking/Shifting Attention. When we **multitask**, we shift our attention from one task to another in an effort to do several tasks at once. The challenge with multitasking and listening is that multitasking forces us to make a choice: What do we pay more attention to? Unfortunately, most of us have been accused by others of selecting a task over the individual who is trying to talk to us. When this occurs, we often have to stop multitasking completely and focus solely on the task of listening to the other person, especially if this individual is important to us. Failure to do so is often problematic for close relationships.

Multitasking-related listening difficulties often occur when we try to manage communication exchanges that are occurring simultaneously via multiple channels. For example, suppose that you are sending one person an email while holding a telephone conversation with someone else. Many people get irritated if they hear you typing on your computer keyboard when they are talking to you on the telephone, since they may feel that you should be giving them your undivided attention. It's almost an unwritten rule: If you are going to multitask and try to listen to others, do so only if the other task does not interfere with the ability to listen to another person. Furthermore, do so quietly so that the other person will not be led to believe that you are not giving her or him your undivided attention.

Pseudolistening. Sometimes we like to give the impression that we are listening to someone when in reality we are not. **Pseudolistening** is pretending to listen to someone; essentially, it is fake listening. There may be times when you really don't want to listen to someone but you don't want to admit it. For example, your friend might be talking about a topic that you care nothing about (e.g., why a contestant on a reality show was asked to leave), so you pretend to listen to what your friend is saying while you think about other things. Other times, our tendency to demonstrate pseudolistening is affected by other listening barriers that are occurring at the same time. For example, if you are thinking about an exam that you have the next day (e.g., preoccupation) and you are trying to get ready to go to work while grabbing something quick to eat (e.g., multitasking), you might try to give the impression that you are listening by making a few head nods of agreement or inserting a few "uh huhs" to keep the conversation going.

It is not very difficult to detect when someone is pseudolistening. Simply look for indicators in how the person communicates and responds to your comments. If someone regularly asks you to repeat yourself or makes comments or responses that are unrelated to the conversation you are having, he or she is probably not fully listening to what you have to say.

Information Overload. When we are bombarded with an excessive number of messages that we consider to be relevant or important, we are most likely experiencing **information overload**. The amount of time and energy needed to process such large quantities of material tends to overwhelm us, and our ability to make sound decisions decreases. In some instances, you might simply shut down and be unable to process anything for the time being. During listening, information overload tends to flood the brain's ability to discriminate what messages to process in what order. As a result, we are more likely to confuse, combine, and misinterpret information that we are trying to understand.

Physiological Distractions. Although we might not consciously focus on messages our body sends to us when interacting with others, these important indicators can influence how well we listen to others.[46] Examples of **physiological distractions** include, but are not limited to, tiredness, fatigue, headaches, hunger, and illness. Simply put, when our bodies are focused on maintaining our basic functioning capacities, secondary functions, such as listening processes, tend to be less effective. As a result, the popular advice about getting a good night's sleep, eating breakfast, and exercising regularly is likely not only to improve your physical health, but also to make you more likely to be an effective listener.

Sometimes we take advantage of the listening gaps that occur when learning, but not always.

Listening Gap. The **listening gap** refers to the time lag that is present when we compare the time it takes to process a message to the maximum potential we have to process inputs.[47] When we listen to others, our brain tends to have a lot of extra "free time" to do other things. In fact, the ratio tends to be around 4:1 or 5:1 in terms of the amount of energy it takes to process a verbal message, compared to the overall amount of brain potential at our disposal at any given time. Therefore, the choices we make regarding how to manage this extra time (e.g., refocus our efforts to listen more critically or thoroughly or daydream until the next interesting piece of information is shared) are important.

As you can see, some listening problems could easily work in combination with one another. For example, we could be both preoccupied and multitasking at the same time. In fact, we may be preoccupied with a task on which we are not actually working at that time. Furthermore, we could be experiencing physiological distractions (e.g., weariness, hunger, illness), compounding the possibility that information-processing barriers are going to negatively influence our ability to listen to someone else.

Listening Barriers Associated with Context Issues

Overcoming context barriers may be a little more challenging, since context barriers are factors outside ourselves over which we often have limited or no control.[48] Many people tend to think of context barriers as environmental barriers that could negatively affect listening. This is not an unreasonable way to think about context barriers. Four context barriers are as follows.

External Noise. **External noise** is any type of interference that occurs outside of the individual's body. Most people think of the sounds that are occurring all around them when they are at home, at work, in their cars, or in public places, such as restaurants. As you know, there are some really loud (and sometimes obnoxious) sounds that can significantly limit our abilities to listen to others, such as pneumatic drills breaking up concrete, vehicle horns being blown continuously during rush hour, or fans shouting during a sporting event.

NATURE/NURTURE intersections

Bring on the Noise?

Noise is typically considered a distraction or nuisance when we are trying to listen to others.[49] In fact, we are often asked to turn down, mute, or shut off whatever device is creating too much noise when others are trying to talk to us. For the majority of us, this strategy is a good one, since these external sounds tend to distract and detract from our ability to process more important messages. However, certain types of noise in moderate amounts can actually help some people to listen better.

Individuals who have attention deficit hyperactivity disorder (ADHD) often have difficulty paying attention and get easily distracted. However, researchers are learning that stochastic resonance (SR), the phenomenon that suggests that moderate noise levels enhance thought processes, may help to explain why some types of noise inducement help those who have ADHD improve their thought processes.[50] In short, participants with low levels of dopamine (a type of neurotransmitter) in their bloodstream, such as individuals who have ADHD, need higher levels of noise in their environments to induce SR, which in turn arouses brain functions and works to improve cognitive thought processes.

People who do not have ADHD already have higher amounts of dopamine in their bloodstreams; therefore, they do not need the help of external noises to modify their brain functions. But we're not just talking about any type of noise. These researchers used "white noise," which is an audio signal that contains sounds at the same level at all frequencies. It is possible to buy white noise machines. In fact, people often purchase these products to mask or limit distracting noises in their environments.

As we learn more about how the brain functions in order to more productively listen and process information, we will be better able to make the decisions about what type of noise, if any, will influence our interactions with others.

Lack of Training. This is actually a tougher barrier to overcome than it might initially seem. Many people believe that listening is a skill that should just come naturally when we speak to others. Unfortunately, we tend to have a **lack of training** in listening—if any at all, for that matter. Since listening is a skill set that is learned, training could be one way to develop or enhance individuals' listening skills.[51]

Listening training is becoming very common in the medical professions. This training may be implemented to improve doctor–patient, nurse–patient, and doctor–nurse communication. Effective listening skills are needed in order to properly diagnose an illness, treat an illness, and maintain successful communication exchanges among all interested parties.[52] Stronger listening skills can also help to reduce the number of medical errors that occur as the result of misinterpreting medical problems or inaccurately comprehending messages that are shared between parties.

Mode/Channel of Communication Used. Sometimes it's not the sender or the sender's message that creates the listening challenge, but the **channels of communication** that the senders and receivers utilize when communicating with one another. Face-to-face communication provides senders and receivers with the greatest number of verbal and nonverbal cues. Thus, face-to-face communication tends to be the preferred channel for interpersonal communication. Unfortunately, face-to-face communication is not always practical or possible. As a result, we continually incorporate new technologies to facilitate our interactions with others. In turn, our communication technology choices may change our listening behaviors.[53]

It is a good idea to be aware of the pros and cons of any communication channel when you are attempting to listen to others. In some instances, you might want to consciously control what channel you choose in an effort to enhance the listening skills of the person you wish to speak to. But if this can't be done or simply isn't very practical, you might want to think about what you want to say and how you want to say it if you think the person's ability to interpret and understand what you are saying may be compromised.

Age and Cultural Factors. As we get older, we sometimes forget that our bodies' sensory systems have aged as well and might not work as effectively as they did when we were younger. Breakdowns in two sensory systems in particular—vision and hearing—become especially important in our ability to listen well to others. It is not uncommon to see people getting hearing aids or wearing glasses with stronger prescriptions or thicker lenses. It is well documented that these vision and hearing issues become more problematic in noisy environments, when there are multiple talkers, when individuals are speaking fast, and when a lot of information is being exchanged.[54] Scholars have also been working on exploring adjustments that our brains make when there are failures in processing auditory inputs.[55]

Some recommended strategies can enhance listening when we are interacting with older individuals.[56] Many points could actually improve anyone's listening, regardless of age. For instance, as we get older, it becomes more difficult to ignore irrelevant or excessive information in a conversation. Therefore, some suggestions include trying to eliminate any excess noise and keeping conversations focused on a limited number of issues before changing topics. Other ideas include talking at a slightly slower rate to allow time for more thought and reflection and taking more time to listen. Perhaps one of our biggest challenges in trying to improve our listening skills is not that we don't want to listen well, but that we want to listen on the basis of the demands of our schedule rather than on the needs of the speaker.

One of the more difficult listening barriers revolves around the role of culture. Researchers have studied the influence of ethnicity on listening predispositions and other communication behaviors.[57] They noted some underlying dynamics affecting how different cultural groups perceive one another's communication skills. In short, the expectations that we have for ourselves as well as for people in other ethnic groups play a significant role in how we perceive actual communication behaviors. It does not appear that one ethnic group listens better than another. Rather, different ethnic groups may communicate and listen differently. "What must be kept in mind is what one perceives as characteristics of a 'good listener' or a 'good communicator' is often determined by subtle, yet powerful influences and rules in one's own ethnic culture."[58]

If you have ever tried to learn a second language, you know that this cannot be accomplished overnight. To complicate matters, not a great deal is known about the role listening plays in developing new language skill sets.[59] Part of the problem is that if you haven't developed a sufficient vocabulary in the new language, your ability to comprehend what others are saying may be limited. This could be especially problematic if you were studying abroad in a country where the language spoken was fairly novel to you and there was a great deal of speaking and listening required of you.[60] To help second language learners, scholars are encouraging instructors to incorporate visual messages to help aid the learners' listening efforts.[61]

Scholars also recommend that instructors incorporate gestures and facial cues when speaking to help reinforce the content of their messages.[62] Although facial cues are not universal and could pose some unforeseen listening barriers for some listeners, watching someone's lips and facial expressions can provide additional information in

It doesn't matter what your age is, everyone wants and deserves to be listened to.

listening to a language that is relatively new. Seeing someone's hand gestures when the person is talking can be even more helpful for focusing attention on the content that is being shared to complete a given task. These could be good ideas for speakers and listeners to apply when communicating in any language.

CHECKING YOUR UNDERSTANDING
Identifying Listening Barriers

Before reading further, take a few minutes to assess your learning by writing your answers to the following items:

1. Five information-processing barriers were mentioned that often occur during listening. Define each of these information-processing barriers, and provide an example of each.
2. Describe what receiver apprehension is and how it influences listening.
3. Four context barriers to listening were discussed. What are the four context barriers, and how does each affect your ability to listen to others?

Improving Listening and Responding Skills

Regardless of your listening preferences or the listening barriers you struggle with, there are things you can do to improve your listening and responding skills. In some respects, the quality of your responses shape people's perceptions of how well you were actually listening.[63] All of these strategies may help you enhance your listening skills with friends, family members, significant others, or coworkers.

Strategies When Listening and Responding to Others

There are specific things you can do to help you effectively listen and respond to others. Although some of these strategies seem obvious or straightforward, you might find the discussion helpful.

Talk Less. Talking less means spending more time listening or receiving messages from someone else than speaking.[64] This allows someone else to contribute to the conversation, thereby creating a dialogue rather than a monologue. In addition, even though you may be refraining from offering verbal messages to the speaker, you can still use nonverbal cues to let the speaker know that you are being attentive to what is being said.

In some instances, talking less is not a problem, since you weren't given much of a chance to say anything in the first place. You might sometimes have felt this way as a child when you were told to keep quiet or that your opinion didn't really matter anyway. When you got older, you might have experienced this in the classroom, when a professor was in the midst of a class lecture, or when your boss called you into the office for a "talk" that really entailed your boss talking and you listening. In these examples, you were probably the one hoping that your parents, the professor, or your boss would be the one who would talk less. There is an adage that states, "Know when to say when." This definitely applies when it comes to listening and responding.

Stay Focused. Staying focused by ignoring outside distractions is a helpful strategy when you want to listen to others.[65] Some of these include, but are not limited to, having background noise such as the television on in the background, individuals doing things that grab your attention, being tired or hungry, or being preoccupied with other things. You might or might not be conscious of things that distract you when you are listening to others. But perhaps the issue is not that you could get distracted when listening or responding to someone, but rather what you do when these distractions are present when you are trying to listen to someone. If you are at least aware that you are being distracted, you can work to address these more obvious cues so that you increase your likelihood of giving the person you are speaking to your (mostly) undivided attention. I've found that I have to turn off the television set when I want to talk to someone, since even irritating commercials on the screen can sidetrack me if I'm not careful.

Paraphrase. Rephrasing or restating what the speaker has said to ensure that you, as a listener, have correctly comprehended what was said is called **paraphrasing**. By paraphrasing, you get a sense of whether or not you really understand what the speaker is trying to say. Sometimes you are correct; at other times, you may be way off base. The focus isn't necessarily on accuracy, although that is always a bonus and the ultimate goal. Rather, did you misunderstand what the person was trying to say? If so, where? Another way to think about paraphrasing is to consider paraphrasing as a type of GPS system reality check. Are you on the right path to comprehending what the person was trying to share, or did you turn left somewhere when you should have turned right? As a result, you might also learn whether you need to be seeking more information, providing support, or offering some type of opinion or guidance to the speaker based on how you have restated what had been shared.

However, restating every thought as soon as someone has shared it tends to irritate the person with whom you were having the conversation. Since the goal is to enhance your understanding of what the person is trying to say, you want to make sure that a sufficient amount of information was shared before you attempt to restate what the person said. Therefore, when paraphrasing, a good strategy is to rephrase what someone said after you feel that the person has shared a main idea or thought. A short summary is all it takes to make sure that you are on the right path to understanding what the person was saying.

Clarify Information. If you are clearly lost or confused when someone is trying to share something with you, you need to **clarify information** or get additional information to understand what was shared.[66] Sometimes we first attempt to paraphrase something, get it wrong, and then ask questions. Other times, we know that we have no idea what someone has said, and we cut to the chase: "I don't get it" or simply "Huh? You lost me." Perhaps the speaker has left out a few details, making it difficult to understand what he or she was attempting to say. If you are hesitant to actually verbalize a question, remember that your nonverbal behaviors may already be sending messages that you are confused.

Look for Key Ideas. One of our goals as listeners is to try to identify the main issues in someone's messages. What seems to be the most important pieces of their message? Sometimes **key ideas** are clearly and easily identifiable. For example, when someone shares that he or she has three things to talk to you about, you know to make sure you can identify these three points by the end of the conversation. Unfortunately, we are often not that direct when interacting with others. Furthermore, we often fall into the trap of assuming that people should just be able to determine the main ideas of our statements when we make them (even if we ourselves may not be entirely sure of our main ideas).

TABLE 6.3

Strategies When Listening and Responding to Others		
Strategy	**Description**	**Example**
Talk less	Spending more time listening, or receiving messages from someone else	Letting someone else talk about his or her day before responding with any remarks
Stay focused	Reducing the problems or barriers that could hinder someone's ability to listen to others	Turning off or muting the television screen, letting any telephone messages go to voicemail
Paraphrase	Trying to assess whether or not the listener has accurately perceived the speaker's message	"So if I heard you correctly, you were really angry when everyone showed up late?"
Clarify information	Asking a speaker for additional information or clarity	"I don't know what some of these terms mean. Could you explain them to me?"
Look for key ideas	Helping to identify the main issues in someone's messages	Listening for speakers' lists or emphasis, start counting ideas

Some helpful strategies when you are trying to determine key ideas are (1) looking for any initial indicators provided by speakers that tell you the number of main ideas they will be discussing, such as hearing them say that there are two main issues bothering them; (2) listening for any themes or topics that are being repeated, which may indicate that this topic is important to the speaker; (3) watching for any nonverbal messages that may give clues as to what is important to the speaker; or (4) in some setting, such as the classroom or during presentations, noticing that the teacher or presenter restates the key ideas at the end of the message, making it easier to determine whether you had identified the same ideas earlier in their presentation or not. Ideally, it is great if you can then share what you believe the key ideas were with the person, but sometimes this is not possible. (See Table 6.3 for a summary of these strategies.)

Strategies for Helping Others to Listen and Respond to You

Sometimes we forget that the things we look for when listening to others are the exact same things that others look for when listening to us. Therefore, if we incorporate strategies to help us develop what we want to say and how we want to say it, we can make it easier for others not only to listen to our messages, but also to understand and remember what we said.

Provide New Information. Most of us are not very patient with people who always seem to say the same thing whenever they talk about a particular subject. We need to remember that **providing new information** is more likely to keep others' attention, thus increasing their likelihood of continuing to listen to us.[67] Granted, this means that we need to have something new to share with others. But whenever we can add new content to what we are sharing about a topic, we are more likely to draw others in. When we fail to do this, others will tend to tune us out over time, diverting their listening energy to other stimuli around them.

Remove or Limit Distractions for Potential Listeners. If individuals who are listening to us are getting distracted by other stimuli, one of the best things to do is to try to **remove or limit distractions for potential listeners.**[68] For example, if the people you want to listen to you tend to look over your shoulder to watch what is on television, it could be a good idea to turn the television off, at least during your conversation. Then you won't have to compete with the television set for their listening attention.

Sometimes we may be our own distraction, especially if we are wearing something that stands out or have some sort of artifact, such as a body piercing or tattoo, that diverts attention to that artifact and away from our comments. If this is the case, then we may want to do what we can to reduce the impact of this artifact, perhaps by either covering it up or removing it for a particular time. Keep in mind that if your primary goal is to be listened to by others, you might have to make a few concessions along the way for your overall goal to be accomplished.

Acknowledge Contextual Limitations. Sometimes the environment is just not conducive to listening successfully in a conversation because of distractions present. If you are able to **acknowledge contextual limitations** in advance, you might want to hold particular conversations in preferred settings. Worst-case scenarios might require you to postpone having conversations in environments where you know it will be difficult for others to be able to listen to you. For example, it is often difficult to hold a conversation in a crowded elevator, but sometimes we forget this and do it anyway.

A different type of contextual barrier worth remembering is whether or not others have the time or sufficient energy to listening to you at that particular moment. Even if you are not ill, tired, hungry, or working to meet a deadline, your listeners could be. If your goal is to have others successfully listen to what you are trying to tell them, then you should look for any signs others are sending that may suggest that they are not at their full potential to listen to your messages. This can be easily addressed by asking people whether this is a good time for you to talk to them. If it is, you are much more likely to be listened to by the other person; if it is not, it is in your best interest to schedule another time to talk to this person.

Provide a Clear, Organized Message. If we don't know what it is that we want to convey to others, we make it difficult for others to be able to successfully listen to us, much less retain the key ideas of our messages. In professional or presentational contexts, the importance of **providing a clear, organized message** is fairly straightforward and easily understood if perhaps sometimes difficult to accomplish. As a speaker, you determine the number of main ideas you would like to share, so keep them within reasonable parameters for your audience members to listen to and retain. In addition, make sure you include transitions between ideas and restate your main ideas at the conclusion of your message. If this sounds a lot like giving a speech, that is correct. In fact, we can extend our understanding of public speaking and message organization to reap the benefits when we interact with others. More important, make it simpler for others to listen to, understand, and perhaps apply our message.[69]

TABLE 6.4

Strategies When Helping Others Listen and Respond to You		
Strategy	**Description**	**Example**
Provide new information	Sharing unknown, relevant, and important information in an effort to attract or keep others' attention, thus increasing their likelihood of listening to you	Inserting current events, discussing content that might not be readily available to others
Remove or limit distractions for potential listeners	Reducing the problems or barriers that could hinder someone's ability to listen to you	Shutting down or reducing access to electronic devices, such as cell phones or computers
Acknowledge contextual limitations	Acknowledging the role the environment or other outside factors may play in the listening process	Staying away from high-traffic areas or avoiding times when others are working to meet a deadline
Provide a clear, organized message	Offering a straightforward and easily understood message	Sharing focused, structured information that is easy to follow

Although it is not difficult to make the connections between speaking and professional communication applications, most of us don't think to apply these same concepts when we talk to friends, family members, or significant others. If we could take some of these basic strategies, such as providing a clear, well-organized message, and apply them when we interact with others in interpersonal settings, we would probably increase the likelihood that others will successfully listen to and process the things that we say to them. (See Table 6.4 for a summary of these strategies.)

 ## CHECKING YOUR UNDERSTANDING

Improving Listening and Responding Skills

Before completing the chapter, take a few minutes to assess your learning by writing your answers to the following items:

1. List the seven different listening responses mentioned, and provide a description and example for each.

2. What are five strategies you could use when listening and responding to others? When would you use each strategy?

3. What are four things you could do if you wanted to make it easier for others to listen and respond to your messages? When would you be most likely to incorporate each strategy?

A Communication Development Plan for Helen

To complete Helen's story, recall that she was upset with her husband, Mark. Helen was trying to make holiday travel plans, but Mark seemed to be more interested in watching the football game. Even though Helen felt that Mark had not been listening to her, Mark's response did address her questions. But Helen still felt that Mark did not understand her concerns, much less the fact that she was frustrated with their conversation.

What do you think?

Was Mark really listening to Helen? What were some of the listening barriers that were getting in the way during this conversation? Should Helen have approached the conversation differently as a result?

Possible explanations:

There are several listening challenges embedded in Helen and Mark's exchange. Helen might want or need Mark to engage in a different listening style when talking to her than he currently applies. When this didn't happen in this conversation, it led to frustration for Helen as well as Mark, since he doesn't seem to think that his listening behaviors were problematic.

Was Mark really listening to what Helen was trying to say to him about the upcoming holiday? At the most basic level, you could argue that Mark did comprehend the basics of Helen's message. The problem was that Mark focused on the specifics of Helen's remarks and missed the emotional uncertainty Helen was feeling.

What types of listening barriers did Helen encounter in this conversation? Numerous listening barriers were present in this scenario, some of which may be more problematic than others. Some of these barriers included preoccupation, multitasking/shifting attention, and external noise. In addition, Helen perceived that Mark had been pseudolistening to her.

Here is some additional advice for Helen and Mark.

1. *Feel free to reduce the number of distractions in the environment.* For example, it would not have been unreasonable if Helen asked to turn off the television or at least mute the sound when she starting talking to Mark. However, it might have been easier for Helen to talk about family travel plans when Mark was not engaged in other activities.

2. *There is nothing wrong with focusing on the facts when listening to others; however, effective listening is not always about providing neutral, objective responses.* It is common for partners to seek out one another's opinions on things, although this type of request is often not openly shared. As a result, there would have been nothing wrong in Mark's asking Helen to clarify how he could help her address the holiday travel concerns.

3. *If possible, try to be mindful of others' listening style tendencies, especially if they are different from your own.* In this case, Helen wanted Mark to demonstrate the people-oriented listening style, while Mark actually demonstrated more of an action- or time-oriented listening style. This can be a challenging problem to overcome, since it is not easy to shift gears to accommodate others' listening needs. However, it is reasonable to share the type of feedback that you desire. Although this is not likely to change someone's listening style, it may be possible for others to adapt a few different listening strategies on occasion.

Take Aways

Listening and responding to others are essential skills in our interactions with virtually everyone we come into contact with. This chapter focused on understanding the listening process, assessing listening preferences, identifying listening barriers, and concluding with strategies for responding to others and helping others listen to what you have to say. The following lists summarize what you have learned in this chapter.

You have increased your understanding and knowledge of the following:

- How verbal and nonverbal messages affect listening.

- How listening styles and your reasons for listening may influence listening behaviors when interacting with others.

- The challenges of information-processing and context barriers and how to apply this knowledge to your own listening behaviors.

- The options people have when providing listening responses to others.

In addition, you are also better able to do the following:

- Explain the relationship between hearing and listening.

- Incorporate listening strategies that could be used to make you a better listener.

- Implement listening strategies that could be used to make you someone who is more likely to be listened to by others.

- Overcome numerous listening barriers that you experience in your interpersonal relationships.

- Understand what your listening preference is and how this affects your communication with others.

Discussion Questions

1. How do verbal and nonverbal messages influence what occurs during the five stages of listening?

2. What are the main characteristics of the four listening styles, and what are some issues that you should be aware of for each listening style?

3. What role does biological sex or gender role orientation play in examining listening styles and personality traits?

4. What are some strategies that could make you a better listener as well as someone who is more likely to be listened to? Which of these strategies are you most likely to use in the future? Why?

Building Your Skills

1. Complete the listening preference profile. Have someone with whom you interact often do the same. How well do your listening style assessments reflect how the two of you listen to one another? Were you surprised by the results, or did they reinforce how you believed that you listen to one another?

2. Keep a log of your conversations for five days. In this log, include whom you spoke to, what your relationship is to this person (e.g., friend, significant other, parent, boss), and when you encountered a listening barrier. At the end of the five days, examine your log to see whether there are any patterns. Is there a particular person (or people) to whom you have a hard time listening? What is your relationship with this person(s)? Were there any patterns that emerged in regards to the listening barriers you exhibited?

3. What are some behaviors that you will continue to demonstrate when you listen to others? What are some behaviors that you will change? Why? On a scale of 1 to 5 (1 being easy and 5 being difficult), how hard do you think it will be for you to consistently apply these changes when you listen to others?

7 Emotions and Communication

Dr. Dasari's Story . . .

Staci sits nervously in the waiting room at Dr. Dasari's office. She has been feeling drained of energy lately and is anxiously awaiting the results of some tests. After what seems like an eternity, she is called into another room. Dr. Dasari enters quickly and motions for Staci to sit. Dr. Dasari glances at Staci's chart while mumbling to herself. Staci is visibly upset, but Dr. Dasari doesn't seem to notice. She seems detached from what is going on around her. After a minute, the doctor looks up from her chart and directly into Staci's eye. Dr. Dasari tells Staci that she has been diagnosed with type 2 diabetes.

The weight of the diagnosis comes crashing down on Staci, who has a hard time focusing as the doctor outlines some new dietary restrictions and discusses the possibility of insulin shots. Staci feels lost and desperate. How will this affect her children, her family? Will she live to see her grandchildren? Staci desperately wants the doctor to help her understand that this disease is manageable, but all she hears is Dr. Dasari's rather curt explanation of the process of checking her blood sugar every day.

Dr. Dasari lacks empathy skills. She does not notice how Staci is dealing with the emotional weight of her diagnosis. Dr. Dasari has seen this type of patient reaction before and is not always in tune with how her patients are feeling. Staci's voice shakes as she finally asks the doctor, "How will this affect my family? My lifestyle?" The doctor is already on her feet and moving toward the door. She stops and pats Staci on the back as she responds, "Don't you worry about that right now. The nurse will be in to answer any questions." Then Dr. Dasari abruptly leaves the room.

Feeling alone and frustrated, Staci fights back tears as the nurse enters to go over her visit. As Staci walks to her car, she is upset with the doctor, but she doesn't really understand why. Dr. Dasari is just doing her job, she tells herself. She can't care about every single sick person who walks into her office.

What do you think? While reading this chapter, consider how you might answer the following questions to help Dr. Dasari and Staci:

CHAPTER OBJECTIVES

AFTER READING THIS CHAPTER, you will understand:

1 The nature of emotions by distinguishing between an emotion and a feeling.

2 How the limbic system, in cooperation with other parts of the brain, works to process and regulate emotion.

3 The eight types of social emotions: happiness/joy, love/affection, pride, anger, fear/anxiety, sadness/grief/depression, jealousy, and guilt/embarrassment.

4 The important functions emotions serve, such as learning and problem solving, being empathic or persuasive, and fulfilling interpersonal needs.

5 The factors that influence emotional communication, such as gender, culture, and emotional intelligence.

6 How current technology has affected the effective communication of emotion through social networking sites and text messages.

- What are some of the reasons why Staci was upset with how Dr. Dasari handled her visit?

- What could Dr. Dasari's have done to make the experience more comfortable for Staci?

- What role did emotion play in the interaction? How was the emotion managed and communicated? Did that emotion affect Staci's ability to focus on what the doctor was saying?

We will revisit Dr. Dasari's story at the end of the chapter and apply the content discussed in this chapter to develop a communication plan to help Dr. Dasari and Staci.

AFTER READING THIS CHAPTER, you will be able to:

1 Use skills to manage and communicate your emotions effectively, including identifying, understanding, and expressing them appropriately.

2 Engage in empathic communication by using active listening skills.

AFTER COMPLETING THE SELF-ASSESSMENTS, you will learn about:

1 Your and your partner's susceptibility to emotional contagion and how that affects your communication with others.

2 How your personality and emotional expressiveness influence your ability to communicate emotion effectively.

Emotion is what gives communication life, according to communication researcher Sally Planalp.[1] Emotions and communication are a part of the human experience; they're resources that fuel relationships and eventually sustain each other. When you feel emotion, you use communication to express to another person how you're feeling. And when you communicate how you're feeling, you sometimes begin to experience stronger emotions. Your emotions and how you communicate about your emotions affect relationships in different ways. For example, feeling joyful, passionate, and happy may enrich and vitalize a relationship, whereas feeling anger, disgust, and jealousy may destroy a relationship.

> Ironically, we probably know more about the rings of Saturn than the emotions we experience every day.
>
> —J. LINDSAY-HARTZ

The purpose of this chapter is to help you understand and communicate emotions in ways that will enhance your interpersonal communication. First, you will learn about the nature of emotions, including the different types and functions of emotions. Second, you will have the opportunity to assess your personality and emotions by learning more about emotional expressiveness, affective orientation, and emotional contagion. Third, you will learn how to develop emotional and empathic communication skills by learning how to interpret emotional messages, manage and communicate emotions, and express empathy. Finally, you'll examine factors that influence how you experience and communicate emotions, including sex and gender, culture, emotional intelligence, and technology.

The Nature of Emotions

Much has been written about **emotional intelligence**, which, in brief, is a person's awareness of and sensitivity to emotions and ability to manage emotions to enhance relational development.[2] Although we will discuss emotional intelligence later in the chapter, you can begin to enhance your emotional intelligence by understanding how emotions, moods, and feelings differ; the different types of emotions that are evoked from your relationships; and how emotions function in your interpersonal communication.

Understanding Emotions

An **emotion** is a mental state that unfolds as a process that includes a cause, an appraisal, physiological responses, expression, and regulation.[3] For example, you experience an emotion when your manager schedules you to work the weekend you requested off for your sister's wedding. The *cause* of your emotion is your manager and the work schedule. When you see the schedule in the break room, you immediately *appraise* or evaluate the situation as negative. Then you begin to sense *physiological* changes in your body; your heart begins to race and you feel your face turning red. Sometimes you *express* how you're feeling at the moment. You might blurt out in a loud voice, "I told him not to schedule me for that weekend!" Finally, you notice that your coworkers are looking at you, and one might even tell you, "Hey, chill," so you gain control or *regulate* your emotions and get on with your day.

According to Antonio Damasio, a leading researcher who studies emotions, a **feeling** occurs when you consciously recognize an emotion or a mood.[4] A feeling is a private recognition of your emotion. No one knows how you're feeling unless you share your feelings with others.[5] Emotional communication occurs when you share your feelings with others. Communication researcher James Dillard suggests three perspectives for examining the relationships between emotions and communication: emotion-motivated communication, emotion-manifesting communication, and emotion-inducing communication.[6]

Emotion-Motivated Communication. When you're driven to express yourself because of how you're feeling, you're using emotion-motivated communication. When you receive good news, such as getting a job or promotion, being accepted into graduate school, or learning that you're going to have a baby, you're motivated to share your joy with other people. At times, you're so motivated to express your happiness to other people that you share your good news with complete strangers. It doesn't matter who is around—you just had to tell someone.

Emotion-Manifesting Communication. When you make your feelings known or reveal them through your communication, you're using emotion-manifesting communication. Some people keep their emotions close.

Even though people mask emotions on occasion, they leak from our faces and bodies. It is clear that this man is upset even though he is trying hard to hide how he is feeling.

These people are very guarded, and it's rare to see an emotional display from them. Others reveal their feelings very easily; they're an open book for all to see. Although some people try to mask how they're feeling, their feelings can leak. There is an old saying that some people are so emotionally sensitive that they wear their feelings on their sleeves for all to see. As you learned in Chapter 5, some people don't hide their emotions well; instead, their emotions leak from their bodies, sometimes without their knowing. For example, suppose that you've just learned some devastating news about your best friend's fiancé. If you were to reveal this information, it would hurt your best friend, and the impending marriage would probably not take place. Although you try to mask your feelings, your concern and worry leak from your body in the form of nonverbal messages. Your face reveals a concerned look. Your shallow, weak voice suggests worry. Your best friend notices these subtle cues because they're not normal for you, and she asks whether anything is wrong.

Emotion-inducing Communication. When your emotional communication elicits a similar emotional response in another person, you're using emotion-inducing communication. Emotions are contagious. Do you cry easily at movies? If so, you understand how one person's emotions can elicit a similar emotional response in you. If you're not careful, you can catch other people's emotions, almost the way you might catch a cold, and they can catch yours. For example, if you're sharing your sadness over a loss of a job or a relationship, it's quite common for the other person, who was feeling happy before communicating with you, to begin feeling sad too. We will discuss this in greater detail below when we discuss the relationships between personality and emotions.

Types of Social Emotions

Although there are a number of ways to organize and talk about emotions, we like how communication researchers Peter Andersen and Laura Guerrero organize emotions.[7] They refer to them as social emotions, or emotions that are generated from interacting with others: happiness/joy, love/affection, pride, anger, fear/anxiety, sadness/grief/depression, jealousy, and guilt/embarrassment. These emotions don't occur by themselves; if they seem to, you're usually thinking about a social interaction that you've had with others. If you've seen someone laughing alone, chances are he or she is remembering a funny conversation or is planning a conversation that should be funny.

One of the reasons for discussing the eight different types of emotions is to increase your own emotional awareness. Numerous research studies have demonstrated the positive relationships between emotional awareness and relationship satisfaction.[8] Put simply, the more aware you and your relational partner are of the emotions you both experience in your relationship, the more likely you are to be satisfied in your relationship. Table 7.1 provides a brief description of these emotions. Try to identify instances in your own life when you have experienced each emotion.

NATURE/NURTURE intersections

Your Brain on Emotions

The brain plays a large role in how you experience, process, and express the emotions that are crucial to your interpersonal communication, which you are learning in this course.[9] Although a number of highly interconnected regions of the brain are responsible for emotional processing, the limbic system, which is buried deep inside the brain, is considered the emotional center of the brain.[10] Figure 7.1 illustrates the brain's Limbic system.

The emotional system is a set of brain structures that is responsible for processing pleasure and pain.[11] At its most fundamental level, the emotional system is similar to a set of light switches. When the emotional system is switched off, you're in approach mode and interact with others. When it's switched on, you're in avoid mode and tend to avoid interacting with others.[12]

Your emotional switches also influence how you experience aggression or what is known as your fight-or-flight response.[13]

When the emotional switch is off, you engage in a flight response—you back down. When the emotional switch is on, you engage in a fight response, or "bring it on."

The two sides of your brain, the left and right hemispheres, also work together to coordinate and process different types of emotional messages. Figure 7.2 shows these two sides of the brain.

The left side of the brain decodes "what is said" or the verbal aspects of an emotional message. The right side of the brain decodes "how it's said" or the nonverbal aspects of an emotional message. When the right and left hemispheres of the brain are functioning properly, a person is able to process and experience emotional messages. When the hemispheres are not working together properly, brain-injured people or individuals with other neurological diseases or disorders may be unable to process emotional messages accurately, resulting in a number of interpersonal communication problems.[14]

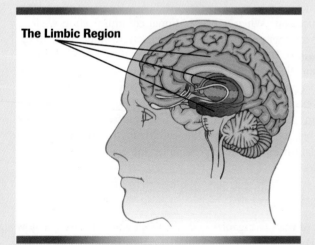

FIGURE 7.1

The Limbic System

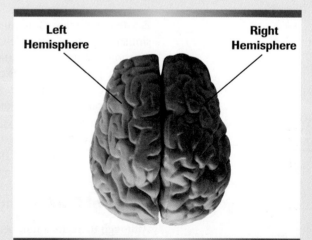

FIGURE 7.2

The Left and Right Brain Hemispheres

Functions of Emotions

Emotions serve a number of important functions in our daily interpersonal communication. Here are just a few of the ways in which emotions function in our lives and relationships.

Learning. Emotions enhance the learning process.[15] Although learning is usually associated with thinking, it is also closely linked with our feelings. Numerous studies show the positive relationship between emotions and learning.[16] Student learning increases if students have a positive emotional connection with the content they're learning. This type of learning, which is referred to as affective learning, is distinctly

TABLE 7.1

Eight Types of Social Emotions

Emotion	Description
Happiness/joy	A feeling of pleasure, goodness, or satisfaction. If you're like most people, you communicate your happiness through smiling and laughter, both of which have been shown to improve your mental health by reducing stress.
Love/affection	A feeling of warmth and fondness that you feel toward another person. It's the feeling that people experience and communicate when they desire to maintain a close relationship with another person.
Pride	The feeling that you experience when another person approves of you and what you're doing and this feeling leads to your evaluating yourself positively.
Anger	The feeling that you experience when you're annoyed, frustrated, irritated, or furious. It is usually triggered when someone behaves in an unexpected manner, as when a person verbally attacks you or acts in rude or inconsiderate manner.
Fear/anxiety	Fear is an emotion caused by threat of some form of harm. Anxiety is an emotional state in which you feel uneasy or apprehensive. People usually experience anxiety about events they cannot control.
Sadness/grief/depression	Sadness usually occurs when you experience an undesirable outcome, such as being laid off from work or when other people reject you. Grief is a special form of sadness and involves the loss of a loved one through death or separation. Depression is a chronic sadness that is not only genetically influenced, but also the result of people who lack social skills, which results in loneliness and depression.
Jealousy	This feeling occurs when an individual perceives that another person poses a threat to a relationship. Jealousy has a tendency to trigger other emotions, such as hurt, anger, sadness, and fear.
Guilt/embarrassment	The feeling that you experience when you hurt someone or fail to help someone. You feel embarrassed when others give you attention that you don't want.

Source: Andersen, P. A., & Guerrero, L. K. (1998). Principles of communication and emotion in social interaction. In P. A. Andersen & L. K. Guerrero (Eds.), *Handbook of communication and emotion: Research, theory, applications, and contexts* (pp. 49-96). New York: Academic Press.

different from cognitive learning. Cognitive learning occurs when you come to understand something new. For example, after reading this book, you will understand the interpersonal communication concepts, theories, and skills that were discussed in the text. Affective learning occurs when you are able to use your new interpersonal communication knowledge and skills in your relationships not because you *have to*, but because you *want to*.[17]

Teaching and learning are not limited to the classroom. Instruction plays a big part in every relationship. Whether you're helping your partner learn how to disclose his or her emotions more easily, teaching your child how to be more verbally assertive without being aggressive at school, or instructing your aging parents in how to take their medication appropriately, learning is more likely to occur if you and your family members have a positive emotional experience related to the lessons you're trying to teach.

Problem Solving. Emotions play an instrumental role in how you solve problems. The old assumption that emotions get in the way of rational thinking is not supported by the research data. Cognitive neuroscientists Mary Helen Immordino-Yang and Antonio Damasio argue that emotions and thinking should not be separated. "Emotional thought" is the term they use to describe how people solve problems. The emotional and reasoning systems in the brain work together in a synthetic manner to solve important problems. For example, if you've ever been dumped by a girlfriend or boyfriend because of something you said that embarrassed this person in front of her or his friends, chances are you felt embarrassment and shame. Because of the intensity of your feelings, they become a part of your emotional memory. The next time you're confronted with a similar problem, you will probably use your emotional memories to solve the problem in a *new* and *different* manner that is more socially appropriate.

Empathy. Emotions allow people to be empathic, which has been shown to be one of the more important predictors of healthy interpersonal relationships. **Empathy** comes from the German word *Einfühling*, meaning "to feel with," which was coined as a translation of the Greek word *empatheia*, which means "passion" or "state of emotion." To empathize with someone is to let the person know, through your communication, that you feel what he or she is feeling rather than just acknowledging the feelings. Being empathic is one way of communicating social support that has been shown to have a number of positive relational outcomes.[18] Empathy occurs when you put yourself in the shoes of the other person; you become emotionally involved. You begin to feel what this person feels.

Not all people experience empathy similarly. A number of factors influence a person's ability to be empathic, including his or her personality and empathic communication skills. We will examine both of these topics more closely later in the chapter. For now, it's important to understand that some people are, by their nature, empathic people. Others have a more difficult time being empathic or emotionally involved with others. Also, one's ability to be empathic can be both a blessing and a curse. Although research suggests that empathic people tend to be relational experts, they also run the risk of emotional burnout, which has a number of relational consequences.[19]

Persuasion and Influence. Emotions are persuasive.[20] Think about the last time you were persuaded. What role did emotions play in the persuasion process? Using emotions to persuade is not a new idea. Aristotle was one of the first communication researchers to talk about the role of emotions in the persuasion process. According to his lectures, which were recorded approximately 300 years before the common era, people are persuaded when their emotions are stirred.[21] Today, advertisers, as well as husbands, wives, and children, know that if you want to persuade someone, you have to get the other person to feel an emotion. Emotions have a tendency to highjack rational thinking. An anonymous author once said, "In the battle between reason and emotion, reason never wins." For example one of your authors, who is allergic to cats, was easily persuaded to adopt a helpless kitten who had been abandoned by her mother. Rationally, it makes no sense to bring a cat into the house when you know you're going to suffer the consequences of such a decision. The emotional attachment he felt toward the abandoned kitten trumped all rational thought. Today, your sneezing author with itchy eyes and throat lives with an adorable cat named Emily.

Fulfilling Interpersonal Needs. According to interpersonal communication researcher John Gottman, our emotions serve as a conduit that allows us to emotionally connect with intimate others, friends, and colleagues and coworkers on the job.[22] These emotional connections allow us to fulfill a number of fundamental interpersonal needs, such as feeling included, controlling and persuading people, and affection. Gottman believes that emotional bonds between a parent and a child can't be overstated, because these bonds serve as the foundation upon which all other life relationships are built. If a child doesn't learn how to connect emotionally with a parent or caregiver, that child will probably encounter difficulty in connecting to people in all sorts of relationships for the rest of his or her life.

CHECKING YOUR UNDERSTANDING
The Nature of Emotions

Before reading further, take a few minutes to assess your learning by writing your answers to the following items:

1. What is the difference between an emotion, a feeling, and a mood? Define each.
2. Summarize the differences between emotion-motivated, emotion-manifesting, and emotion-inducing communication, and provide an example of each.
3. What is the limbic system in the brain? Briefly describe how it works with the two hemispheres of the brain to process and regulate emotion.
4. Andersen and Guerrero talk about social emotions. What makes an emotion social?
5. How do emotions work within our interpersonal relationships? Describe some of the functions emotions can serve.

Personality and Communicating Emotions

Another important factor that influences how you experience and communicate emotions is your personality. We'll look at three communication processes that are strongly related to your personality and interpersonal communication: emotional expressiveness, affective orientation, and emotional contagion.

Emotional Expressiveness

Emotional expressiveness is a personal social style in which people *accurately* encode and convey emotional messages, primarily through the use of nonverbal messages.[23] These are not drama queens or your "high-maintenance" friends but individuals who, because of their personality, are sensitive to others' emotions and express their own emotions well. Researchers agree that emotionally expressive people are considered more interpersonally attractive, better able to develop and maintain constructive relationships, and better liked than emotionally unexpressive individuals.[24]

An emotional personal style is a composite of three factors: expressivity, sensitivity, and control.[25] Emotional expressivity is your ability to express your emotions, such as "I am able to liven up a dull party," and "I have been told that I have expressive eyes." Emotional sensitivity is being attentive to emotional cues, such as "I sometimes cry at sad movies," and "I am often told that I am a sensitive and understanding person." Emotional control is being able to regulate emotional expressions or masking emotions, such as "I am easily able to make myself look happy one minute and sad the next," and "I am very good at maintaining a calm exterior even if I am upset."

Your level of emotional expressivity is related to your personality.[26] For example, your emotional expressiveness is positively related to extraversion. It also appears that your emotional expressiveness remains consistent regardless of the situation you find yourself in and continues to be consistent throughout your life.[27] For example, people who are emotionally expressive at home are also probably emotionally expressive at work. Also, people who are emotionally expressive as adults were also probably emotionally expressive as children.

Affective Orientation

Affective orientation (AO) is the degree to which individuals are aware of and use emotional cues to guide their communication.[28] Communication researchers Melanie Booth-Butterfield and Steve Booth-Butterfield are responsible for identifying this important interpersonal communication variable that is a part of one's personality.[29] The Booth-Butterfields indicate that highly affectively oriented people (high AOs) are very sensitive to their own emotions and use their emotions when making decisions and solving problems. It's not uncommon to hear people saying, when making decisions or solving problems, "Leave your emotions out of this. Let's make a decision in a rational manner." To high AOs, this type of message doesn't make any sense, since they consider their emotions to be important pieces of rational information that should be used when making important decisions or when solving problems. People with low affective orientation (low AOs), on the other hand, tend to be less aware of their emotions and tend to reject their emotions, considering them useless and unimportant. To a low AO, emotions get in the way. When these individuals make decisions or solve problems, they place more weight on factual evidence.[30] Consistent with other research examining sex differences and emotional processing, women tend to self-report higher levels of AO than men do.[31]

Affective orientation is positively related to a number of communication behaviors. For example, high AOs are better able to detect and decode other people's nonverbal behaviors more accurately than low AOs are. Put another way, high AOs can *read* people; they listen to their own instincts. High AOs are aware when people are feeling hurt, disappointed, or awkward in a conversation. They have the ability to change and manage the conversation to make it more comfortable for the person who is not feeling comfortable. Additionally, high AOs are better able to provide comfort to those who are in distress, can make people laugh, and are more easily persuaded by emotional messages.[32]

Emotional Contagion

Emotional contagion (EC) is your tendency to express and feel emotions that are similar to, and influenced by, those of others.[33] Before you read any further, we recommend

NATURE/NURTURE intersections

I Feel Your Pain

Have you ever wondered why some people can "put themselves in another person's shoes" more easily than others can? Perhaps you see others sharing an intense emotional experience that you wish you could be a part of, but you just don't feel the same emotions or the same intensity of emotions. Researchers claim that your ability to empathize with others is partially learned and partially dependent on the action of mirror neurons in your brain.[34]

Mirror neurons are a particular set of circuits that allow you to experience what another person is experiencing by observing or listening to another person's behavior rather than by engaging in the same behavior. In other words, you can emotionally experience what it feels like to play a piano by watching and listening to another person playing the piano.

Figure 7.3 shows two sets of brain scans. The ones on the right are composites of scans of the brains of pianists who were playing the piano. The ones on the left are composites of scans of the brains of pianists who were listening to someone else play the piano. The red areas indicate the neural activity. To a brain researcher, these two sets of brain scans reveal a pattern of similarity:[35] The mirror neurons in the pianist who is listening (left images) are allowing that person to have an emotional experience that is very similar to that of the pianist who is playing (right images).

Mirror neurons allow two people to have a similar emotional experience even when they don't take part in the same activity.[36] Your brain tricks you into feeling what another person is feeling.[37] Researchers argue that people may vary in their ability to be empathic because of differences in their brain structures. For example, people with autism or other brain disorders resulting from injury or disease may struggle with empathic experiences not because they don't want to empathize, but because their mirror neurons malfunction or are less developed owing to injury, disease, or other individual differences.[38]

In addition to learning how to use communication behaviors to be empathic (which will be discussed later in this chapter),

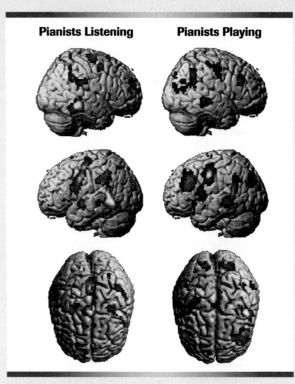

Pianists Listening **Pianists Playing**

FIGURE 7.3

Brain Scans for Pianists Listening to and Playing Music

Source: Bangert, M., Peschel, T., Schlaug, G., Rotte, M., Drescher, D., Hinrichs, H, Heinze, H.J., & Altenmüllera, E. (2006). Shared networks for auditory and motor processing in professional pianists: Evidence from fMRI conjunction. *NeuroImage, 30,* 917–926. This figure has been slightly modified with permission from the author.

your brain plays a role in your ability to be empathic in your communication with others.

that you assess your own susceptibility to emotional contagion by completing the emotional contagion scale, which is located on the next page.

Understanding Your Level of Emotional Contagion. Elaine Hatfield and her colleagues study how people are able to "catch" each other's emotions.[39] We're all susceptible to emotionally contagion to some degree. If you have a tendency to tear up when your best friend tells you about the tragic and unexpected death of her mother or if you feel pain when the doctor or nurse gives your infant daughter or son a shot in the arm, then chances are you have a high level of emotional contagion. If you don't get what all the excitement is about after attending a pep rally at work for meeting your goals or if you're unaffected by other people's anxieties, then you probably have a low level of emotional contagion.

ASSESS YOUR **communication personality**

Doherty's Emotional Contagion Scale[40]

Log onto our self-assessment library, MyPersonalityProfile, found on MyCommunicationLab (www.mycommunicationlab.com), and assess your emotional contagion by completing the interactive assessment. Encourage your relational partner to do the same. This way, you can compare and contrast your scores and begin to understand better how your emotional contagion may influence your interpersonal communication. If you prefer, you can complete the measure below.

Directions:

This is a scale that measures a variety of feelings and behaviors in various situations. There are no right and wrong answers, so try very hard to be completely honest in your answers. Read each question, and indicate the answer that best fits you. Use the following scale:

1 = *Never* applies to me.
2 = *Rarely* applies to me.
3 = *Often* applies to me.
4 = *Usually* applies to me.
5 = *Always* applies to you.

_____ **1.** If someone I'm talking with begins to cry, I get teary-eyed.
_____ **2.** Being with a happy person picks me up when I'm feeling down.
_____ **3.** When someone smiles warmly at me, I smile back and feel warm inside.
_____ **4.** I get filled with sorrow when people talk about the death of their loved ones.
_____ **5.** I clench my jaws and my shoulders get tight when I see the angry faces on the news.
_____ **6.** When I look into the eyes of the one I love, my mind is filled with thoughts of romance.
_____ **7.** It irritates me to be around angry people.
_____ **8.** Watching the fearful faces of victims on the news makes me try to imagine how they might be feeling.
_____ **9.** I melt when the one I love holds me close.
_____ **10.** I tense when overhearing an angry quarrel.
_____ **11.** Being around happy people fills my mind with happy thoughts.
_____ **12.** I sense my body responding when the one I love touches me.
_____ **13.** I notice myself getting tense when I'm around people who are stressed out.
_____ **14.** I cry at sad movies.
_____ **15.** Listening to the shrill scream of a terrified child in a dentist's waiting room makes me feel nervous.

Scoring Instructions:

Add all 15 scores together. Your score should range between 15 and 75. If you score above 45, you are susceptible to emotional contagion. If you score below 45, you have a low susceptibility to emotional contagion.

Unlike a disease or infection, which is always unwanted, there are advantages to being emotionally contagious.[41] Highly emotionally contagious people experience empathy easily, which enhances their ability to understand other people. It enhances relational development. There are also some disadvantages to being highly contagious.[42] Highly emotionally contagious people are susceptible to burnout. This will be discussed in greater detail below.

Watch people closely and you will see them mirroring each other's behaviors. Some researchers argue that by mirroring another person's nonverbal behaviors, we stimulate neurological brain activity that allows us to feel what the other person is feeling.

Your degree of emotional contagion is part of your personality. It's an individual difference that is part of what makes you unique. According to Hatfield and her colleagues, there are two major processes that allow you to feel what another person is feeling.[43] First, you have a tendency to mimic other people's nonverbal behavior. Try it the next time you're talking to a close friend. Fold your arms in a particular manner, and before long, the other person will fold his or her arms in a similar pattern. Your behavior becomes synchronized. It's like a dance.

Second, your bodily movements trigger an emotional reaction in the brain, and you begin feeling what the other person is feeling. In other words, it is your body, not the other person, that causes you to feel. This concept is referred to as the feedback hypothesis. Research has consistently demonstrated that if you smile for a period of time, you will begin feeling happy. Researchers refer to this as the facial feedback hypothesis.[44] These two processes demonstrate one way in which people experience emotional contagion.

If your score on the assessment indicates that you're a high EC (> 45), then you probably benefit from having high-quality relationships. Unfortunately, you may also experience emotional burnout, which can occur in the workplace and in your personal and professional relationships.[45] **Emotional burnout** is emotional exhaustion resulting from the pressures of work and relationships.[46] When you experience burnout, you might feel like a failure and begin to see people as objects rather than humans.[47] You could be on your way to burnout if you experience the following:

- Feeling tired and drained most of the time
- A change in appetite and sleeping habits
- A sense of failure and self-doubt
- Feeling helpless, trapped, and defeated
- Taking out your frustrations on others
- Withdrawing from responsibilities[48]

WHAT CAN I **do now?**

Following are two suggestions that can help highly emotionally contagious (EC > 45) individuals to use their assessment data to reduce burnout and enhance interpersonal communication:[49]

▶ *Set emotional boundaries.* Emotional contagion occurs when you "feel with" another person; empathic concern occurs when you "feel for" another person.[50] To prevent the emotional contagion (feeling with), you must not only avoid the mimicking of nonverbal behaviors, but also distance yourself from the other person's emotions. This is not always an easy process to complete.

▶ *Seek social support.* Surround yourself with people who can provide you with emotional support (letting you know that you're cared for), informational support (providing you with facts and advice), and instrumental support (providing you with physical or material assistance, such as money or an extra set of hands).[51]

Following are a few suggestions that may help low emotionally contagious (EC < 45) individuals to use their assessment data to enhance their interpersonal communication by being more empathic:

▶ *Ask appropriate questions.* To better understand another person's feelings, you might need to ask a number of questions. Most of your questions will serve one of four purposes: (1) to obtain additional information ("Can you tell me more about the problem?"); (2) to check how the person feels ("Are you frustrated because you didn't meet your deadline?"); (3) to ask for clarification ("What did you mean when you said we need to outsource?"); or (4) to verify that you have reached an accurate conclusion about the other person's intent or feeling ("So are you saying you'd rather work at home than at the office?").

▶ *Paraphrase message content.* If you will recall from Chapter 5, **paraphrasing** is restating in your own words what you think the other person is saying. When you paraphrase content, you summarize the details and the main ideas. Here are some common scripts or ways to begin paraphrasing:

"So here is what seems to have happened . . ."

"Let me see if I got this right. You're saying that . . ."

"Here's what I understand you to mean . . ."

"So the point you seem to be making is . . ."

"You seem to be saying . . ."

▶ *Paraphrase emotions.* The most important part about being empathic is to make sure that you understand others' feelings and let them know that you understand. Here are some common ways or scripts for paraphrasing emotions:

"So you feel . . ."

"Emotionally, you're feeling . . ."

"I get a sense that you're feeling . . ."

"Is this how you're feeling? You're feeling . . ."

CHECKING YOUR UNDERSTANDING
Personality and Communicating Emotions

Before reading further, take a few minutes to assess your learning by writing your answers to the following items:

1. How might your own level of emotional expressiveness and your personality traits work together to affect the communication in your interpersonal relationships?

2. What role does affective orientation play in interpersonal relationships? Discuss how a high AO person might have trouble communicating with a low AO person.

3. What does it mean when researchers refer to a person's level of emotional contagion? How might this relate to your ability to understand and communicate emotions effectively?

4. How can a low emotionally contagious person enhance his or her empathic communication skills? Describe the steps that are used to communicate empathy. Why is communicating empathy important?

Developing Emotional Communication Skills

Developing emotional communication skills is another way in which you can enhance the effectiveness of your interpersonal communication. Although you might clearly understand and recognize your own emotions, you still might have a difficult time communicating with others when emotions are involved. This section of the chapter outlines three skills that can help you to identify, understand, and express your emotions.

Identifying Your Emotions

Research clearly suggests that if you can accurately identify how you're feeling, you're one step closer in being able to manage your emotions.[52] For example, if you feel yourself getting angry and you consciously recognize your anger, then you can use this information to help you manage your emotions. To help you accurately identify your emotions, we recommend the following strategies:

Pay Attention to Your Body. What's your body doing? Is your heart beating faster than usual? Are you sweating? How's your breathing? Emotional experience is accompanied by some type of physiological change. You can begin to identify an emotion by paying attention to what your body is doing.

Pay Attention to Your Thoughts. Psychologists Stanley Schachter and Jerome Singer argue that because the physiological responses to some emotions can be similar, such as an increased heart rate in both fear and joy, you should try to understand your physiological response by paying attention to your thoughts.[53] You start by asking, "Why do I feel this way?" As you question yourself, you can begin to assess and interpret the situation.

Pay Attention to Your Vocabulary. Unfortunately, many people don't have a vocabulary for emotions and therefore have a difficult time understanding how they're feeling. Table 7.2 provides an incomplete list of words to describe emotional experience. Once

TABLE 7.2

The Language of Feelings

HAPPY				FEARLESS

HAPPY	Hilarious	Mournful	Pained	Frustrated
Festive	Exhilarated	Dreadful	Suffering	Grumpy
Contented	Jolly	Dreary	Afflicted	Boiling
Relaxed	Playful	Flat	Worried	Fuming
Calm	Elated	Blah	Aching	Stubborn
Complacent	Jubilant	Dull	Crushed	Belligerent
Satisfied	Thrilled	In the dumps	Heartbroken	Confused
Serene	Restful	Sullen	Despair	Awkward
Comfortable		Moody	Torn	Bewildered
Peaceful	**EAGER**	Sulky	Lonely	Independent
Joyous	Keen	Out of sorts	Pathetic	Reassured
Ecstatic	Earnest	Low	Cold	Bold
Enthusiastic	Intent	Discontented	Upset	Brave
Inspired	Zealous	Discouraged		Daring
Glad	Ardent	Disappointed	**ANGRY**	Heroic
Pleased	Avid	Concerned	Resentful	Hardy
Grateful	Anxious	Sympathetic	Irritated	Determined
Cheerful	Enthusiastic	Compassionate	Enraged	Loyal
Excited	Desirous	Choked up	Furious	Proud
Cheery	Excited	Embarrassed	Annoyed	Impulsive
Lighthearted	Proud	Shameful	Inflamed	
Buoyant		Ashamed	Provoked	**FEARLESS**
Carefree	**SAD**	Useless	Infuriated	Encouraged
Surprised	Sorrowful	Worthless	Offended	Courageous
Optimistic	Unhappy	Ill at ease	Sullen	Confident
Spirited	Depressed		Indignant	Secure
Vivacious	Melancholy	**HURT**	Irate	
Brisk	Gloomy	Injured	Wrathful	**INTERESTED**
Sparkling	Somber	Isolated	Cross	Concerned
Merry	Dismal	Offended	Sulky	Fascinated
Generous	Heavy-hearted	Distressed	Bitter	Engrossed
	Quiet			Intrigued

TABLE 7.2 *(continued)*

The Language of Feelings

Absorbed	Powerless	Weak	Bored	**AFRAID**
Excited	Helpless	Sweaty	Hypocritical	Fearful
Curious	Defeated	Breathless	Phony	Frightened
Inquisitive	Pessimistic	**AFFECTIONATE**	Two-faced	Timid
Inquiring	Nauseated	Close	Cooperative	Wishy-washy
Creative	Sluggish	Loving	Impatient	Shaky
Sincere	Weary	Sexy	Nervous	Apprehensive
	Repulsed	Tender	Dependent	Fidgety
DOUBTFUL	Tired	Passionate	Anxious	Terrified
Unbelieving	Alive	Aggressive	Pressured	Panicky
Skeptical	Feisty	Appealing	Worried	Tragic
Distrustful		Warm	Doubtful	Hysterical
Suspicious	**PHYSICAL**		Suspicious	Alarmed
Dubious	Taut	**MISCELLANEOUS**	Hesitant	Cautious
Uncertain	Uptight	Humble	Awed	Shocked
Questioning	Immobilized	Torn	Dismayed	Horrified
Evasive	Paralyzed	Mixed-up	Scared	Insecure
Wavering	Tense	Envious	Cowardly	
Hesitant	Stretched	Jealous	Threatened	
Perplexed	Hollow	Preoccupied	Appalled	
Indecisive	Empty	Cruel	Petrified	
Hopeless	Strong	Distant	Gutless	

Source: Mottet, T. P. (2007). *Fundamentals of human communication: COMM 1310 Guidebook 2006–2007.* San Marcos, TX: Texas State Press.

you're aware of what your body is doing and how you're thinking about an experience, attach the appropriate word to what you're feeling and thinking.

Understanding Your Emotions

To understand your emotions, it's important to have an awareness of your emotional buttons or triggers. Some people have a high emotional threshold, which means that it takes a lot to elicit an emotional response from them. Others have a low threshold; it doesn't take much to elicit an emotion.

People are born with different emotional triggers. Some peoples' triggers are like a light switch or button in that they are turned on or off. Other people's triggers are more like a dimmer switch in that they operate more on a threshold; rather than on/off, they become stronger or weaker.

Understand Your Biological Triggers. Psychologist Jerome Kagan suggests that people are born with different temperaments. A person's temperament is a set of reaction patterns in response to external stimuli.[54] Your temperament is your biological trigger or button. Some people have a long attention span and are approachable, patient, adaptable, and pleasant. Others are just the opposite: They're easily distracted; withdraw from situations; and are impatient, inflexible, and irritable. Such reaction patterns reflect a person's temperament, which affects how the person reacts and interacts with others.

You probably know of people who are in need of anger management. You might say or do something that sets them off. Researchers have found that hostility is an internal angry state. No one knows how angry you are until you communicate your anger. Some people have a high threshold for anger, which means that it takes an intense trigger for the person to express anger. Others have a low threshold for anger, which means that they have sensitive triggers, and even the slightest glance or nonverbal behavior can provoke them into expressing their anger.

What about your own temperament? Are you aware of your own biological triggers? Do you find yourself getting angry easily, or does it take much provoking to get you angry? Once you understand that a part of your temperament is heavily influenced by your biology,[55] meaning that it's stubborn and resistant to change, then you can be more careful not to get yourself into a situation in which your anger could be provoked. When you sense that your anger buttons are being pushed, you can quickly remove yourself from the situation if you have good awareness of your triggers and how you usually react.

Understand Your Environmental Triggers. Communication researcher Melanie Booth-Butterfield recommends locating the emotion in time and space, which means considering the conditions under which you feel this emotion.[56] For example, there may be some situations that have a tendency to make you anxious, such as an invitation to attend a formal event. Social events are often full of uncertainty about how to dress, who will be attending the event, and how you're expected to behave. Because you never know what to expect, you approach formal events with fear and apprehension and usually don't enjoy the events. In many ways, it's not the formal occasion that makes you feel anxious, but the uncertainty surrounding it. If you understand that it is the uncertainty that triggers the emotions, you can attempt to reduce the uncertainty by asking the event planner about what is considered appropriate dress, who will be attending, and the program for the evening. Answers to these questions can minimize the anxious feelings and allow you to enjoy yourself at the event.

Expressing Your Emotions

One way to communicate emotions appropriately is to take responsibility for your emotions. Saying, "I'm feeling mad" rather than saying, "You make me so mad" is an example of taking ownership of emotions. No one can force you to feel in a particular manner without your permission. If the guy you are serious about cheats on you, it's your decision how you're going to feel about learning of his cheating. You may decide to feel hurt, or you may feel relieved. It depends on you and how you process the situation.

A second way to communicate emotions properly is to follow **display rules,** which are guidelines for when, where, and how to manage emotion displays that are appropriate for the situation. Sociologist Erving Goffman argues that people have on-stage and off-stage behavior.[57] For example, the emotions that you display when you're home with family and friends are probably not the same emotions that you display when you're on the job. According to researchers, you learn display rules early in life. Over time, they become habituated, which means that they become so familiar and routine to you that you no longer have to think about how you should behave in a particular situation.[58] Nonverbal communication researcher Paul Ekman identified five different ways in which people manage their emotions in order to communicate them appropriately.[59]

Simulate Emotional Displays. When you **simulate**, you display an emotion when you're not feeling any emotion—you "fake it" to "make it." We alluded to this earlier when discussing ways to avoid emotional burnout, especially if you're susceptible to emotional contagion. Here, we're recommending that you consider simulating an emotion as a way to make the conversation run a bit more smoothly. For example, suppose that you don't have strong emotions, either positive or negative, about an upcoming trip to see family in California. Because your partner is very excited about the trip, you might simulate excitement to maintain the relational harmony.

Inhibit Emotional Displays. When you **inhibit**, you display no emotion when in fact you're feeling an emotion. One of the reasons you might inhibit or hide the emotion is to save face or not to embarrass yourself. For example, suppose that you attended an awards ceremony at which you thought you would receive a prestigious award. Instead, it went to your colleague. Although you were very disappointed, you hid your disappointment in order not to appear to be a bad sport.

Intensify Emotional Displays. When you **intensify**, you create the appearance that you're feeling emotions more strongly than you are. In some situations, you might find yourself feeling happy, but because you believe that your friend expects you to be ecstatic when she tells you that she is getting married, you express more happiness than you really feel. Your lack of 100% enthusiasm might stem from the belief that you're losing your best friend through the marriage or concern that she might not be ready for marriage.

Deintensify Emotional Displays. When you **deintensify**, you give the impression that you're feeling emotions less strongly than you are. Because our emotional displays influence others' emotional displays, we sometimes downplay an emotion in order not to upset another person. For example, suppose that you and your colleague are returning home after working away from home for a month. He is excited that he will be home just in time to celebrate his daughter's first birthday. Unfortunately, the airline canceled the flight at the last minute, and you are both feeling anger and resentment toward the airline. You decide to downplay how angry you're feeling to help your colleague not feel as angry that he will miss his daughter's first birthday.

Mask Emotional Displays. When you **mask**, you show one emotion while feeling a different emotion. Suppose that while you are facilitating a school board meeting, a member of the board rudely criticizes another member who is absent and therefore is unable to defend herself. Even though you're fuming about this situation, you know that if you were to confront the rude member, you would display hostile emotions that

TABLE 7.3

Managing and Communicating Emotions		
Skills	**Strategies**	**Examples of Internal Thoughts**
Identify your emotions	Pay attention to your body.	"I am aware that my heart is beating faster than usual, and I am feeling warm and flushed."
	Pay attention to your thoughts.	"Because of my increased heart rate and body temperature, I am feeling very nervous and anxious."
Understand your emotions	Know your biological triggers.	"I know that I get easily frustrated and impatient when I am tired and hungry. I have the most patience, flexibility, and adaptability in the morning when I'm feeling well rested."
	Know your environmental triggers.	"I know that when I'm in a warm and crowded room, I get irritable. Naturally lit rooms make me feel most comfortable."
Express your emotions by following display rules	Simulate emotions: Display an emotion when you're not feeling an emotion.	"When my husband's team wins, I act happy for him even though I really don't care one way or another."
	Inhibit emotions: Display no emotion when in fact you're feeling an emotion.	"I was very upset when my son confessed that he had lied to me. Because I want to encourage honesty, I am not going to let him see that I am angry."
	Intensify emotions: Create the appearance you're feeling emotions more strongly than you are.	"When my coworker wins a free trip, I act incredibly excited for him when in reality I'm only slightly happy for him."
	Deintensify emotions: Give the impression that you're feeling emotions less strongly than you are.	"I am feeling devastated when my girlfriend informs me that she's pregnant. However, I convey only slight concern to show my support to her."
	Mask emotions: Show one emotion while feeling a different emotion.	"I am showing sadness over the breakup of the relationship even though I am thrilled on the inside."

would hurt your credibility. To get through the meeting, you put on a calm, cheerful face and move the agenda forward.

To summarize, three sets of skills allow you to manage and communicate emotions appropriately. Table 7.3 reviews the skills and strategies and provides examples of each.

 ## CHECKING YOUR UNDERSTANDING

Developing Emotional Communication Skills

Before reading further, take a few minutes to assess your learning by writing your answers to the following items:

1. How would you teach others to identify their emotions? To what should people pay attention, and why are these items important to identifying emotions?

2. Describe how biological and environmental triggers are different. How do these triggers enhance your understanding of your emotions?

3. What did sociologist Erving Goffman mean when he said that people have on-stage and off-stage behavior?

4. Write down the five different ways in which people manage their emotions, according to nonverbal communication researcher Paul Ekman. Provide an original example that illustrates the five methods.

Factors That Influence Emotional Communication

Part of a person's emotional intelligence is being aware of the factors that influence how emotions enhance relational development. To increase your emotional intelligence, we're going to discuss some factors that influence how people experience and express emotions: sex and gender, culture, and technology. Becoming aware of these factors will help you to begin navigating the emotions that are a critical part of all relationships.

Sex Differences and Emotional Communication

According to a number of researchers, it is incorrect to make a blanket statement that women are more emotional than men.[60] However, it is correct to say that women tend to show their emotions more than men do.[61] Research reveals that men and women have similar physiological responses when their emotions are elicited; however, they express and communicate about their emotions differently. Following is a synopsis of some of the research findings:

- Women tend to be better encoders and decoders of emotional information than men are.[62] In other words, women are better able to develop and convey messages about how they're feeling and better able to detect and discern others' emotions.

- Women tend to do a better job than men in noticing micro-level nonverbal behaviors that reveal a person's true emotional state even when the person is attempting to mask emotions.[63]

- Women, more than men, tend to trust their perceptions of others' nonverbal behaviors and to use their perceptions as knowledge to help them better adapt to a variety of different interpersonal situations. So when you say to a woman, "I feel as though you can read my mind," the truth is that she cannot read your mind, but she can intuit what you are thinking on the basis of your nonverbal behavior.

- Women are more likely than men to communicate positive emotions, such as joy and affection, as well as to express sadness and depression.

- Men are more likely than women to express and control anger as well as have more control over all different types of emotional displays.[64]

There are numerous nature/nurture explanations for the sex differences in emotional communication. Some argue that these differences are natural and are due to neurological structural differences in the brain. Men's and women's brains are wired differently; therefore, men and women differ in not only cognitive processes, but also in the ways in which emotions become activated.[65] Others argue that men and women are nurtured or socialized differently and develop gender roles that shape how they process and express emotions. These researchers argue that young children learn to express their emotions according to socially prescribed norms that are reinforced through being punished or rewarded for behaving in sex-appropriate ways, meaning that boys "act like boys" and girls "act like girls."[66]

Within relationships, men and women experience and express emotions differently:

- Men and women manage their sadness differently; women seek out social support, and men engage in more destructive behaviors.[67] It appears that women confront their sadness and reach out to their relational network for social support, whereas men think that reaching out for help is a weakness and bury their feelings by engaging in individual reckless behaviors, such as excessive drinking.[68]

- Men and women respond to jealousy differently. Men are more likely than women to experience sexual jealousy (because of their partners' sexual interaction with another person), whereas women are more likely to experience emotional jealousy (because of their partners' emotional connection with another person).[69]

- When experiencing jealous feelings, women are also more likely than men to report discussing their thoughts and feelings, expressing emotions nonverbally, and enhancing their physical appearance.

- Men are more likely than women to report focusing on the rival and buying gifts or spending money on the partner.[70]

These research findings focusing on jealousy tend to be consistent across cultures, which supports the idea that men and women may have different brain structures when it comes to emotion.[71]

Culture and Emotional Communication

One way to understand the relationship between culture and emotion is to reexamine the cultural values of individualism and collectivism, which we first introduced in Chapter 3. These cultural values affect how people experience and express emotions. People from individualistic cultures more freely and openly expressed emotions, especially positive emotions, than people from collectivistic cultures did.[72] Within individualistic cultures (e.g., the United States, Canada, Australia), people place a higher value on the feelings of individuals, and there is permission for the individual to express how he or she is feeling. Expressing individual feelings is considered culturally appropriate. Within collectivistic cultures (e.g., Indonesia, Malaysia, South Korea), people are more reserved when expressing personal feelings, since it detracts from the focus on the group. Expressing individual feelings is considered culturally inappropriate in collectivistic cultures.

There are also differences in emotional expression within individualistic and collectivistic cultures based on in-group and out-group relationship status.[73] For example, in-group relationships are characterized by people who have a shared history and hope to have a continued relationship in the future. In-group relationships have a culture of familiarity and trust. To get an idea of your in-group relationships, take a look at the contact list in your cell phone. These names probably reflect your in-group. Out-group relationships are characterized by a culture of uncertainty, unfamiliarity, and lack of trust. You communicate out-group status to the individuals that you don't accept as friends on your Facebook or MySpace page.

Some research suggests that you have more freedom to express individual feelings if you're a part of the in-group rather than if you're part of the out-group, regardless of the larger cultural context of individualism or collectivism.[74] In other words, your in-group/out-group status is to some degree more important in determining the appropriateness of expressing individual feelings than is the larger cultural value of individualism and collectivism.

It is rare to see a photo of Vladimir Putin, the Prime Minister of Russia, smiling.

Different cultures also have different display rules. For example, Russians control their expressions of emotions much more than Americans do. Russians adhere to the following display rules for smiling:[75]

- Russians smile only for good reason—and only if the reason is apparent to those around them.

- It's not customary for Russians to smile while helping customers or conducting serious business.

- It's not customary for Russians to smile to lift others' spirits.

Just as Americans mistake Russians' lack of smiling to be surly and miserable, Russians find friendly Americans' smiles to be phony, insincere, and reflecting low intelligence.[76] Moscow subway posters have been trying to change the display rules by encouraging Muscovites to smile as a way to improve their looks. However, it will probably take more than an advertising campaign to change Russia's deep-seated attitudes toward this emotional display.

Emotional Intelligence and Emotional Communication

Your emotional intelligence is your ability to recognize, understand, manage, and ultimately use your emotions and the emotions of others.[77] Although this might seem similar to emotional expressiveness, emotional intelligence is a more comprehensive variable that includes the sending (encoding) and receiving (decoding) of emotional messages. Emotional expressiveness is more limited to the sending (encoding) of emotional messages. How smart are you when it comes to emotions?[78]

Your level of emotional intelligence makes a difference.[79] For example, emotionally intelligent people differ in how they frame problems and make decisions.[80] During a job search, emotionally intelligent individuals consider answers to the question "How satisfied will I be doing this job?" as being more important than answers to the question

"How much money will I make?" Do you know of people who always make decisions by doing the math? For example, a person of lower emotional intelligence might say, "We cannot take this once-in-a-lifetime trip because we can't afford it." A person of higher emotional intelligence might reason differently, saying, "I realize that we cannot afford it, but it's a once-in-a-lifetime opportunity, and we will make it work." It's not that highly emotionally intelligent people are irrational; it's just that they consider the emotional experience of going on a once-in-a-lifetime vacation to have a benefit that might very well outweigh the costs.

Research suggests that emotionally intelligent adults are more satisfied in their relationships with others than are adults with less emotional intelligence.[81] As people become more emotionally intelligent, they also become more effective at being appropriately assertive in relationships.[82] Put simply, they communicate their needs without being demanding or attacking another person. Emotionally intelligent children, too, are more satisfied in their relationships with others, since these children are more likely to be accepted by their peers. Emotionally intelligent children are emotionally responsive and have the emotional self-control needed to relate to other children.[83]

What makes a person emotionally intelligent? We don't know for sure, but like most communication abilities, it's probably part nature (biology), part nurture (environment), and part how the two interact. We do know that women usually score higher on emotional intelligence measures than men do and that your personality doesn't affect your emotional intelligence.[84]

Communication researchers James Keaten and Lynne Kelly suggest that family communication patterns influence the development of emotionally intelligent children. For example, they found that family members who encourage each other to have open conversations about a wide variety of unrestricted topics; share feelings, experiences, and thoughts with each other; and value open exchange of ideas and shared decision making are more emotionally intelligent than are family members who don't encourage this type of family communication.[85]

Technology and Emotional Communication

If you use Facebook, MySpace, Twitter, or any of the other social networking technologies, then you already know how important technology is to your ability to initiate and maintain relationships. In addition to face-to-face interpersonal communication, we carry on numerous relationships through the use of mediated interpersonal communication, which depends on some form of technology, such as a computer or cell phone, to transmit messages.

Interpersonal communication researcher Joe Walther has written extensively about how technology affects interpersonal communication.[86] Walther argues that technology allows relationships to form; however, it takes longer because our current technology does a poor job of transmitting emotional cues. Technology has a way of filtering out of important nonverbal messages, which convey emotional cues, making interpersonal communication more challenging.[87] For example, do people always understand your sense of humor when you text-message or chat online? If the other person doesn't know you well, her or she can easily misinterpret your sarcasm. The message that is sent doesn't equal the message that is received. Other people may decode your text-based messages literally because they can't see your nonverbal messages, such as the grin on your face, or hear the insincerity in your voice that would allow them to interpret the message in the manner you intended. Walther argues that technology allows relationships to develop but that it takes more messages to fully understand another person and his or her social style.

A study conducted in Japan found that Japanese people tend to use communication technologies more than Americans do, and Japanese scored significantly lower than Americans in the ability to recognize anger, disgust, fear, and sadness.[88] A part of this deficiency is attributed to the role that technology plays in today's society. The author of study states that it is common for the modern Japanese family to have minimal face-to-face interaction; instead, family members tend to interact through the use of personal communication technologies. As a result, Japanese people tend to have underdeveloped emotional communication skills.[89]

People have found ways to compensate for the lack of emotional cues in mediated forms of interpersonal communication. For example, you might use all capital letters in a text message to indicate increased volume and anger or use all lowercase to indicate a whisper. Additionally, emoticons (e.g., smiley faces, winks) have been widely adopted as a way to add emotional elements to text-based forms of interpersonal communication.

It is only a matter of time before researchers engineer ways to develop and design communication technologies that allow people to communicate in ways that are more real and emotional. Skype is one Internet-based technology that allows people to see and talk to one other. Other new communication technologies include machine-generated voices that resemble human voices, full of emotion and personality.[90] You may have experienced such a machine-generated voice the last time you called an airline to confirm a reservation or to check on flight information. Not only might the computer-generated voice call you by name, but in some systems, you get a different voice with a different personality each time you make a return call. Researchers have found that humans respond quite positively to these voices and that in some situations, they cannot tell the difference between a human voice and a computer-generated voice.[91]

CHECKING YOUR UNDERSTANDING
Factors That Influence Emotional Communication

Before completing the chapter, take a few minutes to assess your learning by writing your answers to the following items:

1. How do men and women tend to differ in their understanding and communication of emotion?

2. What differences are there in the communication of emotion across cultures?

3. Explain how technology has changed our methods of communication. Has this had any influence on how you communicate emotion? If so, how? If not, why not?

A Communication Development Plan for Dr. Dasari

To complete Dr. Dasari's story, recall how Staci left the doctor's office upset and hurt. Dr. Dasari had failed to notice that Staci was having trouble dealing with the emotional weight of her diagnosis of type 2 diabetes. Rather than taking the time to answer Staci's questions, Dr. Dasari was halfway out the door when she stopped and patted Staci on the back, saying, "Don't you worry about that right now. The nurse will be in to answer any questions."

What do you think?

What was wrong with Dr. Dasari's communication? What was wrong with Staci's communication? How could they have managed this important conversation differently?

Possible explanations:

There are number of ways to explain the communication dynamics that occurred in Dr. Dasari's office. The doctor seemed completely unaware of Staci's emotional state. Dr. Dasari didn't pay attention to Staci, smile at her, or show her any sign of a connection. While Staci struggled to deal with the news of the diagnosis and her emotional reaction, she did not make any effort to communicate these emotions to her doctor. Both Dr. Dasari's lack of empathy and Staci's attempt to hide what she was feeling contributed to the frustration of the office visit.

How will this lack of empathic communication skills affect Dr. Dasari's practice? There is a good chance that if Staci had this kind of experience with Dr. Dasari, others have too. If the doctor wants her practice to thrive and wants to help her patients make healthier decisions, she needs to allow them to react emotionally to their diagnosis, and she needs to respond to their emotions.

How can Dr. Dasari and Staci make adjustments to their communication so that both feel comfortable with the experience? Future visits to Dr. Dasari's office are likely to bring more frustration if Staci does not address what bothered her this time. And Dr. Dasari runs the risk of upsetting more patients unless she can learn to show caring and empathy.

1. *Dr. Dasari can understand the nature of emotions and recognize the role they play in our everyday lives.* For most people, a visit to the doctor's office can be stressful and emotional. If the doctor had been aware of Staci's emotional state as Staci entered the room, Dr. Dasari might have been able to break the news to her in a way that demonstrated caring. In the end, when the doctor walked out and told Staci, "Don't you worry about that right now," her lack of emotion made the comment seem inauthentic and almost condescending.

2. *Dr. Dasari can engage in empathic listening.* If the doctor can show that she cares and has a feel for what her patients are feeling, they may be more comfortable and certainly more at ease asking questions. Some skills for showing empathy include the following:

   - Take some time to take perspective; think about how the other person might be feeling. If it were you or your daughter, how might you feel?

   - Ask questions: Dr. Dasari could have quickly ascertained Staci's emotional state if she had just asked Staci how she was feeling. Perhaps Dr. Dasari's expertise could have calmed Staci's nerves and made her feel more comfortable.

   - Paraphrase the message: When Staci finally did ask how her diagnosis might affect her family and life, the doctor missed a great opportunity to show that she cared. At that point, Dr. Dasari could have taken the time to paraphrase Staci's concerns. This would have showed that Dr. Dasari was listening and cared about Staci.

3. *Staci can allow herself to both feel and express her emotions.* In attempting to hide or mask her emotions, Staci was unable to manage them and allowed her emotions to block out everything her doctor was telling her. If Staci had been able to experience her emotions and communicate them appropriately, she might also have been clear minded enough to listen to the doctor's instructions.

Take Aways

Humans are emotional creatures. We communicate emotional messages constantly. This chapter focused on the emotional messages that we send and receive in our interactions. Following is a list of knowledge claims regarding the nature and function of emotions:

- Emotions and feelings are distinct forms of emotional thought.

- Emotions can be categorized into different types: happiness/joy, love/affection, pride, anger, fear/anxiety, sadness/grief/depression, jealousy, and guilt/embarrassment.

- Emotions serve various functions in our lives, such as helping us to learn, problem-solve, be empathic, be persuasive, and fulfill interpersonal needs.

- Several factors can influence our communication of emotions, including our gender, culture, and emotional intelligence and the technology we use to communicate.

Following are some ways in which you learned more about your emotions:

- By examining affective orientation (AO), you learned how you use emotions as information when solving problems and making decisions.
- By using the emotional contagion (EC) assessment instrument, you learned how you catch other peoples' emotions and how to adapt your communication appropriately.

Following are a list of skills that you can develop to help communicate clearly when emotions are involved:

- Interpret others' emotions accurately, using the cues of pleasure, dominance, and arousal mentioned in this chapter.
- Manage and communicate your emotions clearly and appropriately.
- Be an empathic listener, being aware of the other person's emotional state, asking questions, and paraphrasing answers to show that you are listening.

Discussion Questions

1. What are the differences between emotions, feelings, and moods?
2. How does the limbic system work with the two hemispheres of the brain to process and regulate emotion?
3. What are eight types or categories of social emotions?
4. What functions do emotions serve in our interactions?
5. What factors influence how we communicate emotion?
6. What role have technological changes played in the communication of emotion in our relationships?

Building Your Skills

1. Get together with a friend with whom you tend to share a lot. Make a list of the reasons you think this friend is a good listener. Practice using empathic listening skills with your friend.
2. Think of a recent emotional conversation you have had, such as a conflict with a partner. Examine the emotional messages in the conversation. How did you communicate how you were feeling? What was the other person feeling? What cues did you observe to help you determine your partner's feelings? What skills could you now use to communicate your emotions more effectively?
3. Observe a communication event (a personal conversation or a TV episode). What are some of the display rules you noticed. Discuss how they may be similar to or different from your own.
4. Keep an emotion log for a day. Write down how you are feeling at various points throughout the day. Identify your various moods, feelings, and emotions.
5. After assessing your own and your partner's affective orientations (AO), make a list of the ways in which you could improve communication.
6. Track your technology use for a day. Make specific note of the ways in which you attempt to communicate emotion through technological channels. Compare your notes with your classmates' notes.

8 Conflict in Relationships: Awareness to Resolution

June's Story . . .

June and her daughter Karen frequently experience the "dark side" of the mother–daughter relationship.[1] June wants to be a good mom but feels that her 22-year-old daughter is irresponsible. June knows that her attempts at guidance often lead to arguments that easily spin out of control as both June and Karen say the wrong things. A typical conversation goes like this:

June enters Karen's room on Sunday evening and asks, "What time do you need to get up in the morning to get ready for work? Should I wake you?" Karen remains calm and answers, "I think I'll get up about 9:15. I don't have to be at the gym until 10 anyway." This worries June because she knows Karen's history of being late for work and is certain that 45 minutes is not going to be enough time. She replies, "Are you sure? It takes at least 40 minutes to drive to work." Karen assures her mother, "It will be fine. Monday mornings at the gym are slow, and my first client is always late."

June immediately becomes frustrated with Karen's response. "If I were your boss, consistently arriving late would be unacceptable. In fact, I would probably start looking for a more reliable athletic trainer!" Karen just laughs and shakes her head at her mother's statement. "Whatever, Mom," she finally says, knowing that any more conversation is not going to end well. June persists in telling Karen how she sees things: "It's time for you to be out on your own, and if you lose your job that will never happen." As June begins lecturing Karen on what it means to be a good employee and describes her own past successes, Karen interrupts, stating, "I wish you'd stop worrying about me. It's no big deal. Would you just drop it?"

June begins to raise her voice and says, "Karen, your behavior is lazy and irresponsible." Karen ignores her mother's comments completely. She walks into the bathroom and slams the door. June cannot believe what has just happened. She feels that she deserves more respect from her daughter. At the end of her rope, June shouts through the door, "I'm serious, Karen! You have to admit you've got a pretty cushy life. You don't pay rent, and I don't really ask you to do much around here at all."

Karen finally opens the door and faces her mother. Her fists are clenched, and she is clearly angry. She is determined to

CHAPTER OBJECTIVES

AFTER READING THIS CHAPTER, you will understand:

1 The differences between constructive and destructive conflict and the various types of conflict.

2 Disconfirming messages and their relationship to developing the communication climate and conflict.

3 Positive and negative orientations toward conflict.

4 The differences between approach and avoidance personalities and the impact of conflict on the communication climate.

5 How the need for power can affect conflict and conflict management strategies.

6 How your use of technology can affect the conflict you experience in your relationships.

7 How conflict is different for men and women and for people in individualistic and collectivistic cultures.

8 How conflict is managed in different contexts.

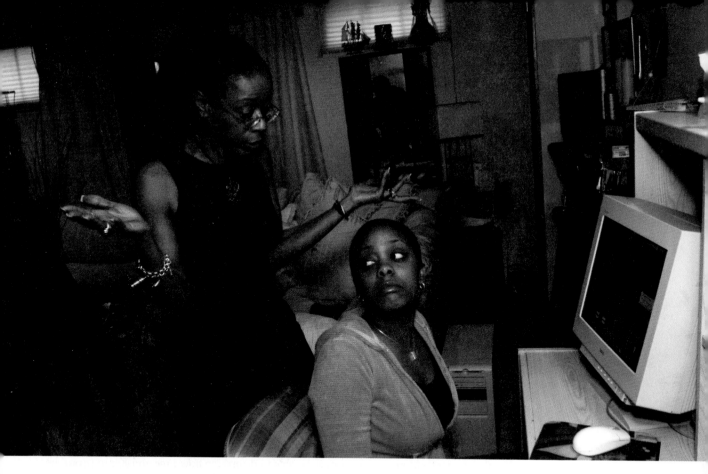

end this conversation once and for all. "You are so obsessive-compulsive it's ridiculous. I'm outta here—I'm sick of listening to this." Karen storms out of the room, heads to the garage to get her luggage, and takes it to her room to begin packing.

What do you think about this interaction? While reading this chapter, consider how you might answer the following questions to help June and Karen:

- Who is the bigger culprit in taking this conversation downhill? At what point in the exchange did you first see it going sour?

- Do you think that power is an issue for either June or Karen in this conflict? If so, where do you see examples of this?

- Do you believe that June and Karen can resolve this conflict?

We will revisit June and Karen at the end of this chapter. As you are reading, look for concepts that might apply to their conflict. Try to develop ways to help June and Karen have this discussion peacefully.

L ike Karen, who ran from the room, most of us hate conflict and try to avoid it at all costs. **Conflict** is defined as an incompatibility of goals between two people who experience different views, opinions, or interests. Let's face it—conflict is messy and typically isn't fun. However, there is really no way around the occasional conflict unless you live in a cave hidden away from the rest of the world. If conflict has been commonplace in the relationships in your life, recall some of the occasions. Your memories most likely go back to a very early time. From the youngest ages, children have been taunting their brothers and sisters. As they become teenagers, they begin arguing with parents over curfews and school grades. Then, as intimate adult relationships develop, a cycle begins in which everyday activities get worked out and are negotiated (e.g., taking out the trash or selecting a movie).

> I argue very well. Ask any of my remaining friends. I can win an argument on any topic, against any opponent. People know this, and steer clear of me at parties. Often, as a sign of their great respect, they don't even invite me.
>
> —DAVE BARRY

This chapter is intended to help you recognize the importance of engaging in and understanding conflict. After all, you are bound to experience conflict at some point in your life. Learning to recognize conflict situations and why they are happening can provide a healthy path to resolving or preventing conflict. Any conflict that affects important relationships in your life must be managed.[2] If it is not, these rifts can have long-lasting effects. By the end of this chapter, you should be much more aware of the characteristics of conflict, how the messages you send influence conflict, and the specific factors that influence your ability to manage conflict. Finally, you should be able to determine how June and Karen (from the case study) can resolve their issues and avoid future conflicts like the one they experienced.

Characteristics of Conflict

Conflict is a familiar concept. When we think about conflict, some common words come to mind: *disagreement, antagonism, tension, defensive communication, arguments,* and so on. Although communication scholars do not agree on a common definition, many of us do accept a definition of conflict from William Wilmot and Joyce Hocker that covers a broad range of interpersonal experiences: Conflict is an expressed struggle occurring between two or more interdependent individuals who feel that the other disagrees or interferes with their goals and provides them few relational rewards.[3] Most of us can easily recall times when we have felt this struggle with another person. In fact, Carolyn Shantz tells us that conflict is so pervasive that it is actually central to every individual's development and a component of virtually every major theory of human development.[4] Other communication professionals have suggested that conflict is required for relational success, even though the type of conflict we choose to engage in can frequently undermine our relationships.[5] Thus, the primary characteristics of conflict that can help us to understand and manage it are that it is natural and inevitable and, depending on the specific type, that it can enhance or damage our relationships with others.

Natural and Inevitable

It is not necessarily the amount of conflict we experience in our relationships that matters; what's important is the way in which we choose to handle the conflict.[6] The conflict that you experience in your relationships is natural, and there is really no escaping it. Because it is inevitable, you should not be afraid to engage in conflict, but you should learn how to manage it. We will discuss some specific techniques later in the chapter.

Interpersonal conflict occurs in any relationship in which two people are interdependent. This means that they rely on one another; their decisions and behaviors affect each other. Imagine the following situation: Your mother decides to invite your repulsive cousin Bill for the holidays. Bill gets to sleep in your room, and you are forced to sleep on a cot in your sister's room. You and your mother are interdependent because her decision affects your sleeping arrangements and your holiday, and your response affects her enjoyment of the holiday. So you stomp around the house and refuse to do anything your mother asks (expressed struggle). Sleeping in your sister's room and being forced to tolerate Cousin Bill were not in your plans. Your mother has interfered with your goal of having the perfect holiday break from school. Where is your reward in all of this?

We often have no control over when and where conflict occurs or who will be involved. Even when you are very close to someone and usually see eye to eye, disagreements happen. High school students, for example, reported experiencing conflict an average of seven times a day. College students reported an average of 2.3 conflicts a week in their dating relationships.[7] A study examining family dinner conversations recorded an average of eighteen disputes, most ending in a standoff.[8] Although it is impossible to avoid conflict, not all conflict is necessarily harmful to your relationships. William Cupach and Daniel Canary assert that engaging in conflict helps people understand how to manage conflict, which, in turn, promotes individual growth.[9] Ultimately, engaging in conflict helps you to learn more about yourself and your relational needs, desires, and goals. Mismanaging conflict, however, can have damaging effects on interpersonal encounters and relationships.

Constructive or Destructive

The effects of conflict can be positive or negative; at times, conflict makes us feel better about ourselves or our relationships. There are other times, however, when conflict can work against our relationships to the point of destruction. On the positive side, when a conflict enhances our positive feelings toward the other person, situation, or relationship, that conflict is considered to be cooperative or constructive. To put it simply, **constructive conflicts** that enhance our interpersonal relationships can be characterized by low levels of emotional intensity, agreeable outcomes, and personal or relational growth.[10] As we discussed in Chapter 4, being argumentative can be a constructive method of dealing with conflict because you refrain from criticizing the person and instead opt to focus on the position or point of view.

Destructive conflicts, on the other hand, negatively influence our relationships. These are represented by intense emotions; frequent coercive behaviors; one party typically giving in; and lasting negative feelings.[11] Verbally aggressive behaviors are often the culprits in destructive conflict. To help you determine whether the effects of conflict you have experienced were constructive or destructive, the following useful indicators or markers have been developed: conflict frequency; conflict issue and associated frequency of aggression; and resolution strategies.[12]

Conflict Frequency. This is self-explanatory but is also very personal, as everyone has his or her own level of tolerance. Only you know when you feel that conflict is occurring too often. Research tells us that siblings experience conflict much more frequently than do other interdependent pairs, such as best friends or a husband and wife. In addition, sibling conflict is typically associated with destructive resolution strategies that seriously injure the relationship—the third marker in identifying whether conflict effects are constructive or destructive.[13]

Though siblings do argue frequently, their conflicts are typically very destructive to their relationships.

Issue and Frequency of Aggression. How often people engage in an aggressive behavior regarding a particular issue helps to determine whether the conflict is constructive or destructive. Issues may fall into one of three categories: concrete issues involving tangible items (e.g., money), abstract issues (e.g., plans, goals, procedures), or behaviors (e.g., annoying social skills). Although these three categories alone do not necessarily destroy a relationship, what can lead to destruction are the level and frequency of aggression expressed within these areas. The more unreasonable people are or the more demanding and coercive they become, the greater is the possibility that they will be perceived as aggressive. As we discussed in Chapter 4, verbal aggression is considered a damaging form of domestic violence, and according to John Gottman, who researches destructive communication among married couples, these specific behaviors are indicators for whether a marriage will fail.[14] We will examine these specific conflict behaviors and messages in greater detail later in this chapter.

Resolution Strategies. The resolution strategy that we select determines whether the effects of conflict are constructive or destructive to the relationship. It is important to remember that this is perception-based and that not everyone views it similarly. In other words, one person may perceive the plan to end the conflict as productive and relationship-enhancing (e.g., negotiation or compromise), while the other may view it as harmful and essentially destructive (e.g., attacking or avoiding). If either of the participants is dissatisfied with the selected resolution strategy or the resolution itself, then the conflict episode can have a detrimental effect on the relationship.[15] What frequently happens is that one or both people will harbor negative feelings toward the other, causing them to create situations that have a cumulative effect. This is an example of what is known as an **escalatory conflict spiral**.[16] You can imagine what happens when you begin adding up all these bad experiences with a person, can't you? A better way to understand how all of this happens is to understand the types of conflict and be able to recognize them in our own lives.

Conflict Types

We've just read about three indicators that help us to understand why conflict affects us in either a positive or negative manner. For many people, winning or having control is so important that they will do whatever it takes to avoid losing, and this makes them feel good. Over the years, scholars have developed a conflict typology made up of both positively and negatively perceived behaviors. Labeling conflict allows us to place a name on our experiences, which can help to create an overall understanding. This is not meant to suggest that you should label everyone's disagreements, but it will help you to recognize what is happening and have a clearer understanding of the effects.

According to William Cupach and Daniel Canary, five types of interpersonal conflict are typically presented in the literature: parallel conflict, displaced conflict, misattributed conflict, latent conflict, and false conflict.[17] In other words, individuals can experience conflict based on real disagreements or incompatibilities, or they can argue over imagined issues. In addition, people can experience conflict over an issue that is not objectively based—a "he-said, she-said" sort of situation.[18]

When the disagreement is evident or objectively based and is understood accurately by both people involved, a **parallel conflict** exists. Both are aware of the issue at odds, and there is no misunderstanding by either party. For instance, if two people in a relationship argue because one of them is late for dinner every evening, they both understand the problem, and the conflict surrounds a clear and objective issue.

When the actual conflict issue is not discussed or perceptions of the actual issue are off base, **displaced conflict** occurs. For example, in the case of a man who is late for dinner, if his partner responds by saying that he doesn't care about her and takes her for granted, the conflict is now about something other than his late arrival for dinner. The conflict issue has become displaced and no longer revolves around an objective issue that can be easily examined and addressed.

When one or both parties incorrectly attributes the conflict to a person, event, or a behavior, this is **misattributed conflict**. Have you ever heard someone say that he or she was fighting with someone because that person "stole" a boyfriend or girlfriend? Why is he or she blaming the third party instead of engaging in conflict with the relational partner who chose to get involved with the third person? Where blame is placed is the **attribution**, and in this instance, conflict is attributed to the wrong person.

Conflict that actually should happen but is consistently avoided is known as **latent conflict**. In this case, there is a real and objective conflict issue that is accurately perceived, but both parties pretend that it doesn't exist. The problem with this is that the conflict does not go away—it festers. Let's say you're married, and your spouse always chuckles when you talk about going back to college. Although you don't like this, you never say anything because your spouse's reaction makes you think that it really may be a zany idea, and you fear an impending argument. What individuals with latent conflict fail to realize, often until it's too late, is that the issue will either rear its ugly head again or create deeper problems down the road. An odd outcome of pretending to agree on a topic is that people often experience greater relational satisfaction than if they actually do agree.[19] Some relationships proceed this way very successfully, suggesting there can be a positive outcome associated with latent conflict.

When the people involved in conflict misunderstand what has created it or what the conflict topic actually is, they are experiencing **false conflict**. For instance, if you accuse a coworker and friend of going behind your back to get the promotion you wanted when, in reality, the coworker did not do this, you are involved in a false conflict. This type of conflict can be very damaging to the friendship because the perceived ideas are without an accurate basis.

CHECKING YOUR UNDERSTANDING

Characteristics of Conflict

Before reading further, take a few minutes to assess your learning by writing your answers to the following items:

1. What are four primary components in the definition of conflict that help us to see it as natural and inevitable in our interpersonal relationships?

2. What are three indicators that can help you to understand whether the conflict you experience in your interpersonal relationships is likely to enhance it or destroy it? Provide your own real-life examples of each of these indicators.

3. What are five types of interpersonal conflict? Provide a brief description of each that clearly shows how they differ from one another.

How Messages Influence Conflict

One way to understand how and why conflict occurs is to dissect the actual language that is used during conversations. In an earlier chapter, you learned about the problems of aggressive language. Also problematic are disconfirming messages that frequently occur in our everyday communication, especially during conflict. It is important to know what these messages are before they create conflict and begin to affect relationships negatively. By being able to recognize the differences between confirming and disconfirming messages and the communication climate they ultimately create, you should be able to construct your interpersonal communication appropriately and avoid conflict.

A **confirmation** message causes another person to feel unique, respected, and important.[20] **Disconfirmation**, by contrast, is sometimes described as the "dark side" of interpersonal communication because it causes another person to feel inferior and unworthy of respect.[21] An important element of any successful relationship is always to be aware of your language choices—not only what you say, but also how you say it. When you were young, you may have heard someone talk about the Golden Rule: "Do unto others as you would have them do unto you." In the case of confirming versus disconfirming messages, we could follow the Golden Rule and say: "Speak to others as you wish to be spoken to." Confirming messages cause another person to feel good about himself or herself.[22]

Confirming Messages

Messages that confirm fall under the three basic positive responses: acknowledging, recognizing, and endorsing. An example of confirmation that ranges from simple acknowledgement to endorsement can be seen in this example: You just found out that you didn't get a job you'd hoped for. Your friend sees your sad face and says, "Wow, you were totally deserving of that job. You really did your homework and nailed the interview. I'm still proud of you, and you should be proud of yourself too. Those people at that company don't know what a terrific employee they just missed." Your friend has acknowledged your sadness, recognized your efforts, and endorsed your abilities. Of course, you still don't have the job, but this is a person with whom you'll most likely share information in the future—a common and beneficial result of confirming messages.

Table 8.1 reveals five specific types of confirmation behaviors that fall within the three overarching functions: *acknowledge, recognize, support, clarify,* and *endorse.* Specific examples of each behavior are included in the table that should help you to understand what types of things you could say to make someone feel more confirmed. You should note that each of these responses within the three functional categories builds upon the previous ones. In other words, as you move up the list of these behaviors,

TABLE 8.1

Confirmation Functions, Types, and Strategies

Confirmation Type	Strategy	Message Sample
Positive endorsement	Demonstrate positive support and agreement of the message and the sender	*I understand totally. If I had worked that hard on an assignment, I'd have expected the same thing. Is there anything I can do to help you figure out what to do next?*
Clarification	Elicit more information from the sender	*So what you're saying is you think you should have gotten an A on the paper because you met all the requirements. Is that what you mean?*
Support	Express understanding and reassure the sender	*I know what you mean. You have to do what is best for you.*
Recognition	Agreement about (not on) the content	*That's an interesting idea, and I can tell you feel very passionate about it.*
Acknowledgement	Noticing and reacting to the other person's message both verbally and nonverbally	*Uh huh . . . right* (as speaker nods head)

ENDORSING

RECOGNIZING

ACKNOWLEDGING

confirmation increases. What develops as you move from acknowledgement of people's feelings and thoughts to actually endorsing them are positive feelings of acceptance and confirmation. You validate them, and this creates a positive and supportive communication climate that can enhance your relationship. Unfortunately, communicating in a disconfirming manner can create the opposite feelings.

Disconfirming Messages

Disconfirming messages cause you to feel badly about yourself and may even cross over into such an extreme level of disconfirmation that someone's words make you feel like a nonperson—as if you don't exist.[23] Consider the earlier job interview example. What if, instead of the confirming remarks made in that example, your friend said, "Oh well—better luck next time. You know, I told you that you didn't really have the qualifications for that job, but you wouldn't listen." How would this make you feel? Do these words suggest that your friend values and respects you? Would you ever tell your friend anything like this again? Imagine the conflict that could result from speaking to another person in this manner.

It is important to understand the types of messages and/or behaviors that contribute to disconfirming communication because a lack of awareness can often lead to relational damage. These communication behaviors fall under three overarching functions of disconfirming messages: indifferent, disqualifying, and impervious.[24] Table 8.2 presents the three functions and indicates that the level or degree of disconfirmation increases as you move up the list of the seven types of disconfirming responses: *incongruous, incoherent, impersonal, tangential, irrelevant, interrupting,* and *impervious.* They become increasingly negative as communication moves from indifferent to impervious and makes you feel disregarded and unwanted. Specific examples of each type of disconfirmation are included

TABLE 8.2

Disconfirmation Functions, Types, and Strategies		
Disconfirmation Type	**Strategy**	**Message Sample**
Impervious	Ignore speaker and message	No verbal or nonverbal response
Interrupting	Cut off the speaker	Interrupt speaker midsentence
Irrelevant	Deliver response unrelated to the original message	Person A: *Honey, I'm making pasta for dinner. Does that sound good?* Person B: *What a crazy day I had today. Do you know what my boss did?*
Tangential	Use speaker's remark to shift conversation to your topic	*I know you need money, but my job isn't going well. I have to get a new one soon or I'm going to go crazy!*
Impersonal	Speak in generalizations or clichés to avoid responding	*Life is tough. No one ever said it was going to be easy!*
Incoherent	Unclear, ambiguous, or rambling responses	*Okay, well, I'll have to think about it and get back to you sometime.*
Incongruous	Nonverbal response contradicts verbal message sent	*Good grief! I said I love you, didn't I?* (said in an irritated tone of voice)

IMPERVIOUS

DISQUALIFYING

INDIFFERENT

ETHICS **in interpersonal communication**

An Experiment about Racism[25]

Communicating disconfirmation may be intentional or unintentional, but no one can discount the negative impact it has. Nowhere perhaps is disconfirming language more harmful than in situations involving discrimination. Consider the following research study.

In an effort to determine just how far the United States has come in overcoming discrimination and racism, ABC News recently conducted an experiment in a New Jersey deli to see how local citizens would react to racist comments aimed at Hispanic customers. When two Hispanic laborers (who were confederates and role-playing in the experiment) attempted to order coffee in broken English, the cashier (also a confederate) launched a host of disconfirming statements at them such as "Get back in your pickup truck with the rest of your family," "Speak English," "Go to Taco Bell," or "Can't help you. I don't speak Mexican."

The goal of the experiment was to determine how patrons at the deli would respond to these unethical, disconfirming, and racist comments. Would they stand up for the rights of all citizens and

come to the aid of these two Hispanic customers? The results of the experiment answer this question very clearly. During the morning of the experiment, eighty-eight people came into the deli. Of this number, forty-nine chose not to get involved at all, and nine customers took the side of the cashier and joined in making disconfirming remarks. One example of this was a black man who called out to the Hispanic men: "If you want me to make you leave, I'll make you leave. So leave. That's all I gotta say. Leave!" When ABC News later questioned the man about the reason for his comments, he responded, "You know what I think? I think they're taking our jobs because we ain't got no jobs." Of the eighty-eight customers in the store, thirty came to the defense of the men.

- What remarks do you find particularly disconfirming?
- How would you describe the effects these comments may have on the receiver?
- Can you think of reasons why the people in this deli engaged in these behaviors? Do you consider them unethical? Why or why not?

in the table to help you understand the types of statements to avoid. Being impervious creates the most negative sort of communication climate because you don't even get a chance to respond or communicate; you are considered a nonperson.

Communication Climate

The social and emotional tone within a relational experience is known as the **communication climate**. This is the way you feel about the relationship and what is currently happening within it. When you are in any type of relationship, your decision to use either confirming or disconfirming messages creates a communication climate. The way you speak to someone sets the emotional and relational tone between the two of you. Disconfirming messages typically cause individuals to become defensive, and this creates a negative communication climate between two people. Within every relationship, there is a communication climate, and it should not surprise you that a positive climate typically in dicates a more upbeat and satisfying relationship. In fact, a positive communication climate has been reported to be one of the best predictors of a happy family and a happy marriage.[26]

Unfortunately, there are people who fight regularly or make snide remarks and ugly faces to others during conversations. When you are with people like this, you probably feel a bit uncomfortable. This is because when they act this way, they are creating a communication climate that has a negative social tone. Once a climate becomes negative, it begins to spin out of control, with both parties fueling and reciprocating each others' negativity. This is often described as an **escalatory conflict spiral**.[27]

On the other hand, it is also possible that one person will simply choose to ignore the other person's comments and avoid getting involved in conflict. This is known as a **de-escalatory conflict spiral** and can be just as damaging to a relationship.[28] Imagine if you never talk constructively about conflict in your relationship. Issues would never be resolved, and this typically causes you to hold a grudge against the other person. The feelings continue to simmer beneath the surface. This example of destructive conflict was discussed earlier. What usually happens as a result is that one or both of the people in the relationship begin to withdraw, and the interdependence that may have existed between them begins to deteriorate. Although it is difficult to predict whether individuals will choose to engage in constructive or destructive forms of conflict, most people have a typical orientation that guides their communication. The next section will help you to determine how you typically deal with the conflict you experience.

Giving up during conflict can often make it worse—especially if this becomes a common pattern in the relationship.

Assessing Your Conflict Orientation

In an attempt to help you recognize whether you tend to participate in escalatory conflict spirals in your interpersonal communication and relationships, the following survey based on Morton Deutsch's research can help you to recognize whether your general **conflict orientation** is constructive or destructive.[29] The conflict orientation scale consists of two extremes: constructive conflict, in which individuals are thinking about the relationship and cooperating with one another, and destructive conflict, which is focused on negative behaviors such as humiliation and shame (disconfirmation). Take a moment to think about how you typically behave during conflict, and answer the twelve questions. The scoring method is included at the end of the instrument. Try not to think about your score or how you are answering the questions. Answer each one as quickly and honestly as possible.

ASSESS YOUR **communication personality**

Deutsch's Conflict Orientation Scale[30]

Log onto our self-assessment library, MyPersonalityProfile, found on MyCommunicationLab (www.mycommunicationlab.com), and assess your conflict orientation by completing the interactive assessment. Encourage someone with whom you've engaged in conflict to do the same. This way, you can compare your scores and begin to understand better how your communication traits may influence your interpersonal communication. If you prefer, you may use the assessment that follows.

Directions:

The following statements concern attitudes about conflict and ways you might choose to deal with it. Indicate how much you agree with each statement. Please circle the number that represents your honest feelings and typical responses.

1 = never true

2 = rarely

3 = sometimes true

4 = often

5 = always true

1. I am careful to avoid attacking a person's intelligence when I critique their ideas.
   1   2   3   4   5
2. When someone is stubborn, I often use insults to soften the stubbornness.
   1   2   3   4   5
3. If a person I am trying to influence really deserves it, I attack their character.
   1   2   3   4   5
4. When I critique a person's ideas, I try not to damage their self-concept.
   1   2   3   4   5
5. When people do things that are mean or cruel, I attack their character in order to correct their behavior.
   1   2   3   4   5
6. When nothing seems to work in trying to influence someone, I yell and scream in order to get some movement from them.
   1   2   3   4   5
7. I am not threatened by conflict.
   1   2   3   4   5
8. When people have conflicts, they should try to work with each other to solve them.
   1   2   3   4   5
9. Physical fighting is an effective way to deal with conflict.
   1   2   3   4   5
10. When I have a conflict with someone, I always discuss it with them as soon as possible.
    1   2   3   4   5

11. Overall, I think I handle conflicts effectively.

 1   2   3   4   5

12. Sometimes physically fighting it out is healthy.

 1   2   3   4   5

Scoring Instructions:

Reverse the score for items 2, 3, 5, 6, 9, and 12, so that if you wrote a 1 you will change it to 5, a 5 will change to a 1, a 2 will become a 4, a 4 will become a 2, and so forth for these 6 items. Once you have reversed the score for these items, now add the values for the twelve items together (including the newly reversed numbers). The lowest possible score is 12. The highest possible score is 60. Higher scores indicate that a person favors constructive or positive conflict; lower scores indicate an inclination to deal with conflict in a negative or destructive manner.

12–27 = Destructive conflict orientation

28–44 = Neither constructive nor destructive conflict is evident

45–60 = Constructive conflict orientation

Understanding Your Conflict Orientation. Your conflict orientation determines whether you choose to engage in positive or negative conflict, and this involves the degree to which your communication confirms or disconfirms the other person. According to Deutsch's research, if you score low ($\leq$ 27), you predominantly use a negative form of conflict resolution.[31] This reflects a competitive orientation in which one person wins and the other loses, and the person who loses typically feels disconfirmed. Whether we want love and acceptance from family, friends, partners, or acquaintances, the desire for confirmation is strong.[32] Yet it sometimes happens that the people we love the most show us the least acceptance and therefore hurt us the most through disconfirming communication. The most typical outcome is that people distance themselves to relieve the pain that has been created.[33] Why would we ever choose to communicate in this way? It may be because we feel safe in the relationship or that this is the one person with whom we feel we can be completely honest. Scholars have suggested that this is more often due to ill will than to poor skill, because dissatisfied individuals tend to disconfirm their partners while utilizing more of their confirming communication skills with strangers.[34] Though disconfirming communication occurs in many types of intimate relationships, it is frequently experienced between mothers and daughters (like June and Karen in the opening case study). This dyad has a unique relationship within the family because mother and daughter typically have a close and interdependent relationship, making them more prone to conflict. It is also more common in relationships in which people strive to integrate their individual goals and behaviors while attempting to maintain a close relationship.[35]

On a more positive note, if your score revealed a cooperative form of conflict resolution ($\geq$ 45), your relational partner likely feels confirmed by you. Those who experience cooperative conflict in their relationships are more open and friendly, and their communication is generally more effective. This is because they take the time to understand one another's goals and view them as valuable and the conflict as a shared problem.

WHAT CAN I **do now?**

If you scored low (≤ 27) on the Conflict Orientation scale, here are a few recommendations that can help you when you are experiencing conflict with someone you care about.

▶ *You could be more aware of times when your conflict is destructive and disconfirming.* This advice might seem obvious, but awareness is the first step toward creating effective communication in your relationships. Without awareness, you can't begin to deal constructively with the conflict you experience in them.

▶ *You could check the nonverbal messages that the person you are in conflict with is sending you.* Can you see the look on the person's face? Those who are feeling disconfirmed typically look down or away, display poor posture, and generally position themselves to avoid the interaction. On the other hand, the person may appear hostile or angry, with glaring eyes and clenched teeth. The moment you become aware of the other person's negative nonverbal messages, they should signal to you that you are not handling the situation well.

▶ *You could practice approaching conflict using a cooperative communication style.* First, reframe the conflict situation itself. Empathize—look through the other person's eyes and ask yourself how you might approach it differently. Second, show support for the other person's ideas, and remain positive and supportive. Finally, practice reciprocity, the give-and-take that is required for an effective and fair exchange. This shows respect for the other person and is tantamount to creating a cooperative resolution to the conflict.

 ## CHECKING YOUR UNDERSTANDING

Impact of Messages on Conflict

Before reading further, take a few minutes to assess your learning by writing your answers to the following items:

1. What are the three primary ways (the factors) in which someone would communicate if they use confirming messages?

2. What are the three primary ways (the factors) to communicate disconfirming messages?

3. What is the definition of a *communication climate*, and why is it important to your relationships?

4. Based on the conflict orientation assessment that you completed, what are two or three behaviors that someone with a destructive conflict orientation might exhibit? What are two or three behaviors that someone with a constructive conflict orientation might exhibit?

Factors That Influence Conflict Interactions

Even though we may have a fairly consistent conflict orientation, elements frequently influence and alter how we deal with conflict. Scholars have begun to examine two individual factors that strongly influence how conflict is handled: personality and the need for power in the relationship. In addition, a third factor that has become critically important to how conflicts are played out in the 21st century is technology. We cannot deny that individuals frequently favor email or text-messaging to confront others with a problem rather than engaging them face to face. It is important to recognize the influence of these three factors if people are to better understand the conflict they experience.

Personality and Conflict

Some models of personality suggest that it is the situation or context that triggers the personality traits. Research has found that personality traits are activated when people encounter competing goals.[36] In other words, when personality traits are activated, they influence the communication and, ultimately, the conflict behaviors. Specific traits that influence conflict and the way in which it is managed fall within two fundamental personality dimensions. The **approach** and **avoidance** dimensions of personality make up the building blocks of our personality traits. Approach and avoidance are biologically based systems of the personality that operate within different structures of the brain.[37] In other words, people can be described as predominantly having either approach or avoidance personality traits.

People who display positive emotions that are more related to the extraversion component of temperament exhibit approach characteristics. They focus their energy on positive and rewarding stimuli. In essence, they are optimistic and have a positive outlook on people, situations, and life in general. An approacher could aptly be described as someone who sees the glass as being "half full." In relationships, an approacher typically looks on the bright side and pays attention to what is working well. Because of this outlook, approachers experience fewer conflicts, so their relationships require less work. Researchers have gone so far as to suggest that approachers have higher-quality relationships and do a better job of managing conflict.

Avoiders either withdraw or exhibit negative emotional reactions to others. The pure avoider sees the glass as being "half empty." Even if there is nothing particularly negative in a conversation or interpersonal encounter, the avoider will impose negativity or even imagine it. It should not be surprising to learn that people with avoidance tendencies experience unsatisfying close relationships and irritation with others. They engage in quarrelsome behaviors that lead to higher incidences of conflict over time. Romantic relationships are problematic for avoiders because they engage in both active and passive destructive conflict behaviors. For example, because they focus on negatives, they tend to provoke disagreements or seek out situations that will likely turn out badly. For whatever reason, the negative section of the brain is stimulated frequently for avoiders. It seems as if they actually experience some kind of reward in these situations.[38]

According to John Gottman, the most unstable couples (dating and married) are those who fall within the avoidance dimension.[39] This, he says, is due to the difference between the way approachers and avoiders listen. When approachers are involved in conflict, they listen to their partners, openly disagree, and confront the conflict issue. Avoidant individuals, by contrast, are dismal conflict participants because they tend to view themselves as the obvious loser, fail to express their opinions completely and openly, and engage in very little listening to their partners' feelings. The avoider's

NATURE/NURTURE intersections

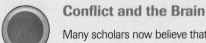

Conflict and the Brain

Many scholars now believe that the two personality dimensions of approach and avoidance are manifestations of temperament that are genetic, inherited, evident in early childhood, and relatively stable throughout life. Allport defines *temperament* as "the characteristic phenomena of an individual's emotional nature, including his susceptibility to emotional stimulation, his customary strength and speed of response, the quality of his prevailing mood, and all peculiarities of fluctuation and intensity of mood."[40] Individual temperaments can be seen in different brain activity within the

prefrontal area of the brain.[41] As we learned in Chapter 2, the Big Five temperament traits that are most frequently depicted are openness to experience, conscientiousness, extraversion, agreeableness, and neuroticism.[42] Hans and Michael Eysenck reduced these to three components: neuroticism, extraversion, and psychoticism.[43] These temperaments are associated with specific brain activity. Extraverts, for example, are more positive and impulsive and therefore have greater left prefrontal activation, which is associated with anticipating rewards. Neurotics experience more right prefrontal activation that has most often been associated with fear of punishment.

conflict falls into two types: hostile (because of negative listening behaviors) and defensive or hostile-detached and emotionally uninvolved. Both hostile or hostile-detached behaviors can have very damaging effects on relationships. Ultimately, these behaviors typically involve a need for power, which influences the way in which conflict is managed.

Need for Power and Conflict

Although most people think that a healthy relationship should be an equal relationship, this is most often not the case. Power differences exist, and individuals need to be aware of how they communicate power to others. The amount of power that is imposed in a relationship has the ability to increase or decrease the stability of the relationship and the overall satisfaction of the relational partners.

In the field of interpersonal communication and the study of relationships, power is most often defined as a person's ability to purposefully influence his or her partner's behaviors, thoughts, and/or feelings.[44] This is frequently the case within marriages, in which the husband traditionally is thought to have more power than the wife. In an effort to better understand whether traditional perceptions of power conflicts in marriage exist, Philip Blumstein and Pepper Schwartz conducted a study of over 3,000 married couples[45] and discovered that 64% of these couples felt that power in their marriages was balanced. Although this is a positive step in our society, since couples who experience shared power have more successful relationships,[46] the need for power differs from person to person and from relationship to relationship. For example, I might feel powerful in my relationship if I can convince my husband that we need to make financial decisions together. Another person might think that evidence of power in a relationship is winning an argument. Since interpretations of power vary, a better way to detect power and its effects on conflict is to understand the need for power.

When we feel a desire to be right and in control, we have **power needs**. William Schutz maintains that to satisfy these needs, we typically choose to take on one of three roles that represent our power personality (see Figure 8.1): *democrat*, *autocrat*, or *abdicrat*.[47] These roles appear to develop early in life and are associated with learned behaviors.[48] Unfortunately, power needs correspond with interpersonal conflict. For example,

FIGURE 8.1

Our Personality Affects Our Need for Power and Conflict

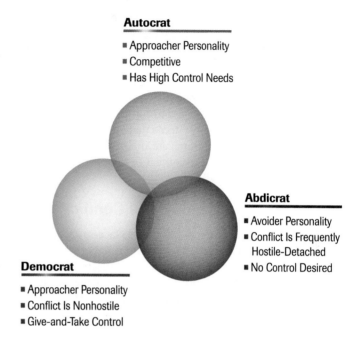

Autocrat
- Approacher Personality
- Competitive
- Has High Control Needs

Abdicrat
- Avoider Personality
- Conflict Is Frequently Hostile-Detached
- No Control Desired

Democrat
- Approacher Personality
- Conflict Is Nonhostile
- Give-and-Take Control

democrats are typically considered to maintain the most positive and desired power response. They maintain approacher personality traits, and they focus on equality and appreciate it when every voice is heard. When democrats engage in conflict, it is not hostile and involves give-and-take conversations. Autocrats handle conflict very differently because they want complete control, and their need for power is high. They are extremely competitive and often hostile; they strive to win, to have the final say, and to make decisions whenever possible.[49] The opposite of this is the abdicrat, who is a follower and maintains the personality traits of an avoider. This person prefers to let others take control even though he or she is not always happy with the decisions. This reflects the hostile-detached behavior that we discussed earlier.

Determining which of these three power needs provides the most accurate description of someone suggests how that person communicates with another, the type of power relationship that exists, and possible conflicts. For example, if Sue is an abdicrat married to Steve, what power balance would enable him to communicate most effectively and deal with their conflicts: democrat, abdicrat, or autocrat? To help you answer this question, examine the following conversation:

Sue: Steve, tomorrow's Friday. Do you want to talk about plans for the weekend?

Steve: I want to go to the Monster Truck Rally they've been advertising on the radio all week.

Sue: Hmmm . . . really? You want to drive all the way into the city when gas is so expensive? What about maybe seeing that new Jean-Claude Van Damme movie that you've been talking about?

Steve: Are you crazy? I've been dying to go to the Monster Truck Rally, and I'm not gonna miss it!

Sue [as she stomps off]: Fine!

On the basis of the above conversation, what need for power does Steve communicate to Sue? As we stated, Sue is an abdicrat. Without directly admitting it, she makes it fairly obvious that she's not interested in the Monster Truck Rally. However, Steve is determined to go, and Sue gives in. What does Steve's response say about his need for power? He doesn't give Sue any options; he states that he's going no matter what, and that's the end of the conversation. Would you say that he is an autocrat? He isn't sensitive to his wife's feelings, and he fails to acknowledge that she is less than enthusiastic. He also fails to notice that she made an alternative suggestion: to see a movie Steve had suggested earlier. Sue doesn't make any attempt to pursue the discussion further; she defers to Steve and completely avoids any sort of confrontation. Steve and Sue have different power needs that align with their personalities (approach versus avoidance), and they communicate differently to deal with the conflict. These patterned methods or responses to conflict become each person's conflict management style.

Technology and Conflict

Conflict is not limited to face-to-face situations. Technology is everywhere, and it plays an important role in our interpersonal communication. We can keep in touch with people in our lives even if they are at work, sitting in class, riding a bus, or watching a movie. Unfortunately, technology use does not always have positive consequences because it is missing some vital components of face-to-face dialogue. Because of this, there are more opportunities for conflict to develop. Researchers have begun to investigate computer-mediated communication through the use of cell phones, email, voicemail, and text messages to create, resolve, and even avoid conflict.

Psychologists tell us that what's missing within electronic communication are the physical cues in the dialogue that represent the other person and your relationship together.[50] These are the tangible cues of actual dialogue (e.g., the smile, the intense look) that spark memories about events and conversations you have shared, and they are important in conflict negotiation. For example, if you send a text message to your best friend Sara telling her that you're irritated that she failed to return your phone call the previous evening and she does not reply for several hours, you might become even more irritated. On the other hand, if you waited to see Sara and tell her how you felt, you would recall past events with her and reflect on what a good friend she has been. In person, you and Sara have many opportunities to connect with one another both verbally and nonverbally as you negotiate your relationship.

Our ability and decision to communicate electronically is increasing. Thus, it is important to understand the mistakes we might make as we deal with touchy situations, recognize why we make them, and know how to avoid them in the future. The telephone is most frequently used to avoid conflict because it's easy to hang up on the other person when arguing on the phone.[51] Other forms of technology can create or exacerbate conflict. Text-messaging has recently been depicted as contributing to relationship failure.[52] It enables individuals to communicate with others without the immediate and visual responses (over hours, days, and weeks), which can have unwanted effects. Think about this example: Janette is irritated with her boyfriend and sends him a text message. She stares at the two-inch screen full of word codes and symbols that attempt to capture both of their thoughts and emotions. Back and forth go the messages over the course of the day, and they look something like this:

U were rude

Look I tried 2b nice but u overreacted

Me? w'evr

W'ever is right btw u said some rude things 2

LOL! ur a jerk!

{Silence—no response}

This rather simple disagreement escalated because there was no shared discussion. The physical elements that help us to create and develop relationships are missing in text messages, so there is considerable opportunity for disaster. What has occurred between Janette and her boyfriend can be described as the **disinhibition effect** in which individuals feel little restraint and choose to express themselves freely.[53] Since electronic communication is not real-time communication, we expect to wait minutes, hours, and even days for a reply. Because this is **asynchronous communication**, or time-lapsed, we are not forced to deal with immediate responses and become disinhibited.[54] This can create terrible conflict in our relationships because we fail to consider the reality of the situation and how our words may be received and interpreted. On the other hand, it may also enable you to be more honest, and this can have certain relational benefits.

Email messages appear to contribute to conflict escalation because of the diminished feedback, minimal social cues, excess attention (e.g., angry thoughts are perceived as angrier, criticism is viewed as more critical), and length of the messages, which are usually more concise than verbal conflict encounters.[55] A recent study reported that college students were guilty of composing hurtful email messages and that the best way to resolve conflicts created in this context was over the telephone or face to face.[56] On the other hand, computer-mediated communication may also give people more time to think and choose their words more carefully.[57]

Recognizing the differences in how you deal with conflict electronically and face to face can be especially enlightening. Read over your electronic messages carefully. Then ask yourself, "Would I use these words and say it this way if I were talking to him or her in person?" Check your communication. If you are using electronic means, then you have the time—use it. We all know that conflict is going to occur, and when it does, we can deal with it more easily if we are aware of our own methods of doing so. The next section will assist you in detecting your style of managing conflict.

Just because you text someone and spell out your feelings, never assume that your message has been clearly received.

CHECKING YOUR UNDERSTANDING

Factors That Influence Conflict Interactions

Before reading further, take a few minutes to assess your learning by writing your answers to the following items:

1. What are the two primary personality dimensions that influence interpersonal conflict? Can you describe how these individuals typically behave?

2. What three terms are used to describe a person's need for power? Can you explain how they are different from one another?

3. Can you describe how electronic communication differs from face-to-face communication? How can it create and worsen conflict? How are text-messaging and email asynchronous and disinhibiting?

Recognizing Your Conflict Management Style

Years of research in interpersonal conflict have produced a variety of descriptions and categories of conflict management. Many textbooks, including this one, subscribe to the five-style perspective; these styles are withdrawal, accommodating, forcing, compromising, and collaborating (see Figure 8.2).[58] The preference for any of these specific styles develops over the course of your life, and some researchers even go so far as to claim that it is genetic. Most scholars describe an individual's conflict management style as emerging from a combination of genetic, cultural, and social influences. What this means is that sometimes you purposefully select your conflict management strategy considering the person and the interaction, and at other times, you opt for what feels most comfortable and natural. For example, think back to a conflict you had with your parents when you were younger. You might really have wanted to argue but knew that arguing would get you into more trouble, so you stepped back. The fact that you stopped, thought about it, and withdrew was wise, but disagreements don't always lend themselves to choices; sometimes

FIGURE 8.2

Conflict Management Strategies at Work: We all develop our own toolbox of strategies to manage our conflict situations.

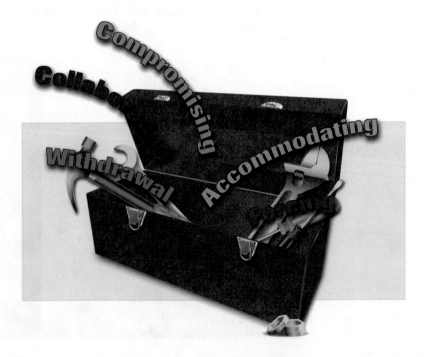

you react almost instinctively. If you feel that you have developed a fairly consistent pattern of managing conflict over the course of your life, it most likely falls within the following five styles of conflict management. See whether you can locate one style that seems to describe your most consistent conflict responses. At the end of this section, you will find a self-assessment that will help you to determine the conflict style that is typical for you as well as a discussion of influential elements: culture, sex differences, and context.

- *Withdrawal.* The style of conflict management in which you physically and psychologically remove yourself from the encounter is known as **withdrawal**. It indicates that you have very little concern for your own goals or those of the other person. So what can happen when you remain this passive during a disagreement? The other person can decide that you are being cooperative and therefore gets his or her way; or the other person can decide that you are being competitive and become frustrated by your lack of engagement and support.

- *Accommodating.* A general lack of concern for your own goals and support for someone else's occurs when you **accommodate**. Most accommodators fail to realize that they are doing this. This style often leads to long-term relational problems as one person may always feel like he or she is giving in to the wishes of the other. Unfortunately, we often assume that when someone consents, that person is feeling positive and favors the decision, but this is certainly not always the case.

- *Forcing.* A competitive and often aggressive conflict style is **forcing**, which is characterized by the exertion of power over others. Excessive use of this conflict management style is often viewed as bullying because when individuals feel strongly about an issue, they will often do whatever is necessary to ensure success, regardless of the effects on others.[59] This aggressive bullying behavior serves to demoralize the other person through frequent put-downs, harassment, and, in some cases, physical violence. Forcing creates a win–lose orientation and places relationships at risk.

- *Compromising.* Viewed most often as a positive conflict management strategy, **compromise** produces a win–win situation. However, in reality, both individuals must give up something. On the positive side, the two who compromise care about the relationship enough to give up or modify their original goals and discover a mutually acceptable outcome. Two items to consider in deciding whether to compromise are time constraints and the importance of the issue. If either of these factors is present in the conflict decision, then compromise is not a good option; in one case, it is much too time-consuming, and in the other, there might simply be too much at stake. Therefore, although compromise is typically seen as positive and productive, it can also be associated with a lose–lose outcome.

- *Collaborating.* One of the most positive and constructive conflict management strategies is **collaborating** because it integrates the goals of both parties. With this strategy, the two of you problem-solve and come up with a mutually satisfying decision that does not involve your having to give up anything, as with compromising. No one wins or loses because neither person is viewed as more powerful than the other. Between the two of you, a new and creative solution is generated by "thinking outside the box." This strategy is typically associated with increased feelings of relational satisfaction because collaboration requires communicating with "we" language instead of "I" language.[60] The downside of this strategy involves effort, motivation, and time—things that people in the throes of conflict rarely stop to consider.

To help you discover your own particular conflict management style, complete the following instrument, and see how you typically deal with interpersonal conflict.

ASSESS YOUR **communication personality**

What Is Your Conflict Management Style?

Log onto our self-assessment library, MyPersonalityProfile found on MyCommunicatonLab (www.mycommunicationlab.com), and assess your Conflict Management Style by completing the interactive assessment. Encourage someone with whom you have engaged in conflict to do the same. This way, you can compare your scores and styles and begin to understand how each of you communicates during conflict situations and why you may or may not be resolving them to your satisfaction. If you prefer, you can use the assessment that follows.

Directions:

Think of a specific person close to you with whom you have had a recent disagreement. Look at the following questions, and fill in the number from the responses below that best describe how you handled, or typically handle, your conflict with this person:

1 = never

2 = rarely

3 = sometimes

4 = frequently

5 = always

1. _____ It is important to me to win an argument with this person.

2. _____ I usually give in during conflict.

3. _____ I am usually stubborn and hold my position when I have a conflict with this person.

4. _____ In conflicts, I give up some points I have in exchange for others in order to resolve our differences.

5. _____ It is important to view conflict as a problem we need to solve together.

6. _____ It is important to me to win an argument with this person.

7. _____ I am willing to compromise to solve a conflict with this person.

8. _____ I try to avoid disagreements with this person.

9. _____ I will give up what I want in order to end a conflict with this person.

10. _____ It is important to discuss both of our points of view in a conflict.

11. _____ I strongly assert my opinions and views in conflict with this person.

12. _____ I withdraw from disagreements with this person.

13. _____ I try to find the middle- or common-ground in a conflict with this person.

14. _____ I will give in to this person in order to end a disagreement.

15. _____ I try to be cooperative and creative in resolving conflict with this person.

16. _____ I shy away from disagreements with this person.

17. _____ I will give up what I want to please this person.

18. _____ I take a powerful stance to win during an argument with this person.

19. _____ I usually will compromise when we are getting nowhere during a conflict.

20. _____ I try to be open and share all my ideas so that we can work together to resolve disagreements.

Scoring Instructions:

Determining Your Conflict Management Style Score: Place the number you selected (1–5) for each of the items below. Then add your scores together to determine each of your style categories. Your total scores can range from 4–20 in each category, and the highest score is the conflict management style you tend to use. You may discover you fall within more than one conflict management style, which is very common. Circle the style(s) where your score was the highest and refer to the following descriptions for a better understanding of how you communicate when you are managing conflict.

1._____	2._____	3._____	4._____	5._____
8._____	9._____	6._____	7._____	10._____
12._____	14._____	11._____	13._____	15._____
16._____	17._____	18._____	19._____	20._____
_____	_____	_____	_____	_____
Withdrawal	Accommodation	Forcing	Compromising	Collaborating

Understanding Your Conflict Management Style.   You should see that one or two of your scores of conflict management style are higher than the others. There are five different styles and four questions that measure each style. For each style, you can earn a possible score of between 4 and 20. The higher your score on a style, the more likely you are to use this style as you are dealing with conflict in your interpersonal relationships. Rarely will anyone score a perfect 20, but it is very likely that your highest score(s) will fall between 15 and 20. Also, remember that your score reflects your conflict style with a specific person. It is possible that the context (and this includes the person) can alter the way in which you handle a particular conflict situation. But also recall that people frequently resort to what feels most comfortable and natural; therefore, you should see one or two styles with higher scores ($\geq$ 15).

- Withdrawal is when you avoid conflict because conflict makes them uncomfortable. When you do this, you don't express your feelings or opinions, and your goals are not realized. If this is you, then the conflict you were thinking about as you were completing the assessment was likely a frustrating experience.

- Accommodators give in to please others. If you scored above 15 in this category, you may be able to recall giving in when you and this person were in conflict. There is a specific reason to accommodate other people. In a work situation, you would probably accommodate your boss because you know that doing this will serve you well in your employment. Even though you lose, the result might not be all bad if it can have a positive impact on your future.

- A high score in the Forcing category should not surprise you if you are a competitive person who hates losing. Verbally aggressive people (as discussed in Chapter 4) will do what it takes to win, and, of course, this can cause relational problems. If you scored high in this category, can you recall how this conflict ended? Do you currently have a successful relationship with this person? Give this some careful thought as you consider this particular conflict episode.

- Compromising can sometimes be viewed as "giving in," though it really can be very positive. If you scored above 15 in this category, then you and the other person must have thought of a mutually acceptable solution. Good for you! On the other hand, you might feel that you got the "short end of the stick," and the compromise didn't necessarily work to your advantage. If this is what happened in your interpersonal conflict situation, you might ask yourself why you compromised. This understanding can help you to realize why you feel positive or negative after a particular conflict has been resolved.

- Although collaborating is thought of as the most positive and constructive conflict management style, people are rarely able to do this consistently. It is time consuming and difficult. But if you earned a high score in this category, then the effort that you had to put forth was important and worth it. You are most likely an open-minded person who is honest, aware, and considerate of others. Now ask yourself whether you would have achieved the same score if you had been thinking of a different person.

 WHAT CAN I **do now?**

Here are a few recommendations that could help you during conflict with someone you care about. The most positive conflict management styles are compromising and collaborating. If you scored low (≤ 8) on those two, you might want to consider these suggestions:

▶ *Practice empathy.* This involves putting yourself in another person's shoes and feeling the way that person does. Instead of focusing on winning, stop and consider what the other person is experiencing. Let's say you are arguing with your girlfriend or boyfriend about spending too much time with his or her friends rather than yours. Your friends are obviously important to you, so you can certainly understand that your boyfriend or girlfriend feels the same about his or her friends. Stop and recognize these feelings. Now attempt a compromise.

▶ *Move slowly and remain calm.* If you jump to conclusions or make impulsive decisions, the outcome will most likely be unpleasant. The key to compromising or collaborating is keeping an open mind and engaging in an open discussion. You must do this calmly and carefully.

▶ *Ask questions and listen carefully to the answers.* If you fail to listen to the other person, the solution will not be based on accurate information and someone is bound to leave dissatisfied. Doing this can help you to reach a compromise or even allow the two of you to come up with new and creative ideas that will satisfy you both. This is a critical step in either compromise or collaboration and an ultimate win–win situation.

Culture and Conflict Management Style

In today's diverse world, individuals from various cultural backgrounds interact on a daily basis. Because research has shown that there are differences in the ways in which people from various countries or racial/ethnic backgrounds manage conflict, it is important to understand these differences. We saw in previous chapters that the level of individualism and collectivism in a culture accounts for some very basic communication differences. This is also true with cultural patterns in conflict strategies. By examining conflict management styles from these two frameworks, we can analyze and understand conflict situations and possibly avoid future destructive encounters.

North America as well as the northern and western regions of Europe are typically described as highly individualistic with an "I focus" rather than a "we focus."[61] This is evident in everyday interactions with friends, family, and coworkers as people use more direct and self-interested conflict strategies. This means that dominating and forcing or competing methods of dealing with conflict are typical. So when conflict arises, individualists voice personal goals and interests and work to see them through. This sends a message of status and success, which is very important to people from a more individualistic culture. Try to imagine two people from individualistic cultures butting heads during a conflict; a win–win outcome is difficult if both people are high on the individualistic continuum. This is not to say that other forms of conflict management are not possible or used; it just means that forcing and competition are prevalent in individualistic cultures.

Collectivistic cultures, by contrast, value the group and what can be accomplished together. This cultural pattern of communication is commonly seen in Asia, Africa, the Middle East, and South America. During conflict, collectivists are accepting of avoidance (withdrawal) behaviors,[62] typically withdraw from conflict, and are more obliging in order to be sensitive to others and allow face-saving. Ultimately, they have a higher expectation that conflict will destroy relationships, and they are more interested in the good of the group.[63]

Americans, who are considered individualistic, frequently encounter problems when disagreements arise during business dealings in China. If these differences in conflict management style are not recognized and understood beforehand, they can be very counterproductive and detrimental to the overall business relationship. The key is to become "conflict fluent" by developing a repertoire of conflict communication skills to adapt to various cultural contexts and maintain harmony.[64]

Sex and Conflict Management Style

Research tells us that men and women do not always use the same conflict management style options, especially in marital relationships. Several theories may help to explain these differences. A physiological explanation suggests that conflict between men and women differs according to a physical need to resolve or escape conflict.[65] Men have a stronger physiological reaction to conflict (e.g., rapid heartbeat or sweating) that causes them to avoid and withdraw from conflict in an effort to reduce feelings of stress. Women, on the other hand, are more prepared to confront conflict and deal with it head-on because they react less stressfully to the conflict they experience.

Another theory, which is based on socialization differences between men and women, says that women are thought to be relationally focused while men are driven by greater independence with a focus on achievement.[66] As a result of this socialization, conflict for men and women plays out very differently. Women tend to be more open and willing to discuss conflict in relationships so that compromise or collaboration of ideas can occur. Men, by contrast, opt to withdraw more frequently, owing to a desire for independence.[67] When men and women are engaged in conflict, the female responds to male withdrawal with demanding behaviors that resemble a forcing conflict management style. In marital contexts, stress appears to be a driving force for these conflict responses; women in stressful conflict situations tend to express more anger and are more confrontational and critical, whereas men withdraw and avoid.[68] What occurs as a result of these conflict interactions is relational dissatisfaction and turmoil, which often destroys the relationship.[69] This should not be new information for couples, however, since research has reported that these demand/withdraw communication patterns between men and women are established and evident very early in both dating and marital relationships.[70] Thus, if you see these patterns early as a couple, it is unlikely that they will change if they are not understood and managed.

So what do married men and women prefer from their partners when it comes to conflict management? Males are reportedly more satisfied with their marriages when they and their wives use a compromising conflict management style; males are least satisfied when they use an accommodating style. When wives are accommodating, however, male satisfaction appears to be the lowest. Married females, by contrast, are more satisfied when they use both compromising and accommodating styles (the style that produces the least satisfaction for husbands). Where research tells us they are in agreement is in regard to a competitive conflict management style; neither sex is satisfied with the relationship if competition is the management style of choice.[71] Though sex differences appear to exist among married women and men, many inconsistent findings have been reported in other relational contexts.

Context and Conflict Management Style

Conflict and the management of it are not the same in every type of relationship. Consider two relationships that you currently are in and in which you sometimes experience disagreements. If these are two very different types of interpersonal relationships (e.g., a significant other and a boss), the conflicts that occur are typically not the same. Because they are different, the way in which you manage the conflict also varies. In this section, we will consider how conflict differs in three interpersonal contexts: committed relationships, friendships, and the workplace.

Committed Relationships. Conflict is important in committed relationships because it conveys the levels of interdependence that exists and provides the means for negotiating vital issues that come up. Daniel Canary, William Cupach, and Susan Messman suggest that the length of couples' confrontations, the decision to avoid or withdraw, and the degree to which they engage in negative behaviors (e.g., sarcasm, put-downs, name-calling) determine their success as a couple.[72] John Gottman focuses on four specific negative behaviors, which he refers to as the **Four Horsemen of the Apocalypse**, that can send relationships into a cascade of isolation and withdrawal: (1) complaining/criticism, (2) contempt, (3) defensiveness, and (4) stonewalling. If a couple is considered stable and strong, they do not consistently engage in these four behaviors—it is as simple as that. According to Gottman, stable and satisfied couples engage in five times as many positive behaviors as negative ones.[73]

Conflict in Friendships. It is much more difficult to describe and analyze conflict within friendships. There are several reasons for this. First, friendships change as people age. During adolescence, friendships often are a central focus and are much more intimate and intense than adult friendships.[74] As we get older, though friendships are not quite as prevalent, the pleasurable experiences within them play a much larger role than the disagreements that might occur. Consistent conflict patterns are not typically evident in these relationships because of these aspects of friendships:[75] they are voluntary; there is a scarcity of rules; inequality or power imbalances can exist;[76] and friendships involve voluntary reciprocity or the choice for mutual reliance.[77] So, in contrast to committed relationships, friendships do not entail specific expectations other than a fair balance of give and take.

Experiencing conflict with a friend helps you to better understand the other person and lets you know where you stand in that relationship, but friendships are delicate and easily broken.[78] The public commitments or contractual agreements that are present in family, marriages, or even in the workplace do not exist in friendships. Thus, when conflicts do occur, it is relatively easy to imagine life without this relationship. Some of the most common conflict issues among friends revolve around topics such as competition for jobs or promotions; the affection of others; and differing attitudes, beliefs, and values.[79] Essentially, if friendships between adults are to be maintained, conflict needs to be avoided. The ease of friendship "breakability" clearly indicates that conflict is risky. On the other hand, conflict can strengthen these relationships (e.g., you know where you stand). This suggests that stable and long-lasting friendships are the ones in which individuals have risked disagreements and have endured them.

Bosses frequently engage in a confrontational conflict style that creates feelings of powerlessness for their employees.

Conflict in the Workplace. Managing conflict in the workplace is very different from managing conflict in committed relationships because a relational future with the people you work with is not optional; as long as you are at the job, you are stuck with them. Two primary forms of interpersonal relationships exist in the workplace: those between superiors and subordinates and those between coworkers. Because of the power differential that exists within these two groups, the conflict that is experienced within them is vastly different. For example, managers in the workplace tend to rely on their power, which means that when conflict ensues, these superiors tend to utilize forceful and competitive styles of management, prompting subordinates to avoid or withdraw.[80] This prevents the development of strong relational bonds.

The patterns of conflict that exist between coworkers are much less clear. Two possible indicators of successful conflict management between coworkers are knowledge of each other's views about the conflict issue and the organizational climate (specifically the organization's history of managing conflict). If an organization has set a precedent for handling conflict, then it is much easier to predict whether employee conflict is likely to be resolved appropriately and effectively. Organizational progress relies on successful conflict management. Although many companies fail to institute formal strategies, being proactive and creating a conflict management plan can prevent future problems from interfering with business. In addition, this can lead to the development of a culture of conflict management that is likely to result in having satisfied employees. The underlying message about workplace conflict is that it must be handled competently, appropriately, and effectively.

CHECKING YOUR UNDERSTANDING
Recognizing Your Conflict Management Style

Before completing the chapter, take a few minutes to assess your learning by writing your answers to the following items:

1. Can you list and describe each of the five conflict management styles? Which style of conflict management is typical for you? How might this affect your current interpersonal communication and relationships?

2. What are the differences between individualistic and collectivistic cultures when it comes to managing conflict? How might these differences affect how people from different cultures do business together?

3. How do men and women communicate differently to manage their conflicts? Describe the differences between conflicts that occur in committed relationships and those that occur in friendships? Why is it important to understand these differences?

4. How are workplace relationships different from other relationships? Why is conflict handled differently in the workplace, and why is this important to understand?

A Communication Development Plan for June

To complete the story of June and her daughter Karen, recall how June spoke to Karen and how this led to a downward spiral of negativity and conflict. June obviously cares about her daughter's future, but the communication climate between them simply doesn't allow for a productive conversation.

What do you think?

Who is the bigger culprit in taking this conversation downhill?

June and Karen are deeply engaged in an escalatory conflict spiral. Because June is relentless in her questions and accusations, Karen's back is against the wall, and becoming defensive is her only recourse. At this point, Karen begins to make her own negative contributions to the conflict. It is important to outline the specific behaviors each of them offers to this unfortunate situation.

What disconfirmation behaviors do June and/or Karen engage in, and does one of them appear to need more power and be more at fault?

June and Karen are both contributors to this escalatory conflict spiral. However, June gets a head start with the disconfirming behaviors that she uses. June uses very disconfirming behaviors with Karen, and one of the primary ways is with her monologue to Karen. She questions Karen over and over again, barely letting her get a word in. When June begins to belittle and name-call (e.g., "lazy and irresponsible"), Karen mirrors her mother's behavior by calling June "obsessive-compulsive."

What power and conflict management strategies are present in June and Karen's conflict?

Overall, it appears that June may have a high need for power as she hopes to control Karen's behavior. She seems more like an autocrat in this relationship. Because of this power need, Karen responds by withdrawing from the situation. You might recall from your reading that withdrawal is one style of conflict management that creates frustration and relational deterioration.

What could have improved the conversation between June and Karen?

Possible explanations:

1. June first needs to understand her own need for power and how her communication affects her relationships. This self-assessment and self-awareness are important because the power role that individuals play (democrat, autocrat, and abdicrat) in relationships is directly related to conflict.[82] If June cannot understand this connection, she will continue to engage in conflict, and Karen is probably not the only recipient of her power

need. Because of this, June attempts to force her opinion on Karen, causing her to withdraw.

2. Karen also must understand her conflict management style. Because June forces, Karen withdraws, and nothing is accomplished. If Karen hopes to have a relationship with her mother, she needs to learn how to deal with June's conflict strategies.

3. June and Karen need to be coached in the behaviors associated with the collaborative conflict management style. June must first accept the fact that collaborating is not giving up her power, keeping in mind that a need for power has most likely been learned over the course of her life.[83] Karen also has work to do in understanding the role she plays in this conflict. By giving up and exiting the conversation, the conflict remains unresolved. The relationship suffers when conflict is allowed to escalate and fester. Therefore, Karen must work with her mother to "think outside the box" and craft a solution that will make them both happy. Collaborating typically leads to stronger, more satisfying relationships.[84]

4. Think about a relationship conflict that you have observed or personally experienced, especially one in which someone has had legitimate power over you. How does this power relationship influence how you handle the relationship and your ultimate conflict management?

Take Aways

This chapter focused on conflict in interpersonal relationships and how to assess, understand, and resolve them. One of the most important ideas to gather from reading this chapter is that conflict is something everyone experiences in all sorts of relationships. Because of this, it is important to have a clear understanding of the type of conflict that is experienced in relationships and why/how it occurred. Without this knowledge, it can rarely be resolved so that both people are satisfied. Understanding and self-assessing is a key component, and this chapter offers assistance in these processes. The following lists summarize what you have learned in this chapter.

You have increased your understanding and knowledge of:

- The differences between constructive and destructive conflict and the various types of conflict.
- Disconfirming messages and their relationship to developing the communication climate and conflict.
- Positive or negative orientations toward conflict.
- The differences between approach and avoidance personalities and the impact of conflict on the communication climate.
- How the need for power can affect conflict and conflict management strategies.
- Conflict orientations and conflict management styles and how conflict management style affects relational satisfaction.

- The way in which conflict can be created through different technologies.
- How conflict occurs and can be managed in different contexts.

Following are some of the ways in which you assessed and learned about how your own conflict style and management strategies influence your interpersonal communication:

- Your own use of constructive and destructive conflict.
- Your particular conflict orientation.
- Your conflict style with someone close to you.

Following are a list of skills you can develop to enhance your interpersonal communication:

- Develop and use a repertoire of constructive conflict strategies.
- Develop and use confirming messages to resolve conflict.
- Compose your electronic messages carefully to assess possible interpretations that could create conflict.
- Adapt your conflict style to take cultural perceptions into account.
- Adapt your conflict management style to various relational contexts.

Discussion Questions

1. Can you explain at least two differences in behaviors that occur during constructive and destructive conflict?

2. How are disconfirming messages related to the communication climate and, eventually, conflict?

3. Can you describe the behaviors of individuals who have a positive conflict orientation and the behaviors of individuals with a negative conflict orientation?

4. How do approach and avoidance personalities differ in their impact on conflict and the communication climate?

5. Can you describe how the need for power affects conflict and the conflict management strategies you might utilize?

6. Why is electronic communication less effective than face-to-face communication in dealing with conflict?

7. In what way should you adapt your conflict style for a collectivist culture versus an individualistic culture?

8. How are conflict and the management of it different in committed relationships, friendships, and the workplace?

9. What are different constructive conflict strategies that you understand how to use after reading this chapter?

10. What are some of the confirming messages that you could use to resolve conflict?

11. What do you now know about your own use of constructive and destructive conflict?

Building Your Skills

1. Meet with a classmate, and share your views of the seven disconfirmation behaviors. Try to think of examples when either of you have used these behaviors during conflict. Can you share how you think this made the other person in the conflict feel? Did the other person do or say anything to confirm your perceptions of his or her feelings? Have you ever had anyone speak to you this way? Who engages in any of these behaviors most often in your life?

2. Read the descriptions of the approach and avoidance personality traits and behaviors. Which do you consider to best describe you? Now think about a time when you experienced a specific conflict with someone in your life. How did being an approacher or avoider affect this conflict episode? Did it help or hurt the outcome, in your opinion?

3. List examples of each of the five types of conflict (parallel, displaced, misattributed, latent, and false). Which one(s) has occurred most often in your relationships? Explain why you think this is by addressing the positive versus negative conflict orientations and the power needs that exist for you and the person with whom you most frequently experience conflict.

4. Meet in a group of three or four students, and engage in a role-play in which each of you enacts a different conflict management style. First develop an issue of conflict. Then each student selects one of the five styles to resolve the conflict issue: withdraw,

accommodate, force, compromise, or collaborate. Take turns serving as the observer and recording specific behaviors within each style that affect the outcome. Do this two or three times and select a different style for each round. Following each enactment, compare what you, as the role-players, noticed with what the observer(s) noticed. Discuss which styles worked best to productively resolve the conflict. Did some people work together better than others? Discuss your observations, and offer an explanation for them.

5. Write down an example of a conflict that could occur in either a committed relationship or a friendship. Then describe how this conflict would be perceived differently and resolved differently within each type of relationship.

6. Select a clip from one of your favorite movies that depicts a common conflict between two people (e.g., friends arguing over a boyfriend or girlfriend, jealousy in a romantic relationship). Analyze the conflict as follows:

   a. Type of conflict

   b. Confirming versus disconfirming messages in the conflict episode

   c. Conflict management style utilized by each person

7. Comment on the resolution of this conflict: Will this particular conflict occur again? Why or why not? Assess the status of this relationship on the basis of your knowledge of how this conflict was addressed.

9 Understanding Relationships

Michaela's Story . . .

Michaela hasn't dated much in college. For the most part, she prefers to hang out with her friends rather than dating anyone in particular. Michaela is attractive and friendly; however, she hasn't met anyone she would be interested in dating seriously. One of Michaela's roommates just got engaged and constantly talks about how wonderful her fiancé is and the great life the two of them are going to have once they get married after graduation. Meanwhile, Michaela was beginning to wonder when, or even whether, she would meet someone special.

Recently, a friend introduced Michaela to Darrell at a party. The two laughed and talked with each other for most of the evening, sharing the usual pieces of information, such as their majors and what they want to do after graduation. From there, they went on to discuss current events and personal interests. When Darrell asked for Michaela's phone number at the end of the night, Michaela was excited at the prospect of spending more time with Darrell.

The next day, Michaela went onto Facebook to learn more about Darrell and liked what she found. Darrell seemed to be a really nice guy with a lot of friends, and there didn't seem to be any negative remarks made about him. Therefore, when Darrell called to invite her to go out with some friends a few nights later, she said yes. Once again, they had a really good time when they were together. The third time Michaela and Darrell went out, the two of them went to a college basketball game and then grabbed something to eat. Before either of them realized it, Michaela and Darrell had started dating.

Now Michaela is starting to get advice from her roommates about what she should do to move her relationship with Darrell "to the next level." She simply wants to enjoy her time with Darrell and get to know him better. But her roommates warn that Michaela should have a discussion with Darrell about making their relationship mutually exclusive, or he might not think she is serious and could begin dating someone else. According to one of Michaela's roommates, the sooner Michaela and Darrell determine

CHAPTER OBJECTIVES

AFTER READING THIS CHAPTER, you will understand:

1 Factors related to the development of social relationships.

2 How two interpersonal communication theories—uncertainty reduction theory and social exchange theories—are related to relationship formation.

3 How relationships of choice and circumstance influence communication across relationship types.

4 How the coming together and coming apart stages of relationship development work.

5 The role that relational maintenance strategies play in sustaining relationships.

6 How personality factors influence the way in which you communicate when developing relationships.

whether each is the "one" for them, the better. After all, there might not be a lot of time left to find a partner while still in school.

What do you think? While reading this chapter, consider how you might answer the following questions:

- Is Michaela and Darrell's relationship developing at the appropriate speed, or should Michaela and Darrell discuss moving the relationship to the next level at this time?

- What are reasonable expectations for Michaela and Darrell to have of each other at this time?

- How important is what other people think when it comes to what should happen and when it should happen in Michaela and Darrell's relationship?

We will revisit Michaela's story at the end of the chapter and use the content discussed in this chapter to develop a communication plan to help Michaela and Darrell.

AFTER READING THIS CHAPTER, you will be able to:

1 Determine how rewards and costs function in relationships.

2 Identify how relational factors (i.e., personality, physical appearance, similarity and complementarity, proximity, and technology) influence how or whether relationships are formed with others.

3 Explain how power and influence are utilized in interpersonal relationships.

4 Use assessment data to address relational maintenance.

AFTER COMPLETING THE SELF-ASSESSMENTS, you will learn about:

1 How you can incorporate relational maintenance strategies into your relationships.

Perhaps it's not surprising that people seem fascinated with watching relationships develop. Dating shows have been on television for decades, ranging from the half-hour matchmaking efforts of "The Dating Game" back in the 1970s to a revamped version in the 1990s called "Love Connection" and progressing to series-long programs such as "The Bachelor." Audiences seem drawn to watching romantic partners select each other; if we get the chance to have a say in the matter, all the better. Furthermore, since we don't have to live with the consequences of these people's choices, it removes a great deal of anxiety we might otherwise experience if *we* were making these relational decisions for our own lives.

This chapter focuses on understanding social relationships and how relationships form. Included in the coverage will be an assessment measure that allows you to reflect on the communication you use to maintain your relationships with others. In addition, several factors that make relationships tricky to navigate are examined. The chapter concludes with an examination of how your personality can influence how you communicate when developing interpersonal relationships.

> When something is missing in your life, it usually turns out to be someone.
>
> —ROBERT BRAULT

Understanding Social Relationships

When people are asked what makes their lives meaningful, they often cite the relationships they have with others.[1] There are many things to consider when examining social relationships. Three main areas that are relevant to understanding social relationships are loneliness and the need to belong, cultural influences, and personal goals and sex differences.

Loneliness and the Need to Belong

We often overlook how friends and family members satisfy our need to feel valued. Unfortunately, unless people are not accessible to us, for either short or sustained periods of time, the loss of these relationships might not be acknowledged or keenly felt, such as leaving a close sibling behind when we go away to college. Not surprisingly, when we encounter problems with our social support systems, we are more likely to experience loneliness.[2]

Having a friend with us can make all the difference in the world.

Belonging to a community allows us to feel less like a number and more like a person who is valued by others. This does not necessarily require face-to-face interactions. More and more, individuals utilize the Internet for email correspondence, Facebook, Twitter, online chat rooms, instant messaging, or other online social contact venues. For example, online gaming communities and topic-specific Web forums appear successful at making their members feel part of something greater than themselves even if people's real identities may not be known.[3] However, substituting online interactions for face-to-face interactions could become problematic because online relationships have the potential to be impersonal.[4] For instance, we might be replacing our stronger face-to-face relationships with weaker online relationships.[5] Whether these relational dynamics lead to social isolation or loneliness remains to be seen. Yet whether in face-to-face or online settings, our interpersonal relationships play a pivotal role in our ability to feel connected to others.

Cultural Influences

Relationships are important for people living in both individualistic and collectivistic cultures (as discussed in Chapter 3), but people in individualistic cultures may tend to think more about their own personal needs, while people in collectivistic cultures may tend to think more about the needs of both parties. For example, scholars have examined how American and Japanese individuals assess the quality of their social relationships in relation to their well-being. Although well-being was more strongly related to the presence of marital relationships and best friendships in Japan than in the United States, the quality of marriages or friendships did not differ between individualistic and collectivistic groups.[6]

Sometimes challenges surface when group or communal identities overlap.[7] In some instances, you may value your relationship to a broad, diverse community. At other times, you may want to separate yourself from the mass collective. Studies of the cultures that are found in neighborhoods or communal dwellings, such as apartment buildings or residence halls, suggest that there is often a balancing act between having individualistic and collectivistic relational goals met.[8] There are many individualistic goals tied to living in communal dwellings, such as having enough hot water in your apartment or access to off-street parking. But collectivistic goals are satisfied when you become friends with other individuals in your building or neighborhood or when important community information is shared (e.g., when building maintenance is scheduled, block parties).

Personal Goals and Sex Differences

Males and females may have more in common than was previously thought. When sex differences are identified, they are more likely based on how well our relational goals or expectations are met or demonstrated.[9] For example, Juan cleaned up the kitchen for Anna, but he failed to take out the garbage or wipe off any of the countertops. There could also be issues related to timing: Do the two parties have the same goals at the same time? When personal goals and expectations are in sync, it is much easier to enjoy the relationship. Sadly, many times, when one person wants one thing, the other person is seeking something else. For instance, whenever Dwayne wants to spend some social time with Nakeesha, she always ends up having some chores they need to do instead. This is when effective communication skills are essential, as both parties need to discuss how and when they will work to satisfy their varied personal needs during the relationship.

Males and females may also differ in the psychological benefits they receive from their social relationships. For example, studies suggest that positive social relationships have more psychological benefits for women than for men.[10] When women have emotionally supportive relationships in their lives, they are less likely to experience depression because they have other people to talk to and confide in.[11] However, when the

NATURE/NURTURE intersections

Come On, Get Happy

A new area of psychology has emerged that focuses on the role of happiness. Appropriately enough, this field of study is called positive psychology, which emphasizes cultivating personality strengths and looks at how and what people do to enhance the level of happiness they experience, without the aid of medications.[12]

Researchers have learned that a person's temperament plays a significant role in the predisposition to be happy. The estimate is that 50% of our happiness tendencies are associated with our genetic makeup.[13] Approximately 40% are associated with our daily thoughts, actions, and behaviors, and the remaining 10% are associated with factors such as where we live, the amount of money we make, our marital status, and our physical appearance (see Figure 9.1).

Researchers are also learning that our ability to develop and nurture relationships with others plays an important role in determining the overall level of happiness we experience. In fact, researchers have learned that taking time to meditate, reflect, and think thoughts of kindness and compassion toward others can actually produce changes in how our brains are wired.[14] But it must be noted that the original subjects had practiced meditation for years.

Constructively reflecting on the relationships in our lives will not, in and of itself, make us happier people. Modifying our genetically predetermined happiness set points is not a simple task and takes more than just dabbling in meditation or winning the lottery.[15] Just the same, it's pretty impressive that being appreciative and reflecting upon the positive relationships that we have on a regular basis, can, over time, increase the likelihood that we can rewire our brains to make us feel more content and fulfilled with the lives we live.

FIGURE 9.1

Where Happiness Comes From

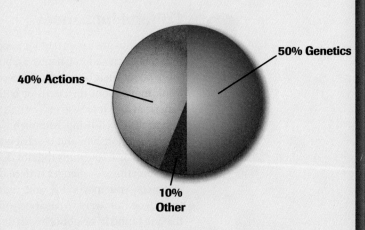

Source: Based on Lykken, D. M., & Tellegen, A. (1996). Happiness is a stochastic phenomenon. *Psychological Science*, *7*, 186–189.

other people in their lives experience difficulties, women may become more susceptible to depression than males. Males may be more sensitive to issues of social isolation rather than social support.[16] Males may not need as many friends as females do, but males may want at least one or two friends to hang out with. Males could also experience greater levels of physiological stress as the size of their social networks increase.[17] While everyone needs social relationships, males and females tend to differ in the type of support they seek and the perceived demands of their relationships.

 ## CHECKING YOUR UNDERSTANDING

Understanding Social Relationships

Before reading further, take a few minutes to assess your learning by writing your answers to the following items:

1. Explain why the need to belong is an important factor in social relationships.

2. What are some examples of cultural influences? How do your examples support the notion that social relationships matter to individuals?

3. How do males and females differ in their perceptions of social relationships?

Why Relationships Form

Scholars across numerous disciplines have been working for decades to comprehend why we form the relationships that we do.[18] The next two sections examine theories relevant to relationship formation and five variables that are often examined when attempting to learn more about relationship formation.

Theories Related to Relationship Formation

A number of different theories examine relational development issues. Historically, the emphasis had been on looking at how relationships advance to deeper levels of involvement—in particular, marriage. More recently, there has been a shift toward studying other relational events that are not exclusive to married couples.[19] The theories that we present here, uncertainty reduction theory and social exchange theories, can be applied to numerous relationship types, ranging from romantic relationships to friendships, giving the theories broad relational appeal.

Uncertainty Reduction Theory. Uncertainty reduction theory, developed by communication scholars Charles Berger and Richard Calabrese,[20] focuses on explaining what occurs during initial interactions with strangers. Because you have never met the other person before, you may consciously (or even subconsciously) experience some apprehension that is unlikely to be reduced until the two of you interact. There are two different types of uncertainty that people try to address: cognitive uncertainty and behavioral uncertainty.[21] **Cognitive uncertainty** refers to the level of uncertainty associated with other people's beliefs and attitudes (e.g., not knowing what their political affiliations are). **Behavioral uncertainty** refers to the uncertainty associated with being unable to predict when or how people are going to act (e.g., not knowing whether, if I extend my hand, the other person will shake it). When talking to others, we might reflect on whether interactions are rewarding, whether exchanges confirm or contradict expectations, and whether we are likely to interact in the future. The degree to which cognitive uncertainty and behavioral uncertainty are present will directly influence how important it is to reduce feelings of uncertainty when communicating with this person.[22]

Three common classes of strategies that people use to get information to help reduce uncertainty are passive, active, and interactive.[23] **Passive strategies** are unobtrusive strategies, such as watching or observing someone's actions. **Active strategies** do not involve direct contact with the person but include strategies such as asking friends for information or going onto Facebook to learn more about someone. **Interactive strategies** are used in speaking or interacting directly with someone, by either holding a conversation, emailing, or text-messaging someone. We may utilize any one or a combination of these strategies when first getting to know others.

Several factors can complicate how people reduce uncertainty:

- Reducing uncertainty in intercultural interactions can be somewhat complicated because perceptions of attraction may shape perceptions of attitude similarity in more developed relationships[24] and people from different cultures may incorporate different strategies in an effort to feel more comfortable interacting with others.[25]

- Certain types of relational uncertainty may involve struggling with what is wanted versus what is expected, which may be the case in long-distance relationships.[26]

- Perceptions of computer-mediated communication could also contribute to uncertainty. For example, the emotional meanings embedded in email messages could be misinterpreted by receivers depending on how senders incorporate nonverbal cues, such as capitalization or emoticons.[27]

Social Exchange Theories. Social exchange theories work from the premise that people want to attain as many rewards or benefits as possible while minimizing the costs or investments from their relationships.[28] A simple calculation is then performed to determine how "profitable" a relationship is:

Rewards – Costs = Net Profit or Net Loss.

First, the rewards and costs need to be identified (see Figure 9.2). There are clear, tangible interpersonal **rewards** such as food, gifts, money, or physical intimacy. Then there are intangible rewards, which could include having someone to hang out with, sharing a favorite interest or pastime, being able to enhance your feelings of happiness when something good happens, and sharing your feelings of sadness or frustration when something doesn't go as planned.

Tangible interpersonal **costs** may include purchasing food, gifts, or lending money. There are also intangible costs, such as doing something that you don't really want to, giving up your free time to help someone else, or taking care of someone else's needs at the risk of neglecting yourself. A third type of cost, known as **communal behaviors**, occur when we take time to help our partners with something they want done. Communal behaviors may be costly, but positive outcomes appear to be associated with such actions unless these actions are unacknowledged or unappreciated.[29] For example, when Tammy fails to appreciate that Chad watched a "chick flick" with her that he had no desire to see but Tammy did, Chad would view his communal actions to be more costly than he would if Tammy had mentioned that she appreciated the time together. Rewards and costs also vary according to the type of relationship you are assessing (e.g., friendship, coworker, family, romantic partner).

Assessing rewards and costs in relationships can get complicated (see Figure 9.2). Here are several things to remember about how rewards and costs operate in relationships:

- *Both rewards and costs are subjective.* What you consider a reward, another person might consider a cost and vice versa (e.g., you love going to the beach, your partner sees it as boring).

- *You cannot simply count up the number of rewards you have and the number of costs and subtract the two totals.* One reward, if it is important enough to you, can mean more than five relatively minimal relational costs.

- *People tend to leave relationships when they feel that the costs significantly outweigh the rewards.* However, rewards and costs can change over time, so you might have to weigh the short-term as well as long-term outcomes.

- *You may desire different rewards and costs depending on the type of relationship you are seeking.* What you find rewarding in a friendship may differ from what you look for in a coworker relationship or a romantic partner.

When people assess relational rewards and costs to determine how satisfied they are with their relationships, two other points are worth discussing: comparison levels and comparison level of alternatives. **Comparison levels** are the minimum expectations,

FIGURE 9.2

Is There a Net Profit or Loss for Lee? Will the Relationship with Pat Last?

Rewards	Costs
■ Lee enjoys time spent with Pat.	■ Pat lives an hour away.
■ Pat has a stable job, nice income.	■ Pat likes to watch a lot of sports. Lee prefers to go to cultural events.
■ Pat gets along with Lee's friends.	■ Pat is only average looking.

desires, or needs we have for our relationships.[30] If these expectations are met or exceeded, you are likely to stay in your relationship; if your comparison levels are not met, you will probably not enter or remain in a relationship. Unfortunately, if our comparison levels are based on perceptions of an ideal other, we may find that few, if any, individuals can meet the comparison levels we have established.[31] Comparison levels may also change as our needs and wants evolve over time.

Comparison level of alternatives is somewhat different. This concept is based on the idea that if another option appears better than your existing choice, you will be more inclined to select the preferred option.[32] If the option is not as good as what you currently have, you will stick with your present choice. For example, some people use comparison level of alternatives to decide whom they wish to date. They may date Caitlin or Kyle until someone else better comes along—say, Eileen or Nick. When that happens, they break up with Caitlin or Kyle and start to date Eileen or Nick instead. Essentially, individuals may be placing a value on their options to help them decide whether to stay in their present relationships or to select an alternative.[33] However, utilizing this strategy can be risky and could backfire; individuals may be labeled as "players" when these actions occur with any frequency in their lives.

Factors Influencing Relationship Formation

Why do we form relationships with some people and not others? Research shows that several factors can explain a great deal about why we form relationships with others.

Personality Traits. Personality traits have been found to significantly influence how relationships develop and evolve. The five personality factors (discussed in Chapter 1) that scholars typically examine are openness, conscientiousness, extraversion, agreeableness, and neuroticism. These five personality traits also affect interpersonal communication and perceptions of relational partners.[34]

When scholars examined how romantic heterosexual relationships developed (whether it was it love at first sight or the couples started out as friends), they found that personality trait similarities surfaced for couples who had taken more time to develop their romantic relationships than for couples who became involved in romantic relationships quickly. People experiencing love at first sight may be placing greater emphasis on perceptions of personality similarity rather than actual personality similarities.[35] Therefore, the role of communication and other relational processes may vary depending on the degrees to which couples have similar or dissimilar personality predispositions, specific personality factors being assessed, and the situations they find themselves in with others.[36]

Physical Appearance. Numerous indicators reinforce the importance of physical appearance in society, ranging from the amount of money spent on products or services to enhance our outward appearances to research findings indicating that physically attractive individuals get paid more, are promoted faster, and receive more positive treatment overall from others and society. In addition, standards of beauty appear to be fairly universal, with most people able to agree with perceptions of physical attractiveness across cultural and ethnic groups.[37]

Many factors need to be considered when assessing the nonverbal communication components of physical appearance.

■ *Some individuals have their partners chosen by others.* The physical appearances of either or both partners might not play a significant role in mate selection in some cultures, which might place a higher premium on features such as social or financial standing.[38]

- *Same-sex partners may have different physical attractiveness preferences than opposite-sex partners do.* Findings suggest that gay and heterosexual men may be more comparable in their preferences for physical attractiveness attributes[39] than lesbian and heterosexual women are.[40]

- *The role of physical attraction may be significantly reduced in online romantic relationships.* We may have to rely more on verbal messages when assessing the potential desirability of partners.[41] As a result, factors other than physical appearance are more dominant in the formation of online relationships when the only type of information exchanged is words.

- *Making comparisons between levels of physical attractiveness (low, medium, high) is complicated.* When researchers studied differences in facial attractiveness, their results suggest that there is a greater negative bias for having low levels of facial attractiveness than a positive bias for having high levels of facial attractiveness. Different neurological processes in the brain may occur in making assessments of facial physical attractiveness.[42]

Similarity-Complementarity. The concept of **similarity** in interpersonal communication suggests that we are more likely to be attracted to people who have more things in common with us, ranging from shared demographics to shared physical characteristics, interests, and attitudes. This idea is also known as perceived homophily (as discussed in Chapter 3). In fact, perceptions of similarity may be even more important than actual, objective similarities. It may be more important that we think we are alike than the fact that we actually are alike in our attitudes or backgrounds.

Complementarity is all about providing balance between ourselves and the other person. Complementarity involves combining opposing forces to attain perceived harmony and overall strength. If your strengths are my weaknesses and vice versa, together we could be stronger than either of us could be by ourselves. For instance, perhaps you like to cook but hate to clean up the mess, while your partner is a lousy cook but is fine with cleaning up the kitchen. Because you are willing to cook and your partner is willing to clean up afterward, you complement each other when it comes to cooking duties.

Although opposites may attract, similarities have their own appeal as well.

Most relationships tend to struggle if there is not a minimal level of perceived similarity to balance out the high degree of complementarity in the relationship. However, distinguishing complementarity from similar perceptions could get murky, especially if relational outcomes are the focus, as opposed to the process taken to get there. Researchers found that "instead of liking someone perceived as similar, they perceived as similar someone whom they liked."[43] As a result, it may be less important whether we demonstrate similar or complementary behaviors and more important whether others' responses to our exchanges are in agreement with our goals.

Proximity. Proximity, which was introduced in Chapter 5, refers to the space and distance, either physical or psychological, between parties. Historically, physical proximity was extremely important when it came to forming relationships, since it was difficult to form a relationship with someone with whom you were not likely to interact face to face. When someone would say that you were likely to marry the boy or girl next door, there had been some merit to this statement. You were less likely to get to know someone who lived much farther away from you.

We value the ability to have close proximity to those we care about. When people say that they are moving back to their hometown to be closer to family and friends, they may be reaffirming the importance of proximity in maintaining family relationships so that routine face-to-face exchanges could occur.[44] Technology has lessened the impact of physical distance, since there are many inexpensive technological means to interact with people ranging from strangers to intimate partners.[45] This is not new, however; a steady stream of advances have been reducing the importance of proximity for interpersonal communication before development of the Internet, such as the development and implementation of mass transit, interstate highways, and the telegraph and telephone.[46]

 Technology. There are conflicting reports about whether the Internet is helpful or detrimental to interpersonal relationships.[47] However, the sheer volume of technological messages sent on any given day suggests that our need to interact with others remains strong. The most frequent explanation for Internet usage has been for interpersonal communication (e.g., emailing friends and family members).[48] Admittedly, the Internet may not always be the preferred or appropriate channel for all types of messages depending on the nature of the relationship (e.g., do we already know the person or are we trying to develop a relationship) and may relate to what we are seeking from the exchange (e.g., entertainment, escape, acquiring information).[49] Preliminary indicators have shown that personality traits, such as extraversion,[50] and preexisting social support networks[51] may be important factors when we examine the impact of the Internet on interpersonal relationships. Furthermore, we tend to forget that access to these technological tools is not available or a daily event for all individuals in the United States, much less the world.

 ## CHECKING YOUR UNDERSTANDING
Why Relationships Form

Before reading further, take a few minutes to assess your learning by writing your answers to the following items:

1. Explain the major concepts associated with uncertainty reduction theory.
2. How do social exchange theories work? Explain other concepts related to social exchange theories and relationship development for different types of relationships.
3. Identify the five factors that influence relationship formation, provide an example for each, and explain how each is related to relationship formation.

Why Relationships Are Messy

Some factors influence our interpersonal relationships even though we don't consciously think about them on a daily basis. In the next section, three factors—relationships of choice and circumstance, relational power and influence, and role and rule expectations— are examined. Your awareness and understanding of these relational features could determine whether your interpersonal exchanges are harmonious or confrontational.

Relationships of Choice and Circumstance

Although we might assume that we should have choices when forming relationships with others, this is often not the case. **Relationships of choice** are relationships that people participate in voluntarily. The most frequently cited relationships of choice would be romantic relationships and friendships.[52] **Relationships of circumstance**, by contrast, are involuntary. We essentially have little or no say in the formation of these relationships, and they may be difficult to terminate. The most frequently cited relationships of circumstance are parents and children, siblings, stepparents and stepchildren, and stepchildren and other stepchildren. There is a mix of choice and circumstance in workplace relationships. If you are in the position of hiring or firing others, you are likely to feel that you are choosing your superior, subordinates, or coworkers (which might or might not be the case). If you are not part of the hiring (or firing) process, you typically have limited say in who you work with or for.

In Western cultures, people like to think that they should have a say in who their partners are going to be and the attributes their partners should possess. However, in many cultures, marriage partners are selected by others, changing the entire mate selection process.[53] There are advantages and disadvantages to romantic relationships of choice as well as to prearranged marriages depending on your own abilities to select prospective partners and circumstances that influence the number of available partners. Some of these are as follows:

- Relationships of choice may be easier to terminate than relationships of circumstance.
- Cultural considerations as well as parties outside of the dyad are often associated with the success or failure of the marriage.
- If we have no say in how our relational partners are chosen, we may be forced to redefine what we are looking for and want in our relationships.

Relational Power and Influence

Have you ever wondered why some people are good at getting others to do things for them? Scholars might explain this behavior as relational power. **Power** may be defined as "the capacity to influence another person to do something he or she would not have done without having been influenced."[54] Two aspects of relational power are often emphasized in interpersonal relationships: power bases and compliance-gaining strategies.

Whether by choice or circumstance, on the wedding day, most couples hope to attain marital happiness.

Power Bases. John French and Bertram Raven's groundbreaking work on power identified five bases of social power individuals may demonstrate in interactions: referent power, reward power, coercive power, legitimate power, and expert power.[55] **Referent power** refers to the characteristics an individual has that make you want to be more like that person (e.g., kind, respectful, brave). **Reward power** refers to an individual's ability to give you things that you want or need (e.g., gifts, a raise, affection). **Coercive power** refers to an individual's ability to punish or withhold resources that you want (e.g., avoiding you, poor performance appraisal). **Legitimate power** is often associated with someone's position or assigned rank and is seen as justified or appropriate on the basis of the position(s) held in the relationship (e.g., boss, significant other). Finally, **expert power** is based on someone's knowledge or expertise on a topic (e.g., strong computer skills).

There are several things to consider when examining the use of power in interpersonal relationships:

- An individual's power bases may vary on the basis of the type of interpersonal relationship (e.g., friendship, workplace, dating, or family).

- There may be times in a relationship when either person could demonstrate power associated with any of the power bases. However, when and how the power is demonstrated could vary.

- Sometimes people don't need to demonstrate their power to their partners; rather, the key is that their partners are aware that the power exists. It may be a matter of perceived power, as opposed to actual power, that is important.[56]

Two main factors should be considered in examining power in the workplace: positional power and relational power.[57] **Positional power** is associated with someone's rank or job title. Positional power can be seen when looking at a company's organizational chart; it identifies who reports to whom and provides a means to visualize how one's position fits into the overall organization. **Relational power** refers to the type of power someone has on the basis of personal relationships with others in the workplace. The saying "It's not what you know, but who you know" refers to elements of relational power. Never underestimate the importance of each type of power, and keep in mind that some individuals may possess both.

Compliance-Gaining Strategies. Compliance-gaining strategies refer to the communication tactics, approaches, or plans that someone uses to get others to do things for them or to act in a certain way. Researchers have identified over sixty possible compliance-gaining strategies that individuals may use in their relationships.[58] Some compliance-gaining strategies may be so subtle that receivers of the compliance-gaining message do not realize that the sender is intentionally trying to influence relational outcomes (e.g., spending time together with mutual friends so that you can get to know someone better). Other strategies are anything but subtle, the intent of the sender being very obvious to the receiver (and other third parties as well) (e.g., taking a horse-drawn carriage ride after dinner on a first date to demonstrate your romantic interest). As a result, the degree of persuasion that is embedded within compliance-gaining strategies could vary. This, in turn, may affect which compliance-gaining strategies are most likely to succeed for individuals.

Effective use of compliance-gaining strategies requires the sender to match particular strategy choices to their relational goals or objectives and their relational partners. Not all strategies work for everyone; therefore, appropriate strategy selection is important.[59] There may also be ethical issues that individuals should consider when selecting strategies. Are you willing to lie or ask other people to lie on your behalf to get a desired outcome? There may be nothing wrong with trying to influence others to agree with us or do things for us in some matters; however, when the stakes are higher, it may be a question of whether it is appropriate for us to do so.

Role and Rule Expectations

The roles we take on (e.g., friend, partner, parent, supervisor) and the rules we are expected to follow (e.g., being loyal, honest, or supportive) play an important part in how we develop and maintain interpersonal relationships. The problem is not that we have these expectations. Rather, the challenge comes because very few of these role and rule expectations are directly communicated between individuals. For example, when we interact within our adult families, we often model the behaviors that are associated with the roles and rules we observed or participated in within our own families while growing up.[60] Rarely are our family roles explicitly written down; observation, early participation, and the communication exchanges that occur during these events are the tools that we typically use to teach roles to other family members. Communication plays an integral part in negotiating family roles, especially if we didn't observe or participate in those roles when growing up. However, financial constraints and/or other obligations, both inside and outside of the family, influence how family members demonstrate familial roles.[61]

The most direct and explicit roles and rules occur in the workplace. Workplace rules are often clearly defined in workplace policies (e.g., employee handbooks). As the size of the organization increases, workplace rules are more likely to be formally documented. Large Fortune 500 companies will have detailed role and rule expectations for their employees to follow, while small businesses tend to have a limited number of roles and rules explicitly spelled out for their employees. Workplace roles are often reflected in someone's job description or duties. As job duties change, it is important for employees to discuss or negotiate any changes in the employee's role within the organization.[62] Conversely, the most indirect and vague roles and rules occur in friendships. Furthermore, there are often differing definitions as to who is a friend, a best friend, or a casual friend. These issues are discussed in greater detail in Chapter 11.

CHECKING YOUR UNDERSTANDING
Why Relationships Are Messy

Before reading further, take a few minutes to assess your learning by writing your answers to the following items:

1. Describe how interpersonal relationships are affected depending on whether they are initiated as a result of circumstance or choice.

2. Explain how power and influence operate in romantic, family, friendship, and workplace relationships.

3. How are role and rule expectations communicated in interpersonal relationships? When are you best able to identify the roles and rules in your interpersonal relationships?

Assessing Communication When Developing Relationships

If someone were to watch a video of the communication exchanges you had with a friend, family member, or significant other, what would your words and actions say about your relationship? In this section, we examine the development and maintenance of relationships. How we communicate verbally and nonverbally with others is a direct reflection of where we are in our relationships and what we are hoping to get from our relationships at any given time.

Coming Together–Coming Apart Stages: One Heck of a Ride

Mark Knapp and Anita Vangelisti's model of relationship stages continues to serve as a basis for how relationships develop over time.[63] Although this model may be used to explore how other types of relationships form (e.g., close friends or mentoring relationships), the emphasis has historically been on romantic heterosexual relationships. These stages are broken down into two primary categories: coming together and coming apart (see Figure 9.3).

Coming Together. The coming together stages begin with the potential for first interaction and progress to public or legal acknowledgement of relationship unions. Specifically, the five coming together stages are initiating, experimenting, intensifying, integrating, and bonding.

FIGURE 9.3

Knapp and Vangelisti's Stages of Relational Development

Source: Knapp, M. L., & Vangelisti, A. (2006). *Interpersonal communication and human relationships* (6th ed.). Boston: Allyn & Bacon.

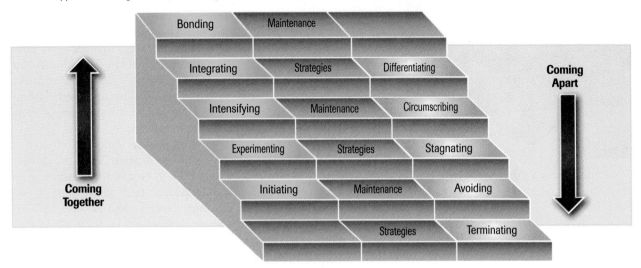

Initiating. The **initiating stage** is the starting point for relationship development. Although an extraverted person may have no difficulty directly walking up to someone and beginning a conversation, there are many people who prefer to do a little bit of background research. The more anxious you are, the more likely you are to gather more information so that you increase your chances of success or at least don't make a fool of yourself. Some people may do a Google search or go onto Facebook to learn more about others. If they find information that is unappealing or unattractive, this could deter them from ever initiating a relationship.

Experimenting. The **experimenting stage** focuses on both parties sharing more about themselves. Although the content that is shared may be relatively public and low risk, the two people are sharing information in much greater quantities. The ultimate goal of the experimenting stage is to determine whether both people want to engage in future exchanges. This is where small talk comes in, allowing you to test out a number of different topics to gauge the other person's interests.[64] The experimenting stage can vary in both length and intensity. This is the stage at which we make preliminary decisions about future friendships, colleagues, or romantic partners.

Intensifying. During the **intensifying stage**, you are really getting to know the other person. You are spending more time with the other person, doing a lot of new and interesting things together, and sharing experiences and thoughts for the first time. For some people, this is the most exciting part of the dating process because everything seems new, vital, energized, and fresh. While there is a lot of excitement associated with the intensifying stage, problems could surface once you feel the newness has worn off.[65] You might see the first signs that boredom or routines are forming. There could also be other factors outside of the relationship that pose problems, such as conflicting schedules or other obligations tied to work or personal commitments that make it difficult to focus significant energy on developing a relationship, whether it is based on romance, work, or friendship. Most relationships do not progress past the intensifying stage.[66]

Integrating. During the **integrating stage**, you and your partner are perceived to be a couple. There are many expressions that are used to convey this sense of togetherness,

The emotions partners share in the integration stage are often easily visible to others.

such as "they're an item" or "joined at the hip." Sharing resources also begins to occur, ranging from sharing the most basic events, such as cooking and eating together, to sharing vehicles or money. If there were a pronoun that could capture what occurs during the integrating stage, it would be "we." There are comparable behaviors demonstrated between friends when they are in the integration stage. They might also refer to each other as best friends and have certain nicknames that the friends use for each other. Mentoring relationships (described in greater detail in Chapter 12) may also demonstrate aspects associated with integration.

The integrating stage is often the one at which you consider the prospect of cohabitation. Some people perceive **cohabitation**, otherwise known as living together, to be a trial run before marriage. In contrast to past practices, the majority of individuals in Western cultures spend some time cohabitating with others. Yet the relational dynamics that are involved with cohabitation might not be the same as the relational dynamics that are involved with being married. Research has shown that cohabitation could later put your marital relationship at greater risk for divorce, especially in the first few years of marriage.[67] However, if you cohabitate with your future spouse and if the two of you participate in premarital education courses or counseling, the likelihood of divorce becomes comparable to that of couples who did not cohabit before marriage.[68]

Bonding. The **bonding stage** is often considered the public capstone event to relational development. The most easily recognized public union is the marriage ceremony and the symbolic gesture of exchanging rings. The ceremony may also have cultural and religious significance and most definitely has legal significance. Controversy surrounds whether the rights, privileges, and responsibilities associated with marriage should be granted only to heterosexual couples. Regardless of your views, the bonding stage and the ability to publicly and symbolically demonstrate commitment between partners appear to be important for virtually all relationship types. It is more difficult to identify the bonding stage in friendships and workplace relationships. This is the time when individuals are likely to make statements such as "friends for life" or "you are part of my family" or go to great lengths to help one another out. Attaining partner status in an organization is one way in which bonding is demonstrated in workplace relationships.

Coming Apart The coming apart stages emphasize how relationships dissolve, need to be repaired, or break down over time. The stages range from retaining your individual identity while still being part of a couple to the relationship ending, sometimes but not always by choice. Specifically, the five coming apart stages are differentiating, circumscribing, stagnating, avoiding, and terminating.

Differentiating. The **differentiating stage** involves dealing with the struggles of maintaining your own identity while remaining part of a couple or dyad. This could get complicated, since so much time and energy have been spent creating a shared identity. One way to identify whether differentiating is occurring is to examine the personal pronouns that are used in conversations. The pronouns "you" and "your" are most likely to show up when you and your partner are in conflicts or disagreements. For couples to thrive, there needs to be a combination of individual and joint identities. When there is an insufficient amount of either, there could be relational difficulties down the road. In friendships, this could occur when one friend's identity seems to be subsumed into the other friend's identity. In the workplace, protégés often want to disengage from their mentors at some point to highlight their own unique workplace contributions.

Circumscribing. The **circumscribing stage** may be a better indicator of possible relational difficulties. In the circumscribing stage, relational partners talk less about issues that matter or have much relational relevance.[69] Conversational content is restricted and restrained. The level and degree of sharing decrease, and partners begin to argue more, even over petty things, as discontent begins to surface. Some problems could be associated with neglect if partners put their relationships on "cruise control" and fail to continue to invest time and energy in their relationships. Circumscribing can be managed, but this often requires an open, honest exchange about the levels of disengagement that are occurring and enacting specific strategies in an effort to reconnect to each other.

Stagnating. During the **stagnating stage**, the relationship has started to become routine, uneventful, and dull. Stagnation also suggests that there has been no relational growth; there is nothing new for you and your partner to experience as a couple. Fortunately, you, your partner, and your relationship are capable of growth, change, and further development. The question becomes one of time and commitment. Do you want to invest the energy necessary to revitalize your relationship? Equally important is whether both of you are interested in making this commitment. If only one of you desires to reenergize the relationship, the likelihood of success is slim. The same holds true for friendships and workplace relationships.

Avoiding. By the time the **avoiding stage** appears, you are on the cusp of ending your relationship. However, before actually doing so, you make efforts to disengage from one another. Four specific types of disengagement strategies have been identified: expressing detachment by openly attempting to avoid your partner, avoiding involvement by leaving the physical environment your partner is in, ignoring or failing to respond to comments or displaying an excessive decorum of politeness, showing antagonism by openly attacking or degrading your partner, and mentally dissociating yourself from your partner by minimizing the significance of your partner's contributions.[70]

Although you may acknowledge that your relationship is in serious trouble, this does not necessarily mean that you will seek to end the relationship. In accordance with comparison level of alternatives discussed earlier,[71] there could be many motivations working to determine how long you are willing to stay in the avoiding stage:

- There could be other relationships to consider.
- There could be financial obligations.
- Either or both of you might not like the alternatives that wait if the relationship were to dissolve.

Terminating. The **terminating stage** happens when either or both parties indicate that they want to end the relationship. Sometimes, this decision is made by only one person. While there is no right way to end a relationship, there are more civil, amicable, or respectful strategies. Some people believe this message should be delivered in person. Others have gone to the extreme of ending their relationships by having someone else share the news, writing a message on a sticky note, or simply serving their relational partners with divorce papers or firing an employee. We may be bad at relational breakups because we don't know how to share this news. Perhaps that explains the often-used line "It's not you, it's me." This may be said as a way to leave the other person with some small measure of dignity. Unfortunately, it can backfire if your partner doesn't feel that "your" issues are insurmountable.

Relationships end for numerous reasons. Some relationships just slowly fade away over time, owing to lack of reinvestment in the relationship, either consciously or unconsciously by partners. Other times, relationships do not end by choice but rather because of unforeseen events such as when a loved one unexpectedly dies. However a relationship ends, there may be challenges in how to share this information with others. **Grave dressing** involves creating a public statement about the termination of your relationship to share with others.[72] Sometimes the statements of both partners coincide; in other cases, the explanations could vary significantly.

How the Stages Work. Although the coming together and coming apart stages logically build on one another, this does not mean that we spend equal amounts of time in every stage or that we follow the progression of stages in order. On the contrary, it is not uncommon to see people spend very brief amounts of time in some stages or skip stages altogether. Here are some things to be mindful of in understanding how relational development stages work:

- *Every relational stage has its purpose.* While skipping a stage or only briefly skimming through one does not doom a relationship to failure, long-term challenges could result.

- *You may go back and forth between stages.* When you discover that there are problems, you may go back to prior stages to reinforce your understanding of each other. This can be a good thing over the long term for relationships and does not necessarily imply that you didn't spend enough time in those stages initially.

- *There may be disagreements between you and your partner about when you have left one stage and have gone on to another.* **Turning points** identify events that transform relationships in some way[73] and often serve as relational markers to help partners remember significant moments in their relationships. The more agreed-upon turning points you and your partner have, the more likely you are to be satisfied with your relationship.[74]

- *Online relational partners might not have the same experiences going through the relational stages as face-to-face partners do.* Some differences may be based on differences that are inherent in the respective mediums.[75] Other differences may be tied to whether the partners' social circles even consider online romances to be valid forms of interpersonal relationships.[76]

- *Although the stages apply to primarily romantic relationships, friendships and workplace relationships often progress through the relational stages in a similar fashion.* However, friendships and workplace relationships may be less likely to advance to the upper levels of relational development (e.g., integration or bonding), and different strategies are used within each stage to address the needs associated with these relationships.

Relational Maintenance: Staying the Course

Relational maintenance is what people do to sustain relationships over time. Relational maintenance is seen as bridging the gap between the coming together and coming apart stages (see Figure 9.4). Maintenance strategies provide hope that you can remain satisfied over time in relationships that are important to you.

Relational maintenance became firmly established as an important relational activity in the early 1990s by Dan Canary and Laura Stafford. The majority of research on relational maintenance has focused on the role of relational maintenance in heterosexual martial couples, although the ideas have been applied to other close relationships as well, such as parent–child and sibling relationships. There are five primary relational maintenance strategies: positivity, openness, assurance, networks, and shared tasks.[77]

FIGURE 9.4

Maintenance Strategies and Relational Development

Source: Knapp, M. L., & Vangelisti, A. (2006). *Interpersonal communication and human relationships* (6th ed.). Boston: Allyn & Bacon.

Positivity. The strategy of exchanging optimistic, friendly messages with your relational partner is called **positivity**. In some ways, positivity strategies are so straightforward, that you might take these messages for granted. For example, common positivity messages include asking how your partner's day went or thanking your partner for completing some type of household task. Inserting more positivity into your relationships takes little time and often encourages continued demonstration of these behaviors. If you are still not convinced about the merits of positivity, consider this. The ratio of positive to negative messages in satisfied marital relationships is 5 : 1.[78]

Openness. This strategy has a lot to do with self-disclosure, which we will talk about in more detail in Chapter 10. The **openness** strategy involves sharing your thoughts, feelings, and opinions with your relational partner. By revealing information about yourself, you let your partner get to know more about you and your wants, needs, and desires. Assuming that there is trust and commitment, openness relational maintenance strategies are invaluable in that your partner feels comfortable agreeing as well as disagreeing with you. Openness relational maintenance strategies enhance feelings not only that your relationship is genuine, but also that the other person cares enough about you to caution you if you might do something you would later regret.

Assurance. Messages that provide affirmation and comfort to your relational partner are called **assurance** strategies. Assurance strategies let you know that someone is there to support you and remind you that even though you may have done something you regret, you are not completely unlovable—foolish, perhaps, but still lovable. Assurance messages can mean a great deal, especially if assurance messages come from someone you respect and love. Assurance messages may occur with greater frequency than you might realize. Examples of assurance messages include such statements as "That's all right," "It will be okay," "You're doing a good job," or "Hang in there." Assurance relational maintenance messages can be incorporated in the day-to-day events of our lives as well as the bigger events that hold greater significance to us.

Sometimes it's just more fun to do things with a group of friends.

Networks. When messages focus on the relationships you and your partner have with others, you are utilizing **network** strategies. Network strategies emphasize the importance of shared relationships outside of your relational dyad. Do you and your partner have shared friends, do your friends at work know your relational partner, and do your relational partner's friends know you? What activities might you do with other people? Shared networks often bring more fun and energy to your relationship and take some of the burden off you and your partner to be the sole (or at least primary) person each of you interacts with socially. However, shared networks may become problematic if there are subsets of your network that do not like your partner (or vice versa).

Shared Tasks. When partners do things together, these messages are called **shared tasks**. The emphasis is on joint participation in activities. These activities can range from you and your partner having similar hobbies or interests to working together raking leaves in the fall. You may actually choose something new that you and your partner want to do as a couple in an effort to participate in the shared pastime. The hobby may become more enjoyable, and both of you could experience less guilt when spending time on the hobby together.

Following is an opportunity for you to assess how likely you are to integrate relational maintenance strategies in a close relationship. As you go through the list, you are encouraged to think about how often you would demonstrate these behaviors. Would any of the strategies become part of a routine with a significant other? Are there any other behaviors that might improve interactions in your family, friend, or workplace relationships?

 ## ASSESS YOUR communication personality

Canary and Stafford's Relational Maintenance Strategies[79]

Log onto our self-assessment library, MyPersonalityProfile, found on MyCommunicationLab (www.mycommunicationlab.com), and assess your relational maintenance strategy usage by completing the interactive assessment. If you currently have a significant other, encourage this person to do the same. This way, you can compare how each of you perceives the relational maintenance behaviors that are occurring in your relationship. If you prefer, you can use the following text-based version.

Directions:

The following items concern things people might do to maintain their relationships. Please indicate the extent to which each of the items describes your current methods of maintaining your relationship (over the past two weeks, for example) with your significant other, a parent, or sibling (just substitute one of your parents or a sibling for "partner" in the questions). Please respond to these items using the following scale:

1 = strongly disagree   5 = slightly agree

2 = disagree   6 = agree

3 = slightly disagree   7 = strongly agree

4 = neutral

_____ 1. I attempt to make interactions with my partner very enjoyable.

_____ 2. I am cooperative in the ways I handle disagreements between us.

_____ 3. I try to build up my partner's self-esteem, including giving him/her compliments, etc.

_____ 4. I ask how my partner's day has gone.

_____ 5. I am very nice, courteous, and polite when we talk.

_____ 6. I act cheerful and positive when I am with my partner.

_____ 7. I do not criticize my partner.

_____ 8. I try to be romantic, fun, and interesting when with my partner.

_____ 9. I am patient and forgiving of my partner.

_____ 10. I present myself as cheerful and optimistic around my partner.

_____ 11. I encourage my partner to disclose thoughts and feelings to me.

_____ 12. I simply tell my partner how I feel about our relationship.

_____ 13. I seek to discuss the quality of our relationship with my partner.

_____ 14. I disclose what I need or want from our relationship with my partner.

_____ 15. I remind my partner about relationship decisions we made in the past (to maintain the same level of intimacy).

_____ 16. I like to have periodic talks about our relationship with my partner.

_____ 17. I stress my commitment to my partner.

_____ 18. I imply that our relationship has a future.

_____ 19. I show my love for my partner.

_____ 20. I show myself to be faithful to my partner.

_____ 21. I like to spend time with our same friends.

_____ 22. I focus on our common friends and affiliations.

_____ 23. I show that I am willing to do things with my partner's friends or family.

_____ 24. I include our friends or family in our activities.

_____ 25. I help equally with tasks that need to be done.

_____ 26. I share in the joint responsibilities that face us.

_____ 27. I do my fair share of the work we have to do.

_____ 28. I do not shirk my duties.

_____ 29. I perform my household responsibilities.

Scoring Instructions:

Positivity: Add the scores for items 1–10 (scores range from 10 to 70)

Openness: Add the scores for items 11–16 (scores range from 6 to 42)

Assurances: Add the scores for items 17–20 (scores range from 4 to 28)

Network: Add the scores for items 21–24 (scores range from 4 to 28)

Tasks: Add the scores for items 25–29 (scores range from 5 to 35)

Understanding Your Relational Maintenance Strategy Usage. There are several factors to consider when assessing someone's relational maintenance strategy usage. Here are some recommendations for how to understand and apply what you are learning about relational maintenance strategies.

- *As your score for each relational maintenance strategy increases (see the range of scores provided for each strategy), you are more likely to intentionally incorporate these communicative behaviors in your relationship.*

- *Some relational maintenance strategies are planned and intentional, while others are embedded in our routine interactions.*[80] If you wish to improve a particular type of maintenance strategy, you might want to consider how to incorporate it into your relationship at both levels.

- *Both you and your partner (parent or sibling) need to perceive that each other is trying to maintain your relationship.* If you don't believe that the other person is also working to maintain your relationship (or vice versa), you minimize the benefits of relational maintenance strategies. This also could be a sign that your relationship is in trouble.[81]

WHAT CAN I **do now?**

▶ *You might want to expand your use of positivity relational maintenance strategies.* Many of these strategies do not require a great deal of time to do, but they do encourage you to be aware of how nice or courteous you are to your partner or family member. But the payoff in both the short and long term could be substantial.

▶ *You might want to reflect on the activities you do with your partner or family member.* You could consider beginning an activity or hobby together, especially if you normally don't have the opportunity for much face-to-face interaction.

▶ *Remember to think about the shared networks that you have with your partner or family member.* Not all of your time together needs to be classified as "alone time." It is okay to do things with others (within moderation). These activities can help to reenergize your relationship.

Personality Patterns: Your Missing Piece

Most scholars believe that if you want to understand why people behave as they do, you should focus on their individual personality traits along with the particular situations in which they find themselves.[82] This approach, known as interactionism,[83] is based on the belief that our behaviors are the result of our personalities and the environment. Not surprisingly, in this view, we tend to choose or modify our environments so that they most closely fit our personality tendencies.[84] Below, we'll look at two of the personality traits that can affect relational development—extraversion and neuroticism—in relation to the situational parameters present within Knapp's developmental stages. However, it must be noted that the relevance of personality trait predispositions may vary by individual, and the dyadic nature of interpersonal communication suggests that individuals may be adapting to their partner's personality predispositions.[85]

Extraversion and Relational Development. Extraversion is a desirable trait to have when forming relationships, since extraverts perceive that there are many rewarding outcomes to be had from interaction with others.[86] Researchers have also found that when both partners are high in extraversion, they are more likely to experience higher levels of marital quality.[87] Extraversion is also associated with positive moods and interpersonal information. It would be common for extraverts to have cheerful or optimistic demeanors when interacting with others.[88] Therefore, when people have higher levels of extraversion, they would be more likely to draw others to them as well as to approach others for interaction. These communicative behaviors may also lead others to consider extraverts as being at least socially attractive if not physically and task attractive as well. Higher levels of extraversion may make it easier to progress through the early stages of Knapp's developmental model.

Neuroticism and Relational Development. Neuroticism is perceived to be a problematic trait when attempting to form relationships with others.[89] In fact, highly neurotic individuals may be caught in a type of lose–lose situation. They tend to have a more difficult time perceiving the benefits from relationships; in addition, their neurotic tendencies tend to generate negative reactions from others.[90] Therefore, it is not surprising that when both partners are high in neuroticism, they may be their own worst enemies because they may also be more inclined to negatively distort their perceptions even if the quality of their marital relationships is high.[91]

Neuroticism is also associated with problematic interpersonal behaviors. It would be common for neurotics to demonstrate panicky or irritable emotions when interacting with others.[92] Therefore, when people have higher levels of neuroticism, they would be less likely to draw others to them and may limit their interactions with others. These communicative behaviors may also lead others to consider neurotics as being unfriendly or difficult to get to know. Neuroticism is not the only personality trait that could cause relational problems. But it appears that neuroticism makes it more difficult to progress through the early stages of Knapp's developmental model.

CHECKING YOUR UNDERSTANDING
Assessing Communication When Developing Relationships

Before completing the chapter, take a few minutes to assess your learning by writing your answers to the following items:

1. What are the five coming together stages, and what type of communication occurs in each stage?

2. What are the five coming apart stages, and what type of communication occurs in each stage?

3. How do each of the five relational maintenance strategies contribute to the maintenance of a relationship?

4. How are extraversion and neuroticism related to relational development? What are some benefits or drawbacks associated with these personality traits and relational development?

A Communication Development Plan for Michaela

To complete Michaela's story, recall that Michaela has recently begun dating Darrell. The relationship is progressing smoothly; however, Michaela is feeling pressure from her roommates to advance the relationship at a faster rate. She wants to continue to get to know him better, while her roommates are telling her that if she does not tell Darrell that she wants a mutually exclusive relationship, she might "lose him" to someone else.

What do you think?

Is Michaela and Darrell's relationship progressing at the right speed? Are Michaela's expectations for her relationship with Darrell reasonable? Does it matter what Michaela's roommates think about her relationship with Darrell?

Possible explanations:

Giving any relationship time to develop takes patience, especially when it comes to romantic relationships. While Michaela is trying to have her relationship with Darrell progress at a rate that she (and probably Darrell) is comfortable with, relationships don't occur in a vacuum. Those around us, whether family members or roommates, often like to have a say in how our romantic relationships develop. This can lead us to second-guess ourselves in addition to reconsidering what is happening in our relationships.

Is Michaela and Darrell's relationship developing at the appropriate speed, or should Michaela and Darrell discuss moving the relationship to the next level at this time? Michaela and Darrell's relationship appears to be at Knapp's intensifying stage. They are experiencing the excitement and joy that often comes when getting to know others. Michaela and Darrell have had only a few dates, so it is reasonable for them to continue to get to know one another at a pace they feel comfortable with.

What are reasonable expectations for Michaela and Darrell to have of each other at this time? It appears that Michaela and Darrell find their relationship to be rewarding. However, it's hard to ignore what other people have to say about our relationships. If Michaela's intuition is telling her to disregard her friends' comments, perhaps she should.

1. *Michaela and Darrell may want to stay in the intensifying stage for at least a few months before deciding whether or not to advance their relationship.* They have known each other only a few weeks. There do not appear to be any factors forcing Michaela to escalate the relationship, so why should she force the issue? If Michaela and Darrell are still in the intensifying stage a year from now, our advice might be different.

2. *Michaela and Darrell's relationship would not be in the intensifying stage if their comparison levels had not been met.* We would conclude that they are finding their relationship to be rewarding and it is likely to continue.

3. *Friends want to help us make good decisions.* Michaela's friends may be assessing how Darrell's and Michaela's personalities mesh in ways that she might not be able to identify at this point in their relationship. However, Michaela shouldn't let anyone push her into something she is not yet ready for. But she might want to reflect on some of her roommates' observations to determine whether there are things she should examine as her relationship develops.

Take Aways

Humans thrive on social interaction. These relationships take several different forms, from friendships to romantic relationships. This chapter focused on increasing your understanding, skills, and knowledge of interpersonal relationships. Following is a list of knowledge claims regarding how and why interpersonal relationships develop.

- It is important to understand factors related to the development of interpersonal relationships. These factors include loneliness and the need for community, intercultural influences, and personal goals and sex differences.

- Two different theories related to relationship formation were examined: uncertainty reduction theory and social exchange theories and how each theory approaches this task.

- Relationships of choice and circumstance influence communication across relationship types.

- Relationships come together and come apart, and numerous stages are involved in the development and decline of relationships.

- Relationships are able to be maintained over time, and there are strategies used to make this happen.

- Personality factors influence the way in which we communicate when developing relationships.

Following are some ways in which you learned more about how relationships develop. You are better prepared to:

- Identify rewards and costs in interpersonal relationships.

- Use personality, physical appearance, similarity and complementarity, proximity, and technology information to influence how relationships develop.

- Troubleshoot challenges that occur in relational development stages.

- Incorporate relational maintenance strategies into relationships.

Discussion Questions

1. Describe three factors that are relevant to understanding social relationships.

2. Describe two theories of interpersonal relationship formation, and explain the key factors of each.

3. How do Knapp and Vangelisti's stages of coming together and coming apart relate to the relational maintenance strategies?

4. How are verbal and nonverbal messages related to detecting relational development challenges in friendships, workplace relationships, and romantic relationships?

Building Your Skills

1. If you owned a matchmaking service, what criteria from this chapter would you emphasize when trying to pair prospective partners? Why did you select these criteria?

2. Break into small groups, and reflect on past times when you saw or experienced the relational development stages in friendships or romantic relationships. Next, practice role-playing the communicative behaviors for the relational development stages. If these role-plays were to be done in the front of the class, would others be able to guess what relational stage you were in on the basis of your verbal and nonverbal messages?

3. Select a movie or one-hour television show, and record whenever partners demonstrate a relational maintenance strategy. What were the most frequently identified strategies? If there was more than one couple, which couple demonstrated the most strategy usage? Which couple seemed the happiest? Was there any relationship between the maintenance strategy usage and happiness for couples?

10 Self-Disclosure and Intimacy in Relationships

Ryan's Story . . .

When Ryan met Jenny three years ago, both were working on their undergraduate degrees. Ryan is pretty easygoing, tends to be quietly confident, and doesn't usually argue or disagree openly with others unless he is really upset; then he gets frustrated, clams up, and leaves the room. It is not uncommon for Ryan to let Jenny do most of the talking when they are having a conversation. As a result, Jenny sometimes underestimates his thoughts and feelings on issues. Jenny tends to be more outgoing, has definite opinions about most things, and voices her thoughts and ideas regularly because she fears being ignored. Although she is willing to listen to what Ryan has to say, she often keeps talking because she believes that he agrees with her remarks, since he doesn't tell her otherwise. Sometimes she comes across as overbearing, but she has good intentions. When Ryan and Jenny started to date, it was pretty natural for Jenny to plan what the two of them would do. Ryan often

didn't voice strong objections to Jenny's ideas, so neither found this pattern problematic. Their relationship developed fairly smoothly, and Ryan and Jenny got married about a year after they started dating.

It is now two years since Ryan and Jenny married. They are both happy with their relationship, but Ryan wishes that Jenny would change some of her communicative tendencies. Ryan wishes that she wouldn't always voice her opinions, since this tends to shut down their conversations, and he starts to tune her out. He is aware that Jenny wishes he would open up and express more of what he is feeling to her and engage in a discussion about some of her ideas. Unfortunately, Ryan is not accustomed to self-disclosing to Jenny, so he often shares very little about what he is thinking or feeling. As a result, Ryan's conversations with Jenny are slowly becoming more generic, and although verbal and nonverbal expressions of intimacy still occur, they do not happen as frequently as they once did.

CHAPTER OBJECTIVES

AFTER READING THIS CHAPTER, you will understand:

1 How two interpersonal theories—social penetration theory and relational dialectics theory—are related to self-disclosure.

2 The factors that shape how and what we self-disclose to others.

3 The elements that guide how intimacy is communicated to others.

4 The influences that affect how intimacy is developed in relationships.

5 The challenges, problems, and dysfunctional communication that can occur when there are difficulties in intimate relationships.

What do you think? While reading this chapter, consider how you might answer the following questions to help Ryan with his relationship with Jenny:

- How are Ryan's and Jenny's different communication tendencies contributing to the problems they are having interacting?

- What effect is Ryan's lack of self-disclosure having on his relationship with Jenny?

- How could Ryan modify how he self-discloses to Jenny to enhance the intimacy they share?

We will revisit Ryan's story at the end of the chapter and use the content discussed in this chapter to develop a communication plan to help Ryan and Jenny's relationship.

AFTER READING THIS CHAPTER, you will be able to:

1 Identify ways to develop and enhance your self-disclosure skills with your friends, family members, or relational partners.

2 Apply self-disclosure theories to help you determine how your self-disclosure patterns change as your relationships develop.

3 Identify how technology affects close relationships in both positive and negative ways.

AFTER COMPLETING THE SELF-ASSESSMENTS, you will learn about:

1 The behaviors you tend to display when you are self-disclosing to a friend or significant other.

What we share about ourselves with our friends, family members, and relational partners and what they share with us provide important indicators about the level of trust and commitment felt by one or both individuals. Therefore, the absence as well as the presence of close, personal disclosures reveals information about how impersonal or intimate relationships may be.

This chapter begins with a discussion of self-disclosure in interpersonal relationships and ways to develop and enhance your self-disclosure skills. An assessment measure is included that you can use to examine how your verbal and nonverbal messages reflect how and what you self-disclose to others. Following this, two popular theories examining self-disclosure—social penetration theory and relational dialectics theory—are discussed. The chapter then explores the nature of intimacy in relationships as well as factors that influence how or whether intimacy develops in your close relationships.

> Passion is the quickest to develop and the quickest to fade.
> Intimacy develops more slowly, and commitment more gradually still.
>
> —ROBERT STERNBERG

Exploring Self-Disclosure

It is hard to foster intimacy if two people aren't willing to share information about themselves. **Self-disclosure** refers to revealing information about ourselves to others that they would otherwise be unlikely to know. Self-disclosure is considered a voluntary expression of information, in contrast to messages that feel coerced, forced, or perceived as unintentional or accidental remarks. Self-disclosure plays an important role in the establishment and maintenance of intimacy in personal relationships. Closeness may be enhanced between people when the nature of the content that is shared is perceived to be private.

The act of self-disclosing is typically associated with **norms of reciprocity**. This is an expectation that comparable information will be exchanged between individuals. For example, if Shannon reveals something personal about herself (e.g., she is afraid of spiders) and Troy responds in a reciprocal fashion, Troy will share a comparable example about

Casual conversations with friends provide us with opportunities to get to know one another better.

himself (e.g., something that he is afraid or nervous about). Normally, reciprocal self-disclosures help to increase intimacy, but sometimes the reverse can happen. Applying the norms of reciprocity to affective communication messages such as "I love you" could be risky and backfire if ulterior motives are present.[1] Perhaps worse still, the person might reciprocate in spirit but not in intent by replying, "I really like you."

Assessing Your Self-Disclosure Skills

Now that you know a little about self-disclosure, we would like to give you an opportunity to learn more about the self-disclosure skills that you most typically apply when communicating with a close friend or significant other.

 ## ASSESS YOUR communication personality

Wheeless's Self-Disclosure Skills Checklist[2]

Log onto our self-assessment library, MyPersonalityProfile, found on MyCommunicationLab (www.mycommunicationlab.com), and assess your self-disclosure skills. Also, encourage someone with whom you communicate regularly (e.g., a friend, roommate, or relational partner) to do the same. This way, you can compare how each of you self-discloses and begin to understand how your self-disclosure skills may influence your interpersonal communication. If you prefer, you may fill in the answers below and calculate the score yourself.

Directions:

Please mark the following statements to reflect how you communicate with a close friend or your current significant other. Indicate the degree to which the statements below reflect how you communicate with this person by using the following scale:

1 = strongly disagree

2 = disagree

3 = moderately disagree

4 = are undecided

5 = moderately agree

6 = agree

7 = strongly agree

Record the number of your response in the space provided. Work quickly, and just record your first impressions.

_____ **1.** When I wish, my self-disclosures are always accurate reflections of who I really am.

_____ **2.** When I express my personal feelings, I am always aware of what I am doing and saying.

_____ **3.** When I reveal my feelings about myself, I consciously intend to do so.

_____ **4.** When I am self-disclosing, I am consciously aware of what I am revealing.

continued

_____ 5. I do not often talk about myself.

_____ 6. My statements of my feelings are usually brief.

_____ 7. I usually talk about myself for fairly long periods at a time.

_____ 8. My conversation lasts the least time when I am discussing myself.

_____ 9. I often talk about myself.

_____ 10. I often discuss my feelings about myself.

_____ 11. Only infrequently do I express my personal beliefs and opinions.

_____ 12. I usually disclose positive things about myself.

_____ 13. On the whole, my disclosures about myself are more negative than positive.

_____ 14. I normally reveal "bad" feelings I have about myself.

_____ 15. I normally "express" my good feelings about myself.

_____ 16. I often reveal more undesirable things about myself than desirable things.

_____ 17. I usually disclose negative things about myself.

_____ 18. On the whole, my disclosures about myself are more positive than negative.

_____ 19. I intimately disclose who I really am, openly and fully in my conversation.

_____ 20. Once I get started, my self-disclosures last a long time.

_____ 21. I often disclose intimate, personal things about myself without hesitation.

_____ 22. I feel that I sometimes do not control my self-disclosure of personal or intimate things I tell `about myself.

_____ 23. Once I get started, I intimately and fully reveal myself in my self-disclosures.

_____ 24. I cannot reveal myself when I want to because I do not know myself thoroughly enough.

_____ 25. I am often not confident that my expressions of my own feelings, emotions, and experiences are true reflections of myself.

_____ 26. I always feel completely sincere when I reveal my own feelings and experiences.

_____ 27. My self-disclosures are completely accurate reflections of who I really am.

_____ 28. I am not always honest in my self-disclosures.

_____ 29. My statements about my feelings, emotions, and experiences are always accurate self-perceptions.

_____ 30. I am always honest in my self-disclosures.

_____ 31. I do not always feel completely sincere when I reveal my own feelings, emotions, behaviors, or experiences.

Scoring Instructions:

You need to reverse your scores for items 5, 6, 8, 11, 13, 14, 16, 17, 24, 25, 28, and 31. This means that any time you scored 1, make it a 7; 2, make it a 6; 3, make it a 5; 5, make it a 3; 6, make it a 2; 7, make it a 1. After successfully recoding the items listed, the following five dimensions of self-disclosure can be calculated.

Intended disclosure: Add items 1–4 (scores range from 4 to 28)

Amount: Add items 5–11 (scores range from 7 to 49)

Positive–negative: Add items 12–18 (scores range from 7 to 49)

Control of depth: Add items 19–23 (scores range from 5 to 35)

Honesty: Add items 24–31 (scores range from 8 to 56)

Understanding Your Level of Self-Disclosure. Much can be learned from reflecting on how you self-disclose, what you self-disclose, and the degree to which you disclose information about yourself to others. Following are a few recommendations for how you can use your assessment data to make the self-disclosures in your interpersonal relationships more effective:

- *If your score for any particular category is at the midway point of the range or lower, you are less likely to agree with or demonstrate these communicative behaviors when self-disclosing.* The midpoints are as follows: intended disclosure: < 16, amount: < 28, positive–negative: < 28, control of depth: < 20, and honesty: < 20.

- *If you want to develop greater intimacy with your close friend or relational partner but your scores on amount, depth, and intended self-disclosure were lower than the midpoints (amount: < 28, depth: < 20, intended: < 16), you would do well to increase the number of subjects you talk about with your partner as well as the degree of self-reflection in the messages shared.* Low scores on these three self-disclosure dimensions may indicate that at the present time, this relationship is not very unique or special.

- *If you scored low on the positive–negative dimension (< 28), the messages that you share about yourself could be negatively biased.* This suggests that you might have a tendency to reveal what you are not so good at, and you might be equally reluctant to share what you are good at. Therefore, the picture that you present of yourself to others emphasizes personal shortcomings while minimizing positive attributes.

 ## WHAT CAN I **do now?**

▶ *You might want to gradually increase the quantity and quality of what you self-disclose to others if you want to develop greater intimacy with a friend or relational partner.* But be careful not to overdo it. Inserting too much quantity and quality of self-disclosures (especially when the change occurs rather suddenly) could overwhelm another person, who might react by withdrawing from the relationship.

▶ *You might want to reflect on what self-disclosure skills are more natural for you to apply and integrate into your conversations with others.* This information lets you know what you should continue to do when self-disclosing. The lower category scores give you some areas to consider enhancing or modifying in future exchanges.

▶ *Remember that you do not need to disclose every shortcoming or problem that you have with others.* There is no need to highlight every flaw you have. For that matter, other people might not even perceive these "issues" if you don't make a point of sharing them.

Social Penetration Theory: Time to Slice Some Onions?

Social psychologists Irwin Altman and Dalmas Taylor developed **social penetration theory** in an effort to explore what we self-disclose and the extent to which we self-disclose as our interpersonal relationships develop over time.[3] There are two key concepts associated with social penetration theory: breadth and depth. **Breadth** refers to the variety of topics that you discuss with someone. As the number of different topics increases, the breadth of your self-disclosures increases. Topics could be very general (e.g., sports, weather) or personal (e.g., dreams, fears). **Depth** refers to the level of intimacy or

FIGURE 10.1

Using Social Penetration Theory to Examine the Breadth and Depth of Self-Disclosure in Relationships

Breadth of Self-Disclosure
(number of topics discussed)

The smallest pieces of the onion represent a topic not often discussed.

The largest piece of the onion represents a topic that is discussed the most.

Depth of Self-Disclosure
(personal significance of information shared)

Outer layers represent content that is fairly general and safe.

As you move toward the center, information shared gets more personal.

If you reach the core, you share your most intimate thoughts.

intensity of the information shared when self-disclosing on a topic. The more personal or unique the material is that is shared, the greater the depth of the self-disclosure.

As relationships develop, both breadth and depth should increase, suggesting that greater intimacy is developing between two individuals. If breadth and depth decrease, this should provide some telling evidence that the bond between these individuals has weakened. To visualize how breadth and depth operate in a relationship, Altman and Taylor created a diagram. This diagram looks like an onion with its many layers wrapped around a core; hence, social penetration theory is often dubbed the "onion model" of self-disclosure (see Figure 10.1).

It is not uncommon for your self-disclosure behaviors to vary across the different relationships you have. The topics that you discuss (breadth) with your parents are likely to differ from the topics that you discuss with your friends. Even among your friends, you might share some pieces of information only with your closest friends (depth), not with more casual friends. For example, Leigh shared with Marie, her close friend, how much her credit card balance was but didn't share this information with her roommates.

In summary, social penetration theory provides a way to examine the quantity (breadth) and quality (depth) of the information that is exchanged in your relationships with others. Changes in the "onions" are likely to reflect changes in your relationships (see Figure 10.2).

FIGURE 10.2

Examining the Breadth and Depth of Self-Disclosure in Two Relationships

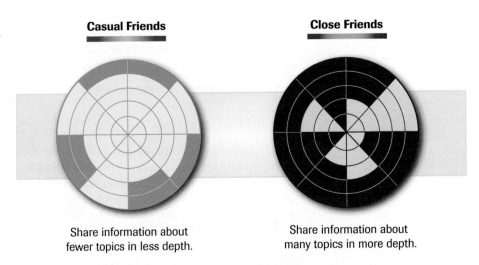

Casual Friends

Share information about fewer topics in less depth.

Close Friends

Share information about many topics in more depth.

Relational Dialectics Theory: A Tug of War

Communication scholar Leslie Baxter developed **relational dialectics theory** as a means to understand how people manage tensions on three fundamental dimensions: connection versus autonomy, openness versus closedness, and predictability versus novelty.[4] When individuals are able to regulate and manage the competing relational needs and desires of each relational partner, both partners may be happier or more satisfied with their relationships. But this can be a difficult task, as relational needs often change over time. Dialectical tensions can occur in virtually any type of relationship, but they have been studied primarily in marital or dating relationships and family relationships (e.g., parent–child dyads).

Dialectical tensions begin as struggles when one person wants something while another person wants the exact opposite. Dialectical tensions can actually occur on several different levels. Dialectics may be internal to a single individual, may be shared across a dyad, or may be between the dyad and the rest of society. Understanding where the tensions are occurring determines how the issues will be managed, the role that communication will play, and ultimately how the relationship will be affected.

Connection–Autonomy. The **connection–autonomy** dialectic focuses on the struggle to be a part of a dyad while simultaneously wanting to be a unique person. Sometimes individuals are not aware of problems associated with the connection–autonomy dialectic. For example, it might take your friends telling you that they never see you since you began dating your new significant other. Other times, parties are well aware of these challenges, especially if partners work different shifts and seldom interact with one another in a face-to-face setting.

Openness–Closedness. Individuals may experience the **openness–closedness** dialectic when deciding whether to reveal or hide parts of their pasts. In many ways, this is about your defining boundaries when deciding whether, or what, you will disclose about yourself to others. For example, you might be open to sharing something with your friend but reluctant to share this same information with one of your parents. This dialectic also includes information that others are open to receiving and processing from outside sources versus messages that individuals prefer to shut themselves off from or deny.

Like any relationship, parents and children need to learn to balance dialectical tensions.

Predictability–Novelty. It is not uncommon for people to struggle with the **predictability–novelty** dialectic. At its best, predictability provides a sense of comfort, because we know that we can count on our significant others, friends, or family members to respond in certain ways. But too much routine is often associated with being boring, dull, or bland. Therefore, inserting some spontaneity into our relationships is generally perceived and received favorably by most people. Two things to be mindful about when incorporating novelty into our relationships are how much or to what degree you are inserting spontaneity and the timing of novelty. There is a tendency to attempt to "think big" and do something out of the ordinary to maximize the impact of the novelty. Therefore, we may assume higher levels of risk in an attempt to maximize our rewards, so we might throw what we consider to be the biggest, best surprise birthday party, even though our partners could feel uncomfortable and overwhelmed by the event.

Although other relational dialectics could surface in our relationships, these three, connection–autonomy, openness–closedness, and predictability–novelty, provide the foundation for understanding that relational tensions may vary in their content and intensity. Therefore, relational partners should individually reflect on and then discuss with each other what they want and need in each of these areas.

CHECKING YOUR UNDERSTANDING

Exploring Self-Disclosure

Before reading further, take a few minutes to assess your learning by writing your answers to the following items:

1. How can understanding your self-disclosure skills help you to improve your interpersonal relationships?

2. What are the main concepts associated with social penetration theory? How do these concepts explain how self-disclosure works and how it changes over time?

3. Describe what takes place within each of the three dialectical tensions of relational dialectics theory and the role that self-disclosure plays in managing these tensions.

Developing and Enhancing Your Self-Disclosure Skills

We need to remember that the messages we exchange about ourselves to our friends, family members, or relational partners are some of the most important. This section examines factors that influence what you self-disclose as well as ways to improve how you self-disclose information to friends, family members, or relational partners.

Factors Associated with Self-Disclosure

There are many things that influence how or whether individuals will self-disclose in their relationships. Four areas that we explore in greater detail are personality, sex differences, cultural differences, and technology.

Personality and Self-Disclosure. Two relational behaviors are often associated with whether or not we self-disclose to our partners: anxiety and avoidance.[5] Recall from Chapter 1 that feelings of anxiety are associated with two personality traits: low levels of extraversion and high levels of neuroticism. Therefore, some of our self-disclosure behaviors are linked to our personality predispositions as well as to behaviors that we have learned and reinforced over time.

When we perceive that our personalities are similar to those of the people with whom we are speaking, we often self-disclose more information.[6] It is hard to determine whether we do this because we actually have more in common with these individuals or because we simply believe that we do because our personalities are similar. In either case, perceptions of personality compatibility could play a role in what we self-disclose or whether we decide to self-disclose to a particular person.

Sex Differences and Self-Disclosure. Communication scholars Kathryn Dindia and Mike Allen have examined how a person's sex (being male or female) affects his or her self-disclosure across a number of research studies.[7] They found that sex differences in self-disclosure are small. In fact, approximately 85% of males and females are similar in their self-disclosure behaviors.[8] This contrasts sharply with many myths about the communicative tendencies of males and females. Here is a brief summary of Dindia and Allen's findings. Remember that these differences, while statistically significant, are small:

- Females tend to disclose more than males to other females.
- Females tend to disclose more than males do to opposite-sex partners.
- Females tend to disclose more to friends, parents, or spouses than males do.
- Females do not disclose more than males to other males.
- Females do not disclose more than males to strangers.
- In examinations of same-sex partner dyads, same-sex female partners report more self-disclosure than same-sex male partners do.

 Cultural Factors Influencing Self-Disclosure. Someone's cultural background could influence what information will or will not be shared with others. For example, people from different cultural groups are more likely to agree on topics that should not be discussed (e.g., family issues, sex) between cultural groups.[9] These areas tend to be **taboo topics** (conversational subjects that are considered to be off limits) for many people,[10] so we could simply be erring on the side of caution by limiting what we talk about. We also tend to self-disclose differently depending on whether we are talking intraculturally (with people from our own culture) or interculturally (with people from different cultures).[11] For example, when Americans talk to other Americans, they tend to demonstrate more conscious intent regarding what they will say as well as how much they will share when self-disclosing. When Americans talk to people from other cultures, they are more likely to limit the depth of what they share. They are also likely to be more positive in what they disclose to others.

When self-disclosure was examined in intercultural friendships, findings showed that the communicative challenges and differences present are more likely to be overcome if people develop relational intimacy with others.[12] By increasing the breadth and depth of what people self-disclose in intercultural relationships, they cultivate relational intimacy. Because they now know one another, it is easier to cope with other relational challenges that are encountered.

 Technology Uses and Self-Disclosure. Some people reveal more private information in their emails or text messages than they do when they talk face to face. This phenomenon has been labeled the **online disinhibition effect**.[13] There are two types of disinhibition: benign disinhibition and toxic disinhibition. In **benign disinhibition**, people share personal information about themselves, such as fears, hopes, or emotions. This also includes acts of kindness and generosity toward others. **Toxic disinhibition** refers to the revealing of less flattering tendencies, such as being rude, overly critical, angry, or threatening. It also includes acts that may be perceived as more dark or inappropriate, such as going to websites that focus on crime, violence, or pornography.

Online communication channels tend to make it more comfortable for shy individuals to communicate with others, but do not completely eliminate someone's shyness. Rather, the effect seems to be to make the shyness more manageable when the person is interacting in a mediated context. As a result, shy individuals may demonstrate behaviors that suggest greater interpersonal competence and a willingness to engage others and get to know them better using online options.[14]

ETHICS **in interpersonal communication**

How Ethical Is Sexting?

One of the more recent trends in online or cell phone communication is "sexting," the electronic sharing, either through videos or pictures, of highly suggestive or openly explicit sexual content. At the present time, teenagers and young adults are the age groups primarily associated with sexting behaviors (either sending or receiving sexually explicit messages). Of the surveys done on sexting behaviors thus far, findings suggest that a sizable percentage of teenagers (over 35%) and young adults (over 55%) had either sent or received sexually explicit messages.[15] One thing that is often overlooked in sexting is the fact that these messages can be easily and widely shared with others.

Sexting poses several ethical dilemmas. First, some people believe that teenagers and young adults engage in sexting as a means to gain social acceptance; they are willing to send sexually explicit messages of themselves to others because they have low self-esteem. But have we as individuals or as a society stooped so low that we have to show naked pictures of ourselves to be accepted? Second, doesn't this compound the potential problem of low self-esteem if others now have extremely sensitive and personal information that they could use against you?

Finally, some view sexting as a "kids will be kids" type of behavior and try to diffuse anxiety or apprehensions others have on the subject. They argue that these behaviors are not new; just the sharing of content via electronic means is new. Yet there have been cases in which fellow classmates have blackmailed other students with these electronic photographs to force them to engage in sexual acts. In other instances, some teenagers have been so traumatized when their messages are shared with others that they have committed suicide. In still other cases, senders and recipients of such photographs have been charged with possession and distribution of child pornography, even when all the participants in the exchanges were friends. Therefore, should we really dismiss or diminish the harm that sexting may cause individuals? What do you think?

Guidelines for Improving Self-Disclosure

There are many things to consider when self-disclosing to others. Four areas are highlighted as you contemplate how and what to self-disclose in your relationships.

Relevance, Clarity, and Timing of Self-Disclosures. Although we may have the best of intentions when sharing information with our partners, the outcomes of our self-disclosures may not be what we had intended. Telling too many stories about previous relationships or childhood mishaps can leave our friends or partners wondering how this information pertains to them. Are we trying to tell them something by sharing this story, or are our friends and partners simply supposed to care about everything we say?

Clarity and timing often work together. When timing is at its worst, there also tend to be clarity problems. For example, have you ever tried to provide a clear explanation for why you are feeling frustrated with your friend when you are both running late for class?

It is not possible to control all aspects associated with when we self-disclose to others. However, we can try to be mindful of what we want to share when we self-disclose. This may mean that we don't self-disclose some information until we are able to articulate what is most important to us. Then we need to be mindful of any time barriers that might compromise our ability to share this message with others. If you can reasonably manage relevance, clarity, and timing, you increase your chances of having your message heard, processed, and understood in the manner that you hoped.

Degree of Risk Involved. When we feel that sharing personal information with others may put us at risk, we are less likely to self-disclose. If we feel that a situation is fraught with intimacy risks, we self-disclose less overall, which in turn leads to reductions in relational quality.[16] To compound matters, when we perceive greater levels of risk, we tend to respond to our friends or partners with less warmth, and we also perceive less warmth from our friends or partners when we are talking to them. Unfortunately, this has the potential to develop into a destructive cycle, since when we perceive greater risk, we disclose less, trust less,

When we whisper to someone, it suggests that this person is special and that we can trust this person with what we are sharing.

experience less intimacy, and have reduced satisfaction with our relationships, which become harder to sustain. Then these problems get reinforced, and we may repeat the destructive communication pattern.

Responding to Someone's Self-Disclosure. People have expectations linked to the feedback that we give them when they self-disclose, whether the feedback is provided in face-to-face or online settings. In particular, when someone discloses information that has a great deal of negative stigma associated with it (e.g., having a mental illness), it is very important not to let our own fears or apprehensions cloud our ability to provide positive feedback to our friends, family members, or partners.[17]

It is just as important to provide positive responses when others share good news. This helps your friends, family members, or partner feel validated, cared for, and understood and enhances their overall relational satisfaction.[18] If you respond passively or destructively to other people's good news, others may experience reduced feelings of trust, intimacy, or satisfaction in their relationship with you.[19] For males, receiving responses for positive events from their partners appears to be especially important; for females, responses to both positive and negative events are important. Therefore, how we respond to the bad things that occur in our partners' lives may involve a different skill set than what is needed for responding to the good things that occur in our partners' lives. Both types of events are worthy of our attention, and neither should be shortchanged when it comes to the effort we put forth when responding.

Having Realistic Expectations. Intimacy between two people does not happen overnight. This does not mean that you may not initially like or be attracted to someone. But you still need to get to know each other. All-night discussions can entail a great deal of self-disclosure. While these discussions can be enlightening, what these all-nighters really do is get us excited about the future. Not every day will include a significant revelation between friends or partners. But if you string together enough days, weeks, months, and years, you substantially increase your odds of having many significant (and, we hope, mostly positive) revelations. If you are patient, you might discover that the journey helps to make the final destination special.

Alternatives to Self-Disclosure

There are other options if you choose not to self-disclose information to others. Some strategies may be more socially acceptable than others, but each provides an alternative to sharing information about yourself (see Table 10.1).

Silence. If you do not know what you want to say or share with another person or you feel that you will get into trouble if you share this information, **silence**, that is, intentionally waiting or reflecting on the message you want to convey, may be a reasonable strategy. It may also be appropriate to refrain from sharing an opinion if you do not have all the facts. However, silence might not be an appropriate strategy if partners, friends, coworkers, or family members are seeking some type of response. If we just sit there and say nothing, this reaction is often misinterpreted as a sign that we do not care or have an opinion rather than being seen as a need for some time to reflect or as a decision to refrain from saying something that could get us into trouble if we voice the sentiment.

TABLE 10.1

Alternatives to Self-Disclosure		
Type of Response	**Description**	**Example**
Silence	The act of refraining from offering a verbal message or response.	"No, I have nothing to add" (or saying nothing).
Lying/Deception	A deliberate act that is undertaken to mislead or misinform others.	"No, I did not purchase any clothes online" (failing to share that you purchased shoes).
Hinting	The act of providing clues to help someone reach a conclusion without explicitly stating a purpose or need.	"Have you thought about how to spend your bonus?"

Lying and Deception. **Lying and deception** are deliberate acts that individuals perform to mislead or misinform others to influence another person's perceptions.[20] There are many different ways to lie as well as different rationales for lying. We may lie by falsifying information, concealing information that we have, or omitting information if someone does not explicitly ask for it. By committing these actions, we could harm others, spare others, or benefit ourselves. What we do with the information when we are lying, as well as what our intentions are when we lie, can skew how "justifiable" we, as well as our partners, consider the lie to be. Although we are more likely to lie to people we are closest to (e.g., relational partners, family members), these lies often go undetected and may even be a part of typical day-to-day interactions (e.g., saying that dinner tastes good even though it does not). If we feel compelled to lie, the perception is that we do it with our partner's best interest at heart (e.g., we don't want our partner to believe that we think he or she is a bad cook). If this is not perceived to be the case, the sentiments toward the liar are often more harsh.

Hinting. **Hinting** is an effort to provide clues to get someone to reach a particular conclusion or objective without intentionally sharing the information with them. Some aspects of hinting can be playful (e.g., "Can you guess what I got you for your birthday?"); other types of hinting are done in an effort to get people to determine what you want without asking. For hinting to be successful, both the sender and the receiver need to be skilled at providing clues or suggestions as well as decoding what these clues or suggestions mean. Unfortunately, some hints are so ambiguous that the receiver reaches one conclusion when another was intended. This can get both parties into trouble, since both can be disappointed in the failed communication attempt.

CHECKING YOUR UNDERSTANDING

Enhancing Your Self-Disclosure Skills

Before reading further, take a few minutes to assess your learning by writing your answers to the following items:

1. What are the four factors that are related to self-disclosure, and how does each factor influence what we share with others?

2. What are four guidelines for self-disclosure, and how can you utilize each to develop how and what you self-disclose in your relationships?

3. Describe three alternatives to self-disclosure, and identify some challenges that are inherent in each option.

The Nature of Intimacy in Relationships

If you were to ask people on the street what intimacy means, it would not be surprising if many of them assumed that by intimacy, you meant sexual intimacy. While this is one type of intimacy, it is certainly not the only way to demonstrate intimacy in close relationships, nor is intimacy limited to romantic relationships. **Intimacy** refers to a type of attachment that arises from a close union, contact, association, or relationship. The following sections explore factors associated with communicating intimacy, love styles, personality, and the significance of prior relational histories.

Factors Associated with Communicating Intimacy

We will discuss three things to help you understand communicating intimacy with your friends, family members, and relational partners: commitment, trust, and expressions of intimacy.

Commitment. When you bind yourself to another person in the form of an allegiance, pledge, or promise, you are making a **commitment**. Commitment demonstrates a desire to stay, not only when things are either going great or not going well at all, but also—and perhaps more—when things are just okay, but not wonderful.[21] Commitments may be demonstrated in public events, such as wedding ceremonies, organizational orientations, or sorority pledges; however, private expressions of commitment also occur and should not be discounted.

Some individuals are perceived to be **commitment-phobic** because they have a serious fear of or apprehension about commitment or intimacy.[22] Other reasons for commitment anxiety are more complex, linked to issues of self-identity or couple identity. There may be challenges inherent in the process of making a commitment to a particular relationship that might overwhelm our existing individual identity.[23] For example, Judy fears that she will lose who she is as a unique person once she marries her fiancé, Keith, because then they will typically be considered part of a dyad rather than two separate individuals. This could be even more challenging for same-sex couples, since partners may be navigating issues tied to their individual sexual identity as well as a broader group identity when they make commitments to one another.[24] For instance, Tom needs to accept his own sexual orientation in addition to how this places him and his relationship with Frank in the broader context of the gay community and the community at large.

Trust. Several factors, such as confidence, honesty, and reliability, play a role in defining trust. Combined, they shape a definition of **trust**: relying upon or placing confidence in another person. It is often difficult to predict whether you will develop trust with another person because trusting another person may make you vulnerable to him or her as well as making the other person vulnerable to you. Some people are also inherently suspicious of others.[25] For instance, if a friend violated your trust and posted something about you on Facebook that was very cruel or critical, you may be reluctant to share information with other friends for fear that the same thing could happen. Conversely, some individuals may doubt that they are worthy of the benefits that come when someone trusts them, such as feelings of acceptance and value. These individuals often act paranoid when around friends or partners even when there is no reason to doubt their sincerity.[26]

If trust violations occur, depending on the nature of the violation and the intent of the violator, one or both individuals may withdraw from the relationship. This may explain why some people exhibit a **truth bias** when processing messages involving those they care about.[27] A truth bias is the tendency for people in close relationships to believe

There are no age limits associated with communicating intimacy to our partners.

that their partners will not lie to them. The closer we are to a person, the less likely it is that we would assume or suspect that this person would lie to us. Relational partners may demonstrate a truth bias if they deny rumors that their partner is cheating.[28] We may also demonstrate a truth bias in our friendships if a friend is lying to us about something but we choose to believe otherwise. In either case, we prefer to deny rather than confront and deal with the issue.

Expressions of Intimacy. We can demonstrate intimacy in our relationships in numerous ways, ranging from physical intimacy to intellectual intimacy or emotional intimacy. All levels of intimacy may be present across the lifespan of our relationships. However, the nature of the relationship (e.g., friend, family member, romantic partner) as well as the age of the individuals involved typically determine what is considered an appropriate display of intimacy. Many expressions of intimacy tend to have common meanings across cultures, such as the different degrees of touch that are used to demonstrate physical expressions in intimacy (e.g., aggression, comfort, love).[29]

Communication scholar Kory Floyd has examined the role of affectionate communication in close relationships. He advocates that "one of the most instrumental communicative behaviors in the development and maintenance of significant personal relationships is the expression of affection."[30] He and his colleagues have found that affectionate communication plays a critical role in maintaining intimacy in established relationships as well as enhancing the physical and psychological well-being of those who engage in affectionate communication. Some findings from this body of work include the following:

- The effects of receiving affectionate messages from our marital partners are more strongly related to healthy stress hormones than are the effects of sending or giving these comments to our partners.[31]

- Marital and cohabiting couples that engage in frequent kissing (with each other) have decreases in total cholesterol and perceived stress. In addition, they report increased relational satisfaction.[32]

- Verbal exchanges containing supportive affectionate communication have the potential to lower resting heart rates and lower the amounts of cortisol that is released into the bloodstream.[33]

Love Styles, Personality, and Communicating Intimacy

One of the most common affective expressions associated with intimacy is love. John Lee began studying different types of love in the 1970s,[34] creating a conceptual typology of love styles that other scholars, such as Clyde Hendrick and Susan Hendrick, measured over the span of more than twenty years.[35] Here is a brief description of the six love styles that they highlighted.[36]

- **Eros** (passionate love): Strongly driven by physical attraction, passion, and emotions, eros lovers often believe in "love at first sight." They have an ideal mate in mind; when they believe that they have met this person, they get very excited.

- **Ludus** (playful love): Not in pursuit of a particular mate, ludus lovers tend to be more in the moment and will have a series of love affairs over time and/or simultaneously. Love is a "game"; it should be "fun" and serves its purpose for that particular moment in time.

- **Storge** (companionate love): Affection and commitment develop over time as storge lovers get to know one another. There is no ideal physical type; perceived similarities and commonalities are more important.

- **Pragma** (practical love): Pragma lovers approach love very practically. Basic characteristics needed in a mate are identified, with compatibility playing an important role in mate selection. The process is comparable to working with an online dating service or writing a classified ad. Pragma lovers are driven by the head more than the heart.

- **Mania** (possessive love): Mania lovers experience an all-encompassing event and take an obsessive attitude toward it. At times, possessiveness can lead to insecurities, and individuals may experience intense jealousy or fear associated with their lover leaving them for another. There is a high degree of dependency tied to their love interests. Ironically, owing to the intensity of the emotions, mania lovers may hold back their emotions from their loved ones for fear of being neglected.

- **Agape** (altruistic love): Considered the most selfless love style and the least common, agape is associated with spirituality and altruistic behaviors, in which a partner is willing to make personal sacrifices for his or her mate. The agape lover will love the other person, even when the partner is demonstrating behaviors that make it difficult to love him or her.

ASSESSING on the web   mycommunicationlab

Log onto our self-assessment library, MyPersonalityProfile, which can be found on MyCommunicationLab (www.mycommunicationlab.com), and complete Lee's Measure of Love-Styles.[37]

Personality traits might not be the best predictor of why one person demonstrates a particular love style while a different person demonstrates another. The interactions that we observed between our parents when we were growing up and then between other romantic couples in adulthood appear to play more important roles in helping us learn both how to love and perhaps what to look for in our own future partners.[38] We may observe both constructive and destructive communication exchanges and note which behaviors get relational results and which do not. Although we may observe dysfunctional relationships, we do not automatically engage in those same destructive behaviors. However, if we regularly observe intimate relationships that integrate destructive communication patterns, this could influence what we might consider to be typical interactions for intimate partners. This finding endorses what others had already believed: that love style preferences are learned.[39]

However, this does not mean that personality traits do not contribute in other ways to shape how we love and what we look for in our intimate partners. Two interesting comparisons pertain to the love styles of storge and eros. As we noted earlier, the storge love style emphasizes partners who begin as friends; getting to know one another before becoming lovers. These individuals share many similarities in personality traits. Conversely, the eros love style involves passionate, physical love and emphasizes "love at first sight." These individuals have fewer personality traits in common, in part because the focus is on mutual physical attraction. It was concluded that "rather than giving rise to *better* relationships, similarity leads to *different* types of relationships."[40] Therefore, it would not be surprising if

NATURE/NURTURE intersections

The "Love" in Your Blood

It is not uncommon to idealize the early periods of relational development, since they tend to be filled with excitement, novelty, and arousal. There is anticipation about what we will share or do next with our partners. We experience a great deal of pleasure when we are with our partners. As a result, we are highly motivated to continue interacting with them. However, as time goes by, we may still want to be with our partners, but the emotions we experience may have changed.[41] While the average person may have experienced these changes as intimacy develops, few of us understand the physiological and cognitive processes that are operating in the shadows of our bodies and brains.

Dopamine and oxytocin are substances synthesized in the brain that are considered to be active contributors in the development and maintenance of intimacy for humans. Although dopamine is involved in several important human processes (e.g., motivation and pleasure), it is primarily linked with rewards. Therefore, to continue to satisfy our relational needs, we may incorporate greater novelty or risk taking in our behaviors.[42] In the process, we get a boost of dopamine. If dopamine acts like an addictive drug within the context of relational develop-ment, this has the potential for negative ramifications in the development of longer-lasting intimacy bonds. This is where oxytocin comes in.

Oxytocin (not Oxycontin, the prescriptive pain medication) is associated with bonding and connections. Oxytocin is released when mutual touch, bonding, intercourse, and/or affection is occurring. This in turns tends to facilitate trust and potential bonds between partners. Oxytocin is also released in females during childbirth and breastfeeding. As a result, oxytocin has been referred to as the "relational maintenance hormone" or the nurturing hormone because establishing or maintaining close physical bonds tends to release more of this hormone into the bloodstream. But this hormone is not limited to females; both sexes have oxytocin in their bloodstream.

Both dopamine and oxytocin are important in the development of human intimacy. This is not to suggest that dopamine is limited to the early stages of intimacy development and oxytocin is limited to the later stages of intimacy. Rather, it helps us to understand why these two periods of intimacy development are often described in very different ways and how our bodies and brains may adjust accordingly to the types of intimacy we experience and nurture over the lifespan.

Sometimes past relationships have a way of affecting present (or future) relationships.

the communicative exchanges that were demonstrated by storge–storge and eros–eros dyads varied as well.

Prior Relational Histories

Whether we realize it or not, we often display patterns of behavior in our close, intimate relationships. Outsiders to our relationships tend to be good at spotting our dating partner patterns. Some people believe that we are destined to keep repeating the same patterns until we have learned the lessons we were supposed to take away from those experiences. Whether or not you believe this, there are indications that we tend to repeat patterns that work for us—or at least are comfortable for us and do not force us to change.

Sadly, sometimes we cast past relational failures onto our present or future relational partners. If our previous partner cheated on us, we automatically assume that our present or future partner will do the same. This is known as **projection**. If it hasn't yet happened, we think, just wait—eventually it will occur. Unfortunately, when we demonstrate projection, we put our present or future relational partners in a no-win situation: We suspect them of behaviors that they might not have done, and we don't seem to want to let them off the hook until our suspicions are confirmed. Projection can be very destructive to developing or maintaining intimacy over time.

CHECKING YOUR UNDERSTANDING

The Nature of Intimacy in Relationships

Before reading further, take a few minutes to assess your learning by writing your answers to the following items:

1. Examine how each factor associated with intimacy contributes to the development of intimacy in friendships, family relationships, and romantic relationships.

2. What are the six love style preferences, and what does a person with each love style look for in a potential partner?

3. How does someone's prior relational history influence the development of intimacy in that person's present or future relationships?

Influences on Interpersonal Intimacy

If someone asked you, "What are you looking for in an intimate relationship?" what would you say? Whether your expectations are attainable may be linked to factors that influence how you and your friends, family members, or partners communicate. Four areas covered that could affect what you are hoping to find in your intimate relationships are sex differences and communicating intimacy, cultural influences on intimacy, technological influences on intimacy, and challenges, problems, and dysfunctional communication.

Sex Differences and Communicating Intimacy

Personal experiences, along with pop culture trends and stereotypes, often oversimplify or magnify sex differences while bypassing less glamorous distinctions. In a comprehensive review of the research, scholars identified several consistently reported sex differences in association with communicating intimacy.[43] The following list provides a sampling of what researchers have learned over several decades:

- *Men tend to receive greater health benefits from their close relationships than women do.* Women tend to promote better health habits for their husbands as well as providing emotional support for their mates. Wives' health is more closely tied to the quality of their marriages.

- *Men and women have different expectations about the amount of time couples should spend together to maintain intimacy and closeness in their relationships.* Women want their husbands to be more responsive and engaged in interactions so that closeness and intimacy can flourish in their relationships. Men report a greater need for autonomy and independence away from their wives.

- *Men and women tend to emphasize the role of sexuality differently in their close relationships.* Women place sexuality within the context of commitment and relational intimacy. Men place sexuality within the realm of physical pleasure and sexual intercourse.

Cultural Influences on Intimacy

Cultural background may affect whether or not a couple discusses matters related to intimacy. There may be cultural norms or expectations associated with whether these matters are discussed openly with others, discussed just between intimate partners, or simply silently enacted.[44] Cultures may also have nonverbal indicators that demonstrate the intimacy between partners. For example, deferring to one's spouse or reserving a particular seat of honor for a partner often demonstrates a level of intimacy and special status between partners for other people to observe. Expressions of intimacy may vary by culture, but expressions of love by partners tend to be universally understood.[45] When individuals have strong concerns about their close interpersonal relationships, they tend to have higher levels of life satisfaction regardless of their country of origin or participants' ages.[46]

Depending on what country you are in, there may be a different set of rules to determine acceptable public displays of affection for heterosexual couples[47] or intimacy in general.[48] For example, it is typically acceptable for heterosexual partners to hold hands in public in North America and Europe. In other parts of the world, these behaviors are less acceptable. In some Middle Eastern countries, two male friends may display more public affection than a married couple can.[49] Acceptance of public displays of affection does not necessarily apply for same-sex romantic couples, even in Europe and North America. Depending on what country (or even region of the country) you are in, there may be a range of acceptability for such displays for same-sex partners.

Technological Influences on Intimacy

Many technologies look at the features that face-to-face communication offers and try to integrate these options into technological advances. For example, instant messaging and text-messaging have the ability to improve the interactive nature of mediated messages because individuals can respond much faster than is typically possible in an email exchange. As a result, we perceive a closeness and stronger link to the person we are speaking to because we are having a more interactive "conversation" that helps to reduce perceptions of distance.

The focus is now shifting from whether partners are able to communicate with one another to emphasizing the navigation of rules or expectations associated with when, where, how, or why to communicate with each other.[50] Research findings indicate that online partners look for some of the same elements as face-to-face romantic partners to

Families are capitalizing on technological advances to stay connected to one another.

enhance their relational satisfaction: intimacy, trust, and communication satisfaction.[51] These issues are particularly noteworthy for intimate relationships that begin online and strive to transfer successfully to face-to-face intimate partnerships.

It has been noted that "the important effects of a new technology may be not to let people do old things more efficiently, but to do new things that were not possible or feasible with old technology (Sproull & Kiesler, 1991)."[52] Some of the latest software applications, such as Skype, allow people to video conference with one another (or a group of people) through the use of web cameras attached to computers. This has become extremely popular with family members or relational partners who are physically separated from one another. Military personnel as well as students studying abroad have used this technology to lessen the negative effects of being apart from their loved ones for extended periods of time. The technology is inexpensive and often the software is free, making it an affordable option for many people to stay connected with those they love.

Challenges, Problems, and Dysfunctional Communication

In 1994, communication scholars William Cupach and Brian Spitzberg edited a book entitled *The Dark Side of Interpersonal Relationships*.[53] This work is often credited with directing more scholarly attention to the problematic side of interpersonal relationships. We discuss three challenges, problems, and dysfunctional exchanges in greater detail: distance and relational intimacy, nonreciprocated intimacy, and verbal and physical aggression.

Distance and Relational Intimacy. Communication scholar Laura Stafford has studied long-distance close relationships[54] and has noted that we tend to modify our expectations of our relational partners if we have only limited access to them (e.g., weekends only). The limited access creates high expectations that partners will do things to maximize their enjoyment with one another in the time they do have together. They tend to avoid discussing conflicts or might set aside more mundane activities that would normally be a part of the relationship if they saw one another more frequently.

It is also becoming more common for marital partners to live in two separate cities because of the demands or restrictions associated with their careers.[55] In such situations, both partners need to have open, regular dialogue as well as strategies they will use to sustain their intimate relationship in spite of physical separation. Although partners may be able to call, email, fax, text, instant message, or Skype each other, these communication channels may be more effective for short-term physical separations than for long-term separations. It is much more problematic if partners believe that these physical barriers are unlikely to be resolved in the foreseeable future.[56] Physical separations may be further complicated if the couple has children, since the children will probably have one primary residence and the family dynamic may start to look like a single-parent household, albeit perhaps with greater financial resources.

A different type of distance problem for intimate partners involves the creation and management of psychological distance. **Relational affiliation** refers to the degree to which individuals feel connected and close to their partners.[57] As they try to manage their psychological distance, some people focus on the differences and perceive that they are worlds apart from their partners on what they want for the relationship. Whether the distance is real or perceived, it will affect the relationship, and their relational affiliation will decrease. Part of the problem is that there are two different relational activities at play in managing psychological distance: trying to engage with your partner to reduce psychological distance and attempting to psychologically distance yourself from a perceived threat.[58] Therefore, partners might need the assistance of a third party to help them address the problems facing their relationship.

Nonreciprocated Intimacy. Unfortunately, our relational partners might not always share the feelings that we have for them. When someone experiences a passionate love for another that is not reciprocated, this is referred to as **unrequited love**. Ultimately, it can make things awkward for both parties—the rejector as well as the person being rejected.[59] In some cases, the feeling of loss is so great for the individuals who must hear that their feelings are not mutually shared that they engage in self-destructive behaviors.[60] In other instances, some people ignore or disregard these disengagement attempts and continue to pursue their hoped-for partners in efforts to convince them to change their minds. This often leads to engaging in problematic behaviors, such as actions based on jealousy.

Jealousy is an emotion that typically gets in the way of establishing or maintaining intimacy. **Jealousy** is an emotional state that is typically experienced when we feel insecure, fearful, or anxious at the thought of losing something or someone important to us, whether this is a friendship, family relationship, or relational partner. In addition, we may try to create jealousy in other people by wanting them to want something that we have (that is typically in scarce supply). Jealousy tends to be linked to the personality trait of neuroticism and an individual's self-esteem. Therefore, as your levels of neuroticism increase, you are more likely to experience jealousy as well as the possibility that your self-esteem will be weakened.[61]

An additional variable that contributes to feelings of jealousy involves perceptions of a **rival**. Rivals can take many different forms. They can be romantic (e.g., someone else is showing a romantic interest in your relational partner), platonic (e.g., your partner spends too much time with his or her friends), or activity-based (e.g., your partner spends too much time working, studying, or attending to other obligations). If you happen to know the rival, rather than the rival being an acquaintance or stranger, you are more likely to feel greater levels of apprehension. When the rival is platonic or activity-based, different challenges may surface, making it imperative that the partners communicate with each other to address these discrepancies. Sometimes people intentionally try to make their partners jealous. While on the surface that might not seem like a good strategy, some people believe that jealousy is one way to show that you care about the relationship; these people might be trying to do some type of relational correction.[62] However, this is a risky strategy and could just as easily erode a relationship.

Verbal and Physical Aggression in Intimate Relationships. Chapter 4 provided a preview of verbal aggression. In the context of this chapter, we are examining verbal and physical aggression in intimate relationships. Verbal aggression occurs when we verbally insult our partners or make hurtful comments to them. Although verbal aggression does not predict physical aggression, the likelihood of physical aggression taking place increases as levels of verbal aggression increase. Communication scholar Dominic Infante and his colleagues have worked to understand what happens when marital partners engage in verbally aggressive exchanges. This led to the development of the **skills deficiency model of interspousal violence**.[63] What occurs when and after marital partners converse is critical to whether events might escalate to physical aggression.

The model contends that the argumentative skills of both marital partners could either provoke or diffuse potentially hostile exchanges. If partners feel ill equipped to respond to verbally aggressive statements, they are more likely to provide a reciprocal negative-valence reply to their spouses and may feel justified in doing so (e.g., if my partner calls me *&@, I can call my partner **&@ in return). If both partners have difficulty arguing constructively, this is particularly problematic. When at least one marital partner is able to talk rationally about issues, the other person may be less likely to reciprocate with a verbally aggressive response, thus reducing the likelihood of escalating the aggressive exchanges. It is important to remember that "verbal aggression is not necessarily a cause for physical violence, but it is always present when physical violence is present."[64] As intimate partners become more accustomed to dealing with verbally aggressive exchanges, they may unwittingly be setting the stage for future physical altercations.

Problems with verbal aggression extend beyond those experienced by marital couples. This type of dysfunctional communication may be present in any relationship but is especially problematic in developing intimacy between parents and their children, siblings, and friends. In all of these instances, verbally aggressive messages affect how or even whether bonds of intimacy are established and maintained. However, because some of these relationships are extremely difficult to disengage from, the consequences of repeated verbally aggressive exchanges can have long-lasting effects on individuals and their relationships.

CHECKING YOUR UNDERSTANDING

Influences on Interpersonal Intimacy

Before completing the chapter, take a few minutes to assess your learning by writing your answers to the following items:

1. How are males and females different in their approaches to intimacy? How are they similar?

2. Explain why cultures might vary in their expressions of intimacy. When might this pose problems for establishing intercultural intimacy in friendships, family relationships, or significant other relationships?

3. In what ways has technology use changed how partners express and maintain intimacy? How do these methods compare to what occurs in face-to-face communication exchanges?

4. Review the challenges, problems, and dysfunctional behaviors that we examined. How are they problematic? How might each be managed? How might they vary on the basis of relationship type?

A Communication Development Plan for Ryan

To complete Ryan's story, recall that Ryan was having difficulty communicating with his wife, Jenny. Ryan tends to "go with the flow" and let Jenny initiate events in their relationship. However, when he gets upset, instead of sharing his thoughts, he refrains from self-disclosing to Jenny. Jenny has the tendency to share more information about her thoughts and feelings and wants Ryan to share more with her, but she perhaps talks too much, often causing Ryan to disengage from their conversations.

What do you think?

How are Ryan's and Jenny's communication tendencies contributing to the problems they have interacting? What effect is Ryan's lack of self-disclosure having on his relationship with Jenny? How could Ryan modify how he self-discloses to Jenny to enhance the intimacy they share?

Possible explanations:

Ryan and Jenny's communication patterns present several self-disclosure challenges. While Ryan might want Jenny to modify her self-disclosure behaviors, he is not helping matters by limiting what he shares with her. As a result, the level of intimacy experienced by both of them is starting to negatively affect the health of their marriage.

How are Ryan and Jenny's different communication tendencies contributing to the problems they are having interacting? Some individuals, such as Jenny, have a greater need to share their thoughts and ideas with others. Others, such as Ryan, do not feel as compelled to share as much information about themselves all the time. Ryan and Jenny have known each other for three years, so these patterns are reasonably well established. However, if nothing changes in how and what they self-disclose to each other, their relationship will be negatively affected.

What effect is self-disclosure (or the lack thereof) having on Ryan and Jenny's relationship? The problems that Ryan and Jenny are having are more complicated than simply saying that Jenny self-discloses too much and Ryan doesn't self-disclose enough. Aside from issues linked with quantity, they have different needs for information.

How could Ryan and Jenny modify how they self-disclose to each other to enhance the intimacy they share? If Ryan and Jenny were to draw their own diagrams of their self-disclosures according to social penetration theory, it would be interesting to compare the breadth and depth of topics each included in their diagrams. This could lead to some interesting insights into how they perceive the communication in their relationship and could pave the way for fruitful discussion.

1. *It is not inherently a problem that Ryan and Jenny have different needs or desires to self-disclose.* However, Jenny's fear of being ignored may be contributing to her excessive self-disclosure. This, in turn, tends to prompt Ryan to withhold more information than he normally would. Jenny needs to trust that Ryan is not going to ignore her. With some encouragement from Ryan, Jenny can work to better manage the quantity of her self-disclosures.

2. *Jenny might want to consider other outlets for some of her comments that may be less relevant to her relationship with Ryan.* There is nothing wrong with sharing information with friends, family members, or colleagues. Our spouses or significant others need not be our only outlet for self-disclosure. Obviously, we need to stay connected to our partners, and self-disclosure is an important tool to be able to do this. But it is healthy and normal to share information with others in our lives as well.

3. *Although Ryan and Jenny have a general sense of the self-disclosure discrepancies in their relationship, they might not have actually discussed the problem with each other.* Although this might feel like a risky thing to do, if Ryan and Jenny work together and both are willing to discuss how this is affecting their relationship, it is a strong step toward addressing the problem.

Take Aways

This chapter focused on increasing your understanding, skills, and knowledge of self-disclosure and intimacy. The following lists summarize what you have learned in this chapter.

You have increased your understanding and knowledge of:

- Two theories—social penetration theory and relational dialectics theory—and how they are related to self-disclosure.

- The factors that shape how and what we self-disclose to others.

- The challenges that are involved in working to manage and improve self-disclosure with friends, family members, and relational partners.

- The elements that guide how intimacy is communicated to others. These elements include factors associated with communicating intimacy; love styles, personality, and communication; and prior relational histories.

- The influences that affect how intimacy is developed in relationships. These influences include sex differences, culture, technology, and difficult communication issues.

  In addition, you are also better able to:

- Identify ways to improve your self-disclosure skills with your friends, family members, or relational partner.

- Apply self-disclosure theories to help you determine how your self-disclosure patterns change as your intimate relationships develop.

- Learn what behaviors you are most likely to display when you are self-disclosing to a friend or significant other.

- Identify how technology can affect close relationships in positive and negative ways.

Discussion Questions

1. Compare and contrast social penetration theory and relational dialectics theory. What do you think are the strengths and weaknesses of each theory? Which theory do you tend to prefer and why?

2. How are the guidelines and suggestions for improving self-disclosure related to the models and theories of self-disclosure? What connections do you see across these two areas?

3. How does technology influence the development of intimacy and self-disclosure in close relationships?

How have you incorporated technology into your communication with friends, family members, and/or your relational partner? Has technology helped or created problems in your interpersonal communication with these individuals?

4. What role should someone's love style preference play in trying to find a relational partner? Should this become a part of any premarital conversations? Why or why not?

Building Your Skills

1. Rank-order the three factors associated with intimacy (commitment, trust, expressions of intimacy) in terms of their importance for you in a close relationship. Compare your rankings to those of a friend or significant other. How similar or different are your rankings? How can you use this knowledge to make any adjustments in your relationship with this person?

2. Where do you think you learned your love style? If you wanted to change or modify your love style, how

would you go about doing this? What challenges would you most likely encounter, and how would you overcome them?

3. Interview three people you have known for over a year, and ask them to share how and what you self-disclose to them and others. Did you find any patterns? How might you use this information to shape future self-disclosures?

11 Family and Friend Relationships

Emily's Story . . .

Emily and Sayuri have been best friends for a long time. When both young women got jobs in the same city after graduation, it was a no-brainer for them to decide to room together. Even though they have very different cultural backgrounds, they have a lot in common. Both were on the soccer team at college, they have similar tastes in music, and they like the same television shows. On top of that, they have many mutual friends and enjoy spending time hanging out together. Although Emily and Sayuri were never roommates in college, they didn't anticipate that this would be a problem.

However, once they got an apartment and started to live together, problems began to surface almost immediately. Emily had never realized how much of a "neat freak" Sayuri is; Sayuri likes the dishes to be done every night before going to bed and complains when this does not happen. Sayuri had not known that Emily is kind of a slob; Emily often leaves her coat and purse on the sofa when she gets home from work and typically leaves the apartment a mess at the end of the night, stating that she will clean in the morning. In

addition, Sayuri likes to have her days planned and structured both before and after she comes home from work (e.g., jogging before work, watching her favorite television shows on Thursday night), while Emily is more open to doing things spontaneously (e.g., making cookies when she has a craving for sweets, getting last-minute tickets to sporting events).

The first two months of living together were pretty rough, and each of the women was thinking of finding another roommate. One night after work, Sayuri talked to a mutual friend about her frustrations with Emily. Unfortunately, Emily learned about this a couple of days later and was really hurt by some of the things Sayuri had said. It was not until one rainy Saturday afternoon, when they were sitting together in the living room, bored, that they really begin to talk about some of the frustrations they were feeling toward each other.

How can Emily ask Sayuri, "Does everything always need to be so tidy and scheduled in advance?" Furthermore, how can Emily share how hurt she was when Sayuri complained about her to someone else? On the other hand, is

CHAPTER OBJECTIVES

AFTER READING THIS CHAPTER, you will understand:

1 The different types of family relationships.

2 The unique features of friendships.

3 The ways in which personality factors and sex differences influence the communication exchanges in family and friend relationships.

4 How friendships evolve over the lifespan.

5 How culture influences family and friend communication.

Emily prepared to hear Sayuri's complaints about her lack of cleanliness or order? These are the challenges facing Emily and Sayuri.

While reading this chapter, consider how you might handle problems similar to the ones that Emily and Sayuri are encountering:

- How are Emily's and Sayuri's perceived similarities and actual differences contributing to the problems they are having as roommates?

- What should Emily do in regard to Sayuri's violation of implicit friendship rules?

- How could Emily modify her interactions with Sayuri to live together successfully while remaining best friends?

We will revisit Emily's story at the end of the chapter and use the content discussed in this chapter to develop a communication plan to help Emily and Sayuri's friendship.

AFTER READING THIS CHAPTER, you will be able to:

1 Explain the role of personality in family and friend relationships.

2 Distinguish between what it means to be a friend and what it means to be a roommate.

3 Apply your knowledge of sex differences when interacting with others in your personal relationships.

4 Identify how technology affects family and friend relationships in both positive and negative ways.

5 Identify characteristics associated with family strengths.

6 Enhance your communication in family and friend relationships.

AFTER COMPLETING THE SELF-ASSESSMENTS, you will learn:

1 How you perceive the strength of your friendship network.

2 The degree to which friendship strength, reciprocity, and mutual influence are demonstrated in your friendships.

The word "family" tends to generate strong emotions. Many people consider family relationships to be the most important interpersonal relationships a person can have. Although our families may not be perfect, we will defend them mightily if others are overly critical of our kin. This may help to explain the appeal of referring to some groups or teams as "families." Members are there for each other and have staunch loyalty that leads them to protect the interests of group or "family" members.

> Lots of people want to ride with you in the limo, but what you want is someone who will take the bus with you when the limo breaks down.
>
> —OPRAH WINFREY

Our friends can be equally important to us. Although some people say that friends fill the interpersonal gaps that are missed by our partners or families, this characterization minimizes the importance of the friendship relationship. When someone says something like "I'm marrying my best friend" or "This person is more than a brother/sister—this person is my friend," that person is implying that being someone's friend may be the ultimate compliment one person could pay another.

The first half of this chapter focuses on family relationships. The second half of the chapter examines friendships. Specifically, we'll examine the unique features of family relationships and friend relationships along with personality and sex differences, cultural factors, and the role of technology in maintaining family and friend relationships. There is also an opportunity to assess the strength of your friendships. Finally, we'll examine three problematic areas for family and friend relationships: secrets, hurtful messages, and deception.

Communication in Families

Family interactions provide the foundation for the relationships we have with others. By interacting in our families, we learn who we are as individuals and how we fit into a larger social unit. We also learn how we should interact with others both in and outside our families. Next, we'll discuss some of the types of family relationships and the role that personality factors, sex differences, culture, and technology play in these relationships. Then we'll explore ways in which we can enhance our family relationships.

Types of Family Relationships

There are many types of family relationships. Some emphasize the biological connections between members; others are based on the voluntary, mutual acceptance of the relationship between members. The four types of family relationships that we'll review here are some of the most common: spousal or partner, parent–child, sibling, and intergenerational relationships.

Spousal or Partner Relationships. Early family communication research focused on the communication between marital partners. Clearly, this is an important family dyad and heavily influences the communication patterns in other family dyads. An overview of marital and family research found that happy marriages and happy families share three characteristics: effective communication, common interests, and religion.[1] Furthermore, studies have repeatedly found that strong, healthy marital dyads tend to lead to stronger, healthier family relationships. Therefore, one of the best things

Healthy, happy marriages play a critical role in developing healthy, happy families.

parents can do for their children is to have a healthy, happy marriage. That, of course, is easier said than done. When my husband and I were going through required religious premarital counseling, our priest told us that marriages should not follow a 50–50 rule but rather a 0–100 rule. He said that we should not think of ourselves but only of our partner's needs. When both partners do this, everyone's needs and desires are met. This implies that both parties embrace the love style of agape (discussed in Chapter 10). My husband and I have yet to master the 0–100 rule. But on a more practical note, although couples may vary in what it takes to sustain marital happiness, spending quality time together and having shared interests, hobbies, values, and personalities were behaviors that happy couples typically identified.[2] Underlying these suggestions would likely be open communication, active listening, constructive conflict resolution skills, and humor demonstrated by both partners.

Today, marital relationships can be complicated to study. One reason is that one or both partners may have been married before. Statistics examining divorce rates around the world indicate that the United States has one of the highest divorce rates for first marriages, at 41% (only Canada's divorce rate for first marriages was higher, at 50%).[3] Approximately 75% of these individuals remarry.[4] Unfortunately, the divorce rates only go up for second or third marriages. An explanation could be that the added stressors placed on these marital dyads from either within or outside the relationship (e.g., children or former spouses) make successful martial communication more challenging.[5]

Parent–Child Relationships. There are four possible parent–child dyads: mother–daughter, mother–son, father–daughter, and father–son. Mother–child dyads have been studied the most extensively. Mothers have often taken on the primary nurturing role in raising children. This could explain why we know more about how mothers interact with their children than about how fathers and children interact. Parent–child relationships evolve as children get older and their abilities to interact with their parents change. For instance, as children learn to talk and share their thoughts, feelings, and ideas, parents are better able to understand and meet their children's needs. Parents and children also have the ability to influence one another.[6] Furthermore, the effects that parents have on their children and that children have on their parents can and do occur across the lifespan.[7] Whenever parents move to a new residence, for example, their children have to make some sort of adjustment, whether this is attending a different school and making new friends or having to travel if their parents move farther away. Comparable adjustments are made when adult children start careers or families in a different location. Life events (e.g., puberty, returning home to live after college graduation, marriages or remarriages, health problems) can also influence when, how, or why the communication dynamics of parent–child relationships change.[8]

Changes in the family's structure or membership also affect parent–child relationships. For example, when an individual with a child or children remarries, a stepfamily or blended family is formed. As a result, there is a newly created marital dyad as well as a newly formed parent–stepchild dyad(s). When both partners have children from previous relationships, even more parent–stepchild dyads, as well as stepchild–stepchild dyads, form. Therefore, a lot of adjustments are taking place, ranging from morning routines or eating meals together to developing new family traditions. Parents as well as children may be struggling to adjust to these changes.[9] If the children didn't want or request the change but are forced to live with it, this could create greater stress on parent–child relationships. Building a strong family unit requires time, patience, and communication. New relational bonds shouldn't be forced. However, blended families have the potential to build strong family traditions and rituals of their own to form a new collective identity.

Sibling Relationships. Sibling relationships have three stages: childhood through adolescence, early to middle adulthood, and old age.[10] As young children, there are expectations that siblings will interact with each other whether or not they like each other.[11] In the second stage, siblings offer one another companionship, emotional support, and resources (e.g., financial or emotional) when needed. In the later years, ideally, rivalries are resolved, reminiscing occurs, emotional bonds are enhanced, and resources continue to be shared when possible. As siblings get older, some relationships also demonstrate characteristics of close friendships. It is less about *having* to communicate with each other about practical matters and more about *wanting* to communicate to provide emotional support to one another.[12] For example, Margo and Jacob are siblings who are approximately two years apart in age. When they were younger, Margo and Jacob often played together and sometimes fought with each other over who got to make decisions about what they would do. When they got older and started dating, they gave each other advice, teased each other, and typically scrutinized each other's dates. Now that they are in their mid-thirties, they listen to each other talk about their jobs and families, and they work hard to get both of their families together for social gatherings.

Researchers have identified three different dimensions that help to explain the intricate dance that often occurs in sibling relationships; they have found that sibling relationships typically contain elements of affection, hostility, and rivalry.[13] The first element, affection, is probably the most straightforward and assumed. Brothers and/or sisters are supposed to like one another. Siblings help one another to remember their past and are often there to create or share family memories. However, the very things that build closeness in sibling relationships also have the potential to create rivalry, especially if comparisons are made between siblings (e.g., who is the better student or athlete) or if any of the siblings feel that they are not getting enough support or attention. Then siblings may do things to one another to give themselves a competitive advantage, such as hiding sports equipment so that their sibling can't practice or becoming moody if they believe that their sibling is getting all the attention from others.

Hostility can occur if the expectations we have of our siblings are not met. We might demand more from our brothers or sisters than we would from others in part because we expect family members to support and be there for one another. If we don't feel that our siblings are doing their fair share, we might start to feel resentment. This problem is magnified if other family members don't see this inequity or dismiss it as trivial (e.g., "It's okay if Terry is not helping you to clean up the kitchen because Terry needs some rest"). In short, affection, hostility, and rivalry all play a role in how siblings communicate with each other across the lifespan.

Intergenerational Relationships. At various times in the past, it was not uncommon for multiple generations to be living under the same roof (e.g., grandparents, parents, and grandchildren). In some countries and cultures, this living arrangement is still common. Such an arrangement could be set up voluntarily, for financial reasons, or to manage health concerns. However, when people are raised in different time periods (e.g., your grandparents grew up in the 1940s and 1950s, your parents grew up in the 1970s, you are growing up in the late 1990s and 21st century), perceptions of what is or is not important in relationships could vary. For example, it is more common for children to question or talk back to their parents than in years past. This could lead to some interesting communication challenges between family members.

Naturally, if family members live near one another, this increases the chances for intergenerational relationships to develop. But physical proximity is becoming less of an issue for families. Family members live longer, and improved travel options and technologies have made it more likely as well as easier for grandparents to communicate with their grandchildren. In fact, many grandparents use email or are on Facebook to make it easier to stay connected to family members. Video technologies such as Skype allow people to see each other as they converse even when thousands of miles apart. These new possibilities have led to enhanced intergenerational relationships.[14]

As more couples with children divorce and the number of single-parent households increases, along with the number of dual-career couples, the role that grandparents play in their adult children's and grandchildren's lives has become more important and integrated into family interactions.[15] Many grandparents take care of their grandchildren during the day or baby-sit so that the parent(s) can run errands or simply have some "alone time." While these tasks benefit the adult child, the grandchildren also benefit. Grandchildren may build a strong bond with their grandparents as they learn how to do things and spend some high-quality one-on-one time with an adult who cares for them. Finally, grandparents may also reap rewards by helping to nurture and teach younger family members and feeling an important part in their grandchildren's lives.

More families are taking advantage of opportunities to develop intergenerational relationships.

Personality, Sex Differences, and Family Communication

Psychologists have typically examined identical twins to learn more about the role of biology and genetic predispositions in forming family members' personalities. Communication scholar Cary Horvath's research was one of the earliest communication studies to examine the biological predispositions of identical and nonidentical twins to learn what impact personality has on a child's communication traits. Her results indicate that a large portion of someone's communicator style is inherited. The identical twins were significantly more similar to one another in communicator style than the nonidentical twins were, with genetics providing the dominant explanation.[16] Additional twin studies on communication variables have identified strong genetic linkages to social composure (e.g., staying calm when interacting with others in social situations) and wit (e.g., telling jokes or inserting humor when responding to others) and moderate genetic linkages to social confirmation (e.g., making others feel valued or validated).[17]

Although our genetic makeup may come from our biological parents, the family environment in which we are raised is also important. In our families, we learn what behaviors are considered appropriate and how to manage our communication tendencies when interacting with others. Sometimes behavioral expectations for children are influenced by the gender expectations parents have for their sons and daughters. However, it may be just as important to know whether it is the mother or the father communicating with the child. For instance, researchers found that mothers tend to communicate more feminine gender role messages (e.g., being soft-spoken, sympathetic, compassionate, or cheerful) to both their daughters and sons. In fact, mothers communicated more feminine gender role messages to their sons than fathers did to their daughters. Not surprisingly, fathers were likely to communicate more masculine gender role messages (e.g., being self-reliant, dominant, aggressive, competitive, or ambitious) to their sons than their daughters. Mothers' usage of masculine gender role messages did not differ between their sons and daughters.[18]

In addition, different expectations are often found when researchers examine how families teach male and female children what they should do and how they should interact with others. While little girls and little boys may have similar personality tendencies, the types of play in which each sex engages tend to support or limit certain communicative tendencies. Differences in temperament appear to be less important than societal expectations of gender roles that enforce or discourage how parents play with their children and the toys they select.[19]

NATURE/NURTURE intersections

The Mind of a Teenager

If you were to ask most teenagers, they would say that the decisions they make while driving or spending time with their friends are logical and rational. However, their parents or insurance companies would paint a very different picture. Are parents and insurance companies unjustly picking on teenagers, or is there some evidence to suggest that the decision-making skill sets of teens are not as advanced as the teens would like to believe?

As researchers have learned more about how the human brain develops and processes information, we have learned that significant changes are occurring during the developmental stage known as adolescence that extend beyond puberty. When it comes to our brains, the prefrontal cortex plays an important role in developing moral reasoning as well as planning. There are also linkages between this part of the brain and risk-taking and decision-making behaviors. However, the prefrontal cortex is still being developed in teens.[20]

Although some people have a tendency to blame their bad choices on their genes or DNA in an attempt to deflect any personal responsibility,[21] there is an interesting twist in the case of adolescent behaviors. Many parents are actually grateful that there is some type of brain developmental explanation for why their teenage children do the seemingly crazy things that they do.[22] It's not *really* their children's fault, from a physiological and cognitive perspective, and the parents can hope that the child will grow out of it.

Culture and Family Communication

Ethnic and religious factors influence family interactions. For instance, are family members of African American, Asian, European American, Latino, Native American, or Middle Eastern ethnic descent? Every ethnic culture has strong views about the roles of family members, normative behaviors for family members, and expectations for males and females within the family. However, the degree and extent to which each of these views is incorporated into family interactions varies. Every ethnic group demonstrates positive communication in families. Following are examples of differences associated with family ethnicity and communication exchanges between parents and their children:

- African American, Asian, and Latino parents demonstrate greater levels of behavioral control (e.g., degrees of strictness) with their children than European American parents do.[23]

- Latino parents exhibit more monitoring behaviors (e.g., asking, "Where are you going?" or "Is your homework done?") than European American parents do.[24]

- European American parents incorporate more messages demonstrating warmth (e.g., smiling at their children, providing praise) than Asian American and African American parents do.[25]

- African American mothers practice and reinforce beliefs associated with ethnic pride and representing one's ethnic group more effectively to others than European American mothers do.[26]

When families comprise individuals from two or more ethnic groups or if members are experiencing challenges with acclimating to the norms and practices of a new culture, the roles, norms, and expectations could conflict. This makes it difficult for individuals to adhere to any one set of guidelines. This may force couples to develop their own, shared guidelines[27] or to make parental decisions when the cultures clash.[28]

Religious guidelines and practices may influence both behavioral (e.g., who should do what) and communicative (e.g., how family members should talk to one another) norms in families. Teenage sons' and daughters' perceptions of their parents' religious beliefs are often similar to their own perceived religious beliefs. When it comes to parents' actual religious beliefs, children's behaviors are more closely aligned with their mothers' religious belief systems.[29] When mothers and their older adolescent children shared their views and questions about religious topics with one another, their relationships were strengthened.[30] It is unclear whether strong mother–child relationships increase the likelihood of self-disclosures about religion or whether self-disclosures about religion lead to healthier mother–child relationships. Even less is known about the role fathers play in the exchange of religious disclosures with their children.

When family members engage in and practice different religious teachings, this may complicate which religious customs are observed and the religious education children receive. A person's religious orientation also plays a role in how family members manage these differences.[31] When individuals have an intrinsic religious orientation, their faith is internally centered, and is used as a central driving force in the things they say and do. Individuals who have an extrinsic religious orientation demonstrate their religious practices in social or public settings; therefore, attending religious services together may be important to them.

Technology and Family Communication

Family members continually look for new ways to stay connected. Although advancements in technology may have their roots in improving business practices or social networks,[32] people have been quick to see the merits of incorporating these tools into their personal lives. Email, cell phones, and Facebook are just some of the options available for family members to stay connected. Others capitalize on visual technologies such as webcams, YouTube videos, or digital pictures to enhance how and what messages family members share with one another.

While technology offers choices for how family members communicate, there may be drawbacks. The first challenge pertains to access. If only a portion of the family has access to a certain technology, the result can be to unintentionally limit the flow of messages to and from some family members. Another challenge involves the possibility of less shared family time and increases in parent–child conflicts about Internet usage.[33] Parents may perceive that children are sharing family information that should remain private; parents may also worry that the children will be at risk of becoming victims of the deviant online behaviors of others. Because adolescents rely extensively on the Internet to communicate with others,[34] it can be more complicated than simply limiting the amount of time children can spend on the Internet while at home.

Identifying Family Strengths and Enhancing Family Relationships

The characteristics that make families strong and healthy have a lot in common with what you learned about how to have strong, healthy interpersonal relationships. Table 11.1 highlights several common attributes of strong, healthy families as reported by scholars

---

ETHICS in interpersonal communication

Helicopter Parents

Over the last several years, universities have encountered parents who want to speak directly to faculty members, university administrators, and now even employers at college job fairs about events affecting their children. Parents who demonstrate these behaviors have been given a label: **helicopter parents**.[35] These parents "hover" over their children, often speaking on their children's behalf even though their children might be right next to them. While no one is disputing a parent's right to care about his or her child's well-being, many people speculate that helicopter parents' overbearing behaviors are more problematic than helpful to their adolescent and young adult children.[36]

Several different problems are embedded in the behaviors of helicopter parents. First, when do parents need to step back and let their children stand up and represent themselves as independent adults, even though these children might not have the established skill sets or knowledge base that their parents have? Second, when do adult children need to take personal responsibility for their actions and professional futures and not have their parents intervene? Third, the Family Education Rights and Privacy Act (FERPA) was designed to protect the privacy of students' education records.[37] As a result, although parents may have access to their children's educational records before their children reach the age of 18, once their children turn 18 or attend school beyond the high school level, access to academic records now transfers directly to the students themselves. Academic institutions then cannot share academic information with parents unless the students provide written consent to do so.

■ When do you think parents cross the line when it comes to intervening in their college students' lives?

■ Is it wrong for adult children to allow their parents to be so actively engaged in their educational and professional pursuits, such as meeting with their professors or attending college job fairs with them?

There are no clear answers for establishing boundaries in parent–adult child relationships. However, the desire of parents to care about, or even control, the events in their adult children's lives has the potential to backfire in ways that have yet to be identified.[38]

TABLE 11.1

Common Characteristics of Strong, Healthy Families	
Ability to Talk to Each Other	**Demonstrate Constructive Communication Skills**
Share feelings	Demonstrate active listening
Give honest feedback to one another	Use I-Messages
Provide confirming responses	Don't interrupt each other
Desire to Spend Time Together	**Offer Encouragement and Support**
Spend quality time in great quantity	Care for each other emotionally or financially
Enjoy each other's company	Help manage and solve problems
Emphasize excitement and positivity	Offer praise and encouragement
Deal Constructively with Conflict	**Able to Deal with Stress and Crisis**
Be open to different perspectives or opinions	View crises as challenges and opportunities
Be willing to take personal responsibility	Be willing to change or adapt
Work together to manage and solve problems	Demonstrate resilience and patience

over decades of research. As you will see, most of these characteristics were addressed in earlier chapters. Furthermore, many of these qualities are often noted by cultures around the world; it is not just families in the United States that value constructive communication or effective conflict resolution skills.[39] This is not to suggest that families around the world (or just across the street) are identical to each other, because they are not. However, strong, healthy families around the world may have more, rather than less, in common with one another.

Family relationships lay the foundation for how we interact with others both inside and outside the family. Therefore, to improve our family relationships, we need to remember the following:

- *Family members influence one another.* It is easy to see how parents' behaviors influence how their children respond. But we often forget that children's behaviors also influence how parents respond.[40] If you want to improve how you get along with a family member, your choice of verbal and nonverbal messages is just as important as theirs in changing the dynamics of your relationship.

In today's busy world, people place a high priority on shared family time.

- *As family relationships change over time, communication patterns may also need to change.* Role changes as well as power changes typically occur as family members get older. Therefore, family members need to understand that communication dynamics might need to be adjusted to reflect or accommodate these changes.

- *Manage how technology is used between family members.* Family members should discuss how, when, and why to use particular technologies when communicating with each other. Then everyone will have shared expectations and be less likely to get frustrated when someone is overly engaging with some technological tools while another family member is not.

 ## CHECKING YOUR UNDERSTANDING

Communication in Families

Before reading further, take a few minutes to assess your learning by writing your answers to the following items:

1. What are the different types of family relationships, and how does communication function in each?

2. What role does personality play in family communication? Describe the role of sex differences in family communication.

3. How does culture influence family interactions?

4. Describe the pros and cons associated with family usage of technologies.

5. What are some of the primary characteristics of strong families? What role does interpersonal communication play in helping families become stronger?

Communication in Friendships

Friendships provide us with opportunities to make connections with others that can last a lifetime. Perhaps one of the reasons we value our friendships is that our friends accept us for who we are. Former radio host Bernard Meltzer remarked, "A true friend is someone who thinks that you are a good egg even though he knows that you are slightly cracked." This next section examines the unique features of friendships and the effects of personality, sex differences, lifespan considerations, and technology on friendship communication. Finally, it provides an instrument and discussion to assess our friendship strengths.

Unique Features of Friendships

If you were to stop and reflect on the friendships that you have, what would stand out for you? Would it be that your friends make you laugh? Or that your friends get you to try new things that you would never do if you were by yourself? Perhaps they just like you for who you are. Following are three attributes that make friendships unique:

- *Friendships are voluntarily formed.* No one can force you to be friends with someone. You may have to interact with a person, but you don't have to like him or her. Friendships are wonderful examples of relationships of choice (as discussed in Chapter 9).

- *Friends have the ability to influence one another.* Friends have the ability to encourage as well as to criticize us (within reason), and we are able to give them the same types of messages in return.

- *Friendships are often developed with our **peers** (people who have status or power comparable to ours).* This appears to give us a common framework to build the friendship. But friendships can also develop between individuals who are different in rank, age, race, or religion. In fact, by getting to know others and becoming their friends, we are often better able to manage these differences.

But just because you want to be friends with someone, does not mean it will automatically happen. Developing strong friendships involves both parties investing time and energy in the friendship. Some people might say that this is a combination of quantity *and* quality. They would argue that you need to spend time together. Furthermore, the time needs to include face-to-face time and not just online conversational time. For example, when my good friend's dog died, she stopped by my house a couple days later. We both cried, and I gave her a hug and tried to comfort her. It would have been virtually impossible to try to share those sentiments or the physical comfort I gave her using electronic communication channels. It does not mean that you can't use electronic communication to stay connected to friends. But many people would argue that literally being there for our friends helps to solidify the friendship. Investing time and energy in our friendships is particularly important if the friendship is going to last for an extended period of time.[41]

There are various life transitions that often test friendships. For example, research has shown that the transition from high school to college is very challenging for best friends. By the completion of the first year of college, approximately half of the "best" friendships examined in the study had been reclassified to either close or casual friendships. The problem was less an issue of proximity than one of having to try to maintain existing friendships while simultaneously trying to establish new friendships. Communication proved to be the critical factor for the best friends who were able to

Sometimes, simply hanging out with a friend can improve your day.

stay close during this period of transition. In particular, frequent exchanges as well as continued self-disclosures and maintenance behaviors (such as positivity) helped best friends to stay close.[42] However, there are no set patterns or events that determine whether friendships will flounder or flourish.[43]

Friendship Rules and Guidelines. The rules for friendship are linked to behavioral expectations or shared sentiments about friendship. We might learn how friendships should function by observing others, by trial and error, or from interactions we have had with siblings. However, you seldom see friends sit down and discuss the rules for their relationship. Instead, friendship rules tend to be implied and stated indirectly if at all. Some **implied friendship rules** include standing up for each other, trusting each other, helping one another, criticizing each other only in private, keeping each other's secrets, offering emotional support to each other, respecting one another's privacy, and not being jealous of one another.[44]

When friends break the implied rules, there may be a range of reactions. One friend could simply disregard the violation (e.g., "Yeah, whatever"), directly confront the friend (e.g., "Why did you say that? I trusted you!"), or, in extreme cases, end the friendship (e.g., because one friend stole large sums of money from the other). Forgiveness in friendships also tends to occur indirectly, particularly if the rule violation is not extreme or does not have significant negative ramifications. A joke, nudge, hug, or glance exchanged between friends may indicate that all is forgiven.[45]

Distinguishing Friends from Roommates. It is certainly possible for friends to be roommates and for roommates to be friends. However, what we desire as well as tolerate in our friends might not be identical to what we desire and are willing to tolerate in roommates. Part of the challenge stems from the original goals of each relationship. In friendships, we often seek compatibility and social interaction. With roommates, we may also want compatibility and social interaction, but on the most basic level, we are looking for another person or people with whom to share our living arrangement. This is the space where we sleep, eat, and relax. There may be more practical criteria that come into play, such as sharing financial burdens (e.g., rent, utilities), managing shared resources (e.g., taking out the garbage, buying shared household items such as toilet paper), and demonstrating courtesy to one another (e.g., turning down the television when our roommate is sleeping, cleaning up after ourselves).

Perhaps the "secret ingredient" to successful roommate relationships is consideration. Are roommates mindful and respectful of each other? Are they aware that if they leave the kitchen a mess after cooking a meal (intending to clean it up later), this could be the dirty environment that greets their roommate every time the roommate comes home from school or work? Although people might not intend to be inconsiderate, this is just one example of how roommates can drive one another crazy.

In contrast to friendships, roommates are encouraged to establish formal rules before moving in together, such as expectations associated with noise, food, public spaces, and private spaces. This requires open, honest communication between roommates. This type of communication exchange may be even more important if friends are going to be roommates, because friends may be more likely to take advantage of each other when sharing living arrangements or to think that because they are friends, things will somehow just work out.

Personality, Sex Differences, and Friendships

What we look for in friendships might not be identical to what we find appealing or attractive in our intimate relationships, but some characteristics are consistent. Perceived homophily (as was discussed in Chapter 9) occurs when our friends are similar to us in their personalities, likes and dislikes, or strengths and weaknesses. In sum, our similarities bring us together. If we like something about our personality and communication predispositions, for instance, if we like to smile and tell jokes to make people feel more comfortable, we are likely to admire these qualities in our friends. However, our perceptions of friendship similarities are more important than actual similarities. If we *perceive* that others are similar to us, we are more likely to become friends with them, regardless of whether they actually *are* similar to us.[46]

Complementary relationships (also discussed in Chapter 9) occur when our friends have aspects of themselves that differ from us. If we are good at something, perhaps they are weaker, and vice versa. Complementary friendships often provide opportunities for growth and appreciation beyond our existing knowledge base or comfort zone. Furthermore, complementary friendships allow us to see how our weaknesses can be strengths for one another. These friendships give us opportunities for our communication tendencies to be valued in others who do not have these same attributes. For example, when Carly is feeling somewhat introverted, she appreciates it when her more extraverted friend, Monique, is willing to engage in conversations and plan things to do together.

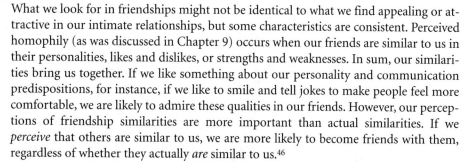

Intercultural friendships offer a mix of perceived similar and different characteristics. On the surface, differences in cultural backgrounds could serve as a deterrent to friendship development. Communication barriers are significant challenges to overcome in intercultural friendships. However, if individuals can overcome language difficulties, intercultural friendships can be very rewarding.[47] Furthermore, cultural differences can actually facilitate friendships. **Sensation seeking** is a personality characteristic that focuses on the individual's needs for novelty, thrills, or adventure. When given the opportunity to develop intercultural friendships, individuals who reported higher levels of sensation seeking were more likely to develop intercultural friendships than were individuals who reported low levels of sensation seeking.[48] Getting to know someone who is culturally different from you may be perceived as positive social risk taking.

A commonly cited difference between male and female same-sex friendships is the way in which the friends interact.[49] Same-sex female friends often spend the majority of their time together conversing; same-sex male friends often spend the majority of their time together participating in shared activities. When individuals were asked which of their friendships were more satisfying, both males and females reported friendships that consisted of at least one female; either male–female or same-sex female friendships. Same-sex male friendships were perceived to be the least satisfying.[50] However, when same-sex male friends increase the amount of self-disclosures in their interactions, they felt increased levels of closeness toward one another.[51] Unfortunately, there also tends to be increased levels of competition in same-sex male friendships, which could negatively affect the ability to maintain close same-sex male friendships.[52]

Some friendships last for the majority of our lives.

Lifespan Considerations

Friendships are some of the longest-lasting relationships individuals will have outside of sibling relationships. You might have friendships that began as early as childhood. Some friendships have such a profound impact on us that we consider these individuals to be "family." We care greatly about what happens in these friends' lives, and they feel the same way about us. Thus, when one of our close friends dies, its impact can be significant. We have lost a close confidant, a "partner in crime," or someone who accepted us for who we are. Losing a friend may feel similar to losing a loved one; for some, they are one and the same.

Several factors shape how friendships develop and are maintained over a lifetime:

- The size of our friendship networks decreases with age.[53] Although there is not a limited time frame within which to build a friendship, most people find that from middle age on, they begin to target their energies and put more emphasis on a smaller number of closer, more intimate friendships.[54]

- Friends to whom we are closest over time tend to have similar thoughts, engage in similar behaviors, and often reflect a great deal of time and energy put into the relationship.[55]

- Friends who are closer to us in age are likely to experience similar life events at similar points in their lives. This increases perceptions of similarity between same-aged friends.[56]

Technology and Friendship Communication

Technology provides opportunities to reunite with friends from earlier in our lives as well as to create new friendships with individuals to whom we might not otherwise have had access.[57] MySpace and Facebook have served as a means to reconnect long-lost friends from around the world as well as to develop new friendships. The speed with which these networks can be established can be quite astounding. However, maintaining friendships, whether face-to-face or online, takes a significant amount of time if you want these relationships to be meaningful. In one study, students reported spending at least three hours per day on their own or someone else's MySpace or Facebook account.[58] Furthermore, simply "friending" others so that it appears that you have lots of friends does not mean that all of these relationships are strong, well-developed friendships. Also, just because someone wants to be your online friend does not necessarily mean that you want to be theirs.[59] In any medium, trying to convey your lack of interest in developing a friendship can be tricky.

As people become more comfortable exchanging messages online, personal information may be shared that is not truly relevant to the intent of that particular venue, such as sharing problems about your roommate or relational partner with friends you made on a web forum for one of your hobbies. However, even if you think you are sharing prudently, you might unknowingly share private information when others examine your friendship associations. For example, when researchers examined the friendship networks on individuals' Facebook profiles, they were often able to identify individuals' sexual orientation on the basis of the sexual orientations of their online friends.[60] In other words, our online social networks may reveal information about us that we don't wish to make public but can't control. It didn't require any interaction to examine someone's social network. This information was all publicly available.

Assessing the Strength of Friendships

Your views about friendships in general and your friendship network in particular could reveal what characteristics you look for in your friends as well as what you expect of yourself in the friendships you have with others.[61] Before you continue reading, we recommend that you assess the behaviors in which you and your friends engage with one another by completing the assessment on page 298.

Understanding Your Friendship Strengths. When our friends' and our own friendship expectations are in agreement and we and our friends respond to those expectations similarly, we are more likely to perceive that our friendships are healthy and strong. This increases the likelihood that we will continue these friendships. If the expectations are not in sync, we might want to examine where our perceptions are in agreement or disagreement.

Now that you have some indication about how you perceive the strength of your friendships, here are a few suggestions to help you interpret your friendship score and increase your understanding of friendships:

- *If your score on Patterson and Bettini's friendship inventory is at or above 33, you perceive your friendships to be generally strong, reciprocal in nature, and mutually beneficial.* You are more likely to depend on your friends, and they on you. This increases the likelihood that you would be comfortable helping them and vice versa. Individuals who believe that they have a strong friendship network are also less likely to be depressed than are those with weaker friendship networks.[62]

ASSESS YOUR **communication personality**

Patterson and Bettini's Friendship Inventory[63]

Log onto our self-assessment library, MyPersonalityProfile, found on MyCommunicationLab (www.mycommunicationlab.com), and assess your friendships by completing the interactive assessment. Encourage one of your friends to do the same. This way, you can compare how each of you perceives your friendship. This may help you to identify things that you can continue to do or change in your communication with your friend. If you prefer, you can use the following text-based version.

Directions:

Please read each statement carefully, and indicate the extent to which you agree with it, using the following scale:

1 = strongly disagree

2 = disagree

3 = undecided

4 = agree

5 = strongly agree

_____ 1. If I ever need help, my friends are there.

_____ 2. If I have any problems, my friends will help.

_____ 3. If my friends have any problems, I'll try to help.

_____ 4. My friends have been pretty nice to me.

_____ 5. My friends love me.

_____ 6. I think my friends would do anything for me.

_____ 7. My friends and I have a great deal in common.

_____ 8. My friends care for me and I care for my friends.

_____ 9. My friends and I enjoy each other talking.

_____ 10. I count on my friends for fellowship.

_____ 11. My friends do many nice things for me.

_____ 12. My friends and I have common interests.

Scoring Instructions:

Please add your total score. Scores range from 12 to 60.

- *If your score on Patterson and Bettini's friendship inventory is below 33, you may perceive your friendship network to be less strong or established overall.* Lower scores could also be an indication that you and your friends are less consistent in reciprocating behaviors. You do things for your friends, but they don't always do things for you (or vice versa). Just because you have a low score (32 or lower) does not mean that you don't value your friendships. This measure does not assess friendship intimacy or other qualitatively based relational aspects of friendships.[64]

- *If your score on Patterson and Bettini's friendship inventory is not what you anticipated, there are several things to consider.* This score pertains to your friendship network in general, not to any specific friendship. It could be that a particular friendship you have is biasing your overall score (e.g., overly high or overly low). You might want to reflect on actual interactions you have with your friends. As you reflect on the specific verbal and nonverbal exchanges you have with your friends, you enhance your understanding of how you and your friends interact.

WHAT CAN I **do now?**

▶ *You could keep a journal of the actual behaviors you exhibit in your friendships and the actual behaviors demonstrated by your friends.* This will help you to assess whether you are underestimating, overestimating, or accurately estimating the behaviors exhibited between you and your friends.

▶ *Remember to be willing to ask for assistance from your friends and to return the favor when your friends ask as well.* People often prefer to help others rather than asking for help themselves. It is not a sign of weakness when you ask your friends to assist you on something. It makes them feel good that they could help you and opens the door for you to help them in return. The demonstration of reciprocal behaviors is also one way to develop and maintain strong friendships.

▶ *You may need to spend more time with your friends.* Sometimes we don't interact enough with our friends. This could be due to conflicting schedules or the fact that some friendships are relatively new. In either case, it may be a good idea to invest more time and energy into your friendships if you are interested in forming long-lasting friendship bonds. This may also increase your level of commitment and caring for one another.

Enhancing Friendships

There are many things we can do to enhance the friendships we have. Here are three suggestions to enhance the friendships you have as well as to make new friends:

- *If you want stronger friendships, be a better friend.* If you feel that your friendships are not as strong as you would like them to be, three aspects you could work on are dependability, reciprocity, and mutual influence.[65] Demonstrate to your friends that they can count on you. If your friend does a favor for you, do a favor for your friend. In addition, change how and what you communicate to your friends, and they might change how and what they communicate back to you.

- *Online friendships need to be maintained if they are going to develop and become strong.* Social networking sites have made it easier to become virtual friends with countless individuals. However, if you want to develop and strengthen these relationships, they are likely to take as much time as face-to-face friendships.

- *Remember that your perceptions are subjective and could be wrong.* We might sometimes make mistakes when perceiving whether we could develop a friendship with someone. Be willing to give someone a second chance. You might find that you have more in common than you initially thought. Also, be prepared to find that there are times when you thought someone was your friend and it turns out that he or she is not.

CHECKING YOUR UNDERSTANDING
Communication in Friendships

Before reading further, take a few minutes to assess your learning by writing your answers to the following items:

1. Why are friendships different from other interpersonal relationships? How do rules work in friendships? What distinguishes friends from roommates?
2. Describe the roles that personality and sex differences play in friendships.
3. Describe how friendships change across the lifespan.
4. How is technology changing the ways in which we communicate with our friends?

The Dark Side of Family and Friend Relationships

The choices that family members and friends make when communicating with those they care about significantly affect the future health or struggles encountered. Three areas where communication plays a pivotal role in how families and friends manage challenging interpersonal issues are secrets, hurtful messages, and deception. Although some people may consider these topics to be "black or white" issues, there are often shades of grade involved in the use of secrets, hurtful messages, and deceptive messages in relationships. Furthermore, these issues may call into question the popular notion that if we could just communicate more—or better—our relationships would improve.[66]

Privacy and Secret Issues

When you have a secret, you are keeping information from people who might have a legitimate reason for having access to the information.[67] Furthermore, when someone shares a secret with you, that gives you control over that person's private information. In this case, you are what scholars refer to as a **secret keeper**. Secret keepers are typically presented with two challenges: learning the content of the secret and refraining from sharing the secret with others.[68] This can be a double-edged sword. Sometimes it is a good thing to reveal a secret; at other times, sharing someone's secret has serious personal and relational consequences.[69] This often forces secret keepers to assess the risks associated with whether or not to reveal the secret.[70] If there are serious risks involved, individuals may be more likely to conceal information even if this becomes emotionally draining for the secret keepers. For example, when children are forced to keep a secret about a family member's illness from people outside the family, including their own friends, this can be very stressful for children.[71]

Sharing secrets or highly personalized information with close friends varies somewhat from doing the same in family relationships. Friends often assume that they can share just about anything with one another. However, when the content of the message involves sex and sexuality, traumatic life experiences, or illegal activities, even friends may become reluctant secret keepers.[72] It is not that our friends will not respond in a supportive manner, since most of the time they will. However, there are times when friends may consider some of our secrets to be "TMI"—too much information. Furthermore, depending on the friendship, if the content is considered to be extreme enough or too burdensome for the friends to manage, friendships may be significantly altered or may end.

Although the general feeling is that secrets have the potential to be problematic for interpersonal relationships, there are several caveats worth noting:[73]

- Individuals may conceal family secrets if they perceive that there are possible punishments, negative sanctions, or judgments for sharing the information.
- There may be times when individuals withhold information because they are trying to protect themselves, their relational partners, and/or their relationships.
- Cultures may differ in how problematic or appropriate it is to have secrets.

Mean and Hurtful Messages

People experience **hurtful messages** when they believe that another person said or did something that caused pain, anger, or disappointment. When we believe that others are intentionally trying to hurt us with their remarks, we often respond by attempting to create distance between ourselves and our partners through physical or psychological means. But our relationships are often changed as a result, and we feel less satisfied and close to these people.[74] When family members make hurtful remarks to one another, it may become more difficult for them to remain close, especially if we think that they are intentionally trying to hurt us by their words and behaviors.[75] Therefore, it becomes very important to examine what happens after the hurtful statement has occurred to see how family members attempt to repair any damage that has been done. Preliminary research in this area suggests that marital couples tend to justify why they engaged in the hurtful behavior, often finding some reason external to themselves to explain why they did what they did (e.g., "It's not my fault that this occurred" or "You made me do it this way"). If a hurtful comment is geared toward a specific behavior (e.g., "You're driving me crazy"), these remarks tend to be hard to misinterpret; therefore, apologies are often used to begin to correct the relational damage that occurred.[76]

Understanding how hurtful messages affect sibling relationships can be more complicated. It is not a question of whether siblings say hurtful things to each other, because they often do; rather, there tend to be undercurrents of verbal aggression associated with siblings' hurtful comments. Typically, one sibling is made to feel less important or

It may take more than flowers to repair a relationship, especially if the person hurt does not fully believe you regret your actions.

significant to the other sibling.[77] It is difficult to fully understand the impact that hurtful remarks have on siblings. This could be for any of the following reasons:

- Siblings may become desensitized or immune to hurtful remarks if they occur on a regular basis.

- Siblings may feel that there is no relational alternative; they are "stuck" with their siblings whether they like it or not.

- Siblings interpret the hurtful comments as simply being part of who their siblings are, so they are able to discredit or disregard some of the statements that are made.

A dilemma occurs if we believe that someone needs to know something even if it may be painful to hear. These exchanges are referred to as **honest but hurtful (HBH) messages**. Communication scholars Shuangyue Zhang and Laura Stafford have studied HBH messages in close relationships. Here are some of their findings:

- *There are distinct differences based on whether you are the sender of the HBH message or the receiver of the HBH message.* When we are the recipients of these messages, we are more likely to remember the HBH message; however, if we are the one that initiated the HBH message, we may be less inclined to remember that we made the remark.[78]

- *The content of the HBH message matters.* When HBH messages are associated with the state of our relationship with our partners, these messages are considered to be more threatening than messages linked to personal characteristics, such as our personality, personal appearance, or behaviors.[79]

- *The impact of HBH messages for our friendships and significant other relationships tends to vary.* While friends and romantic partners are equally worried that they might get hurt again if the HBH message was especially painful, the negative ramifications of HBH messages for romantic relationships (e.g., increased perceptions of distrust, dislike of the other person, the relationship is weakened) appear to be more significant.[80]

Trust and Deception Violations

There are many reasons why we might deceive family members. Sparing family members pain is often one reason for withholding bad news (e.g., when someone in the family is getting a divorce) or problematic matters (e.g., a smaller family budget). This is often the case when parents use deceptive messages in communicating with their children. Although the parents' intent may be admirable, children might not perceive it that way. For example, when parents are planning to get a divorce, children often feel deceived if they did not have any prior indicators that there were problems between their parents. This can cause children to trust their parents less and could lead to more problematic exchanges between parents and their children later in life.[81]

When they are young, children often lie to their parents to avoid being punished. As they get older, they might also lie to get some type of reward or to protect their friends. Although it may be normal for children to lie once in a while to their parents, of greater concern is persistent or habitual lying by children to their parents.[82] This erodes trust between parents and their children and often negatively affects parent–child communication. If parents fear that every time their children talk to them, the children are simply making things up, it might become easier to simply reduce the amount of conversations they have with one another. As a result, the ability to demonstrate productive parenting behaviors is affected. Regular lying by adolescents to their parents affects the adolescents as well. Adolescents who regularly lie to their parents are more likely to have emotional problems such as stress, depression, and low self-esteem.[83]

As adolescents get older, a common motivation for lying to parents is the need to establish autonomy. Many adolescents believe that this explanation provides reasonable justification for the lies.[84] Once adolescents enter college, they report lying to their parents less, but will still do so to avoid conflicts and to protect what they believe is their right to make decisions independently of their parents. As parents feel more comfortable trusting their children's decision-making abilities, this in turn, may reduce the perceived need their children feel to lie to parents about their behaviors or choices.

Friends are likely to encounter some of their biggest challenges with deception when they have to decide whether to share information about a friend's significant other with the friend. Although most friends justify expressing or withholding their dislike out of a desire to protect or not upset their friends, the explanation for using deception (through concealment) is more complicated. When friends share information about a friend's significant other, the emphasis appears to be to protect the friend from an external force (the partner). However, when friends withhold information, this appears to be linked to a desire to protect their friends and perhaps themselves from encountering problems internal to their friendship.[85] In fact, researchers noted that negative disclosures about a friend's significant other can have negative ramifications for the friendship later. This suggests that deception in friendship may be loaded with numerous factors to consider.

CHECKING YOUR UNDERSTANDING
The Dark Side of Friend and Family Relationships

Before completing the chapter, take a few minutes to assess your learning by writing your answers to the following items:

1. What are some of the challenges faced by secret keepers? Why are family secrets complicated?

2. How do hurtful messages vary for marital couples and siblings? Explain how honest but hurtful messages work in families and friendships.

3. Explain how deceptive messages affect family relationships and friendships. What do they have in common? How might they differ?

A Communication Development Plan for Emily

To complete Emily's story, recall that Emily and her best friend and roommate, Sayuri, are encountering problems. Emily and Sayuri have different expectations of each other and how they would like their apartment maintained. In addition, Sayuri complained to a friend about Emily, and Emily found out about this conversation and was very hurt by Sayuri's comments.

What do you think?

Are Emily and Sayuri's perceived similarities and actual differences at the heart of their problems as roommates? How should Emily respond to Sayuri's violation of implicit rules? Is there a way to reach a solution that will make it possible for Emily and Sayuri to stay best friends and roommates?

Possible explanations:

How are Emily and Sayuri's perceived similarities and actual differences contributing to the problems they are having as roommates? Emily and Sayuri thought that they had enough things in common that the transition to being roommates would be uneventful. Unfortunately, what they don't have in common is creating difficulties for their friendship.

What should Emily do in regard to Sayuri's violation of implicit friendship rules? Although Sayuri might not have intended to hurt Emily's feelings, talking to a mutual friend instead of going directly to Emily to discuss her concerns may have made matters worse. Now Emily is unsure what she should say to Sayuri. The problem is not likely to be corrected by ignoring it. Therefore, it would be best for their friendship to directly confront the problem.

How could Emily modify her interactions to live together successfully with Sayuri while remaining best friends? Emily and Sayuri's friendship has hit a rough patch. Emily has to decide what she wants to address directly and what she wants to ignore or tolerate in Sayuri's behaviors. Her choices are likely to influence whether the two continue to be roommates as well as the long-term implications for their friendship.

1. *Friends are rarely identical in their likes, dislikes, and preferences.* Furthermore, there is a different set of rules for living with another person than for being someone's friend. The problems that Emily and Sayuri face do not center on their friendship. Rather, the problems are about how to manage living with one another. Setting up shared rules and expectations regarding household duties is the most logical step at this time.

2. *Sometimes friends vent to other friends when they are frustrated.* Although this is understandable, it can be painful to learn that your best friend is talking behind your back. We recommend that Emily speak directly to Sayuri about this event. Emily might still feel hurt, but she is more likely to forgive Sayuri for this friendship violation, especially if Sayuri has not done this in the past and apologizes. Because they are best friends, their relationship should be able to move forward, but both will now be aware of the importance of talking directly to one another when there is a problem.

3. *Emily and Sayuri are best friends. Therefore, they owe it to each other to take the time to address their roommate problems.* If Emily openly talks about the behaviors that are frustrating her and is also open to hearing Sayuri's concerns, they should be able to reach a workable solution (e.g., Emily cleans up more in the public spaces they share; Sayuri learns to live with a little more clutter). Then they should touch base with each other in a few weeks to find out whether there are other issues that still need to be resolved. Finally, Emily and Sayuri should plan some time to spend with each other. In the midst of their differences, they might need to be reminded that they really do enjoy each other's company.

Take Aways

Some of our most important interpersonal relationships are those that we have with family members and friends. This chapter focused on increasing your understanding, skills, and knowledge of friend and family relationships.

You have increased your understanding and knowledge of:

- The factors that affect different types of family relationships.
- The unique features of friendships.
- The ways in which personality factors and sex differences influence the communication exchanges in family and friend relationships.
- How friendships evolve over the lifespan.
- How culture influences family and friend communication.

In addition, you are also better able to:

- Explain the role of personality in family and friend relationships.
- Distinguish between what it means to be a friend and what it means to be a roommate.
- Apply your knowledge of sex differences when interacting with others in your personal relationships.
- Identify how technology affects family and friend relationships in both positive and negative ways.
- Identify characteristics associated with family strengths.
- Enhance your communication in family and friend relationships.
- Assess the strength of your friendship network and make modifications as needed.

Discussion Questions

1. How are friendships different from other relationships we have in our lives?

2. In what ways does personality influence family and friend relationships?

3. What opportunities and challenges has technology usage generated for family and friend relationships?

4. What are the pros and cons of sharing honest but hurtful messages with friends and family members?

Building Your Skills

1. Keep a journal for one week. During that time, record every time you communicate with a family member. With whom are you communicating? What communication channel was used (e.g., face-to-face, email, texting)? What type of content was being shared? At the end of the week, examine the journal to see whether any patterns surface. What does this information tell you about how and with whom you communicate in your family? Would you have changed anything about how you communicated with each other? If so, what and why?

2. Think about the information that you share about yourself when you are interacting on a social networking site such as Facebook or MySpace. Is there anything that you share with friends online that you are not sharing with them when you are face to face or vice versa? Do the rules of friendship change when you communicate online with friends rather than face to face?

3. Think about the last time someone told you a family secret. As a secret keeper, what was your initial reaction after hearing the secret? How did knowing this family secret affect your interactions with family members? Would you like to be told more family secrets, or would you prefer not to know someone's family secret? Explain.

12 Workplace Relationships

Jacquie's Story . . .

Jacquie recently graduated from college, where she earned a degree in organizational communication with a minor in marketing. She feels fortunate to have landed a position in her field at a large corporation, and she has just completed the mandatory three-week training program at corporate headquarters. She is now at the regional office, where she will be stationed permanently, and she realizes that she is the only new hire at this location. Jacquie is assigned to her cubicle and tries to familiarize herself with her new surroundings, boss, and coworkers. Jaedyn is Jacquie's new boss. He has heard good things about Jacquie's performance in the training program and is happy to have her join the department, since there is plenty of work to be done. Jacquie's new coworkers are also glad to see her, as they have been putting in long hours to make up for the shortage of workers in the department.

Now two months have gone by, and Jacquie has settled into her daily work routine. Her coworkers have invited her to join them for their regular lunch outings, but she has

done so only once or twice, preferring to have a "working lunch" in an attempt to spend more time getting her work done and make a good impression. Her coworkers also encouraged Jacquie to attend the company picnic, but she got nervous when she arrived and didn't see anyone she knew, so she left a short time afterward. As a result of her actions, Jacquie's coworkers don't really know much about her, so they are starting to leave her alone. Jacquie doesn't know why she is not more social at work, but she still feels so overwhelmed on most days that she doesn't allow herself much time to think about it.

Four months have gone by, and Jacquie is starting to feel more comfortable with the work she is doing, but she is somewhat lonely. She doesn't interact with others in the office as often as she thought she would. She responds to plenty of email messages but otherwise feels somewhat isolated from her coworkers. In addition, other than a friendly "hello" from Jaedyn, she doesn't seem to talk a great deal to him. A couple of times, she has approached him, and this has worked well. But she doesn't want to feel

---

CHAPTER OBJECTIVES

AFTER READING THIS CHAPTER, you will understand:

1 The features of superior–subordinate, coworker, mentor–protégé, and worker–customer/client workplace relationships.

2 The ways in which personality factors and sex differences influence the communication exchanges in workplace relationships.

3 How culture influences workplace communication.

4 How office romances, workplace bullying, and work–life balance issues affect employees as well as organizations.

like a burden, so she tries to work through any problems she encounters.

Jacquie is now beginning to wonder whether or not she wants to start looking for another position. She heard about a job opening where one of her college friends works. It would mean less money and a longer commute, but she is starting to feel stressed about the way things are going and knows she needs to do something.

While reading this chapter, consider how you might handle problems similar to those that Jacquie is encountering:

- What is Jacquie doing or not doing that affects how she perceives her new job?

- How could Jacquie modify her workplace interactions to make her feel better about her job and perhaps the company?

- Should Jacquie consider alternative places of employment?

We will revisit Jacquie's story at the end of the chapter and use the content discussed in this chapter to develop a communication plan to help Jacquie.

AFTER READING THIS CHAPTER, you will be able to:

1 Explain the role of personality in workplace relationships.

2 Apply your knowledge of sex differences when interacting with others in your professional relationships.

3 Identify how technology affects professional relationships in both positive and negative ways.

4 Improve your communication in workplace relationships.

AFTER COMPLETING THE SELF-ASSESSMENTS, you will learn:

1 How you perceive your level of organizational assimilation.

2 The degree to which you are connecting to and accepting the people and culture of the organization where you work.

A large portion of most adults' lives will be spent in the workplace. For this reason, some people decide to work with their relationship partners, family members, or friends as a way to make sure they interact with people they like and care about throughout the day instead of having only limited interactions in the morning and evening or on weekends. However, this is not the preferred choice for everyone. That doesn't mean that the rest of us don't care about who we work with. Our job satisfaction is likely to be affected by the people with whom we interact at work.[1] We simply might need a little bit more separation from our friends, partners, or family members.

This chapter provides an overview of workplace relationships and the features that make workplace relationships different from the other interpersonal relationships in our lives. We'll address key communication features of workplace relationships, ranging from the types of interpersonal relationships you may develop in the workplace to what you can do to enhance your workplace relationships. In addition, we'll examine three factors associated with workplace relationships: office romances, workplace bullying, and work–life balance issues, which may influence how you perceive and manage your workplace relationships.

> I'm not the smartest fellow in the world, but I can sure pick smart colleagues.
>
> —FRANKLIN D. ROOSEVELT

Understanding Communication in Workplace Relationships

Workplace communication can be physically, emotionally, or psychologically draining if we don't like the people with whom we need to interact on a regular basis to perform our jobs.[2] In this section, we examine several types of workplace relationships and the ways in which messages are exchanged between employees. In addition, personality, sex differences and workplace communication, cultural factors influencing workplace communication, and technological impacts on workplace relationships are examined. There is also an opportunity to assess how your communication may be related to workplace relationships. The section concludes with suggestions for enhancing your workplace relationships.

Types of Workplace Relationships

Workplace relationships tend to have elements of both relationship-focused content and task-focused content. **Relationship-focused content** focuses on information related to your personal backgrounds or interests. It could include sharing things about events occurring in your personal relationships (e.g., a family member has been in a car accident) as well as your hobbies or interests (e.g., the latest movie you have seen). **Task-focused content** emphasizes information tied to your job duties or obligations. It highlights content that is necessary to complete your or others' work assignments (e.g., the report will be completed by the end of the day, everyone needs to get their requests for vacation into human resources by Friday). A continuum helps us to visualize this balancing act (see Figure 12.1).

FIGURE 12.1

Workplace Relationship Continuum

Relationship-Focused Content ←——————————————————→ Task-Focused Content

Depending on the nature of the relationship (e.g., being supervised or supervising others, interacting with coworkers, working with customers, or being mentored); the focus could shift from one side of the continuum to the other. Where individuals place each of their professional relationships on the continuum says a great deal about the types of interactions that occur between parties.

Superior–Subordinate Relationships. The vast majority of us will always have someone to whom we need to report in our professional lives. Therefore, your ability to communicate effectively with your supervisor will be extremely important to your long-term employment success. The same thing holds true for our bosses; their ability to lead and motivate others plays an important role in their long-term career success as well. **Superior–subordinate relationships** are dyadic relationships that incorporate hierarchical ranking in which one person in the organization reports to another. It is common for many people to report to the same boss. Unfortunately, this makes it more challenging to get the time and attention from our superior that we feel we need and deserve to do our jobs well. Limited one-on-one time with superiors may be especially problematic for new employees, who are trying to acclimate to a new position and a new organization. Although superiors need to be aware of this factor, their job responsibilities often require superiors to attend to other duties. Superior–subordinate relationships tend to emphasize task-focused content.

The messages that are exchanged between superiors and subordinates tend to travel in two directions. **Downward communication** involves messages that are sent from supervisors or others higher up in the organization to their employees. Downward messages tend to be formal. The message is communicated from the sender to the receiver and then typically ends. As a result, there is limited opportunity for subordinates to provide direct feedback to their superiors. Examples of downward messages are memos about company policies or rules, statements about job duties or assignments, and announcements about future events or changes. However, there are times when employees want to share information with their superiors. Then employees engage in upward communication. **Upward communication** involves messages that employees send up to their supervisors or others higher up in the organization. These messages may start out as informal requests or suggestions but could become more formalized if employees were to draft written documents. Examples of upward messages are sharing ideas to improve or solve a workplace problem and asking questions to clarify a task or issue.

When employees and supervisors are able to effectively interact, everyone wins.

Communication plays a critical role in determining the quality of superior–subordinate relationships. When superiors focus on the person they are speaking to rather than the position a person holds, subordinates, superiors, and organizations benefit. Positive bonds are being established between employees and their bosses. There are potential benefits for both parties (e.g., monetary rewards or career progression), and employees are more likely to stay and demonstrate commitment to the organization.[3] When individuals have a high-quality relationship with their supervisors, they are more likely to engage in upward communication and directly share what their concerns are. However, if the quality of the relationship is poor, employees are more likely to refrain from addressing or reporting their concerns to their supervisors.[4]

First-time supervisors (especially those who have been promoted from within their departments) may notice significant adjustments in workplace interactions. From a communicative standpoint, when you are promoted to a supervisory position, there are numerous changes that signal that you are no longer an insider in the coworker group but have become an outsider, now part of the management team. The communication changes include employees waiting for you to speak, changing topics when you enter a room, or providing you with overly critical or hurtful feedback or comments that are difficult to comprehend.[5] Demonstrating your desire to learn from your employees by listening to them and being open to considering alternative ways of approaching a task rather than simply persuading them or directing them to do things is one way to encourage feedback and improve your job performance as a supervisor.

Coworker Relationships. Whom you work with is as important as whom you work for. **Coworker relationships** focus on the people who work next to you while you both wait on customers, who have an office across the hall from you, or with whom you interact on a daily basis. These are sometimes referred to as peer or collegial relationships, since you and your coworker(s) could have similar ranks in the organization. Coworker relationships often involve large amounts of relationship-focused content; however, coworkers often provide task-based support to one another, especially if the boss is unavailable. Collegial relationships may also include your relationships with people in positions similar to yours, but at different companies. For example, Sue, a buyer for her organization, has colleagues who are also buyers for their respective retail stores. Because of the quantity of interactions we have with our coworkers as well as the experiences we share with them, we increase our likelihood of developing interpersonal relationships that transcend the boundaries of work.[6] For some people, their coworkers and friends are one and the same.

While messages that are exchanged between superiors and subordinates tend to be directed either downward or upward, depending on who sends the messages, the direction of communication exchanges between coworkers is typically horizontal. **Horizontal communication** refers to the messages exchanged between individuals having similar rank and status. Horizontal messages may also take place between departments in an organization. Examples of horizontal messages are exchanges between coworkers when working on a task or the communication that takes place when the accounting department asks for an invoice from the purchasing department.

Mentor–Protégé Relationships. **Mentor–protégé relationships** provide opportunities for individuals to learn from others who have advanced knowledge or understanding of workplace practices. At their best, these relationships can be transformative.[7] In simplistic terms, mentors are perceived to be "experts," while protégés (or mentees) are considered to be "apprentices." Mentoring relationships are found primarily in the workplace, but the idea of an older, wiser person helping a younger individual has also been incorporated into the philosophies of many nonprofit organizations, such as Big Brothers Big Sisters. You are likely to see both downward and upward communication exchanges between mentors and protégés because the developmental nature of these relationships dictates that there are often as many questions asked as there are answers given. Although some mentoring relationships involve primarily task-focused information, it is common for mentoring relationships to include both task-focused and relationship-focused exchanges.

Mentoring tends to address two different sets of functions: **career functions** (e.g., advancing someone's career success by having greater workplace visibility or getting more challenging job assignments) and **psychosocial functions** (e.g., enhancing perceptions of competence or one's professional identity, often achieved by getting personalized feedback or reinforcement from others).[8] Individuals who have a mentor in the workplace are more likely to succeed than are those who do not. There could also be times when mentors and protégés switch roles, and protégés teach their mentors skill sets in which the protégés have expertise. When this occurs, mentors, protégés, and the organizations they work for prosper.[9]

Worker–Customer/Client Relationships. Worker–customer/client relationships are relationships between a service provider and a customer. The first three workplace relationship types typically occur within the same organization. Worker–customer/client relationships are relationships that capture a different dynamic. Worker–customer/client relationships are relationships in which one party has something (perhaps a good or a service) in which the other party is interested. Worker–customer/client relationships are equally important to an organization's success, since each side has something the other wants: a high-quality good or service and prompt payment for the good or service. When these relationships are successful, it is not uncommon for some relationships to take on attributes of friendships.[10] When this happens, the messages that are exchanged extend beyond task-focused content to include relationship-focused information as well.

When customers are considering whether to buy a product, both task- and relational-focused information may influence if an item is purchased.

The communication exchanges in worker–customer/client relationships may involve elements of downward, upward, or horizontal communication. The direction of communication depends on the nature of the exchange and whether third parties get involved. When the two parties are trying to establish and maintain a relationship, they are likely to utilize horizontal communication. No one is trying to pull a power play, and they are treating one another with respect. For example, in sales, the salesperson is friendly and respectful to the customer, and the customer is attentive and respectful to the salesperson. However, if the customer makes a request that requires supervisory approval (e.g., wanting to return an excessive amount of ordered paper products), a form of downward communication could result (e.g., the salesperson's supervisor determines whether this return will be accepted or denied). If a customer asks whether it is possible to produce a particular product (e.g., "Could you make this shirt without the stitching on the side?"), a form of upward communication takes place, as the salesperson needs to check with production.

Table 12.1 lists the different types of workplace relationships and the typical direction of communication in each.

TABLE 12.1

Communication in Workplace Relationships		
Type of Relationship	**Direction of Communication**	**Example**
Superior–Subordinate	Downward: Superior to Subordinate	Downward: "These are the guidelines for overtime."
	Upward: Subordinate to Superior	Upward: "Here is an idea to improve quality."
Coworker–Coworker	Horizontal: Coworker to Coworker	Horizontal: "Do you remember what we should do with these old receipts?"
Mentoring	Downward: Mentor to Protégé	Downward: "This is why it is important to volunteer."
	Upward: Protégé to Mentor	Upward: "How long should I wait before applying for a promotion?"
Worker–Customer/Client	Horizontal: Worker to Customer/Client	Horizontal: "How did you like that last shipment we sent you?"
	Horizontal: Customer/Client to Worker	Horizontal: "What can you tell me about the latest version of this product?"
	Downward: Worker's Supervisor to Customer/Client	Downward: "I'm sorry, but we cannot meet your request."
	Upward: Customer/Client to Worker's Coworker or Supervisor	Upward: "Let me ask our shipping department if we can do that."

NATURE/NURTURE intersections

Balancing the Young with the Old

Research about how the human brain processes information has found that our abilities to reason and solve novel problems decline as we age.[11] As a result, we might not be able to incorporate new ideas as fast as we could when we were younger. On the surface, this can lead some people to conclude that older employees are simply not as quick and innovative as their younger counterparts. But this could be a very "slippery slope" to stand on.

The challenges associated with interacting with people who differ from one another on the basis of some demographic, such as age, is nothing new.[12] Group members have a tendency to overemphasize the skill sets they bring to the table while perhaps minimizing the value that others have to offer. But a better mix for organizations could be to consider how both young employees and older employees can bring important, but not identical, contributions to the workplace that extend beyond their abilities to process new amounts of information. These interactions can be further enhanced if there is a sense of shared norms and cooperative interdependence between members.[13]

Although younger individuals may contribute more innovative ideas, as we age, we become more adept at applying our existing knowledge bases, demonstrating self-control, and capitalizing on our social skills when working with others.[14] This may help to explain why the successful implementation of ideas often requires someone who has the understanding, knowledge, and frame of reference to overcome potential obstacles. This tends to be difficult for younger employees, who, in their enthusiasm to embrace the concept, might not yet fully understand the steps that must be taken to move the concept across the workplace finish line. This also could explain some of the chaos that ensues in many organizations when a large number of older employees retire, are laid off, or are let go as part of "corporate downsizing." The organization could still have new ideas coming in, but might not operate effectively. As Eleanor Roosevelt said, "It takes as much energy to wish as it does to plan."

Often, we assume that the higher-ranking individual is also the older individual. When managers are younger than their employees, the challenges can multiply—for everyone.[15] Therefore, it becomes important for everyone to overlook the biological age factor and think instead about what cognitive strengths everyone brings to the table to help accomplish workplace goals.

Personality, Sex Differences, and Workplace Communication

Companies have not shied away from using personality data in their efforts to maximize workplace productivity. Recruiters might look for specific personality traits during the interview process. Sometimes organizations require their employees to complete a personality assessment (often before any hiring decisions) in an attempt to match the person's personality predispositions with the appropriate job.[16] Some companies have actually put their employees' personality profiles into some type of composite visual display for other employees to see so that everyone has some data to help them determine how to interact with their coworkers.

Personality testing has also been used to assess who is most likely to be a good protégé in the workplace. Two personality traits, extraversion and openness to new experiences, were positively linked with someone's likelihood of being successfully mentored. One personality trait, neuroticism, was negatively related to being mentored. When individuals are willing to engage in new experiences and are able to control their levels of anxiety or worry, they are more likely to be selected for and benefit from mentoring relationships.[17]

The extraversion trait is associated with a range of positive as well as problematic workplace outcomes. Some of these include the following:[18]

- Extraversion is positively correlated with job performance in positions that require social interaction (e.g., sales, customer service). However, in positions that require limited social interaction (e.g., computer programming, working on an assembly line), high levels of extraversion could lead to decreases in workplace productivity.

- Extraverts who are new to the workplace tend to be absent from work more frequently.

- In workplace teams, a 50/50 mix of extraverts and introverts may be optimal. When there are too many extraverts on a team, there may be problems as individuals jockey to gain control of the group.

Often, sex differences in the workplace are less about actual differences in individual behaviors based on biology and more about the gender roles we expect people to play. For example, when males communicate to complete a task in a clear, direct fashion (which is very masculine-based), their coworkers perceive them as communicating assertively. However, when females communicate to complete a task in a clear, direct fashion, their demonstration of masculine gender behaviors is often perceived by their coworkers as domineering, demanding, or pushy. The males and females actually communicated in a similar manner; there were no differences based on the person's sex. However, the behaviors were perceived differently. These gender-influenced differences are often less substantial for individuals who have more than a high school education.[19]

Three issues continue to underlie workplace gender role challenges:

- Assigning stereotypically masculine or feminine social roles on the basis of someone's biological sex is a habit that some people have difficulty breaking (e.g., a woman serving as secretary/note taker at meetings).

- Biologically speaking, women can give birth to children and men cannot. That fact cannot be changed regardless of the amount of social concern or conversations held.

- Women want respect from men. They want to be recognized for their knowledge, contributions, stability, sound judgment, and skills demonstrated in the workplace. These are often perceived to be masculine workplace attributes. This issue goes beyond being respected as a human being; it involves the respect that people earn as a result of the work and outcomes they have successfully accomplished.[20]

Cultural Factors Influencing Workplace Communication

One way to distinguish one group of people from another is to examine each group's culture. To do this, we often examine the beliefs, values, assumptions, rules, and norms that people in each group share. The concept of culture can also be applied to organizations. It has been said, "Organizations exist within cultures, and cultures exist within organizations."[21] Another way to think about organizational culture is to ask what it would feel like to be in or work for this organization. How do people talk to one another? What is the dress code? Do people interact more formally or informally? In this section, we'll focus on three approaches to culture and workplace communication: the culture that is present within an organization, individualistic versus collectivistic approaches to work, and considerations of intercultural communication diversity.

Organizational Culture. In simplistic terms, a culture consists of people who have similar backgrounds and act, think, and communicate in similar ways.[22] In defining an organization's culture, several elements of culture are emphasized. Organizational culture includes the following:

- Group interactions—you cannot have a culture by yourself.

- Patterns and consistencies—looking for what is shared between organizational members.

Some of the best organizational ideas surface when there is a diverse group of people working on a task.

- Basic beliefs and values that are shared, such as trying to be eco-friendly, or "green."
- Continued emphasis on developing and evolving—members change, and new information needs to be learned over time.[23]

An organizational culture is something that an organization *is*. It is imbued in the messages that organizational members exchange. It also goes beyond an organization's boundaries to let outsiders know what that organization is about, what is important to that organization, and what it means to work for that company. Finally, every organizational culture is unique. It is extremely difficult to replicate an organizational culture, even if it just involves going from one fast-food store to another run by the same company. The workers ultimately guide how an organization's culture develops and emerges.[24]

 Individualistic versus Collectivistic Approaches to Work. Organizations often require employees to work both individually and in groups. But for workers to be productive, different mindsets are needed in completing individual tasks and in completing group tasks. Successful completion of individual tasks often requires self-motivation, determination, and having the necessary skill sets to complete a task without significant outside assistance. Successful completion of group tasks often requires collaboration, joint decision making, effectively managing communication between group members, and a desire to work with others on a joint project.

Organizations vary in their assessment of individual and group performance outcomes. When most of us receive our annual performance reviews at work, we are assessed on the basis of how we, as individuals, underperformed, met, or exceeded workplace goals or objectives. When your job involves a great deal of teamwork or collaboration, the emphasis may shift to how your contributions affected the performance outcomes of the group or team. This is a very different mindset to accept or embrace. If you are a fan of professional sports, you hear players (and sometimes coaches) mention individualistic versus collectivistic goals. It is customary for players to first talk about "team outcomes."

If the team does well, individual awards and accolades will follow. For other players, it may be all about what their own final statistics are, especially if their contracts are on the verge of being renegotiated. As fans, we are able to learn more by listening to the pronouns individuals use. Are players inserting the word "me" or the word "we" in their remarks?

Intercultural Communication Diversity. Intercultural business communication is a reality for much of the world. Working with colleagues from across the globe may be a part of day-to-day operations. Yet cultural diversity in the workplace exists without having to cross national borders. For example, companies hire employees who may differ from one another on the basis of race or ethnicity, biological sex, sexual orientation, physical abilities, or age.

There are many virtues associated with intercultural workplace communication. Some of the most common arguments for promoting intercultural communication in the workplace are the following:[25]

- Increased creativity and innovation emerging when different voices are contributing to problem solving or goal setting.
- Decreased likelihood that groupthink will occur. **Groupthink** refers to a shared mindset that occurs when there is excessive cohesion and similarity between group members that limits the sharing of alternative perspectives.

When organizations are committed to implementing diversity principles, they may reap competitive advantages ranging from high-quality research and development to enhanced customer service.

Yet successful integration of diversity practices requires time and energy on the part of top management as well as all employees. Challenges that organizations encounter when engaged in intercultural workplace practices include the following:

- *Employees having insufficient language skills to successfully share their ideas with others.* For example, informal exchanges, such as those that occur when groups brainstorm, often incorporate subtle details that might not translate easily from one language to another.[26]
- *Understanding when to use different modes of communication (e.g., email, videoconferencing, telephone, face-to-face) to facilitate communication between employees.*[27] This is particularly important when employees are working in virtual teams.
- *Employees being insensitive to the cultural backgrounds of others.* This may occur by mistake or be done intentionally to marginalize others.[28]

Technological Impacts on Workplace Relationships

Historically, some of the earliest consumers of new technologies were individuals who were seeking to improve their job performance, work more efficiently, and advance within the organization.[29] Corporations also had the funds to invest in new technologies to advance workplace operations. As a result, how people work and when people work continue to change and reflect advances in communication technologies.

There is often a ripple effect when new technologies are adopted into the workplace. First, new technologies may be initially expensive. Once a technology becomes mainstream, prices go down. However, some companies (and employees) are unable or unwilling to wait for significant price reductions to occur before purchasing products. For example, when the iPhone first became available, the cost to consumers was $600. The number went down significantly within six months to a year. Second, technology training needs to occur (for the physical device and/or for software packages). This requires additional time and resources. Third, although technologies may make it faster to complete some tasks, they may increase the number of different tasks individuals need to do. Fourth, when the technology is used for communication purposes (e.g., email), responding to information requests can become cumbersome as the number of messages received per day (or hour) increases. Fifth, people need to learn when it is appropriate to use the technology and when it is likely to become problematic. There is a time and place for every technology.

Appropriate use of technological tools continues to be a challenge for employees as well as organizations. Following are some challenges that employees and organizations face:

■ *Determining when a particular communication channel is appropriate for the type of message being shared.* When supervisors must give bad news to employees, getting the message via email is not the way most employees want to receive such information.[30]

■ *Separating work time from personal time.* As more technologies become mobile, individuals are able to literally take their offices home with them. While this gives employees freedom to work in environments that are most productive for them, it also means that they are more likely to be accessible 24/7. Therefore, they may feel as though they are, or may actually be, "on call" whether they are technically working or not.[31]

■ *Monitoring and managing what employees are doing with the technology to which they have access at work.* **Cyberslacking** refers to using a computer for non-work-related activities while on the job. Are employees playing computer solitaire, looking up sports scores, purchasing personal items online, checking their friends' Facebook updates, or browsing questionable websites when they are supposed to be working?[32] Some organizations monitor their employees' Internet use and may block certain websites in an effort to control cyberslacking.

Workplace technologies can be both a blessing and a curse.

Assessing Communication in the Workplace

Although we might not realize it, the messages that we send and receive in the workplace may be an important indicator in assessing how well we fit in or are accepted in the workplace. **Organizational assimilation** has traditionally focused on how well employees become integrated into an organization's culture.[33] However, this puts the primary emphasis on what employees do to fit in and be accepted into the workplace. A more integrated approach to organizational assimilation refers to the interactive events that occur in the workplace that demonstrate how well there is mutual acceptance of new employees to and with the organization they work for.[34] When organizational assimilation goes poorly, individuals often make the decision to find employment elsewhere if they can. Employers may respond by limiting promotion opportunities or assigning these employees the least desired tasks.

You are encouraged to complete the organizational assimilation self-assessment on page 318 to learn more about the degree to which you are integrated into the culture of your place of employment as well as the degree to which you accept your coworkers and the organization in which you work.

ASSESS YOUR communication personality

Myers and Oetzel's Organizational Assimilation Assessment[35]

Log onto our self-assessment library, MyPersonalityProfile, found on MyCommunicationLab (www.mycommunicationlab.com), and complete the interactive assessment. If you prefer, you may fill in the answers below and calculate the score yourself.

Directions:

Please respond to a series of questions about feeling a part of your organization. For this measure, the term "organization" refers to your place of work. There are no right or wrong answers to this survey; it is simply a way to learn what you think about and feel about your organization. For each statement, indicate the degree to which it reflects how you communicate at your organization, using the following scale:

1 = strongly disagree

2 = disagree

3 = neutral

4 = agree

5 = strongly agree

_____ 1. I feel that I know my supervisor pretty well.

_____ 2. My supervisor sometimes discusses problems with me.

_____ 3. My supervisor and I talk together often.

_____ 4. I understand the standards of the company.

_____ 5. I think I have a good idea about how this organization operates.

_____ 6. I know the values of my organization.

_____ 7. My supervisor recognizes when I do a good job.

_____ 8. My supervisor listens to my ideas.

_____ 9. I think my supervisor values my opinions.

_____ 10. I think my superior recognizes my value to the organization.

_____ 11. I talk to my coworkers about how much I like it here.

_____ 12. I volunteer for duties that benefit the organization.

_____ 13. I talk about how much I enjoy my work.

_____ 14. I feel involved in the organization.

_____ 15. I often show others how to perform our work.

_____ 16. I think I'm an expert at what I do.

_____ 17. I have figured out efficient ways to do my work.

_____ 18. I can do others' jobs, if I am needed.

_____ 19. I have offered suggestions for how to improve productivity.

_____ 20. I have helped to change the duties of my position.

Scoring Instructions:

The following six dimensions of organizational assimilation can be calculated:

Supervisor familiarity: Add items 1 through 3 (scores range from 3 to 15)

Acculturation: Add items 4−6 (scores range from 3 to 15)

Recognition: Add items 7−10 (scores range from 4 to 20)

Involvement: Add items 11−14 (scores range from 4 to 20)

Job competency: Add items 15−18 (scores range from 4 to 20)

Role negotiation: Add items 19−20 (scores range from 2 to 10)

Understanding Your Level of Organizational Assimilation. Here is a brief description of Myers and Oetzel's six dimensions of organizational assimilation to help you identify how well you are interacting with your fellow employees as well as how well you may be adapting to your organization's culture:[36]

- **Supervisor familiarity:** Getting to know and becoming better acquainted with one's supervisors. Considered the first step toward fitting into an organization. Whether these interactions are positive or negative often influences employees' feelings about where they work.

- **Acculturation:** Accepting and being willing to make adjustments to integrate into an organization's culture. When this occurs, employees tend to feel more familiar with, and share a greater understanding of, their organization's goals and values with their coworkers.

- **Recognition:** Feeling acknowledged for one's contributions to the organization by one's superiors. It also includes experiencing a personal awareness of one's own contributions to the goals and mission of the organization.

- **Involvement:** Demonstrating a level of commitment and connection to the organization by volunteering for assignments or helping to come up with solutions to organizational problems. This, in turn, may help to increase employees' productivity.

- **Job competency:** Employees' beliefs that they are able to perform tasks associated with their jobs in a satisfactory manner.

- **Role negotiation:** Interactions involving new employees and experienced coworkers in an effort to determine how a role should be performed in the workplace.

How you communicate and what you communicate at work as well as the degree to which you show others that you understand your position, can competently perform your job responsibilities, and are engaged in the goals of your organization are indicators of your organizational assimilation. Following are a few recommendations for how you can interpret your assessment data to add to, modify, or enhance your relationships and work performance as you make your organizational assimilation journey:

- *It is not uncommon to assimilate faster into some aspects of organizational life than others.* Category subscores suggest areas in which you could continue, enhance, or modify how or what you communicate when interacting with others at work.[37] In addition, assimilation levels can change throughout someone's time at an organization for a variety of reasons, such as a change in leadership, a change in policies, or changes in relationships with coworkers.

- *It is important to reflect on your work history when examining your organizational assimilation dimensions.* Organizational assimilation subscores tend to be the highest and occur across the most dimensions overall if you have not switched jobs and have continued to work for the same company. They tend to be the least consistent if you have regularly changed jobs.[38]

- *It is important to realize that most of these organizational assimilation dimensions require some level of interpersonal communication.* If you are encountering challenges with any of these dimensions, there could be deeper issues tied to the individuals with whom you are interacting at work. There could be concerns linked to perceptions of trust, competency, or credibility.

WHAT CAN I do now?

▶ *You might want to take greater advantage of opportunities to interact with your coworkers.* Your coworkers might want to get to know you as much as you want to get to know them. However, if you never accept their invitations (e.g., join them for lunch, attend company outings), at some point, they will stop asking you to join them.

▶ *Remember to take your job seriously and do it to the best of your ability.* No one wants to work with or manage someone who is a slacker. This does not mean you cannot ask questions if you are unsure about how to do something. But make a point to listen to the answer. If you keep asking the same question over and over, your boss or coworkers could start to question your competence.

▶ *Don't get discouraged if you are not getting as much praise as you would like.* Your supervisor might have many issues that demand his or her immediate attention. Therefore, your supervisor could overlook telling you when you are doing something well. Perhaps touch base with your supervisor in a quieter moment to talk about how you are progressing. You don't want to come across as too needy, so be mindful of how often you seek feedback.

Enhancing Workplace Relationships

There are many ways to enhance workplace relationships. The following three suggestions allow you to improve workplace relationships by focusing on your relationships with others, career potential, and technology usage at work:

- *Actively engage in getting to know your coworkers, supervisor, and organization as a whole.* Getting to know the people with whom you work can make the workday more enjoyable. It also helps you to acquire information to which you might not otherwise have access. In addition, it doesn't hurt to learn more about the history of your organization. Learning the origins of a company also helps you to understand how and perhaps why the organizational culture has developed and evolved.

- *By participating in a mentoring relationship, you can improve your professional success as well as your social network.* Working with someone who has "been there and done that" provides you with opportunities to learn how to succeed as well as how to avoid failing.[39] In addition, mentors typically introduce their protégés to other people inside and outside of the workplace. This increases the protégé's network and feelings of connection to the organization.

- *Understand the expectations associated with access to workplace technology, hours worked, and relationship responsibilities.* Companies use technologies to help improve worker productivity. Once you get these technological tools, you may be expected to be accessible for longer periods of time extending beyond the typical workday or workweek. This may complicate the boundaries of when you are expected to be "working" and available to your supervisors and coworkers and when you are not.

? CHECKING YOUR UNDERSTANDING
Understanding Communication in Workplace Relationships

Before reading further, take a few minutes to assess your learning by writing your answers to the following items:

1. Describe the different types of workplace relationships, and explain the features of each.

2. How do personality factors and sex differences influence workplace communication?

3. What are the benefits and challenges of intercultural communication in the workplace?

4. How has technology affected workplace communication? What are three challenges that employees and organizations face when managing workplace technology usage?

5. What are three things that you can do to enhance your workplace relationships? Can you think of any other ideas?

Managing Workplace Relationship Challenges

Workplace relationships have many things in common with other types of interpersonal relationships. However, the organizations in which we work influence our interpersonal relationships in several unique ways. Three important areas associated with workplace interpersonal relationships are office romances, workplace bullying, and balancing work–life issues.

Office Romances

The workplace often provides opportunities to meet other people who may have similar academic backgrounds and attitudes to yours. We may also end up spending more time with our coworkers than we do with our friends and acquaintances. Therefore, it is not surprising that people could find potential partners within their workplace.[40] **Office romances** are the romantic relationships that develop between workers who are employed by the same company.

Although workplace romances are common, they are often perceived as negative.[41] Some organizations even have formal policies regarding workplace dating because of the

It is becoming more common for individuals to meet their significant others at work.

inherent challenges that such relationships may present to more people than just the dating couple.[42] This may be because individuals who are engaging in workplace romances are not always motivated by love. Some individuals date their bosses, peers, or subordinates to fill ego needs (e.g., excitement, adventure, sexual experience) or for job-related motives (e.g., advancement, money, job security).[43] Following are some of the primary issues associated with workplace dating:

- *What is the rank of each person?* If a superior and a subordinate are dating one another, there could be concerns about each person's real motives (e.g., the superior is demonstrating power over the subordinate, the subordinate is using sex as a means to get a promotion).[44] Other workers could also feel jealous or suspect that the subordinate has an unfair advantage.[45]

- *Are individuals working in the same department?* When two workers in the same department date one another, this could make it awkward for the rest of the people in the department, especially if the workplace romance is negatively affecting the workplace and coworkers.[46] Furthermore, it can be tricky to determine when coworkers consider the two people to be separate individuals and when they are considered a united couple.[47]

- *What happens if the relationship ends?* When office romances end, this may be problematic for more people than just the two employees who had been in the relationship.[48] Relationships with other coworkers may also be affected. In addition, the organization may have to invest additional resources if individuals are transferred or terminated or if there are legal issues associated with the breakup.[49]

One of the biggest concerns organizations have about office romances relates to accusations of **sexual harassment**, which occurs when advances or behaviors of a sexual nature are unwanted by the receiver of the message(s).[50] When individuals claim that sexual harassment took place, they typically say that it involved a quid pro quo or a hostile work environment. **Quid pro quo** is a Latin phrase meaning "this for that." An example of quid pro quo involving sexual harassment would be a situation in which you will receive a raise if you have sex with your boss, but if you do not have sex with your boss, your boss will not give you a raise. This type of sexual harassment is most likely to occur between superiors and subordinates. The majority of workplace romances are between higher-status men and lower-status women.[51] This may explain why workplace sexual harassment claims are typically made by women.

When claims are made that sexual harassment occurred the result of a **hostile work environment**, this refers to unwanted sexual advances or inappropriate verbal comments or nonverbal behaviors of a sexual nature that occur repeatedly. This type of sexual harassment could occur between superiors and subordinates as well as between coworkers. As a result, in an attempt to manage sexual harassment claims, some organizational policies forbid any dating relationships between employees, set restrictions on the types of employees who are allowed to date one another (e.g., you cannot date someone who reports to you, you cannot date someone who is in the same department or division of the organization), and mandate all employees participate in sexual harassment prevention programs.

Workplace Bullying

"Some might believe that bullying is confined to the playground, but unfortunately, it is all too common in the workplace."[52] In fact, the same people who bullied others in school often continue to demonstrate those behaviors at the places where they work when they get older.[53] **Workplace bullying** involves intentionally negative communication behaviors that are not welcomed or desired; occur repeatedly; escalate over an extended period of time; and are potentially harmful physically, psychologically, or emotionally to the target of the behaviors.[54] Common behaviors displayed by workplace bullies include making insults or threats, targeting individuals for gossip, publicly humiliating others, excluding or ostracizing someone from groups, or persistently criticizing someone.

Although there is often a power disparity between bullies and their targets, it is not necessary to hold a superior rank within an organization to bully others. The power disparity could be associated with the resources or relationships the bully has with others in the organization.[55] As a result, just about anyone can be the target of workplace bullying. For instance, victims of workplace bullying may have a strong work history, be well-educated, and be perceived as cooperative and kind.[56] Men and women report being bullied in approximately equal rates. The profile of workplace bullies suggests that they tend to be male, but it is not uncommon for the bully to be female; the percentages found in research were 60% male and 40% female. However, bullies are most likely to be in a higher-ranking position than their targets are. Peer-to-peer bullying does occur but with much less frequency.[57]

Researchers are discovering differences in how people experience and respond to workplace bullying. Communication scholar Pamela Lutgen-Sandvik found that a worker's biological age played a role in the amount of bullying behaviors they experienced, the type of bullying behavior they experienced, and how they responded to the bullying behavior. Here are some differences she found when comparing the bullying experiences of workers who were 25 years of age and younger and those who were 26 and older:[58]

- Those who were 25 and younger encountered more bullying behaviors than did those who were 26 and older.

- Those who were 25 and younger received significantly more verbally aggressive messages when being bullied than did those who were 26 and older.

- Those who were 25 and younger experienced less peer-to-peer bullying than did those who were 26 and older.

- Those who were 25 and younger were more likely to quit their jobs as a result of workplace bullying. Those who were 26 and older were more likely to make internal and external reports about the bullying exchanges.

Workplace bullying is not necessarily a private communication interaction. Unfortunately, more people may be involved in workplace bullying than just the bully and the target. Coworkers as well as supervisors (assuming that they are not the actual bullies) may be witnesses to bullying exchanges. Approximately 49% of the adults in a national survey indicated that they had direct or indirect exposure to bullying.[59] A 2010 study asked over 3,000 respondents to report whether bullies worked alone or with others. While approximately 68% perceived that the bully worked alone, 27% of the respondents perceived that there was more than one person doing the bullying (5% reported not being sure).[60] Furthermore, approximately 60% of respondents perceived that bullies received some type of support through reinforcement or experienced minimal consequences for the bullying behavior from within the organization. Whether or not senior managers, peers of the bully, human resource departments, or the target's peers actually support the behaviors of bullies, organizations across the United States still need to address or manage the problem of workplace bullying.

ETHICS **in interpersonal communication**

Are You an Accomplice to Workplace Bullying?

Scholars who research workplace bullying have historically put their emphasis on two people: the bully and the target of the bullying. However, a third group—those who witness workplace bullying—is now being studied as researchers discover that the effects of workplace bullying have the potential to affect organizations on a larger scale. Recent scholarship suggests that some witnesses to workplace bullying help to reinforce or support workplace bullying behaviors. In fact, some people could actually be accomplices to workplace bullying.[61]

Understanding the actions of those who witness workplace bullying poses several ethical challenges. First, if you witness workplace bullying, are you required to respond in some way? Or is it inappropriate to intervene in workplace disputes in which you are not an active participant? Another way to think about this would be to ask yourself whether it is your business to stop or intervene when someone is being bullied. Second, if you do not respond to someone being bullied in the workplace, are you, at minimum, passively supporting the bully? Is your failure to act a sign of quiet support or consent for the bully to continue to act in this fashion toward the target?

Some people might say that if you defend a target of workplace bullying, you will simply be providing the bully with a new target: you. In your desire to help someone else, you present yourself as the one who will receive the onslaught of negative, demoralizing behaviors. Therefore, how should people respond or react when they witness workplace bullying? What do you think?

Work–Life Balance

A common complaint is that there are not enough hours in the day to juggle the demands that our jobs place on us and the demands of our personal lives. Researchers have studied these dilemmas, and this body of knowledge is often called **work–life balance** scholarship. Work–life balance scholarship examines how and why individuals make the choices they do when trying to satisfy their professional and personal needs and obligations, as well as what these choices are. Clearly, this also involves examining what organizations do to assist their employees, such as providing on-site daycare or

Some people find that the decision to keep working or to stop for the night is never easy.

workout facilities. The rationale is that these services will help employees to stay focused and help to relieve stress, but some people speculate that what organizations really want is to increase employees' thoughts about work, if not actual work production.[62]

Many different factors come into play in examining work–life issues. Three of the most common factors are marital or partner status, the employment status of both partners, and whether the individual or couple has any children. The first factor, marital or partner status, is important because the choices we might make when we are single (e.g., lots of work-related travel) might not be the same choices we would make if we had a partner to take into consideration (e.g., travel being less attractive because it might mean seeing our partner only on weekends). The second factor pertains to whether the partners are both employed and whether the employed partner(s) works full or part time. In **dual-career couples**, both people are actively engaged in their respective careers. Each person may work well over 40 hours per week and often feels very committed to attaining his or her professional goals. When both partners are deeply engaged in their careers, this tends to create tensions because the two people are putting so much time and energy into their professional lives, leaving limited time to attend to their relationship, let alone the routine duties associated with maintaining their home and other personal obligations. The final factor is whether the individual or couple has any children (especially below the age of 18). If so, the needs of the child (or children) also must be taken into consideration. These concerns range from preparing meals and arranging for childcare to having solutions if the child becomes ill and needs to stay home from school or daycare. This third factor has been studied the most extensively.[63]

People have many different strategies for balancing professional and personal demands. Some strategies may be more effective than others, but here is a sampling of what some people have done to deal with the daily grind of balancing work and home:

- *Consider setting up clear boundaries around when you will and will not work.* Knowing when (or if) you can stop looking at your email messages or stop working on a project at the end of the day is important to allow some space between your personal life and your professional one. But there is no "one size fits all." These are going to have to be decisions you make to fulfill your own professional and personal obligations.[64]

- *Examine what is and is not getting done in your professional life and your personal life.* Work–life balance does not necessary mean an equal balance. What is and is not occurring? What changes would need to take place for things to become more balanced? If you have a partner, how could this person help to make things more manageable? If you wish to seek help from your employer, do so with caution and after careful reflection, since your employer may perceive your requests for assistance in ways that you had not intended (e.g., the employer might think that you are unable to successfully complete your job obligations as opposed to simply needing some short-term job flexibility).[65]

- *Do something that you really love in your professional life.* If you can do this, it will not feel as though you are constantly "working," since if you had the choice, you would still engage in the activity even when you had left work at the end of the day.

- *Make some serious choices about what you do and do not want in both the short and long term.* Even Oprah Winfrey noted, "I've learned that you can't have everything and do everything at the same time." Your professional and personal needs will vary over time and perhaps even on a daily basis. Understanding what you want your priorities to be could help in making professional as well as personal decisions.

CHECKING YOUR UNDERSTANDING

Managing Workplace Relationship Challenges

Before completing the chapter, take a few minutes to assess your learning by writing your answers to the following items:

1. What are three primary issues associated with office romances? Why are these issues potentially problematic for people who wish to date someone where they work?

2. How is workplace bullying defined? What behaviors do workplace bullies tend to exhibit toward their targets? How does the experience potentially vary for younger targets versus somewhat older targets?

3. What are three factors that influence how individuals attempt to attain work–life balance? How does each factor influence someone's ability to manage work–life balance issues?

A Communication Development Plan for Jacquie

To complete Jacquie's story, recall that Jacquie has just started her first position after graduating from college. Although she is starting to feel more comfortable performing her job duties, she has often declined invitations to have lunch or get together with her new coworkers, preferring to put her focus on her work. Unfortunately, now that Jacquie is becoming more comfortable with her job duties, she is feeling somewhat disconnected from her coworkers and the organizational culture. As a result, she is contemplating looking for a different position.

What do you think?

Was Jacquie making wise decisions about how she spent her time at work? How could Jacquie modify her behaviors to change how she feels about her coworkers and her place of employment? Should Jacquie be looking for a position at a different company?

Possible explanations:

What is Jacquie doing or not doing that affects how she perceives her new job? Jacquie is trying to be a good employee, even eating her lunch at her desk in an effort to get more work done. Unfortunately, Jacquie is underestimating the value of having lunch with her colleagues. She could be getting to know them better, and they could be getting to know her better as well without taking significant time away from her job duties.

How could Jacquie modify her workplace interactions to make her feel better about her job and perhaps the company? Jacquie has not developed a personal connection either to her coworkers or to the company where she works. While there are things that others could be doing to help her out, Jacquie also has to think about her own behaviors. Since she has declined her coworkers' invitations in the past, she might need to initiate some exchanges to re-energize these relationships.

Should Jacquie consider alternative places of employment? Changing positions will solve the problem of feeling disconnected at this company. However, the pattern is likely to be repeated if Jacquie does not take time to recognize and understand how workplace relationships can affect professional success. These issues can be fixed, but Jacquie needs to be willing to change some of her own behaviors to help make this possible.

1. *Jacquie needs to realize that people don't dislike her where she works; they simply don't know her.* Jacquie's coworkers are open to her joining them for lunch and probably other social functions as well, but they need to feel that Jacquie also wants to get to know them. Jacquie's coworkers could also be resources if she has any questions at work that she does not want to ask her boss. Some individuals have the problem of letting relational development override the work that needs to be done. Just the reverse is occurring with Jacquie.

2. *Jacquie should make more of an effort to attend informal social gatherings with her coworkers.* A lot can be learned about an organization and its employees by attending company functions. Admittedly, these can be intimidating events if Jacquie feels that she doesn't know anyone, so she could try attending the event with

at least one or two other coworkers in the beginning to help her start to get to know others. Jacquie could also look for opportunities to get involved in any volunteer work in which the organization may be involved. She doesn't need to help with every event, but if there is one that she finds interesting, this is another way to extend her circle of acquaintances in the company.

3. *Jacquie may want to reflect on what she wants out of her career.* The transition from college to entry-level career position can be challenging. If she really is unhappy, Jacquie might need to decide what she is seeking from her career and then consider whether the personal changes would make it worthwhile to change jobs.

Take Aways

This chapter focused on increasing your understanding, skills, and knowledge of professional relationships.

You have increased your understanding and knowledge of:

- The features of superior–subordinate, coworker, mentor–protégé, and worker–customer/client workplace relationships.
- The ways in which personality factors and sex differences influence the communication exchanges in workplace relationships.
- How culture influences workplace communication.

- How office romances, workplace bullying, and work–life balance issues affect employees as well as organizations.

In addition, you are also better able to:

- Explain the role of personality in workplace relationships.
- Apply your knowledge of sex differences when interacting with others in your professional relationships.
- Identify how technology affects professional relationships in both positive and negative ways.
- Improve your communication in your workplace relationships.
- Assess the level of your organizational assimilation and make modifications as needed.

Discussion Questions

1. How does the type of workplace relationship influence the communication exchanges that occur between two people?
2. In what way does personality influence workplace relationships?

3. How does an organization's culture influence workplace communication? What role does culture play in someone's ability to assimilate into the organization in which he or she works?
4. What opportunities and challenges has technology usage generated for workplace relationships?

Building Your Skills

1. Keep a journal for one week. During that time, keep a daily record of how you spend your time. Are you at work? Commuting to or from work? Cleaning your apartment? Running personal errands? Playing video games? At the end of the week, examine the journal to see whether any patterns surface. What does this information tell you about how you spend your time? Were there any surprises? What are you likely to keep doing? What are you interested in changing so that you can maintain the work–life balance you are seeking?
2. Think about the behaviors and communication exchanges you had when you first started attending college.

What are some of the things you did or didn't do to settle in on campus? Did you do anything in particular to try to fit in with your new surroundings? What worked or failed, and why? What would you share with high school students to help them assimilate into college?

3. If your supervisor were to ask you to develop a day-long workshop on improving workplace diversity in your company, what type of content would you emphasize? Because you are not likely to be able to cover everything, what are you going to have to exclude? Why? What do you hope individuals will take away from the workshop when it is over?

13 Interpersonal Communication Research

CHAPTER OBJECTIVES

AFTER READING THIS CHAPTER, you will understand:

1 The four steps in the research process: asking questions, collecting data, analyzing data, and interpreting data.

2 The differences between primary and secondary sources of research and between popular and academic research.

3 The peer-review process that ensures that the research you read in academic journals is of the highest quality.

AFTER READING THIS CHAPTER, you will be able to:

1 Identify titles of academic journals that showcase interpersonal communication research.

2 Locate interpersonal communication research using online search engines.

3 Evaluate interpersonal communication research applying the following criteria: primary or secondary source of research, academic or popular research, peer-review process, and appropriate credentials.

4 Begin conducting interpersonal communication research by working with a faculty member or research team or by conducting your own research.

Interpersonal communication researchers are problem solvers. Verbal and nonverbal messages are to a communication researcher what blood is to a biologist. Messages and communication allow relationships to survive. Without communication, there is no relationship. The purpose of this chapter is to take the mystery out of the research process in the hope that you might see yourself as a researcher and actually begin solving interpersonal communication problems.

This chapter is divided into three main sections. First, we want you to understand the research process. We want you to know how research is conducted and introduce you to topics that interpersonal communication researchers actually study. Second, we want you to be able to use research. We want you to become more comfortable in locating and evaluating research. Finally, we want you to be able to conduct your own research by working with a faculty member or as a member of a research team.

Understanding Research: How Do We Know What We Know?

Research can be an intimidating topic. It's a bit scary because many students have never been informed about the research process. Wouldn't you agree that your fear about a topic increases when you don't know much about the topic? For example, scuba diving is a scary adventure for many people until they receive appropriate training in how to scuba dive. With appropriate knowledge and skills, the fear goes away. Knowledge is empowering. The same is true about the process of conducting research. Once you understand the process, you begin feeling more confident in your ability to conduct research.

One of the ways in which you can begin to understand research is by asking yourself this important question: How do you know what you know? There are a number of ways to answer this question, but two obvious ones are the following:

- *You learn from your experiences.* You know that something is real and true because you have personally experienced it firsthand. It actually happened to you or to someone close to you.

- *You learn from studying a particular topic such as interpersonal communication.* You know that something is real and true because you have read about it in a textbook and you trust the authors to be accurate and trustworthy.

Another way to approach the question "How do I know what I know?" is to begin conducting your own research. It's never too early (or too late) to become a communication researcher.

> Research is formalized curiosity.
> It is poking and prying with
> a purpose.
>
> —ZORA NEALE HURSTON

How Is Research Conducted?

Research is the process of discovery. As communication researcher Joanne Keyton explains, "research is a process of asking questions and finding answers."[1] You're already quite familiar with the research process because you probably used it to find the university that you attend. It's the same scientific method that you learned in junior high, and it includes four basic steps, which are illustrated in Figure 13.1.

1. *Ask a question*: What do you want to know. For example, of the three colleges to which I have been admitted, which one should I attend?
2. *Collect data*: Gather information about the question. For example, you visit and tour the three schools, collecting a variety of information about programs, financial aid, rankings, and other pertinent data.
3. *Analyze the data*: Study the data. How do the data help you to answer your question. For example, after visiting the three colleges, you sit down and compare and contrast the three schools, listing the advantages and disadvantages of each school.
4. *Interpret the data*: Make sense of the answers. For example, you make a decision about the colleges on the basis of your needs and inform the schools of your decision with regard to their acceptances.

FIGURE 13.1

The Research Process

FIGURE 13.2

Example of an Interpersonal Communication Research Study Published in
Communication Quarterly

> ## The Role of Sexual Orientation in Predicting Outcome Value and Anticipated Communication Behaviors
>
> Timothy P. Mottet
>
> *The purpose of this study was to (1) examine the role of sexual orientation in determining a positive or negative predicted outcome value during an initial interaction, and (2) to test whether the predicted outcome value (POV) was related to anticipated communication behaviors. Participants (N = 284) completed one of two surveys. The surveys differed only in terms of the opening scenario, which introduced a fictitious target those sexual orientation was manipulated. The data from this study suggest that learning of an individual's sexual orientation during an initial encounter negatively influences predicted outcome value and anticipated communication behaviors. Additionally, men continue to predict outcome values that are significantly more negative than those predicted by women. The results from this study remain important especially in light of recent research in which interpersonal contact with gays and lesbians has been shown to influence positively heterosexuals' attitudes toward this minority group.*
>
> **KEY CONCEPTS** Predicted Outcome Value, Sexual Orientation, Gay and Lesbian Identification, Identity Management Strategies, Heterosexual Attitudes, Gender Differences
>
> **Timothy P. Mottet** (Ed.D., West Virginia University, 1998) is Assistant Professor and Basic Course Director, Department of Speech Communication, Southwest Texas State University, San Marcos, Texas. This paper was presented at the annual conference of the Eastern Communication Association in Saratoga, New York, April 1998. The author would like to thank the following for their review and assistance with this manuscript Melanie Booth-Butterfield, Matt Martin, Phil Salem, Paul Raffeld, and two anonymous reviewers.
>
> Communication theorists and researchers suggest that individuals attempt to reduce uncertainty in initial encounters in order to increase predictability in relationships (Berger & Calabrese, 1975; Sunnafrank, 1986). Additionally, reducing uncertainty during initial interactions allows individuals to make evaluative decisions regarding future interactions. What happens to future interactions when individuals obtain information they perceive to be negative and inconsistent with their attitudes, beliefs, and values? Predicted outcome value theory (Sunnafrank,
>
> *Communication Quarterly*, Vol. 48, No. 3, Summer 2000, pages 223–239.

Source: Mottet, T. P. (2000). The role of sexual orientation in predicting outcome value and anticipated communication behaviors. *Communication Quarterly, 48*(3), 223–239.

We're all social scientists to some degree. **Social science** is the systematic study of social life. The difference between you and a trained social scientist is the degree of precision that is used in conducting research. For example, suppose you notice an interesting phenomenon when your friend, who is gay, meets new people. In one situation, when meeting a group of possible new friends, he immediately informed them that he was gay. When this happened, he was not included as a part of the group. In another situation, he waited to disclose his sexual orientation until after the group had gotten to know him as a person. When this happened, he was included in the friendship group. As you observe these interactions, you begin to suspect that the timing of his gay self-disclosure could make a difference.

Rather than relying only on his or her personal experiences, a social scientist would conduct an experiment to determine how learning of someone's gay identity affected friendship development. To illustrate the research process, we're going to quickly walk you through a published research study, which is featured in Figure 13.2 (opposite page).

Ask a Question. The general purpose of this study was to answer the following question: Does learning of someone's sexual orientation during an initial meeting affect the development of a friendship? The literature is inconclusive. Some of the research suggests that if you have regular contact with gay people, then learning of someone's gay identity is no big deal.[2] Other research suggests that it depends on the timing. For example if you know someone and later find out that he or she is gay, then the relationship is more than likely to continue. If you learn of someone's sexual orientation first without knowing the person, then chances are that the relationship will never fully form.[3]

Collect Data. To answer the question, one of your authors conducted an experiment with college students using a questionnaire. Half of the students read the passage in Figure 13.3 with the word *boyfriend*, and half of the students read the passage with the word *girlfriend*. After reading the passage, all students were asked to complete a questionnaire that asked questions about their likelihood of developing a friendship with Steve.

FIGURE 13.3

This part of the description was manipulated. Half of the students read "boyfriend." Half of the students read "girlfriend."

You recently met your new neighbor Steve. During this initial conversation, you learned a lot about Steve. It appears that you are going to be neighbors for some time. You and Steve both grew up in similar neighboring towns, you are the same age, you practice the same faith, and you share the same interest in music. Steve has a boyfriend and seems rather intelligent. He comes from a close-knit family and has one older brother and one younger sister.

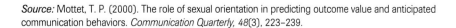

Source: Mottet, T. P. (2000). The role of sexual orientation in predicting outcome value and anticipated communication behaviors. *Communication Quarterly, 48*(3), 223–239.

Analyze the Data. After the data were collected, they were entered into a statistical software program in which a series of statistical tests were computed to determine whether Steve's having a boyfriend or a girlfriend made a difference in whether a friendship would form.

Interpret the Data. The results indicated that the sexual orientation mattered. Students who learned that Steve was homosexual were less likely to form a friendship with him than were students who learned that Steve was heterosexual. The data also suggested that men, more than women, had a difficult time with Steve's being homosexual.

What Do Researchers Study?

Researchers investigate interpersonal communication from a variety of different perspectives. Many researchers are interested in how people use communication to get into relationships, manage relationships, and end or get out of relationships. Each of these three stages of relational development is unique and involves different types of communication processes. We first discussed the stages of relational development in Chapter 9.

Another way in which researchers study interpersonal communication is by focusing on a particular type of relationship. For example, the communication that takes place between husbands and wives is quite different from the communication that takes place between teachers and students or between doctors and patients. As you will recall from Chapters 10, 11, and 12, different relationship types affect communication in their own ways. Table 13.1 provides an incomplete list of topics that interest interpersonal communication researchers.

Researchers are sometimes interested in communication trait variables that influence interpersonal communication, such as a person's communication apprehension, verbal aggression, and argumentativeness. All three of these communication traits, which we discussed in Chapter 4, have been shown to influence interpersonal communication. Other researchers are interested in examining communication skills that have been shown to influence interpersonal communication, such as conflict management, listening, and self-disclosure skills.

Another topic that researchers study is interpersonal perceptions. In Chapter 3, you learned about how you perceive others and how others perceive you, both of which are psychological processes that affect the communication that occurs in a relationship. Interpersonal communication researchers are particularly interested in how perceptions of credibility, homophily, and attraction, as well as trust and solidarity, influence how people get into, manage, and get out of relationships.

A number of important factors that affect interpersonal communication are woven throughout this textbook, including sex and gender, culture, technology, and emotion. Interpersonal communication researchers want to know how men and women are similar and how they are different in their communication. Although popular research would indicate that men and women communicate so differently that they sometimes seem to come from different planets (Mars and Venus perhaps),[4] the academic research suggests that there are more similarities than differences.[5]

Communication researchers also investigate what is referred to as the dark side of interpersonal communication. "The **dark side of interpersonal communication** is concerned with the dysfunctional, distorted, distressing, and destructive aspects of human action."[6] Put simply, the dark side examines what happens when communication and relationships take a turn for the worse. Researchers examine such topics as gossip, jealousy, envy, and anger, as well as sexual coercion, stalking, and "fatal attraction" dynamics.

TABLE 13.1

Partial List of Interpersonal Communication Types, Variables, and Skills	
Relationship Types	
Friends	Supervisors and subordinates
Families	Students and teachers
Husbands and wives	Patients and doctors
Dating and romantic partners	
Communication Trait Variables That Affect Interpersonal Communication	
Communication apprehension	Assertiveness and responsiveness
Verbal aggression	Affective orientation
Argumentativeness	Humor
Interpersonal communication motives	
Interpersonal Communication Skills	
Conflict management	Impression management
Listening and empathy	Affinity seeking
Self-disclosure	Negotiating
Nonverbal immediacy and responsiveness	Conversational skills
	Compliance gaining
Interpersonal Perceptions	
Credibility	Trust
Homophily	Solidarity
Attraction	
Factors That Affect Interpersonal Communication	
Emotion	Culture
Gender and sex	Technology
Ethnicity	Sexual orientation
Dark Side of Interpersonal Communication	
Aggressive communication	Stalking
Sexual harassment	Sexual coercion and resistance
Deception	

CHECKING YOUR UNDERSTANDING
How Do We Know What We Know?

Before reading further, take a few minutes to assess your learning by answering the following questions. Feel free to use the text or talk out your answers with the person sitting next to you.

1. List and explain the four steps of the research process. To reinforce your understanding, apply each of the steps to something you recently purchased that cost you a lot of money.

2. Explain how social scientific research is different from other forms of research.

3. Differentiate relationship type, communication trait, and perception variables that interpersonal communication researchers study.

4. Researchers are interested in examining how sex and gender differences, cultural differences, and technology factors affect interpersonal communication. Provide one research finding from your reading of this textbook that illustrates how each of these factors influences interpersonal communication.

Using Research: Is It Fact or Fiction?

With the explosion of information that is available on the Internet as well as from other sources, it is becoming more and more important for people to be critical consumers of research. It's important to always ask the question "Is this fact or fiction?" Do you know the difference? As you already know, the quality of information that you get from reading the tabloids located in the checkout line of your local supermarket is quite different from the quality of information that you get from reading the academic journals in your college or university library. But what about something less obvious, such as the difference between downloading information that you found by using Google versus information that you found via Google Scholar or Communication and Mass Media Complete? In this section, we're going to help you to find and evaluate research.

Where Do I Find Research?

The obvious place to find interpersonal communication research is in your college or university library. Most academic libraries contain a collection of scholarly books and journals that include interpersonal communication research. Table 13.2 provides a partial listing of some of the Communication discipline's journals. Most college and university libraries have many of these titles in their collections. In these journals, you will find academic research that was conducted by using the research process described earlier.

Another way to locate scholarly research is to use your college library's online search engines. As a student, you probably have access to a number of online search engines by visiting your library's website and then selecting an "online database" menu option. This will probably take you to a menu of online search engines. There are three popular search engines that you will find particular helpful as you search for interpersonal communication research: Communication and Mass Media Complete, PsycINFO, and Google Scholar.

TABLE 13.2

Partial Listing of Academic Journals Showcasing Interpersonal Communication Research

Specific Types of Relationships

Communication Education (teacher–student relationships)	*Journal of Health Communication* (physician–patient relationships)
Health Communication (physician–patient relationships)	*Management Communication Quarterly* (superior–subordinate relationships)
Journal of Family Communication (family relationships)	

General Interpersonal Communication

Communication Monographs	*Journal of Communication*
Communication Quarterly	*Journal of Intercultural Communication Research*
Communication Reports	
Communication Research	*Journal of Nonverbal Behavior*
Communication Research Reports	*Journal of Social and Personal Relationships*
Communication Review	*Qualitative Research Reports in Communication*
Communication Studies	
Human Communication Research	*Southern Communication Journal*
Journal of Applied Communication Research	*Western Journal of Communication*

The advantage to using Communication and Mass Media Complete and PsycINFO is that they will allow you to download academic journal articles, if they're available, without a charge. This is one of the library services that you receive for paying your student service fees at your college or university. Google Scholar is an online search engine that is available to the general public, and many of the articles you may want to download will cost you a fee.

If you use online search engines to locate your research, you will need to pay particular attention to the search terms you use. Your online search is only as good as your search terms. Table 13.3 provides a partial listing of common search terms that are used in interpersonal communication research. You may find some of these terms helpful when conducting your own online searches.

For example, if you're interested in locating research that examines how a physician's emotional support of his or her patient enhances the doctor–patient relationship, you would enter two sets of search terms "physician-patient relationship" and "emotional support"—into the Communication and Mass Media Complete search engine.

TABLE 13.3

Partial Listing of Common Search Terms for Interpersonal Communication Research Using Online Search Engines	
Interpersonal communication	Personality and interpersonal communication
Relational communication	Empathy
Relationship satisfaction	Interpersonal attraction
Relationship commitment	Stages of relational development
Language and interpersonal communication	Relational maintenance behaviors
Nonverbal communication	Social penetration theory
Culture and interpersonal communication	Uncertainty reduction theory
Technology and interpersonal communication	Self-concept/self-esteem and communication
Gender and interpersonal communication	Relational control
Emotional support	Trust and communication
Power and dominance	Conflict management styles
Emotions in interpersonal communication	Interpersonal perceptions
Communication competence	Affinity-seeking behaviors
Relational communication competence	Compliance-gaining behaviors
Social and personal relationships	Communication styles
Interpersonal control and deception	Parenting styles
Deception	Marital conflict communication
Confirmation	Demand-withdrawal communication
Defensiveness	Student-teacher relationship
	Physician-patient relationship

How Do I Evaluate Research?

Once you find the research, it's important that you evaluate it to make sure that it is of the highest quality. Again, our goal is to help you become a critical consumer of research. The evaluation process includes your asking the following four questions.

Is It Primary or Secondary Research? **Primary research** is a published work that comes directly from the author of the original research. After the researcher conducts a study, he or she describes the research process and the results in a research paper. The goal for the researcher is to get the paper published in an academic journal so that other researchers can use the results from the study to help them solve the communication problems they're investigating. If you refer to the back of this book, you will see a long lists of references. There is one list for each chapter. Most of these references are primary sources of research.

Secondary research is a published work that summarizes and interprets primary research done by others. A secondary source is similar to secondhand information. If I tell you something, I am the primary source. If you tell someone else what I told you, you become the secondary source. The textbook that you're reading is a secondary source of research. It's a summary of over approximately 1,000 different pieces of primary research that have been synthesized into this review of research. Put another way, we are interpreting other researchers' work and using their work to tell a story about interpersonal communication.

Both primary and secondary research have advantages and disadvantages. The advantage of primary research is that the person writing the research is the person who conducted the research. It's not secondhand information. The disadvantage is that sometimes primary research is not as accessible as secondary research, in terms of being able to locate it and being able to read it and understand it. The advantages of secondary research are that it is sometimes easier to locate and that it has been translated for you. Someone has read the primary research and is interpreting it for you making it easier for you to understand. The disadvantage is that sometimes the author doesn't interpret the research adequately or correctly.

Is It Popular or Academic Research? Most **popular research**, which is a form of secondary research, is written for the nonacademic audience. Popular research books are written in an accessible manner so that a person without formal academic training can read the book and understand the concepts and ideas. You will see these books at your local bookstore such as Barnes and Noble. Dr. Deborah Tannen, from Georgetown University in Washington, D.C., is an example of an academic researcher who has made her research available to the popular audience. Her book titled, *You Just Don't Understand*, was on the *New York Time's* bestseller list for four years and was ranked #1 for eight months. This book is a summary of Dr. Tannen's primary research examining gender differences in communication.

Academic research, by contrast, is written for an audience of men and women who have formal training in a particular area of study. Because you're a college student, you fall into this category. You are being formally trained in interpersonal communication. Although not always, much of the academic research is primary research. It comes directly from the researcher who conducted the study, and in the published work, the researcher details the research process and the findings from the study.

In the academic setting, we recommend that you use academic rather than popular research. We make this recommendation for a couple of reasons. First, the interpersonal communication research that you read about in *Cosmopolitan* or even *Psychology Today* is not the same research that you read about in a textbook, scholarly book, or academic journals. Popular magazine publishers are trying to sell as many copies of their magazine as possible, so they use research to tell a story that will appeal to buyers (i.e., the *Cosmo* quizzes) and do not pay rigorous attention to accuracy, detail, and thoroughness.

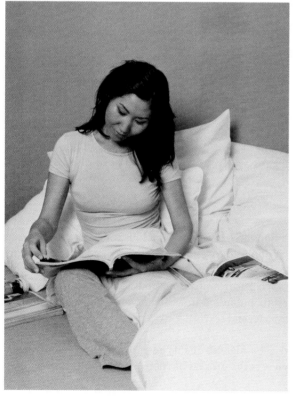

Although self-report quizzes found in many popular magazines are fun to complete, they lack many of the features needed in order for an assessment instrument to be valid, reliable, and therefore useful.

FIGURE 13.4

Academic Credentials
and University Affiliation

Communication Research Reports
Vol. 24, No. 4, November 2007, pp. 361–372

Are Children Communicated with Equally? An Investigation of Parent–Child Sex Composition and Gender Role Communication Differences

Sean M. Horan, Marian L. Houser, & Renee L. Cowan

Parents play a pivotal role in the gender development and sex-typing of children. It is important to discover whether gender role communication differences exist based on the sex of the child or parent. The present study aimed to discover differences in gender role messages communicated between mother–daughter, mother–son, father–daughter, and father–son dyads. Participants (n = 630) completed a modified version of Bem's Sex Role Inventory. Two key results were discovered: mothers communicate significantly more feminine messages to children, regardless of child sex; and the modified BSRI identifies respondents as weak vs. strong gender identity rather than masculine, feminine, androgynous, or undifferentiated.

Keywords: Gender; Gender Identity; Gender Role Messages; Parent–Child Gender Communication

Researchers in the social sciences have spent years investigating sex differences in communication (Barry, Bacon, & Child, 1957; Eisenberg & Lennon, 1983; Ford & Beach, 1951). This has resulted in numerous studies reporting a polarization in communication behaviors based on sex, with scholars claiming different behaviors between men and women (Canary & Hause, 1993; Tannen, 1995). This obsession with sex differences is pervasive in society, and can be seen in books like *Men Are*

Sean M. Horan (M.A., Texas State University, 2005) is a doctoral student at West Virginia University. Marian L. Houser (Ph.D., University of Tennessee) is an Assistant Professor at Texas State University-San Marcos. Renee L. Cowan (M.A., Texas State University, 2005) is a doctoral student at Texas A&M University. *Correspondence:* Dr. Marian L. Houser, Department of Communication Studies, Texas State University San Marcos, 601 University Drive, San Marcos, TX 78666-2165. Tel.: Office (512) 245-3137; Fax: (512) 245-3138; E-mail: mh53@txstate.edu

ISSN 0882-4096 (print)/ISSN 1746-4099 (online) © 2007 Eastern Communication Association
DOI: 10.1080/08824090701624262

Biographical information is included at the bottom of the title page that includes earned degrees and college and university affiliations.

Source: Horan, S. M., Houser, M. L., & Cowan, R. L. (2007). Are children communicated with equally?: An investigation of parent–child sex composition and gender role communication differences. *Communication Research Reports, 24*, 361–172.

By contrast, academic publications are know for scrupulous concern with accuracy. The purpose of academic research publications, such as textbooks and academic journals, is to showcase the research. Furthermore, academic research is conducted by using the scientific research process, which ensures precision and accuracy. Because future research may be based on the results published in academic journals, it is important that the information be clear, complete, and correct.

Is It Peer-Reviewed Research?   The highest-quality research is always going to be peer-reviewed research. **Peer review** is the process of subjecting an author's scholarly work, research, or ideas to the scrutiny of others who are experts in the same field. Here's a brief review of how the process works. Researchers submit their manuscript to an editor of an academic journal or book with the hope that their work will be published. Once the editor receives it, the manuscript is forwarded to two or three other academic researchers who are considered specialists in this particular research area. The author's name is usually removed from the manuscript, making it a blind review. This ensures that the reviewers don't let any bias they might have for or against a particular author influence their appraisal of the manuscript. The reviewers evaluate the research and determine whether it is of the highest quality. If so, they make a recommendation to the editor of the academic journal or book who ultimately makes the decision to publish or reject the manuscript. Reviewers may also make suggestions for improvements that could make the article more suitable for publication. Academic journals, scholarly books, and even textbooks are peer-reviewed. For the most part, popular research is not peer-reviewed. With popular research, the editor makes all the decisions, and the peer group is rarely consulted about the quality of the work.

Is the Researcher Credentialed? Another way to evaluate research is to find out whether the researcher is **credentialed**, which is a certification that the person is a professional. Put simply, does the researcher have the knowledge and skills needed to make him or her a credible or believable researcher? In most academic research publications, the author or author team is featured on the title page, and their degrees and university affiliations are included somewhere on the title page. See Figure 13.4 (on facing page) for an example.

Although not always, if the researchers have a doctoral degree (PhD, EdD) or are in the process of acquiring one, they probably have the skills and knowledge needed to conduct high-quality research. If the researchers are affiliated with a college or university, chances are they also have the knowledge, skills, and resources needed to conduct research.

CHECKING YOUR UNDERSTANDING
Is It Fact or Fiction?

Before reading further, take a few minutes to assess your learning by writing your answers to the following items:

1. Assume that the person sitting next to you has never conducted a search for academic research. How would you advise this person to begin the process? Discuss three or four critical steps in locating academic research.

2. Describe three online search engines that people use to locate scholarly research. Where can you find these search engines? Which one do you prefer and why? What are the differences between the three search engines?

3. What are the differences been primary and secondary sources of research? How does academic research differ from popular research? What do people mean when they say that research is peer-reviewed? What are credentials, and why are they important to how you evaluate research?

Conducting Research: How Do I Get Started?

If you're curious and have questions that you want to have answered, then you're ready to begin conducting research. You can get involved in the process in a number of different ways, including partnering with a faculty member, working as a member of a research team, and developing your own research study.

Working with a Faculty Member or Research Team

The easiest way for you to begin doing research is to become a research assistant for one of your professors. Ask your faculty members whether they're doing research, and let them know that if they need help, you would like to assist them. At some colleges and universities, you can work as a paid undergraduate research assistant. If monies are not available, you might be able to work as a research assistant as part of an internship or as independent study in which you get course credit for the work you complete.

If you work as an undergraduate research assistant, we recommend that your supervising faculty member provide you with a list of expectations for the research assistantship so that you know what will be expected of you. Before you begin, you will want to know your job duties as a research assistant, the requirements for the position, and how much you will be paid in addition to the number of hours you are expected to work per week. It's important that you review the expectations and communicate with the supervising faculty member whether you feel you will be able to meet the expectations. If not, then you will need to ask your supervising faculty member for appropriate training and guidance. It's important to openly communicate what you can and cannot do and the areas in which you will need training. Your faculty member will appreciate your being candid about your abilities.

You might also have the opportunity to work as a member of a research team. The team may include other faculty members or students who share an interest in the

Assisting a faculty member with a research project is one of the best ways to help you develop your own research skills. Not only will you learn how to become a researcher, but you will also develop a stronger relationship with your faculty member

research study. When you're a part of a research team, your supervising faculty member serves as the project manager and usually assigns each member of the team a specific research task. For example, you might be assigned to locate research articles. Or you might be assigned to help collect data by administering surveys or conducting interviews. Most research teams meet regularly to share status reports on the team members' respective assignments and to receive new assignments.

Working as a research assistant or as a member of a research team will give you an inside look at the research process and will help you to develop new research skills. These skills will benefit you in a couple of different ways. First, your new skills will help you to be a better student. You will feel more comfortable and be more proficient in locating, evaluating, and using academic research. Second, your new research skills will make you a more competitive candidate as you conduct your job search. Research skills are highly valued among hiring managers, and including your new research skills on your résumé will enhance your marketability.[7]

Working on Your Own Research

Another way of conducting research is to develop your own research study. Many colleges and universities have capstone courses, which are courses that are designed to allow students to synthesize their learning. To finish a capstone course, students usually have to complete a rather extensive paper, project, or presentation. Conducting a research study would be the perfect project for a capstone course. Another way in which you could conduct your own study is to do an independent study. Most departments allow you to work with a faculty advisor on an independent study. You propose a research study and then carry out the proposal while enrolled in the independent study.

Another college and university initiative that is gaining popularity is the undergraduate research conference.[8] Some colleges and universities set aside one day of the academic year to allow students to present their research in a format similar to that of the annual academic conferences that professors attend.[9] The undergraduate research conference has become so popular that there is a professional organization specifically devoted to this endeavor. The National Conferences on Undergraduate Research (NCUR) promotes undergraduate research, scholarship, and creative activity in all fields of study by sponsoring an annual conference for students.[10] The conference welcomes students from all colleges and universities. Through their annual conference, the NCUR encourages undergraduate student achievement and provides models of exemplary research and scholarship.

To develop your own study, use the social scientific research process outlined in Figure 13.1: ask a question, collect data, analyze the data, and interpret the data. To give you some idea of how you might do this, consider the following examples of real student projects that were conducted under the direction of the authors of your textbook.

Monica's Question. How do military couples pick up where they left off after one spouse has been away on active duty for an extended period of time? To answer this research question, Monica collected data using the interview method. She developed an interview guide, which is a consistent set of questions that she asked ten different military couples after they were reunited. With the couples' permission, Monica tape-recorded the interviews and took notes. She analyzed her data by reviewing her interview notes and listening to the audio files numerous times, listening for themes. She interpreted the data using key concepts from Chapter 9, especially the stages of coming together and coming apart and relational maintenance strategies.

Max's Question. Do male waiters who appropriately touch their male and female customers get more tips? To answer this research question, Max collected data by conducting a field experiment at the local Chili's restaurant where he worked as a waiter.[11] With the permission of the restaurant manager, Max involved a good friend, Sean, who also waited tables at Chili's. Max kept Sean in the dark about his research question; however, he did instruct Sean to briefly touch the shoulder of the male or female customer who was paying the bill. At the end of the evening, Max asked Sean for the total amount of dollars he had earned in tips. The following week, on the same day of the week during the same shift, Max again invited Sean to be a part of his research study. This time, Sean was instructed not to touch the customer who was going to pay the bill. At the end of the evening, Max again asked Sean for the amount of his earned tips. Max analyzed the data by comparing the amount of tips earned and interpreted his findings using many of the concepts from Chapter 5, especially the discussion focusing on haptics and the functions of nonverbal messages.

Patricia's Question. Is there a relationship between using social networking sites and social skill development? To answer this research question, Patricia collected data using a survey that she developed. Her survey included a number of items that assessed how much time per day students used social networking sites, such as MySpace and Facebook. The survey also included a social skills inventory that measured how socially skilled the person perceived himself or herself to be. Patricia administered her survey to fifty students. With the help of a faculty member, Patricia analyzed her data using SPSS, which is a statistical software program. She interpreted her findings using many of the ideas and concepts from Chapter 1, including the section on using communication technologies appropriately.

 ## CHECKING YOUR UNDERSTANDING
How Do I Get Started?

Before completing the chapter, take a few minutes to assess your learning by discussing the following questions with the person next to you.

1. What does it mean to work with a faculty member as an undergraduate research assistant? How would you explain your new job to your parents?

2. How does working as a member of a research team differ from working as a research assistant?

3. What are the benefits of working as an undergraduate research assistant or as a member of a research team?

4. What is the National Council of Undergraduate Research? What are its goals and objectives?

5. If you were to conduct your own research study, what would you study? Why?

Take Aways

Interpersonal communication researchers are problem solvers. They study the communication processes that allow relationships to exist. The purpose of this chapter was to take the mystery out of the research process in the hope that you might see yourself as a researcher and actually begin the process of discovering what works and doesn't work in your relationships.

Following is a list of knowledge claims regarding interpersonal communication research:

- The research process includes four steps: asking questions, collecting data, analyzing data, and interpreting data.

- Academic research is a form of research written for a specialized audience of men and women who have formal training in a particular area of study, whereas popular research is written for the nonacademic audience.

- Primary research is a published work that comes directly from the author of the research, whereas secondary research is a published work that summarizes and interprets original research done by others.

- The peer-reviewed process occurs when an editor of an academic book or journal asks other equally qualified researchers to review a researcher's manuscript. If this panel of judges considers the research to be of the highest quality, then the editor of the publication may decide to publish the work.

Following is a list of questions you can now answer to assess the quality of published interpersonal communication research:

- Is the research primary or secondary source material?
- Is it popular or academic research?
- Is the researcher credentialed?
- Was the research process followed?

Discussion Questions

1. Describe each of the four steps in the research process: asking questions, collecting data, analyzing data, and interpreting data.

2. Explain the differences between academic and popular research. Why is academic research considered to be more credible or believable than popular research?

3. Describe the importance of the peer-review process and how it insures that the academic research you read is of the highest quality?

4. Describe the significance of a researcher's credentials? Where do you find the researcher's credentials in a published piece of academic research?

Building Your Skills

1. Locate and bring to class a sample of social scientific academic research. Using a highlighter, identify the four steps in the research process: questions asked, data collected, data analyzed, and data interpreted. Now, answer the following questions. What was the question? How were the data collected? How were the data analyzed? How were the data interpreted?

2. Locate and bring to class samples of academic and popular research. Now discuss the following evaluation criteria: Is it considered primary or secondary research? Why is this distinction important? Is the author of the

work credentialed? How do you know this? Can you tell if the research process was followed: questions asked, data collected, data analyzed, and data interpreted.

3. Identify an interpersonal communication problem or issue that you're currently having. Conduct a search using one of the online search engines you learned about in this chapter. Locate a research study that you believe may help you work through the problem. After reading the study, discuss with a friend how you might use the new information to help with your problem.

Glossary

Academic research: A form of research written for a specialized audience of men and women who have formal training in a particular area of study.

Accent: The way a word is spoken, using a particular pronunciation and stressing a particular syllable.

Accommodating: A conflict management style in which a person shows support of another person's goals with no concern for his or her own.

Acculturation: A dimension of organizational assimilation that emphasizes an employee's acceptance and willingness to make adjustments to integrate into an organization's culture.

Acknowledge contextual limitations: A listening strategy that is recommended if the environment or other outside factors play a factor in the listening process.

Action-oriented listening style: A listening style that focuses on the tasks and goal(s) that needs to be accomplished.

Active strategies: Uncertainty reduction strategies that do not involve direct contact with the person with whom you are interested in interacting.

Affection: When you communicate to express love or to be loved by others.

Affective orientation: The degree to which individuals are aware of and use emotional cues to guide their communication.

Agape: A love style associated with spirituality and altruistic behaviors, in which a partner is willing to make personal sacrifices for his or her mate. Also known as altruistic love.

Agentic: A common masculine gender stereotype that Western culture associates with active, instrumental, and competent personality traits.

Agreeableness: A personality trait where people tend to be positive, considerate, friendly, generous, and willing to extend a helping hand when needed.

Agreeableness personality trait: Refers to an individual's tendency to be positive; get along with others; and be considerate, friendly, and generous.

Amiable social style: Considered to be relationship specialists, high on responsiveness and low on assertiveness.

Analytical social style: Considered to be technical specialists, low on responsiveness and low on assertiveness.

Androgyny: A gender-role category that describes an individual who exhibits a combination of highly masculine and highly feminine characteristics.

Appearance: Refers to the personal visual items that people use to shape an image of another, such as clothing, jewelry, makeup, and tattoos.

Approach dimension: A fundamental personality dimension in which a person displays positive emotions, thus encountering fewer conflicts. During conflict, approachers willingly discuss and confront the issue.

Argumentativeness: A communication trait by which people have a desire to advocate a position on an issue and criticize other people's positions.

Arousal: One of the three dimensions of nonverbal immediacy with behaviors that exhibit interest.

Artifacts and the environment: The nonverbal category that involves items and objects external to physical appearance and the mind. Examples are items such as clothing and jewelry, the color of artifacts, and the way in which the rooms are arranged.

Assertiveness: The ability to express needs, wants, and desires in a firm but polite manner.

Assertiveness: An individual's ability to make requests; actively disagree; express personal rights and feelings; initiate, maintain, or disengage from conversations; and stand up for oneself without attacking others.

Assurance: A relational maintenance strategy that provides affirmation and comfort to your relational partner.

Asynchronous communication: A form of communication in which a time lapse occurs between the sending and receiving of messages.

Attending: A listening stage that centers on giving further attention or focus to the sounds that individuals have selected.

Attribution: The process of attempting to determine the cause for someone else's behavior.

Attributional confidence: The level of confidence we have in evaluating the facts about people.

Attributions: The reasons we create in our minds for why other people engage in certain behaviors.

Auditory association: The ability to establish connections or relationships between new incoming sounds to ones with which we are already familiar.

Auditory discrimination: The ability to distinguish one sound from another.

Avoidance dimension: A fundamental personality dimension in which a person either withdraws from conflict or exhibits negative emotional reactions toward others. Avoiders fail to fully engage in the conflict, thus exacerbating the negative situation.

Avoiding stage: The fourth coming apart stage, in which you are on the cusp of ending your relationship.

Back channel cues: Nonverbal cues such as "uh huh" or head nods that indicate an interest in having the speaker continue speaking.

Behavioral uncertainty: The uncertainty associated with being unable to predict when or how people are going to act.

Benign disinhibition: People's tendency to freely share personal information about themselves online, such as fears, hopes, dreams, or emotions.

Biased language: Language that makes assumptions about people, groups, or organizations and categorizes them.

Big Five personality model: A model of personality developed by psychologists Robert McCrae and Paul Costa that includes five factors: openness, conscientiousness, extraversion, agreeableness, and neuroticism.

Biological time: A time orientation that relates to our own body clocks and the way in which individuals respond to time.

Bonding stage: The fifth coming together stage, often considered the public capstone event to relational development. You and your partner make some type of symbolic public gesture to recognize your union.

Breadth: The variety of topics that you discuss with someone.

Career functions: Aspects of mentoring relationships that emphasize advancing someone's career success by having greater workplace visibility or getting more challenging job assignments.

Certain verbal messages: Those messages that contain specific information that allow you to comfortably predict that something will happen.

Channel: The pathway by which verbal and nonverbal messages are transmitted from source to receiver, usually including our senses: visual/sight, auditory/hearing, tactile/touch, and olfactory/smell.

Channel of communication: A listening barrier that occurs when senders and receivers utilize modes of communication that hinder the ability to listen effectively.

Choice theory: A theory that posits that although we might not be able to alter the behaviors of others, we can change the way we perceive others.

Chronemics: The study of time and how time communicates.

Circumscribing stage: The second coming apart stage, in which relational partners are not only talking less in general, but also talking less about issues that matter or have much relational relevance.

Clarifying information: Acquiring additional information to understand the message someone has shared with you.

Co-cultural group: A cultural group within a larger culture.

Coercive power: An individual's ability to punish or withhold resources that you want (e.g., avoiding you, receiving a poor performance appraisal).

Cognitive dissonance: A feeling of imbalance in our perceptions that impedes our desire for consistency in our perceptions.

Cognitive restructuring: The process that one goes through when one replaces debilitating irrational beliefs with empowering rational beliefs.

Cognitive schemata: Our mental frameworks, or mental file folders, that are filled with our past knowledge and experiences.

Cognitive self-esteem: A self-evaluation regarding an individual's ability to learn, process, and use information and knowledge.

Cognitive uncertainty: The level of uncertainty associated with others' beliefs and attitudes.

Cohabitation: Two relational partners living together without being married.

Collaborating: A conflict management style that is viewed as the most constructive and positive because it integrates the goals of both parties involved in the disagreement as they come up with a new and creative solution.

Collectivistic culture: A culture in which value is placed on interdependence, with a focus on group and social norms.

Commitment: Binding oneself to another in the form of an allegiance, pledge, or promise.

Commitment-phobic: A serious fear of or apprehension about commitment or intimacy.

Communal: A common feminine gender stereotype that Western culture associates with warm, emotional, and nurturing personality traits.

Communal behaviors: A type of cost that occurs when we take time to help our partners with something they want done. This type of cost could have positive outcomes for your relationship.

Communication apprehension: An individual's level of fear or anxiety associated with either real or anticipated communication with another person or persons.

Communication climate: The social tone within a relational experience. It is how you feel about what has been said or done between you and another person.

Communication traits: Enduring consistencies and differences in message-sending and message-receiving behaviors among individuals.

Communicator reward valence: The positive or negative status assigned to a person who has violated our nonverbal expectations.

Comparison level: The minimum expectations, desires, or needs that we have for our relationships.

Comparison level of alternatives: If another relational option appears better than your existing choice, you would select the preferred option. If the option is not as good as what you currently have, you will stick with your present choice.

Complementarity: Providing balance to another person. Combining opposing forces to attain perceived harmony and overall strength.

Compromising: A conflict management style that is typically viewed as positive but in which you give up your original goals and negotiate a solution that is mutually acceptable.

Confirmation: This behavior involves the use of words that cause another person to feel unique, respected, and important.

Conflict: An incompatibility of goals between two people. A simpler definition suggests that conflict is an interaction in which the people involved have differing views, opinions, or interests.

Conflict orientation: A generalized view or orientation toward conflict that is either constructive/positive or destructive/negative.

Connection–autonomy: A dialectical tension that is associated with being either too close or enmeshed or too independent and separate.

Connotative meaning: Interpretation of words in a subjective manner, according to an individual's personal experiences.

Conscientiousness: A personality trait where people are goal-driven and work hard to achieve their goals.

Conscientiousness personality trait: Refers to an individual's tendency to be goal-driven, develop plans, and work hard to achieve personal goals.

Constructive conflict: A positive conflict orientation in which individuals think of the other people around them and the relationship. This view of conflict typically involves cooperation or collaboration behaviors.

Contamination: A form of encroachment where territory or space is made useless, unclean, or impure.

Content level: The information, ideas, or suggested actions that the speaker wishes to express in a message.

Content-oriented listening style: A listening style that highlights the desire to look for details and to analyze problems or situations.

Context: The physical, historical, and psychological communication environment.

Control: When you communicate to have others perform tasks for you, to tell others what to do, or to acquire things you need.

Conversational rituals: Routine scripts that we have learned to use when talking and responding to others.

Costs: Tangible or intangible investments or drawbacks associated with relationships, such as purchasing food, gifts, lending money, or doing things that you really don't want to.

Coworker relationships: Sometimes referred to as peer or collegial relationships, since you and your coworker(s) could have similar ranks in the organization. Coworker relationships may also include the relationships you have with people in positions that are similar to yours but at different companies.

Credentialed: Having the knowledge, skills, and training needed to make a researcher credible or believable.

Cultural time: A time focus that relies on cultural values to determine whether a group views time as technical, formal, informal, or displaced/diffused.

Culture: A learned system of knowledge, behavior, attitudes, beliefs, values, and norms that is shared by a group of people.

Cyberslacking: Using a computer for non-work-related activities while on the job.

Dark side of interpersonal communication: Research that is concerned with the dysfunctional, distorted, distressing, and destructive aspects of human action.

De-escalatory conflict spiral: A form of destructive conflict in which one person chooses to ignore another and to ignore the conflict altogether. The typical results are grudges, withdrawal from the relationship, and deteriorating interdependence.

Decoding: The process of interpreting and evaluating the other person's message.

Defense mechanisms: The four perceptual filters we use to alter or distort the intended meaning of the multiple messages we receive (selective exposure, selective attention, selective perception, and selective retention). They are used to keep our perceptions orderly and stable.

Deintensify: To give the impression that emotions are felt less strongly than they really are.

Denotative meaning: Interpretation of words in a literal manner, using a dictionary definition.

Depth: The level of intimacy or intensity of the information that is shared when self-disclosing on a topic.

Destructive conflict: A conflict orientation that is negatively focused on behaviors such as humiliation and shame. This view of conflict typically involves forcing or withdrawal.

Devil's advocate role: A role that is taken when someone criticizes or opposes something purely to provoke a discussion or argument.

Dialect: A regional variation in a language, including vocabulary and grammar.

Differentiating stage: The first coming apart stage, which deals with the struggles of maintaining your own identity while remaining part of a couple.

Differentiation: The first step of the phase model of conflict involves three stages: raise the conflict issue, clarify positions, and acknowledge severity of positional differences.

Direct verbal messages: Messages that immediately and explicitly make a request, ask a question, or state a comment using specific information, and leave no doubt as to the intended meaning.

Disconfirmation: This behavior involves the use of words that cause another person to feel inferior, unworthy of respect, and a nonperson.

Disinhibition effect: This occurs when certain contexts or circumstances cause individuals to feel little restraint during communication and choose to express themselves openly.

Displaced conflict: Type of interpersonal conflict in which the actual conflict issue fails to get discussed and perceptions of the actual issue are incorrect.

Display rules: Guidelines for when, where, and how to manage emotion displays that are appropriate for the culture or situation.

Dominance: One of the three dimensions of nonverbal immediacy with behaviors that exhibit status.

Downward communication: Messages that are typically sent from supervisors or others higher up in the organization to their employees.

Driver social style: Considered control specialists and are low on responsiveness and high on assertiveness.

Dual-career couples: Couples in which both partners are actively engaged in their respective careers.

Ectomorphs: A nonverbal code of body shape that depicts a person who is thin, skinny, or frail.

Emotion: A mental state that unfolds as a process, including a cause, appraisal, physiological response, expression, and regulation.

Emotional burnout: Emotional exhaustion resulting from the pressures of work and relationships.

Emotional contagion: An individual's tendency to express and feel emotions that are similar to and influenced by those of others.

Emotional expressiveness: A personal social style in which people accurately encode and convey emotional messages, primarily through the use of nonverbal signals.

Emotional intelligence: An individual's level of awareness of and sensitivity to emotions and ability to manage emotions to enhance relational development.

Empathy: The action of feeling what another person is feeling another's emotions rather than just recognizing them.

Encoding: The process of putting your thoughts and feelings into words and nonverbal cues.

Encroachment: A nonverbal behavior of invasion, violation, or contamination of one's territory.

Endomorphs: A nonverbal code of body shape that depicts a person who is soft, chubby, or fat.

Entropy: The chaos we feel when bombarded with perceptual stimuli.

Equilibrium theory: A theory that explains an inverse relationship between mutual eye gaze, intimacy, and space during social interactions.

Eros: A love style that is strongly driven by physical attraction, it is passionate, emotional and often associated with the phrase "love at first sight." Also known as passionate love.

Escalatory conflict spiral: This occurs when disconfirming messages are repeated during conflict until a full-fledged battle ensues.

Escape: When you communicate to avoid other activities and worries by communicating with someone.

Ethic: A belief, value, or moral principle by which one determines what is right and wrong.

Ethnocentric: An attitude that a particular culture and its cultural representations are superior to others.

Expectancy violation theory: A theory that is intended to explain our thoughts about the nonverbal communication we anticipate having with others.

Experimenting stage: The second coming together stage, which focuses on getting both parties to share more about themselves.

Expert power: Power associated with someone's knowledge or expertise on a topic (e.g., strong computer skills).

Expressive social style: Considered social specialists and are high on responsiveness and high on assertiveness.

External noise: A listening barrier that refers to any type of interference occurring outside of the individual's body.

Extraversion: A personality trait where people tend to be high-energy and action-oriented individuals who are receptive to exciting opportunities.

Extraversion personality trait: Refers to an individual's tendency to be high-energy, action oriented, and sociable.

False conflict: A type of interpersonal conflict that occurs because both parties involved misunderstand what it is that is creating the conflict or what the conflict topic actually is.

Feed-forward messages: Messages that inform others of how to process information.

Feedback: The receiver's response to a message.

Feeling: A conscious recognition of an emotion.

Forcing: A conflict management style that is aggressive and conflict is seen as a competition with power over others desired.

Formal verbal messages: Messages that recognize status differences and titles and in which language is used in its proper form.

Four Horsemen of the Apocalypse: Four behaviors among married couples that, according to Gottman's research, reveal that the relationship is doomed: criticizing, defensiveness, stonewalling, and contempt.

Fundamental attribution error: A perception problem that occurs when we determine that someone is behaving a certain way because of internal causes or personality factors inherent within them.

Gender: The cultural and psychological characteristics that are associated with being masculine and feminine that are learned or develop over time.

Grave dressing: Creating a public statement about the termination of your relationship to share with others.

Groupthink: A shared mindset bias that occurs when there is excessive cohesion and similarity between group members that limits the sharing of alternative perspectives.

Halo effect: A principle, common within the primacy effect, that occurs when individuals are judged favorably based upon a single positive characteristic.

Haptics: A nonverbal message type that is conveyed through touch.

Hearing: The physiological processing of sound waves.

Hedge: A statement that limits the speaker's responsibility and softens or weakens the meaning of the idea.

Helicopter parents: Label given to parents who "hover" over their children, often speaking on their children's behalf even though their children could be right next to them.

High-context cultures: Cultures in which nonverbal cues are extremely important in interpreting messages.

Hinting: An effort to provide clues to get someone to reach a particular conclusion or objective without intentionally sharing the information with them.

Homophily: This element of the interpersonal perception process that describes the degree to which we believe we are similar to someone.

Honest but hurtful (HBH) messages: Information that someone believes another person needs to know even if it may be painful to hear.

Horizontal communication: Messages exchanged between individuals who have similar rank and status.

Hostile work environment: A type of sexual harassment that is associated with undue and unwanted sexual advances or inappropriate verbal comments or nonverbal behaviors of a sexual nature that occur repeatedly.

Hurtful messages: Something that a person says or does that caused pain, anger, or disappointment for someone else.

Ideal self: What an individual strives to become.

Identity: A set of characteristics that an individual recognizes as belonging uniquely to him or her and to no one else.

Identity management: Also known as impression management, refers to the ways in which people try to control the impressions others have of them.

Implied friendship rules: Rules often applied in friendships that tend to be stated indirectly, if at all, such as standing up for each other, trusting each other, helping one another, criticizing only in private, keeping secrets, offering emotional support to each other, respecting one another's privacy, and not being jealous of one another.

Inclusion: When you communicate to be a member of a group, to be affiliated with others, or to have friends and companions.

Indirect verbal message: Messages that make a request, ask a question, or state a comment in an implicit, hidden or incomplete manner, allowing the context of the conversation to fill in the blanks.

Individualistic culture: A culture in which primary value is placed on the individual with a focus on self-reliance and personal achievement.

Informal verbal messages: Casual, overly familiar messages that don't always recognize the status difference in the relationship.

Information overload: A listening barrier that occurs when you are bombarded with an excessive number of messages.

Inhibit (emotional displays): To hide or fail to display an emotion an individual is feeling.

Initiating stage: The starting point for relationship development. It is the first coming together stage.

Integrating stage: The fourth coming together stage, which emphasizes you and your partner being perceived as a couple.

Intensifier: A word that is evaluative and emotive.

Intensify: To create the appearance that an emotion is felt more strongly than it really is.

Intensifying stage: The third coming together stage, which involves really getting to know the other person.

Interaction schemata: Our mental classification of people according to their social behaviors or how they interact with others (assertive, aggressive, etc.).

Interactive strategies: Uncertainty reduction strategies that are used in speaking or interacting directly with someone.

Intercultural communication: A process that occurs when individuals or groups from different cultures or co-cultural groups attempt to communicate.

Interpersonal communication: A transactional process that occurs when two people use verbal and nonverbal messages to create understanding and to influence each other to manage the relationship.

Interpersonal communication motives: Relatively stable personal characteristics that explain why people communicate with others and how people communicate to satisfy their needs.

Interpersonal deception theory: A theory that was developed to help explain why people lie and why they utilize nonverbal messages to do so.

Interpersonal perceptions: The process of observing the verbal and nonverbal communication of people around us and making sense of them through our own frame of reference.

Interpreting: The third stage of the perceptual process, in which we evaluate information and determine what it means to us and how we feel about it.

Intimacy: A type of attachment that arises from a close union, contact, association, or relationship. This attachment may occur in a variety of relationships.

Invasion: A territorial encroachment behavior that alters the territory's meaning.

Involvement: A level of organizational assimilation that includes demonstrating commitment and connection to the organization by volunteering for assignments or helping to come up with solutions to organizational problems.

Jealousy: An emotional state that is typically experienced when we feel insecure, fearful, or anxious at the thought of losing something or someone important to us, whether this is a friendship, family relationship, or relational partner.

Job competency: A dimension of organizational assimilation that examines employees' beliefs about whether they are able to perform tasks associated with their jobs in a satisfactory manner.

Key ideas: A listening strategy that is used to help identify the main issues in someone's messages.

Kinesics: A nonverbal message type that includes gestures, body movements, and facial expressions.

Lack of training: A listening barrier that occurs when individuals have not received any instruction or guidance in how to listen effectively.

Language: A system of symbols governed by rules that we use to stimulate meaning in the mind of others.

Latent conflict: A type of interpersonal conflict that fails to occur because individuals pretend that it does not exist. As a result, conflict fails to disappear and irritation grows.

Leakage hypothesis: A hypothesis that was developed to explain the small nonverbal signals that unconsciously escape or "leak out" of the body and, when grouped, provide very reliable indicators of lying.

Learned helplessness: A term that is used to explain a person's inclination to use stable or consistent/repetitive causes to explain why bad things happen to them.

Legitimate power: Power that is associated with someone's position or assigned rank and is seen as justified or appropriate on the basis of the position(s) held in the relationship (e.g., boss, parent).

Listening: The process of receiving, constructing meaning from, and responding to spoken and or nonverbal messages.

Listening gap: A listening barrier that involves the time lag we find when we compare the time it takes to process a message to the maximum potential we have to process inputs.

Listen to build and maintain relationships: A reason for listening that highlights our intent to get to know another person or to sustain existing relationships.

Listen to evaluate: A reason for listening that focuses on attempts to critically process what someone is saying.

Listen to help others: A reason for listening that is used when we hope to give others some form of assistance.

Listen to understand: A reason for listening that is applied when we are trying to comprehend the content of someone's message.

Low-context cultures: Cultures that rely more explicitly on language and the meanings of words and use fewer contextual cues to send and interpret information.

Ludus: A love style that does not involve pursuit of a particular mate but rather tends to be more in the moment, involving a series of affairs over time and/or simultaneously. Also known as playful love.

Lying and deception: Deliberate acts that individuals perform to mislead or misinform others to influence another person's perceptions or actions.

Mania: A love style that approaches love as an all-encompassing event and takes on an obsessive quality to it. Also known as possessive love.

Mask: To show one emotion while feeling a different emotion.

Mentor–protégé relationships: Relationships primarily found in the workplace in which a more advanced individual in the workplace assists a younger individual in his or her career.

Mesomorphs: A nonverbal code of body shape that describes someone who is lean, muscular, and athletic.

Misattributed conflict: A type of interpersonal conflict in which one or both parties involved in the conflict incorrectly blame another person, another situation, or another event rather than the actual cause of the conflict.

Monochronic: Behavior emphasizing punctuality, task organizing, and doing one thing at a time.

Multitasking: A listening barrier that involves trying to do several tasks at once.

Negatively valenced: A negative interpretation of a violated nonverbal expectation.

Networks: A relational maintenance strategy that emphasizes the importance of shared relationships outside of your relational dyad.

Neurocultural theory: A theory that contends that since all humans are born with the same neuromuscular structure, all humans must encode and decode emotions similarly.

Neuroticism: A personality trait where people tend to experience feelings of anxiety, anger, and depression.

Neuroticism personality trait: Refers to an individual's tendency to be emotionally reactive and to experience feelings of anxiety, anger, and depression.

Noise: Anything that distorts or interferes with the communication process.

Nonverbal immediacy: Behaviors that exhibit interest, attention, and closeness to others.

Nonverbal messages: Any messages other than verbal ones.

Norms of reciprocity: The expectation is that comparable behaviors or messages will be exchanged between individuals.

Office romances: Romantic relationships that develop between workers who are employed by the same company.

Online disinhibition effect: Getting people to share things about themselves online that they might not normally reveal in face-to-face relationships.

Openness: A personality trait where people tend to be intellectually curious, aware of their feelings, and tend to be imaginative and creative.

Openness strategy: A relational maintenance strategy that involves sharing your thoughts, feelings, and opinions with your relational partner.

Openness–closedness: A dialectical tension that is associated with being very receptive to sharing information or receiving information and being very restrictive to sharing information or receiving information.

Openness personality trait: Refers to an individual's tendency to be intellectually curious, have an appreciation for art, and be imaginative and creative.

Organizational assimilation: The interactive events that occur in the workplace that demonstrate how well there is mutual acceptance of new employees in their place of employment, as well as acceptance of new employees to and with the organization they work for.

Organizing: The second stage of the perceptual process, in which we find ways to make sense of the stimuli we have recognized.

Orienting response: The response from a violated nonverbal expectation that leads to a shift in attention from the conversation to the person in order to interpret or evaluate the unexpected behavior.

Other-expectations: The standards we set for others or how we believe others should behave in certain situations.

Overattribution: A perceptual attribution error that occurs when two or three traits are blamed for and used to explain all the negative experiences in someone's life.

Parallel conflict: A type of conflict in which the problem is evident and accurately understood by parties involved in the conflict.

Paraphrasing: a listening response that occurs when listeners try to assess whether or not they have accurately perceived speakers' messages.

Passive strategies: Unobtrusive uncertainty reduction strategies, such as watching or observing someone's actions.

Peer group influence: A reflection of the impact that an individual's friends and social group have on the individual's self-concept development.

Peer review: The process that occurs when an editor of an academic book or journal invites other equally qualified researchers to review a researcher's manuscript before the editor makes a decision to publish or reject the manuscript.

Peers: People who have status or power comparable to ours.

People-oriented listening style: A listening style that focuses on the relational factors that are present between a listener and speaker.

Perception: The process of observing things around us and making sense of them through our own frame of reference.

Personality: The total psychological makeup of an individual, a profile that reflects experiences, motivations, attitudes, beliefs, values, and behaviors.

Personality traits: Distinguishable and relatively enduring ways in which one individual differs from another.

Phonological rules: Rules that govern how words sound when spoken.

Physical appearance: A nonverbal code that sends a message of the "look" or physique that is more acceptable in a specific culture.

Physical schemata: Our mental classification of people we meet based on their physical appearance—related to our previous experiences.

Physical self-esteem: Self-evaluation regarding an individual's body image and attractiveness.

Physiological distractions: The type of listening barriers that occur when our bodies are tired, fatigued, hungry or otherwise preoccupied so that we listen less effectively.

Pleasure: One of the three dimensions of nonverbal immediacy with behaviors that exhibit liking.

Pleasure motive: When you communicate to be entertained.

Polychronic: A chronemic structure of time for individuals who have several things going on simultaneously and avoid rigid time structures.

Popular research: A form of secondary research, written for the nonacademic audience.

Positional power: Power that is associated with someone's rank or job title.

Positive violation valence: A positive interpretation of a violated nonverbal expectation.

Positivity: A relational maintenance strategy that emphasizes the importance of exchanging optimistic, friendly strategies with your relational partner.

Power: The capacity to influence another person to do something he or she would not have done without having been influenced.

Power needs: An individual's level of desire to be right and in control, depicted by three general roles: democrat, autocrat, and abdicrat.

Powerful language: Language that is characterized by assertiveness; stereotypically masculine.

Powerless language: Language that is characterized by an emphasis on relationship and connection; stereotypically feminine.

Pragma: A love style that takes a very practical approach to love. Basic characteristics needed in a mate are identified, with compatibility playing an important role in mate selection. Also known as practical love.

Pragmatic rules: Rules that govern how verbal messages should be interpreted in a given context.

Pragmatic self: A perception of self in which identity is flexible and adaptable to the situation and context.

Predictability–novelty: A dialectical tension that is associated with being very routine and consistent or very spontaneous and random.

Prejudice: Beliefs or behavior associated with positive or negative judgments of a specific group of people.

Preoccupation: A listening barrier that occurs when we focus on things other than the person we are listening to.

Primacy: A principle that enables us to make instant judgments about who someone is. They are the first impressions we create for others.

Primary research: A published work that comes directly from the author of the original research.

Principle of consistency: A principle created by scholar Leon Festinger that describes humans' strong desire to keep things, especially perceptions, basically the same.

Principled self: A perception of self in which identity is something that should not be altered or adapted to fit situations.

Private identity: The person you believe yourself to be in moments of honest self-examination.

Projection: Casting past relational failures or difficulties onto our present or future relational partners.

Prophecy: A prediction about a future event.

Providing a clear, organized message: A listening strategy that emphasizes the importance of offering a straightforward, easily understood message.

Providing new information: A listening strategy that is suggested to attract or keep others' attention, thus, increasing their likelihood of listening to us.

Proxemics: The nonverbal message type that focuses on the study of space.

Pseudolistening: Pretending to listen to someone; fake listening.

Psychological schemata: Our mental classification of people according to their personal dispositions and mental states (nervous, worried, etc.).

Psychological time: A time focus that relies on the value we assign to the past, present, and future.

Psychosocial functions: Aspects of mentoring relationships that enhance perceptions of competence or one's professional identity, often achieved by getting personalized feedback or reinforcement from others.

Public identity: The person you present yourself to be in public; the way you want others to view you.

Quid pro quo: A Latin phrase meaning "this for that." In the case of sexual harassment, quid pro quo would be requiring some type of sexual behavior in exchange for some type of work-related outcome.

Rapport talk: Language that focuses on sharing information about relationships.

Real self: An individual's honest assessment of his or her own current abilities.

Receiver: The person listening to the message.

Recency: A principle of the perception process in which we assign greater weight to the most current information we encounter in another person.

Recognition: A dimension of organizational assimilation that targets whether employees feel acknowledged by their superiors for their contributions to the organization.

Referent power: The characteristics an individual possesses that make you want to be more like them (e.g., kind, respectful, brave).

Reflected appraisals: The assessments an individual makes about him or herself based on the perception of how others see and behave toward that individual.

Relational affiliation: The degree to which individuals feel connected and close to their partners or disengaged and separate from their partners.

Relational dialectics theory: A theory that examines how partners manage relational tensions on three fundamental issues: connection versus autonomy, openness versus closedness, and predictability versus novelty.

Relational level: Focuses not on what is said, but on how it is said. Usually conveyed and interpreted through nonverbal communication, such as tone of voice, eye contact, and posture.

Relational power: The type of power someone has on the basis of personal relationships with others in the workplace.

Relationship-focused content: Focuses on information related to your personal backgrounds or interests. It could include sharing things about events occurring in your personal relationships as well as your hobbies or interests.

Relationships of choice: Relationships in which people voluntarily participate.

Relationships of circumstance: Relationships that are involuntary in nature; not freely chosen by individuals.

Relaxation: When you communicate to unwind, rest, or feel less tense.

Remembering: A listening stage that is focused on retaining information that has been gained from processing the message so that the listener can refer to it (and the outcome that was reached) at a later point in time.

Removing or limiting distractions: A listening strategy that encourages reducing the distractions that could hinder your ability to listen to someone.

Report talk: Language that focuses on sharing factual or statistical information.

Responding: A listening stage that looks at the type of reaction or feedback that individuals provide to a message.

Responsiveness: An individual's ability to be sensitive to the communication of others to be seen as a good listener, make others comfortable in a conversation, and recognize the needs and desires of others.

Reverse halo effect: A principle, common within the primacy effect, that occurs when individuals are judged negatively on the basis of a single negative characteristic. It is also often referred to as the *devil effect*.

Reward power: An individual's ability to give you things that you want or need (e.g., gifts, a raise, affection).

Rewards: Tangible or intangible benefits that are associated with relationships, such as food, gifts, money, spending time together, or sharing a favorite interest or pastime.

Rival: Individuals with whom we or others compare ourselves that tend to make us insecure, typically on the basis of features such as physical attractiveness or status cues.

Role negotiation: A dimension of organizational assimilation that focuses on interactions involving new employees with experienced coworkers in an effort to determine how a role should be performed in the workplace.

Role schemata: Our mental classification of the communication behaviors of individuals who fulfill specific roles or social positions.

Secondary research: A published work that summarizes and interprets original research done by others.

Secret keeper: A person who is told a secret by another person.

Selecting: The first stage of the perceptual process, in which we opt to focus on a specific stimulus in the environment and, consequently, tune out other stimuli.

Selecting: A listening stage in which choices about what auditory inputs to pay attention to and what auditory inputs to ignore occur.

Selective attention: A perceptual defense mechanism that occurs when we pay attention only to messages that reinforce our beliefs.

Selective exposure: A perceptual defense mechanism that occurs when we seek out and allow ourselves to only be exposed to messages that reinforce our existing attitudes and beliefs.

Selective perception: A perceptual defense mechanism that occurs when messages we receive are understood through our current frame of reference, sometimes to the point of changing the intent of the message.

Selective retention: A perceptual defense mechanism that occurs when we remember only those parts of the message that reinforce and are consistent with our beliefs.

Self-concept: The sum total of a person's knowledge and understanding of his- or herself.

Self-disclosure: Our willingness or intent to reveal information about ourselves to others that they would be unlikely to otherwise know.

Self-efficacy: An individual's assessment of his or her ability to perform in a certain manner and ability to reach his or her own goals.

Self-enhancing bias: An attribution error that occurs when a person takes credit for the success or the positive outcome that he or she experiences.

Self-esteem: A reflection of a person's overall self-appraisal of his or her own worth.

Self-expectations: The goals a person sets for himself or herself regarding how he or she ought to behave.

Self-fulfilling prophecy: The idea that what one believes about oneself often comes true because one expects it to come true.

Self-monitoring: An internal process of being aware of oneself and how one is coming across to others.

Self-perception: A person's assessment of his or her own abilities and talents.

Self-protecting bias: An attribution error that occurs when a person attempts to explain that the things that have gone wrong or have failed are out of his or her control.

Self-serving attribution bias: An attribution error that occurs when we select either internal or external factors to explain communication behaviors on the basis of what is in our best interest.

Semantic rules: Rules that govern the ways in which people assign meanings to words.

Sensation seeking: A personality characteristic that focuses on an individual's need for novelty, thrills, or adventure.

Setback: Something that reverses or delays an individual's progress in reaching his or her goal.

Sex: The biological characteristics that are present from the time of birth including the body's reproductive organs that identify a person as male or female.

Sexual harassment: Refers to any advances or behaviors of a sexual nature that are unwanted or desired by the receiver of the message(s).

Shared tasks: A relational maintenance strategy that focuses on messages that involve doing things together with your partner.

Signs: A natural representation that signals the presence of something else.

Silence: Intentionally waiting and reflecting on the message if you do not know what you want to say or share with another person or you feel that sharing this information will be problematic.

Similarity: When individuals have many things in common with us, ranging from shared demographics to shared physical characteristics, interests, and attitudes.

Simulate: To display an emotion an individual is not feeling.

Skills deficiency model of interspousal violence: A model that examines the argumentative skills of both marital partners to determine if their skill sets either provoke or diffuse potentially hostile exchanges.

Small talk: A brief, informal conversation about matters of little importance that allows people to relate to each other.

Social capital: How valuable an individual is perceived to be in terms of interpersonal connections.

Social comparison: The process or a person comparing himself or herself to others.

Social desirability bias: When we believe something about ourselves that others would find to be attractive or desirable, even if it may not be true.

Social intelligence: A sense of self-knowing that fosters competent perceptions and the ability to act wisely in human relationships.

Social penetration theory: A theory that explores what we self-disclose and the extent to which we self-disclose as our interpersonal relationships develop over time.

Social science: The systematic study of social life.

Social self-esteem: Self-evaluation regarding one's ability to interact and relate to others as well as the ability to develop and maintain friendships.

Social style: The patterns of communication behaviors that others observe when one interacts with them.

Socio-communicative orientation (SCO): How one perceive one's levels of responsiveness and assertiveness when communicating with others.

Source: The person who has a thought or a feeling and wants to express the idea and feeling to another person.

Stagnating stage: The third coming apart stage, in which the relationship has started to become routine, uneventful, and dull.

Staying focused: Working to limit or ignore outside distractions so that we will be better able to listen to others.

Stereotypes: The categories in which we place people on the basis of the groups to which the people belong. Stereotypes help us to make sense of the world and plan our communication with others.

Storge: A love style involving the belief that affection and commitment develop over time as individuals get to know one another. Also known as companionate love.

Superior–subordinate relationships: Dyadic relationships that incorporate hierarchical ranking in which one person in the organization reports to another.

Supervisor familiarity: A dimension of organizational assimilation that focuses on employees getting to know and getting better acquainted with their supervisors.

Symbol: An artificial representation of an idea or an object.

Syntactic rules: Rules that govern the grammar of a language, which is the system of rules by which words are formed and put together to form sentences.

Taboo topics: A conversational subject that is considered to be off limits by many people, so we err on the side of caution by discussing other subjects instead.

Tag question: A combination of a sentence and a question, treated as a single unit.

Talking less: A listening strategy that entails spending more time listening, or receiving messages from someone else.

Task-focused content: Emphasizes information tied to job duties or obligations. It highlights content necessary to complete your or others' work assignments.

Terminating stage: The fifth coming apart stage, which pertains to the ending of the relationship.

Territory: The space that we own or desire to own and protect.

Time-oriented listening style: A listening style that emphasizes the role of time management when communicating with others.

Touch avoidance: A trait that reflects your apprehension and personal like or dislike of touching or being touched by others.

Toxic disinhibition: Being rude, overly critical, angry, or threatening when communicating online. It also includes acts that may be perceived as more dark or inappropriate, such as going to websites that focus on crime, violence, or pornography.

Traits: Distinguishable ways in which one individual differs from others.

Trust: Relying upon or placing confidence in another person.

Truth bias: The tendency for people in close relationships to believe that their partners will not lie to them. The closer we are to a person, the less likely it is that we would assume or suspect that this person would lie to us.

Turning points: Events that transform relationships in some way and often serve as relational markers to help partners remember significant moments in their relationships.

Ultimate attribution error: A perception problem that is common when observed communication behaviors are negative and we decide that they are due to internal causes.

Uncertain verbal messages: Messages that are incomplete or vague and from which the listener cannot comfortably predict that something will happen.

Uncertainty avoidance: A measure of how accepting a culture is of a lack of predictability; a culture's level of tolerance for uncertainty and ambiguity.

Understanding: The process of making sense out of the message or sounds on which you have chosen to focus.

Unrequited love: A passionate love for another person that is not reciprocated.

Upward communication: Messages that employees send up to their supervisors or others higher up in the organization.

Verbal aggression: The tendency to attack the self-concept of another person instead of, or in addition to, attacking the other person's arguments.

Verbal messages: A system of symbols governed by rules that we use to stimulate meaning in the minds of others; the words and language that we use to communicate with others.

Verbal message style: The way in which an individual uses language to communicate.

Violation: A form of encroachment where someone's territory is taken or used without permission.

Vocalics: The sounds of the voice, often referred to as paralanguage, including speaking rate, volume, pitch, etc.

Withdrawal: A conflict management style in which one party is physically and psychologically removed from the conflict, indicating little concern for the goals of either party.

Worker–customer/client relationships: Relationships that occur between a service provider and a customer.

Work–life balance: Refers to how and why individuals make the choices they do when trying to satisfy their professional and personal needs and obligations, as well as what these choices are.

Workplace bullying: Intentionally negative communication behaviors that are not welcomed or desired; occur repeatedly; escalate over an extended period of time; and are potentially harmful physically, psychologically, or emotionally to the target of the behaviors.

References

Chapter 1

[1] This idea is attributed to Dr. Jim McCroskey. When teaching undergraduate students at West Virginia University, Dr. McCroskey used this simple equation to illustrate the difference between communication and miscommunication.

[2] Watzlawick, P., Bavelas, J. B., & Jackson, D. D. (1967). *Pragmatics of human communication*. New York: Norton & Company.

[3] Condit, C. M. (2000). Culture and biology in human communication: Toward a multi-causal model. *Communication Education, 49*, 7–24; Beatty, M. J., & McCroskey, J. C. (2000). A few comments about communibiology and the nature/nurture question. *Communication Education, 49*, 25–28.

[4] Daly, J. A., & Bippus, A. M. (1998). Personality and interpersonal communication: Issues and directions. In J. C. McCroskey, J. A. Daly, M. M. Martin, & M. J. Beatty (Eds.) *Communication and personality: Trait perspectives* (pp. 1–40). Cresskill, NJ: Hampton Press.

[5] Beatty, M. J., McCroskey, J. C., w/ Valencic, K. M. (2001). *The biology of communication: A communibiological perspective*. Cresskill, NJ: Hampton Press.

[6] Beatty, M. J., Heisel, A., Hall, A., Levine, T., & LaFrance, B. (2002). What can we learn from the study of twins about genetic and environmental influences on interpersonal affiliation, aggressiveness, and social anxiety?: A meta-analytic study. *Communication Monographs, 69*, 1–18; Beatty, M. J., McCroskey, J. C., & Heisel, A. (1998). Communication apprehension as temperamental expression: A communibiological paradigm. *Communication Monographs, 65*, 197–219.

[7] Beatty, M. J., McCroskey, J. C., w/ Valencic, K. M. (2001). *The biology of communication: A communibiological perspective*. Cresskill, NJ: Hampton Press.

[8] Smith, A. G. (Ed.) (1966). *Communication and culture*. New York: Rinehart &Winston.

[9] Condit, C. M. (2000). Culture and biology in human communication: Toward a multi-causal model. *Communication Education, 49*, 7–24.

[10] Floyd, K., & Morman, M. T. (2000). Affection received from fathers as a predictor of men's affection with their own sons: Tests of the modeling and compensation hypotheses. *Communication Monographs, 67*, 347–361.

[11] *Behavior matters: Communication research and human connections*. (2002). Washington, DC: National Communication Association; Ayres, J. (1988). Loneliness and interpersonal communication patterns. *Journal of the Northwest Communication Association, 16*, 39–60; Duran, R. L. (1992). Communication adaptability: A review of conceptualization and measurement. *Communication Quarterly, 40*, 253–268.

[12] Wilson, C. M., & Oswald, A. J. (2005, May). *How does marriage affect physical and psychological health? A survey of the longitudinal evidence*. IZA Discussion Paper Series No. 1619. Bonn Germany: The Institute for the Study of Labor.

[13] Burleson, B. R., Delia, J. G., & Applegate, J. L. (1995). The socialization of person-centered communication: Parental contributions to the social-cognitive and communication skills of their children. In M. A. Fitzpatrick & A. L. Vangelisti (Eds.), *Explaining family interactions* (pp. 34–76). Thousand Oaks, CA: Sage.

[14] Noveck, J., & Tompson, T. (2007, August 20). Poll: Family ties key to youth happiness. The Associated Press. Reported in *The Washington Post* and retrieved on November 9, 2008, from http://www.washingtonpost.com/wp-dyn/content/article/2007/08/20/AR2007082000451.html

[15] Muris, P., Meesters, C., van Melick, M., & Swambag, L. (2001). Self-reported attachment style, attachment quality, and symptoms of anxiety and depression in young adolescents. *Personality and Individual Differences, 30*, 809–818.

[16] Ohlemacher, S. White Americans no longer a majority by 2042. Retrieved on August 14, 2008, from http://abcnews.go.com/Politics/wireStory?id=5575766.

[17] DiMeglio, F. (2007, August 14). New role for business school research. *Business Week Online*.

[18] DiMeglio, F. (2007, August 14). New role for business school research. *Business Week Online*.

[19] Watzlawick, P., Bavelas, J. B., & Jackson, D. D. (1967). *Pragmatics of human communication*. New York: Norton & Company.

[20] Funder, D. C. (2006). *The personality puzzle* (4th ed.). New York: W. W. Norton & Company.

[21] Guilford, J. P. (1959). *Personality*. New York: McGraw-Hill.

[22] McCrae, R. R., & Costa, P. T., Jr. (1987). Validation of the five-factor model of personality across instruments and observers. *Journal of Personality and Social Psychology, 52*, 81–90.

[23] Funder, D. C. (2006). *The personality puzzle* (4th ed.). New York: W. W. Norton & Company; Golsing, S. D., Rentfrow, P. J., & Swann, W. B. (2003). A very brief measure of the big-five personality domains. *Journal of Research in Personality, 37*, 504–528; Goldberg, L. R. (1990). An alternative "description of personality": The big-five factor structure. *Journal of Personality and Social Psychology, 59*, 1216–1229; McCroskey, J. C., Daly, J. A., Martin, M. M., & Beatty, M. J. (Eds.). (1998). *Communication and personality: Trait perspectives*. Cresskill, NJ: Hampton Press.

[24] McCroskey, J. C., & Beatty, M. J. (1998). Communication apprehension. In J. C. McCroskey, J. A. Daly, M. M. Martin, and M. J. Beatty (Eds.), *Communication and personality: Trait perspectives* (refer to discussion on pp. 219–220). Cresskill, NJ: Hampton Press.

[25] Funder, D. C. (2006). *The personality puzzle* (4th ed.). New York: W. W. Norton & Company.

[26] Christie, R., & Geis, F. L. (1970). *Studies in Machiavellianism* (p. 312). New York: Academic Press.

[27] Christie, R., & Geis, F. L. (1970). *Studies in Machiavellianism.* New York: Academic Press.

[28] McIlwain, D. (2003). Bypassing empathy: A Machiavellian theory of mind and sneaky power. In B. Repacholi & V. Slaughter (Eds.), *Individual differences in theory of mind: Implications for typical and atypical development* (pp. 39–66). New York: Psychology Press.

[29] Walter, H. L., Anderson, C. M., & Martin, M. M. (2005). How subordinates' Machiavellianism and motives related to satisfaction with superiors. *Communication Quarterly, 53,* 57–70.

[30] Beatty, M. J., McCroskey, J. C., & Floyd, K. (Eds.). (2009). *Biological dimensions of communication: Perspectives research and methods.* Cresskill, NJ: Hampton Press.; Beatty, M. J., McCroskey, J. C., & Valencic, K. M. (2001). *The biology of communication: A communibiological perspective.* Cresskill, NJ: Hampton Press.

[31] Beatty, M. J., McCroskey, J. C., & Valencic, K. M. (2001). *The biology of communication: A communibiological perspective.* Cresskill, NJ: Hampton Press; Beatty, M. J., McCroskey, J. C., & Pence, M. E. (2009). Communibiological paradigm. In Beatty, M. J., McCroskey, J. C., & Floyd, K. (Eds.), *Biological dimensions of communication: Perspectives, research, and methods* (pp. 3–32). Cresskill, NJ: Hampton Press.

[32] Beatty, M. J., McCroskey, J. C., & Valencic, K. M. (2001). *The biology of communication: A communibiological perspective.* Cresskill, NJ: Hampton Press.

[33] This story is an illustration that is supported by a number of empirical studies: Valencic, K. M., Beatty, M. J., Rudd, J. E., Dobos, J. A., & Heisel, A. D. (1998). An empirical test of a communibiological model of trait verbal aggressiveness. *Communication Quarterly, 46,* 327–341; McCroskey, J. C., & Heisel, A. D. (1998). Communication apprehension as temperamental expression: A communibiological paradigm. *Communication Monographs, 65,* 197–220; McCroskey, J. C., Richmond, V. P., Heisel, A. D., & Hayhurst, J. L. (2004). Eysenk's big three and communication traits: Communication traits as manifestations of temperament. *Communication Research Reports, 21,* 404–410.

[34] McCroskey, J. C., & Richmond, V. P. (1993). Identifying compulsive communicators: The talkaholic scale. *Communication Research Reports, 10,* 107–114; Bostrom, R. N., & Harrington, N. G. (1999). An exploratory investigation of characteristics of compulsive talkers. *Communication Education, 48,* 73–80.

[35] Beatty, M. J., McCroskey, J. C., & Valencic, K. M. (2001). *The biology of communication: A communibiological perspective.* Cresskill, NJ: Hampton Press; Valencic, K. M., Beatty, M. J., Rudd, J. E., Dobos, J. A., & Heisel, A. D. (1998). An empirical test of a communibiological model of trait verbal aggressiveness. *Communication Quarterly, 46,* 327–341.

[36] Begley, S. (2007). *Train your mind, change your brain.* New York: Ballantine Books.

[37] Valencic, K. M., Beatty, M. J., Rudd, J. E., Dobos, J. A., & Heisel, A. D. (1998). An empirical test of a communibiological model of trait verbal aggressiveness. *Communication Quarterly, 46,* 327–341; Beatty, M. J., McCroskey, J. C., & Heisel, A. D. (1998). Communication apprehension as temperamental expression: A communibiological paradigm. *Communication Monographs, 65,* 197–219.

[38] Hane, A. A., & Fox, N. A. (2006). Ordinary variations in maternal caregiving influence human infants' stress reactivity. *Psychological Science, 17,* 550–556.

[39] Fries, A. B., Ziegler, T. E., Kurian, J. R., Jacoris, S., & Pollak, S. D. (2005, November). Early experience in humans is associated with changes in neuropeptides critical for regulating social behavior. *Proceedings of the National Academy of Sciences, 102,* 17237–17240.

[40] Rubin, R. B., Perse, E. M., & Barbato, C. A. (1988). Conceptualization and measurement of interpersonal communication motives. *Human Communication Research, 14,* 602–628; Paulsel, M. L., & Mottet, T. P. (2004). Interpersonal communication motives: A communibiological perspective. *Communication Quarterly, 52,* 182–195.

[41] Rubin, R. B., Perse, E. M., & Barbato, C. A. (1988). Conceptualization and measurement of interpersonal communication motives. *Human Communication Research, 14,* 602–628.

[42] Rubin, R. B., Perse, E. M., & Barbato, C. A. (1988). Conceptualization and measurement of interpersonal communication motives. *Human Communication Research, 14,* 602–628.

[43] Burleson, B. R., & Caplan, S. C. (1998). Cognitive complexity. In J. C. McCroskey, J. A. Daly, M. M. Martin, & M. J. Beatty (Eds.), *Communication and personality: Trait perspectives* (pp. 233–286). Cresskill, NJ: Hampton Press.

[44] Osborn, J. (2005, May). *Predicting need fulfillment and satisfaction in romantic relationships: Defining and testing interpersonal need compatibility.* Paper presented at the annual meeting of the International Communication Association, New York.

[45] Ling, C., & Cegala, D. J. (1994). Topic management, shared knowledge, and accommodation: A study of communication adaptability. *Research on Language and Social Interaction, 27,* 389–418; Rubin, R. B., & Martin, M. M. (1994). Development of a measure of interpersonal communication competence. *Communication Research Reports, 11,* 33–44.

[46] Tannen, D. (1990). *You just don't understand: Women and men in conversation.* New York: Morrow; Tannen, D. (2003). The relativity of linguistic strategies: Rethinking power and solidarity in gender dominance. In C. B. Paulston, & G. R. Tucker (Eds.), *Sociolinguistics: The essential readings* (pp. 208–219). Hoboken, NJ: Wiley-Blackwell.

[47] Gray, J. (2004). *Men are from mars, women are from venus: The classic guide to understanding the opposite sex.* New York: Harper.

[48] Canary, D. J. & Dindia K. (Eds.). (1998). *Sex differences and similarities in communication: Critical essays and empirical investi-*

gations of sex and gender in interaction. Mahwah, NJ: Lawrence Erlbaum Associates; see also La France, B. H., Henningsen, D. D., Oates, B., & Shaw, C. M. (2009). Social-sexual interactions? Meta-analyses of sex differences in perceptions of flirtatiousness, seductiveness, and promiscuousness. *Communication Monographs, 76*, 263–285.

49 Timmerman, L. M. (2002). Comparing the production of power in language on the basis of sex. In M. Allen, R. W. Preiss, B. M. Gayle, & N. Burrell (Eds.), *Interpersonal communication research: Advances through meta-analysis* (pp. 73–88), Mahwah, NJ: Lawrence Erlbaum; Wood, J. T. (2010). Gendered lives: Communication, gender, and culture. New York: Wadsworth.

50 Smith, A. G. (Ed.). (1966) *Communication and culture*. New York: Rinehart & Winston.

51 Leap, W. L. & Boellstorff, T. D. (2004). *Speaking in queer tongues: Globalization and gay language*. Urbana: University of Illinois Press.

52 *Let's talk annual cell phone etiquette survey: More people find cell phone use in cars and supermarkets acceptable*. Retrieved on January 7, 2009, from http://www.letstalk.com/company/release_031406.htm; Haig, M. (2002). *Mobile marketing: The message revolution*. London: Kogan Page Ltd.; Reid, D., & Reid, F. (2004). *Insights into the social and psychological effects of SMS text messaging*. Retrieved on September 27, 2008, from www.160characters.org/documents/SocialEffectsOfTextMessaging.pdf.

53 Ellison, N. B., Steinfield, C., & Lampe, C. (2007). The benefits of Facebook "friends": Social capital and college students' use of online social network sites. *Journal of Computer-Mediated Communication, 12*, 1143–1168.

54 Adapted from Lipscomb, T. J., Totten, J. W., Cook, R. A., & Lesch, W. (2005). Cellular phone etiquette among college students. *International Journal of Consumer Studies, 31*, 46–56; Wel, R., & Leung, L. (1999). Blurring public and private behaviors in public space: Policy challenges in the use and improper use of the cell phone. *Telematics and informatics, 16, 11–26. Let's talk announces cell phone etiquette guidelines based on 6 years of etiquette research*. Retrieved on January 7, 2009, from http://www6.letstalk.com/company/release_031406.htm.

55 Adapted from Miller, C. A. (2004) *Communications of the ACM-Special Issue: Human-computer etiquette, 47*, 30–61.

56 Adapted from Miller, C. A. (2004) *Communications of the ACM-Special Issue: Human-computer etiquette, 47*, 30–61.

57 Rosen, C. (Fall 2004/Winter 2005). The age of egocasting. *The New Atlantis: Journal of Technology and Society*. Retrieved on January 14, 2009, from www.thenewatlantis.com; Crane, R. M. (2005). Social distance and loneliness as they relate to headphones used with portable audio technology. Retrieved on January 14, 2009, from http://hdl.handle.net/2148/28.

Chapter 2

1 Hamachek, D. E., (1978). *Encounters with the self* (2nd ed.). New York: Holt, Rinehart, and Winston; this description of self-concept was also influenced by James, W. (1890). *Principles of psychology*. New York: Henry Holt and Company.

2 James, W. (1890). *The principles of psychology* (Vol. 1). Cambridge, MA: Harvard University Press.

3 Rosenberg, M. (1965). *Society and the adolescent self-image*. Princeton, NJ: Princeton University Press.

4 Rosenberg, M. (1972). *Society and the adolescent self-image* (p. 5). Princeton, NJ: Princeton University Press.

5 Markus, H., & Wurf, E. (1987). The dynamic self-concept: A social psychological perspective. *Annual Review of Psychology, 38*, 299–337.

6 Markus, H., & Wurf, E. (1987). The dynamic self-concept: A social psychological perspective. *Annual Review of Psychology, 38*, 299–337.

7 Bandura, A. (2001). Social cognitive theory: An agentic perspective. *Annual Review of Psychology, 52*, 1–26.

8 Taylor, S. E., Wood, J. V., & Lichtman, R. R. (1983). It could be worse: Selective evaluation as a response to victimization. *Journal of Social Issues, 39*, 19–40.

9 Harris, J. R. (2007). *No two alike: Human nature and human individuality*. New York: W. W. Norton; also refer to Harris, J. R., & Pinker, S. (1999). *The nurture assumption: Why children turn out the way they do*. New York: Free Press.

10 Harris, J. R., & Pinker, S. (1999). *The nurture assumption: Why children turn out the way they do*. New York: Free Press.

11 Cooley, C. H. (1912). *Human nature and the social order*. New York: Scribner's.

12 Swann, W. B., Jr., & Read, S. J. (1981). Self-verification processes: How we sustain our self-conceptions. *Journal of Experimental Social Psychology, 17*, 351–372; Hardy, L., & Moriarty, T. (2006). Shaping self-concept: The elusive importance effect. *Journal of Personality, 74*, 377–402.

13 Savin-Williams, R. C., & Demo, P. (1983). Situational and transitional determinants of adolescent self-feelings. *Journal of Personality and Social Psychology, 44*, 820–840.

14 Markus, H., & Kunda, Z. (1986). Stability and malleability of the self-concept. *Journal of Personality and Social Psychology, 51*, 858–866.

15 Cooper, B. S. (2007). The politics of homeschooling. *Educational Policy, 21*, 110–131.

16 Scharrer, E. (2005). Hypermasculinity, aggression, and television violence: An experiment. *Media Psychology, 7*, 353–376; Klein, J. (2006). An invisible problem: Everyday violence against girls in schools. *Theoretical Criminology, 10*, 147–177; Swann, W. B., Jr., & Read, S. J. (1981). Self-verification processes: How we sustain our self-conceptions. *Journal of Experimental Social Psychology, 17*, 351–372.

17 Markus, H., & Cross, S. (1990). The interpersonal self. In L. A. Pervin (Ed.), *Handbook of personality* (pp. 576–608). New York: Guilford Press; see also Markus, H. R., Chen, S., Boucher, H. C., & Tapias, M. P. (2006). The relational self revealed: Integrative conceptualization and implications for interpersonal life. *Psychological Bulletin, 132*, 151–179.

18 Kelly, G. A. (1963). *A theory of personality: The psychology of personal constructs*. New York: W. W. Norton.

19 This example was developed after reading Jandt, F. E., & Darsey, J. (1981). Coming out as a communicative process. In J. W. Chesebro (Ed.), *Gayspeak: Gay male and lesbian communication* (pp. 12–27). New York: Pilgrim Press.

[20] Goffman, E. (1963). *Stigma: Notes on the management of spoiled identity.* Englewood Cliffs, NJ: Prentice-Hall.

[21] Rill, L., Baiocchi, E., Hopper, M., Denker, K., & Olson, L. N. (2009). Exploration of the relationship between self-esteem, commitment, and verbal aggressiveness in romantic dating relationships. *Communication Reports, 22,* 102–113.

[22] Neiss, M. B., Sedikides, C., & Stevenson, J. (2006). Genetic influences on level and stability of self-esteem. *Self and Identity, 5,* 247–266.

[23] Sahlstein, E., & Allen, M. (2002). Sex differences in self-esteem: A meta-analytic assessment. In M. Allen, R. W. Preiss, B. M. Gayle, & N. Burrell (Eds.), *Interpersonal communication research: Advances through meta-analysis* (pp. 59–72). Mahwah, NJ: Lawrence Erlbaum. See also Birndor, S., Ryan, S., Auinger, P., & Aten, M. (2005). High self-esteem among adolescents: Longitudinal trends, sex differences, and protective factors. *The Journal of Allergy and Clinical Immunology, 37,* 194–201.

[24] Neiss, M. B., Sedikides, C., & Stevenson, J. (2006). Genetic influences on level and stability of self-esteem. *Self and Identity, 5,* 247–266; Roy, M. A., Neale, M. C., & Kendler, K. S. (1995). The genetic epidemiology of self-esteem. *The British Journal of Psychiatry, 166,* 813–820; Kendler, K. S., Gardner, C. O., & Prescott, C. A. (1998). A population-based twin study of self-esteem and gender. *Psychological Medicine, 28,* 1403–1409.

[25] Garber, J. & Flynn, C. (2001). Predictors of depressive cognitions in young adolescents. *Cognitive Theory and Research, 25,* 353–376.

[26] Mann, M., Clemens, M. H., Schaalma, H. P., & de Vries, N. K. (2004). Self-esteem in a broad-spectrum approach for mental health promotion. *Health Education Research, 19,* 357–372; Garber, J., & Flynn, C. (2001). Predictors of depressive cognitions in young adolescents. *Cognitive Theory and Research, 25,* 353–376.

[27] Sadker, M., & Sadker, D. (1994). *Failing at fairness: How America's schools cheat girls.* New York: Simon & Schuster; see also Sadker, D., Sadker, M., & Zittelman, K. R. (2009). *Still failing at fairness: How gender bias cheats girls and boys in school and what we can do about it.* New York: Simon & Schuster.

[28] Sax, L. (2007). *Boys adrift: The five factors driving the growing epidemic of unmotivated boys and underachieving young men.* New York: Basic Books; Sommers, C. H. (2001). *The war against boys.* New York: Simon & Schuster.

[29] McCroskey, J. C., & McCroskey, L. L. (1988). Self-report as an approach to measuring communication competence. *Communication Research Reports, 5,* 108–113.

[30] Richmond, V. P., McCroskey, J. C., & McCroskey, L. L. (1989). An investigation on self-perceived communication competence and personality orientations. *Communication Research Reports, 6,* 28–36.

[31] Merton, R. K. (1968). *Social theory and social structure.* New York: Free Press.

[32] Downey, G., Freitas, A. L., Michaelis, B., & Khouri, H. (2004). The self-fulfilling prophecy in close relationships: Rejection sensitivity and rejection by romantic partners. In H. T. Reis & C. E. Rusbult (Eds.), *Close relationships* (pp. 435–455). New York: Psychology Press.

[33] Goss, B. (1995). *The psychology of human communication* (2nd ed.). Prospect Heights, IL: Waveland Press.

[34] Walker, C. O., Greene, B. A., & Mansell, R. A. (2005). Identification with academics, intrinsic/extrinsic motivation, and self-efficacy as predictors of cognitive engagement. *Learning and Individual Differences, 16,* 1–12.

[35] Shimotsu, S. (2008). *The relationships between student self-reported perfectionism, communication apprehension, temperament, and learning outcomes.* Unpublished master's thesis, University of Texas-Pan American, Edinburg, Texas; Hill, R. W., & Zrull, M. C. (1997). Perfectionism and interpersonal problems. *Journal of Personality Assessment, 69,* 81–103.

[36] Brophy, J. E., & Good, T. L. (1974). *Teacher-student relationships: Causes and consequences.* New York: Holt, Rinehart, & Winston.

[37] Edwards, R., & Pledger, L. (1990). Development and construct validation of the sensitivity to feedback scale. *Communication Research Reports, 7,* 83–89.

[38] Gass, R. H., & Seiter, J. S. (2006). *Persuasion: Social influence and compliance gaining* (3rd ed.). Boston: Allyn and Bacon.

[39] Mann, M., Clemens, M. H., Schaalma, H. P., & de Vries, N. K. (2004). Self-esteem in a broad-spectrum approach for mental health promotion. *Health Education Research, 19,* 357–372.

[40] Mottet, T. P., & Thweatt, K. S. (1997). The relationships between peer teasing, self-esteem, and affect for school. *Communication Research Reports, 14,* 1–8; Hay, I., Ashman, A. F., & van Kraayenoord, C. E. (1998). Educational characteristics of students with high or low self-concept. *Psychology in the Schools, 35,* 391–400.

[41] Bandura, A. (1977). *Social learning theory.* Englewood Cliffs, NJ: Prentice-Hall.

[42] Ellis, A., Abrams, M., & Abrams, L. (2008). *Theories of personality.* New York: Sage Press.

[43] For example: Glasser, W. (1999). *Choice theory.* New York: HarperCollins; Ledley, D. R., Marx, B. P., & Heimberg, R. G. (2005). *Making cognitive-behavioral therapy work: Clinical process for new practitioners.* New York: Guilford Press; Neenan, M. (2002). *Life coaching: A cognitive behavioural approach.* New York: Routledge.

[44] Shimotsu, S., & Mottet, T. P. (2009). The relationships among perfectionism, communication apprehension, and temperament. *Communication Research Reports, 26,* 188–197.

[45] Adapted from Schiraldi, G. R. (2001). *The self-esteem workbook.* Oakland, CA: New Harbinger Publications.

[46] Infante, D. A., Rancer, A. S., & Womack, D. F. (2003). *Building communication theory* (4th ed.). Prospect Heights, IL: Waveland Press.

[47] Beatty, M. J., McCroskey, J. C., & Floyd, K. (2009). *Biological dimensions of communication: Perspectives, research, and methods.* Cresskill, NJ: Hampton Press; McCroskey, J. C., Daly, J. A., Martin, M., & Beatty, M. J. (Eds.) (1998). *Communication and personality: Trait perspectives.* Cresskill, NJ: Hampton Press.

[48] McCroskey, J. C. (1978). Validity of the PRCA as an index of oral communication apprehension. *Communication Monographs, 45,* 192–203.

[49] From Richmond, V. P., & McCroskey, J. C. (1998). *Communication: Apprehension, avoidance, and effectiveness.* (5th ed.). Boston: Allyn and Bacon.

[50] McCroskey, J. C. ,& Beatty, M. J. (1998). Communication apprehension. In J. C. McCroskey, J. A. Daly, M. M. Martin, & M. J. Beatty (Eds.), *Communication and personality: Trait perspectives,* (pp. 215–231). Cresskill, NJ: Hampton Press.

[51] Lippert, L., Titsworth, B. S., & Hunt, S. K. (2005). The ecology of academic risk: Relationships between communication apprehension, verbal aggression, supportive communication, and students' academic risk status. *Communication Studies, 56,* 1–21; Limon, M. S., & France, B. H. (2005). Communication traits and leadership emergence: Examining the impact of argumentativeness, communication apprehension, and verbal aggressiveness in work groups. *Southern Communication Journal, 70,* 123–133; Wheeless, L. R., & Parsons, L. A. (1995). What you feel is what you might get: Exploring communication apprehension and sexual communication satisfaction. *Communication Research Reports, 12,* 39–45; Kim, M., & Storm, R. (2000). A test of a cultural model of patients' motivation for verbal communication in patient-doctor interactions. *Communication Monographs, 67,* 262–284; Lucchetti, A., Powers, W. G., & Love, D. E. (2002). The empirical development of the child-parent communication apprehension scale for use with young adults. *Journal of Family Communication, 2,* 109–131.

[52] Discussed on pages 67–78 in Richmond, V. P., & McCroskey, J. C. (1998). *Communication: Apprehension, avoidance, and effectiveness.* (5th ed.). Boston: Allyn and Bacon.

[53] Schwartz, C. E., Wright, C. I., Shin, L. M., Kagan, J., & Rauch, S. L. (2003). Inhibited and uninhibited infants grown up: Adult amygdala response to novelty. *Science, 300,* 1952–1953.

[54] Beatty, M. J., & Friedland, M. H. (1990). Public speaking state anxiety as a function of selected situational and dispositional variables. *Communication Education, 39,* 142–147.

[55] McCroskey, J. C., & Beatty, M. J. (2000). The communibiological perspective: Implications for communication in instruction. *Communication Education, 49,* 1–6.

[56] Kelly, L., & Keaten, J. A. (2000). Treating communication anxiety: Implications of the communibiological paradigm. *Communication Education, 49,* 45–57.

[57] Ayers, J., & Hopf, T. S. (1985). Visualization: A means of reducing speech anxiety. *Communication Education, 34,* 318–323; Ayres, J., & Heuett, B. L. (1999). An examination of the impact of performance visualization. *Communication Research Reports, 16,* 29–39.

[58] Kelly, L., & Keaten, J. A. (2000). Treating communication anxiety: Implications of the communibiological paradigm. *Communication Education, 49,* 45–57.

[59] Brown, B. L., Shwalb, D. A., Godfrey, K., & Larcher, A. M. (2007). The efficacy of selective serotonin reuptake inhibitors in adult social anxiety disorder: A meta-analysis of double blind, placebo-controlled trials. *Journal of Psychopharmacology, 21,* 102–111.

[60] Richmond, V. P., & McCroskey, J. C. (1998). *Communications: Apprehension, avoidance, and effectiveness.* (5th ed.). Boston: Allyn and Bacon.

[61] Richmond, V. P., & McCroskey, J. C. (1998). *Communication: Apprehension, avoidance, and effectiveness* (5th ed.). Boston: Allyn and Bacon.

[62] Richmond, V. P., & McCroskey, J. C. (1998). *Communication: Apprehension, avoidance, and effectiveness* (5th ed.). Boston: Allyn and Bacon.

[63] Modified from Richmond, V. P., & McCroskey, J. C. (1992). *Organizational communication for survival.* Englewood Cliffs, NJ: Prentice Hall. See also Thomas, K. W., & Kilmann, R. M. (1974). *Thomas-Kilmann conflict mode instrument.* Tuxedo, NY: Xicom.

[64] Richmond, V. P., & McCroskey J. C. (1992). *Organizational communication for survival.* Englewood Cliffs, NJ: Prentice Hall. See also Thomas, K. W., & Kilmann, R. M. (1974). *Thomas-Kilmann conflict mode instrument.* Tuxedo, NY: Xicom.

[65] Adapted from Bolton, R., & Grover-Bolton, D. (2009). *People styles at work: Making bad relationships good and good relationships better.* New York: American Management Association.

[66] Rosenfeld, P. (1997). Impression management, fairness, and the employment interview, *Journal of Business Ethics, 16,* 801–808.

[67] Schlenker, B. R., & Pontari, B. A. (2000). The strategic control of information: Impression management and self-presentation in daily life. In A. Tesser, R. Felson, & J. Suls (Eds.), *Perspectives on self and identity* (pp. 199–232). Washington, DC: American Psychological Association.

[68] Ellison, N., Heino, R., & Gibbs, J. (2006). Managing impressions online: Self-presentation processes in the online dating environment. *Journal of Computer-Mediated Communication, 11,* 415–441.

[69] Ellison, N., Heino, R., & Gibbs, J. (2006). Managing impressions online: Self-presentation processes in the online dating environment. *Journal of Computer-Mediated Communication, 11,* 415–441.

[70] Vilela, B. B., Gonzalez, J. A., Ferrin, P. F., & del Rio Araujo, M. L. (2007). Impression management strategies and affective context: Influence on sales performance appraisal. *European Journal of Marketing, 5/6,* 624–639.

[71] Schlenker, B. R., & Pontari, B. A. (2000). The strategic control of information: Impression management and self-presentation in daily life. In A. Tesser, R. Felson, & J. Suls (Eds.), *Perspectives on self and identity* (pp. 199–232). Washington, DC: American Psychological Association.

[72] Goffman, E. (1959). *The presentation of self in everyday life.* New York: Anchor Books.

[73] Goffman, E. (1959). *The presentation of self in everyday life.* New York: Anchor Books.

[74] Snyder, M., & Campbell, B. H. (1982). Self-monitoring: The self in action. In J. Suls (Ed.), *Psychological perspectives on the self* (Vol. 1. pp. 185–230). Hillsdale, NJ: Lawrence Erlbaum.

[75] Gifford, R., Ng, C. F., & Wilkinson, M. (1985). Nonverbal cues in the employment interview: Links between applicant qualities and interviewer judgments, *Journal of Applied Psychology, 70,* 729–736.

[76] From p. 528 of Snyder, M. (1974). Self-monitoring of expressive behavior. *Journal of Personality and Social Psychology, 30,* 526–537.

[77] Gangestad, S. W., & Snyder, M. (2000). Self-monitoring: Appraisal and reappraisal. *Psychological Bulletin, 126,* 530–555.

78 Leone, C., & Hawkins, L. B. (2006). Self-monitoring and close relationships. *Journal of Personality, 74,* 739–778.

79 Falomir-Pichastor, J. M. (2009). "I'm not gay . . . I'm a real man!": Heterosexual men's gender self-esteem and sexual prejudice. *Personality and Social Psychology Bulletin, 35,* 1233–1243; Herek, G. M., & Glunt, E. K. (1993). Interpersonal contact and heterosexuals' attitudes toward gay men: Results from a national survey. *Journal of Sex Research, 30,* 239–244; Kite, M. E., & Whitley, B. E. (1996). Sex differences in attitudes toward homosexual persons, behaviors, and civil rights: A meta-analysis. *Personality and Social Psychological Bulletin, 22,* 336–353.

80 Woods, J. D. (1994). *The corporate closet: The professional lives of gay men in America.* New York: The Free Press; Griffin, P. (1992). From hiding out to coming out: Empowering lesbian and gay educators. In K. M. Harbeck (Ed.), *Coming out of the classroom closet* (pp. 167–196). New York: Harrington Park Press.

81 Brewer, M. B., & Miller, N. (1984). Beyond the contact hypothesis: Theoretical perspectives on desegregation. In N. Miller & M. B. Brewer (Eds.), *Groups in contact: The psychology of desegregation* (pp. 281–302). Orlando, FL: Academic Press.

82 Seiter, J. S., & Sandry, A. (2003). Pierced for success?: The effects of ear and nose piercing on perceptions of job candidates' credibility, attractiveness, and hirability. *Communication Research Reports, 20,* 287–298. This information was adapted from "Dressing for success in interviews," n.d., retrieved on March 27, 2007, from http://www.wetfeet.com/Content/Articles/d/dressing%20for%20success%20in%20interviews.aspx.

83 Gladwell, M. (2005). *Blink: The power of thinking without thinking.* New York: Little, Brown, and Company.

84 Chaplin, W. F., Phillips, J. B., Brown, J. D., Clanton, N. R., & J. L. Stein, J. L. (2000). Handshaking, gender, personality, and first impressions. *Journal of Personality and Social Psychology, 79,* 110–117.

85 For a review of the research, see Burgoon, J. K., Birk, T., & Pfau, M. (1990). Nonverbal behaviors, persuasion, and credibility. *Human Communication Research, 17,* 140–169. Also refer to Pearce W. B., & Conklin, F. (1971). Nonverbal vocalic communication and perception of speaker. *Speech Monographs, 38,* 235–241; Street, R. L., & Brady, R. M. (1982). Speech rate acceptance ranges as a function of evaluative domain, listener speech rate, and communication context. *Communication Monographs 49,* 290–308.

86 Leathers, D. G. (1988). Impression management training: Conceptualization and application to personal selling. *Journal of Applied Communication Research, 16,* 126–145.

87 Mottet, T. P., Beebe, S. A., & Fleuriet, C. (2006). Students' influence messages. In T. P. Mottet, V. P. Richmond, & J. C. McCroskey (Eds.), *Handbook of instructional communication: Rhetorical and relational perspectives* (pp. 143–166). Boston: Allyn and Bacon.

88 Walther, J. B., Van Der Heide, B., Kim, S., Westerman, D., & Tong, S. T. (2008). The role of friends' appearance and behavior on evaluations of individuals on Facebook: Are we known by the company we keep? *Human Communication Research, 34,* 28–49.

89 Rodriguez, K. (2007, Feb. 4). Kids can find what principals can't on a prospective teacher's character. *San Antonio Express-News,* B-1, B-3; see also Ferguson, T. (2007, March 28). Want a job? Clean up your Web act. Retrieved on March 30, 2007 from http://news.zdnet.com/2102-9588_22-6171187.html.

90 Kleck, C. A., Reese, C. A., Behnken, D. Z., & Sundar, S. S. (2007, May). *The company you keep and the image you project: Putting our best face forward in online social networks.* Paper presented at the meeting of the International Communication Association, San Francisco, CA.

91 Elisson, N. B., Steinfield, C., & Lampe, C. (2007). The benefits of Facebook "friends": Social capital and college students' use of online social network sites. *Journal of Computer-Mediated Communication, 12,* 1143–1168.

92 Some of these suggestions were recommended in RoAne, S. (2007). *How to work a room: Your essential guide to savvy socializing.* New York: HarperCollins.

Chapter 3

1 Glasser, W. (1998). *Choice theory: A new psychology of personal freedom.* New York: HarperCollins.

2 Phipps, C. J. (n.d.). Social intelligence: The heart and science of human relationships. Retrieved September 14, 2009, from http://www.innovativehumandynamics.com/pdfs/social_intelligence.pdf.

3 Albrecht, K. (2006). *Social intelligence: The new science of success.* San Francisco: Jossey-Bass.

4 Thorndike, E. L. (1920). Intelligence and its use. *Harper's Magazine, 140,* 227–235.

5 Houser, M. L., Horan, S. M., & Furler, L. A. (2008). Dating in the fast lane: How communication predicts speed dating success. *Journal of Social and Personal Relationships, 25,* 749–768.

6 Ambady, N., & Rosenthal, R. (1992). Thin slices of expressive behavior as predictors of interpersonal consequences: A meta-analysis. *Psychological Bulletin, 11,* 256–274.

7 Rock, D. A. (2006). Brain-based approach to coaching. *International Journal of Coaching in Organizations, 4(2)* 32–43.

8 Burgoon, J. K., & Hale, J. L. (1988). Nonverbal expectancy violations theory: Model elaboration and application to immediacy behaviors. *Communication Monographs, 55,* 58–79.

9 Shannon, C. E. (1948, July/October). A mathematical theory of communication, *Bell System Technical Journal, 27,* 379–423, 623–656.

10 Andersen, P. A. (1999). *Nonverbal communication: Forms and functions.* Palo Alto, CA: Mayfield.

11 Burgoon, J. K., & Burgoon, M. (2001). Expectancy theories. In P. Robinson & H. Giles (Eds.), *The new handbook of language and social psychology* (2nd ed.). Sussex, U.K.: Wiley.

12 Heider, F. (1958). *The psychology of interpersonal relations.* New York: Wiley.

13 Heider, F. (1958). *The psychology of interpersonal relations.* New York: Wiley.

14 Clary, E., & Tesser, A. (1983). Reactions to unexpected events: The naive scientist and interpretive activity. *Personality and Social Psychology Bulletin, 9,* 609–620.

15 Weiner, B. (2000). Intrapersonal and interpersonal theories of motivation from an attributional perspective. *Educational Psychology Review, 12,* 1–14.

[16] Pascarella, E. T., Edison, M., Hagedorn, L., Nora, A., & Terenzini, P. T. (1995). *Influences on students' internal locus of attribution for academic success in the first year of college.* University Park, PA: National Center on Postsecondary Teaching, Learning, and Assessment. (ERIC Document Reproduction Service No. ED 384283).

[17] Peterson, C., Maier, S., & Seligman, M.E.P. (1993). *Learned helplessness: A theory for the age of personal control.* New York: Oxford University Press

[18] Weiner, B. (1995). *Judgments of responsibility: A foundation for a theory of social conduct.* New York: Guilford.

[19] Rothblum, E., & Solovay, S. (Eds.). (2009). *The fat studies reader.* New York: New York University Press.

[20] Bargh, J. A., Lombardi, W. L., & Higgins, E. T. (1988). Automaticity of chronically accessible constructs in person × situation effects on person perception: It's just a matter of time. *Journal of Personality and Social Psychology, 49,* 1129–1146; Sekikides, C., & Skowronski, J. J. (1990). Toward reconciling personality and social psychology; A construct accessibility approach. *Journal of Social Behavior and Personality, 5,* 531–546; von Hippel, W., Hawkins, C., & Narayan, S. (1994). Personality and perceptual expertise: Individual differences in perceptual identification. *Psychological Science, 5,* 401–406; O'Mahony, J. F. (1984). Knowing others through the self-influence of self-perception on perception of others: A review. *Current Psychology, 3,* 48–62.

[21] Cuperman, R., & Ickes, W. (2009). Big five predictors of behavior and perceptions in initial dyadic interactions: Personality similarity helps extraverts and introverts, but hurts "disagreeables." *Journal of Personality and Social Psychology, 97,* 667–684.

[22] Robins, R. W., & Oliver, P. J. (1997). Toward a broader agenda for research on self- and other perception, *Psychological Inquiry, 7,* 279–287.

[23] Cuperman, R., & Ickes, W. (2009). Big five predictors of behavior and perceptions in initial dyadic interactions: Personality similarity helps extraverts and introverts, but hurts "disagreeables." *Journal of Personality and Social Psychology, 97,* 667–684.

[24] Weaver, J. B., III (1998). Personality and self-perceptions about communication. In J. C. McCroskey, J. A. Daly, M. M. Martin, & M. J. Beatty (Eds.), *Communication and personality: Trait perspectives* (pp. 95–131). Cresskill, NJ: Hampton Press.

[25] American Psychological Association. (2001, February 9). Personality influences the brain's responses to emotional situations more than thought: Extraverts show more brain reactivity to positive images than introverts. *Science Daily.* Retrieved October 10, 2009, from http://www.sciencedaily.com/releases/2001/02/010205080513.htm.

[26] Cooley, C. H. (1912). *Human nature and the social order.* New York: Scribner's.

[27] Graham, S. M., & Clark, M. S. (2006). The "Jekyll and Hyde"-ing of relationship partners. *Journal of Personality and Social Psychology, 90,* 652–656.

[28] Bem, S. (1974). The measurement of psychological androgyny. *Journal of Consulting and Clinical Psychology, 42,* 155–162.

[29] Brown, C. D., & Nelson, A. (2009). *Code Switching: How to Talk So Men Will Listen.* New York: Alpha Books.

[30] Brescoll, V. L., & Uhlmann, E. L. (2005). Attitudes toward traditional and nontraditional parents. *Psychology of Women Quarterly, 29,* 436–445; Williams, J. C., & Cooper, H. C. (2004). The public policy of motherhood. *Journal of Social Issues, 60,* 849–865.

[31] Wu, S., & Keysar, B. (2007). The effect of culture on perspective taking. *Psychological Science, 18,* 600–606.

[32] Decety, J., & Sommerville, J. A. (2003). Shared representations between self and other: A social cognitive neuroscience view. *Trends in Cognitive Sciences, 7,* 527–533.

[33] Hedden, T., Ketay, S., Aron, A., Markus, H. R., & Gabrieli, J. D. E. (2008). Cultural influences on neural substrates of attentional control. *Psychological Science, 19,* 12–17.

[34] Swim, J. K., & Hyers, L. I. (2009). Sexism. In T. D. Nelson (Ed.), *Handbook of prejudice, stereotyping, and discrimination* (pp. 407–430). New York: Psychology Press.

[35] Jussim, I. (2005). Accuracy in social perception: Criticisms, controversies, criteria, components, and cognitive processes. *Advances in Experimental Social Psychology, 37,* 1–93.

[36] Butcher, E. (2009, May 29). "What are you?": Biracial perceptions of persistent identity questions when bodily appearances signify race. Paper presented at the annual meeting of the International Communication Association, Sheraton New York, New York City. Retrieved from http://www.allacademic.com/meta/p14097_index.html.

[37] Collins, E. C., Biernat, M., & Eidelman, S. (2009). Stereotypes in the communication and translation of person impressions. *Journal of Experimental Social Psychology, 45,* 368–374.

[38] Klein, O., Demoulin, S., Licata, L., & Lambert, S. (2004). "If you know he is an engineer, I don't need to tell you he is smart": The influence of stereotypes on the communication of social knowledge. *Current Psychology of Cognition, 22,* 463–478.

[39] Ruscher, J. B. (1998). Prejudice and stereotyping in everyday communication. In M. P. Zanna, (Ed.), *Advances in experimental social psychology* (Vol. 31, pp. 241–307). San Diego: Academic Press.

[40] Elias, M. (2006, August). USA's Muslims under a cloud. *USA Today.* Retrieved from http://www.usatoday.com/news/nation/2006-08-09-muslim-american-cover_x.htm.

[41] The Associated Press. (2009, October). Hotelier to Hispanic workers: Change names. *MSNBC.com.* Retrieved from http://www.msnbc.msn.com/id/33479833/ns/us_news-race_and_ethnicity?GT1=43001.

[42] Willis, J., & Todorov, A. (2006). First impressions: Making up your mind after 100 ms exposure to a face. *Psychological Science, 17,* 592–598.

[43] Stone, V. A. (1969). A primacy effect in decision-making by jurors. *Journal of Communication, 19,* 239–247.

[44] Asch, S. E. (1946). Forming impressions of personality. *Journal of Abnormal and Social Psychology, 41,* 258–290.

[45] Duffy, S., & Crawford, L. E. (2008). Primacy or recency effects in forming inductive categories. *Memory & Cognition, 36,* 567–577.

[46] Wixted, J. T., & Ebbesen, E. B. (1991). On the form of forgetting. *Psychological Science, 2,* 409–415.

[47] Cook, G. I., Marsh, R. L., & Hicks, J. L. (2003). Halo and devil effects demonstrate valence-based influences on source-monitoring decisions. *Consciousness and Cognition, 12,* 257–278.

[48] van Leeuwen, M. L., & Macrae, C. N. (2004). Is beautiful always good?: Implicit benefits of facial attractiveness. *Social Cognition, 22,* 637–649.

[49] McCroskey, J. C., Richmond, V. P., & Daly, J. A. (1975). The development of a measure of perceived homophily in interpersonal communication. *Human Communication Research, 1,* 323–332.

[50] Festinger, L. (1957). *A theory of cognitive dissonance.* New York: Row, Peterson.

[51] McCroskey, J. C., Richmond, V. P., & Stewart, R. A. (1986). *One on one: The foundations of interpersonal communication.* Englewood Cliffs, NJ: Prentice-Hall.

[52] Ross, L. (1977). The intuitive psychologist and his shortcomings: Distortions in the attribution process. In L. Berkowitz (Ed.), *Advances in experimental social psychology* (Vol. 10, pp. 173–220). New York: Academic Press.

[53] Gilbert, D. T., & Osborne, R. E. (1989). Thinking backward: Some curable and incurable consequences of cognitive busyness. *Journal of Personality and Social Psychology, 57,* 940–949.

[54] Green, S. K., Lightfoot, M. A., Bandy, C, & Buchanan, D. R. (1985). A general model of the attribution process. *Basic & Applied Social Psychology, 6,* 159–179.

[55] Holtzworth-Munroe, A., & Jacobson, N. S. (1985). Causal attributions of married couples: When do they search for causes? What do they conclude when they do? *Journal of Personality and Social Psychology, 48,* 1398–1412.

[56] Kelsey, D. M., Kearney, P., Plax, T. G., Allen, T. H., & Ritter, K. J. (2004) College students' attributions of teacher misbehaviors. *Communication Education, 53,* 40–55.

[57] Clatterbuck, G. W. (1979). Attributional confidence and uncertainty in initial interaction. *Human Communication Research, 5,* 147–157.

[58] Clatterbuck, G. W. (1979). Attributional confidence and uncertainty in initial interaction. *Human Communication Research, 5,* 147–157.

[59] Gudykunst, W. B. (1985). The influence of cultural similarity, type of relationship, and self-monitoring on uncertainty reduction processes. *Communication Monographs, 52,* 203–217.

[60] Gardner, H. (1993). *Multiple intelligences: The theory in practice.* New York: Basic Books.

[61] Goleman, D. (2007). *Social intelligence: The new science of human relationships.* New York: Random House.

[62] Ekman, P. (1992). *Telling lies: Clues to deceit in the marketplace, politics, and marriage.* New York: Norton.

[63] Fujishin, R. (2009). *Creating communication: Explaining and expanding your fundamental communication skills* (2nd ed.). Lanham, MD: Rowman & Littlefield.

Chapter 4

[1] Levine, T. R., Aune, K. S., & Park, H. S. (2006). Love styles and communication in relationships: Partner preferences, initiating, and intensification. *Communication Quarterly, 54,* 465–486; Keeley, M. P., & Yingling, J. M. (2007). *Final conversations: Helping the living and the dying talk to each other.* Acton, MA: Vander Wyk & Burnham.

[2] Keeley, M. P., & Yingling, J. M. (2007). *Final conversations: Helping the living and the dying talk to each other.* Acton, MA: Vander Wyk & Burnham.

[3] Gottman, J. M., Gottman, J. S., & DeClaire, J. (2006). *Ten lessons to transform marriage.* New York: Random House; Gottman, J. M. (2001). *The relationship cure.* New York: Three Rivers Press.

[4] Jacobs, S. (1994). Language and interpersonal communication. In M. L. Knapp & G. R. Miller (Eds.), *Handbook of interpersonal communication* (2nd ed., pp. 199–228). Thousand Oaks, CA: Sage; Chomsky, N. (1957). *Syntactic structures.* The Hague, Netherlands: Mouton.

[5] Chomsky, N. (1957). *Syntactic structures.* The Hague, Netherlands: Mouton.

[6] Patai, D. (1999). *Heterophobia: Sexual harassment and the future of feminism.* Lanham, M. D.: Rowman and Littlefield, pp. 17–19.

[7] See Chesebro, J. L., & Wanzer, M. B. (2006). Instructional message variables. In T. P. Mottet, V. P. Richmond, & J. C. McCroskey (Eds.), *Handbook of instructional communication: Rhetorical and relational perspectives* (pp. 89–116). Boston: Allyn and Bacon; see also, Kenton, S. B. (1989). Speaker credibility in persuasive business communication. *Journal of Business Communication, 26,* 143–157.

[8] Salter, M. M., Weider-Hatfield, D., & Rubin, D. L. (1983). Generic pronoun use and perceived speaker credibility. *Communication Quarterly, 31,* 180–184; see also Greene, K., & Rubin, D. L. (1991). Effects of gender inclusive/exclusive language in religious discourse. *Journal of Language and Social Psychology, 10,* 81–98.

[9] Adapted from Maggio, R. (2001). *How to say it: Choice words, phrases, sentences, and paragraphs for every situation.* New York: Prentice Hall.

[10] Wheeless, L. R., Frymier, A. B., & Thompson, C. A. (1992). A comparison of verbal output and receptivity in relation to attraction and communication satisfaction in interpersonal relationships. *Communication Quarterly, 40,* 102–115; Norton, R. W. (1977). Communicator style as an effect determinant of attraction. *Communication Research, 4,* 257–283.

[11] Chiu, C., Krauss, R. M., & Lau, I. (1998). Some cognitive consequences of communication. In S. R. Fussell & R. J. Kreuz (Eds.), *Social and cognitive approaches to interpersonal communication* (pp. 259–278). Hillsdale, NJ: Erlbaum; see also Hoijer, H. (Ed.). (1954). *Language in culture: Conference on the interrelations of language and other aspects of culture,* Chicago: University of Chicago Press; Carroll, J. B. (Ed.), (1956). *Language, thought, and reality: Selected writings of Benjamin Lee Whorf.* Boston: MIT Press.

[12] Brown, R. W., & Lenneberg, E. H. (1954). A study in the language and cognition. *Journal of Abnormal and Social Psychology, 49,* 454–462; Davies, I. R. L., Sowden, P. T., Jerrett, D. T., Jerrett, T., & Corbett, G. G. (1998). A cross-cultural study of English and Setswana speakers on a colour triads task: A test of the Sapir-Whorf hypothesis. *British Journal of Psychology, 89,* 1–15.

[13] Chiu, C., Krauss, R. M., & Lau, I. (1998). Some cognitive consequences of communication. In S. R. Fussell & R. J. Kreuz (Eds.), *Social and cognitive approaches to interpersonal communication* (pp. 259–278). Hillsdale, NJ: Erlbaum. See also Eiser, J. R., & Pancer, T. C. (1971). Attitudinal effects of the use of evaluatively biased language. *European Journal of Social Psychology, 9,* 39–47.

[14] Personal conversations with Mr. George Kalorgridis, general manager of Disneyland Resort Paris in Paris, France.

[15] Cann, A., & Calhoun, L. G. (2001). Perceived personality associations with differences in sense of humor: Stereotypes of hypothetical others with high or low senses of humor. *International Journal of Humor Research, 14,* 117–130; Thorson, J. A., & Powell, F. C. (1993). Sense of humor and dimensions of personality. *Journal of Clinical Psychology, 49,* 799–809.

[16] Adapted from Norton, R. (1983). *Communicator style: Theory, application, and measures.* Beverly Hills, CA: Sage.

[17] Cardello, L. L., Ray, E. B., & Pettey, G. R. (1995). The relationship of perceived physician communicator style to patient satisfaction. *Communication Reports, 8,* 27–37.

[18] Martin, D. M., & Gayle, B. M. (1999). It isn't a matter of just being funny: Humor production by organizational leaders. *Communication Research Reports, 16,* 72–80.

[19] Myers, S. A., Mottet, T. P., & Martin, M. M. (2000). The relationships between student communication motives and perceived instructor communicator style. *Communication Research Reports, 17,* 161–170.

[20] Burkel-Rothfuss, N. L., & Bell, R. A. (1987). Validity of the affinity-seeking instrument. *Communication Research Reports, 4,* 24–37.

[21] Graham, E. E., Barbato, C. A., & Perse, E. M. (1993). The interpersonal communication motives model. *Communication Quarterly, 41,* 172–186.

[22] Horvath, C. W. (1995). Biological origins of communicator style. *Communication Quarterly, 43,* 394–407.

[23] Lenhart, A., Arafeh, S., Smith, A., & Macgill, A. R. (2008, April 24). *Writing, technology, and teens.* Washington, DC: Pew Internet & American Life Project,. Retrieved September 28, 2008, from http://www.pewinternet.org/PPF/r/247/report_display.asp.

[24] Lenhart, A., Arafeh, S., Smith, A., & Macgill, A. R. (2008, April 24). *Writing, technology, and teens.* Washington, DC: Pew Internet & American Life Project. Retrieved September 28, 2008, from http://www.pewinternet.org/PPF/r/247/report_display.asp.

[25] Thurlow, C., & Poff, M. (2009). The language of text-messaging. In S. C. Herring, D. Stein, & T. Virtanen (Eds.), *Handbook of the pragmatics.* New York: Mouton de Gruyter.

[26] These characteristics were discussed extensively in Thurlow, C., & Poff, M. (2009). The language of text-messaging. In S. C. Herring, D. Stein, & T. Virtanen (Eds.), *Handbook of the pragmatics.* New York: Mouton de Gruyter.

[27] Lenhart, A., Arafeh, S., Smith, A., & Macgill, A. R. (2008, April 24). *Writing, technology, and teens.* Washington, DC: Pew Internet & American Life Project. Retrieved September 28, 2008, from http://www.pewinternet.org/PPF/r/247/report_display.asp.

[28] Thurlow, C., & Poff, M. (2009). The language of text-messaging. In S. C. Herring, D. Stein, & T. Virtanen (Eds.), *Handbook of the pragmatics.* New York: Mouton de Gruyter.

[29] Thurlow, C., & Poff, M. (2009). The language of text-messaging. In S. C. Herring, D. Stein, & T. Virtanen (Eds.), *Handbook of the pragmatics.* New York: Mouton de Gruyter.

[30] Reid, D., & Reid, F. (2004). *Insights into the social and psychological effects of SMS text messaging.* Retrieved September 27, 2008, from www.160characters.org/documents/SocialEffectsOfTextMessaging.pdf.

[31] Reid, D., & Reid, F. (2004). *Insights into the social and psychological effects of SMS text messaging.* Retrieved September 27, 2008, from www.160characters.org/documents/SocialEffectsOfTextMessaging.pdf.

[32] Reid, D., & Reid, F. (2004). *Insights into the social and psychological effects of SMS text messaging.* Retrieved September 27, 2008, from www.160characters.org/documents/SocialEffectsOfTextMessaging.pdf.

[33] Lenhart, A., Arafeh, S., Smith, A., & Macgill, A. R. (2008, April 24). *Writing, technology, and teens.* Washington, DC: Pew Internet & American Life Project. Retrieved September 28, 2008, from http://www.pewinternet.org/PPF/r/247/report_display.asp.

[34] Rosen, L., Chang, J., Erwin, L., Carrier, L. M., & Cheever, N. A. (2010). The relationship between "textisms" and formal and informal writing among young adults. *Communication Research, 37,* 420–440.

[35] Rosen, L., Chang, J., Erwin, L., Carrier, L. M., & Cheever, N. A. (2010). The relationship between "textisms" and formal and informal writing among young adults. *Communication Research, 37,* 420–440.

[36] The results of this study were described in Needleman, S. E. (2008, 29 July). "Thx for the IView! I Wud ❤ 2 Work 4 U!!" *Wall Street Journal,* D, pp. 1, 4.

[37] Grohol, J. M. (2008. 1 March). SMS addiction and texting addiction. Retrieved September 28, 2008 from http://psychcentral.com/blog/archives/2008/03/01sms-addiction-and-texting-addiction/.

[38] Rutland, J. B., Sheets, T., & Young, T. (2007). Development of a scale to measure problem use of short message service: The SMS problem use diagnostic questionnaire. *CyberPsychology & Behavior, 10,* 841–843; see also http://www.clearsms.com/blog/2008/1/30/sms-text-addictionwhen-you-just-cant-stop-texting.html.

[39] Tannen, D. (1990). *You just don't understand: Women and men in conversation.* New York: Morrow; Tannen, D. (1994). *Talking from 9 to 5: How women's and men's conversational styles affect who gets heard, who gets credit, and what gets done at work.* New York: Morrow.

[40] Lakoff, R. (1975). Language and woman's place, *Language in Society, 2,* 45–80; Lakoff, R. (1975). *Language and woman's place.* New York: HarperCollins.

[41] Wood, J. (2001). *Gendered lives: Communication, gender, and culture* (4th ed.). Belmont, CA: Wadsworth.

[42] Timmerman, L. M. (2002). Comparing the production of power in language on the basis of sex. In M. Allen, R. W. Preiss, B. M. Gayle, & N. Burrell (Eds.), *Interpersonal communication research: Advances through meta-analysis* (pp. 73–88). Mahwah, NJ: Erlbaum.

[43] Timmerman, L. M. (2002). Comparing the production of power in language on the basis of sex. In M. Allen, R. W. Preiss, B. M. Gayle, & N. Burrell (Eds.), *Interpersonal communication*

research: Advances through meta-analysis (pp. 73–88). Mahwah, NJ: Erlbaum; Hackman, M. Z., Hills, M. J., Paterson, T. J., & Furniss, A. H. (1993). Leaders' gender-role as a correlate of subordinates' perceptions to effectiveness and satisfaction, *Perceptual and Motor Skills 77*, 671–674; Griffin, B. Q. (1992). *Perceptions of managers: Effects of leadership style and gender.* Paper presented at the Annual Meeting of the Southeastern Psychological Association, Knoxville, TN.

44 Quina, K., Wingard, J. A., & Bates, H. G. (1987). Language style and gender stereotypes in person perception, *Psychology of Women Quarterly 11*, 111–122; Haleta, L. L. (1996). Student perceptions of teachers' use of language: The effect of powerful and powerless language on impression formation and uncertainty. *Communication Education 45*, 16–28.

45 Hackman, M. Z., Hills, M. J., Paterson, T. J., & Furniss, A. H. (1993). Leaders' gender-role as a correlate of subordinates' perceptions to effectiveness and satisfaction, *Perceptual and Motor Skills 77*, 671–674; Griffin, B. Q. (1992). *Perceptions of managers: Effects of leadership style and gender.* Paper presented at the Annual Meeting of the Southeastern Psychological Association, Knoxville, TN.

46 Tannen, D. (2005). *Conversational style: Analyzing talk among friends.* New York: Oxford University Press; Tannen, D. (1999). Women and men in conversations. In R. S. Wheeler (Ed.), *The workings of language: From prescriptions to perspectives* (pp. 211–216). New York: Greenwood Publishing Group.

47 Tannen, D. (1995, September–October). The power of talk: Who gets heard and why, *Harvard Business Review, 73*, 138–148.

48 Tannen, D. (1995, September–October). The power of talk: Who gets heard and why, *Harvard Business Review, 73*, 138–148.

49 Tannen, D. (1994). *Talking from 9 to 5: How women's and men's conversational styles affect who gets heard, who gets credit, and what gets done at work.* New York: Morrow.

50 Tannen, D. (1994). *Talking from 9 to 5: How women's and men's conversational styles affect who gets heard, who gets credit, and what gets done at work.* New York: Morrow; see also Reis, H. T. (1998). Gender differences in intimacy and related behaviors: Context and process. In D. J. Canary and K. Dindia (Eds.), *Sex differences and similarities in communication* (pp. 203–231). Mahwah, NJ: Erlbaum.

51 Tannen, D. (1995, September–October). The power of talk: Who gets heard and why, *Harvard Business Review, 73*, 138–148.

52 Tannen, D. (1994). *Talking from 9 to 5: How women's and men's conversational styles affect who gets heard, who gets credit, and what gets done at work.* New York: Morrow.

53 Gluszek, A., & Dovidio, J. F. (2010). Speaking with a non-native accent: Perceptions of bias, communication difficulties, and belonging in the United States. *Journal of Language and Social Psychology, 29*, 224–234; see also Gil, M. M., & Badzinksi, D. M. (1992). The impact of accent and status on information recall and perception formation. *Communication Reports, 5*, 99–106.

54 Ellis, D. S. (1967). Speech and social status in America. *Social Forces, 45*, 431–437.

55 Dixon, J. A. (2002). Accents of guilt. *Journal of Language and Social Psychology, 21*, 162–168.

56 Hunter, A. (2008, July 28). Attractive voice may speak volumes about desirability. Retrieved July 28, 2008, from http://abcnews.go.com/Health/story?id=5449438&page=1; Evans, S. Neave, N., & Wakelin, D. (2005). Relationships between vocal characteristics and body size in human males: An evolutionary explanation for a deep male voice. *Biological Psychology, 72*, 160–163.

57 DeShields, O. W., Kara, A. Kaynak, E. (1996). Source effects in purchase decisions: The impact of physical attractiveness and accent of salesperson. *International Journal of Research in Marketing, 13*, 89–101.

58 Hall, E. T. (1976). *Beyond culture.* Garden City, NY: Doubleday

59 Hofstede, G. (1980). *Culture's consequences: International differences in work-related values.* Beverly Hills, CA: Sage; Hofstede, G. (1991). *Cultures and organizations: Software of the mind.* London: McGraw-Hill.

60 Hofstede, G. (1980). *Culture's consequences: International differences in work-related values.* Beverly Hills, CA: Sage; Hofstede, G. (1991). *Cultures and organizations: Software of the mind.* London: McGraw-Hill.

61 Andrews, E. L. (2000, January 4). Walmart lowers its prices at stores across Germany. *New York Times.* Retrieved on July 31, 2008, from http://query.nytimes.com/gst/fullpage.html? res= 9F0DE1DF1F38F937A35752C0A9669C8B63; see also Williams, C. J. (1999, August 15). Not all ways Walmart as chain takes on Germany. *Los Angeles Times,* C1.

62 Rancer, A. S., & Avtgis, T. A. (2006). *Argumentative and aggressive communication: Theory, research, and application.* Thousand Oaks, CA: Sage.

63 Richmond, V. P., & McCroskey, J. C. (1998). *Communication: Apprehension, avoidance, and effectiveness* (5th ed.) Boston: Allyn and Bacon.

64 Rathus, S. A. (1974). A thirty item schedule for assessing assertive behavior. In E. J. Thomas (Eds.), *Behavior modification procedure* (pp. 257–266). Chicago: Aldine.

65 Impett, E. A., Gable, S. L., & Peplau, E. A. (2005). Giving up and giving in: The costs and benefits of daily sacrifice in intimate relationships. *Journal of Personality and Social Psychology, 89*, 327–344.

66 Rill, L., Baiocchi, E., Hopper, M., Denker, K., & Olson, L. N. (2009). Exploration of the relationship between self-esteem, commitment, and verbal aggressiveness in romantic dating relationships. *Communication Reports, 22*, 102–113; Wigley, C. J. (1998). Verbal aggressiveness. In J. C. McCroskey, J. A. Daly, M. M. Martin, and M. J. Beatty (Eds), *Communication and personality: Trait perspectives* (pp. 191–214). Cresskill, NJ: Hampton Press; see also Infante, D. A., & Rancer, A. S. (1982). A conceptualization and measure of argumentativeness, *Journal of Personality Assessment, 46*, 72–80.

67 Richmond, V. P., & McCroskey, J. C. (1998). *Communication: Apprehension, avoidance, and effectiveness* (5th ed.). Boston: Allyn and Bacon.

68 Rakos, R. F. (2000). Asserting and confronting. In O. Hargie (Ed.), *A handbook of communication skills* (pp. 289–319). New York: Routledge.

[69] Hamilton, M. A., Buck, R. W., Beatty, M. J., Chory, R. M., & Patrylak, L. A. (2009). Individualistic and cooperative affect systems as determinants of aggressive or collaborative message choice. In Beatty, M. J., McCroskey, J. C., & Floyd, K. (Eds.), *Biological dimensions of communication: Perspectives, research, and methods* (pp. 227–250). Cresskill, NJ: Hampton Press; Beatty, M. J., Heisel, A. D., Hall, A. E., Levine, T. R., & La France, B. H. (2002). What can we learn from the study of twins about genetic and environmental influences on interpersonal affiliation, aggressiveness, and social anxiety?: A meta-analytic study. *Communication Monographs, 69,* 1–18.

[70] Crockett, M. J., Clark, L., Tabibnia, G., Lieberman, M. D., & Robbins, T. W. (2008). Serotonin modulates behavioral reactions to unfairness. *Science, 320,* 1739; Best, M., Williams, J. M., & Coccaro, E. F. (2002). Evidence for a dysfunctional prefrontal circuit in patients with an impulsive aggressive disorder. *PNAS, 99,* 8448–8453.

[71] Infante, D. A., & Rancer, A. S. (1982). A conceptualization and measure of argumentativeness. *Journal of Personality Assessment, 46,* 72–80.

[72] Infante, D. A., & Rancer, A. S. (1982). A conceptualization and measure of argumentativeness. *Journal of Personality Assessment, 46,* 72–80; see also Rancer, A. S., & Avtgis, T. A. (2006). *Argumentative and aggressive communication: Theory, research, and application* (pp. 255–256). Thousand Oaks, CA: Sage.

[73] Rancer, A. S. (1998). Argumentativeness. In J. C. McCroskey, J. A. Daly, M. M. Martin, & M. J. Beatty (Eds), *Communication and personality: Trait perspectives* (pp. 149–170), Cresskill, NJ: Hampton Press.

[74] Infante, D. A., & Gorden, W. I. (1987). Superior and subordinate communication profiles: Implications for independent-mindedness and upward effectiveness. *Central States Speech Journal, 38,* 73–80; Infante, D. A., & Gorden, W. I. (1989). Argumentativeness and affirming communicator style as predictors of satisfaction/dissatisfaction with subordinates. *Communication Quarterly, 37,* 81–89; Infante, D. A., & Gorden, W. I. (1991). How employees see the boss: Test of an argumentative and affirming model of superiors' communicative behavior, *Western Journal of Speech Communication, 55,* 294–304.

[75] Johnson, A. J. (2009). A functional approach to interpersonal argument: Differences between public-issue and personal-issue arguments. *Communication Reports, 22,* 13–28. Rancer, A. S., & Avtgis, T. A. (2006). *Argumentative and aggressive communication: Theory, research, and applications.* Thousand Oaks, CA: Sage.

[76] Infante, D. A., Chandler, T. A., & Rudd, J. E. (1989). Test of an argumentative skill deficiency model of interspousal violence. *Communication Monographs, 56,* 163–177.

[77] Rudd, J. E., Burant, P. A., & Beatty, M. J. (1994). Battered women's compliance gaining strategies as a function of argumentativeness and verbal aggression. *Communication Research Reports, 11,* 13–22; Sabourin, T. C., Infante, D. A., & Rudd, J. E. (1993). Verbal aggression in marriages: A comparison of violent, distressed but nonviolent, and nondistressed couples. *Human Communication Research, 20,* 245–267.

[78] Center for Educational Research and Innovation. (2007). *The understanding the brain: The birth of a learning science.* Paris: Center for Educational Research and Innovation.

[79] Gray, J. A. (1991). The neuropsychology of temperament. In J. Strelau & A. Angleitner (Eds.), *Explorations in temperament* (pp. 105–128). New York: Plenum.

[80] Gray, J. A. (1990). Brain systems that mediate both emotion and cognition. *Cognition and Emotion, 4,* 269–288; Beatty, M. J., & McCroskey, J. C. (1997). It's in our nature: Verbal aggressiveness as temperamental expression. *Communication Quarterly, 45,* 446–460.

[81] Wigley, C. J. (1998). Verbal aggressiveness. In J. C. McCroskey, J. A. Daly, M. M. Martin, & M. J. Beatty (Eds.), *Communication and personality: Trait perspectives* (p. 192). Cresskill, NJ: Hampton Press; see also Infante, D. A., & Rancer, A. S. (1982). A conceptualization and measure of argumentativeness, *Journal of Personality Assessment, 46,* 72–80.

[82] Rancer, A. S., & Avtgis, T. A. (2006). *Argumentative and aggressive communication: Theory, research, and application.* Thousand Oaks, CA: Sage.

[83] Rancer, A. S., & Avtgis, T. A. (2006). *Argumentative and aggressive communication: Theory, research, and applications.* Thousand Oaks, CA: Sage.

Chapter 5

[1] Burgoon, J. K. (1994). Nonverbal signals. In M. L. Knapp & G. R. Miller (Eds.), *Handbook of interpersonal communication* (2nd ed., pp. 229–285). Thousand Oaks, CA: Sage.

[2] Guerrero, L. K., Hecht, M. L., & DeVito, J. A. (2008). Perspectives on defining and understanding nonverbal communication. In L. K. Guerrero & M. L. Hecht (Eds.), *The nonverbal communication reader* (3rd ed., pp. 3–20). Long Grove, IL: Waveland Press.

[3] Richmond, V. P., McCroskey, J. C., & Hickson, M. L. (2008). Communication and nonverbal behavior. In *Nonverbal behavior in interpersonal relations* (6th ed., pp. 1–14). Boston: Allyn & Bacon.

[4] Watzlawick, P., Beavin, J. H., & Jackson, D. D. (1967). Some tentative axioms of communication. In *Pragmatics of human communication: A study of interactional patterns, pathologies, and paradoxes* (pp. 48–71). New York: W. W. Norton.

[5] Mehrabian, A. (1972). *Nonverbal communication.* Chicago: Aldine.

[6] Guerrero, L. K., Hecht, M. L., & DeVito, J. A. (2008). Perspectives on defining and understanding nonverbal communication. In L. K. Guerrero & M. L. Hecht (Eds.), *The nonverbal communication reader* (3rd ed., pp. 3–20). Long Grove, IL: Waveland Press.

[7] DePaulo, B. M., & Rosenthal, R. (1979). Ambivalence, discrepancy, and deception in nonverbal communication. In R. Rosenthal (Ed.), *Skill in nonverbal communication: Individual differences* (pp. 204–248). Cambridge, MA: Oelgeschlager, Gunn, & Hain.

[8] Zuckerman, M., DePaulo, B. M., & Rosenthal, R. (1981). Verbal and nonverbal communication of deception. In L.

Berkowitz (Ed.), *Advances in experimental social psychology* (Vol. 14, pp. 1–59). San Diego: Academic Press.

9 Ekman, P., & Friesen, W. V. (1969). The repertoire of nonverbal behavior: Categories, origins, usage, and coding. *Semiotica, 1*, 49–98.

10 Hall, E. T. (1969). *The hidden dimension.* Garden City, NY: Doubleday.

11 Argyle, M., & Dean, J. (1965). Eye contact, distance, and affiliation. *Sociometry, 28*, 289–304.

12 Aiello, J. R. (1977). A further look at equilibrium theory: Visual interaction as a function of interpersonal distance. *Journal of Nonverbal Behavior, 1*, 122–140.

13 DeVito, J. A. (1989). *The nonverbal communication workbook.* Prospects Heights, IL: Waveland Press.

14 Cromwell, P. F. and Birzer, M. (2007). *Effects of police response to emotional reactions of victims of burglary.* Paper presented at the annual meeting of the American Society of Criminology, Atlanta, Georgia. Retrieved from http://www.allacademic.com/meta/p200337_index.html,

15 Browne, J. (2004). Early relationship environments: Physiology of skin-to-skin contact for parents and their preterm infants. *Clinics in Perinatology, 31*(2), 287–298.

16 Kim, T., Shin, Y., & White-Traut, R. (2003). Multisensory intervention improves physical growth and illness rates in Korean orphaned newborn infants. *Research in Nursing and Health, 26*(6), 424–433.

17 Jones, S. E., & Yarbrough, A. E. (1985). A naturalistic study of the meanings of touch. *Communication Monographs, 52*, 19–56.

18 Levine, R. V. (1990). The pace of life. *American Scientist, 78*, 450–459.

19 Bruneau, T. (1977). Chronemics: The study of time in human interaction. *Communication, 6*(2), 1–30; DeVito, J. A. (1989). *The nonverbal communication workbook.* Prospects Heights, IL: Waveland Press.

20 Workman, J. E. (1984). Effects of appropriate and inappropriate attire on attributions of personal dispositions. *Clothing and Textile Research Journal, 3*, 20–23.

21 Roach, D. K. (1997). Effects of graduate teaching assistant attire on student learning, misbehaviors, and ratings of instruction. *Communication Quarterly, 45*, 125–141.

22 Morris, T. L., Gorham, J., Cohen, S.H., & Huffman, D. (1996). Fashion in the classroom: Effects of attire on student perceptions of instructors in college classes. *Communication Education, 45*, 135–148.

23 Mehta, R., & Zhu, R. (2009). Blue or red?: Exploring the effect of color on cognitive task performances. *Science Magazine, 323*, 1226–1229.

24 Smith, V. M., & Stewart, B. L. (2006). *Feng shui: A practical guide for architects and designers.* Chicago, IL: Kaplan Publishing–AEC Education.

25 Chen, G. M. (2007). The impact of *feng shui* on Chinese communication. *China Media Research, 3*(4), 102–109.

26 Buslig, A. L. (1999). "Stop" signs: Regulating privacy with environmental features. In L. K. Guerrero, J. A. DeVito, & M. L. Hecht (Eds.), *The nonverbal communication reader* (2nd ed., pp. 241–249). Long Grove, IL: Waveland Press.

27 Goffman, E. (1967). *Interaction ritual: Essays on face-to-face behavior.* Garden City, NY: Doubleday.

28 Peterson, D. R. (1992). Interpersonal relationships as a link between person and environment. In W. B. Walsh, K. H. Craik, & R. H. Price (Eds.), *Person-environment psychology.* Hillsdale, NJ: Erlbaum.

29 Griffin, A. M., & Langlois, J. H. (2006). Stereotype directionality and attractiveness stereotyping: Is beauty good or is ugly bad? *Social Cognition, 24*, 187–206.

30 Bloch, P. H., & Richins, M. L. (1993). Attractiveness, adornments, and exchange. *Psychology & Marketing, 6*, 467–470.

31 Mealey, L., Bridgstock, R., & Townsend, G. C. (1999). Symmetry and perceived facial attractiveness: A monozygotic co-twin comparison. *Journal of Personality and Social Psychology, 76*, 151–158.

32 Sheldon, W. H. (1954). *Atlas of man: A guide for stereotyping the adult male at all ages.* New York: HarperCollins.

33 BeautifulPeople.com (n.d.). *What is BeautifulPeople.com?* Retrieved from http://www.beautifulpeople.com/about.

34 BBC News (2010, January 4). *Dating site axes 5,000 'fatties.'* Retrieved from http://news.bbc.co.uk/go/pr/fr/-/hi/technology/8439495.stm.

35 Daily News. (2010, January 4). Savvy business decision? BeautifulPeople.com expels 5,000 people for gaining weight over holidays. Retrieved from http://www.nydailynews.com/fdcp?1268267706503

36 BBC News (2010, January 4). *Dating site axes 5,000 'fatties.'* Retrieved from http://news.bbc.co.uk/go/pr/fr/-/hi/technology/8439495.stm.

37 Burgoon, J. K., Buller, D. B., & Woodall, W. G. (1996). *Nonverbal communication: The unspoken dialogue.* New York: McGraw Hill.

38 Bull, P. (1983). *Body movement and interpersonal communication.* New York: John Wiley.

39 Ekman, P. (1973). Cross-cultural studies of facial expression. In P. Ekman (Ed.), *Darwin and facial expression: A century of research in review* (pp. 169–122). New York: Academic Press; Ekman, P. (1997). Expression or communication about emotion. In N. L. Segal, G. E. Weisfeld, & C. C. Weisfeld (Eds.), *Uniting psychology and biology: Integrative perspectives on human development* (pp. 315–338). Washington, DC: American Psychological Association.

40 Collins, S. A. (2000). Male voices and women's choices. *Animal Behavior, 60*, 773–780; Feinberg, D. R., Jones, B. C., Little, A. C., Burt, D. M., & Perrett, D. I. (2005). Manipulations of fundamental and formant frequencies influence the attractiveness of human male voices. *Animal Behavior, 69*, 561–568; Saxton, T. K., Caryl, P. G., & Roberts, S. C. (2006). Vocal and facial attractiveness judgments of children, adolescents and adults: the ontogeny of mate choice. *Ethology, 112*, 1179–1185.

41 Collins, S. A. (2000). Male voices and women's choices. *Animal Behavior, 60*, 773–780; Feinberg, D. R. (2004). Fundamental frequency perturbation indicates perceived health and age in male and female speakers. *Journal of Acoustical Society of America, 115*, 2609.

[42] Collins, S. A., & Missing, C. (2003). Vocal and visual attractiveness are related in women. *Animal Behavior, 65,* 997–1004.

[43] Ambady, N., & Rosenthal, R. (1992). Thin slices of expressive behavior as predictors of interpersonal consequences: A meta-analysis. *Psychological Bulletin, 11,* 256–274; Mehrabian, A. (1966). Immediacy: An indicator or attitude in linguistic communication. *Journal of Personality, 34,* 26–34.

[44] Houser, M. L., Horan, S. M., & Furler, L. A. (2008). Dating in the fast lane: How communication predicts speed-dating success. *Journal of Social and Personal Relationships, 25,* 749–768.

[45] Ekman, P., & Friesen, W. V. (1969). Nonverbal leakage and clues to deception. *Psychiatry, 32,* 88–106.

[46] Dew, A. M., & Ward, C. (1993). The effects of ethnicity and culturally congruent and incongruent nonverbal behaviors on interpersonal attraction. *Journal of Applied Social Psychology, 23,* 1376–1389.

[47] Hall, E. T., & Hall, M. R. (1987). *Hidden differences: Doing business with the Japanese.* Garden City, NY: Anchor.

[48] Samovar, L. A., Porter, R. E., & McDaniel, E. R. (2007). *Communication between cultures.* Belmont, CA: Thomson.

[49] Guerrero, L. K., & Andersen, P. A. (2008). Public touch behavior in romantic relationships between men and women. In L. K. Guerrero & M. L. Hecht (Eds.), *The nonverbal communication reader* (3rd ed., pp. 217–225). Long Grove, IL: Waveland Press.

[50] Guerrero, L. K., & Andersen, P. A. (2008). Public touch behavior in romantic relationships between men and women. In L. K. Guerrero & M. L. Hecht (Eds.), *The nonverbal communication reader* (3rd ed., pp. 217–225). Long Grove, IL: Waveland Press.

[51] Lee, J. W., & Guerrero, L. K. (2001). Type of touch in cross-sex relationships between coworkers: Perceptions of relational and emotional messages, inappropriateness, and sexual harassment. *Journal of Applied Communication Research, 29,* 197–220.

[52] Hall, J. A. (1998). How big are nonverbal sex differences?: The case of smiling and sensitivity to nonverbal cues. In D. J. Canary & K. Dindia (Eds.), *Sex differences and similarities in communication* (pp. 155–178). Mahwah, NJ: Erlbaum.

[53] Hall, J. A. (1998). How big are nonverbal sex differences?: The case of smiling and sensitivity to nonverbal cues. In D. J. Canary & K. Dindia (Eds.), *Sex differences and similarities in communication* (pp. 155–178). Mahwah, NJ: Erlbaum; Thunberg, M., & Dinberg, U. (2000). Gender differences in facial reactions to fear-relevant stimuli. *Journal of Nonverbal Behavior, 24,* 45–51.

[54] Rice, R. E., & Love, G. (1987). Electronic emotion: Socioemotional content in a computer-mediated network. *Communication Research, 14,* 85–108; Sarbaugh-Thompson, M., & Feldman, M. S. (1998). Electronic mail and organizational communication: Does saying "hi" really matter? *Organization Science, 9,* 685–698.

[55] Derks, D., Fischer, A. H., & Bos, E. R. (2007). The role of emotion in computer-mediated communication: A review. *Computers in Human Behavior, 24*(3), 1–17.

[56] Derks, D., Fischer, A. H., & Bos, E. R. (2007). The role of emotion in computer-mediated communication: A review. *Computers in Human Behavior, 24*(3), 1–17.

[57] Doering, N., & Poeschl, S. (2007). *Nonverbal cues in mobile phone text messages: The effects of chronemics and proxemics.* Paper presented at the annual meeting of the International Communication Association conference, San Francisco, CA.

[58] Liu, Y., Ginther, D., & Zelhart, P. (2001). How do frequency and duration of messaging affect impression development in computer-mediated communication? *Journal of Universal Computer Science, 7*(10), 893–912.

[59] Hall, J. A. (2006). Women's and men's nonverbal communication. In V. Manusov & M. L. Patterson (Eds.), *The sage handbook of nonverbal communication* (pp. 201–218). Thousand Oaks, CA: Sage.

[60] Wilson, E. V., & Zigurs, I. (2001). Interpersonal influence goals and computer-mediated communication. *Journal of Organizational Computing and Electronic Commerce, 11*(1), 59–76.

[61] Byron, K., & Baldridge, D. C. (2007). E-mail recipients' impressions of senders' likability: The interactive effect of nonverbal cues and recipients' personality. *Journal of Business Communication, 44*(2), 137–160.

[62] Svoboda, E. (2008, January/February). Solving the mystery of gaydar. *Psychology Today.* Retrieved from http://www.psychologytoday.com/rss/index.php?term=pto-20080214-000009&print=1.

[63] Liu, Y., Ginther, D., & Zelhart, P. (2001). How do frequency and duration of messaging affect impression development in computer-mediated communication? *Journal of Universal Computer Science, 7*(10), 893–912.

[64] Bauerlein, M. P. (2009, August 28). Why Gen-Y Johnny can't read nonverbal cues. *The Wall Street Journal,* p. W15.

[65] Gilroy, M. (2004). Invasion of the classroom cell phones. *Education Digest, 69,* 56–60.

[66] Bauerlein, M. P. (2009, August 28). Why Gen-Y Johnny can't read nonverbal cues. *The Wall Street Journal,* p. W15.

[67] Burgoon, J. K., & Hoobler, G. D. (2002). Nonverbal signals. In M. L. Knapp & J. A. Daly (Eds.), *The handbook of interpersonal communication* (3rd ed., pp. 240–299). Thousand Oaks, CA: Sage.

[68] Burgoon, J. K., & Hoobler, G. D. (2002). Nonverbal signals. In M. L. Knapp & J. A. Daly (Eds.), *The handbook of interpersonal communication* (3rd ed., pp. 240–299). Thousand Oaks, CA: Sage.

[69] Mehrabian, A. (1971). *Silent messages.* Belmont, CA: Wadsworth.

[70] Andersen, P. A., & Andersen, J. F. (2005). Measurements of perceived nonverbal immediacy. In V. Manusov (Ed.), *The sourcebook of nonverbal measures: Going beyond words* (pp. 113–126). Mahwah, NJ: Erlbaum.

[71] Cole, J. G. (2000), Temperament and perceptions of nonverbal behavior. *Communication Research Reports, 17,* 9–94.

[72] Dabbs, J. M., Jr., Strong, R., & Milan, R. (1997). Exploring the mind of testosterone: A beeper study. *Journal of Research in Personality, 31,* 57–587.

[73] Depue, R. A., Luciana, M., Arbisi, P., Collins, P., & Leon, A. (1994). Dopamine and the structure of personality: Relation of agonist-induced dopamine activity to positive emotionality. *Journal of Personality and Social Psychology, 67,* 485–498.

[74] Richmond, V. P., McCroskey, J. C., & Johnson, A. E. (2003). Development of the Nonverbal Immediacy Scale (NIS): Measures

of self- and other-perceived nonverbal immediacy. *Communication Quarterly, 51,* 50–515.

[75] Andersen, P. A., & Andersen, J. F. (2005). Measurements of perceived nonverbal immediacy. In V. Manusov (Ed.), *The sourcebook of nonverbal measures: Going beyond words* (pp. 11–126). Mahwah, NJ: Erlbaum; Floyd, K., & Mikkelson, A. C. (2005). The affectionate communication index. In V. Manusov (Ed.), *The sourcebook of nonverbal measures: Going beyond words* (pp. 11–126). Mahwah, NJ: Erlbaum; Montagu, A. (1971). *Touching: The human significance of the skin.* New York: Columbia University Press.

[76] Andersen, J. F., Andersen, P. A., & Lustig, M. W. (1987). Opposite-sex touch avoidance: A national replication and extension. *Journal of Nonverbal Behavior, 11,* 89–109.

[77] Patterson, M. L. (1973). Stability of nonverbal immediacy behaviors. *Journal of Experimental Social Psychology, 9,* 97–109; Patterson, M. L. (1978). The role of space in social interaction. In A. W. Siegman and S. Feldstein (Eds.), *Nonverbal Behavior and Communication* (265–290). Hillsdale, NJ: Erlbaum.

[78] Andersen, J. F., Andersen, P. A., & Lustig, M. W. (1987). Opposite-sex touch avoidance: A national replication and extension. *Journal of Nonverbal Behavior, 11,* 89–109.

[79] Harper, R. G., Wiens, A. N., & Matarazzo, J. D. (1978). *Nonverbal communication: The state of the art.* New York: John Wiley and Sons; Patterson, M. L. (1978). The role of space in social interaction. In A. W. Siegman and S. Feldstein (Eds.), *Nonverbal Behavior and Communication* (265–290). Hillsdale, NJ: Erlbaum.

[80] Malandro, L. A., & Barker, L. (1983). *Nonverbal communication.* Reading, MA: Addison-Wesley; Patterson, M. L. (1978). The role of space in social interaction. In A. W. Siegman and S. Feldstein (Eds.), *Nonverbal Behavior and Communication* (265–290). Hillsdale, NJ: Erlbaum.

[81] Andersen, P. A., & Sull, K. K. (1985). Out of touch, out of reach: Tactile predispositions as predictors of interpersonal distance. *Western Journal of Speech Communication, 49,* 57–72.

[82] Goldberg, L. R. (1990). An alternative "description of personality": The Big-Five factor structure. *Journal of Personality and Social Psychology, 59,* 1216–1229.

[83] Dorros, S., Hanzal, A., & Segrin, C. (2008). The Big Five personality traits and perceptions of touch to intimate and nonintimate body regions. *Journal of Research in Personality, 42,* 1067–1073.

[84] Richmond, V. P., & McCroskey, J. C. (2008). *Nonverbal behavior in interpersonal relations* (6th ed.). Boston: Allyn & Bacon.

[85] Martin, M. M., & Anderson, C. M. (1993). Psychological and biological differences in touch avoidance. *Communication Research Reports, 10,* 141–147.

[86] Pisano, M. D., Wall, S. M., & Foster, A. (1986). Perceptions of nonreciprocal touch in romantic relationships. *Journal of Nonverbal Behavior, 10,* 29–50.

[87] Sorenson, G., & Beatty, M. J. (1988). The interactive effects of touch and touch avoidance on interpersonal evaluations. *Communication Research Reports, 5,* 84–90.

[88] Burgoon, J. K., & Hoobler, G. D. (2002). Nonverbal signals. In M. L. Knapp & J. A. Daly (Eds.), *The handbook of interpersonal communication* (3rd ed., pp. 240–299). Thousand Oaks, CA: Sage.

[89] Goleman, D. (1981). The 7000 faces of Dr. Ekman. *Psychology Today, 15,* 43–49.

[90] DePaulo, B. M. (1992). Nonverbal behavior and self-presentation. *Psychological Bulletin, 111,* 203–243.

[91] Gudjonsson, G. H., & Sigurdsson, J. F. (2004). The relationship of suggestibility and compliance with self-deception and other-deception. *Psychology, Crime and Law, 19,* 447–453.

[92] Christie, R., & Geis, F. L. (1970). *Studies in Machiavellianism.* New York: Academic Press.

[93] McLeod, B. A., & Genereux, F. L. (2008). Predicting the acceptability and likelihood of lying: The interaction of personality with type of lie. *Personality and Individual Differences, 45,* 591–596.

[94] Burgoon, J. (1978). A communication model of personal space violations: Explication and an initial test. *Human Communication Research, 4,* 129–142; Burgoon, J. K. (1983). Nonverbal violations of expectations. In J. M. Wieman & R. P. Harrison (Eds.), *Nonverbal interaction* (pp. 77–111). Beverly Hills, CA: Sage.

[95] Mehrabian, A. (1981). *Silent messages: Implicit communication of emotions and attitudes.* Belmont, CA: Wadsworth.

[96] Mehrabian, A. (1981). *Silent messages: Implicit communication of emotions and attitudes.* Belmont, CA: Wadsworth.

[97] Houser, M. L., Horan, S. M., & Furler, L. (2008). Dating in the fast lane: How communication predicts speed-dating success. *Journal of Social and Personal Relationships, 25,* 749–768.

[98] Burgoon, J. K., & Hoobler, G. D. (2002). Nonverbal signals. In M. L. Knapp & J. A. Daly (Eds.), *Handbook of interpersonal communication* (3rd ed., pp. 240–299). Thousand Oaks, CA: Sage.

[99] Afifi, W. A., & Burgoon, J. K. (2000). The impact of violations on uncertainty and consequences for attractiveness. *Human Communication Research, 26,* 203–233; Andersen, P. A., & Guerrero, L. K. (1998). Principles of communication and emotion in social interaction. In P. A. Andersen & L. K. Guerrero (Eds.), *Handbook of communication and emotion: Research, theory, applications, and contexts* (pp. 49–96). San Diego: Academic Press.

[100] Burgoon, J. K., & Hoobler, G. D. (2002). Nonverbal signals. In M. L. Knapp & J. A. Daly (Eds.), *Handbook of interpersonal communication* (3rd ed., pp. 240–299). Thousand Oaks, CA: Sage.

[101] Burgoon, J. K., & Le Poire, B. A. (1999). Nonverbal cues and interpersonal judgments: Participant and observer perceptions of intimacy, dominance, composure, and formality. *Communication Monographs, 66,* 105–124.

[102] Burgoon, J. K. (1983). Nonverbal violations of expectations. In J. M. Wiemann & R. P. Harrison (Eds.), *Nonverbal interaction* (pp. 77–111). Beverly Hills, CA: Sage.

[103] Burgoon, J. K., & Hale, J. L. (1988). Nonverbal expectancy violations: Model elaboration and application to immediacy behaviors. *Communication Monographs, 55,* 58–79.

[104] Burgoon, J. K., & Hale, J. L. (1988). Nonverbal expectancy violations: Model elaboration and application to immediacy behaviors. *Communication Monographs, 55,* 58–79.

[105] Burgoon, J. K., & Hale, J. L. (1988). Nonverbal expectancy violations: Model elaboration and application to immediacy behaviors. *Communication Monographs, 55,* 58–79.

[106] Floyd, K., Ramirez, A., & Burgoon, J. K. (1999). Expectancy violations theory. In L. K. Guerrero, J. A. DeVito, & M. L. Hecht (Eds.), *The nonverbal communication reader: Classic and contemporary readings* (pp. 437–444). Prospect Heights, IL: Waveland.

Chapter 6

[1] Brownell, J. (2006). *Listening: Attitudes, principles, and skills* (3rd ed.). Boston: Pearson.

[2] Brownell, J. (2006). *Listening: Attitudes, principles, and skills* (3rd ed.). Boston: Pearson.

[3] Brownell, J. (2006). *Listening: Attitudes, principles, and skills* (3rd ed.). Boston: Pearson.

[4] *Human body.* (2004). London: Quantum.

[5] Brownell, J. (2006). *Listening: Attitudes, principles, and skills* (3rd ed.). Boston: Pearson.

[6] *ABC's of the human body: A family answer book.* (1987). Pleasantville, NY: Reader's Digest Association.

[7] Taken from the International Listening Association's definition of listening, which may be found on their web site at http://www.listen.org.

[8] Wolvin, A., & Coakley, C. G. (1996). *Listening* (5th ed.). Madison, WI: Brown & Benchmark.

[9] Brownell, J. (2006). *Listening: Attitudes, principles, and skills* (3rd ed.). Boston: Pearson.

[10] Brownell, J. (2006). *Listening: Attitudes, principles, and skills* (3rd ed.). Boston: Pearson.

[11] Brownell, J. (2006). *Listening: Attitudes, principles, and skills* (3rd ed.). Boston: Pearson.

[12] Wolvin, A., & Coakley, C. G. (1996). *Listening* (5th ed.). Madison, WI: Brown & Benchmark.

[13] Wolvin, A., & Coakley, C. G. (1996). *Listening* (5th ed.). Madison, WI: Brown & Benchmark.

[14] Brownell, J. (2006). *Listening: Attitudes, principles, and skills* (3rd ed.). Boston: Pearson.

[15] Brownell, J. (2006). *Listening: Attitudes, principles, and skills* (3rd ed.). Boston: Pearson.

[16] Bullard, B., & Carroll, K. (1999). *Communicating from the inside out.* Dubuque, IA: Kendall/Hunt.

[17] Murphy, J. (2008). *The power of your subconscious mind.* New York: Prentice Hall.

[18] Murphy, J. (2008). *The power of your subconscious mind.* New York: Prentice Hall.

[19] Emanuel, R., et al. (2008). How college students spend their time communicating. *International Journal of Listening, 22,* 13–28.

[20] Wolvin, A., & Coakley, C. G. (1996). *Listening* (5th ed.). Madison, WI: Brown & Benchmark.

[21] Barker, L., Edwards, R., Gaines, C., Gladney, K., & Holley, F. (1980). An investigation of proportional time spent in various communication activities by college students. *Journal of Applied Communications Research, 8,* 101–109.

[22] Emanuel, R. et al. (2008). How college students spend their time communicating. *International Journal of Listening, 22,* 13–28.

[23] Lawson, M., & Winkelman, C. (2003). The social desirability factor in the measurement of listening skills: A brief report. *Counseling Psychology Quarterly, 16,* 43–45.

[24] Nichols, M. P. (1995). *The lost art of listening.* New York: Guilford Press.

[25] Watson, K. W., Barker, L. L., & Weaver, J. B. III. (1995). The listening styles profile (LSP-16): Development and validation of an instrument to assess four listening styles. *International Journal of Listening, 9,* 1–13.

[26] Barker, L., & Watson, K. (2000). *Listen up: How to improve relationships, reduce stress, and be more productive by using the power of listening* (p. 21–34). New York: St. Martin's Press.

[27] Watson, K. W., Barker, L. L., & Weaver, J. B. III. (1995). The listening styles profile (LSP-16): Development and validation of an instrument to assess four listening styles. *International Journal of Listening, 9,* 1–13.

[28] Worthington, D. L. (2003). Exploring the relationship between listening style preference and personality. *International Journal of Listening, 17,* 68–87.

[29] Watson, K. W., Barker, L. L., & Weaver, J. B., III. (1995). The listening styles profile (LSP-16): Development and validation of an instrument to assess four listening styles. *International Journal of Listening, 9,* 1–13.

[30] Watson, K. W., Barker, L. L., & Weaver, J. B., III. (1995). The listening styles profile (LSP-16): Development and validation of an instrument to assess four listening styles. *International Journal of Listening, 9,* 1–13.

[31] Watson, K. W., Barker, L. L., & Weaver, J. B., III. (1995). The listening styles profile (LSP-16): Development and validation of an instrument to assess four listening styles. *International Journal of Listening, 9,* 1–13.

[32] Worthington, D. (2008). Exploring the relationship between listening style and need for cognition. *International Journal of Listening, 22,* 46–58.

[33] Worthington, D. L. (2003). Exploring the relationship between listening style preference and personality. *International Journal of Listening, 17,* 68–87.

[34] Wolvin, A. D., & Coakley, C. G. (1994). Listening competency. *International Journal of Listening, 8,* 148–160.

[35] Brownell, J. (2006). *Listening: Attitudes, principles, and skills* (3rd ed.). Boston: Pearson.

[36] Brownell, J. (2006). *Listening: Attitudes, principles, and skills* (3rd ed.). Boston: Pearson.

[37] Barker, L., & Watson, K. (2000). *Listen up: How to improve relationships, reduce stress, and be more productive by using the power of listening.* New York: St. Martin's Press.

[38] Wolvin, A., & Coakley, C. G. (1996). *Listening* (5th ed.). Madison, WI: Brown & Benchmark.

[39] Weaver, J. B., III, Watson, K. W., & Barker, L. L. (1996). Individual differences in listening styles: Do you hear what I hear? *Personality and Individual Differences, 20,* 381–387.

40 Weaver, J. B., III, Watson, K. W., & Barker, L. L. (1996). Individual differences in listening styles: Do you hear what I hear? *Personality and Individual Differences, 20,* 381–387.

41 Villaume, W. A., & Bodie, G. D. (2007). Discovering the listener within us: The impact of trait-like personality variables and communicator styles on preferences for listening style. *International Journal of Listening, 21,* 102–123.

42 Tannen, D. (1990). *You just don't understand: Women and men in conversation.* New York: Ballantine Books.

43 Weaver, J. B., III, Watson, K. W., & Barker, L. L. (1996). Individual differences in listening styles: Do you hear what I hear? *Personality and Individual Differences, 20,* 381–387.

44 Johnson, M. K., Weaver, J. B., III, Watson, K. W., & Barker, L. L. (2000). Listening styles: Biological or psychological differences? *International Journal of Listening, 14,* 32–46.

45 Villaume, W. A., & Bodie, G. D. (2007). Discovering the listener within us: The impact of trait-like personality variables and communicator styles on preferences for listening style. *International Journal of Listening, 21,* 102–123.

46 Burley-Allen, M. (1995). *Listening: The forgotten skill* (2nd ed.). New York: John Wiley & Sons.

47 Burley-Allen, M. (1995). *Listening: The forgotten skill* (2nd ed.). New York: John Wiley & Sons.

48 Burley-Allen, M. (1995). *Listening: The forgotten skill* (2nd ed.). New York: John Wiley & Sons.

49 Broadbent, D. E. (1958). *The effects of noise on behaviour.* Elmsford, NY: Pergamon Press.

50 Soderlund, G., Sikstrom, S., & Smart, A. (2007). Listen to the noise: Noise is beneficial for cognitive performance in ADHD. *Journal of Child Psychology and Psychiatry, 48,* 840–847.

51 Janusik, L. A. (2002). Teaching listening: What do we do? What should we do? *International Journal of Listening, 16,* 5–39.

52 Wanzer, M. B., Booth-Butterfield, M., & Gruber, K. (2004). Perceptions of health care providers' communication: Relationships between patient-centered communication and satisfaction. *Health Communication, 16,* 363–384.

53 Bentley, S. C. (2000). Listening in the 21st century. *International Journal of Listening, 14,* 129–142.

54 Murphy, D. R., Daneman, M., & Schneider, B. A. (2006). Why do older adults have difficulty following conversations? *Psychology and Aging, 21,* 49–61.

55 Martin, J. S., Jerger, J. F. (2005). Some effects of aging on central auditory processing. *Journal of Rehabilitation Research & Development, 42,* 25–44.

56 Giordano, J. A. (2000). Effective communication and counseling with older adults. *International Journal of Aging and Human Development, 51,* 315–324.

57 Dillon, R. K., & McKenzie, N. J. (1998). The influence of ethnicity on listening, communication competence, approach, and avoidance. *International Journal of Listening, 12,* 106–121.

58 Dillon, R. K., & McKenzie, N. J. (1998). The influence of ethnicity on listening, communication competence, approach, and avoidance. *International Journal of Listening, 12,* 106–121.

59 Seo, K. (2005). Development of a listening strategy intervention program for adult learners of Japanese. *International Journal of Listening, 19,* 63–78.

60 Huang, J. (2006). English abilities for academic listening: How confident are Chinese students? *College Student Journal, 40,* 218–226.

61 Seo, K. (2002). The effect of visuals on listening comprehension: A study of Japanese learners' listening strategies. *International Journal of Listening, 16,* 57–81.

62 Sueyoshi, A., & Hardison, D. M. (2005). The role of gestures and facial cues in second language listening comprehension. *Language Learning, 55,* 661–699.

63 Brownell, J. (2006). *Listening: Attitudes, principles, and skills* (3rd ed.). Boston: Pearson.

64 Burley-Allen, M. (1995). *Listening: The forgotten skill* (2nd ed.). New York: John Wiley & Sons.

65 Britton, M. E. (2005). Keys to improving your listening skills. *Family Practice Management, 12*(4), 1.

66 Paternostro, J. M. (1993, November). Improving your listening skills. *Nursing, 23*(11), 84–86.

67 Goss, B. (1995). *The psychology of human communication* (2nd ed.). Prospect Heights, IL: Waveland Press.

68 Wolvin, A. D., Berko, R. M., & Wolvin, D. R. (1993). *The public speaker/the public listener.* Boston: Houghton Mifflin.

69 Wolvin, A. D., Berko, R. M., & Wolvin, D. R. (1993). *The public speaker/the public listener.* Boston: Houghton Mifflin.

Chapter 7

1 Planalp, S. (1999). *Communicating emotion: Social, moral, and cultural processes.* Cambridge, UK: Cambridge University Press.

2 Goleman, D. (1995). *Emotional intelligence.* New York: Bantam; Salovey, P. & Meyer, J. M. (1998). Emotional intelligence. In J. M. Jenkins, K. Oatley, & N. L. Stein (Eds.), *Human emotions* (pp. 313–319). Malden, MA: Blackwell.

3 Planalp, S. (1999). *Communicating emotion: Social, moral, and cultural processes.* New York: Cambridge University Press; Russell, J. A., & Barrett, L. F. (1999). Core affect, prototypical emotional episodes, and other things called emotion: Dissecting the elephant. *Journal of Personality and Social Psychology, 76,* 805–819; Hatfield, E., Cacioppo, J. T., & Rapson, R. L. (1994). *Emotional contagion.* New York: Cambridge University Press.

4 Damasio, A. (1999). *The feelings of what happens: Body and emotion in the making of consciousness.* New York: Harcourt.

5 Damasio, A. (1999). *The feelings of what happens: Body and emotion in the making of consciousness.* New York: Harcourt.

6 Dillard, J. P. (1998). The role of affect in communication, biology, and social relationships. In P. A. Andersen & L. K. Guerrero (Eds.), *Handbook of communication and emotion: Research, theory, applications, and contexts* (pp. xvii–xxxii). New York: Academic Press.

7 Andersen, P. A., & Guerrero, L. K. (1998). Principles of communication and emotion in social interaction. In P. A. Andersen & L. K. Guerrero (Eds.), *Handbook of communication and emotion: Research, theory, applications, and contexts* (pp. 49–96). New York: Academic Press.

8 For a review of this research, see Croyle, K. L., & Waltz, J. (2002). Emotional awareness and couples' relationship satisfaction. *Journal of Marital and Family Therapy, 28,* 435–444.

[9] Gazzaniga, M. S., Ivry, R. B., & Mangun, G. R. (2002). *Cognitive neuroscience: The biology of the mind* (2nd ed., pp. 572–575). New York: W. W. Norton & Company; Floyd, K., & Mikkelson, A. C. (2003). Effects of brain laterality on accuracy of decoding facial displays of emotions. *Communication Quarterly, 51,* 419–437.

[10] Gazzaniga, M. S., Ivry, R. B., & Mangun, G. R. (2002). *Cognitive neuroscience: The biology of the mind* (2nd ed.). New York: W. W. Norton & Company, pp. 545–546; Beatty, M. J., & McCroskey, J. C. (2001). *The biology of communication: A communibiological perspective.* Cresskill, NJ: Hampton Press.

[11] Damasio, A. (1999). *The feelings of what happens: Body and emotion in the making of consciousness.* New York: Harcourt; Le Doux, J. E. (1992). Emotion and the amygdala. In J. P. Aggleton (Ed.), *The amygdala: Neurobiological aspects of emotion, memory, and mental dysfunction* (pp. 339–351). New York: Wiley-Liss.

[12] Damasio, A. R. (1994). *Descartes' error: Emotion, reason, and the human brain.* New York: G. P. Putnam; MacLean, P. D. (1949). Psychosomatic disease and the "visceral brain": Recent developments bearing on the Papez theory of emotion. *Psychosomatic Medicine, 11,* 338–353; Gray, J. A. (1991). The neuropsychology of temperament. In J. Strelau & A. Angleitner (Eds.), *Explorations in temperament* (pp. 105–128). New York: Plenum; Davidson, R. J., Ekman, P., Saron, C. D., Senulis, J. A., & Friesen, W. V. (1990). Approach-withdrawal and cerebral asymmetry: Emotional expression and brain physiology: I. *Journal of Personality and Social Psychology, 58,* 330–341.

[13] Gazzaniga, M. S., Ivry, R. B., & Mangun, G. R. (2002). *Cognitive neuroscience: The biology of the mind* (2nd ed.). New York: W. W. Norton & Company.

[14] Godfrey, H. P. D. & Shum, D. (2000). Executive functioning and the application of social skills following traumatic brain injury. *Aphasiology, 14,* 433–444; Karow, C. M., & Connors, E. C. (2003). Affective communication in normal and brain-damaged adults: An overview. *Seminars in Speech and Language, 24,* 69–91; McDonald, S. (2003). Traumatic brain injury and psychosocial function: Let's get social. *Brain Impairment, 4,* 36–47.

[15] Mottet, T. P., & Beebe, S. A. (2002). Relationships between teacher nonverbal immediacy, student emotional response, and perceived student learning. *Communication Research Reports, 19,* 77–88; Byrnes, J. P. (2001). *Minds, brains, and learning.* New York: Guilford Press; Zull, J. E. (2002). *The art of changing the brain.* Sterling, VA: Stylus; Immordino-Yang, M. H., & Damasio, A. (2007). We feel, therefore we learn: The relevance of affective and social neuroscience to education. *Mind, Brain, and Education, 1,* 3–10.

[16] Crossman, J. (2007). The role of relationships and emotions in student perceptions of learning and assessment. *Higher Education Research & Development, 26,* 313–327; Dirkx, J. M. (2008). The meaning and role of emotions in adult learning. *New Directions for Adult and Continuing Education, 120,* 7–18; Zembylas, M., Theodorou, M., & Pavlakis, A. (2008). The role of emotions in the experience of online learning: Challenges and opportunities. *Educational Media International, 45,* 107–117.

[17] Mottet, T. P., & Richmond, V. P. (1998). New is not necessarily better: A reexamination of affective learning measurement. *Communication Research Reports, 15(4),* 370–378; Krathwohl, D. R., Bloom, B. S., & Masia, B. B. (1964). *Taxonomy of educational objectives: Handbook II: Affective domain.* New York: McKay; Mottet, T. P., & Beebe, S. A. (2006). Foundations of instructional communication. In T. P. Mottet, V. P. Richmond, & J. C. McCroskey (Eds.), *Handbook of instructional communication: Rhetorical and relational perspectives* (pp. 3–32). Boston: Allyn and Bacon.

[18] Adams, J. C. (2008). The effects of out-of-class social support on student satisfaction and motivation to learn. *Communication Education, 57,* 373–388; Pauley, P. M., & Hess, C. (2009). The effects of social support, depression, and stress on drinking behaviors in a college student sample. *Communication Studies, 60,* 493–508; Xu, Y., & Burleson, B. R. (2004). The association of experienced spousal support with marital satisfaction: Evaluating the moderating effects of sex, ethnic culture, and type of support. *Journal of Family Communication, 4,* 123–145.

[19] Snyder, J. (2009). The role of coworker and supervisor social support in alleviating the experience of burnout for caregivers in the human-service industry. *Southern Communication Journal, 74,* 373–389; Miller, K. I., Stiff, J. B., & Ellis, B. H. (1988). Communication and empathy as precursors to burnout among human service workers. *Communication Monographs, 55,* 250–266.

[20] Jorgensen, P. F. (1998). Affect, persuasion, and communication processes. In P. A. Andersen & L. K. Guerrero (Eds.), *Handbook of communication and emotion: Research, theory, applications, and contexts* (pp. 403–422). New York: Academic Press.

[21] Aristotle (1991). *The art of rhetoric* (H. C. Lawson-Tancred, Trans.). New York: Penguin Books.

[22] Gottman, J. M., & Notarius, C. I. (2002). Marital research in the 20th century and a research agenda for the 21st century. *Family Process, 41,* 159–197; see also Gottman, J. M. (2001). *The relationship cure.* New York: Three Rivers Press.

[23] Riggio, H. R., & Riggio, R. E. (2002). Emotional expressiveness, extraversion, and neuroticism: A meta-analysis. *Journal of Nonverbal Behavior, 26,* 195–218.

[24] Riggio, H. R., & Riggio, R. E. (2002). Emotional expressiveness, extraversion, and neuroticism: A meta-analysis. *Journal of Nonverbal Behavior, 26,* 195–218.

[25] Riggio, R. E. (2005). The social skills inventory (SSI): Measuring nonverbal and social skills. In V. Manusov (Ed.), *The sourcebook of nonverbal messages: Going beyond words* (pp. 25–33). Mahwah, NJ: Erlbaum.

[26] Riggio, H. R., & Riggio, R. E. (2002). Emotional expressiveness, extraversion, and neuroticism: A meta-analysis. *Journal of Nonverbal Behavior, 26,* 195–218.

[27] Allport, G. W., & Vernon, P. E. (1933). *Studies in expressive movement.* New York: Hafner; Kagan, J., Reznick, J. S., Snidman, N., Gibbons, J., & Johnson, M. O. (1988). Childhood derivatives of inhibition and lack of inhibition to the unfamiliar. *Child Development, 59,* 1580–1589.

[28] Booth-Butterfield, M., & Booth-Butterfield, S. (1998). Emotionality and affective orientation. In J. C. McCroskey, J. A. Daly, M. M. Martin, & M. J. Beatty (Eds.), *Communication and personality: Trait perspectives* (pp. 171–189). Cresskill, NJ: Hampton Press; see also Booth-Butterfield, M., & Booth-Butterfield, S. (1990). Conceptualizing affect as information in communication production. *Human Communication Research, 16,* 451–476; Booth-Butterfield, M., & Booth-Butterfield, S. (1994). The affective orientation to communication: Conceptual and empirical distinctions. *Communication Quarterly, 42,* 331–344.

[29] Booth-Butterfield, M., & Booth-Butterfield, S. (1998). Emotionality and affective orientation. In J. C. McCroskey, J. A. Daly, M. M. Martin, & M. J. Beatty (Eds.), *Communication and personality: Trait perspectives* (pp. 171–189). Cresskill, NJ: Hampton Press.

[30] Booth-Butterfield, M., & Booth-Butterfield, S. (1998). Emotionality and affective orientation. In J. C. McCroskey, J. A. Daly, M. M. Martin, & M. J. Beatty (Eds.), *Communication and personality: Trait perspectives* (pp. 171–189). Cresskill, NJ: Hampton Press.

[31] Booth-Butterfield, M., & Booth-Butterfield, S. (1998). Emotionality and affective orientation. In J. C. McCroskey, J. A. Daly, M. M. Martin, & M. J. Beatty (Eds.), *Communication and personality: Trait perspectives* (pp. 171–189). Cresskill, NJ: Hampton Press.

[32] Booth-Butterfield, M., & Booth-Butterfield, S. (1998). Emotionality and affective orientation. In J. C. McCroskey, J. A. Daly, M. M. Martin, & M. J. Beatty (Eds.), *Communication and personality: Trait perspectives* (pp. 171–189). Cresskill, NJ: Hampton Press.

[33] Hatfield, E., Cacioppo, J. T., & Rapson, R. L. (1994). *Emotional contagion.* New York: Cambridge University Press.

[34] Rizzolatti, G., & Craighero, L. (2004). The mirror-neuron system. *Annual Review of Neuroscience, 27,* 169–192; Carr, L., Iacoboni, M., Dubeau, M. C., Mazziotta, J. C., & Lenzi, G. L. (2003). Neural mechanisms of empathy in humans: A relay from neural systems to imitation to limbic areas. *Proceedings of the National Academy of Sciences (PNAS), 100,* 5497–5502.

[35] Bangert, M., Peschel, T., Schlaug, G., Rotte, M., Drescher, D., Hinrichs, H., Heinze, H.J., & Altenmüllera, E. (2006). Shared networks for auditory and motor processing in professional pianists: Evidence from fMRI conjunction. *NeuroImage, 30,* 917–926.

[36] Gazzola, V., Aziz-Zadeh, L., & Keysers, C. (2006). Empathy and the somatotopic auditory mirror system in humans. *Current Biology, 16,* 1824–1829.

[37] Gazzola, V., Aziz-Zadeh, L., & Keysers, C. (2006). Empathy and the somatotopic auditory mirror system in humans. *Current Biology, 16,* 1824–1829.

[38] Bangert, M., Peschel, T., Schlaug, G., Rotte, M., Drescher, D., Hinrichs, H., Heinze, H. J., & Altenmüllera, E. (2006). Shared networks for auditory and motor processing in professional pianists: Evidence from fMRI conjunction. *NeuroImage, 30,* 917–926.

[39] Hatfield, E., Cacioppo, J. T., & Rapson, R. L. (1994). *Emotional contagion.* New York: Cambridge University Press.

[40] Doherty, R. W. (1997). The emotional contagion scale: A measure of individual differences. *Journal of Nonverbal Behavior, 21,* 131–154.

[41] Hatfield, E., Cacioppo, J. T., & Rapson, R. L. (1994). *Emotional contagion.* New York: Cambridge University Press; Mottet, T. P., & Beebe, S. A. (2000, November). *Emotional contagion in the classroom: An examination of how teacher and student emotions are related.* Paper presented at annual conference of the National Communication Association, Seattle, WA. [ERIC ED 447 522]; Homburg, C., & Stock, R. M. (2004). The link between salespeople's job satisfaction and customer satisfaction in a business-to-business context: A dyadic analysis. *Journal of the Academy of Marketing Science, 32,* 144–158.

[42] Miller, K. I., Stiff, J. B., & Ellis, B. H. (1988). Communication and empathy as precursors to burnout among human service workers. *Communication Monographs, 55,* 250–265; Hochschild, A. (1983). *The managed heart.* Berkeley: University of California Press.

[43] Hatfield, E., Cacioppo, J. T., & Rapson, R. L. (1994). *Emotional contagion.* New York: Cambridge University Press

[44] Cappella, J. N. (1993). The facial feedback hypothesis in human interaction: Review and speculation. *Journal of Language and Social Psychology, 12,* 13–29; Laird, J. D. (1974). Self-attribution of emotion: The effects of expressive behavior on the quality of emotional experience. *Journal of Personality and Social Psychology, 29,* 475–486; Hatfield, E., Hsee, C. K., Costello, J., Schalenhamp, M., & Denney, C. (1995). The impact of vocal feedback on emotional experience and expression. *Journal of Social Behavior & Personality, 10,* 293–312.

[45] Hochschild, A. (1983). *The managed heart.* Berkeley: University of California Press; Hochschild, A. (1997). *The time bind.* New York: Henry Holt.

[46] Freudenberger, H. J. (1974). Staff burn-out. *Journal of Social Issues, 30,* 159–165.

[47] Cordes, C. L., & Dougherty, T. W. (1993). A review and integration of research on job burnout. *Academy of Management Review, 18,* 621–656; Maslach, C. (1982). *Burnout: The cost of caring.* Englewood Cliffs, NJ: Prentice Hall.

[48] See Miller, K. (2009). *Organizational communication: Approaches and processes* (5th ed., p. 207). Boston: Wadsworth Cengage Learning; see also *Preventing burnout: Signs, symptoms, causes, and coping strategies.* Retrieved June 24, 2009, from http://www.helpguide.org/mental/burnout_signs_symptoms.htm.

[49] This model was partially adapted from *Preventing burnout: Signs, symptoms, causes, and coping strategies.* Retrieved June 24, 2009, from http://www.helpguide.org/mental/burnout_signs_symptoms.htm.

[50] See Miller, K. (2009). *Organizational communication: Approaches and processes* (5th ed., p. 207). Boston: Wadsworth Cengage Learning; see also Miller, K. I., Stiff, J. B., & Ellis, B. H. (1988). Communication and empathy as precursors to burnout among human service workers. *Communication Monographs, 55,* 250–265

[51] For a review of this research, see Albrecht, T. L., Burleson, B. R., & Goldsmith, D. (1995). Supportive communication. In M. Knapp & G. R. Miller (Eds.), *Handbook of Interpersonal Communication* (pp. 419–449). Thousand Oaks, CA: Sage.

[52] Barrett, L. F., Gross, J., Christensen, T., & Benvenuto, M. (2001). Knowing what you're feeling and knowing what to do about it: Mapping the relation between emotion differentiation and emotion regulation. *Cognition and Emotion, 15,* 713–724

[53] Schachter, S., & Singer, J. (1962). Cognitive, social, and physiological determinants of emotional state. *Psychological Review, 69,* 379–399.

[54] Kagan, J. (1992). Temperamental contributions to emotion and social behavior. In M. S. Clark (Ed.), *Emotion and social behavior* (pp. 99–118). Newbury Park, CA: Sage; Chess, S., & Thomas, A. (1989). Temperament and its functional significance. In S. I. Greenspan & G. H. Pollock (Eds.), *The course of life: Early childhood* (Vol. 2, pp. 163–228). Madison, CT: International Universities Press.

[55] Bates, J. E. (1987). Temperament in infancy. In J. D. Osofsky (Ed.), *Handbook of infant development* (2nd ed., pp. 1101–1149). New York: Wiley; Bates, J. E., & Wachs, T. D. (Eds.). (1994). *Temperament: Individual differences at the interface of biology and behavior.* Washington, DC: American Psychological Association.

[56] Booth-Butterfield, M. (2002). *Interpersonal essentials.* Boston: Allyn and Bacon.

[57] Goffman, E. (1959). *The presentation of self in everyday life.* New York: Doubleday.

[58] Hayes, J. G., & Metts, S. (2008). Managing the expression of emotion. *Western Journal of Communication, 72,* 374–396; Burgoon, J. K. (1993). Interpersonal expectations, expectancy violations, and emotional communication. *Journal of Language and Social Psychology, 12,* 30–48.

[59] Ekman, P. (1978). Facial expression. In A. W. Siegman & S. Feldstein (Eds.), *Nonverbal behavior and communication* (pp. 97–116). Hillsdale, NJ: Erlbaum.

[60] Kring, A. M., & Gordon, A. H. (1998). Sex differences in emotion: Expression, experience, and physiology. *Journal of Personality and Social Psychology, 74,* 686–703.

[61] Kring, A. M., & Gordon, A. H. (1998). Sex differences in emotion: Expression, experience, and physiology. *Journal of Personality and Social Psychology, 74,* 686–703.

[62] For a review of this research, see Guerrero, L. K., & Reiter, R. L. (1998). Expressing emotion: Sex differences in social skills and communicative responses to anger, sadness, and jealousy. In D. J. Canary & K. Dindia (Eds.), *Sex differences and similarities in communication* (pp. 321–350). Mahwah, NJ: Erlbaum; Croyle, K. L., & Waltz, J. (2002). Emotional awareness and couples' relationship satisfaction. *Journal of Marital and Family Therapy, 28,* 435–444; Ciarrochi, J., Hynes, K., & Crittenden, N. (2005). Can men do better if they try harder?: Sex and motivational effects on emotional awareness. *Cognition and Emotion, 19,* 133–141; Lane, R. D., Quinlan, D. M., Schwartz, G. E., Walker, P. A., & Zeitlin, S. B. (1990). The levels of emotional awareness scale: A cognitive-developmental measure of emotion. *Journal of Personality Assessment, 55,* 124–134.

[63] Rosip, J. C., & Hall, J. A. (2004). Knowledge of nonverbal cues, gender, and nonverbal decoding accuracy. *Journal of Nonverbal Behavior, 28,* 267–286.

[64] Burgoon, J. K., & Bacue, A. E. (2003). Nonverbal communication skills. In J. O. Greene & B. R. Burleson (Eds.), *Handbook of communication and social interaction skills* (pp. 179–219). Mahwah, NJ: Erlbaum; Floyd, K. (2006). *Communicating affection: Interpersonal behaviors and social context.* Cambridge, UK: Cambridge University Press; Blier, M. J., & Blier-Wilson, L. A., (1989). Gender differences in sex-rated emotional expressiveness. *Sex Roles, 21,* 287–295; Riggio, R. E. (1993). Social interaction skills and nonverbal behavior. In R. S. Feldman (Ed.), *Applications of nonverbal behavioral theories and research* (pp. 3–30). Hillsdale, NJ: Erlbaum.

[65] Gur, R. C., Turetsky, B. I., Matsui, M., Yan, M., Bilker, W., Hughett, P., & Gur, R. E. (1999). Sex differences in brain gray and white matter in healthy young adults: Correlations with cognitive performance. *The Journal of Neuroscience, 19,* 4065–4072; see also Brody, L. R. (1985). Gender differences in emotional development: A review of theories and research. *Journal of Personality, 53,* 102–149.

[66] For a review of this research, see Guerrero, L. K., & Reiter, R. L. (1998). Expressing emotion: Sex differences in social skills and communicative responses to anger, sadness, and jealousy. In D. J. Canary & K. Dindia (Eds.), *Sex differences and similarities in communication* (pp. 321–350). Mahwah, NJ: Erlbaum

[67] Guerrero, L. K., & Reiter, R. L. (1998). Expressing emotion: Sex differences in social skills and communicative responses to anger, sadness, and jealousy. In D. J. Canary & K. Dindia (Eds.), *Sex differences and similarities in communication* (pp. 321–350). Mahwah, NJ: Erlbaum.

[68] Burleson, B. R. (2003). Emotional support skill. In J. O. Greene & B. R. Burleson (Eds.), *Handbook of communication and social interaction skills* (pp. 551–594). Mahwah, NJ: Erlbaum

[69] Guerrero, L. K., & Reiter, R. L. (1998). Expressing emotion: Sex differences in social skills and communicative responses to anger, sadness, and jealousy. In D. J. Canary & K. Dindia (Eds.), *Sex differences and similarities in communication* (pp. 321–350). Mahwah, NJ: Erlbaum.

[70] Guerrero, L. K., & Reiter, R. L. (1998). Expressing emotion: Sex differences in social skills and communicative responses to anger, sadness, and jealousy. In D. J. Canary & K. Dindia (Eds.), *Sex differences and similarities in communication* (pp. 321–350). Mahwah, NJ: Erlbaum.

[71] Buss, D. M., Shackelford, T. K., Kirkpatrick, L. E., Choe, J. C., Hang, K. L., Hawegawa, M., Hawegawa, T., & Bennett, K. (1999). Jealously and the nature of beliefs about infidelity: Tests of competing hypotheses about sex differences in the United States, Korea, and Japan. *Personal Relationships, 6,* 125–150; Takahashi, H., Matsuura, M., Yahata, N., Koeda, M., Suhara, T., & Okubo, Y. (2006). Men and women show distinct brain activations during imagery of sexual and emotional fidelity. *Neuroimage, 32,* 1299–1307.

[72] All of the findings in this section are published in Matsumoto, D. (2008). Mapping expressive differences around

the world: The relationship between emotional display rules and individualism and collectivism. *Journal of Cross-Cultural Psychology, 39,* 55–72.

[73] Matsumoto, D. (2008). Mapping expressive differences around the world: The relationship between emotional display rules and individualism and collectivism. *Journal of Cross-Cultural Psychology, 39,* 55–72.

[74] Matsumoto, D. (2008). Mapping expressive differences around the world: The relationship between emotional display rules and individualism and collectivism. *Journal of Cross-Cultural Psychology, 39,* 55–72.

[75] Refer to Krakovsky, M. (2009, January 1). *Global psyche: National poker face.* Retrieved June 29, 2009, from http://www.psychologytoday.com/node/20211.

[76] Krakovsky, M. (2009, January 1). *Global psyche: National poker face.* Retrieved June 29, 2009, from http://www.psychologytoday.com/node/20211.

[77] Mayer, J. D., & Salovey, P. (1997). What is emotional intelligence. In P. Salovey & D. Sluyter (Eds.), *Emotional development and emotional intelligence: Implications for educators* (pp. 3–31). New York: Basic Books; Salovey, P., & Mayer, J. D. (1990). Emotional intelligence. *Imagination, Cognition, and Personality, 9,* 185–211.

[78] As with other social scientific constructs, researchers question whether emotional intelligence meets the traditional "intelligence" standards. To understand their arguments, see Roberts, R. D., Zeidner, M., & Matthews, G. (2001). Does emotional intelligence meet the traditional standards for an intelligence?: Some new data and conclusions. *Emotion, 1,* 196–231; Brody, N. (2004). What cognitive intelligence is and what emotional intelligence is not. *Psychological Inquiry, 15,* 234–238.

[79] Salovey, P., & Grewal, D. (2005). The science of emotional intelligence. *Current directions in psychological science, 14,* 6.

[80] Salovey, P., & Meyer, J. M. (1998). Emotional intelligence. In J. M. Jenkins, K. Oatley, & N. L. Stein (Eds.), *Human emotion: A reader* (pp. 313–319). Malden, MA: Blackwell.

[81] Lopes, P. N., Salovey, P., & Straus, R. (2003). Emotional intelligence, personality, and the perceived quality of social relationships. *Personality and Individual Differences, 35,* 641–658.

[82] Zeidner, M., Matthews, G., Roberts, R. (2004). Emotional intelligence in the workplace: A critical review. *Applied psychology: An International Review, 53,* 371–399.

[83] Gottman, J. (1997). *Raising an emotionally intelligent child.* New York: Simon and Schuster (pp. 39–40).

[84] Brackett, M. A., Mayer, J. D., & Warner, R. M. (2004). Emotional intelligence and its relation to everyday behavior. *Personality and Individual Differences, 36,* 1387–1402; Lopes, P. N., Salovey, P., & Straus, R. (2003). Emotional intelligence, personality, and the perceived quality of social relationships. *Personality and Individual Differences, 35,* 641–658.

[85] Keaten, J., & Kelly, L. (2008). Emotional intelligence as a mediator of family communication patterns and reticence. *Communication Reports, 21,* 104–116.

[86] Walther, J. B., Loh, T., & Granka, L. (2005). Let me count the ways: The interchange of verbal and nonverbal cues in computer-mediated and face-to-face affinity. *Journal of Language & Social Psychology, 24,* 36–65; Walther, J. B., Van Der Heide, B., Kim, S. Y., Westerman, D., & Tong, S. T. (2008). The role of friends' appearance and behavior on evaluations of individuals on Facebook: Are we known by the company we keep? *Human Communication Research, 34,* 28–49.

[87] Culnan, M. J., & Markus, M. L. (1987). Information technologies. In F. M. Jablin, L. L. Putnam, K. H. Roberts, & L. W. Porter (Eds.), *Handbook of organizational communication: An interdisciplinary perspective* (pp. 420–443). Newbury Park, CA: Sage; Mottet, T. P., & Stewart, S. L. (2002). Teacher communication in the distance education context. In J. L. Chesebro & J. C. McCroskey (Eds.), *Communication for teachers* (pp. 157–171). Needham Heights, MA: Allyn and Bacon; Mottet, T. P. (2000). Interactive television instructors' perceptions of students' nonverbal responsiveness and their influence on distance teaching. *Communication Education, 49,* 146–164.

[88] Matsumoto, D. (2007). Playing catch with emotions. *Journal of Intercultural Communication, 10,* 39–49; Matsumoto, D., Consolacion, T., Yamada, H., Suzuki, R., Franklin, B., Paul, S., et al. (2002). American-Japanese cultural differences in judgments of emotional expressions of different intensities. *Cognition and Emotion, 16,* 721–747.

[89] Matsumoto, D. (2007). Playing catch with emotions. *Journal of Intercultural Communication, 10,* 39–49

[90] Lee, K. M., & Nass, C. (2005). Social-psychological origins of feelings of presence: Creating social presence with machine-generated voices. *Media Psychology, 7,* 31–45.

[91] Lee, K. M., & Nass, C. (2005). Social-psychological origins of feelings of presence: Creating social presence with machine-generated voices. *Media Psychology, 7,* 31–45.

Chapter 8

[1] Spitzberg, B. H., & Cupach, W. R. (Eds.). (2007). *The dark side of interpersonal communication.* Mahwah, NJ: Erlbaum.

[2] Cupach, W. R., & Canary, D. J. (1997). *Competence in interpersonal conflict.* Long Grove, IL: Waveland Press.

[3] Wilmot, W. W., & Hocker, J. L. (2007). *Interpersonal conflict* (7th ed.). New York: McGraw-Hill.

[4] Shantz, C. U. (1987). Conflicts between children. *Child Development, 58,* 283–305.

[5] Hocker, J. L., & Wilmot, W. W. (1991). *Interpersonal conflict* (3rd ed.). Dubuque, IA: William C. Brown.

[6] Markman, J. J., Stanley, S. M., Blumberg, S. I., Jenkins, N., & Whiteley, C. (2004). *Twelve hours to a great marriage.* San Francisco: Jossey-Bass.

[7] Laursen, B. (1993). The perceived impact of conflict on adolescent relationships. *Merrill-Palmer Quarterly, 39,* 535–550; Lloyd, S. A. (1987). Conflict in premarital relationships: Differential perceptions of males and females. *Family Relations, 36,* 290–294.

[8] Vuchinich, S. (1984). Sequencing and social structure in family conflict. *Social Psychology Quarterly, 47,* 217–234.

[9] Cupach, W. R., & Canary, D. J. (1997). *Competence in interpersonal conflict.* Long Grove, IL: Waveland Press.

[10] Dunn, J. (1993). *Young children's close relationships: Beyond attachment.* Newbury Park, CA: Sage; Shantz, C. U., & Hartup, W. W. (1992). *Conflict in child and adolescent development.* New York: Cambridge University Press.

[11] Emery, R. E. (1992). Family conflicts and their developmental implications: A conceptual analysis of meanings for the structure of relationships. In C. U. Shantz & W. W. Hartup (Eds.), *Conflict in child and adolescent development.* New York: Cambridge University Press.

[12] Furman, W., & McQuaid, E. L. (1992). Intervention programs for the management of conflict. In C. U. Shantz & W. W. Hartup, (Eds.), *Conflict in child and adolescent development.* New York: Cambridge University Press.

[13] Rinaldi, C., & Howe, N. (1998). Siblings' reports of conflict and the quality of their relationships. *Merrill-Palmer Quarterly, 44,* 404–422.

[14] Gottman, J. M. (1999). *The marriage clinic: A scientifically based marital therapy.* New York: W. W. Norton and Company.

[15] Deutsch, M. (1973). *The resolution of conflict: Constructive and destructive processes.* New Haven, CT: Yale University Press.

[16] Wilmot, W. W., & Hocker, J. L. (2007). *Interpersonal conflict* (7th ed.). New York: McGraw-Hill.

[17] Cupach, W. R., & Canary, D. J. (1997). *Competence in interpersonal conflict.* Long Grove, IL: Waveland Press.

[18] Deutsch, M. (1973). *The resolution of conflict: Constructive and destructive processes.* New Haven, CT: Yale University Press.

[19] Sillars, A. L., Weisberg, J., Burggraf, C. S., & Zietlow, P. H. (1990). Communication and understanding revisited: Married couples' understanding and recall of conversations. *Communication Research, 17,* 500–532.

[20] Cissna, K. N., & Sieburg, E. (1981). Patterns of interactional confirmation and disconfirmation. In C. Wilder-Mott & J. H. Weakland (Eds.), *Rigor and imagination: Essays from the legacy of Gregory Bateson* (pp. 253–282). New York: Praeger; Sieburg, E. (1976). Confirming and disconfirming organizational communication. In J. L. Owen, P. A. Page, & G. I. Zimmerman (Eds.), *Communication in organizations* (pp. 129–149). St. Paul, MN: West.

[21] Spitzberg, B. H. & Cupach, W. R. (Eds.). (2007). *The dark side of interpersonal communication.* Mahwah, NJ: Erlbaum.

[22] Sieburg, E., & Larson, C. (1971 April). *Dimensions of interpersonal response.* Paper presented at the International Communication Association convention, Phoenix, AZ.

[23] Sieburg, E., & Larson, C. (1971 April). *Dimensions of interpersonal response.* Paper presented at the International Communication Association convention, Phoenix, AZ.

[24] Dailey, R. M. (2006). Confirmation in parent-adolescent relationships and adolescent openness: Toward extending confirmation theory. *Communication Monographs, 73,* 434–458; Sieburg, E. (1985). *Family communication: An integrated systems approach.* New York: Gardner Press.

[25] Hanan, E., & Schwartz, Y. (2009, January 5). Confronting racism in America: Customers react very differently when Hispanics denied service at N.J. deli. *abcNEWS.* Retrieved January 10, 2009, from http://abcnews.go.com/WhatWouldYouDo/story?id= 6551048&page=1.

[26] Gottman, J. (2006). Why marriages fail. In K. M. Galvin & P. J. Cooper (Eds.), *Making connections: Readings in relational communication,* 4th ed. (pp. 228–236). Los Angeles: Roxbury.

[27] Wilmot, W. W., & Hocker, J. L. (2007). *Interpersonal conflict* (7th ed.). New York: McGraw Hill.

[28] Wilmot, W. W., & Hocker, J. L. (2007). *Interpersonal conflict* (7th ed.). New York: McGraw Hill.

[29] Deutsch, M. (1973). *The resolution of conflict: Constructive and destructive processes.* New Haven, CT: Yale University Press.

[30] Deutsch, M. (2000). Cooperation and competition. In M. Deutsch & P. T. Coleman (Eds.), *The handbook of conflict resolution: Theory and practice.* (pp. 21–40). San Francisco: Jossey-Bass.

[31] Deutsch, M. (2000). Cooperation and competition. In M. Deutsch & P. T. Coleman (Eds.), *The handbook of conflict resolution: Theory and practice.* (pp. 21–40). San Francisco: Jossey-Bass.

[32] Maslow, A. (1970). *Motivation and personality.* New York: HarperCollins; Schutz, W. C. (1980). *FIRO: A three dimensional theory of interpersonal behavior.* New York: Holt, Rinehart and Winston.

[33] Vangelisti, A. L., & Young, S. L. (2000). When words hurt: The effects of perceived intentionality on interpersonal relationships. *Journal of Social and Personal Relationships, 17,* 393–424.

[34] Birchler, G.R., Weiss, R. L., & Vincent, J. P. (1975). A multimethod analysis of social reinforcement exchange between martially distressed and nondistressed marital dyads. *Journal of Personality and Social Psychology, 31,* 349–376; Noller, P. (1984). *Nonverbal communication and marital interaction.* New York: Pergamon Press.

[35] Dixon, S. V., Graber, J. A., & Brooks-Gunn, J. (2008). The roles of respect for parental authority and parenting practices in parent–child conflict among African American, Latino, and European American families. *Journal of Family Psychology, 22,* 1–10.

[36] Reis, H. T., Capobianco, A., & Tsai, F. F. (2002). Finding the person in personal relationships. *Journal of Personality, 70,* 813–850.

[37] Elliot, A. J., & Thrash, T. M. (2002). Approach-avoidance motivation in personality: Approach and avoidance temperaments and goals. *Journal of Personality and Social Psychology, 82,* 804–818; Watson, D., Wiese, D., Vaidya, J., & Tellegen, A. (1999). The two general activation systems of affect: Structural findings, evolutionary considerations, and psychobiological evidence. *Journal of Personality and Social Psychology, 76,* 820–838.

[38] Keltner, D., Gruenfeld, D. H., & Anderson, C. (2003). Power, approach and inhibition. *Psychological Review, 110,* 265–284.

[39] Gottman, J. M. (1993). The roles of conflict engagement, escalation, and avoidance in marital interaction: A longitudinal view of five types of couples. *Journal of Consulting and Clinical Psychology, 61,* 6–15.

[40] Allport, G. W. (1937). *Personality: A psychological interpretation.* New York: Holt.

[41] Sutton, S. K., & Davidson, R. J. (1997). Pre-frontal brain asymmetry: A biological substrate of the behavioral approach and inhibition systems. *Psychological Science, 8,* 204–210.

[42] Digman, J. M. (1990). Personality structure: Emergence of the five-factor model. *Annual Review of Psychology, 41,* 417–440; John, O. P. (1990). The "Big Five" factor taxonomy: Dimensions of personality in the natural language in questionnaires. In L. A. Pervin (Ed.), *Handbook of personality: Theory and research* (pp. 66–100). New York: Guilford Press.

[43] Eysenck, H. J., & Eysenck, M. W. (1985). *Personality and individual differences: A natural science approach.* New York: Plenum Press.

[44] Impett, E. A., & Peplau, L. A. (2006). "His" and "her" relationships?: A review of the empirical evidence. In A. L. Vangelisti & D. Perlman (Eds.). *The Cambridge handbook of personal relationships* (pp. 273–291). New York: Cambridge University Press.

[45] Blumstein, P., & Schwartz, P. (1983). *American couples.* New York: Pocket Books.

[46] Impett, E. A., & Peplau, L. A. (2006). "His" and "her" relationships?: A review of the empirical evidence. In A. L. Vangelisti & D. Perlman (Eds.). *The Cambridge handbook of personal relationships* (pp. 273–291). New York: Cambridge University Press.

[47] Schutz, W. C. (1980). *FIRO: A three-dimensional theory of interpersonal behavior.* New York: Holt, Rinehart and Winston.

[48] Brown, C. T., & Keller, P. W. (1973). *Monologue to dialogue.* Englewood Cliffs, N J: Prentice Hall.

[49] Gottman, J. M. (1993). The roles of conflict engagement, escalation, and avoidance in marital interaction: A longitudinal view of five types of couples. *Journal of Consulting and Clinical Psychology, 61,* 6–15.

[50] Singer, J. (2008, July). Texting leaves out more than the vowels. *Psychology Today.* Retrieved from http://www.psychologytoday.com/node/1448.

[51] Chang, S. (2003). *Communication technologies and long-distance romantic relationships.* Paper presented at International Communication Association, San Diego, pp. 1–31. doi:ica_proceeding_11995.PDF; (*AN 16028227*).

[52] Weingartner, N. (2008, July 30). Ending that relationship is easier than you think: Text arguing. *Digital Journal.* Retrieved from http://www.digitaljournal.com/article/258023.

[53] Suler, J. (2004). The online disinhibition effect. *CyberPsychology & Behavior, 7*(3), 321–326.

[54] Suler, J. (2010). Interpersonal guidelines for texting. *International Journal of Applied Psychoanalytic Studies, 7,* 358–361.

[55] Friedman, R. A., & Currall, S. C. (2003). Conflict escalation: Dispute exacerbating elements of e-mail communication. *Human Relations, 56,* 1325–1347.

[56] Chang, S. (2003). *Communication technologies and long-distance romantic relationships.* Paper presented at International Communication Association, San Diego, pp. 1–31. DOI:ica_proceeding_11995.PDF; (*AN 16028227*).

[57] Shapiro, E., & Allen, B. J. (2001). Why fight on the net?: Conflict on e-mail. *Journal of the Northwest Communication Association, 30,* 40–61.

[58] Rahim, M. A., & Magner, N. R. (1995). Confirmatory factor analysis of the styles of handling interpersonal conflict: First-order factor model and its invariance across groups. *Journal of Applied Psychology, 80,* 122–132.

[59] Lutgen-Sandvik, P., Tracy, S. J., & Alberts, J. K. (2007). Burned by bullying in the American workplace: Prevalence, perception, degree, and impact. *Journal of Management Studies, 44,* 835–860.

[60] Greeff, A. P., & De Bruyne, T. (2000). Conflict management style and marital satisfaction. *Journal of Sex and Marital Therapy, 26,* 321–334.

[61] Hofstede, G. (2001). *Culture's consequences: Comparing values, behaviors, institutions, and organizations across cultures* (2nd ed.). Thousand Oaks, CA: Sage.

[62] Hofstede, G. (2001). *Culture's consequences: Comparing values, behaviors, institutions, and organizations across cultures* (2nd ed.). Thousand Oaks, CA: Sage.

[63] Friedman, R. A., Chi, S., & Liu, L. A. (2006). An expectancy model of Chinese-American differences in conflict-avoiding. *Journal of International Business Studies, 37,* 76–91.

[64] LeBaron, M. (2003). *Bridging cultural conflicts: A new approach for a changing world.* San Francisco: Jossey-Bass.

[65] Gottman, J. & Levenson, R. W. (1986). Assessing the role of emotion in marriage. *Behavioral Assessment, 8,* 31–48.

[66] Gilligan, C. (1982). *In a different voice: Psychological theory and women's development.* Cambridge, MA: Harvard University Press; Rubin, L. B. (1983). *Intimate strangers: Men and women together.* New York: Harper & Row.

[67] Christensen, A. (1987). Detection of conflict patterns in couples. In K. Hahlweg & M. J. Goldstein (Eds.), *Understanding major mental disorders: The contribution of family interaction research* (pp. 250–265). New York: Family Process Press.

[68] Brody, L. (1999). *Gender, emotion, and the family.* Cambridge, MA: Harvard University Press.

[69] Christensen, A., & Shenk, J. L. (1991). Communication, conflict, and psychological distance in nondistressed, clinic, and divorcing couples. *Journal of Counseling and Clinical Psychology, 59,* 458–463.

[70] Noller, P., Feeney, J. A., Bonnell, D., & Callan, V. J. (1994). A longitudinal study of conflict in early marriage. *Journal of Social and Personal Relationships, 11,* 233–252; Vogel, D. L., Wester, S. R., & Heesacker, M. (1999). Dating relationships and the demand/withdraw pattern of communication. *Sex Roles, 41*(314), 297–306.

[71] Greeff, A. P., & de Bruyne, T. (2000). Conflict management style and marital satisfaction. *Journal of Sex and Marital Therapy, 26,* 321–334.

[72] Canary, D. J., Cupach, W. R., & Messman, S. (1995). *Relationship conflict: Conflict in parent–child, friendship, and romantic relationships.* Thousand Oaks, CA: Sage.

[73] Gottman, J. M. (1994). *What predicts divorce?: The relationship between marital processes and marital outcomes.* Hillsdale, NJ: Erlbaum.

[74] Weiss, R. S. (1986). Continuities and transformations in social relationships from childhood to adulthood. In W. W. Hartup & Z. Rubin (Eds.), *Relationships and development* (pp. 95–110). Hillsdale, NJ: Erlbaum.

[75] Dykstra, P. A. (1990). *Next of (non)kin.* Lisse, Netherlands: Swets & Zeitlinger.

[76] Hartup, W. W. (1992). Conflict and friendship relations. In C. U. Shantz & W. W. Hartup (Eds.), *Conflict in child and adolescent development* (pp. 186–215). New York: Cambridge University Press.

[77] Claes, M. E. (1992). Friendship and personal adjustment during adolescence. *Journal of Adolescence, 15*, 39–55.

[78] Rawlins, W. K. (1994). Being there and growing apart: Sustaining friendships during adulthood. In D. J. Canary & L. Stafford (Eds.), *Communication and relational maintenance* (pp. 275–296). San Diego: Academic Press.

[79] Argyle, M., & Furnham, A. (1983). Sources of satisfaction and conflict in long-term relationships. *Journal of Marriage and the Family, 45*, 481–493.

[80] Morley, I., & Shockley-Zalabak, P. (1986). Conflict avoiders and compromisers: Toward and understanding of their organizational communication style. *Group and Organizational Behavior, 11*, 387–402.

[81] Schutz, W. C. (1958). *The interpersonal underworld.* Palo Alto, CA: Science and Behavior Books.

[82] Brown, C. T., & Keller, P. W. (1979). *Monologue to dialogue: An exploration of interpersonal communication* (2nd ed.). Englewood Cliffs, NJ: Prentice Hall.

[83] Greeff, A. P., & de Bruyne, T. (2000). Conflict management style and marital satisfaction. *Journal of Sex and Marital Therapy, 26*, 321–334.

Chapter 9

[1] Perlman, D., & Vangelisti, A. L. (2006). Personal relationships: An introduction. In A. L. Vangelisti & D. Perlman (Eds.), *The Cambridge handbook of personal relationships* (pp. 1–7). New York: Cambridge University Press.

[2] Bell, R. A., & Gonzalez, M. C. (1988). Loneliness, negative life events, and the provisions of social relationships. *Communication Quarterly, 36*, 1–15.

[3] Steinkuehler, C. A., & Williams, D. (2006). Where everybody knows your (screen) name: Online games as "third places." *Journal of Computer-Mediated Communication, 11*, 885–909.

[4] Sun, S., Mathews, R. M., Hughes, I., & Campbell, A. (2008). Internet use and loneliness in older adults. *Cyberpsychology and Behavior, 11*, 208–211.

[5] Kraut, R., Patterson, M., Lundmark, V., Kiesler, S., Mukopadhyay, T., & Scherlis, W. (1998). Internet paradox: A social technology that reduces social involvement and psychological well-being? *American Psychologist, 53*, 1017–1031.

[6] Kraut, R., Patterson, M., Lundmark, V., Kiesler, S., Mukopadhyay, T., & Scherlis, W. (1998). Internet paradox: A social technology that reduces social involvement and psychological well-being? *American Psychologist, 53*, 1017–1031.

[7] Witteborn, S. (2004). Of being an Arab woman before and after September 11: The enactment of communal identities in talk. *Howard Journal of Communication, 15*, 83–98.

[8] Foth, M., & Hearn, G. (2007). Networked individualism of urban residents: Discovering the communicative ecology in inner-city apartment buildings. *Information, Communication & Society, 10*, 749–772.

[9] Impett, E. A., & Peplau, L. A. (2006). "His" and "her" relationships?: A review of the empirical evidence. In A. L. Vangelisti & D. Perlman (Eds.), *The Cambridge handbook of personal relationships* (pp. 273–291). New York: Cambridge University Press.

[10] Elliott, M. (2001). Gender differences in causes of depression. *Women and Health, 33*, 183–198.

[11] Kendler, K. S., Myers, J., & Prescott, C. A. (2005). Sex differences in the relationship between social support and risk for major depression: A longitudinal study of opposite-sex twin pairs. *American Journal of Psychiatry, 162*, 250–256.

[12] Paquette, M. (2006). The science of happiness. *Perspectives in Psychiatric Care, 42*(1), 1–2.

[13] Lykken, D. M., & Tellegen, A. (1996). Happiness is a stochastic phenomenon. *Psychological Science, 7*, 186–189.

[14] Davidson, R. J. (2005). Emotion regulation, happiness, and the neuroplasticity of the brain. *Advances in Mind-Body Medicine, 21* (3), 25–28.

[15] Sheldon, K. M., & Lyubomirsky, S. (2006). Achieving sustainable gains in happiness: Change your actions, not your circumstances. *Journal of Happiness Studies, 7*, 55–86.

[16] Bloor, L. E., Uchino, B. N., Hicks, A., & Smith, T. W. (2004). Social relationships and physiological function: The effects of recalling social relationships on cardiovascular reactivity. *Annals of Behavioral Medicine, 28*, 29–38.

[17] Hughes, B. M. (2007). Social support in ordinary life and laboratory measures of cardiovascular reactivity: Gender differences in habituation-sensitization. *Annals of Behavioral Medicine, 34*, 166–176.

[18] Surra, C. A., Gray, C. R., Boettcher, T. M., Cottle, N. R., & West, A. R. (2006). From courtship to universal properties: Research on dating and mate selection, 1950 to 2003. In A. L. Vangelisti & D. Perlman (Eds.), *The Cambridge handbook of personal relationships* (pp. 113–130). New York: Cambridge University Press.

[19] Surra, C. A., Gray, C. R., Boettcher, T. M., Cottle, N. R., & West, A. R. (2006). From courtship to universal properties: Research on dating and mate selection, 1950 to 2003. In A. L. Vangelisti & D. Perlman (Eds.), *The Cambridge handbook of personal relationships* (pp. 113–130). New York: Cambridge University Press.

[20] Berger, C. R., & Calabrese, R. J. (1975). Some explorations in initial interaction and beyond: Toward a developmental theory of interpersonal communication. *Human Communication Research, 1*, 99–112.

[21] Berger, C. R., & Bradac, J. J. (1982). *Language and social knowledge: Uncertainty in interpersonal relations.* London: Edward Arnold.

[22] Berger, C. R. (2005). Interpersonal communication: Theoretical perspectives, future prospects. *Journal of Communication, 55*, 415–447.

[23] Berger, C. R. (1995). Inscrutable goals, uncertain plans, and the production of communicative action. In C. R. Berger & M. Burgoon (Eds.), *Communication and social processes* (pp. 1–28). East Lansing: Michigan State University Press.

[24] Gudykunst, W. B. (1985). The influence of cultural similarity, type of relationship, and self-monitoring on uncertainty reduction processes. *Communication Monographs, 52*, 203–217.

25 Gudykunst, W. B., & Nishida, T. (1984). Individual and cultural influences on uncertainty reduction. *Communication Monographs, 51*, 23–36.

26 Maguire, K. C. (2007). "Will it ever end?": A (re)examination of uncertainty in college student long-distance dating relationships. *Communication Quarterly, 55*, 415–432.

27 Byron, K., & Baldridge, D. C. (2007). E-mail recipients' impressions of senders' likability: The interactive effect of nonverbal cues and recipients' personality. *Journal of Business Communication, 44*, 137–160.

28 Roloff, M. E. (1981). *Interpersonal communication: The social exchange approach.* Beverly Hills, CA: Sage.

29 Clark, M. S., & Grote, N. K. (1998). Why aren't indices of relationship costs always negatively related to indices of relationship quality? *Personality and Social Psychology Review, 2*, 2–17.

30 Thibaut, J. W., & Kelley, H. H. (1959). *The social psychology of groups.* New York: Wiley.

31 Sternberg, R. J., & Barnes, M. L. (1985). Real and ideal others in romantic relationships: Is four a crowd? *Journal of Personality and Social Psychology, 49*, 1586–1608.

32 Roloff, M. E. (1981). *Interpersonal communication: The social exchange approach.* Beverly Hills, CA: Sage.

33 Molm, L. D., Peterson, G., & Takahashi, N. (2001). The value of exchange. *Social Forces, 79*, 159–185.

34 Barelds, D. P. H., & Dijkstra, P. (2006). Reactive, anxious and possessive forms of jealousy and their relation to relationship quality among heterosexuals and homosexuals. *Journal of Homosexuality, 51*, 183–198.

35 Barelds, D. P. H., & Barelds-Dijkstra, P. (2007). Love at first sight or friends first?: Ties among partner personality trait similarity, relationship onset, relationship quality, and love. *Journal of Social and Personal Relationships, 24*, 479–496.

36 Daly, J. A., & Bippus, A. M. (1998). Personality and interpersonal communication: Issues and directions. In J. C. McCroskey, J. A. Daly, M. M. Martin, & M. J. Beatty (Eds.), *Communication and personality: Trait perspectives* (pp. 1–40). Cresskill, NJ: Hampton Press.

37 Cunningham, M. R., Roberts, A. R., Barbee, A. P., Druen, P. B., & Wu, C.-H. (1995). "Their ideas of beauty are, on the whole, the same as ours": Consistency and variability in the cross-cultural perception of female physical attractiveness. *Journal of Personality and Social Psychology, 68*, 261–279.

38 Anderson, S. L., Adams, G., & Plaut, V. C. (2008). The cultural grounding of personal relationship: The importance of attractiveness in everyday life. *Journal of Personality and Social Psychology, 95*, 352–368.

39 Swami, V., & Tovee, M. J. (2008). The muscular male: A comparison of the physical attractiveness preferences of gay and heterosexual men. *International Journal of Men's Health, 7*, 59–71.

40 Bassett, J., Pearcey, S., & Dabbs, J. M. Jr. (2001). Jealousy and partner preference among butch and femme lesbians. *Psychology, Evolution, & Gender, 3*, 155–165.

41 Levine, D. (2000). Virtual attraction: What rocks your boat. *Cyberpsychology & Behavior, 3*, 565–573.

42 Grinnin, A. M., & Langlois, J. H. (2006). Stereotype directionality and attractiveness stereotyping: Is beauty good or is ugly bad? *Social Cognition, 24*, 187–206.

43 Dryer, D. C., & Horowitz, L. M. (1997). When do opposites attract? Interpersonal complementarity versus similarity. *Journal of Personality and Social Psychology, 72*, 592–603.

44 Neyer, F. J., & Lang, F. R. (2003). Blood is thicker than water: Kinship orientation across adulthood. *Journal of Personality and Social Psychology, 84*, 310–321.

45 Kraut, R., Patterson, M., Lundmark, V., Kiesler, S., Mukopadhyay, T., & Scherlis, W. (1998). Internet paradox: A social technology that reduces social involvement and psychological well-being? *American Psychologist, 53*, 1017–1031.

46 Boase, J., & Wellman, B. (2006). Personal relationships: On and off the Internet. In A. L. Vangelisti & D. Perlman (Eds.), *The Cambridge handbook of personal relationships* (pp. 709–723). New York: Cambridge University Press.

47 Boase, J., & Wellman, B. (2006). Personal relationships: On and off the Internet. In A. L. Vangelisti & D. Perlman (Eds.), *The Cambridge handbook of personal relationships* (pp. 709–723). New York: Cambridge University Press.

48 Kraut, R., Kiesler, S., Boneva, B., Cummings, J., Helgeson, V., & Crawford, A. (2002). Internet paradox revisited. *Journal of Social Issues, 58*, 49–74.

49 Bessiere, K., Kiesler, S., Kraut, R., & Boneva, B. S. (2008). Effects of internet use and social resources on changes in depression. *Information, Communication, & Society, 11*, 47–70.

50 Kraut, R., Kiesler, S., Boneva, B., Cummings, J., Helgeson, V., & Crawford, A. (2002). Internet paradox revisited. *Journal of Social Issues, 58*, 49–74.

51 Bessiere, K., Kiesler, S., Kraut, R., & Boneva, B. S. (2008). Effects of internet use and social resources on changes in depression. *Information, Communication, & Society, 11*, 47–70.

52 Rawlins, W. K. (1992). *Friendship matters: Communication, dialectics, and the life course.* New York: Aldine De Gruyter.

53 Anderson, S. L., Adams, G., & Plaut, V. C. (2008). The cultural grounding of personal relationship: The importance of attractiveness in everyday life. *Journal of Personality and Social Psychology, 95*, 352–368.

54 Richmond, V. P., McCroskey, J. C., & McCroskey, L. L. (2005). *Organizational communication for survival: Making work, work* (3rd ed). Boston: Allyn and Bacon, p. 132.

55 French, J. R. P., & Raven, B. H. (1959). The bases of social power. In D. Cartwright (Ed.), *Studies in social power* (pp. 150–167). Ann Arbor: University of Michigan.

56 Sprecher, S. (2005). Sex differences in bases of power in dating relationships. In W. Dragon & S. Duck (Eds.), *Understanding research in personal relationships: A text with readings* (pp. 114–121). London: Sage Publishing.

57 Miller, K. (2006). *Organizational communication: Approaches and processes* (4th ed.). Belmont, CA: Thomson Wadsworth.

58 Kellerman, K., & Cole, T. (1994). Classifying compliance-gaining messages: Taxonomic disorder and strategic confusion. *Communication Theory, 4*, 3–60.

[59] Ifert, D. E., & Roloff, M. E. (1997). Overcoming expressed obstacles to compliance: The role of sensitivity to the expressions of others and ability to modify self-presentation. *Communication Quarterly, 45,* 55–67.

[60] Paradise, R., & Rogoff, B. (2009). Side by side: Learning by observing and pitching in. *ETHOS, 37,* 102–138.

[61] Galvin, K. M., Bylund, C. L., & Brommel, B. J. (2004). *Family communication: Cohesion and change* (6th ed.). Boston: Pearson.

[62] Miller, K. (2006). *Organizational communication: Approaches and processes* (4th ed.). Belmont, CA: Thomson Wadsworth.

[63] Knapp, M. L., & Vangelisti, A. (2006). *Interpersonal communication and human relationships* (6th ed.). Boston: Allyn & Bacon.

[64] Coupland, J. (2003). Small talk: Social functions. *Research on Language and Social Interaction, 36,* 1–6.

[65] Beatty, M. J. (1986). *Romantic dialogue: Communication in dating and marriage.* Englewood, CO: Morton Publishing.

[66] Dunbar, R. I. M. (2008). Cognitive constraints on the structure and dynamics of social networks. *Group Dynamics: Theory, Research, and Practice, 12,* 7–16.

[67] Coontz, S. (2005). *Marriage, a history: From obedience to intimacy or how love conquered marriage.* New York: Penguin Books.

[68] Coontz, S. (2005). *Marriage, a history: From obedience to intimacy or how love conquered marriage.* New York: Penguin Books.

[69] Duck, S. (1987). How to lose friends without influencing people. In M. E. Roloff & G. R. Miller (Eds.), *Interpersonal processes: New directions in communication research* (pp. 278–298). Beverly Hills, CA: Sage.

[70] Hess, J. A. (2000). Maintaining nonvoluntary relationships with disliked partners: An investigation into the use of distancing behaviors. *Human Communication Research, 26,* 458–488.

[71] Roloff, M. E. (1981). *Interpersonal communication: The social exchange approach.* Beverly Hills, CA: Sage.

[72] Duck, S. (1982). A topography of relationship disengagement and dissolution. In S. W. Duck (Ed.), *Personal relationships 4: Dissolving personal relationships* (pp. 1–29). London: Academic Press.

[73] Baxter, L. A., & Bullis, C. (1986). Turning points in developing romantic relationships. *Communication Research, 12,* 463–493.

[74] Baxter, L. A., & Pittman, G. (2001). Communicatively remembering turning points of relational development in heterosexual romantic relationships. *Communication Reports, 14,* 1–17.

[75] Levine, D. (2000). Virtual attraction: What rocks your boat. *Cyberpsychology & Behavior, 3,* 565–573.

[76] Wildermuth, S. M., & Vogl-Bauer, S. (2007). We met on the Internet: An exploratory study of how online romantic relationship partners define and describe their relationships. *Southern Communication Journal, 72,* 211–227.

[77] Stafford, L., & Canary, D. J. (1991). Maintenance strategies and romantic relationship type, gender, and relational characteristics. *Journal of Social and Personal Relationships, 8,* 217–242.

[78] Gottman, J. M. (1994) *What predicts divorce?: The relationship between marital processes and marital outcomes.* Hillsdale, NJ: Erlbaum.

[79] Canary, D. J. & Stafford, L. (1992). Relational maintenance strategies and equity in marriage. *Communication Monographs, 59,* 243–267.

[80] Stafford, L., Dainton, M., & Haas, S. (2000). Measuring routine and strategic relational maintenance: Scale revision, sex versus gender roles, and the prediction of relational characteristics. *Communication Monographs, 67,* 306–323.

[81] Canary, D. J., & Stafford, L. (2001). Equity in maintaining personal relationships. In J. H. Harvey & A. E. Wenzel (Eds.), *Close romantic relationships: Maintenance and enhancement* (pp. 133–150). Mahwah, NJ: Erlbaum.

[82] Daly, J. A., & Bippus, A. M. (1998). Personality and interpersonal communication: Issues and directions. In J. C. McCroskey, J. A. Daly, M. M. Martin, & M. J. Beatty (Eds.), *Communication and personality: Trait perspectives* (pp. 1–40). Cresskill, NJ: Hampton Press.

[83] Magnusson, D., & Endler, N. S. (Eds.). (1977). *Personality at the crossroads: Current issues in interactional psychology.* Hillsdale, NJ: Erlbaum.

[84] Daly, J. A., & Bippus, A. M. (1998). Personality and interpersonal communication: Issues and directions. In J. C. McCroskey, J. A. Daly, M. M. Martin, & M. J. Beatty (Eds.), *Communication and personality: Trait perspectives* (pp. 1–40). Cresskill, NJ: Hampton Press.

[85] Daly, J. A. (2002). Personality and interpersonal communication. In M. L. Knapp & J. A. Daly (Eds.), *Handbook of interpersonal communication* (3rd ed., pp. 133–180). Thousand Oaks, CA: Sage.

[86] Simpson, J. A., Winterheld, H. A., Chen, J. Y. (2006). Personality and relationships: A temperament perspective. In A. L. Vangelisti & D. Perlman (Eds.), *The Cambridge handbook of personal relationships* (pp. 231–250). New York: Cambridge University Press.

[87] Barelds, D. P. H. (2005). Self and partner personality in intimate relationships. *European Journal of Personality, 19,* 501–518.

[88] de Raand, B., Sullot, E., & Barelds, D. P. H. (2008). Which of the big five factors are in need of situational specification? *European Journal of Personality, 22,* 269–289.

[89] Simpson, J. A., Winterheld, H. A., Chen, J. Y. (2006). Personality and relationships: A temperament perspective. In A. L. Vangelisti & D. Perlman (Eds.), *The Cambridge handbook of personal relationships* (pp. 231–250). New York: Cambridge University Press.

[90] Simpson, J. A., Winterheld, H. A., & Chen, J. Y. (2006). Personality and relationships: A temperament perspective. In A. L. Vangelisti & D. Perlman (Eds.), *The Cambridge handbook of personal relationships* (pp. 231–250). New York: Cambridge University Press.

[91] Barelds, D. P. H. (2005). Self and partner personality in intimate relationships. *European Journal of Personality, 19,* 501–518.

[92] de Raand, B., Sullot, E., & Barelds, D. P. H. (2008). Which of the big five factors are in need of situational specification? *European Journal of Personality, 22,* 269–289.

Chapter 10

[1] Floyd, K. (1997). Knowing when to say "I love you": An expectancy approach to affectionate communication. *Communication Research Reports, 14,* 321–330.

[2] Wheeless, L. R. (1978). A follow-up study of the relationships among trust, disclosure, and interpersonal solidarity. *Human Communication Research, 4*, 143–157.

[3] Altman, I., & Taylor, D. A. (1973). *Social penetration: The development of interpersonal relationships.* New York: Holt, Rinehart & Winston.

[4] Baxter, L. A. (1988). A dialectical perspective on communication strategies in relationship development. In S. Duck (Ed.), *Handbook of personal relationships: Theory, research, and interventions* (pp. 257–273). Chichester, UK: Wiley & Sons.

[5] Bradford, S. A., Feeney, J. A., & Campbell, L. (2002). Links between attachment orientations and dispositional and diary-based measures of disclosure in dating couples: A study of actor and partner effects. *Personal Relationships, 9*, 491–506.

[6] Skoe, E. E., & Ksionzky, S. (1985). Target personality characteristics and self-disclosure: An exploratory study. *Journal of Clinical Psychology, 41*, 14–21.

[7] Dindia, K., & Allen, M. (1992). Sex differences in self-disclosure: A meta-analysis. *Psychological Bulletin, 112*, 106–124.

[8] Dindia, K. (2006). Men are from North Dakota, women are from South Dakota. In K. Dindia & D. J. Canary (Eds.), *Sex differences and similarities in communication* (2nd ed., pp. 3–20). Mahwah, NJ: Erlbaum.

[9] Horenstein, V. D., & Downey, J. L. (2003). A cross-cultural investigation of self-disclosure. *North American Journal of Psychology, 5*, 373–386.

[10] Baxter, L. A., & Wilmot, W. (1985). Taboo topics in close relationships. *Journal of Social and Personal Relationships, 2*, 253–269.

[11] Allen, J. L., Long, K. M., O'Mara, J., & Judd, B. B. (2003). Verbal and nonverbal orientations toward communication and the development of intracultural and intercultural relationships. *Journal of Intercultural Communication Research, 32*, 129–160.

[12] Chen, Y., & Nakazawa, M. (2009). Influences of culture on self-disclosure as relationally situated in intercultural and interracial friendships from a social penetration perspective. *Journal of Intercultural Communication Research, 38*, 77–98.

[13] Suler, J. (2004). The online disinhibition effect. *Cyberpsychology & Behavior, 7*, 321–326.

[14] Stritzke, W. G. K., Nguyen, A., & Durkin, K. (2004). Shyness and computer-mediated communication: A self-presentational theory perspective. *Media Psychology, 6*, 1–22.

[15] The National Campaign to Prevent Teen and Unplanned Pregnancy. (2008). Sex and tech. Retrieved on March 29, 2010, from http://www.thenationalcampaign.org/sextech/PDF/SexTech_Summary.pdf; Beatbullying. (2009).Truth of Sexting amongst UK teens. Retrieved March 29, 2010, from http://www.beatbullying.org/docs/media-centre/news-archive/August%2009/truth_of_sexting.html.

[16] Brunell, A. B., Pilkington, G. D., & Webster, G. D. (2007). Perceptions of risk in intimacy in dating couples: Conversation and relationship quality. *Journal of Social and Clinical Psychology, 26*, 92–119.

[17] Dietz-Uhler, B., Bishop-Clark, C., & Howard, E. (2005). Formation of and adherence to a self-disclosure norm in an on-line chat. *Cyberpsychology & Behavior, 8*, 114–120.

[18] Gable, S. L., Reis, H. T., Impett, E. A., & Asher, E. R. (2004). What do you do when things go right?: The intrapersonal and interpersonal benefits of sharing positive events. *Journal of Personality and Social Psychology, 87*, 228–245.

[19] Gable, S. L., Gonzaga, G. C., & Strachman, A. (2006). Will you be there for me when things go right?: Supportive responses to positive event disclosures. *Journal of Personality and Social Psychology, 91*, 904–917.

[20] Knapp, M. L. (2006). Lying and deception in close relationships. In A. L. Vangelisti & D. Perlman (Eds.), *The Cambridge handbook of personal relationships* (pp. 517–532). New York: Cambridge University Press.

[21] Rusbult, C. E., Coolsen, M. K., Kirchner, J. L., & Clarke, J. A. (2006). Commitment. In A. L. Vangelisti & D. Perlman (Eds.), *The Cambridge handbook of personal relationships* (pp. 615–636). New York: Cambridge University Press.

[22] Traeen, B., & Sorensen, D. (2000). Breaking the speed of the sound of loneliness: Sexual partner change and the fear of intimacy. *Culture, Health & Sexuality, 2*, 287–301.

[23] Seginer, R., & Noyman, M. S. (2005). Future orientation, identity and intimacy: Their relations in emerging adulthood. *European Journal of Developmental Psychology, 2*, 17–37.

[24] Potoczniak, D. J., Aldea, M. A., & DeBlaere, C. (2007). Ego identity, social anxiety, social support, and self-concealment in lesbian, gay, and bisexual individuals. *Journal of Counseling Psychology, 54*, 447–457.

[25] Levine, T. R., & McCornack, S. A. (1991). The dark side of trust: Conceptualizing and measuring types of communicative suspicion. *Communication Quarterly, 39*, 325–340.

[26] Lemay, E. P., Jr., & Clark, M. S. (2008). "Walking on eggshells": How expressing relationship insecurities perpetuates them. *Journal of Personality and Social Psychology, 95*, 420–441.

[27] Ickes, W., Dugosh, J. W., Simpson, J. A., & Wilson, C. L. (2003). Suspicious minds: The motive to acquire relationship-threatening information. *Personal Relationships, 10*, 131–148.

[28] Knapp, M. L. (2006). Lying and deception in close relationships. In A. L. Vangelisti & D. Perlman (Eds.), *The Cambridge handbook of personal relationships* (pp. 517–532). New York: Cambridge University Press.

[29] Hertenstein, M. J., Verkamp, J. M., Kerestes, J. M., & Holmes, R. M. (2006). The communicative functions of touch in humans, nonhuman primates, and rats: A review and synthesis of the empirical research. *Genetic, Social, and General Psychology Monographs, 132*, 5–94.

[30] Floyd, K., Mikkelson, A. C., Tafoya, M. A., Farinelli, L., La Valley, A. G., Judd, J., Haynes, M. T., Davis, K. L., & Wilson, J. (2007). Human affection exchange XIII: Affectionate communication accelerates neuroendocrine stress recovery. *Health Communication, 22*, 123–132; Floyd, K. (1997). Communicating affection in dyadic relationships: An assessment of behavior and expectancies. *Communication Quarterly, 45*, 68–80; Floyd, K. (2006). *Communicating affection: Interpersonal behavior and social context.* Cambridge, UK: Cambridge University Press.

[31] Floyd, K., & Riforgiate, S. (2008). Affectionate communication received from spouses predicts stress hormone levels in healthy adults. *Communication Monographs, 75*, 351–368.

[32] Floyd, K., Boren, J. P., Hannawa, A. F., Hesse, C., McEwan, B., & Veksler, A. E. (2009). Kissing in marital and cohabiting relationships: Effects on blood lipids, stress, and relationship satisfaction. *Western Journal of Communication, 73*, 113–133.

[33] Floyd, K., Mikkelson, A. C., Tafoya, M. A., Farinelli, L., La Valley, A. G., Judd, J., Davis, K. L., Haynes, M. T., & Wilson, J. (2007). Human affection exchange. XIV: Relational affection predicts resting heart rate and free cortisol secretion during acute stress. *Behavioral Medicine, 32*, 151–156.

[34] Lee, J. A. (1973). *Colours of love: An exploration of the ways of loving.* Toronto, Canada: New Press.

[35] Hendrick, C., & Hendrick, S. (1986). A theory and method of love. *Journal of Personality and Social Psychology, 50*, 392–402; Hendrick, C., Hendrick, S. S., & Dicke, A. (1998). The love attitudes scale: Short form. *Journal of Social and Personal Relationships, 15*, 147–159.

[36] Lee, J. A. (1988). Love-styles. In R. J. Sternberg & M. L. Barnes (Eds.), *The psychology of love* (pp. 38–67). New Haven, CT: Yale University Press.

[37] Lee, J. A. (1988). Love-styles. In R. J. Sternberg & M. L. Barnes (Eds.), *The psychology of love* (pp. 38–67). New Haven, CT: Yale University Press.

[38] Waller, N. G., & Shaver, P. R. (1994). The importance of non-genetic influences on romantic love styles: A twin-family study. *Psychological Science, 5*, 268–274.

[39] Lee, J. A. (1988). Love-styles. In R. J. Sternberg & M. L. Barnes (Eds.), *The psychology of love* (pp. 38–67). New Haven, CT: Yale University Press.

[40] Barelds, D. P. H., & Barelds-Dijkstra, P. (2007). Love at first sight or friends first?: Ties among partner personality trait similarity, relationship onset, relationship quality, and love. *Journal of Social and Personal Relationships, 24*, 479–496.

[41] Beatty, M. J. (1986). *Romantic dialogue: Communication in dating and marriage.* Englewood, CO: Morton.

[42] Zald, D. H. (2008). Midbrain dopamine receptor availability is inversely associated with novelty-seeking traits in humans. *Journal of Neuroscience, 28*, 14372–14378.

[43] Impett, E. A., & Peplau, L. A. (2006). "His" and "her" relationships?: A review of empirical evidence. In A. L. Vangelisti & D. Perlman (Eds.), *The Cambridge handbook of personal relationships* (pp. 273–291). New York: Cambridge University Press.

[44] Ribner, D. S., & Kleinplatz, P. J. (2007). The hole in the sheet and other myths about sexuality and Judaism. *Sexual and Relationship Therapy, 22*, 445–456.

[45] Lee, J. A. (1988). Love-styles. In R. J. Sternberg & M. L. Barnes (Eds.), *The psychology of love* (pp. 38–67). New Haven, CT: Yale University Press.

[46] Hofer, J., Chasiotis, A., & Campos, D. (2006). Congruence between social values and implicit motives: Effects on life satisfaction across three cultures. *European Journal of Personality, 20*, 305–324.

[47] Hewitt, J., & Alqahtani, M. A. (2003). Differences between Saudi and U.S. students in reaction to same- and mixed-sex intimacy shown by others. *Journal of Social Psychology, 143*, 233–242.

[48] Argyle, M., Henderson, M., Bond, M., Iizuka, Y., & Contarello, A. (1986). Cross-cultural variations in relationship rules. *International Journal of Psychology, 21*, 287–315.

[49] Hewitt, J., & Alqahtani, M. A. (2003). Differences between Saudi and U.S. students in reaction to same- and mixed-sex intimacy shown by others. *Journal of Social Psychology, 143*, 233–242.

[50] Baker, A. (2002). What makes an online relationship successful? Clues from couples who met in cyberspace. *Cyberpsychology & Behavior, 5*, 363–375.

[51] Anderson, T. L., & Emmers-Sommer, T. M. (2006). Predictors of relationship satisfaction in online romantic relationships. *Communication Studies, 57*, 153–172.

[52] Anderson, T. L., & Emmers-Sommer, T. M. (2006). Predictors of relationship satisfaction in online romantic relationships. *Communication Studies, 57*, 153–172.

[53] Cupach, W. R., & Spitzberg, B. H. (Eds.). (1994). *The dark side of interpersonal communication.* Hillsdale, NJ: Erlbaum.

[54] Stafford, L. (2005). *Maintaining long-distance and cross-residential relationships.* Mahwah, NJ: Erlbaum.

[55] Goodman, S. (2005). From the loneliness of long-distance love to the practicality of new relocation services, Sally Goodman looks at solutions to the two-body problem. *Nature, 433*(7025), 552–553.

[56] Maguire, K. C. (2007). "Will it ever end?": A (re) examination of uncertainty in college student long-distance dating relationships. *Communication Quarterly, 55*, 415–432.

[57] Hess, J. A., Fannin, A. D., & Pollom, L. H. (2007). Creating closeness: Discerning and measuring strategies for fostering closer relationships. *Personal Relationships, 14*, 25–44.

[58] Hess, J. A., Fannin, A. D., & Pollom, L. H. (2007). Creating closeness: Discerning and measuring strategies for fostering closer relationships. *Personal Relationships, 14*, 25–44.

[59] Young, S. L., Paxman, C. G., Koehring, C. L. E., & Anderson, C. A. (2008). The application of a face work model of disengagement to unrequited love. *Communication Research Reports, 25*, 56–66.

[60] Emanuele, E. (2009). Of love and death: The emerging role of romantic disruption in suicidal behavior. *Suicide and Life-Threatening Behavior, 39*, 240.

[61] Dijkstra, P., & Barelds, D. P. H. (2008). Self and partner personality and responses to relationship threats. *Journal of Research in Personality, 42*, 1500–1511.

[62] Barelds, D. P. H., & Dijkstra, P. (2006). Reactive, anxious and possessive forms of jealousy and their relation to relationship quality among heterosexuals and homosexuals. *Journal of Homosexuality, 51*, 183–198.

[63] Infante, D. A., Chandler, T. A., & Rudd, J. E. (1989). Test of an argumentative skill deficiency model of interspousal violence. *Communication Monographs, 56*, 163–177.

[64] Rancer, A. S., & Avtgis, T. A. (2006). *Argumentative and aggressive communication: Theory, research, and application.* Thousand Oaks, CA: Sage.

Chapter 11

[1] Billingsley, S., Lim, M., Caron, J., Harris, A., & Canada, R. (2005). Historical overview of criteria for marital and family success. *Family Therapy, 32,* 1–14.

[2] Mitchell, B. A. (2010). Midlife marital happiness and ethnic culture: A life course perspective. *Journal of Comparative Family Studies, 41,* 167–183.

[3] Divorce rate (2010, August 14). Divorce rate in America. Retrieved from http://www.divorcerate.org/.

[4] Top54u. (2010, February 12). Remarriage statistics and facts will shock you. *Home & Family Ezine.* Retrieved on August 14, 2010, from http://home-family.top54u.com/post/Remarriage-Statistics.aspx.

[5] Afifi, T. D., & McManus, T. (2006). Investigating privacy boundaries: Communication in post-divorce families. In K. Floyd & M. T. Morman (Eds.), *Widening the family circle: New research on family communication* (pp. 171–187). Thousand Oaks, CA: Sage.

[6] Stafford, L., & Bayer, C. L. (1993). *Interaction between parents and children.* Newbury Park, CA: Sage.

[7] Ambert, A. (2001). *The effect of children on parents* (2nd ed.). New York: Haworth Press.

[8] Vogl-Bauer, S. (2009). When the world comes home: Examining internal and external influences on communication exchanges between parents and their boomerang children. In T. J. Socha & G. H. Stamp (Eds.), *Parents and children communicating with society: Managing relationships outside of home* (pp. 285–304). New York: Routledge.

[9] Afifi, T. D., & McManus, T. (2006). Investigating privacy boundaries: Communication in post-divorce families. In K. Floyd & M. T. Morman (Eds.), *Widening the family circle: New research on family communication* (pp. 171–187). Thousand Oaks, CA: Sage.

[10] Goetting, A. (1986). The developmental tasks of siblingship over the life cycle. *Journal of Marriage and the Family, 48,* 703–714.

[11] Myers, S. A., & Goodboy, A. K. (2006). Perceived sibling use of verbally aggressive messages across the lifespan. *Communication Research Reports, 23,* 1–11.

[12] Voorpostel, M., & van der Lippe, T. (2007). Support between siblings and between friends: Two worlds apart? *Journal of Marriage and Family, 69,* 1271–1282.

[13] Stocker, C. M., & McHale, S. M. (1992). The nature and family correlates of preadolescents' perceptions of their sibling relationships. *Journal of Social and Personal Relationships, 9,* 179–195; Tseung, C. N., & Schott, G. (2004). The quality of sibling relationships during late adolescence: Are there links with other significant relationships? *Psychological Studies, 49,* 20–30.

[14] Waites, C. E. (2007). Grandparents communicating with grandchildren: Fostering Intergenerational understanding. *Journal of Health & Social Policy, 22* (3–4), 149–165.

[15] Antonucci, T. C., & Jackson, J. S. (2007). Intergenerational relations: Theory, research, and policy. *Journal of Social Issues, 63,* 679–693; Soliz, J. (2008). Intergenerational support and the role of grandparents in post-divorce families: Retrospective accounts of young adult grandchildren. *Qualitative Research Reports in Communication, 9,* 72–80.

[16] Horvath, C. W. (1995). Biological origins of communicator style. *Communication Quarterly, 43,* 394–407.

[17] Beatty, M. J., Marshall, L. A., & Rudd, J. E. (2001). A twins study of communicative adaptability: Heritability of individual differences. *Quarterly Journal of Speech, 87,* 366–377.

[18] Horan, S. M., Houser, M. L., & Cowan, R. L. (2007). Are children communicated with equally?: An investigation of parent–child sex composition and gender role communication differences. *Communication Research Reports, 24,* 361–372.

[19] Caldera, Y. M., & Sciaraffa, M. A. (1998). Parent–toddler play with feminine toys: Are all dolls the same? *Sex Roles, 39,* 657–668.

[20] Aamodt, S., & Wang, S. (2008). *Welcome to your brain: Why you lose your car keys but never forget how to drive and other puzzles of everyday life.* New York: Bloomsbury.

[21] Begley, S. (2010, June 13). My alleles made me do it: The folly of blaming bad behavior on wonky DNA. *Newsweek.* Retrieved on June 14, 2010, from http://www.newsweek.com/blogs/the-human-condition/2010/06/13/my-alleles-made-me-do-it.

[22] Aamodt, S., & Wang, S. (2008). *Welcome to your brain: Why you lose your car keys but never forget how to drive and other puzzles of everyday life.* New York: Bloomsbury.

[23] Chao, R., & Kanatsu, A. (2008). Beyond socioeconomics: Explaining ethnic group differences in parenting through cultural and immigration processes. *Applied Developmental Science, 12*(4), 181–187.

[24] Chao, R., & Kanatsu, A. (2008). Beyond socioeconomics: Explaining ethnic group differences in parenting through cultural and immigration processes. *Applied Developmental Science, 12*(4), 181–187.

[25] Chao, R., & Kanatsu, A. (2008). Beyond socioeconomics: Explaining ethnic group differences in parenting through cultural and immigration processes. *Applied Developmental Science, 12*(4), 181–187.

[26] Hill, N. E., & Tyson, D. F. (2008). Excavating culture: Ethnicity and context as predictors of parenting behavior. *Applied Developmental Science, 12*(4), 188–197.

[27] Foeman, A., & Nance, T. (2002). Building new cultures, reframing old images: Success strategies of interracial couples. *Howard Journal of Communications, 13,* 237–249.

[28] Ceballo, R., & Hurd, N. (2008). Neighborhood context, SES, and parenting: Including a focus on acculturation among Latina mothers. *Applied Developmental Science, 12*(4), 176–180.

[29] Milevsky, I. M., Szuchman, L., & Milevsky, A. (2008). Transmission of religious beliefs in college students. *Mental Health, Religion & Culture, 11,* 423–434.

[30] Brelsford, G. M., & Mahoney, A. (2008). Spiritual disclosure between older adolescents and their mothers. *Journal of Family Psychology, 22,* 62–70.

[31] Hughes, P. C., & Dickson, F. C. (2005). Communication, marital satisfaction, and religious orientation in interfaith marriages. *Journal of Family Communication, 5,* 25–41.

[32] Seybold, A. M. (2008). The convergence of wireless, mobility, and the Internet and its relevance to enterprises. *Information Knowledge Systems Management, 7*, 11–23.

[33] Mesch, G. S. (2006). Family relations and the Internet: Exploring a family boundaries approach. *Journal of Family Communication, 6*, 119–138.

[34] Subrahmanyam, K., & Lin, G. (2007). Adolescents on the net: Internet use and well-being. *Adolescence, 42*, 659–677.

[35] Coburn, K. L. (2006, July–August). Organizing a ground crew for today's helicopter parents. *About Campus, 11*, 9–16.

[36] Manos, M. A. (2009). Helicopter parents: Empathetic or pathetic? *Phi Kappa Phi Forum, 89*(3), 21.

[37] U.S. Department of Education. Family Education Rights and Privacy Act (FERPA). Retrieved from http://www2.ed.gov/policy/gen/guid/fpco/ferpa/index.html.

[38] U.S. Department of Education. Family Education Rights and Privacy Act (FERPA). Retrieved from http://www2.ed.gov/policy/gen/guid/fpco/ferpa/index.html.

[39] DeFrain, J., & Asay, S. M. (2007). Strong families around the world: An introduction to the family strengths perspective. *Marriage and Family Review, 41*, 1–10; Noller, P., & Fitzpatrick, M. A. (1993). *Communication in family relationships.* Englewood Cliffs, NJ: Prentice Hall; Otto, H. A. (1962). What is a strong family? *Marriage and Family Living, 24*, 77–80; Royse, D. D., & Turner, G. T. (1980). Strengths of Black families: A Black community's perspective. *Social Work, 25*, 407–409.

[40] Ambert, A. (2001). *The effect of children on parents* (2nd ed.). New York: Haworth Press.

[41] Ledbetter, A. M., Griffin, E., & Sparks, G. G. (2007). Forecasting "friends forever": A longitudinal investigation of sustained closeness between best friends. *Personal Relationships, 14*, 343–350.

[42] Oswald, D. L., & Clark, E. M. (2003). Best friends forever?: High school best friendships and the transition to college. *Personal Relationships, 10*, 187–196.

[43] Johnson, A. J., Wittenberg, E., Villagran, M. M., Mazur, M., & Villagran, P. (2003). Relational progression as a dialectic: Examining turning points in communication among friends. *Communication Monographs, 70*, 230–249.

[44] Argyle, M., & Henderson, M. (1984). The rules of friendship. *Journal of Social and Personal Relationships, 1*, 211–237.

[45] Merolla, A. J. (2008). Communicating forgiveness in friendships and dating relationships. *Communication Studies, 59*, 114–131.

[46] Selfhout, M., Denissen, J., Branje, S., & Meeus, W. (2009). In the eye of the beholder: Perceived, actual, and peer-rated similarity in personality, communication, and friendship intensity during the acquaintanceship process. *Journal of Personality and Social Psychology, 96*, 1152–1165.

[47] Sias, P. M., Drzewiecka, J. A., Meares, M., Brent, R., Konomi, Y., Ortega, M., & White, C. (2008). Intercultural friendship development. *Communication Reports, 21*, 1–13.

[48] Morgan, S. E., & Arasaratnam, L. A. (2003). Intercultural friendships as social excitation: Sensation seeking as a predictor of intercultural friendship seeking behavior. *Journal of Intercultural Communication Research, 3*, 175–186.

[49] Elkins, L. E., & Peterson, C. (1993). Gender differences in best friendships. *Sex Roles, 29*, 497–508.

[50] Elkins, L. E., & Peterson, C. (1993). Gender differences in best friendships. *Sex Roles, 29*, 497–508.

[51] Bowman, J. M. (2008). Gender role orientation and relational closeness: Self-disclosive behavior in same-sex male friendships. *Journal of Men's Studies, 16*, 316–330.

[52] Fife. E. M. (2007). Male friendship and competition: A dialectical analysis. *Ohio Communication Journal, 45*, 41–64.

[53] Ledbetter, A. M., Griffin, E., & Sparks, G. G. (2007). Forecasting "friends forever": A longitudinal investigation of sustained closeness between best friends. *Personal Relationships, 14*, 343–350.

[54] Wright, K. B., & Patterson, B. R. (2006). Socioemotional selectivity theory and the macrodynamics of friendship: The role of friendship style and communication in friendship across the lifespan. *Communication Research Reports, 23*, 163–170.

[55] Ledbetter, A. M., Griffin, E., & Sparks, G. G. (2007). Forecasting "friends forever": A longitudinal investigation of sustained closeness between best friends. *Personal Relationships, 14*, 343–350.

[56] Patterson, B. R. (2007). Relational development revisited: A preliminary look at communication in friendship over the lifespan. *Communication Research Reports, 24*, 29–37.

[57] Raacke, J., & Bonds-Raacke, J. (2008). MySpace and Facebook: Applying the uses and gratifications theory to exploring friend-networking sites. *CyberPsychology & Behavior, 11*, 169–174.

[58] Raacke, J., & Bonds-Raacke, J. (2008). MySpace and Facebook: Applying the uses and gratifications theory to exploring friend-networking sites. *CyberPsychology & Behavior, 11*, 169–174.

[59] Boyd, D. (2006). Friends, friendsters, and top 8: Writing community into being on social network sites. *First Monday, 11*(12). Retrieved October 30, 2009, from http://firstmonday.org/issues/issue11_12/boyd/index.html.

[60] Jernigan, C., & Mistree, B. F. T. (2009). Gaydar: Facebook friendships expose sexual orientation. *First Monday, 14*(10). Retrieved October 30, 2009, from http://firstmonday.org/issues/issue14_10/jernigan/index.html.

[61] Patterson, B. R., & Bettini, L. A. (1993). Age, depression, and friendship: Development of a general friendship inventory. *Communication Research Reports, 10*, 161–170.

[62] Patterson, B. R., & Bettini, L. A. (1993). Age, depression, and friendship: Development of a general friendship inventory. *Communication Research Reports, 10*, 161–170.

[63] Patterson, B. R., & Bettini, L. A. (1993). Age, depression, and friendship: Development of a general friendship inventory. *Communication Research Reports, 10*, 161–170.

[64] Patterson, B. R., & Bettini, L. A. (1993). Age, depression, and friendship: Development of a general friendship inventory. *Communication Research Reports, 10*, 161–170.

[65] Patterson, B. R., & Bettini, L. A. (1993). Age, depression, and friendship: Development of a general friendship inventory. *Communication Research Reports, 10*, 161–170.

66 Spitzberg, B. H., & Cupach, W. R. (2007). Disentangling the dark side of interpersonal communication. In B. H. Spitzberg & W. R. Cupach (Eds.), *The dark side of interpersonal communication* (2nd ed., pp. 3–28). New York: Routledge.

67 Afifi, T. D., Caughlin, J., & Afifi, W. (2007). The dark side (and light side) of avoidance and secrets. In B. H. Spitzberg & W. R. Cupach (Eds.), *The dark side of interpersonal communication* (2nd ed., pp. 61–92). New York: Routledge.

68 Frijns, T., Finkenauer, C., Vermulst, A. A., & Engels, R. C. M. E. (2005). Keeping secrets from parents: Longitudinal associations of secrecy in adolescence. *Journal of Youth and Adolescence, 34,* 137–148.

69 Vangelisti, A. L., Caughlin, J. P., & Timmerman, L. (2001). Criteria for revealing family secrets. *Communication Monographs, 68,* 1–27.

70 Afifi, T. D., & Steuber, K. (2009). The revelation risk model (RRM): Factors that predict the revelation of secrets and the strategies used to reveal them. *Communication Monographs, 76,* 144–176.

71 Murphy, D. A., Roberts, K. J., & Hoffman, D. (2002). Stigma and ostracism associated with HIV/AIDS: Children carrying the secret of their mothers' HIV + serostatus. *Journal of Child and Family Studies, 11,* 191–202.

72 McBride, M. C., & Bergen, K. M. (2008). Communication research: Becoming a reluctant confidant: Communication privacy management in close friendships. *Texas Speech Communication Journal, 33,* 50–61.

73 Afifi, T., Caughlin, J., & Afifi, W. (2007). The dark side (and light side) of avoidance and secrets. In B. H. Spitzberg & W. R. Cupach (Eds.), *The dark side of interpersonal communication* (2nd ed., pp. 61–92).

74 Vangelisti, A. L., & Young, S. L. (2000). When words hurt: The effects of perceived intentionality on interpersonal relationships. *Journal of Social and Personal Relationships, 17,* 393–424.

75 Vangelisti, A. L., Maguire, K. C., Alexander, A. L., & Clark, G. (2007). Hurtful family environments: Links with individual, relationship, and perceptual variables. *Communication Monographs, 74,* 357–385.

76 Dunleavy, K. N., Goodboy, A. K., Booth-Butterfield, M., Sidelinger, R. J., & Banfield, S. (2009). Repairing hurtful messages in marital relationships. *Communication Quarterly, 57,* 67–84.

77 Myers, S. A., & Bryant, L. E. (2008). Emerging adult siblings' use of verbally aggressive messages as hurtful messages. *Communication Quarterly, 56,* 268–283.

78 Zhang, S. (2009). Sender-recipient perspectives of honest but hurtful evaluative messages in romantic relationships. *Communication Reports, 22,* 89–101.

79 Zhang, S., & Stafford, L. (2008). Perceived face threat of honest but hurtful evaluative messages in romantic relationships. *Western Journal of Communication, 72,* 19–39.

80 Zhang, S., & Stafford, L. (2009). Relational ramifications of honest but hurtful evaluative messages in close relationships. *Western Journal of Communication, 73,* 481–501.

81 Thomas, C. E., Booth-Butterfield, M., & Booth-Butterfield, S. (1995). Perceptions of deception, divorce disclosures, and communication satisfaction with parents. *Western Journal of Communication, 59,* 228–245.

82 Engels, R. C. M. E., Finkenauer, C., & van Kooten, D. C. (2006). Lying behavior, family functioning and adjustment in early adolescence. *Journal of Youth and Adolescence, 35,* 949–958.

83 Engels, R. C. M. E., Finkenauer, C., & van Kooten, D. C. (2006). Lying behavior, family functioning and adjustment in early adolescence. *Journal of Youth and Adolescence, 35,* 949–958.

84 Jensen, L. A., Arnett, J. J., Feldman, S. S., & Cauffman, E. (2004). The right to do wrong: Lying to parents among adolescents and emerging adults. *Journal of Youth and Adolescence, 33,* 101–112.

85 Zhang, S., & Merolla, A. J. (2006). Communicating dislike of close friends' romantic partners. *Communication Research Reports, 23,* 179–186.

Chapter 12

1 Winstead, B. A., Derlega, V. J., Montgomery, M. J., & Pilkington, C. (1995). The quality of friendships at work and job satisfaction. *Journal of Social and Personal Relationships, 12,* 199–215.

2 Beebe, S. A., & Mottet, T. P. (2010). *Business and professional communication: Principles and skills for leadership.* Boston: Allyn & Bacon.

3 Fix, B., & Sias, P. M. (2006). Person-centered communication, leader-member exchange, and employee job satisfaction. *Communication Research Reports, 23,* 35–44.

4 Kassing, J. W. (2000). Investigating the relationship between superior-subordinate relationship quality and employee dissent. *Communication Research Reports, 17,* 58–70.

5 Jentz, B. (2009, September). First time in a position of authority. *Phi Delta Kappan, 91*(1), 56–60.

6 Sias, P. M., & Cahill, D. J. (1998). From co-worker to friends: The development of peer friendships in the workplace. *Western Journal of Communication, 62,* 273–300.

7 Ragins, B. R., & Kram, K. E. (2007). The roots and meaning of mentoring. In B. R. Ragins & K. E. Kram (Eds.), *The handbook of mentoring at work: Theory, research, and practice* (pp. 3–15). Los Angeles: Sage.

8 Turban, D. B., & Lee, F. K. (2007). The role of personality in mentoring relationships: Formation, dynamics, and outcomes. In B. R. Ragins & K. E. Kram (Eds.), *The handbook of mentoring at work: Theory, research, and practice* (pp. 21–50). Los Angeles: Sage.

9 Wagner, C. G. (2009, January–February). When mentors and mentees switch roles. *The Futurist,* 6–7.

10 Adelman, M. B., Ahuvia, A., &\Goodwin, C. (1994). Beyond smiling. In R. T. Rust & R. L. Oliver (Eds.), *Service quality: New directions in theory and practice* (pp. 139–171). Thousand Oaks, CA: Sage.

11 Begley, S. (2010, June 28, July 5). This is your brain. Aging. *Newsweek,* 64–68.

12 Flynn, F. J., Chatman, J. A., & Spataro, S. E. (2001). Getting to know you: The influence of personality on impressions and performance of demographically different people in organizations. *Administrative Science Quarterly, 46,* 414–442.

[13] Flynn, F. J., Chatman, J. A., & Spataro, S. E. (2001). Getting to know you: The influence of personality on impressions and performance of demographically different people in organizations. *Administrative Science Quarterly, 46*, 414–442.

[14] Begley, S. (2010, June 28, July 5). This is your brain. Aging. *Newsweek*, 64–68.

[15] Shore, L. M., Cleveland, J. N., & Goldberg, C. B. (2003). Work attitudes and decisions as a function of manager age and employee age. *Journal of Applied Psychology, 88*, 529–537.

[16] Ryan, A. M., & Kristof-Brown, A. (2003). Focusing on personality in person-organization fit research: Unaddressed issues. In M. R. Barrick & A. M. Ryan (Eds.), *Personality and work: Reconsidering the role of personality in organizations* (pp. 262–288). San Francisco: Jossey-Bass.

[17] Turban, D. B., & Lee, F. K. (2007). The role of personality in mentoring relationships: Formation, dynamics, and outcomes. In B. R. Ragins & K. E. Kram (Eds.), *The handbook of mentoring at work: Theory, research, and practice* (pp. 21–50). Los Angeles: Sage.

[18] Lucas, R. E., & Diener, E. (2003). The happy worker: Hypotheses about the role of positive affect in worker productivity. In M. R. Barrick & A. M. Ryan (Eds.), *Personality at work: Reconsidering the role of personality in organizations* (pp. 30–59). San Francisco: Jossey-Bass.

[19] Barbuto, J. E., Jr., Fritz, S. M., Matkin, G. S., & Marx, D. B. (2007). Effects of gender, education, and age upon leaders' use of influence tactics and full range leadership behaviors. *Sex Roles, 56*, 71–83.

[20] Thompson, R. E. (2005, January–February). The changing face of gender issues in the 21st century workplace. *The Physician Executive, 31*(1), 64–65.

[21] Richmond, V. P., McCroskey, J. C., & McCroskey, L. L. (2005). *Organizational communication for survival: Making work, work* (3rd ed., p. 152). Boston: Pearson.

[22] Richmond, V. P., McCroskey, J. C., & McCroskey, L. L. (2005). *Organizational communication for survival: Making work, work* (3rd ed.). Boston: Pearson.

[23] Schein, E. H. (1992). *Organizational culture and leadership* (2nd ed.). San Francisco: Jossey-Bass.

[24] Miller, K. (2006). *Organizational communication: Approaches and processes* (4th ed.). Belmont, CA: Thomson Wadsworth.

[25] Lauring, J. (2007). Obstacles to innovative interaction: Communication management in culturally diverse organizations. *Journal of Intercultural Communication, 15*, 1–5.

[26] Lauring, J. (2007). Obstacles to innovative interaction: Communication management in culturally diverse organizations. *Journal of Intercultural Communication, 15*, 1–5.

[27] Grosse, C. U. (2002). Managing communication within virtual intercultural teams. *Business Communication Quarterly, 65*(4), 22–38.

[28] Grosse, C. U. (2002). Managing communication within virtual intercultural teams. *Business Communication Quarterly, 65*(4), 22–38.

[29] Seybold, A. M. (2008). The convergence of wireless, mobility, and the Internet and its relevance to enterprises. *Information Knowledge Systems Management, 7*, 11–23.

[30] Timmerman, P. D., & Harrison, W. (2005). The discretionary use of electronic media: Four considerations for bad news bearers. *Journal of Business Communication, 42*, 379–389.

[31] Ladner, S. (2008). Laptops in the living room: Mobile technologies and the divide between work and private time among interactive agency workers. *Canadian Journal of Communication, 33*, 465–489.

[32] Garrett, R. K., & Danziger, J. N. (2008). Disaffection or expected outcomes: Understanding personal Internet use during work. *Journal of Computer-Mediated Communication, 13*, 937–958; Garrett, R. K., & Danziger, J. N. (2008b). On cyberslacking: Workplace status and personal Internet use at work. *CyberPsychology & Behavior, 11*, 287–292.

[33] Jablin, F. M. (2001). Organizational entry, assimilation, and exit. In F. M. Jablin & L. L. Putnam (Eds.), *The new handbook of organizational communication* (pp. 732–818). Thousand Oaks, CA: Sage.

[34] Myers, K. K., & Oetzel, J. G. (2003). Exploring the dimensions of organizational assimilation: Creating and validating a measure. *Communication Quarterly, 51*, 438–457.

[35] Myers, K. K., & Oetzel, J. G. (2003). Exploring the dimensions of organizational assimilation: Creating and validating a measure. *Communication Quarterly, 51*, 438–457.

[36] Myers, K. K., & Oetzel, J. G. (2003). Exploring the dimensions of organizational assimilation: Creating and validating a measure. *Communication Quarterly, 51*, 438–457.

[37] Jablin, F. M. (2001). Organizational entry, assimilation, and exit. In F. M. Jablin & L. L. Putnam (Eds.), *The new handbook of organizational communication* (pp. 732–818). Thousand Oaks, CA: Sage.

[38] Chao, G., O'Leary-Kelly, A., Wolf, S., Klein, H., & Gardner, P. (1994). Organizational socialization: Its content and consequences. *Journal of Applied Psychology, 79*, 730–743.

[39] Ragins, B. R., & Kram, K. E. (2007). The roots and meaning of mentoring. In B. R. Ragins & K. E. Kram (Eds.), *The handbook of mentoring at work: Theory, research, and practice* (pp. 3–15). Los Angeles: Sage.

[40] Riach, K., & Wilson, F. (2007). Don't screw the crew: Exploring the rules of engagement in organizational romance. *British Journal of Management, 18*, 79–92.

[41] Horan, S. M., & Chory, R. M. (2009). When work and love mix: Perceptions of peers in workplace romances. *Western Journal of Communication, 73*, 349–369.

[42] Cleveland, J. N., Stockdale, M., & Murphy, K. R. (2000). *Women and men in organizations: Sex and gender issues at work.* Mahwah, NJ: Erlbaum; Powell, G. N., & Foley, S. (1998). Something to talk about: Romantic relationships in organizational settings. *Journal of Management, 24*, 421–448.

[43] Quinn, R. E. (1977). Coping with cupid: The formation, impact, and management of romantic relationships in organizations. *Administrative Science Quarterly, 22*, 30–45.

[44] Horan, S. M., & Chory, R. M. (2009). When work and love mix: Perceptions of peers in workplace romances. *Western Journal of Communication, 73*, 349–369.

[45] Pierce, C. A., Aguinis, H., & Adams, S. K. R. (2000). Effects of a dissolved workplace romance and rater characteristics on

responses to a sexual harassment accusation. *Academy of Management Journal, 43,* 869–880.

46 Cole, N. (2009). Workplace romance: A justice analysis. *Journal of Business and Psychology, 24,* 363–372.

47 Powell, G. N., & Foley, S. (1998). Something to talk about: Romantic relationships in organizational settings. *Journal of Management, 24,* 421–448.

48 Horan, S. M., & Chory, R. M. (2009). When work and love mix: Perceptions of peers in workplace romances. *Western Journal of Communication, 73,* 349–369.

49 Cleveland, J. N., Stockdale, M., & Murphy, K. R. (2000). *Women and men in organizations: Sex and gender issues at work.* Mahwah, NJ: Erlbaum.

50 Pierce, C. A., Aguinis, H., & Adams, S. K. R. (2000). Effects of a dissolved workplace romance and rater characteristics on responses to a sexual harassment accusation. *Academy of Management Journal, 43,* 869–880.

51 Cleveland, J. N., Stockdale, M., & Murphy, K. R. (2000). *Women and men in organizations: Sex and gender issues at work.* Mahwah, NJ: Erlbaum.

52 Davies, N. (2010). A workplace menace. *Nursing Standard, 24*(42), 64.

53 Magnuson, S. & Norem, K. (2009). Bullies grow up and go to work. *Journal of Professional Counseling, Practice, Theory, and Research, 37*(2), 34–51.

54 Cowan, R. L. (2009). "Rocking the boat" and "Continuing to fight": Un/productive justice episodes and the problem of workplace bullying. *Human Communication, 12,* 283–302.

55 Cowan, R. L. (2009). "Rocking the boat" and "Continuing to fight": Un/productive justice episodes and the problem of workplace bullying. *Human Communication, 12,* 283–302.

56 Magnuson, S. & Norem, K. (2009). Bullies grow up and go to work. *Journal of Professional Counseling, Practice, Theory, and Research, 37*(2), 34–51.

57 Namie, G., & Lutgen-Sandvik, P. E. (2010). Active and passive accomplices: The communal character of workplace bullying. *International Journal of Communication, 4,* 343–373.

58 Lutgen-Sandvik, P. (2007). But words will never hurt me: Abuse and bullying at work, a comparison between two worker samples. *Ohio Communication Journal, 45,* 81–105.

59 Namie, G., & Lutgen-Sandvik, P. E. (2010). Active and passive accomplices: The communal character of workplace bullying. *International Journal of Communication, 4,* 343–373.

60 Namie, G., & Lutgen-Sandvik, P. E. (2010). Active and passive accomplices: The communal character of workplace bullying. *International Journal of Communication, 4,* 343–373.

61 Namie, G., & Lutgen-Sandvik, P. E. (2010). Active and passive accomplices: The communal character of workplace bullying. *International Journal of Communication, 4,* 343–373.

62 Hoffman, M. F., & Cowan, R. L. (2008). The meaning of work/life: A corporate ideology of work/life balance. *Communication Quarterly, 56,* 227–246.

63 Hoffman, M. F., & Cowan, R. L. (2010). Be careful what you ask for: Structuration theory and work/life accommodation. *Communication Studies, 61,* 205–223.

64 Tremblay, D., & Genin, E. (2008). Permeability between work and non-work: The case of self-employed IT workers. *Canadian Journal of Communication, 33,* 701–720.

65 Hoffman, M. F., & Cowan, R. L. (2010). Be careful what you ask for: Structuration theory and work/life accommodation. *Communication Studies, 61,* 205–223.

Chapter 13

1 Keyton, J. (2006). *Communication research: Asking questions, finding answers* (2nd ed.). Boston: McGraw-Hill.

2 Mottet, T. P. (2000). The role of sexual orientation in predicting outcome value and anticipated communication behaviors. *Communication Quarterly, 48,* 223–239.

3 Mottet, T. P. (2000). The role of sexual orientation in predicting outcome value and anticipated communication behaviors. *Communication Quarterly, 48,* 223–239.

4 Gray, J. (2004). *Men are from Mars, women are from Venus: The classic guide to understanding the opposite sex.* New York: Harper.

5 Canary, D. J., & Dindia, K. (1998). *Sex differences and similarities in communication.* Mahwah, NJ: Erlbaum; Timmerman, L. M. (2002). Comparing the production of power in language on the basis of gender. In M. Allen, R. W. Preiss, B. M. Gayle, & N. Burrell (Eds.), *Interpersonal communication research: Advances through meta-analysis* (pp. 73–88). Mahwah, NJ: Erlbaum.

6 Spitzberg, B. H., & Cupach, W. R. (1998). Introduction. In B. H. Spitzberg and W. R. Cupach (Eds.), *The dark side of close relationships* (pp. xi–xxii). Mahwah, NJ: Erlbaum.

7 Johnson, D. D. (2008). *Research methods for everyday life: Blending qualitative and quantitative approaches.* San Francisco: Jossey Bass.

8 Dabney, M. (2005, August 25). A taste of the scholarly life: Undergrads from across the country present findings at UCSD summer research conference. Retrieved July 15, 2009, from http://ucsdnews.ucsd.edu/newsrel/general/AEP082505.asp.

9 Guterman, L. (2007, August 17). What good is undergraduate research, anyway? *Chronicle of Higher Education.* Retrieved July 15, 2009, from http://chronicle.com/weekly/v53/i50/50a01201.htm.

10 For more information, you can find the National Council for Undergraduate Research on the web at http://www.ncur.org/index.htm.

11 Replication of study by Crusco, A. H., & Wetzel, C. G. (1984). The Midas touch: The effects of interpersonal touching on restaurant tipping. *Personality and Social Psychology Bulletin, 10,* 512–517; see also Crusco, A. H., & Wetzel, C. G. (2008). The Midas touch: The effects of interpersonal touch on restaurant tipping. In L. K. Guerrero & M. L. Hecht (Eds.), *The nonverbal communication reader: Classic and contemporary readings* (3rd ed., pp. 226–231). Long Grove, IL: Waveland Press.

Credits

Photo Credits

2, © Simon Marcus/Corbis; **5,** iStockphoto.com/Joey Boylan; **10,** © Photos 12/Alamy; **14,** © GlowImages/Alamy; **17,** YAKOBCHUK VASYL/Shutterstock; **17,** Terry Chan/Shutterstock; **17,** Yuri Arcurs/Dreamstime; **17** iStockphoto.com/Catherine Yeulet; **26,** Apollofoto/Shutterstock; **26,** GLYPHstock/Shutterstock; **26,** © ICP/Alamy; **30,** Fred Sweet /Shutterstock; **39,** Andresr/Shutterstock; **40,** Tim Mottet; **48,** Yuri Arcurs/Shutterstock; **48,** Yuri Arcurs/Shutterstock; **48,** wavebreakmedia ltd/Shutterstock; **48,** AVAVA/Shutterstock; **55,** © Corbis; **60,** Kelly Redinger/Design Pics/Kelly Redinger/Design Pics/Newscom; **63,** Hans Neleman/Riser/Getty Images; **66,** Jeff Kravitz/FilmMagic/Getty Images; **69,** Purestock/Getty Images; **72,** © Citizen Stock/SuperStock; **75,** Jon Feingersh Photography Inc/Blend Images/Getty Images; **88,** © Golden Pixels LLC/Alamy; **94,** Jupiterimages/Thinkstock; **97** © Image Source/Corbis; **97,** Cheryl E. Davis/Shutterstock; **99,** © Radius Images/Alamy; **109,** BananaStock/Thinkstock; **117,** Doug Menuez/Getty Images; **129,** Chris Haston/NBCU Photo Bank via AP Images; **131,** © Rex/Alamy; **133,** Irina Mozharova/Shutterstock; **133,** © Daniel Hambury/Reuters/Corbis; **144,** © Cultura Limited/SuperStock; **151,** stefanolunardi/Shutterstock; **153,** © Nucleus Medical Art, Inc./Alamy; **154,** © Blend Images/Alamy; **162,** © Blend Images/Alamy; **164,** © Editorial Rights Managed/Alamy; **168,** UpperCut Images/Getty Images; **170,** D. Anschutz/Thinkstock; **179,** © Belinda Images/SuperStock; **181,** © Luciano Leon/Alamy; **182,** iStockphoto.com/James Arrington; **182,** tatniz/Shutterstock; **182,** iStockphoto.com/James Arrington; **182,** tatniz/Shutterstock; **189,** © Hill Street Studios/Blend Images/Corbis; **194,** © fStop/Alamy; **199,** ALEXEI NIKOLSKY/AFP/Getty Imagezs/Newscom; **205,** Copyright © Peter Byron/Photo Edit; **208,** © ACE STOCK LIMITED/Alamy; **213,** Supershoot images/Getty Images; **221,** Nancy Ney/Getty Images; **221,** CREATISTA/Shutterstock; **229,** Jupiterimages/Thinkstock; **235,** © Tetra Images/Alamy; **235,** © kevin finch/Alamy; **242,** Michelle Pedone/Getty Images; **244,** Vitaly Mikhaylov/Dreamstime; **249,** © Blend Images/SuperStock; **251,** © Anton Vengo/SuperStock; **259,** © Radius Images/Alamy; **260,** © Glow Asia RF/Alamy; **265,** Daly and Newton/Getty Images; **269,** © Adam Burn/Corbis; **272,** © Blend Images/SuperStock; **274,** Jace Tan/Shutterstock; **276,** © MIXA/Alamy; **283,** Image Source/Getty Images; **285,** © Design Pics Inc./Alamy; **287,** © Image Source/Corbis; **292,** David Ellis/Digital Vision/Getty Images; **293,** Photodisc/Thinkstock; **296,** © Hill Street Studios/Blend Images/Corbis; **301,** © Panorama media/Alamy; **307,** © UpperCut Images/Alamy; **309,** © Blend Images/Alamy; **311,** © Frances Roberts/Alamy; **315,** Yuri Arcurs/Shutterstock; **317,** © moodboard/SuperStock; **322,** © Radius/SuperStock; **324,** Glovatskiy/Shutterstock; **337,** © Corbis Cusp/Alamy; **340,** © Purestock/SuperStock/Corbis; **341,** StockLite/Shutterstock; **342,** Creatas/Thinkstock; **342,** michaeljung/Shutterstock

Text

Page 16: Reprinted from *Journal of Research in Personality, Vol. 37*, Issue 6, Gosling, S. D., Rentfrow, P. J., & Swann, W. B., A very brief measure of the big-five personality domains, 504–528, Copyright 2003, with permission of Elsevier. http://www.sciencedirect.com/science/journal/00926566 **Page 20:** Rubin, R. B., Perse, E. M., & Barbato, C. A. (1988). Conceptualization and measurement of interpersonal communication motives. *Human Communication Research, 14,* 602–628. Reprinted by permission of John Wiley and Sons. **Page 26 (Table 1.4):** Letstalk announces cell phone etiquette guidelines based on 6 years of etiquette research. Press Release dated March 16, 2006. Retrieved January 7, 009 from http://www6.letstalk.com/company/release_031406 **Page 26 (Table 1.4):** From Text etiquette: How to avoid pushing the wrong buttons. (2006, January 29). *USA Today*. Retrieved on January 8, 2009 from http://www.usatoday.com/tech/news/techinnovations/2006-01-29-safe-texting-sidebar_x.htm; and **Page 26 (Table 1.4):** Text messaging etiquette. The Emily Post Institute. Retrieved January 8, 2009 from http://www.emilypost.com/lifething/tips/text_messaging.htm. Adapted from the following sources: University of York website. Retrieved January 9, 2009 from http://www.york.ac.uk/weboffice/policies/social-networking.htm; Conlin, M. (2006, March 27) You are what you post, *Business Week*; Flesher, J. (2006, January 12). How to clean up your digital dirt before it trashes your job search. *The Wall Street Journal*, p. 4A. **Page 40 (Table 2.2):** Adapted from: Schiraldi, G. R. (2001). *The self-esteem workbook*. Oakland, CA: New Harbinger Publications. **Page 42:** Richmond, Virginia P.; McCroskey, James C. *Communication: Apprehension, Avoidance, and Effectiveness*, 5th edition, © 1998. Reprinted by permission of Pearson Education, Inc., Upper Saddle River, NJ. **Page 46:** Richmond, Virginia P.; McCroskey, James C. *Communication: Apprehension, Avoidance, and Effectiveness*, 5th edition, © 1998. Reprinted by permission of Pearson Education, Inc., Upper Saddle River, NJ. **Page 47 (Figure 2.2):** Richmond, V. P., & McCroskey, J. C. (1990). Reliability and separation of factors on the assertiveness and responsiveness scale. *Psychological Reports, 67,* 449–450. **Page 78:** McCroskey, J. C., Richmond, V. P., & Daly, J. A. (1975). The development of a measure of perceived homophily in interpersonal communication. *Human Communication Research, 1,* 323–332. Reprinted with permission of John Wiley and Sons. **Page 82:** Clatterbuck, G.W. (1979). Attributional confidence and uncertainty in initial interaction. *Human Communication Research, 5,* 147–157. Reprinted with permission of John Wiley and Sons. **Page 95 (Table 4.1):** Adapted from Norton, R. (1983). *Communicator style: Theory, application, and measures*. Beverly Hills, CA: Sage. **Page 103 (Figure 4.1):** Based on Hall, E. T., & Hall, M. R. (1990). *Understanding Cultural Differences*. Yarmouth, ME: Intercultural Press Inc. **Page 107:** *Behavior modification procedure: a sourcebook* by Thomas, Edwin J. Copyright 1974. Reproduced with permission of

Index

Note: Authors cited in the text are indexed to the page where the citation is made. Authors whose works are referenced without in-text citations are indexed to the end-of-text references.